THE PROCESSING OF MEMORIES:
Forgetting and Retention

THE EXPERIMENTAL PSYCHOLOGY SERIES

Arthur W. Melton · *Consulting Editor*

THE PROCESSING
OF MEMORIES:
Forgetting and Retention

NORMAN E. SPEAR

STATE UNIVERSITY OF NEW YORK
AT BINGHAMTON

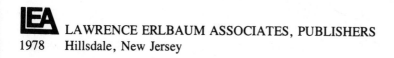 LAWRENCE ERLBAUM ASSOCIATES, PUBLISHERS
1978   Hillsdale, New Jersey

DISTRIBUTED BY THE HALSTED PRESS DIVISION OF
JOHN WILEY & SONS
New York   Toronto   London   Sydney

Lawrence Erlbaum Associates, Inc., Publishers
62 Maria Drive
Hillsdale, New Jersey 07642

Distributed solely by Halsted Press Division
John Wiley & Sons, Inc., New York

Library of Congress Cataloging in Publication Data

Spear, Norman E.
   The processing of memories.

   Bibliography: p.
   Includes indexes.
   1. Memory. I. Title. [DNLM: 1. Memory.
2. Psychophysiology. BF371.S741p]
BF371.S74   153.1'2   77-19113
ISBN 0-470-26290-7

Printed in the United States of America

To
Jesse B. Spear and *Florence Eberman Spear,*
Dedicated Parents and Educators.

Contents

STM

LTM

Preface

The fate of a memory has always been a more fascinating question to me than how the memory was acquired originally. The information represented by a memory—the events of your first day at kindergarten, where you caught your largest fish or hit your first home run, how you determined the solution to a particular class of differential equations, the major points critical to an argument with the Dean—sometimes is so clearly remembered that it seems the episode just occurred and the associated information just acquired. Yet on other occasions, the information is so difficult to pry out of its storage place that for practical purposes it might never have been learned originally.

What factors determine what is and what is not remembered? By what principles can we predict when an episode, once learned, will be remembered well and when not at all? In their ultimate, final form, such principles are not at hand; but neither are they far away. The purpose of this book is to present the evidence that seems to me of greatest importance for understanding forgetting and retention, and to consider issues that must be resolved if we are to establish these principles.

The study of learning, transfer, and retention (generally, the processing of memories) has proceeded along two major fronts: investigations of how normal humans retain or forget verbal materials, and those psychobiological studies that test retention and forgetting in animals under conditions in which it would be impossible, or very inconvenient, to use human subjects. Information acquired on these two fronts should have mutual benefit toward understanding retention and forgetting. But, there has been little interaction between investigators taking these two approaches, and virtually no integration of knowledge or identification of common issues solvable by each group. This seems to me to have retarded progress.

Failure of communication among scientists investigating a common topic is unfortunate because it precludes valuable integration among diverse ideas and methods of study, and in this case the practical consequences also are quite real. Pertinant to examples of the latter are the day-to-day application in medical practice of a patient's forgetting as a diagnostic indicator and the critical importance of long-term retention for certain psychiatric therapies. It is for such practical circumstances that we need to understand the relationship between physiological function (and malfunction) and forgetting, and a key to such understanding may come through the classical application of the animal model for solution of human health problems.

One might reasonably ask, however, whether human retention and forgetting of verbal materials actually has anything in common with the retention and forgetting observed in animals. I obviously believe that it does, but I also can see that this remains an empirical question. Part of the purpose of this book is to collect and organize the empirical evidence as an aid in answering this question.

The book is organized in terms of problem areas and issues I find particularly pertinent to understanding retention and forgetting. For certain problems and issues, research to date has dealt almost exclusively with human subjects, while for others animals have nearly always been the experimental subjects. The issue of "mnemonic preparation" (Chapter 8), for example, is addressed almost exclusively by studies with human subjects, and maybe this seems obvious; perhaps less obvious, the influence of brain damage on forgetting also has been studied more effectively with human subjects, even though a complete analysis will require the use of animal subjects. On the other hand, effects such as state-dependent retention and the amnesic or hypermnesic influence of certain drugs has been studied almost exclusively with animal subjects. And finally, topics such as the influence of a retention interval or the interfering effects of a conflicting memory on forgetting have been studied a good bit with animals and also with humans.

From this it should be clear that the book has not been organized in terms of "effects on animals" compared with "effects on humans." At the same time reference to empirical evidence will never be made without regard to the species tested. Within these bounds the attempt simply has been to apply the best evidence available for the problem area or issue under consideration.

The book excludes two major topics that might reasonably be considered within the title "Processing Memories." One of these is transfer from an established memory to acquisition of another; I have made no attempt to review or analyze what is known about transfer, and except for its use as an index of retention, the topic is not considered. The second is subject matter relevant to "semantic memory," the store of permanent knowledge not directly traced to a discrete set of events or episode. The concern of this book is for retention and forgetting of specifiable episodes known in the jargon as "learning tasks."

As to specific organization, this book includes first an introductory chapter that defines the topic and considers its historical development, and second, a chapter that describes the theoretical orientation and emphasizes it through consideration of contextual influences on retention and forgetting. Probably these two chapters should be read first, but after that the reader may skip about and not lose the thread, since each chapter considers particular issues and problem areas. Chapter 3 concerns the influence of short retention intervals; Chapters 4 and 5 deal mainly with relatively long intervals between the acquisition of a memory and the test for retention. Chapters 6 and 7 review and analyze the retention and forgetting associated with abnormal physiological conditions, and Chapters 8 and 9 consider a variety of general issues.

Completion of this book depended upon the invaluable editorial guidance of Arthur W. Melton. His suggestions and comments were directed with precision and insight and a level of wisdom that was somewhat awesome to me and yet expected from this eminent leader of experimental psychology. It is a pleasure to note my gratitude for this opportunity to work with Art Melton and for his important contribution to this book.

It is a pleasure to acknowledge also the intellectual leadership and inspiration of Benton J. Underwood. The professional and personal model he has provided since my graduate school years is a continuing inspiration and challenge to my behavior, and his specific encouragement to write this book kept me at it during difficult periods.

I am indebted to several other colleagues for their personal exchanges of ideas pertinent to this book. These primarily include Byron Campbell, John Capaldi, George Collier, Michael D'Amato, William K. Estes, William C. Gordon, Werner Honig, Donald J. Lewis, Ralph Miller, Jack Richardson, Endel Tulving, Michael Watkins, and Lawrence Weiskrantz; but so many others have been similarly helpful that I cannot acknowledge them all by name. My wife, Linda Patia Spear, has provided not only astute professional advice, but personal encouragement as well. The patience of my daughters Mandy and Jennifer Spear also was helpful. Completion of the book was made possible by the effectiveness with which my research associate, colleague, and friend, Norman G. Richter, directed most of the operations in our laboratory. Funds for our research mentioned throughout this book were provided by a grant from the National Science Foundation (BMS24194), a place to study the literature and to work was provided by Rutgers University, the Department of Experimental Psychology at Oxford University, and SUNY Binghamton, and my time for this project was facilitated by a Research Scientist Development Award from the National Institute of Mental Health (MH 47359).

In their preliminary stages, the chapters in this book benefited greatly from the astute editorial suggestions of Charlotte Pastore. I am grateful also to the exceptional secretaries who facilitated the completion of this book, Annette Goldstein, Muriel Cohn, Margaret Reich, Susan Digby-Firth, Debra Ditkovich, and Alida Camp. Finally, I am pleased to acknowledge the thoroughly professional work of the staff of LEA in producing this book, and the cheerful patience, understanding and expertise of Lawrence Erlbaum and Sondra Guideman in directing it to completion.

Norman E. Spear

1

Introduction and Historical Perspective

"Blackouts" may result when too much alcohol is ingested. Blackouts are a symptom associated with alcoholism, although they occur in nonalcoholics as well. This symptom is a special kind of forgetting that is abnormally severe and attributed to a source not usually encountered in nature, which may qualify it as a case of "amnesia."

The term *blackout* is misleading because its occurrence does not necessarily involve loss of consciousness. A person suffering a blackout does not appear abnormal to most observers, and in fact some victims have been said to appear less intoxicated during a blackout than otherwise (Goodwin, 1971).

Neither the functional nor the organic basis of blackouts is understood, and their study is impeded by their irregularity. Blackouts occur sometimes in alcoholics, but neither exclusively nor inevitably. They often follow if large amounts of alcohol are consumed at a rapid rate, but not always, even among persons for whom blackouts are common. In addition, there appear to be two very distinct types of blackouts: the more severe *en bloc* type and a mild type. The latter case of blackout is so similar to normal bouts of forgetting that often the same memory deficit may occur when no alcohol has been consumed, in which case the diagnosis "blackout" or "amnesia" may be superfluous.

The topics to be discussed in this book are not the sorrier consequences of ingesting alcohol or any other drug, as the title indicates. However, the blackout phenomenon is a convenient vehicle for introducing some issues of memory processing because the associated memory deficit is perhaps the most common severe instance of abnormal forgetting. Many of us either have experienced, or thought we experienced, a blackout. This case of amnesia may be used to illustrate some general features of memory processing. As with most cases of forgetting, persons experiencing the less severe case of blackout may not realize

1

that they have lost their memory of specific events unless they are made aware that these events did in fact occur. As with more common forgetting, memories of these events may return if the subject is "reminded" by the appropriate hints or cues, that is, by real or vicarious exposure to associated events. One similarity between blackouts and instances of common forgetting is especially intriguing: In spite of apparently adequate sensation and perception of prior events and reasonable intent to learn them, there is utter failure to account for them later. Whenever perception of certain events is inadequate, the study of their retention usually is uninteresting. To study retention and forgetting, we have to compare differences in performance, and we can only draw the conclusions we seek if the performance differences are not due to uncontrolled differences in sensation, perception and motivation. Indeed, we must also exclude contamination by differences in learning, a measure that seems especially difficult to control. More on this later.

The more severe *en bloc* type of blackout has limited counterparts in normal memory. This is characterized by an inability to recall events that occurred throughout entire periods of time, from a few hours to a few days. Recall for these events often cannot be recovered, in spite of intense prompting. A few instances of common forgetting are this extreme—for example, you might try to recall events in your own history prior to reaching the age of two or three—but it is rare for events not too remote in time.

Our stored representations ("memories") of personal experiences are relatively permanent. In this book, we will find it useful to assume that ordinarily memories are absolutely permanent once stored. We will be concerned here with the circumstances under which a memory comes to influence our behavior and the circumstances under which it does not. Blackouts are one of many specific behavioral phenomena that provide an experimental preparation for use in studying this question, but we now consider more general issues concerning the processing of memories.

BASIC CONCEPTS

Memory and Its Processing

If an organism is to make use of the internal representation—the memory—of events encountered, two steps are required. Though only preliminary to our concerns here, these steps in themselves have enormous significance for behavior. First, the events must be perceived, coded at the receptor level in terms of neurochemical activity, and further modified in the central nervous system in light of prior experience with similar events. This process of perception is quite beyond the scope of this book, and we will have little more to say about it. It is notable, nevertheless, that it is by no means simple to determine whether certain phenomena often considered to be aspects of "short-term memory" are in fact separable from perception, and vice versa.

The second preliminary process is the encoding that occurs beyond perception, in which representations of events are "stamped into" an organism for future reference and consequent modification of behavior. The set of representations of events—collectively, the memory—must be "stored" or "consolidated" neurochemically. Storage of the memory may be accomplished simultaneously with perception, but not usually. Because memory storage more commonly proceeds beyond initial perception, we are led to consider the principles of learning and conditioning in order to understand the environmental determinants of memory storage.

By learning and conditioning we mean the portion of memory processing that functions when an organism is exposed, usually repetitively, to certain episodes (an "episode" being a set of events). If the separable events of an episode are related (e.g., if those events are contiguous, predictive, etc.), then this group of environmental events may be represented in the organism by a group of corresponding "memory attributes," which collectively constitute the "memory" for that episode.

When we say "I remember a bell and I remember the end of a lecture period," we imply only separately stored memory attributes representing the concepts "bell" and "lecture period." But when we say "I remember that a bell indicates the end of a lecture period," we describe the memorial consequences of conditioning—a joint representation of "bell and lecture period" together with attributes that represent the general stimulus context in which this relationship has been acquired. Further, if we say "I remember that the bell indicates the end of the lecture on experimental psychology," the contextual attribute of the memory is still more specific.

Of course, the consequences of conditioning and learning need not be verbalizable. The point is, however, that learning and conditioning are processes by which a relationship between events becomes stored as a memory together with specific attributes representing the context of those events. A good share of our attention will be given to the hypothetical consolidation process that may be viewed as responsible for initial storage of a memory. For our purposes, consolidation is interesting to the extent that it may be separated from perception. If the consolidation process actually proceeds so rapidly as to fall within the duration of the perceptual processes, then it may be more effective to consider it together with other phenomena of perception, which we shall not discuss in this book. Later we shall discuss further the concept of consolidation, especially in considering abnormal memory processing. Certainly, we must consider the events that *follow* initial consolidation—the elaboration of the basic memory through integration with previously established memories of similar content, an interaction that hardly can be denied in view of the dynamic quality of memory processing. But for the most part the focus of this book will be on the behavioral manifestation of established, "well-consolidated" memories. Thus, for our purposes perception will be assumed and the characteristics and determinants of original learning are of only secondary interest.

What is a "Memory"?

It was first realistic, then useful, and now customary to take a multidimensional view of a memory. A memory is a conglomerate of attributes, characteristics, or dimensions that uniquely define an event. Although "memory" often is used also with reference to the entire process of learning and remembering, it is used here only as the individual's representation of events. It is a hypothetical construct for what is remembered. The memory of a human child's scratchy encounter with an impatient cat may be represented not only as a startling, claw-induced pain from a previously soft, furry object but also as the yowl of the cat, the scream of the mother, the child's own internal sympathetic response to these exciting or noxious stimuli, the sequence of "cat teasing" that preceded the scratch and whether the episode occurred in the living room or on the patio, and more. A rat confronted with the task of leaving one compartment and entering another within five seconds to avoid footshock may represent this episode collectively in terms of separate memory attributes (apart from the immediate experimental contingencies governing the footshock): the odor of the room, the sensation of the experimenter's hand, the rat's internal hormonal state based on time of day or point in estrous cycle or state of adrenal depletion, the rat's physical or emotional state (illness, fatigue, hunger, or fear), the severity of the footshock, the structure of the grid floor, and perhaps the sequence of just-preceding events in its home cage leading up to its predicament.

Similarly, as Underwood (1969) has described, the memory of a verbal unit by an adult human may include attributes that define the unit's orthographic characteristics, its acoustical characteristics, its relative frequency in a given context or absolute frequency in the language, and the general context in which the verbal unit was presented.

Serving as a subject in a verbal learning experiment, a student instructed to memorize a list of words may include as part of her memory not only the words-as-presented but perhaps also some features of the room, the color of the paper on which the words were written, the odor of the experimenter's perfume, and whether the student is nervous about appearing stupid or is irritated at having been coerced into serving in the experiment. The complexity of the memory—the number of separate events represented for an episode—will vary depending on a variety of circumstances, such as how familiar the subject is with the environment of learning, whether the task or material to be learned has been practiced before, and so on.

Each representation of a psychologically separable event is called a memory attribute. When we speak of "memory" processing, we are referring hypothetically to the entire set of memory attributes formed during original learning. In actual fact, these attributes may function rather independently. If you are asked to recall the latest portion read of the novel you are now reading, you may immediately respond with the gist of the recent events in the story, and perhaps the general portion of the book in which it belongs. However, you are unlikely to remember the precise page numbers, the first word on the page you are now reading, or the precise time at which you picked up the novel, even though you may have registered this information originally. The point is that different attributes of a memory may be forgotten at different rates. If so (we shall consider this question later), it would appear that attributes of a memory should be treated as mutually independent. A further point is that subjects may select for retrieval only one aspect of a memory, depending on what they believe is required. It is not necessary at this point to make precise assumptions about these theoretical aspects of a memory. It is useful, however, to think of a memory as a multidimensional representation.

This multidimensional characteristic of memory is quite obvious in any educational enterprise. A former student once carefully reported to me that he remembered the names my infant daughter had assigned two of her dolls. As an anecdotal illustration of infantile amnesia, I had described in a lecture how my daughter, now grown to age five, did not recognize the names "Darfy" and "Lub-Lub" as the names she earlier had assigned these dolls (which she had played with constantly at age two, but since were stored away). Moreover, she had thought her father a bit weird for suggesting such absurd names. The point is that while the former student readily produced the words "Darfy" and "Lub-Lub" and remembered my daughter's disappointment with her father's silly behavior, he sheepishly admitted that he forgot *why* I had told that story. Although trivial details of the episode were remembered, the major point was forgotten.

Finally, the concept of "coding" is intrinsic to understanding the nature of a memory. What is stored is not the external "stimuli" but the organism's responses to those stimuli. The nominal stimulus is therefore not usually the functional stimulus. The difference between them depends on the external context of the nominal stimulus and the internal state of the organism, as well as response biases due to past learning or biological dispositions. These factors determine this elementary form of coding, which occurs in animals and humans alike to yield the multidimensional representation termed a *memory*.

Memory Storage and Memory Retrieval

Memory "storage" and memory "retrieval" are hypothetical constructs. Storage is the process of representing events initially and thus establishing the memory for potential future reference. Retrieval is the process that takes the stored representations (memories) of events and manifests them in terms of behavior, with the understanding that "behavior" in this case might include further covert processing of the memory that may be inferred from subsequent overt behavior (an empirical example of the latter is "implicit reactivation," described in Chapter 7; see also Spear, 1973, 1976).

Perhaps the most ubiquitous reference to memory processing is not how representations of episodes are stored initially but how and when a memory influences behavior after it has been stored. How can we *retrieve* the information that has been stored as a memory? Under what circumstances will a memory be retained or forgotten?

In common usage, *memory* is most often applied as if it were the retrieval process. If John Doe says "I have a poor memory for names," he does not mean that he cannot learn the name of a woman he is meeting for the first time. Nor does John mean that he cannot refer to the woman's name during the next few minutes or hours of conversation with her. Instead, the reference is to what happens after John has stopped active processing, "thinking" of that particular episode; then, when John later sees the now-familiar face, he cannot produce her name. Notice that John probably can retrieve *some* representation of that woman. For instance, in addition to recognizing her face from among strangers, other physical characteristics may be remembered, and, probably, John will remember to a large extent what her name is not.

The problem of memory retrieval may be addressed by considering any instances in which an animal or human engages in an episode (a set of events) and learns it. Let us say there is evidence that behavior has been modified as a consequence of the episode. Can we now be certain that the individual's retrieval process will cause the "new" behavior to recur when appropriate conditions call for it? For example, if you should learn to recite this paragraph verbatim, could we be certain that you would recite it perfectly next year? Of course not.

The reasons for our uncertainty are at the same time obvious and obscure. It is obvious that acquired information is not inevitably available for use (i.e., "remembered"). Your parents could tell you how at the age of two or three you had learned quite well the names of your dolls, the location of hidden cookies, and several road signs on the way to Grandma's. Yet it is unlikely that you can recall this information today.

The obscure aspect is reflected in how widely the likelihood of recalling acquired information may differ, yet how effectively this recall may be controlled. Equally obscure is a clear understanding of the basic processes underlying such recall and why their effectiveness varies. Differences in the accuracy of remembering among individuals equal in many other skills can be astounding. Mr. S. was reported by Luria (1968) to recall perfectly a matrix of 20 randomly chosen numbers that had been presented to him on a single occasion 16 years earlier. In contrast, certain victims of brain damage, whose basic IQ nevertheless may be equal to that of Mr. S., may be quite unable to remember the name of their doctor within a few seconds after he has left the room (see, e.g., Barbizet, 1970). Equally wide variability may be found in terms of experimental tests of memory processing in animals. For example, certain drugs that act as neural stimulants, when given shortly after learning a problem, may negate later remembering; other drugs with similar effects on the central nervous system may be given to another animal to enhance remembering of the same problem.

The obscurity of the reasons for forgetting may be illustrated further by simple treatments that seem to alleviate forgetting. Adults instructed to stand in front of a group of other adults and shout loudly "No, I won't!" may spontaneously recall forgotten events of childhood or adopt childish postures (Tompkins, 1970). Tompkins also reports that the idiosyncratic nature of the adult signature may be lost and childish handwriting assumed when adults are instructed to write their names slowly, at the rate of about three seconds per letter. It often is reported that through hypnotic suggestion adults may be made to recall verifiable events of childhood that apparently otherwise were not remembered (e.g., Reiff & Scheerer, 1959). Humans or animals given treatments that induce amnesia for specific learning can be made to recover from that amnesia by the simple passage of time or by the presentation of some portion of the circumstances that governed the original learning (e.g., Bickford, Mulder, Dodge, Svien, & Rome, 1958; Lewis, 1969; Spear, 1973, 1976).

The point I wish to emphasize is that following its acquisition a memory continues to be subject to psychological processes that determine ultimately whether this information will influence behavior at any given moment. These memory processes that occur following learning will occupy much of our attention in the following chapters. But before we can discuss this topic meaningfully, we must identify more specifically how we may measure the product of the retrieval process—specifically, what is meant by retention and forgetting. The bulk of the current chapter then will explore the history of the study of memory processing.

Retention and Forgetting

Two terms associated with the study of memory processing—*retention* and *forgetting*—will be used in a strictly operational sense. To assess the extent to which a memory may be manifested in behavior, some index (test) of one or more attributes of the memory must be selected. An index must be some form of measurable behavior that is known, or believed, to be related to the memory attribute in question. The index used for human subjects may be simply a vocal or written description of exactly, or approximately, what they had learned. But the index for animals is, of course, less symbolic and may be the emitting of a response whose representation was stored as a memory attribute, that is, one of the events that defined the original episode. For example, if a hungry rat turns left in a T-maze and finds food, its memory representing that episode may be indexed by a left turn. Alternately, the index may be the effect on some contrary or dissimilar behavior; for example, the memory acquired by the hungry rat just mentioned also may be indexed by how difficult it is, after a left turn led to food, to train the rat to turn right instead.

In terms of such indexes of a memory, "forgetting" caused by a specified event is defined by a decrement relative to the same index assessed when that event is absent. The source of forgetting most frequently considered is a relatively undisturbed interval between training and testing. In this case, forgetting is assessed relative to performance immediately after the last training trial (where "immediately" is defined by an interval identical to the previous intertrial interval). Similarly, retention is defined by the difference in the indexes of animals that had acquired the memory and animals that had not.

In contrast to storage and retrieval, "forgetting" and "retention" are defined quite objectively and imply nothing about the underlying processes. If an organism's test performance is poorer than that found on the earlier, immediate test, and if motivational, perceptual, and simple performance factors may be discounted by proper controls, then we say that the animal has forgotten. We say that retention has occurred when a trained animal's performance differs from the performance obtained in a comparable untrained animal; more generally, retention is the difference between the performance of an organism exposed to an episode and that of one not exposed.

We implicitly exclude trivial effects on performance per se. For example, if an animal has learned a discrimination in order to obtain a food reinforcer and later is tested for retention just after a big meal, or if an animal is trained to move quickly to avoid a shock and then is tested after an injection of a barbituate or a lesion in the motor area of the cortex, it obviously would be ridiculous to call the performance decrement "forgetting." Unfortunately, the circumstances separating performance and memorial effects are not always so obvious, and one of the major methodological issues in the study of memory is separation of these factors. A similar methodological problem, and a fundamental issue in interpretation of memory phenomena as well, is the separation of memory storage from memory retrieval as differential sources of forgetting.

Measurement of Retention

A variety of measurement techniques can provide an index of retention—evidence that the process of memory retrieval has been effective and the residue of previous experience has been contacted. The most direct technique with humans is to instruct them to reproduce—to "recall"—something about the critical episode. A parallel procedure with animal subjects is to reexpose the animal to the circumstances of memory storage and then measure responses that occur prior to the introduction of the reinforcer. A related measure is recognition, the index of discrimination between the episode-to-be-remembered and another episode.

Other measures are more indirect than the recall or recognition measures in that the effectiveness of the process of memory retrieval must be inferred from the organism's performance in a second task bearing some known relation to the episode represented by the critical memory. The second tasks are termed *transfer tasks*, implying the utilization of the critical memory. Transfer is either positive or negative, depending on whether acquisition of the critical memory helps or hinders the performance of the second task (i.e., the retention test). It is conventional to assess positive transfer between the critical memory and the retention test. For this purpose specific response measures include rate of relearning the events of the original episode, or the extent of positive transfer to a generally new task known to benefit from acquisition of the critical memory, or savings (i.e., the proportional reduction in practice required to accomplish relearning, relative to that required for original learning).

Although less common, it often is useful strategically to assess retention in terms of negative transfer—performance on a task for which learning is slower if individuals have just acquired the critical memory than if they have not. For example, suppose that you had spent six months in England driving on the left side of the road. Upon your return to the United States or to continental Europe, the extent to which you deviate from the right side to the left side of the road when driving would be an index of retention of your driving experience in England. However elementary this may appear, there are cases in which retention may be assessed more sensitively in terms of negative transfer than otherwise. A common instance is when performance on a relearning or recall task is "perfect" among all experimental conditions and more subtle differences in retention might be masked by the performance imposed by this measurement.

In short, retention is measured and memory retrieval implied by any change in performance that reflects the residue of an earlier experience, and there are many ways to assess this change. The sensitivity of these measures may vary from one set of circumstances to another. But whatever the exact measure, appropriate controls are required so that the clear inference can be drawn that it is the acquired memory, and not some contemporary demands on the organism, that is influencing performance.

Forgetting is Rarely "Complete"

That forgetting is partial rather than complete is an important point. Rarely will an episode be forgotten totally in the sense that *none* of the events can be recalled or recognized (if *all* could be assessed). A student asked to remember a poem may be unable to recite a single line but nevertheless may remember the circumstances under which the poem was assigned, the part of the book in which it is found, the person who assigned the poem, what it was about, and so forth. A rat trained to emit certain behaviors in order to avoid footshock may behave no differently than an untrained rat in terms of the particular avoidance behavior, but may show more fear in other ways when returned to the experimental situation than a naive rat.

The essential point is that we assess forgetting by measuring *selected* aspects of behavior. We cannot measure everything. Sometimes we may measure only the aspect of behavior that is indeed "forgotten," while on other occasions we may measure only the behaviors that are "retained." We shall return to this point in later pages.

Epistemological Note

Knowledge concerning the processing of memories comes from a variety of sources. The primary source for the material presented here is information gathered by the experimental method. Many of the experiments that we will cite have been conducted with animals, but data gathered from humans, primarily with regard to memories largely verbal in content, also will be considered. We shall see that a good portion of the conceptual advances made in the study of memory processing have been proposed by investigators working with the latter data.

For the purpose of understanding the structure and function of memory processing, there are some clear advantages in studying humans. The most obvious is our subjective experience in dealing with memory processing—our personal examples of forgetting and retention. As a result of these experiences, we are prepared a good deal better to casually observe and understand the memorial behavior of other humans than that of lower animals. Krech (1972) notes this advantage in his criticism of the frequently insular research on memory processing conducted by scientists trained in neurochemistry (not unlike the insular research on neurochemistry sometimes conducted by scientists trained in memory processing). As an illustration, Krech cites the opinion held by some observers that more rapid advances in understanding may occur in the brain chemistry of mental disorders than in the brain chemistry of memory processing. Krech agrees with this opinion, he says, because scientists working on the former problem more often have had intimate experience in carefully observing and considering mental disorders in their patients. In contrast, Krech continues, those working on the brain chemistry of memory processing have tapped only rarely the systematic knowledge already gathered on human and animal memory, and perhaps also are less inclined to ponder memory processing routinely during casual thinking. Krech presents this charge to psychobiologists studying memory processing: "Go constantly to look at memory in people. Know what you are studying, and whence came your question, and before whom your work will be judged" (1972, p. 223).

A further advantage in studying human memory is the clinical evidence concerning abnormal memory processing in humans. Characteristics of a broad spectrum of amnesias have been catalogued and have had great influence on theories of memory processing. Recently, the intriguing features of persons who exhibit abnormally effective memory processing have begun to have similar influence.

Why, then, is so much attention given here to data gathered on lower animals? The answer, quite familiar to psychologists and biologists, is that a greater variety of experimental manipulations are possible with animals and better control over extraexperimental experience may be exerted. By using animals, for example, (1) the neurophysiological control of memory may be studied experimentally without resort to clinical inference; (2) the ontogeny of memory may be studied, without restriction, from conception to old age, and the control of past and contemporary experience—variables of immense importance for forgetting and retention—may be complete; (3) the events presented to subjects in the laboratory for storage as memories may be made richer in content—require a broader range of memory attributes for representation—when the subjects are animals, especially in terms of attributes representing the subject's motivational condition or its general internal state, including hormonal and neurophysiological conditions. Still other advantages will become apparent later. Also, history is quite clear on the value of using animals as models in the study of any number of biological processes, pathological or normal, for the purpose of medicine or "pure science."

Finally, in his analysis of human memory, Tulving (1972) argues that two classes of memorial processes should be dealt with independently. One is "semantic memory," which depends on stores of symbolic, linguistic information and possibly is uniquely human. The other, "episodic memory," is memory for explicit events, and this process, or at least some classifiable portion of the memory processing in humans, must be shared in some approximated form by animals of all phylogenetic levels.

We shall be sensitive to methodological problems among the studies to be discussed. Experimental errors are likely to be subtle and rapidly can lead to misconceptions in this area of memory. We must pay constant attention to whether, on the basis of the method that has been applied, a conclusion is justified. In this respect, there is one general danger that is worth emphasizing at this early point. Before drawing a conclusion about retention and forgetting, one must be sure that experimental treatments are not confounded by differences in degree of original learning. As Underwood (1964) has shown for human learning, this is hazardous business indeed because of the subtle means by which degree of learning may differ. Confounding between ultimate degree of learning and variables introduced before completion of learning is especially likely, for example, when the limits of performance have been reached by all animals at the conclusion of training. This procedure often may mask differences in overtraining. Of course, it is not always sufficient simply to hold the number of training trials constant or to take all animals to a common criterion of learning. Underwood has demonstrated such methodological pitfalls, and solutions for avoiding them, for some tests of human verbal learning, but similar problems remain unsolved in tests of animal memory. We shall return to this problem later, together with considerations of the meaning of "degree of learning." For now, our intention is to induce some caution through awareness that this is indeed a problem.

HISTORY

Memory as Art and Entertainment

Long before anyone considered studying it experimentally, the value of skill in processing memories was well appreciated. The art of memory was studied and practiced at least as early as the Roman Empire. Cicero considered memory to be one of the five components of rhetoric, and for many years memory remained a standard topic taught as a technique by which orators could deliver long speeches without reference to notes. The practice of memory as an art continued through Europe until relatively recent times. Even as Bacon, Descartes, and Leibnitz were furthering the revolution toward science and the experimental method, they discussed the application of memory skill as an important tool toward gathering and organizing knowledge without considering its analysis through the experimental method.

The basic technique preferred by these philosophers for efficient storage and retrieval of memories differed little from that taught in ancient Rome. An informative source, apparently written in Rome between 86 and 82 B.C., considered two kinds of memory. " 'Natural memory' . . . is ingrafted in our minds, born simultaneously with thought." However, this natural memory could be improved, it was thought, by the refinement of " 'artificial memory,' . . . a memory strengthened or confirmed by training" (Yates, 1966, p. 5). Cicero identified the originator of this notion of artificial memory as Simonides, a Greek poet. The core of the story is that Simonides encountered a basic mnemonic device while presenting his poems at a banquet. Part way through the banquet, Simonides was called out of the banquet hall, and while he was gone the roof fell in, killing all those in attendance. Roofs were a good deal thicker in those days, and as a consequence most of the victims were crushed quite beyond recognition. However, Simonides found that he could remember the location of each guest at the table and thereby identify the bodies. He thus realized the mnemonic advantage of the orderly location of each person around the table and so, wrote Cicero, ". . . inferred that persons desiring to train this faculty [of memory processing] must select places and form mental images of the things they wish to remember and store these images in the places . . ." (Cicero, from Yates, 1966, p. 2).

From this, practitioners and teachers of the art of memory evolved a basic mnemonic technique. First, a series of loci, places that can be readily ordered in some spatiotemporal manner, is developed and learned. For example, one may imagine oneself taking a familiar and constant path throughout the house and thus establish as loci various tables, window sills, spots on the floor, doorknobs, and the like located along the way. Next, material to be remembered is coded into discrete images of things placed in the appropriate order at the various loci. For example, to establish a memory such as a speech, the main points are coded as concrete objects and mentally "placed" in order at each successive locus. Finally, when the material is desired or the speech is to be delivered, all that is necessary is to imagine oneself revisiting each of the loci in order.

For hundreds of years, there were polemic confrontations concerning how such mnemonic devices could be improved or employed to maximum utility. The issues were, for example, how one might most effectively establish loci—when memory is heavily loaded and the usual loci are exhausted, should one have a "second house" in one's imagination or simply another room, or perhaps move one's mind into a completely new establishment involving a new set of loci—and by what sensory modality could the most effective images be established. Only relatively recently (e.g., Wood, 1967) have such issues been studied in a systematic experimental fashion.

Today, at least in the United States, there is little practice of the art of memory, except for some mnemonists employed in the entertainment industry. Because of the recent interest in the analysis of mnemonic techniques, however, some professional and amateur mnemonists have come under study. It is interesting, and perhaps also significant, that two of the more famous of these cases, Luria's "S" (Luria, 1968) and Hunt and Love's "VP" (Hunt & Love, 1972), both spent the early part of their childhood among a culture in Eastern Europe in which rote memory is valued highly among schoolchildren, more so than is typically the case in the United States. It is notable that "VP" attributes his capacity for memorization to the emphasis given the skill in his early training. We shall return to "S" and "VP" later and will find that the bases of the mnemonic expertise of the two subjects actually appear to be quite different.

Conceptualizing "Memory"

A young Polish scholar, Bronislaw R. Gomulicki, completed in 1953 an interesting little book—actually his thesis, written at Cambridge University—concerned with the history of conceptualizations of memory. This book was the outgrowth of a study conducted by Gomulicki as an undergraduate at Cambridge under the direction of Professor O. L. Zangwill. In the following historical material, we have borrowed often from Gomulicki's work.

Gomulicki observed that memory theories prior to 1950 concerned the following eight aspects of a memory:

1. Localization of the memory in terms of its anatomical characteristics
2. Form of the memory trace (whether physiological or spiritual)
3. Temporal aspects of the formation of the memory trace, including consideration of the initial duration necessary for establishing the trace, whether repetitions are required, and whether after the trace is established it continues to change qualitatively
4. Durability of the trace (whether it becomes stronger or weaker with time or does not change at all)
5. "Internal organization," a term used by Gomulicki to refer to the conditions necessary for initially establishing the memory trace and for its subsequent modification, if possible
6. "External organization," used by Gomulicki to refer to the extent to which a memory trace is dependent on affective or emotional factors
7. Reactivation of traces and the necessary and sufficient conditions for memory retrieval
8. Varieties of memory, of which a large number have been suggested

These topics have a contemporary sound, and we shall hear their echo in later portions of this book. For our immediate purposes, we concentrate on the historical aspects of the first two items.

Form and Localization of a Stored Memory

In ancient times, it was a rather radical concession to admit that the basis of memory really might be vitalistic, actually located in the body in some material form. Because of the belief in a spiritual basis of memory, it is not surprising that physiological localization of the memory store or memory trace was not studied with intensity. Some relevant hypotheses were formed, nevertheless. In the sixth century B.C., Parmenides viewed memory as a unique relationship between the light or heat and dark or cold in the body. Forgetting occurred when this unique relationship was disturbed. In the fifth century B.C., Diogenes of Apollonia noticed a tendency for persons to breathe more easily when a forgotten event was recalled. This suggested to him an explanation similar to that of Parmenides, but with the memory represented in terms of an appropriate distribution of air throughout the body (Gomulicki, 1953).

In the fourth century B.C., Plato suggested that memory was like a wax tablet into which representations of events could be etched, but subsequently was easily impaired, as by effacement of the etching. He suggested further that different individuals possessed "tablets" of differing size or consistency, which might determine both ease in acquiring the original representation and its subsequent permanence. Gomulicki notes that Plato clearly intended this analogy, still often employed by writers in many disciplines, to have no literal application.

Aristotle, also in the fourth century B.C., was a good deal more specific physiologically. He was approximately correct about many functions of the central nervous system, but he located the seat of control of these functions in the heart rather than the brain. Those of us who, since childhood, have heard the expression "learn by heart" might wonder if growth of knowledge regarding the function of the brain ended with Aristotle. Not so. In fact, Aristotle's own grandson, Erasistratus, working in the third century B.C. with Herophilus, actually dissected the human brain, being perhaps the first to do so (Gomulicki, 1953). They recognized that the heart was physiologically critical, but believed that "animal spirits," which controlled mental processes, were located in the brain.

Progress in this direction seems to have been slowed in the Roman-controlled civilization. Scholars like Cicero were very much interested in techniques for efficient processing of memories, but they apparently were less concerned with the underlying basis of memory function. Progress in the latter respect was further suppressed, together with scientific inquiry generally, by the authority of the Church.

In the second century A.D., Galen suggested a more detailed account of how the "animal spirits" functioned in the brain to control mental processes. The critical sites, he believed, were the lateral ventricles, because it was here that the animal spirits presumably were manufactured. Subsequently, these animal spirits were distributed to sensory and motor nerves by the action of the brain, which Galen believed had diastolic and systolic movements like the heart. As Gomulicki has noted, this advance toward neuroanatomical specificity was rather a mixed blessing, because Galen was held in such good favor by the Church that for many centuries it discouraged other scholars from disputing Galen's views.

With the passing of the Dark Ages into the scientific revolution, new conceptions of memory appeared. In the seventeenth century Descartes viewed the pineal gland as a homunculus-like control center that emitted animal spirits through "pores" of the brain until they reached the locus of the critical memory trace. These animal spirits then returned to the pineal gland, and this organ, in turn, transmitted the representation to the mind (Descartes being a mind–body dualist). An interesting aspect to this thesis is that Descartes believed that once the spirits had taken a certain path through the pores, these particular pores would "open more readily." This is the same basic conception as that used by more modern theorists who believe that memory depends on synaptic transmission and that the synapse becomes more easily crossed by neural impulses with successive crossings (e.g., Hebb, 1949).

In the eighteenth century, some skepticism arose about the concept of "animal spirits." The control of nervous function increasingly became viewed as due to some relatively more innocuous, clearly inanimate substance. At least one scholar, Zanotti, suggested that electrical or magnetic forces might be responsible.

In the nineteenth century, Gall and Spurzheim developed the popular notion of "phrenology" through nonsystematic observation. Gomulicki (1953) notes that Gall's discovery of the center of verbal memory was prompted by his acquaintance with two schoolmates who both were good memorizers and had protruding eyes. From this he concluded that the faculty of verbal memory must be located in the frontal cortex behind the eyes. However, phrenology was soon followed by empirical research like that of Flourens, who conducted careful experiments very much like those conducted by Lashley in the twentieth century, including systematic extirpation of parts of the animal brain and observation of the consequent changes in behavior.

Throughout the second half of the nineteenth century, Charles Darwin's theory of evolution had its inevitable impact on the thinking of memory theorists. One of the most influential papers of the time was read by Ewald Hering at meetings of the Imperial Academy of Science at Vienna in 1870 (Gomulicki, 1953). Hering presented two main points, the first of which, reflecting a Lamarckian reaction against Darwinism, was that acquired memories may be transmitted genetically to offspring. Hering's historically more important point was that the property of "memory" (processing) should not be restricted to special areas of the central nervous system of higher animals only. Rather, these properties were basic to all animal life. Hering asserted, furthermore, that species differences in the characteristics of memory processing and content were quantitative rather than qualitative. The last point undoubtedly encouraged physiological and behavioral work on memory processing in lower animals and increased the prestige of already completed work of this sort. This previously completed work included that of Paul Broca, who located the "speech center" (an area of the brain that still bears his name) through studies of his aphasic patients. A contemporary of Broca's, the famous physiologist Hitzig, previously had used electrical stimulation to study the motor area of the cortex in collaboration with Fritsch, and agreed with Broca's contention that essentially all parts of the brain were potential sites of memory stores. He believed, though, that the site of more abstract memories must be the frontal cortex, because stimulation of this area had produced neither sensory nor motor responses.

Two other memory theorists of the nineteenth century should be mentioned because the influence of their ideas is still with us today. The first, Theodule A. Ribot, is important because of his "law of regression." This "law" stated, briefly, that older memories are more stable, less subject to disruption—stronger—than more recently acquired memories. He evolved this view from his studies of amnesia, contending that the previously accepted view of the role of repetition in strengthening memories, a view supported by intuition and a priori argument, was not buttressed by evidence of an empirical sort. Ribot observed that his amnesic patients were inclined to lose their newer, more complex, or more poorly organized memories before the older, simpler, or better-organized ones and that the latter reappeared first during recovery from amnesia. As a mechanism to explain this effect, he appealed to a structural theory by Delboeuf that had described memory as the rearrangement of molecular structures within neurons (for elaboration of this mechanism, see Gomulicki, 1953). "Ribot's law" remains among the concerns of memory theory (e.g., Wickelgren, 1972), and the role of repetition in learning and memory, together with clarification of the concept of "memory strength," is a basic issue that needs attention in any theory of memory processing.

Finally, the views of William James are important because of their early and continuing influence. James believed that the formation of an association occurred when any two simultaneously active areas of the cortex became connected, or "drained" into each other. Subsequently, excitation of either of these cortical points would induce excitation of the other. Some additional assumptions were added to account for the association between successive events; James also emphasized the affective properties of memory formation. Of perhaps greatest significance today, James suggested a distinction between "primary" and "secondary" memory, providing the precedent for later theorists who elaborated a possible disjunction of two systems—one for processing memories for a short period following acquisition ("short-term memory") and another for their subsequent processing ("long-term memory"). We shall return to each of these points in later discussion.

Concerning the Neurological Locus of Memories

A tendency among clinical neurologists during the early part of the twentieth century, especially in analyzing the consequences of the many cases of brain damage incurred during World War I, was to map the location of certain mental functions in accordance with the site of the lesion and the corresponding functional disruption. Caution against such an approach had been urged by many biologists, including the eminent John Hughlings Jackson. The simple error in this approach, particularly for localizing memory stores, is that if memories were stored in single locations their arousal might be impaired by damage to afferent fibers and their expression impaired by damage to efferent fibers. No known behavioral tests could differentiate these sorts of damage from actual disruption of the hypothetical memory stores.

Gomulicki cites as examples of investigators who did not heed these cautions two important German neurologists, Henschen and Kleist (1934). These men were not at all hesitant to assign specific locations to mental functions such as memory processes. Neurologists in the United States were equally guilty of this practice (as an example, see Cobb, 1946).

However, there were equally important physiological psychologists who saw the danger in such a specific localization approach, especially when based solely on clinical evidence. Loeb (1900) noted as an example the case of one brain-damaged individual who could not recognize numbers above 3. Loeb pointed out that it would be ridiculous to suppose that the store of memories for all numbers except 1, 2, and 3 had been destroyed. Moreover, his own experiments with dogs, in which he removed various combinations of the areas of the brain that other investigators had labelled "association centers," resulted in no detectable effects on their learning and problem-solving behavior. It requires a great deal of self-confidence to evolve principles on the basis of negative results (and the sensitivity of Loeb's behavioral tests, as with others of that era, may easily be questioned today); nevertheless, Loeb used these results to develop ideas having a good deal in common with the theorizing of later physiological psychologists such as Lashley. Loeb called attention to the dynamic nature of an "association" and the likelihood that the storehouse of such "associations" probably would be found in all parts of the hemispheres, including the possibility that they might be localized subcortically.

Perhaps also contributing to Lashley's thinking were the writings of von Kries (1901). Von Kries suggested that the static models of neural representation prevalent at the turn of the century were quite inadequate to deal with psychological phenomena such as generalization. He cited the familiar example of a melody being recognizable in many different keys, even though different keys must stimulate different neurons. However, it was Lashley who phrased these questions and potential answers with the most effective psychological insight and physiological plausibility. Perhaps more than any other scientist in the early portion of the twentieth century, Lashley promoted the wedding between neurophysiology and psychological theories of memory processing, especially through his own research on the physical locus of memories. For full appreciation, Lashley's own papers should be read (see Beach, Hebb, Morgan, & Nissen, 1960, for selected papers by Lashley). For our purposes, it is well to return to the attention given memory processing by contemporary psychologists concerned primarily, or exclusively, with behavior.

Experimental Study of Memory Processing Prior to 1950

The experimental study of memory processing was more profitable within the context of human verbal learning than with experiments using animals, at least until about 1950. One of the earliest problems in this area was the manner in which thoughts or ideas occur in relatively regular sequences. This concern was expressed by Hobbes in the seventeenth century, by Locke in the eighteenth century, and by other British "associationists." About 200 years after Locke died, Hermann Ebbinghaus devised the technique described in the following section for studying the nature of the thought sequences that Locke had termed *association of ideas*.

Studies of the Processing of Verbal Memories

Ebbinghaus, an energetic and brilliant ex-soldier of the German army, completed his Ph.D. dissertation on the philosophy of the unconscious when he was only 23 years old, in those days an unusual accomplishment. As items to be memorized in his now-familiar experiments, Ebbinghaus took pronounceable sets of three (sometimes four) letters, discarding any that formed a real word. Thus, he invented new "words," "nonsense syllables," which he initially believed would be equally difficult to learn and unfamiliar to all subjects. He treated lists containing 10 or 12 of these "nonsense syllables" as the analog of strings of ideas, and learned each list in a prescribed order. Once a given list was learned, Ebbinghaus set it aside and proceeded to learn other lists until some later time when his schedule indicated that he should bring the first list out again and test himself for retention. He found that he forgot rapidly, losing up to 75% of the memory for a list after only 24 hours (a loss that would have been still greater, we now know, had he measured his retention in terms of a recall procedure rather than by his indexes of relearning and savings). This observation, along with many others and the general finding that memory could be studied systematically and objectively, was to have a profound influence on American psychology.

By the time Ebbinghaus' work was published in English and made available in the United States in 1913, American psychologists already were comparing the merits of two theories of forgetting. According to the "perseveration" theory suggested by Müller and Pilzecker (1900), memory processing ordinarily would continue following learning to strengthen the memory and permit better subsequent retention; forgetting occurred whenever an event subsequent to learning disrupted the continuity of this memory processing. The other interpretation, the "law of disuse" suggested by Thorndike (1913) and others, held that memory simply faded away and decayed over time if not reemployed, just as muscles atrophy when not in continual use.

Both theories were later criticized severely in an important paper by McGeoch (1932). This paper was important for its brilliant defense of McGeoch's interpretation of retroactive interference to explain forgetting and also because it helped establish McGoech, his functionalistic approach to understanding the processing of memories, and the interference interpretation of forgetting in particular as dominant forces. Taking paired-associate learning as a model—and thus assuming the presence of a specific stimulus item at the test for retention—McGoech argued that forgetting was a consequence of either of two factors: (1) the acquisition of competing associations between original learning and the retention test; or (2) changes in the stimulus context that occurred between learning and the retention test. However, his theoretical and empirical focus was on the former factor, the role of interference in forgetting and, specifically, *retroactive* interference. Although McGoech died at a relatively young age in 1942, his influence on the study of memory processing remained strong. His posthumous textbook (McGeoch, 1942; McGeoch & Irion, 1952) continued for several years to have a profound direct influence on students of learning and retention, and one of his last graduate students, B. J. Underwood, quickly became recognized as the leading authority in human learning and retention.

Within the next 20 years, three guiding principles became empirically established. The first concerned retroactive interference, which is indexed by the retention decrement resulting from new materials learned between memory storage and retrieval. McGeoch (e.g., 1932, 1942) saw that in order to understand the precise mechanisms through which learning of new verbal associations impaired retention of previously learned ones, it would be necessary first to understand the converse—how learning of the interfering associations themselves was affected by the previous learning, that is, transfer of training. In other words, because the fundamental determinant of interference presumably is the degree of similarity between two conflicting tasks, it is necessary first to understand how the learning of one such task transfers to the learning of another. A second guiding principle, also concerning the analysis of retroactive interference, was established by Melton and Irwin (1940). They discovered that the interfering effects on retention did not inevitably result in overt mixups between the alternative verbal associations. Interference in retention could occur covertly, quite apart from those more obvious instances in which the subject simply said the wrong word at the wrong time. It became clear that more subtle behavioral aberrations were involved that would require more subtle techniques of assessment. The third principle established proactive interference as a source of forgetting (Whitely & Blankenship, 1936). Melton and VonLackum (1941) established that proactive interference was like retroactive interference in being sensitive to the degree of similarity between sets of verbal items, though in their tests, proactive interference caused less forgetting than did retroactive interference. Under other circumstances, Underwood (e.g., 1945) demonstrated that conflicting associations acquired before original learning—proactive interference—could contribute dramatically to subsequent forgetting. Clearly, for forgetting to occur the interference need not take place between original learning and the retention test.

A parallel line of analysis, which unfortunately did not receive equal experimental attention, was initiated by Bartlett (1932). Bartlett's book, initiated as part of his Ph.D. dissertation in 1916, continues to be read today (see Zangwill, 1972) because of its consideration of the forgetting of entire sentences or stories, a more complex case of forgetting than that dealt with by McGeoch. Bartlett, and later Koffka (e.g., 1935), were concerned particularly with the way in which perceptual principles might account for forgetting, and they were interested in the influence of general techniques or cognitive frameworks, or "schemata," used by subjects at the time of original learning in comparison with those applied at the retention test. Perhaps because of the complexity of the topic, it was difficult to frame testable questions from this loose theoretical framework. This may account for the lesser influence of these ideas at that point in the history of the science of memory processing. (For a more recent, and much more effective, study of retention for sentence and paragraphs, see Kintsch, 1974.)

Contemporary Events in the Study of Memory Processing in Animals

The same year that the translation of Ebbinghaus' work appeared, a monograph concerning memory processing in animals was published by the eminent Walter S. Hunter (1913). Two graduate students, Hough and Reed, at the University of Chicago had tried out a technique for the study of retention and forgetting in animals, and Hunter applied it systematically toward fundamental issues of animal behavior (see Tinklepaugh, 1928). This technique, the delayed-response test, is still used today in any of several variations. The task is simple to instrument, although Hunter did it the hard way initially. For Hunter's first experiments, the animal was placed in front of three doors above each of which was a lightbulb. One bulb was turned on to indicate that a food reward could be obtained behind that door. After preliminary training, however, the light was turned off *before* the animal was permitted to choose among the three doors. By varying the interval between offset of the light and release of the animals, Hunter hoped to discover how the capacity for symbolic processes differed for different species of animals. For the simpler procedure in his later experiments (Hunter, 1913), the light was not used and the location of the food merely was shown to the animal instead, prior to the retention interval. The major result that some animals tolerate longer delays than others need not be discussed here. Of more interest is Hunter's approach. Working within a behavioristic framework that characterized the initial reactions against mentalism and anecdotal comparative psychology, Hunter was by no means ready to consider "memory" in animals. This term was reserved for humans, who alone were presumed to have a capacity for "voluntary recall." Instead, animals that showed some evidence for symbolic processing by responding accurately in spite of long delays following offset of the light were described as having "sensory thought" or "sensory recognition." Such a capacity was presumed to be based on some unknown, intraorganic cue and was viewed as intermediate between the highest level of cognitive capacity (i.e., "thought," including "imagery" found in humans) and the lowest (i.e., "overt orienting attitudes," e.g., setter-like behavior) that could be used for accuracy in delayed responding.

Hunter's view that animals had qualitatively different symbolic processing than humans represented a bias held at least since the writings of Aristotle; this prejudice was preserved in behavioral science as a protection against mentalism (Winograd, 1971). The idea was that a beagle resting by the fireplace cannot recall, and so has no memory of, the best locations for hunting rabbits, but if taken to familiar fields, the dog readily discriminates rabbit-rich from rabbit-poor spots on the basis of sensory recognition. This notion that lower animals do not possess recallable memorial representations of episodes, which in our view is unlikely to be correct, seems to be derived from the misleading assumption that *humans* have a capacity for "spontaneous recall." More likely, all retrieval of memories, whether by humans or by animals, is cued by explicit stimuli. These stimuli may be random events that occur internally or externally, verbal instructions, releasing stimuli, or whatever, but they certainly are not "free will" or a homunculus residing in our hippocampus. Also, the general orderliness found in memory processing argues against "spontaneous" retrieval. While the latter might be supported on the basis of apparent spontaneous firing of neurons in the central nervous system, this reasoning easily can become circular, and spontaneous firing involves an unimportant qualification in any case. We shall see that some cases of recognition may not require the same processes as recall, and animals may be limited in terms of the latter; but recall in either case must be under stimulus control.

Hunter had an interesting view of the operation of sensory thought. In his testing situation, he assumed that some internal cue was aroused by the light, then waned during the retention interval, and finally was rearoused when a response was permitted. It is unfortunate that these ideas were not tested systematically in later years. Nevertheless, some important consequences were evolved from Hunter's innovative work with the delayed response. For example, this task provided a valuable clinical techinque, a basic behavioral index. Fletcher (1965) has noted that the delayed response task "reveals phylogenetic, ontogenetic, and sex differences; it detects, where other tests fail to detect, the effects of brain lesions, drugs, radiation, and deprivation" (p. 129). Also, although the delayed-response task is deficient in clearly separating the effects of memory processing from simple performance effects, it has led to the development of a similar but more efficient instrument, the delayed-matching-to-sample task. Using these two tasks, especially the latter, psychologists have learned much about short-term retention in subhuman primates, as we shall see in Chapter 3.

In spite of these benefits, however, there was a paradoxical negative consequence of Hunter's pioneering work. It diverted a good deal of the research energy of various psychologists into the study of two unproductive questions. One was based upon Hunter's tentative conclusion that raccoons and human children could employ sensory thought while rats and dogs depended on physical orientation (''overt orienting attitudes'') to bridge the interval between the signal and their response. Studies of this topic investigated which kinds of animal could and which could not give evidence for a symbolic capacity (i.e., independent of bodily orientation). The other set of studies sought a simple ordering of species in terms of the maximal length of retention interval tolerable before retention no longer was evident. However interesting these questions may appear, the fact is that the methodological pitfalls associated with their investigation are enormous, and there has yet to be a convincing set of studies published concerning either question. As phrased, these questions simply were not sufficiently analytical. In addition to these unfortunate cul-de-sacs that resulted from Hunter's work, two other factors acted to relegate the study of ''animal memory'' to secondary status throughout the first half of the twentieth century. First, Pavlov, whose behavioral work had enormous impact on American psychology, never demonstrated much interest in questions of retention and forgetting. Second, laboratory animals appeared to forget so little that there was no point in studying it.

Pavlov and animal memory.   Apparently, Pavlov never experimentally manipulated length of retention interval. He did conduct, however, at least one set of tests after an interruption of two months had occurred between conditioning and testing. In a lecture delivered in 1928, Pavlov described such a case for five dogs. Some deficits in the dogs' performance clearly occurred after the retention interval, but Pavlov attributed these largely to emotional factors. In one dog, the conditioned salivation to food ''disappeared'' and then ''reappeared'' only after differential conditioning was conducted. A second dog performed in accordance with a discrimination that had been established but apparently ''lost'' prior to the retention interval [because of a treatment which ''proved to be too great a strain for the nervous system of our animal'' (Pavlov, 1928, p. 351)]. Performance by this animal was better *after* the interruption than before. For two other dogs, previously conditioned reflexes ''disappeared'' over the retention interval. For each of these four dogs, conditioning was reestablished rapidly after the initial retention deficit. (For the fifth dog, there was no retention deficit on the first day following the retention interval, but after that, behavioral control was strangely lost and the animal could not be reconditioned.)

Like other experimental psychologists of the time, Pavlov was inclined to be more impressed by the retention than by the forgetting demonstrated by these animals. Accordingly, he concluded that "these observations show that the presence or the absence of such and such conditioned or unconditioned factors determines exactly and continuously the behavior of the animal" (Pavlov, 1928, p. 352). In other words, Pavlov believed that conditioning is permanent provided that there is maintenance of the circumstances of original training.

Perhaps one reason why Pavlov paid so little attention to forgetting was that he did so little of it himself. He seemed to exemplify what is commonly called "total recall." Pavlov was known to recall explicit details of experimental protocols shown to him only once by his collaborators and students, especially remarkable in view of the enormous number of ongoing experiments produced in his laboratory, sometimes involving as many as 30 coworkers, each working on individual experiments. His capacity for remembering remained remarkable even as he became quite old. Once when he was 75 he commented on a medal worn by a collaborator. The medal had been awarded in conjunction with a running event in a track meet and Pavlov, being interested in athletics generally, casually asked what the winning time had been. Several months later someone else asked the collaborator the same questions and he hesitated in answering, but Pavlov, standing nearby, promptly provided the answer to the nearest fifth of a second: "10 min 11 4/5 sec." Pavlov was known to astonish people by recalling their names along with the occasion on which they had met 20 or 30 years before.

Pavlov's predecessor, Sechenov, described by Pavlov as "the father of Russian physiology," did provide some conjectures about the processing of memories after their acquisition, although he conducted no systematic experiments on the topic. With reference to the maintenance of acquired behavioral change over retention intervals of relative inactivity, he believed that memory processing was so important as to be "the force upon which all psychical development is based" (Sechenov, 1863, p. 68). He viewed memory as a trace, analogous to a visual afterimage but lasting longer. Sechenov saw no reason to assume that neural excitation representing a memory ceased upon cessation of a visual sensation. He believed that the main property of memory processing was to preserve sensations in "a latent state" (1863, p. 71), and he identified its primary determinants as frequency and recency, characteristics that remain perhaps the most important parameters of memory processing even today. Said Sechenov: "The memory of a vivid sensation is stronger than that of a weak one, and the more recent the sensation (the fresher the impression), the stronger the memory of it" (1863, p. 71).

Do laboratory animals forget?   The capacity of laboratory animals for remarkably efficient retention over very long intervals became evident during the first half of the twentieth century. Scientists who thought forgetting was caused by the acquisition of competing habits or associations that interfere with the retention of the prior learning were not at all surprised by this; after all, the isolated and restrictive environments in which laboratory animals live provide little opportunity for interfering learning. On the other hand, the antimnemonic bias held by comparative psychologists, as exemplified by Hunter, led other investigators to be so astounded by the retention shown by animals that they ignored the forgetting that occurred. Evidence for excellent retention by pigeons, dogs, or rats may indeed by found, with only slight evidence of decline over a large portion of an animal's lifetime. The question is whether these demonstrations really are representative of the level of retention to be found commonly in animals or whether these represent restricted circumstances that are especially conducive to efficient retention.

In humans, for example, the alphabet rarely is practiced in its entirety after the first or second year of elementary school, yet it can be recited without error 80 or 90 years later, often in spite of a variety of behavioral and neural deficiencies. While you will have no difficulty remembering the alphabet, you may find it a great deal harder to retrieve the memory of the schoolmate who sat beside you when you last practiced the alphabet. The difference is that your memory for the alphabet was both heavily overlearned originally and often reactivated in later years when use of its parts was required.

Like memory of the alphabet, memories for which animals have been tested after long intervals often were well overlearned. An example is Wendt's (1937) study, often cited for the remarkable retention of conditioned foot withdrawal shown by a dog tested after a retention interval of 2.5 years. During conditioning in this study, the onset of a tone was followed after 1 sec by shock to the forepaw, and both shock and tone terminated .5 sec later. During the first session of 25–30 pairings, the dog's leg began to move in response to the tone (sufficient movement of the leg prevented or terminated shock). This conditioned response was stable by the seventh session. Nevertheless, 18 additional sessions were given prior to the retention interval, and still more training involving the same response apparently was given to the dog with a light as the conditioned stimulus. Wendt does not report the details or consequences of the latter portion of the training, but it is likely that it added, in effect, to the overtraining that preceded the retention interval. The 2.5-year retention test consisted of 20 presentations of the tone unaccompanied by shock. Prior to this test, the dog was given three shocks to its forepaw. Later we shall see that such presentations of the reinforcer prior to a retention test probably facilitate retrieval of the memory and so improve test performance. Test performance by this dog was impressive indeed: Conditioned foot withdrawal occurred on 16 out of 20 tone presentations. This test score compares favorably with the score of 29 withdrawals among 30 presentations given during the last training session 2.5 years earlier, indicating considerable retention (though some forgetting, with a reduction of 17%). Nevertheless, the average *magnitude* of foot withdrawal on the retention test was four times greater than it had been in the last training session. Later we shall consider why this increase in magnitude of response might represent considerable forgetting, because the magnitude of the response had declined to a low level at the termination of original training. Furthermore, seven months after the first test no conditioned foot withdrawal occurred at all upon initial presentations of the conditioned stimulus (relearning was rapid, however).

In an influential paper often cited for this particular result, Skinner (1950) reported some remarkable retention by pigeons. Four years after the pigeons had been trained to peck a key whenever it was illuminated with a pattern, they were returned to the experimental apparatus and tested for retention. Remarkably, no pigeons pecked the key until it was lighted with the visual pattern, and then they responded quickly. The bird showing the best retention responded within 2 seconds of the appearance of the pattern. But in terms of toal responding this bird gave only about 25–50% as many pecks as would have been given without the retention interval. In other words, this aspect of performance indicated that the bird forgot 50–75% over the four-year period. The point of these examples is this: However remarkable such cases of long-term retention in animals may seem (under the assumption that they are really simple organisms with no ''memory'' capacity as such), the fact is that the forgetting also may be substantial, certainly not negligible. In spite of much training, even ''overtraining,'' and in spite of the very limited opportunity for these animals to acquire interfering memories, substantial forgetting occurred. Part of our task will be to understand why this magnitude of forgetting occurs and under what conditions it increases or decreases.

Absence of theory concerning retention and forgetting.   The study of memory processing in animals also was retarded by the absence of theories emphasizing this aspect of behavior as opposed to theories emphasizing the initial acquisition of memories and the influence of motivation on learned behavior. The absence of a theoretical orientation concerning the processing of acquired memories is illustrated in a paper published by Corey (1931).

Corey reported the following study, which clearly was conducted with care and at considerable expense in terms of materials, time, and effort. First, 186 rats were trained in a multiple-choice maze until they made no errors for five consecutive trials. Fourteen days later, the rats were retrained on the same task. This describes the entire exercise; it was not an experiment because there was only one condition. To say that the study was not sufficiently analytical to warrant its cost is to understate excessively. Corey's study was devoid of direction from any theory or conceptual framework as to how memory processing might determine retention and forgetting. At best, the study was demonstrational, not intended to answer any of many substantial questions concerning retention and forgetting that might be posed today.

How can one explain production of such a study, which inadequately estimated forgetting and tested no ideas about memory processing nor produced much information of any kind? This is especially puzzling because at about the same time exciting ideas about learning and motivational processes were being exchanged by some of the most creative scientists to have studied behavior—Pavlov, Tolman, Hull, and Lashley. This lack of analysis and conceptual depth concerning retention and forgetting becomes especially paradoxical when we recall that during the same period, within the realm of human verbal learning, transfer and retention were issues of fundamental concern and systematic investigation. While one can question whether the work on verbal transfer and retention was oriented around theory, there is no doubt that its direction was determined by a fairly coherent conceptual framework that unfortunately made little contact with the animal laboratory. There were some attempts to assess systematically the rate of associative interference in forgetting by animals (e.g., Marx, 1944), but these did not lead to new principles, perhaps because the wrong questions were asked or the wrong techniques applied (for analysis of these problems, see Gleitman, 1971; Spear, 1971; Winograd, 1971). Another answer may be that in studying the learning process in animals investigators became sidetracked by the promise of relatively global theories of behavior, referred to at times as learning theory.

The rise and fall of learning theory. By "learning theory" we refer to no specific theory of learning but, rather, to an idealized promise of a set of principles through which behavior can be predicted from selected parameters of learning and motivation. Learning theory is used here more as caricature than reality, but we believe it represents an attitude that might be termed, according to conventional wisdom, a scientific "paradigm" (cf. Kuhn, 1962, 1970).

The evolution of theory toward understanding behavior through learning principles is vastly important. Why, then, should such a significant object of study as learning theory first blossom widely, then wither away with such rapidity? While selective theories of learning still are prevalent and clearly needed (e.g., Capaldi, 1966, 1971), why are they given less attention now as a group, with little reference to a far more global learning theory? A brief analysis, somewhat oversimplified and biased, may provide some perspective of learning theory against which issues in "memory theory" may be evaluated.

Watson (e.g., 1917) proposed a comprehensive theory of learning as part of the behavioristic reaction against introspection and anthropomorphism, and contrary to certain schools of psychology such as the Gestaltists. In retrospect, Watson's theory was a behavioristic exaggeration, but overstatement is not uncommon among influential ideas. Part of its value lay in restricting the number of principles to which one must appeal to account for learning. No longer was it necessary to deal with nebulous, experimentally intractable concepts like "will" and "images," which introspective philosophers previously had used in the attempt to understand learning. Moreover, this behaviorism was supported in the studies and interpretations of instrumental learning by Thorndike and of classical conditioning by Pavlov.

Learning, under controlled circumstances at least, seemed simple enough to be understood using only a few principles. Moreover, with the reasonable assumption that all learning has a common base, it seemed a relatively elementary matter to extrapolate such principles to more complex circumstances through all levels of behavioral plasticity. The task was to discover the principles.

The search for the proper principles, the proper learning theory, grew between 1920 and 1950, perhaps reaching an apex with the theories of Tolman, Hull, and Spence. These theorists employed the philosophically attractive "intervening variable" approach to theorizing. Skinner (1938) began his search for principles along very similar lines, but quickly abandoned this approach, turning instead to exert his important influence in the direction of methodology and principles of *how* behavior should be studied, instead of being concerned with the principles per se of general behavior.

Armed with the firm conviction that the capacity of an organism for behavioral plasticity was the most important determinant of the ultimate behavioral product (rather than, for example, the genetic control of species-specific behavior), researchers often viewed these theories as a means for encompassing and predicting all behavior. Many systems were developed in precisely this direction, as "behavior theories." With the isolation of critical parameters such as habit strength (amount of practice) and motivation (degree of deprivation or amount of reward) and the evolution of principles such as the reinforcing effect of drive reduction, these theories began to be applied confidently in global fashion. For example, Dollard and Miller (1950; see also Miller & Dollard, 1941) provided one ingenious application of these principles toward understanding personality development and abnormal behavior, with considerable influence on the practice of clinical psychology.

Difficulties with learning theory.   Prematurely, learning theory came to be regarded by educators, sociologists, and the general public as a unitary and precise tool for understanding behavior. Experimental psychologists, however, were well aware of its limitations, and readily recognized a number of technical problems, both philosophical and empirical (see e.g., Estes, Koch, MacCorquodale, Meehl, Mueller, Schoenfeld, & Verplanck, 1954). A foremost concern was that the empirical base of learning theory was insufficient.

Might the influence of these theories of learning have been more durable had more experiments been done? Probably not. More experiments dealing with learning were conducted between 1950 and 1960 than ever before, yet it was during this period that the global-theories approach to learning began to be abandoned. The reason, in our view, is that the research base of these theories was misdirected in three respects. The first two concern limitations of the tests employed. First, the animals tested in this research, such as the laboratory rat, from which the bulk of the data were derived, were not well understood behaviorally. Although relatively well studied physiologically, the animals' biological dispositions for certain behaviors, controlled through the interaction between their inherited biological equipment and early experience, were little recognized and less appreciated. Of course, these factors were acknowledged implicitly in the construction of experimental learning tasks, which had to be designed so the animal would emit, from the start, enough behavior to measure and yet would learn slowly enough to yield differences among experimental treatments but not so slowly as to overtax the experimenter's patience. Tasks that rats could master immediately or never master were ignored, but unfortunately so were the biological dispositions or environmental factors that contributed to these interesting behavioral extremes.

The second difficulty concerns which determinants of learned behavior were studied. In the very early days of theory building, complex mazes provided the learning task; later, simpler and more analytical straight runways or single-choice apparatuses were employed. When applied to the rat, all of these tests were very sensitive to motivational effects. Consequently, theory building began to emphasize the importance of motivational parameters in learning because it was the manipulation of these factors—magnitude of the reinforcer, level of deprivation, and so forth—that yielded the biggest differences in behavior. Of course, the amount of practice on the task made a difference, but even this difference often was slight when such simple apparatuses were used. Moreover, when motivation was controlled, alterations in performance through learning did indeed appear to be permanent, at least in view of the few tests of retention that were conducted. The extinction process was well studied, but its analysis also was dominated by motivational concerns.

A third experimental misdirection contributing to the decline in concern with a broad learning theory was the failure of theorists to widen the empirical base by appealing to data gathered outside the animal laboratory. For example, an abundance of data and ideas about learning, transfer, and retention were produced during this time in studies of human (motor and verbal) learning. Why were these findings not incorporated more thoroughly into the construction of learning theory? Perhaps it was because the critical parameters of motivation, so important to learning theory, were relatively ineffective in human learning. More probably, because of the constant reminder of the behavioristic revolution and the fear of offending Morgan's canon by applying human characteristics to animals, scientists were reluctant to risk unwarranted generalization between the principles governing human and animal behavior; and rightly so.

There were some important attempts to apply the models and concepts of the principal learning and behavior theories to human learning. One notable example is the application of the Hull–Spence theory to studies of eyelid conditioning and paired-associate learning. In these studies, generalized anxiety of the human subjects was considered to be a generalized drive state (e.g., Spence & Taylor, 1951; Spence, Taylor and Ketchel, 1956; Taylor, 1951; Taylor & Spence, 1952). A second example is the application of inhibition constructs derived from Hullian theory to interpretations of the effects of distributed practice on human perceptual–motor learning (e.g., Ammons, 1947; Kimble, 1949). A third example includes the several attempts to extend reinforcement theory to paired-associate verbal learning (e.g., Goss, Morgan, & Golin, 1959) and the analysis that led to the general conclusion that the consequences of outcomes (confirming or disconfirming; "yes" or "no"; "good," "bad," or no response) were effective because of their informational content rather than as relatively automatic reinforcers (see Hilgard & Bower, 1974).

These attempts to understand human learning and behavior through principles based on the characteristics of basic conditioning were only marginally successful and perhaps limited to paradigmatic value. Yet there remained a reluctance to incorporate experimental results and concepts of verbal learning—especially those concerning retention and forgetting—toward the modification of general theories of learning and behavior. This was also in spite of the fact that the research on transfer and retention with human subjects used tasks—simple motor learning and rote verbal memory tasks—that were so elementary and uncomplicated as to seem quite as applicable to memory processing in general as experiments in animal learning.

It is easy enough to criticize in retrospect the building of learning theories. The fact is, nevertheless, that the ideas of the superb scholars who contributed to the more important learning theories—Hull, Tolman, Spence, Lashley—not only were inventive, productive, and excellent in their day but are still quite viable. To fully appreciate these theorists, it is important to read what they actually wrote rather than paraphrases of what they wrote or the caricatures of their ideas that are too often applied by contemporary theorists seeking new directions.

The power and influence of learning theory should not be underestimated. This influence is reflected in the astounding portion of published experiments that were directed toward testing alternative versions of learning theory (e.g., Hull, 1943; Spence, 1956; Tolman, 1932) during the years 1940–1960. This influence also may be detected by reading the ideas of educators or social scientists during these years, prior to 1970, and even today. In fact, perhaps one reason for the demise of this sort of theory building is that the "learning theory" that existed, or was presumed to have existed, was consumed, disseminated, and applied incautiously by scholars of many disciplines with perhaps little appreciation for its limited scope.

In contrast to the dramatic influence of theories of learning during this period, memory processing in animals following initial training was not subjected directly to such a massive theoretical and experimental investigation. Indeed, the causes of forgetting and determinants of retention were not really considered in these theories. The reasons are many; some have already been mentioned. For example, with motivation well controlled there apparently was little loss in retention to be concerned about. Thus, whatever was important about something termed *memory processing*—and the term *memory* was rarely, if ever, used in the writings of learning theorists unless accompanied by *trace*—was presumed to be encompassed by the subject matter of the learning theories. However, somewhat of a psychobiological subculture did exist that may be said to have been concerned with theories of how the processing of memories leads sometimes to retention and other times to forgetting. This "subculture" seemed to have more influence relative to learning theory outside of the United States, and it was more likely to be found among physiologists, philosophers, and psychiatrists than among experimental psychologists. The influence of the question of further processing of acquired memories began to increase sharply just prior to 1950.

Developments Since 1950 in the Study of Memory Processing by Animals

Just prior to 1950, two classes of events converged to stimulate the investigation of memory processing in animals. The first class included the spinoff from medical technology developed through the war effort both in the field of technological advances and in basic knowledge of neurophysiology. The second, not entirely independent of the first, ensued from the development of new theories and specific questions about memory processing in general.

If there can be any favorable outcome from war, it must be the knowledge of physiology and associated technology derived from the treatment of war's unfortunate victims. Such new knowledge was placed at the disposal of science just after World War II and soon exerted a powerful influence on the directions taken by investigators of memory processing. With these new insights into neurophysiological functions, scientists no longer found it necessary to depend on a "conceptual nervous system," nor could they overlook the dramatic discoveries about the neurophysiological basis of behavior. Whether the form of theorizing was a formalized set of intervening variables and postulates of their interaction or a loose conceptual framework with less commitment, certain facts concerning the relationship between physiological and behavioral functioning could not be ignored. A pertinent example is the analysis by Russell and Nathan (1946) of the relative consequences of general brain concussion and discrete gunshot wounds in the head.

For a number of years both before and after World War II, Russell had studied the relationship between physiological trauma and failures in memory processing (amnesia). He was fully acquainted with the general syndrome: the variability from case to case in how long memory processing was impaired following trauma; the frequent uncertainty regarding when memory processing actually returns to normal; the alleviation of the abnormal forgetting as time passes, often with a dramatically sudden improvement in retention; the occasional appearance of extraordinarily effective memory processing for events associated with a trauma (which contrasts so sharply with the more typical deficit in memory processing); the existence of isolated intervals following the trauma during which memory processing appears quite normal, only to have the patient once more slip back into defective processing; and the fact that the general amnesic syndrome is more likely to occur following general concussion of the brain than following relatively localized gunshot wounds or minor hemorrhaging. Russell encountered many cases of amnesia among the large number of injured in Great Britain during World War II. He and Nathan analyzed over 1,000 of these cases for characteristics of a particularly interesting aspect of amnesia, relating to events occurring *prior* to the trauma:

> The curious phenomenon of retrograde amnesia which is so well known in head injury is also found after electric convulsion therapy, status epilepticus, meningitis and acute cerebral anoxia as in hanging, CO poisoning, and severe loss of blood. R.A. (retrograde amnesia) is for events which occurred before the injury while the patient was still fully conscious. The events occurring during this period were often dramatic and must have been registered by the normally acting sensorium, yet the injury intervenes and these events are thereby prevented from being retained, or if they are retained they cannot be recalled. (Russell & Nathan, 1946, p. 292).

Retrograde amnesia holds unusual interest for two reasons. First, the retention deficit is clearly separated from any deficit in sensation or perception. The deficit is for events that occurred *prior* to the brain trauma and so, as Russell and Nathan mentioned, "must have been registered by the normally acting sensorium." Second, events more temporally contiguous with the trauma are more likely forgotten. The 30 minutes immediately preceding the trauma seemed to be especially critical in the cases studied by Russell and Nathan. Among 1,029 persons having head injuries (which did not include the relatively discrete effects of gunshot wounds), 69% were unable to recall events that occurred during the 30 minutes immediately prior to trauma, but *could* recall earlier events; in contrast, only 13% were unable to recall events occurring just prior to the 30 minute pre-trauma period. In other words, of the 82% with retrograde amnesia for events during at least the 30 minutes prior to the trauma, more than four out of every five cases *could* recall events that had occurred just prior to 30 minutes before the trauma. Apparently, something very important for memory processing occurs during the 30-minute period. Closer analysis of this 30-minute period indicated that events during the 1-minute period just prior to the trauma were most susceptible to processing deficits.

Russell and Nathan were keenly aware that their analysis could only *suggest* a temporally dependent, postperceptual memory process. The very existence of amnesia admittedly was "roughly estimated": They could not be certain that a similar retention deficit might not have occurred without the trauma; the measurements of temporal relationships were imprecise; and the permanence of the amnesia was not considered in this analysis. Nevertheless, these cases did indeed suggest dramatically that the more closely events precede brain trauma, the less likely their retention; or in other words, memory processing of events is abnormally deficient the sooner physiological disruption follows the events. The implication was that memory processing is not instantaneous. An account was necessary of what goes on during the period of memory processing during which the memory apparently is stored.

A model of such processing was suggested by Hebb (1949) in his influential book *The Organization of Behavior*. Hebb suggested two stages of memory formation: an initial stage, believed to be active, temporary, labile, and fragilely susceptible to disruption or even destruction, and a second stage, supposedly passive, permanent, and relatively robust. Because the internal representation of events—the memory—does not enter directly into a stable state, Hebb suggested, it may during the initial labile period be destroyed or prevented from being stored as a faithful representation of the external events (e.g., if the neurological system responsible for its formation is distorted by traumatic head injury). Hebb's fundamental idea was not new. To account for normal memory-processing phenomena such as retroactive interference, Müller and Pilzeker had suggested a similar principle 50 years earlier. However, McGeoch (1932) had shown this sort of explanation to be defective, at least in the case of human verbal learning. Nevertheless, Hebb's arguments, beautifully written and supported by intriguing examples of behavior as well as new knowledge and educated guesses as to how the brain might work, were convincing and influential. The influence of Hebb's ideas probably was enhanced by independent conclusions of Hebb's former teacher, Lashley, presented at about the same time that Hebb's book was published. Nearing retirement, Lashley had formulated his principles of "mass-action" (total amount of brain cortex removed is critical for memory processing) and "equipotentiality" (locus of the tissue removed from cortex is unimportant for memory processing) to conclude his extensive research effort aimed at identifying the locus of memory storage in the brain. Lashley's classic and facetious conclusion that learning must not be possible was a consequence not only of the inadequate neurophysiological evidence of the day but also of the inadequacy of the existing models of memory processing. It was time for the new, more dynamic model of memory with a physiological basis provided by Hebb.

The publication of certain experiments by Duncan (1949) provided additional support for Hebb's ideas in the form of systematically derived experimental support. Duncan's work (begun four years earlier) suggested that if electroconvulsive shock were administered to a rat soon after training, memory processing of the events of that training was impaired. After each of several learning trials, the rat was shocked through the head with an electrical current with an intensity sufficient to produce a convulsion. The sooner the electroconvulsive shock followed each trial, the less increment in performance resulted from that trial. Translated into terms more consistent with the Russell–Nathan analysis, memory processing for events that occurred prior to the trauma appeared more likely to be impaired the closer the trauma followed the events.

In the following decade, further experiments were directed at the disruption of memory processing by electroconvulsive shock or by other means of modifying the central nervous system, but these were scattered efforts. About 1960, researchers accelerated experimental attention to the "consolidation" concept in Hebb's theory. This increase in interest was due to several factors: new information concerning a chemical basis of neurotransmission and a protein basis of memory storage; an instructive review of the problems by Glickman (1961); and energetic leadership, both experimental and theoretical, provided by a physiologically oriented student of Tolman, James L. McGaugh (e.g., McGaugh, 1966).

Research on the role of a "consolidation" in memory processing by animals was enhanced further by general technical accomplishments in biochemistry and psychopharmacology. In the United States, such advances were particularly rapid in the late 1950s and 1960s as a consequence of the general increase in federal funding of research prompted by Russia's launching of Sputnik and the impetus provided by behavioral research laboratories developed within pharmaceutical companies. Immense profits were to be made from drugs; the various barbiturates and amphetamines, for example, rapidly were becoming popular as modifiers of behavioral states. Might these drugs not have effects on memory processing as well as on emotion and perception? As we shall see, certain drugs administered following learning seemed to impair later retention, and others to enhance it.

The study of memory processing in animals, especially retention and forgetting, proceeded along other lines as well, as we shall see. However, for about 20 years following 1950, studies of memory processing were concentrated on the consolidation concept and tests of its validity and generality.

Developments Since 1950 in the Study of Human Memory Processing

The study of human memory processing throughout the first half of the twentieth century was largely functionalistic, an approach that helped tie pretheoretical concepts more closely to the data than was the case for animal memory. Other advantages, too, were inherent in the study of human learning and permitted clearer statements about verbal memory processing than could be made for relationships concerning memory processing by animals. For example, human memory-processing experiments are influenced less by nonmemorial variables than are animal memory-processing experiments. A prime example of a nonmemorial variable is motivation, a critical determinant of performance in animal learning but rarely effective in human verbal learning. Also, whereas the study of memory processing in animals involved a wide variety of tasks and subject variables (e.g., species or strain), verbal memory processing was studied almost exclusively with college sophomores and with tests largely restricted to the learning and retention of unique pairings or orderings of verbal items.

This limited scope had clear disadvantages, but it may be argued that this was a necessary stage in the understanding of human memory processing. These narrow boundaries of study did permit some crisp answers regarding the determinants of verbal learning and retention. For example, differences in the rate of learning of a paired-associate list could be accounted for almost exclusively in terms of meaningfulness or intralist similarity of the items, differences (unspecified) among humans' learning ability, and the nature of any prior learning the subject had acquired in the laboratory. Other variables of potential interest—motivational variables and methods of presentation such as distribution of practice—clearly had little effect. Similarly, retention was shown in these tests of verbal memory processing to depend quite clearly on degree of learning and prior or subsequent learning of similar materials in the laboratory, but to be relatively unaffected by the meaningfulness or intralist similarity of the verbal materials, how rapidly the subject learned originally, or motivational variables (for reviews, see Hall, 1966; Jung, 1968; Spear, 1970; Underwood, 1966a; Underwood & Schulz, 1960). An astounding portion of the advances in this area that occurred between 1950 and 1960 was contributed by one laboratory, that of Benton J. Underwood. Moreover, this early work paved the way for variation in methodology and an increased spectrum of issues in human memory in the 1960s and 1970s, and Underwood continued to supply many of the technical innovations and conceptual advances needed for the new problem areas. During the latter period especially, Tulving and Postman must also be credited with an extraordinary share of the scholarly output, experimental and theoretical, concerning retention and forgetting. Thus prepared, we may expect many references to Underwood's work, and to Postman's and Tulving's work, in the pages ahead.

Four developments of special significance toward the understanding of human retention occurred between 1950 and 1960. Three of these originated in Underwood's laboratory. First, Underwood and his associates developed a method that permitted more accurate assessment of factors controlling rate of forgetting. Earlier studies of verbal learning and retention lacked proper control of degree of final learning prior to the retention interval. By applying carefully derived techniques for separating the influence of learning from that of retention, and by focusing on individual items rather than treating the list of items as a whole, Underwood and others evolved more correct statements of what does and what does not determine rate of simple forgetting. Previously it had been concluded that retention of nonsense syllables was better the higher their degree of meaningfulness, and also that subjects who learned a list of verbal items more rapidly than other subjects also had better retention. Underwood's better technique indicated that neither conclusion was justified.

Second, Underwood (1957) discovered a methodological oversight in earlier studies of the source and magnitude of forgetting following the learning of a single set of verbal items in the laboratory. These studies had been conducted under the implicit assumption that forgetting is due to new, conflicting learning that occurs during the period *following* training, but for reasons of economy and convenience the subjects used were well experienced in the learning and recall of verbal materials in laboratory settings. The results had led to the conclusion that about 75% of verbal learning is forgotten after 24 hours. However, Underwood (1957) demonstrated that *previous* learning experience in the laboratory was an important determinant of the subsequent rate of forgetting; for subjects new to such a task, the rate of forgetting after 24 hours is closer to 25% than 75%. Because the 50% greater forgetting by the well-practiced subjects clearly was due to proactive sources of interference, this emphasized, together with other work by Underwood, the importance of proactive interference as a determinant of retention.

Also during this period, Underwood and his associates (e.g., Barnes & Underwood, 1959; McGovern, 1964) began to analyze the mechanisms of retroactive interference, a powerful influence on retention. With the assumption that paired-associate learning could be analyzed in terms of two empirically separable processes, response learning and the association of the response with its stimulus item, Underwood's laboratory proceeded to develop techniques for isolating and evaluating retroactive interference with three kinds of associations: between the general context and the response, between the stimulus and the response, and "backward" between the response and the stimulus.

A fourth development of considerable impact was initiated almost simultaneously in both England (Brown, 1958) and the United States, at Indiana University (Peterson & Peterson, 1959). This was a technique permitting analysis of the forgetting of a single verbal item over very short retention intervals. The Brown–Peterson technique (see Chapter 3) was simple, efficient, and easily applied. It was rapidly adopted by many students of memory processing, and psychological journals soon became flooded with new studies of retention and forgetting in humans, this time concerning "short-term memory" (cf. Melton, 1963; Wickelgren, 1973).

The spectrum of developments in the study of human memory processing broadened drastically after 1960. New directions, conceptual and technical, included topics of special relevance to retention and forgetting. A few selected examples may be mentioned briefly. First, a relatively formalized and specifically testable version of interference theory was devised to explain the forgetting of verbal units learned in the laboratory and tested after intervals of a day or longer (Underwood & Postman, 1960). The theory was admirably testable, and as with any new theory that undergoes rigorous examination, a series of tests revealed that the theory needed shoring up, as we shall see. Second, an analysis by Underwood (1963) of human learning concurred with that by Lawrence (1963) of animal learning, in the view that organisms "code" stimuli in a manner not always consistent with the experimenter's designation; in short, the nominal stimulus is not always the functional stimulus, and Underwood and Lawrence foresaw important implications of this fact for transfer, retention, and forgetting. Third, computerized techniques for presenting materials and processing behavioral data in terms of mathematical models increasingly refined the analysis of short-term retention. It is somewhat ironic that as computers provided innovative means for studying information processing, reaction time (a procedure earlier deemed old-fashioned and rarely used in experimental psychology) was revived as a major behavioral index in this work. However, this new understanding of information processing was accompanied by a growing complexity—as time-dependent features of perception were identified, the distinction between perception and short-term memory became correspondingly blurred. Fourth, rehearsal and other mnemonic operations on materials to be learned were recognized as important aspects of memory processing and were studied directly. Also, with the increased use and understanding of computers, a distinction became common between the operations influencing memory storage and those influencing memory retrieval. Concurrently, a general trend began toward emphasizing aspects of memory processing that appear to be "uniquely human." These aspects include a variety of memorial processes: stages that are conceptually and functionally distinct in paired-associate learning, such as stimulus encoding, selection, and discrimination; response learning, which may or may not involve transformations through coding mechanisms; learning of associations through a variety of mediational schemes; various organizational mechanisms with which humans operate on verbal materials for convenience in storage and subsequent retrieval; special mnemonic techniques; and linguistic influences on learning, transfer, and retention.

Although considerable information has been obtained as to how memories are acquired and retained concurrently with other activities by normal human subjects, a good deal more awaits discovery concerning the nature of forgetting. Beyond this, analysis of memory processing in general is relatively restricted when only normal human subjects are considered. We can expect to acquire a good deal more information about memory processing from psychobiological research with animals and abnormal human subjects.

ORIENTATION OF THE FOLLOWING CHAPTERS

The intent of this book is to discuss issues fundamental to retention and forgetting. Inevitably, my selection of what is and what is not fundamental is tinted by bias, perhaps less than I really would have liked but more than others will tolerate. It is hoped that constraints imposed by the data, from which we shall not stray far, will minimize such bias. Further protection from bias is provided by an approach that reflects at most only a loose conceptual framework, and more often a sort of atheoretical neofunctionalism.

I hold the view that the two major general issues are to identify the sources of forgetting and the factors regulating these sources. At an operational level, we actually can identify several sources of forgetting and several of their regulating factors. Among the clearest sources of forgetting subject to experimental control are the following:

1. The interval that elapses between acquisition of a memory and a test of its retention (with the understanding that it is unidentified or unspecified events occurring during the retention interval that ultimately are responsible for the forgetting)
2. Interference, the acquisition of memories having some attributes in common but some critically different compared with the memory being tested
3. A change in the context, internal or external to the learner, between that which surrounded acquisition of the memory and that prevailing at the time of the test for retention
4. Normal changes in the physiology of the organism, such as aging
5. Abnormal changes in the physiology of the organism, such as traumatic insult to the central nervous system
6. Directed or intentional forgetting.

Regulating factors are more diffuse, defying a potential listing, but we shall encounter many.

At this point, we shall not attempt to clarify or justify any of these sources of forgetting, but these are the sources to which we most often will refer in the following pages, or those that we believe responsible for any given case of forgetting. Bear in mind that these sources may not function independently to produce forgetting in a given circumstance and may have a common underlying basis. It may be noted that the book is not organized in terms of these sources, which reflects a certain lack of confidence in considering them very seriously as even potentially independent. Among the factors apparently regulating these sources are three that seem sufficiently important and general to justify fairly extensive consideration in a later chapter. These factors are (1) events that alleviate forgetting by a mechanism facilitating memory retrieval, (2) the content of a memory, and (3) the "mnemonic preparation" (behaviors to enhance retention or alleviate forgetting) in which an individual engages at some point during or following storage of the memory. By proper analysis, we expect that each of these sources ultimately may be a consequence of a Grand Source (perhaps only one), and similarly, we may end with only a single Grand Regulator of that source. We shall not accomplish this here, to no one's surprise.

What we shall try to accomplish is to consider the sources of forgetting and regulatory factors that promise greatest generality. The hope is to work toward principles of retention and forgetting that may apply equally to the behavior of humans or subhuman species when memory processing occurs under either normal or abnormal circumstances. The generality actually achieved will be disappointing to novice psychologists; and perhaps the term *generality* is itself an overstatement when applied to what actually is accomplished in the following pages. It would not be unfair to say that much of what follows is little more than a discussion of the behavior of college sophomores, monkeys, and rats involving apparently shared requirements of memory processing. Furthermore, one might continue, the behavioral phenomena (and governing principles) involving these and other species are really rather disparate, although considered with more spatial contiguity (i.e., within the same chapters) than usual. I happen to take a rather different view of what is accomplished; and surely each reader must judge for himself or herself. These chapters do represent, nevertheless, an attempt to rectify the problem of seriously inadequate communication among investigators of memory processing who may happen to be working on different aspects of the same topic.

A variety of other issues frequently are raised as fundamental to understanding memory processing and may have considerable bearing on retention and forgetting. These include whether more than one kind of memory processing exists and where in the central nervous system memory processing takes place. These and other issues will arise frequently in our discussion, so some preliminary consideration relating them to our conceptual framework of retention and forgetting is presented later. First, however, we shall discuss briefly why forgetting occurs, in a more general sense than is intended when addressing specific sources of forgetting.

Why Does Forgetting Occur?

If there were no forgetting at all, most other issues concerning memory processing would disappear. The concept of memory still would be needed, but only to distinguish what is learned from among all events encountered. Because we view "forgetting" operationally—as any decrement in the predisposition or immediate capacity to employ what was learned—absence of forgetting would mean that an organism could apply all stored memories with equal probability at any time.

Basically, forgetting may occur for either of two reasons: (1) The memory is no longer present in the precise form it took at original storage, or (2) although it is still maintained in storage with undiminished integrity since original learning, the memory cannot be retrieved. In other words, the cause of forgetting is either that the memory is no longer stored in its original form, or if it is, that it cannot be retrieved as readily as before. Theories assuming the former state attribute the failure in storage to either spontaneous decay or active impairment of the memory by events that follow learning. Theories that account for forgetting in terms of retrieval failure most often view the acquisition of interfering memories as the basis of the retrieval difficulties. Our bias is that forgetting is a failure in retrieval, and we view the theoretical source of forgetting as more general than interference—in this view, forgetting typically is a consequence of the failure of stimulus events noticed at the time of retrieval to match the attributes of the memory, and forgetting induced by interfering learning is encompassed as a special case. Alternative interpretations of forgetting combine storage and retrieval factors. For example, in one, retrieval probability is assumed to decrease and interfering memories to become more likely to dominate as the decay of the target memory proceeds; in another, a stored memory is thought to be dynamic rather than static, and the structure of the memory is constantly changing with each input of information, thus rendering the original memory irretrievable. We shall consider these interpretations later.

We shall find it helpful to consider what sorts of mechanisms organisms have evolved to counteract forgetting. Operationally, forgetting and retention are reciprocal processes and so cannot be defined independently, but we still can look into the mechanisms an organism may employ to oppose forgetting or to compensate for forgetting that is unavoidable. Homeostatic mechanisms are, after all, the rule in nature.

Postman (1963) has discussed conservatory mechanisms that oppose interference with retention of verbal materials. Possibly these conservatory mechanisms are specific to the forgetting of these particular kinds of memories. However, we shall consider mechanisms with similar function that have wider applicability, such as the following: Forgetting generally may be lessened by overlearning, perhaps by providing redundant sources for effective retrieval of memories in spite of some forgetting; memories for certain events in certain organisms seem remarkably resistant to the forces of forgetting, which perhaps is attributable to some special structural disposition of the organism, for example, the memory for a novel gustatory experience when a subsequent noxious visceral event, such as poisoning, occurs; and certain types of events following learning seem to be likely sources to maintain retrieval of a memory in opposition to forgetting—these include varieties of overt and covert rehearsal and occurrence of events that may reactivate the memory to permit such recycling.

Is There More Than One Kind of Memory?

The most parsimonious view of memory would consider only one fundamental store through which memories are processed and catalogued for subsequent retrieval. By such a view, all memories are processed through this store, whether old or new and regardless of the set of receptors and central neural structures through which the information has been coded. This interpretation may not seem consonant with intuition. For instance, after reading any sentence on this page your efficiency in recalling it verbatim will dissipate rapidly, and after a few seconds only the gist of the sentence will remain, although it will remain retrievable in about the same form for some time. Does this mean that the formal, verbatim structure of the sentence is held in a different, more transient memory store than the meaning of the sentence? Or try sampling any new phone number, then recall your own current number and a previous one, and then write down all three. Was your failure in recalling the first number due to its loss from a more transient and fragile memory store than the others? Was it because the first number was sampled only by the visual modality while the other numbers have been heard or spoken from time to time and so are represented in more different forms in your head? Or was it simply due to the difference in the number of times you thought about it, regardless of how or why?

A feature that varies among the many theories or pretheoretical ideas about memory is whether one, two, three, or more stores of memory exist. Some theories assign separate stores of memory to accommodate different forms of information held by a memory; but more often the theoretical basis of separate stores is differences in the temporal characteristics of one's experience with the information, whether the information has been processed for a few seconds or for many weeks. For simplicity, we shall refer to the two most widely used classifications, short-term memory (STM) and long-term memory (LTM). Melton (1963) wrote an especially insightful discussion of such a classification, framed with clear historical perspective, to guide much of the important work that followed on this topic.

Even if they are based only on operational differences, which is our preference, the terms STM and LTM provide a convenient shorthand. STM typically refers to memory for which retrieval is requested after intervals no more than a few minutes in length and sometimes as short as a few seconds. Because experimental inferences cannot be made if all conditions show perfect retention, an STM paradigm must allow a low degree of learning at the beginning of the retention interval. The study of STM with humans is complicated further by the need to occupy subjects enough during the retention interval to prevent them from rehearsing the material. Some interpolated activity that subjects may be required to do clearly interferes with retention, while other activity may have little or no effect, depending on the activity's similarity with the critical material and how much it precludes further processing (e.g., "consolidation," rehearsal) of the material. In a typical LTM study, after learning a task the subject leaves the laboratory and goes about daily activities until tested a day or several days later. So for LTM the subject does not experience any distractor task. Another operational distinction between procedures for studying STM and LTM with humans arises from the scientifically trivial matter of economy. A subject usually is exposed to many more experiences of learning and recall during tests of STM than during tests of LTM, and the simple reason is that a large number of STM tests can be given in a very short time, while the learning time alone required for LTM is considerable. These points illustrate that the study of STM employs a variety of procedures (other than simple retention interval) that are quite different from those used in testing LTM, and these apparently incidental procedural differences actually are important. Differences we observe between STM and LTM may therefore be due to these procedural differences and not to differences in the processing of memories after short and long intervals.

Direct tests of STM in animals obviously do not require procedural measures to control rehearsal, although comparing STM and LTM is difficult in other respects, as with humans. Except for several varieties of the delayed-matching-to-sample task, there are relatively few satisfactory tests of STM with animals. Most information concerning STM in animals has been obtained inferentially through techniques that disrupt memory; for example, an agent that induces amnesia is administered after either short or long intervals following learning and the effects compared.

Conceptual distinctions between STM and LTM reflect related biases. Scientists who believe STM to be a process different from LTM have to consider how they are different. Whereas those who accept only one memory process may hold that interference is responsible for all forgetting, those who believe that there are two stores of memory, STM and LTM, may say that physical perturbation or simple distraction during the period shortly after input accounts for all STM forgetting and that interference applies only to LTM. As the kinds of postulated memory processing increase, so must the postulation of associated mechanisms, and we shall see how this factor expands the divergence among theories of memories.

How Is a Memory Represented Physiologically?

This question has been a constant concern of psychologists having a biological orientation. An answer also is important to physiologists and medical practitioners for two obvious reasons: first, for understanding the total physiology of the organism, and second, for diagnosis and treatment of diseases linked to physiological processes responsible for the control of memory processing. In addition, knowing the physiological basis of a memory and its processing may help in understanding the interrelationship between memory processing and behavior. However, because psychologists are not in agreement on this issue, it is insufficient simply to assert this. Some maintain that memorial behavior may be understood best by analyzing total behavior and its consequences in relation to the environment, without regard to the underlying physiological mechanisms. For example, if one is interested in predicting the rate of learning mathematics in a classroom setting, it is not obvious how it helps to know precisely where the knowledge accumulates in the student's body.

It is difficult, nevertheless, to deny the potential for more rapid understanding of memorial behavior once the issue of physiologic representation is resolved. This resolution would permit the relatively rapid alteration or rejection of ideas, hypotheses, models, and theories of memory. For purposes of illustration, suppose that one could identify specifically a biological entity that is equivalent to an attribute or unit of memory. If so, the knowledge of the temporal flow of modifications in that biological representation immediately would give direction to theories of memory storage and retrieval. If exposure to a new event results in complete formation within milliseconds of a new biological representation, the notion of a temporally dependent and automatic consolidation process becomes relatively unimportant for determining the permanence of learning. However, if the form of the biological representation continues to change for an hour or so, it would be most unwise to omit such a consolidation process from a memory theory. Similarly, if the biological representation is observed to die or otherwise to lose its structural integrity while the animal still is living, then theories of memory should entertain the notion of spontaneous decay of memories. Unfortunately, we are far from reaching this level of physiological knowledge. Even if the possibilities just mentioned were fact, the ultimate behavioral consequences concerning memory could not be derived so simply, as we shall see later. What can be said, though, is that if everything were known about the physiological representation of memory, the work of psychologists in this area would become more like engineering than science.

Ideas of how a memory may be represented physiologically may be considered in terms of an example. Suppose that an organism is exposed to a bell that is followed closely by a puff of air to the eye, inducing a blink. After a number of such sequences, the organism will blink when the bell sounds, whether the air puff is presented or not. The question is, How is the memory for this episode represented? Because it was known that discrete elements of behavior are more influenced by damage to the brain than damage to other parts of the anatomy, the brain seemed the reasonable general location for a physiological representation of memory. This is almost certainly correct. In modern times, the simplest conception of a physiological model of memory is that some sort of connection or groove develops between the cells in the brain that represent the bell and those that represent the blink. Models of this type, called "switchboard theories" (John, 1967, 1972), are quite inadequate, for reasons that we will consider later.

Lashley has been perhaps the most influential individual scientist concerned with the physiological basis of learning in the history of psychology. From a wide spectrum of studies that included extensive inquiry into the physiological locus of memory, Lashley concluded that the simple reflex model of memory that treated a memory as a single bond or connection simply would not do. He took instead a view of memory as "a reorganization of a vast system of associations involving the interrelations of hundreds of thousands or millions of neurons" (Lashley, 1950, p. 474). Lashley came to view memory as a matter of multiple representations in the brain, possibly unique patterns of excitation or activity among a group of neurons. This view has been given elegant elaboration by John (1967, 1972), who has the advantage of more sophisticated data than Lashley's.

At a somewhat different level of inquiry are questions concerning the specific structural changes that take place, perhaps in a single neuron, when a memory is stored. Probably the action takes place at the synapse and involves either a chemical or a morphological change that modulates some electrochemical modification in the substance that controls transmission of neural impulses. Some special protein, which is more important for memory than any other protein, is suspected to be the molecular-level basis of these events. Finally, a very pertinent question is whether physiological representations of memories take the same form throughout their existence. For example, recently acquired memories may be stored in electrochemical form, while memories that have been maintained for longer periods may have more permanent structural representation.

Few principles concerning the structural representation of memories may be described as well established. Indeed, it is not certain that all memories are stored in neurons—it is quite possible, for example, that glial cells serve a similar storage function. At present, however, these sorts of issues are largely the province of biochemists and neuroanatomists, and at present they make relatively little contact with the behavioral issues of memory processing to be discussed in this book.

What Conditions are Conducive to Remembering: When Will Stored Memories Be Retrieved?

In this book, we place considerable emphasis on the retrieval of memories, which in my view is a major process that is insufficiently understood. For both humans and animals, the probability of retrieving stored information depends on a number of specific critical factors. These factors may be classified generally as enhancing the similarity between the organism's environment (internal and external) during memory storage and at the time when the memory is to be retrieved. A "memory to be retrieved" includes information not only about a specific response to a particular stimulus but also about the context in which that response was paired with that stimulus.

It is no accident that the introduction began with a brief statement on the influence of alcohol on memory, because many effects on memory processing of this and other common drugs can be attributed to changes in internal state induced by their ingestion. Simply, such changes in the internal environment may cause events occurring under inebriation to be irretrievable when the subject is sober, and vice versa. We shall return to this issue in Chapter 2.

Simple Retention

Common reference to "memory" implies the maintenance of stored information for periods of varying length following a memory's initial acquisition—for years on some occasions, for only seconds on others—and that the length of the retention interval will help determine the influence of a stored memory on behavior. We know that forgetting occurs regardless, or in spite of, experimental operations. Thus, we define studies of "simple retention" as memory experiments invoking no extratask manipulations (other than differing retention intervals) to modify retention. Such experiments may be contrasted with those in which the subject acquires conflicting memories, either prior to or subsequent to the material that later is to be remembered, or with circumstances in which the animal's physiology is modified.

Although one may acquire interesting normative data with tests of simple retention, analysis of memory processing is very limited when the sole variable is length of retention interval. Therefore, we will treat the retention interval associated with simple retention as one of several empirically determined sources of forgetting and examine it, and others, in terms of how its effect is modified or regulated by orthogonal factors. The fundamental features of the effects of retention interval length are well known. For example, forgetting is most rapid soon after learning; retention is usually, but not always, a monotonic decreasing function of the retention interval; and some characteristics of retention are different after a short interval (a few seconds or minutes) than after a long interval (a few days or years). We shall see that such basic relationships have had central importance in the analysis of memory processing.

Forgetting Caused by Interfering Memories

Although there is widespread agreement that the most general source of forgetting is interference caused by other learning, disagreement arises in identifying the specific mechanisms of the interference and exactly what constitutes an interfering memory. Psychologists generally admit, however, that interference in retention is caused by both previously acquired memories (proactive interference, or "PI") and subsequent learning (retroactive interference, or "RI"). The role of interfering memories in retention depends on a number of factors. Two factors are especially notable: the degree of similarity between the material to be remembered and the interfering material; and certain temporal relationships among the occasion of acquiring the interfering memory, that of acquiring the memory to be retrieved, and that at which retention is assessed. There is a paradox of which we must be aware regarding the effect of similarity. Typically, the greater decrement in retention is found when interfering memories are similar to the critical memory. Yet under some circumstances retention may be increased by the occurrence of events similar to those that constitute the critical memory, and the greater the similarity, the larger the effect. No satisfactory simple resolution is in sight, but a number of memory phenomena seem less mysterious if we are aware of the paradox.

The effect of interference on forgetting has been analyzed most extensively in terms of memories of isolated verbal units. Interference with memories of more complex verbal material (sentences, paragraphs, or stories), and with memories of discrete motor movements also has been studied with humans, but these experiments are relatively few and rarely analytical enough to influence theory (an exception is Kintsch, 1974).

The limited study of interference in animal memory also has rarely been analytical. However, a substantial number of studies in the literature may qualify as investigations of the influence of interference on forgetting in animals if we take the view that an animal must acquire new memories in order to adapt successfully to changes in task contingencies. Thus, any experiments that test animals following experimental extinction, reversal, or other change in reinforcement conditions are, to some extent, tests of the effect of interference on retention. As an example, suppose that an animal learns to discriminate a circle from a square when a food pellet is paired with the circle and nothing is paired with the square. If the circle and square are presented again but the food is paired with the square, not the circle (or perhaps food is not present at all), we may expect that retention of the first memory, circle–food and square–no food, will be subject to interference from a second memory that represents the new reinforcement contingencies.

Compared to the study of interference and forgetting in humans, these animal investigations have an inherent peculiarity that the reader already may have observed: Unlike humans, animals obviously cannot be instructed exactly what they are to remember. So if the animal first learns that food is paired only with the circle, and later learns that it is paired only with the square, we cannot know which of these two memories the animal is "trying" to retrieve when the circle and square are presented for a test. In other words, with animals we sometimes cannot know what is interfering with what, so we cannot distinguish PI and RI. We shall see, however, that the flexibility possible in manipulating conditions of retrieval in animal memory experiments compensates for this apparent disadvantage. Because instructions about what is to be remembered are potential retrieval cues, their use causes the loss of a degree of freedom from the experimental manipulation of retrieval. While a human subject would be pretty suspicious if he or she were not instructed what to do in the retention test, a rat or monkey would not give the absence of such instructions a second thought.

SUMMARY AND CONCLUSIONS

This chapter introduced the orientation that guides the analysis of retention and forgetting in subsequent chapters. Included were a few basic definitions: "memory" as an organism's multidimensional representation of an episode (and not as a process), "retention" and "forgetting" defined operationally, and "memory storage" and "memory retrieval" as the hypothetical processes responsible for input and output of information about an episode. Joint consideration of research on humans and animals was emphasized as basic to the orientation of this book, as was joint consideration of ideas derived from these areas. Also emphasized were the evolution of modern concepts from ideas put forth during pre-science history, when memory processing was studied for its application as a skill, and the empirical and theoretical background of the science of memory processing.

The early neglect of psychological studies and theories concerning retention and forgetting was discussed in relation to several factors: the apparent belief of Pavlov in the essential permanence of conditioning and his inclination to apply inhibition constructs to account for changes in the probability of manifestation of a particular acquired behavior; the utilization of behavioral tasks insensitive to detection of forgetting among lower animals; and the preoccupation with developing global theories of learning and behavior, the emphasis on motivational constructs in these theories, and an apparent reluctance to incorporate in these theories functional characteristics of transfer and forgetting derived from experiments in human verbal learning.

Among the factors that ultimately enhanced the psychobiological study of memory storage and memory retrieval were the appearance of experimental techniques for studying a wider variety of sources of forgetting (e.g., drugs, electroconvulsive shock, and other "amnesic agents"), theories linking the consequences of these sources to newly discovered facts about neurophysiology, and a number of conceptual and technical advances in the study of human memory processing.

Finally, a few basic issues of memory processing were discussed briefly to illustrate the conceptual framework underlying the remainder of the book. From this point of view, the task is to develop principles for identifying sources of forgetting and factors regulating these sources, through analysis of retention and forgetting among all organisms. Within this framework, emphasis is given to the hypothetical process of memory retrieval as the most fundamental determinant of retention and forgetting.

2
Contextual Determinants of Retention

Historically, students of memory processing have accepted a broad determinant of retention: the degree of similarity between the context of learning (memory storage) and the context of the retention test (memory retrieval). In this book, we treat this general determinant as a principle of memory processing and orient our interpretation of the facts of memory processing around it. The clear intention, though, is to use it—this ancient principle of the importance of stimulus similarity—in the interpretation of memory retrieval, but to apply it only as a pretheoretical conceptual framework, a point of view not yet formalized as theory.

There is nothing new in the suggestion that stimulus context is intimately involved in the development and retrieval of a memory. This suggestion reverberates through the writings of leading theorists who may differ widely in research orientation. Both Lashley (1950) and Underwood (1966b) noted that associations generally must be contextually dependent. Postman (1968) also considered associations involving stimulus context important in his analysis. When Skinner (1938) described the function of the discriminative stimulus in instrumental learning as "setting the occasion for a response" (p. 241), he implicated contextual factors as further determinants of the response (when the discriminative stimulus already is present).

Thorndike (1931) noted that "if I attempt to analyze a man's entire mind, I find connections of varying strength between (a) situations, elements of situations, and compounds of situations and (b) responses, readiness to respond, facilitations, inhibitions and directions of responses" (p. 133). McGeoch (1932, 1942) considered one of two major sources of forgetting to be differences in the contexts of learning and testing (the other, of course, was retroactive interference). Guthrie (1952), commenting on Pavlov's alimentary conditioning of dogs, notes that "the dog is responding not only to the food and to the bell, not only to his state of hunger with its attendent stomach contractions and general muscular tension, but to his posture, and to his own movements through the movement-produced stimuli in which they result" (p. 83).

Contemporary scholars concerned with human retention increasingly have emphasized the role of retrieval in general and the role of contextual cues in particular (e.g., Anderson & Bower, 1972, 1974; Norman & Rumelhart, 1970, pp. 25–27; Postman, 1971, p. 68; Tulving, 1968; Tulving & Thomson, 1973; Watkins & Tulving, 1975). Keppel (1972) and Postman (1971) note instances in which retention of verbal materials has declined as a consequence of changes in surprisingly mundane features of the environment, such as the nature of the experimental room and the color of the ink used to print the words. Rand and Wapner (1967) reported that a change between a human's physical position during learning and his position during the retention test (standing vs. lying down) was accompanied by a retention deficit. Because of such data, Underwood (1969) has suggested that important attributes of a memory may be contextual in nature.

Estes (1955) introduced a particularly influential model, perhaps the earliest systematic analysis incorporating contextual features as an explicit determinant of retention. Subsequently, significant evolution and application of this model were achieved by Bower in terms of verbal memory processing (Bower, 1967, 1972). In a more general consideration of memory processing, Estes (1970, p. 12) has suggested that changes in the stimulus context are likely to result in a retention deficit (cf. Estes, 1955), but cautions, however, that such stimulus change effects will be dependent on the organism's attention to general context (p. 19). Shortly we shall consider further cautions in assessing the role of context in retention. Estes' (1970) description of the mechanism of anticipation also is interesting for its similarity to expressions used here and elsewhere to describe the role of contextual cues in memory retrieval. Estes states that "if the sight of food has preceded the taste on an earlier occasion, then the sight of food will lead to reinstatement of memory of a representation of the unconditioned stimulus, which will in turn initiate facilitatory feedback, thus increasing the likelihood that the response sequence leading from the sight of food to ingestion will again run off without interruption" (p. 11). Heron (1951) considered similar issues concerning the role of stimulus context in the memory of lower animals in a delayed-response task.

The precise manner in which contextual features may determine one's memorial representation of an episode has not been established. There seem to be two major alternatives. Either an event is represented differently when it occurs in different contexts, or a common representation is maintained for separate occurrences of an event, with its occurrence in different episodes delineated by memory attributes (or "tags") representing the unique features of the context. This distinction has been drawn most clearly in terms of verbal memory processing, perhaps because homographs provide a more convenient tool for empirical tests of these notions than is available for more biologically oriented studies. By illustration, suppose that CARDINAL occurring in a cleric-related episode is less likely to be recalled in a context concerning birds. Is this because the subject's memorial representation of the word is different and quite separate in these two cases owing to the semantic–affective variance of the individual's code for this word, and so what is aroused for retrieval is not precisely what was stored? Or is it because the constellation of cleric-related contextual attributes makes no contact with that concerning birds? This issue, sometimes termed the question of transsituational identity (Tulving & Thomson, 1973; Watkins & Tulving, 1975), will reappear frequently in this book.

Many researchers, therefore, have suggested that contextual stimuli may determine retention, and it hardly could be otherwise. Moreover, lower animals are especially dependent on contextual stimuli to identify what must be remembered, in a manner analogous to human dependence on instructions.

A framework for studying the role of context in memory retrieval is presented next, followed by consideration of boundary conditions delimiting the influence of contextual cues on memory retrieval and separating these influences from effects on other aspects of behavior.

A CONCEPTUAL FRAMEWORK FOR DISCUSSING MEMORY PROCESSING

In our view, a memory is a representation of the collection of events that constitute an episode of an organism's experience. The structure of this representation is multiple, including a collection of relatively independent attributes of the memory, corresponding to events of the episode. For any given organism, the specific nature of these attributes will depend on the particular means of encoding information that happen to be dominant for that organism. For humans, especially adults, much encoding is verbal, and otherwise more attributes probably are visual or auditory rather than tactual or gustatory. Of course, some memories for humans would seem to include olfactory attributes, especially for memories representing childhood episodes or a particularly strange environment. Many animals, on the other hand, are likely to be dominated by olfactory attributes that help represent aversive and appetitive episodes or distinguish home trails from those of predators.

Clearly, a potentially large number of isolated events for any given episode may be recognized and attended to by the organism. Of the events noticed by the organism, how many actually become encoded as a part of the memory for that episode? The answer depends on the past history of that organism in combination with its perceptual capacities. Although it is not necessary for us to know for each organism and each memory precisely what the attributes are in order to apply this principle toward understanding memory processing, some characteristics of the interaction among these attributes must be isolated for more effective interpretation. As a first step in this regard, we assume that memory attributes may function independently. Thus, to retrieve a special target attribute or a complete memory, one need not arouse the unique combination of all attributes that may represent collectively the stimulus "compound" that is identical to the external and internal world that existed during learning. Rather, any of a variety of separate attributes may act independently in a variety of different combinations to retrieve the memory. In other words, we view stimulus selection as generally more germane than stimulus compounding for memory storage and retrieval.

An important implication of this view is that the retrieval cues for a given memory need not include the nominal conditioned stimulus or discriminative stimulus. Instead, it is probable that portions of the stimulus context that are redundant for learning the task may be effective agents in retrieving the episode of the learning experience, including the solution to the task. For example, a subject taught in a particular room in the psychology building to blink her eye upon hearing a tone, or to say DXZ whenever LMN appears on the screen, may retrieve the memory of that lesson together with its specific contingencies merely upon reexposure to that room.

A Broad Mechanism of Memory Retrieval

Now we may state the general pretheoretical framework within which we view the process of memory retrieval (also see Spear, 1971, 1973, 1976). The memory is stored as a collection of separate attributes corresponding to separate events that constitute an episode registered by the organism. For the memory to be retrieved, a sufficient number (or kind) of the memory's attributes must be aroused contiguously. A given attribute will be aroused when the organism notices an event in its internal or external environment that is sufficiently similar to the event originally represented by that attribute. Attributes (including the target attribute in particular) also will be aroused when the entire memory is retrieved. It is possible that an individual attribute may be aroused following the arousal of another individual attribute without arousing the entire memory. We will address this "redintegration" issue, and others like it, in later portions of this book.

The Process and the Effectiveness of Memory Retrieval

We may distinguish variables that influence the *effectiveness* of retrieval from those that influence the retrieval *process* itself. Like any process, the ultimate act of retrieving a memory in order to influence behavior involves a systematic series of component actions. For memory retrieval, these actions undoubtedly are physiological, occurring largely in the neural and endocrine systems of an organism. If any of these component actions malfunctions, retrieval of a memory will not occur because the process has been disrupted. Alternatively, the retrieval process may function adequately, but retrieval of a given memory may fail nevertheless: such ineffective retrieval may occur whenever the organism notices an insufficient number of events that correspond to, and hence evoke, attributes of that memory.

Suppose, for example, a rat is conditioned to jump onto a ledge at the sound of a bell in order to avoid a shock. If the rat is treated with a hypothetical drug that alters the threshold of firing for all neurons controlling auditory memories, it may not retrieve the memory of the original training episode (and hence the target attribute of jumping onto the ledge), regardless of how similar all circumstances are to that episode, because the processing of all memories involving an auditory component has been disrupted. Compare this malfunction of processing with a situation in which appropriate stimuli are insufficient or ineffective. A similar rat in a normal physiological state (i.e., no drug) presented with the same bell and ledge, but in a different laboratory, may retrieve the memory too slowly to avoid the shock, or it may fail totally in retrieving the memory. Here the failure is not in the process but simply because the odors, sounds, and sights of the new laboratory do not correspond sufficiently to the events represented as attributes of the original memory. We may say that the retrieval process probably is intact, but the effectiveness of retrieval is deficient because of insufficient retrieval cues.

For our purposes, a contextual cue is any event noticed by an organism, *with the specific exclusion of the features that are required to define evidence of memory acquisition (original learning)*. In experimental tests of memory, this would exclude, for example, the specific stimulus for a response in a paired-associate task, the specific conditioned stimulus (CS) for classical conditioning, or the discriminative stimulus in instrumental conditioning. Where a discrimination is involved, both the CS+ and CS−, or correct and incorrect stimuli (S+ and S−), would be excluded. Except for the response used as the index of learning, all other events noticed by an organism would be contextual stimuli, including the proprioceptive stimuli that are consequences of the response. Of special importance here is the fact that a contextual cue has latent capacity for retrieval.

Contemporary context and prior cueing to influence memory retrieval. Differences between the context accompanying acquisition of the memory and the context present when retrieval of the memory is required may cause forgetting. For a variety of reasons, such differences become more likely as the interval between acquisition and retrieval of a memory lengthens:

1. Sensory consequences of training dissipate (rapidly), neurochemical and hormonal consequences dissipate (somewhat more slowly), and in certain cases internal homeostatic responses to these two physiological effects may add to the stimulus change.
2. The internal environment also changes on the basis of preprogrammed factors that may be progressive (e.g., aging) or cyclical (e.g., estrous).

3. The external environment changes because of either rhythmic (e.g., daily or seasonal) or irregular (e.g., the weather) factors.
4. New memories may be acquired that, though different in certain critical respects, may have attributes in common with the memory to be retrieved and so may compete (interfere) at the time of retrieval.
5. Idiosyncratic responses that preceded acquisition of the memory, including some caused by the preceding factors, may be less likely to recur prior to the occasion of memory retrieval.

Such changes in context may produce forgetting for either of two general reasons. First, a sufficient number, or the proper kind, of memory attributes may fail to be activated because of the absence during testing of stimuli that were present during learning. Second, through notice of stimuli during the retention test that were not present during learning, attributes of conflicting memories may be aroused: Retrieval of a conflicting memory may interfere with retrieval of the critical memory through competition.

As noted earlier, a common consequence of changes in the stimulus context is the introduction of novel stimuli, which, in turn, elicit unconditioned behaviors, such as attentional or investigatory responses, which may have the effect of decreasing retention performance. The control and isolation of such effects is important for the analysis of memory processing, but they are not considered a portion of the memorial consequences of contextual change.

The implication of this reasoning is that forgetting might be alleviated by modifying the context that exists at the time of the retention test in such a way as to make it more similar to the context of memory acquisition. Thus two classes of observations could provide evidence favorable to this point of view: if forgetting either is increased by contextual change or is decreased by eliminating contextual change.

The important changes in exteroceptive stimuli are those that are noticed at the time of the retention test. This is also the case for interoceptive contextual stimuli. Manipulations providing the latter, however, may also be initiated in the animal or person prior to the retention test through a technique that we term *prior cueing*.

By "prior cueing," we refer to the presentation of events to an individual prior to the retention test, events that cease before the test itself. For example, suppose a rat has learned that upon the occurrence of a tone, it must jump a hurdle to avoid receiving a footshock. Suppose further that this rat then is exposed to a source of forgetting (e.g., a long retention interval) such that a test would reveal retention decrement. We may find that presenting this animal with a footshock in a neutral apparatus 5 minutes before a retention test lessens the retention decrement. Assuming that through proper control we have eliminated performance factors of a trivial (i.e., non-memorial) nature arising from this footshock, there appear to be two possible reasons for its influence. The first is that the internal state or context of the animal at the time of the retention test may have become more like that which prevailed during learning because of physiological consequences (e.g., hormonal) that persisted from the time of the footshock until the time of the retention test, thus increasing the effectiveness of memory retrieval. The second possibility is that footshock alone may have been sufficient to cause memory retrieval and, because of the relatively short 5-minute interval, the memory continued to be accessible at the time of the retention test. We will enlarge upon this distinction later, but mention it here to point out the possibility that to influence memory retrieval, prior cueing may act through the same or different mechanisms as changes in the contemporary context.

A major advantage of the prior-cueing technique is that consequential unconditioned responses (e.g., investigatory or arousal) are less likely to be elicited (and more easily controlled if elicited) than when the contemporary context of testing is modified.

Intratask and extratask contextual stimuli.   To consider the operations of contextual stimuli, we should discuss both intratask and extratask stimuli. Intratask stimuli are events to which subjects must attend during storage of the memory because these events are intrinsic to the episode being learned (though not necessary for measurement of the learning, as mentioned earlier). A rat that learns to jump a hurdle in order to avoid a shock must attend to the shock; a human given a series of sentences from which she must later recall the direct object of each is effectively required to attend to other portions of each sentence as well. Extratask contextual stimuli, in contrast, are explicitly redundant to learning. Attention to these stimuli does not benefit performance on the learning task and could impair performance; in any case, such attention is not necessary for effective learning. For example, the rat learning to avoid shock by hurdle jumping may always experience these contingencies in a *humid room* with a *musty smell*; a human may learn a list of words in a *cold room*, instructed to do so by a *grouchy professor who coughs* continually.

An issue of central importance is whether intra- and extratask contextual stimuli combine with the nominal CS or discriminative stimulus to form a unique stimulus compound. Alternatively, if no such compound is formed, the subject may ignore other stimuli and select, for functional purposes, the signal (or restricted combination of signals) that best predicts the occurrence of some critical consequence. I prefer the latter interpretation: The role of contextual stimuli in memory retrieval is determined by a stimulus selection process where the contextual stimuli function independently. In fact, stimulus selection has been well analyzed empirically, and is a ubiquitous phenomenon observed in both animals and humans (for reviews, see D'Amato, 1970; Lawrence, 1963; Richardson, 1972a, 1976; Rudy, 1974; Underwood, 1963). In spite of its seeming omnipotence, however, stimulus selection is not inevitable and is rarely, if ever, complete (Farthing & Hearst, 1970). Also, there is good evidence for stimulus compounding (e.g., Rescorla, 1973; Weiss, 1972; Whitlow & Wagner, 1972). The existence of stimulus compounding as such is not damaging to our view of memory retrieval unless one holds the extreme interpretation that *all* contextual events combine with the CS to form a single compound. Aside from this unlikely position, compounding—and indeed, some degree of compounding cannot be denied—may be accommodated in our framework by simply altering the estimated number of psychologically independent contextual stimuli for a given situation. The issue of whether contextual stimuli act through memory storage as part of a stimulus compound or as independent attributes of a memory is the general case of the question of transsituational identity, alluded to earlier (cf. Watkins & Tulving, 1975).

It is difficult to make a general statement concerning which episodic stimuli the organism must heed at the time the memory of an episode enters storage. Separate consideration of each individual episode being stored is inefficient, however. For our purposes, we may estimate that contextual stimuli include events that formally define the laboratory learning task: Typically, stimuli that are included or implied in published descriptions of experimental method are prime examples. In animal learning, this encompasses aspects of the discriminanda, training compartment, manipulanda, reinforcer, experimental room, and handling procedures. For humans, contextual stimuli include the experimenter, the location and apparatus for the task, instructions given the subject, and all events to which the subject must respond during the task.

Limits on the Influence of Contextual Cues on Retention

There must inevitably be some change in the stimulus context between acquisition of behavior and the test of retention. However, this change does not always mean that the subject will fail to retrieve the memory required in this situation. Consequently, some brief comments are appropriate concerning probable limits on the role of stimulus change in memory retrieval.

1. Performance deficits caused by stimulus change are not all memory deficits. Performance deficit also may result from the disruptive effects of stimulus change on responding or on perceptual processing of critical stimuli. Bindra (1959, 1961) considered the former in his analysis of decrements in instrumental responding accompanying change in contextual cues. Such response decrement, according to Bindra, is primarily a consequence of the introduction of new stimuli—perhaps with unconditioned exploratory responses. Such unconditioned investigatory behavior often impairs performance by competing with the desired instrumental response. Alternatively, change in contextual stimuli might increase orienting behavior toward new stimuli and divert attention from the stimuli that previously controlled behavior (e.g., Veronin, Leontiev, Luria, Sokolov, & Vinogradova, 1965), hence disrupting the input of stimuli. We must exclude both of these sources, disruption of response output and stimulus input, if per-

formance deficits induced by stimulus change are to be interpreted as memory effects.

2. Humphrey (1933) reported a classic example of how memory retrieval may be impaired dramatically by changes in context. Human subjects experiencing a shock paired with a specific tone were conditioned to raise their hands to that tone. Subjects tested with the melody "Home Sweet Home" (in which the particular tone occurs 14 times) showed poor performance. This effect has been called the arpeggio paradox and may be viewed as a retrieval failure. Hull (1943, p. 372) interpreted this effect as an instance of stimulus compounding caused by the persistent aftereffects of preceding tones at the time the critical tones occurred during the melody.

Two cautions are appropriate here. First, certain changes in contextual stimuli in fact may alter perceptual coding of the conditioned or discriminative stimulus. This is consistent with the view from some studies of verbal memory processing that the coded meaning of an item depends on its context (e.g., strawberry *jam* vs. traffic *jam*). In this respect, the interpretations of theorists such as Tulving and Martin (e.g., Martin, 1975; Tulving & Thomson, 1973; Watkins & Tulving, 1975; see Chapter 8) are like that of Hull. But if contextual stimuli were stored as independent attributes of a memory, one might prefer to treat such changes in perception independently of forgetting and memory retrieval. Second, we must be cautious in interpreting the influence of contextual change on recognition (the measure used to define the arpeggio paradox) because the role of retrieval processes in recognition performance is unclear and may be minimal (see Underwood, 1972). We shall return frequently to these points, especially in Chapter 8.

3. Not all stimuli are equally likely to yield memory decrements when changed. Contextual stimuli that are attended to and hence influence behavior when changed may be selected readily if the experimenter is familiar with the species he is testing (cf. Asratian, 1965, Chap. 4). However, one cannot expect to be perfectly accurate in assessing a priori which stimuli are crucial to maintaining behavior. Depending on the organism and the task, some drastic changes in contextual stimuli may leave performance undisturbed. In tests on both the grain beetle and the salamander, for example, surprisingly little forgetting has been attributed to the dramatic physical changes that define metamorphosis. Planaria reportedly have shown significant retention of habituation, classical conditioning, and discrimination following regeneration of 50% or so of tissue that had been removed. Although debated by some, this interpretation is held firmly by several scientists (see Dyal, 1971). Similar results are reported for phylogenetically higher animals. Chen, Aranda, and Luco (1970) trained cockroaches to avoid shock by lifting their legs to a certain height. After achieving a criterion of 100% avoidances in a 10-trial session, two of the cockroaches had their heads cut off. On intuitive grounds, it seems reasonable to expect that the loss of one's head would cause some retention loss due (at least) to severe alteration of the

perceived stimulus context (although not necessarily alteration in the perception of the CS and UCS; in this case, the CS was light footshock, the UCS a strong footshock). Nevertheless, when these two cockroaches were tested 24 hours later they still avoided on 100% of their test trials. It is notable that naive headless cockroaches do not "avoid" 100% of the time, although they can be trained to do so.

The point is that, first, change in contextual stimuli will affect forgetting only if these stimuli had been attended to during learning, and second, even though attended to, different contextual stimuli may differ in their saliency for control of memory retrieval.

4. For certain contextual stimuli, the effects of stimulus change are conditional on other factors in the experimental situation—performance decrements occur under some circumstances but not under others. For example, slight modifications of the apparatus used for conditioned fear in rats have been found to decrease test performance when introduced shortly after training but not after a longer retention interval (McAllister & McAllister, 1971). A similar effect has been reported in retention of appetitive conditioning (Perkins & Weyant, 1958; Steinman, 1967).

The remainder of this chapter is a selective review and evaluation of information exemplifying conditions under which contextual stimuli may influence memory processing.

Summary

Let us summarize the basic beliefs and conclusions discussed earlier before examining empirical evidence concerning contextual stimuli. Contextual stimuli are those that are noticed by an individual during the acquisition of a memory, with the exclusion of stimuli such as conditioned or discriminative stimuli that are necessary to determine that the memory was acquired. Viewing memory as a multidimensional conglomerate of attributes, we expect retrieval to occur when the individual notices a sufficient number or an appropriate kind of events that correspond to the attributes of the memory to be retrieved. The effectiveness of memory retrieval depends on the similarity between events noticed at the time of retrieval and those represented previously as attributes of the critical memory. The greater the similarity, the better the retention. Memory retrieval still may fail, however, if the *process* of retrieval is not functioning properly.

Retention and forgetting may be modified by altering the context of the retention test. Retention may be improved by prior cueing, the technique where the subject is exposed to certain relevant stimuli prior to the retention test. Contextual stimuli of importance to retrieval may be external or internal to the animal and intrinsic or separable from the learned task. Probably the effect of contextual change also may depend on degree of learning, especially if stimulus selection is altered as degree of learning increases (Richardson, 1976). While factors such as retention interval and degree of learning may help determine the extent to which contextual change influences retention and forgetting, they may equally be viewed as important empirical questions about contextual change.

INTRATASK STIMULUS CONTEXT

Effects on Memory Retrieval in Animals

Riccio, Urda, and Thomas (1966) varied an incidental feature of the apparatus between training and testing and obtained results suggesting that context influences memory retrieval. Hungry pigeons obtained seed (on a VI–120-sec schedule) by pecking an illuminated disk on the wall. Quite incidentally to this task, the floor of the apparatus was tilted at a 30° angle for some pigeons while they were learning; for other pigeons, the floor was level (0° tilt). Twenty-four hours after training was completed, the pigeons were given a generalization test in which all aspects of the task remained constant, except that the floor was tilted to an angle of 0°, 10°, or 30°. The results indicated that retrieval of the memory representing the training episode was more effective the more similar the tilt of the floor at the time of testing to the tilt at the time of training: Pigeons trained with the floor tilted at 30° responded most at the same angle and progressively less at smaller angles; those trained with a 0° tilt responded most when tested at 0° and progressively less with steeper angles.

Obviously, alternative interpretations may be applied to the observations made by Riccio and his associates. For instance, the pigeons may have acquired specific body orientations to accommodate the particular angle of the floor during training, and any change in angle during testing may have required adjustment of the body position, which, in turn, may have retarded pecking efficiency. The interpretation we prefer, however, is that these results provide a particularly vivid example of how the degree of similarity between the intratask contextual cues present during learning and those present during the retention test influence memory retrieval: As similarity between test and learning context decreased, so did pecking performance.

Reinforcement conditions as contextual stimuli. It has been observed that there is an appropriate level of behavior associated with a given reinforcer magnitude. For example, rats trained to run to a goal for one pellet of food tend to stabilize at a particular running speed. Similarly, rats trained to run for a nine-pellet reward tend to stabilize at a different, slightly faster speed. Spear (1967) reviewed studies that investigated the effects of changing the magnitude of the reinforcer between learning (memory storage) and testing (memory retrieval). Rats trained to run to either of two magnitudes of reinforcer required about the same amount of practice to stabilize at the level of behavior appropriate to their particular magnitude of reinforcer. When switched to a common low-level reinforcer or no reinforcer at all, the performance of the two groups of rats declined to a common level. Finally—and this is the key result—when both groups were presented the same (higher) magnitude of reinforcer, but it was a magnitude that one of the groups had previously trained on, the group that had previously received that magnitude reached the appropriate level of performance sooner than the other group. The magnitude of the reinforcer functioned as a contextual stimulus, facilitating memory retrieval for the group of rats that had experienced that particular magnitude during learning. Thus, performance appropriate to current reinforcer magnitude is attained more readily by rats that previously have received that magnitude. But if another, new reinforcer magnitude is presented instead of reinstating the original, animals do not differ in their rates of approach speed, regardless of their original reinforcer magnitude.

A comprehensive theory encompassing this and similar effects of reinforcement schedules has been elaborated by Capaldi (e.g., 1971). One fundamental idea underlying this theory is that performance following a given number of nonrewarded trials will depend on the number of previous occasions on which the animal encountered a similar number of nonreinforced trials followed by a food reward on the next trial. As a very general summary of this aspect of Capaldi's theory, one may say that performance during an extinction treatment depends on the similarity between the sequential circumstances of that treatment and corresponding attributes of similar, previously acquired memories that, however, had included a reinforcer attribute.

Equally common are data indicating that the occurrence of negative reinforcers also may constitute an important contextual cue. In Chapter 8, we shall discuss examples in which punishing footshock may maintain or facilitate retrieval of memories that include such punishment as an attribute. For now, it provides an opportunity to emphasize the boundaries of generalization regarding contextual cues. We want to call attention to the existence of studies showing results inconsistent with the degree of significance of contextual cues claimed in this chapter. We generally view these studies as unconvincing, but shall find it useful to describe them on occasion, together with positive evidence.

A simple test of the notion that stimulus consequences of punishment may serve as effective contextual cues to facilitate retrieval of memories that involve similar punishment would be the following: First, train animals on a task using appetitive reinforcers, giving half of the animals intermittent punishment; at the retention test, test half of each of these groups with intermittent presentation of the punishment source and half without. If the internal (physiological) consequences of the punishment served as a contextual cue, we would expect better retention for animals punished during both training and testing and for animals given punishment on neither occasion, compared with animals punished during training but not testing or vice versa.

An experiment by Ni (1934) approached these conditions but yielded results inconsistent with our interpretation. Ni, a student of Lashley, was interested in the absolute effects of providing punishment for errors during training and testing. He trained 120 food-deprived rats to run a complex maze with seven choice points for milk-soaked bread as a reinforcer, with half the rats given footshock each time they made an incorrect turn at a choice point and half not given footshock. Relearning trials were given 30 days later, with half of each of the original groups punished by footshock for errors and half not punished. Ni found, however, that the animals trained and tested without punishment required nearly twice as many trials as the animals given punishment during either acquisition or the retention test, and eight times as many trials as the animals both trained and tested with punishment. This result may be reconciled with our conceptual framework on the basis of a number of factors: Throughout the retention interval, all the rats were given trials in a straight alley for food reward, and because no punishment was presented during this interpolated experience, the consequential interference with retention may have been greatest for the animals trained and tested without punishment; the degree of original learning may have been too high (later in this chapter, see the effect of degree of learning on state-dependent learning); the influence of contextual cues may depend on the length of the retention interval; and so on. Also, we shall discuss later results consistent with the notion that punishing footshock during appetitive conditioning can serve as a contextual cue and promote retention. Nevertheless, Ni's results are based on a substantial study, and because of their inconsistency with the argument presented here they warrant mention.

General apparatus features as contextual stimuli. It is known that whenever an apparatus is changed, however insignificant the change may appear to the experimenter, and however slight or negligible the change in the CS or discriminative stimulus that presumably controls the behavior, the performance of even a well-trained animal may be disrupted dramatically (see McAllister & McAllister, 1971). There can be no doubt that much of this disruption may be traced to the animal's response to novelty, as discussed earlier. However, it is likely that memory retrieval also is disrupted, perhaps particularly in cases involving less well-established memories. For example, two studies have been published in which rats first learned to turn in a particular direction in a T-maze, then were tested in a different T-maze after various retention intervals (Chiszar & Spear, 1969; Zentall, 1970). These studies show that even when the same turn continues to be reinforced, a previously acquired memory of the proper turn is less likely to be manifested in behavior if the apparatus is changed. Similarly, Miller (1960) found that rats' prior experience in receiving footshocks made the shocks less effective as punishment, but only if this prior experience occurred in the identical apparatus used for testing; if the same type of footshocks were administered in a different apparatus, their potential as punishment was hardly affected. Perhaps the rats acquired a memory representing particular devices for minimizing the effects of shock and this memory was retrieved less effectively under the unfamiliar circumstances of the new apparatus.

Proprioceptive feedback as a contextual stimulus.   The importance of proprioceptive feedback as a cue probably is restricted. For example, animals that have a well-established memory of a discrimination task, such as running through a maze, will show nearly perfect retention when they must swim through the same maze or even when they must "roll" through it when their coordination has been impaired by lesions in the cerebellum (Lashley & Franz, 1917).

The application of potassium chloride to the cortex impairs retention when the consequent "spreading depression" is present during storage but not during retrieval of the memory, or vice versa. One interpretation of this effect is that proprioceptive feedback is altered when the spreading depression influences the motor and sensory areas of the cortex (Schneider, 1967, 1973). In turn, the differences in proprioceptive feedback between memory storage and memory retrieval, for animals trained with depressed cortices but tested without, may yield differences in the intratask contextual stimuli to disrupt memory retrieval. However, the interpretation that the retention deficit accompanying spreading cortical depression is due to deviation in the proprioceptive stimuli at testing compared to training has not been completely successful (see Mayes & Cowey, 1973). Thus, except for certain cases of less well-established memories, modification of proprioceptive feedback probably has little influence on memory retrieval.

The examples of reinforcement, apparatus change, and proprioceptive feedback obviously are not conclusive evidence of the range of effect of intratask context on memory retrieval. Indeed, it is unlikely that completely convincing evidence for these effects will be gathered by measuring retention after a modification of intratask contextual cues, because it is so difficult to factor out the nonmemorial effects of stimulus change in such an experimental design. Later we shall examine two types of more compelling evidence for an influence of contextual stimuli on memory retrieval, one type indicating that such stimuli may serve as a special case of discriminative stimuli, and the other indicating that the addition of such stimuli may facilitate memory retrieval (in that pretest exposure to them produces better retention scores). In discussing the latter, we shall return to additional examples of the influence of intratask contextual stimuli, especially reinforcement conditions, on memory retrieval.

Effects on Memory Retrieval in Humans

Brain-damaged people suffering from "aphasia" (generally, a disturbance in verbal communication) are particularly unable to recall the appropriate word to fit certain occasions. This deficit is most apparent for words unconstrained by aspects of verbal context such as syntax. Thus, these persons are most likely to have difficulty recalling proper names or the names of objects in isolation. For prepositions and other terms dictated by sentence structure, their memory processing may appear quite normal. Of secondary importance here, but relevant to a point to be discussed later, is the observation that aphasics are more likely to recall well-established memories, that is, highly familiar objects or frequently used words (Hecaen, 1969).

When normal humans are confronted with a list of words that they must recall later without regard to order of presentation, they also may benefit from the reappearance of other verbal items incorporated in the task. A vivid example is seen in the dramatic aid to recall provided by presenting a stimulus word with which the word to be recalled was paired during learning. As another, we know that if category names are presented along with category exemplars during learning (e.g., PEACH, PLUM, FRUIT, APPLE, ORANGE), subjects provided the category names when tested recall as many as 50–100% more of the other items than subjects without these recall cues (See Chapter 8).

Generally speaking, humans have a remarkable ability to segregate, probably on the basis of intratask features of contemporary context, a list of verbal items presented for later recall. For example, although not all items may be recalled correctly, only rarely will an item from outside the list intrude into the subject's list of recalled words. Underwood (1964) reports that of 1,424 overt errors made in a paired-associate task, only one of these, the expression of the word *yellow* instead of the correct response, *canary*, was a word that did not appear elsewhere in the list. This capacity to exclude common words because they do not appear in the list (i.e., do not occur in the same intratask context as similar words presented for later recall) has been termed the *selector mechanism* (Underwood & Schulz, 1960; see also Chapters 4 and 8).

There are a variety of cases in which verbal retention has been facilitated by reproducing intratask context at the recall test. A few examples follow. These examples may reflect benefit to memory retrieval, but in these cases the number of alternative mechanisms might also account for this facilitation in retention.

Coding items within a sentence may facilitate retention. Rohwer (1973) and his colleagues (e.g., Rohwer, Schuell, & Levin, 1967) conducted a variety of experiments with children and adults and found that a given pairing of words may be learned more efficiently if the pair is embedded in a sentence when first presented to subjects. Recall of the words was best when the sentences were presented during testing exactly as they were presented during original learning, but similar facilitation was not found when the context of the words-to-be-recalled consisted of material "less meaningful" than a complete sentence, and still less facilitation was found when a conjunctive phrase formed the context of the words (Rohwer et al., 1967). Perhaps part of the benefit may be attributed to some unique advantages of linguistic structure, but an explanation in terms of general facilitation of memory retrieval by intratask context remains plausible (cf. Rohwer 1973, pp. 27–30). An important question to which we shall return frequently is whether the essence of this context is linguistic–conceptual (the subject's own interpretation of what is presented) or the physical appearance of the words presented.

Intratask verbal context and the "spacing effect."   An effective technique for facilitating recall of words, the "spacing effect," has been interpreted, paradoxically, in terms of the decreased effectiveness in retrieval of a word when the verbal context changes. The spacing effect is found when subjects are presented a list of words to be recalled in any order: Recall of a word is better the more often it has been repeated within the list, and this benefit of frequency is far greater when other items are interpolated between repetitions of a given word.

Each time a word is presented with a different word or words preceding it, we say that it has appeared within a different verbal context. Each time a word appears in such a new context, retrieval of the previous encoding of that word will be relatively unlikely and the word may become encoded differently than before; or even if it is encoded as before, the second occurrence may enter into a different interitem organization than the first. With the word thus accessible from more than one encoding or organizational scheme, the probability of subsequent retrieval increases and that word becomes more likely to be given at recall. Although we tend toward a somewhat different explanation of the spacing effect, some knowledgeable theorists have viewed favorably an explanation concerning contextual influences (for further discussion, see Crowder, 1976, pp. 288–291; Melton, 1967; Madigan, 1969; see also Chapter 8).

Recognition of verbal items that appear in different verbal contexts. What, you may ask, defines a different verbal context? We have mentioned, with reference to the selector mechanism, that humans are quite adept at sorting out "different" verbal contexts. This ability is verified further in an experiment by Jacoby (1972), which addressed the question of what constitutes a difference in verbal context and also included a test relevant to the spacing effect.

Jacoby presented 72 simple sentences to subjects. A sentence such as *The weary slave was working* shared with other sentences the same core idea but differed in adjectives and verbs (e.g., *The tired slave was laboring*). Subjects were exposed to a core idea one, two, or four times: Some subjects saw the idea expressed (one or more times) in only a single form, and others saw the idea in a different way on each presentation. Retention was measured by subjects' reports of how often a given sentence and a given noun had appeared.

In one sense, it may be said that subjects viewed each of the slight variations of this sentence as a different verbal context: The frequency of actual repetitions of a given sentence was judged rather accurately, and when asked how often a specific sentence occurred when three variants of it had been presented also, subjects usually judged correctly that it had occurred only once. However, when repetitions of an idea were consecutive (i.e., massed rather than spaced), subjects judged a given noun to have occurred more frequently when it was repeated in slightly different sentences than when it was repeated in identical sentences. Similarly, subjects judged a noun as having appeared more frequently in identical sentences that were spaced (i.e., in which ten other items intervened between repetitions) rather than massed.

We might conclude from Jacoby's study that when the same noun was repeated in successive sentences expressing the same idea but in slightly different words, subjects viewed the noun as having occurred in different contexts. Subjects also viewed the same noun as having occurred in different contexts when the noun was repeated within identical sentences that were spaced by sentences with other themes. Therefore, just as we may expect a word to be retrieved more readily when it appears in the same sentence at both learning and recall, we also may expect it to be retrieved poorly when it appears in a different sentence or a number of intervening items occur to disrupt accessibility to that word. However, as discussed in the previous section on the spacing effect, such changes in the context of repetitions of a word probably have an ultimate advantage in causing the word to enter into different memories, thus increasing the probability of its retrieval on any given occasion.

The influence of context on recognition has become an important issue in theories of how the recognition process works. One of the more successful theories of recognition holds that, generally, the semantic context in which a word appears should be relatively unimportant because recognition proceeds primarily on the basis of the relative frequency with which verbal units have appeared in a particular situation (Ekstrand, Wallace, & Underwood, 1966; Underwood, 1971, 1974, 1976; Underwood & Freund, 1970). Empirical support for this position has been impressive, and we shall consider this theory later in comparison to alternative positions. For now, the intention is to sample briefly the empirical evidence concerning whether a change in context occurring between the presentation of an item and the retention test ever influences the probability of the item's recognition.

When linguistic changes in the context of a word are such that the meaning of the word differs between the presentation and the test, recognition may be affected. The pioneer study by Light and Carter-Sobell (1970) is exemplary. They presented subjects with nouns accompanied by a modifying adjective; later they asked for recognition of these nouns when presented alone or when presented with the same or a different modifying adjective. Recognition performance was best when the noun was presented with precisely the same adjective as during presentation, somewhat poorer if the noun was presented alone or with a different adjective (expressing the same meaning as the adjective paired with the noun during presentation), and poorest when presented with an adjective that altered the noun's meaning.

Results reported by Winograd and Conn (1971) also indicate that the manner in which a subject interprets or encodes nouns during presentation could influence the probability of their later recognition, depending on the context of testing. They presented subjects with 50 nouns having potentially different meanings (e.g., *back,* which could be either a part of the body or a position on a football team; *cardinal,* which could be either a bird or a member of the clergy). Subjects were tested for recognition of these nouns presented alone as before, or presented within a sentence that biased toward the most familiar meaning of the word, or within a sentence that biased toward the relatively unfamiliar meaning of the word. Results indicated slight (but insignificant) superiority of recognition for subjects who were presented items for testing just as they had been during original learning in comparison with subjects biased by sentence context toward the familiar meaning. Recognition in both of these conditions, however, was superior to that of subjects who were presented the items in sentence contexts that biased toward the relatively unfamiliar meaning of the word.

An influence of another sort of semantic context is implied in the results of Tulving and Thompson (1971). After subjects had been presented with pairs of words that they were to associate—that is, give one of the words when presented with the other—recognition of one of those items was impaired if the word appeared either without its original partner or with a different, associatively related word. The interpretation of this interesting study, and of Tulving and Thompson (1973), requires consideration of additional factors, to which we shall turn in Chapter 8.

On the other hand, an extensive study by Underwood, Patterson, and Freund (1972) indicates that linguistic context in general, of the sort that may not necessarily alter the associative relationships of a particular word, has no influence on recognition. In this study, the number of unrelated words that accompanied a critical word during a test of recognition, relative to the number of words that had accompanied the critical word during presentation, did not influence the accuracy with which that word was recognized. This manipulation, however, was not intended to analyze the influence of associative context that might alter the semantic coding of the word to be recognized.

Later we shall return to the evaluation of the influence of semantic context on recognition because it is part of the basic issue of whether the same processes underlie retention assessed in terms of recognition compared with recall. For now, it is notable that changes in the context of words may occur not only in altered orthographic features but also in altered semantic features, and associative semantic features seem the more important for recognition when the test biases subjects toward consideration of semantic attributes. The latter qualification concerning biasing toward semantic analysis by subjects may be unnecessary. Melton suggests that from a coding viewpoint semantic attributes are always involved when subjects are presented words for storage or test, although individuals will differ in the consistency of their encoding at presentation and test. Furthermore, this usual variability in encoding suggests that if Winograd and Conn (1971, see earlier discussion) had included a condition in which subjects were biased toward the familiar encoding at *both* presentation and test, recognition performance in that condition would have surpassed performance in all other conditions, including an unbiased condition (Melton, personal communication, 1976).

Recognition of verbal items following a change in physical form.   When we alter the way a verbal item is presented, its orthographic features as well as others such as color of print or modality (visual or acoustical), presentation may be varied independently of its linguistic identity. If the process of recognition involves matching the stimulus presented at the retention test against a perfect physical replica stored by the subject to represent the words previously seen, then we expect that recognition would suffer if, for example, the orthographic chracteristics of the letters in the words differed between the presentation and the test.

As part of a much more extensive experiment, Hintzman, Block, and Inskeep (1972) tested subjects for recognition of common three-letter nouns (such as DOG and HAT) that had been presented typed in uppercase block letters for some subjects and in lowercase script letters for other subjects. Half of the subjects were tested with words presented in the same form (script or block) as during original presentation, and half in the form different from the one they had seen initially. Some superiority of recognition was found when the physical form of the letters was the same at presentation and test. However, this was a relatively weak effect. The superiority was statistically significant in one experiment and not in another, and where significant, the effect was restricted in that it did not appear in all possible instances. With symbolic events such as words, it appears unlikely that minor orthographic changes in their form have much influence on recognition.

Incidental learning and contextual similarity.   Humans presented verbal units to examine may learn something about them and be capable of recalling them accurately, even without instructions to do so. This is termed *incidental learning,* distinguishing it from *intentional learning,* in which subjects are specifically instructed to learn (see Postman, 1964, for a review of this phenomenon; also see Craik & Lockhart, 1972). The amount of incidental learning of verbal items is increased, and the difference between incidental and intentional learning correspondingly is decreased, if subjects are required to emit the same overt and covert responses to the items as those made by intentional learners (Mechanic, 1964).

During recall, subjects inevitably expose themselves to a substantial verbal context by the simple act of recalling the items and by applying whatever covert verbal mnemonic mechanisms they might use to facilitate their performance. Perhaps by obliging incidental learners to respond to verbal items during presentation, the verbal context is made more similar to the context during the subsequent recall test, and so retrieval of the memory of presentation is enhanced.

Verbal context induced by "filler" tasks. Just as instructions from the experimenter are an inevitable source of verbal context in many studies of memory, so are "filler" tasks, intended to prevent the subject from rehearsing, a source of verbal context. Experiments reported by Falkenberg (1972) illustrated that such tasks may create a stimulus context during storage of a memory that must be replicated for more effective retrieval.

Falkenberg conducted an extensive study of short-term retention of groupings of three consonants ("consonant trigrams," or "CCCs"). His procedure included the conventional "Brown–Peterson paradigm" (see Chapter 3), in which the subject is presented the verbal item to be remembered and then is immediately given a filler task to occupy him and prevent rehearsal during the retention interval. For example, between learning and recall the subject may be presented a three-digit number and asked to count backward by threes until recall is requested. Falkenberg was concerned that while the filler task was reducing rehearsal it also might create a different context preceding recall (counting backward) than preceding original learning (no counting backward). He reasoned that perhaps such a contextual change could impair memory retrieval and thus enhance forgetting.

Falkenberg's initial test of this hypothesis replicated the basic experiment by Peterson and Peterson (1959), but added conditions in which the context prior to learning was more similar to that prior to retrieval. Subjects were required to count backward both prior to seeing the consonant trigram and prior to recalling it. As illustrated in Figure 2.1, subjects given identical "counting" contexts prior to learning and recall had significantly better retention scores. To add generality to the conditions under which this contextual similarity effect could be produced, Falkenberg completed two additional experiments in which the filler task was adding pairs of numbers. In these two experiments, Falkenberg showed that retention was progressively better as the number of identical pairs added prior to learning approached the number of pairs added between learning and the cue to recall.

Subsequent experiments by Falkenberg tested alternative interpretations of this effect. He concluded, however, that the best explanation was the simple one— recall of a verbal unit after a short interval is better when the contextual events that precede recall are identical to those that preceded learning, even when these events are redundant.

Cueing by predetermined members of verbal context. One of the most obvious methods for studying the influence of verbal context on verbal retention is "cueing." With this technique, a verbal item ("cue") is presented together with a word that later is to be recalled; retention performance in the presence of that cue word is compared with performance found in the absence of the cue word. There is no doubt that presentation of a cue word during both memory storage and retrieval can be beneficial to retention. The extent of the benefit has

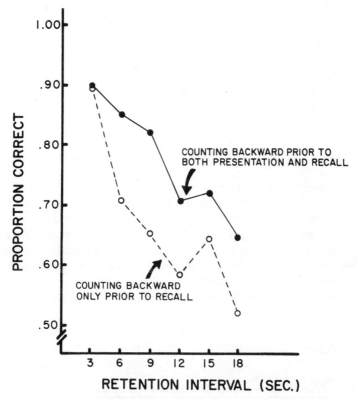

Figure 2.1   Proportion correct recall of consonant trigrams after differing lengths of retention interval. Between presentation of the trigram and the test for its recall, subjects were required to count backward from a specified number. This figure indicates that less forgetting occurred for subjects that were also required to count backward prior to presentation of the trigram.

ranged from "clear" to "dramatic" in various studies. We shall postpone discussion of this phenomenon until later, when we shall consider in depth these and other instances in which memory retrieval may be facilitated by the occurrence of certain stimuli (see Chapter 8).

Other influences of context on retention of verbal materials.   Context may influence learning and retention of verbal units in several ways in addition to our current concern with the role of absolute changes between acquisition and retrieval of memory.

If each verbal stimulus item (to which a response item must be associated) is accompanied by a unique nonverbal context, learning may be influenced. For example, if stimulus word A always appears against a blue background, stimulus word B always appears against a yellow background, and so forth, subjects may find it advantageous to ignore the verbal stimulus and apply instead the contextual background as the functional stimulus (see Richardson, 1972a; Underwood, 1963). This issue of stimulus selection—and its opposite member, stimulus compounding—is not of concern here, although it is obviously of immense general significance for learning, whatever its role in retention.

Similarly, a context may serve as a mediator if pairs of items to be associated are presented always within a unique context. If stimulus A and response B both appear always against a yellow background, and stimulus C and response D are always against a purple background, a subject may facilitate learning if she employs the background color as a mediating device (e.g., Birnbaum, 1966). Again, this is largely irrelevant to our present concern with retention and forgetting.

Finally, the particular context in which memory is acquired may serve not only a retrieval function of the sort we have emphasized here, but also a discriminative function to resist potential interference in retention. Such a function appears to account for the reduction in retroactive interference that occurs if the original learning and the conflicting interpolated learning are presented in different physical contexts (see Strand, 1970), and for the similar effect that appears in situations where proactive interference occurs (Dallett & Wilcox, 1968). Within the Brown–Peterson paradigm for testing short-term retention, certain kinds of contextual changes also may alleviate proactive interference in retention (Wickens, 1970). The discriminative function of contextual cues is a particularly important matter for retention and memory retrieval, and we shall be discussing it again.

EXTRATASK STIMULUS CONTEXT

Effects on Memory Retrieval in Animals

In spite of the caricature of "S-R psychology," few scientists have ever suggested that learning results in the inevitable production of a response whenever the stimulus previously associated with it is presented. The very underpinnings of the reflex model of learning made it evident that such an inescapable bond is unlikely. Sechenov, working on the simple preparation of the spinal frog in the nineteenth century, found that an identical stimulus applied to the digits of a limb might produce extension or flexion, depending on the initial position of the limb. Similarly, Lashley and others have shown that identical stimulation to the same portion of the motor area of the cerebral cortex often results in differing motor responses from occasion to occasion. Moreover, the specific response elicited depends on a number of uncontrolled (and possibly some unknown) factors, including the initial position of the limb that is being controlled.

Furthermore, specific conditioned or discriminative stimuli that nominally control behavior appear quite dependent on the contemporary context to determine the probability that the associated response will be elicited. This dependence is on extratask environmental events both external and internal to the organism. Potentially, all such events may be represented as attributes of a given memory, and memory retrieval may be facilitated to the extent that these events recur.

We will examine control over responding exerted by external environmental events that also are redundant to, and usually independent of, the learning task. This control may be mediated by the influence of these events on memory retrieval. We will consider also the similar influence of internal contextual stimuli. Although in some respects the evidence for the influence of internal stimuli is more dramatic, we shall see that to a large extent it has been disregarded, especially concerning human memory processing.

Pavlovian conditioning. Among the more systematic studies of the control of learned behavior by external contextual stimuli, mediated perhaps by the latter's influence on memory retrieval, has been that conducted by Asratian and his colleagues, who investigated the "switching" phenomenon. An experiment reported by Asratian (1965, pp. 126–127) illustrates an instance of "switching." Metronome clicks paired with food were presented to hungry dogs by one experimenter at a given time of day; at another time of day, a different experimenter gave the same animals pairings of footshock and the same metronome clicks. Ultimately, the metronome clicks became a CS and came to elicit salivation without foot withdrawal in the former case, and foot withdrawal without salivation in the latter case. In this particular study, the experimenters themselves apparently were the critical contextual stimuli: The experimenter who had administered appetitive conditioning continued to obtain unambiguous appetitive responses regardless of time of day, and the experimenter who had administered aversive conditioning elicited the avoidance response (even though the identical CS, clicks, occurred in both instances). When both experimenters were present, however, "the result was considerable confusion in conditioned reflex activity, i.e., the dogs reacted to the stimuli sometimes as to a food signal, sometimes as to an electric defence signal, and sometimes their reactions were mixed" (Asratian, 1965, p. 127).

Asratian and his colleagues have found that other contextual cues, including the experimental room and equipment, the particular sequence in which experiments are conducted, and the time of testing, can be similarly effective. For example, in one experiment a CS was paired with electrical stimulation of a dog's left leg in the morning and its right leg in the afternoon. As the dog's switching became more efficient, increased EEG activity was measured in the cortical area believed to integrate the postural reflexes of the leg being conditioned at that particular time of day. Moreover, this EEG pattern became evident immediately upon preparation for that session's training; the change was detected as soon as the animal was set in the apparatus and EEG was measured (see also John, 1967).

Asratian has interpreted these contextual stimuli—the "switching agents"—as a special case of conditioned stimuli (see also Lashley, 1958, p. 8). Such contextual stimuli, Asratian (1965) asserts, gradually develop into "constantly acting conditioned stimuli which can evoke conditioned reflexes . . . and create a definite functional background" (p. 137). For these "switching" results considered in isolation, one cannot readily determine whether they are better interpreted as an instance in which retrieval of a memory is elicited by a contextual stimulus or as an instance in which retrieved memories are discriminated on the basis of contextual stimuli (conditional discrimination) or simple stimulus selection, or a case of stimulus compounding among contextual and conditioned stimuli. Asratian clearly prefers the stimulus compounding interpretation, but the memory-retrieval function of the contextual stimuli is not easily dismissed (for further consideration of such alternative interpretations, see Spear, 1976).

Instrumental conditioning. Although the studies by Asratian and his group included only classical (Pavlovian) conditioning, similar phenomena have been found with instrumental learning. Overton (1964) trained rats to turn in a particular direction, depending on external contextual stimuli, to avoid footshock in a T-maze. Within about 150 trials, Overton's rats learned to turn right when the shock level was 2.0 milliamperes, the 100-watt bulb over the choice point was lighted, and a loud tone sounded intermittently; when the shock was 0.6 milliamperes and the light and tone were off, the rats turned left. Subsequent experiments by Overton (1971) indicated that the most effective of these contextual stimuli was illumination. Rats given ten trials per day of training to turn in one direction when the entire maze was illuminated and ten trials on other days to turn the opposite direction without illumination subsequently behaved as if retrieval of the target memory (turning right or turning left) was determined by degree of illumination. This effect, however, was relatively weak. Perhaps this is to be expected in view of the number of possible contextual cues to which the rat is exposed in these early training trials. That is, the contextual illumination cues may have been overshadowed by more salient stimuli and not noticed by the rats during the relatively short training sessions. Nevertheless, Moffett and Ettlinger (1967) have reported a similar influence of contextual illumination on retention with monkeys.

Generally, there is little doubt that environmental features quite separate from the task to be learned may become represented as attributes of the memory for a particular learning episode. The lore of behavioral-testing laboratories includes anecdotes of dramatic effects on learned behavior as a consequence of incidental changes in contextual features, effects not satisfactorily explained by trivial investigatory behaviors or simple changes in general activity. John (1967) reported the consequences of either moving the training apparatus from one experimental room to another or changing some apparently insignificant aspect of the apparatus. In such cases, he notes, "it has been commonplace in our experience that previously well-trained cats display a decrement in performance after these changes, minor though they may seem to us. Such deterioration has been observed in a variety of behavioral situations involving both approach and avoidance tasks" (John, 1967, pp. 68–69). Welker, Tomie, Davitt, and Thomas (1974) report that occasionally "when the masking noise generator malfunctioned during an experimental session in our laboratory, we have observed pigeons to cease responding entirely until the noise has been reinstated" (p. 550). With the belief that such effects may be explained, at least in part, in terms of the stimulus control that may be acquired by contextual stimuli and is useful for memory retrieval, we will now consider problems regarding the precise origin and characteristics of such control.

Interpretations.   The observations just described indicate that the presence of certain contextual events may increase the probability of a particular response (and decrease that of another) by virtue of the events' correlation with certain reinforcement contingencies involving responding to other, often more informative stimuli. In other words, a particular response has a higher probability of being reinforced in the presence of a certain contextual event than in its absence, although this difference may be less than that involving presence *versus* absence of a specific CS. As such, control acquired by contextual stimuli may be viewed as no different in kind from control acquired by discriminative stimuli. Certain characteristics of contextual stimuli are not conducive to rapid acquisition of stimulus control. For example, a contextual stimulus typically remains present regardless of the animal's response, thus providing no information as to whether the response emitted was correct or incorrect. In the case of instrumental conditioning such as in Overton's paradigm, contextual stimuli become correlated with reinforcement only after the basic discrimination has been at least partially acquired. In Asratian's Pavlovian switching paradigm, the reinforcer (UCS) is perfectly correlated with the contextual stimuli from the start, but the response attribute of the memory (i.e., the CR) is not; both responses often occur to the CS in either context until switching is perfected. Eventually, the conditional discriminations studied by Asratian and Overton provide the sort of circumstances needed for the acquisition of discriminative stimulus control in general: Given a particular stimulus, the probability of a particular response's being reinforced is higher than in the absence of that stimulus. But I am suggesting something different. In my view, contextual stimuli acquire a capacity for memory retrieval even without explicit or implicit discrimination training, although this capacity may be enhanced by discriminative training. The only necessary condition is that a contextual stimulus be noticed together with other events that constitute the memory, such as the response, the reinforcer, and any particular (internal) stimulus correlated with the occurrence of the reinforcer.

This is an old issue in the study of learning (cf. Lashley & Wade, 1946). More recently, Sutherland and Mackintosh (1971) and others (e.g., Terrace, 1966) have maintained that stimulus control, at least in the case of operant (instrumental) conditioning, requires discrimination learning, whether explicit or implicit.

This stand is not easily refuted. If a pigeon is presented a lighted key that produces a food reward when pecked, it may be inferred that characteristics of the light have acquired control over the pigeon's behavior because responding is observed to be less likely with a brighter or dimmer light than with the original. One can argue that this is a consequence of an implicit discrimination acquired by the pigeon: By responding to the key per se, rather than to some dimmer or brighter object elsewhere in the training apparatus, the pigeon developed an implicit discrimination (see Terrace, 1966). This issue is extensive and complex, as evidenced by the mass of relevant information provided in the entire book by Sutherland and Mackintosh (and, more recently, by Mackintosh, 1974), and this is not the place to reiterate and reexamine their arguments. Much of the evidence cited in this chapter, from humans and animals, is general support for our position, but it is largely indirect. A study by Welker, Tomie, Davitt, and Thomas (1974) provides direct support for our position that contextual stimuli may acquire stimulus control in the absence of discrimination training.

The Welker et al. (1974) experiment.   Welker and his associates trained pigeons to peck a standard unilluminated pigeon key (a round disk 2.9 cm in diameter) in order to obtain food. While the animals were in the training apparatus, the houselight was on and a 1,000-Hertz tone occurred. The houselight and the tone therefore are regarded collectively as the contextual stimulus. Accordingly, this contextual stimulus was present all the time the bird was pecking, eating, hopping, cooing, or whatever, and at no time was this contextual stimulus absent in correspondence with the animal's failure to be reinforced on the prescribed schedule.

Following 17 daily sessions in which the hungry birds obtained food on a VI schedule by pecking the plain response key, with the contextual stimulus (houselight and tone) present continuously, a discrimination task was introduced. For this task, the key was sometimes lighted with a green color (555 nm) and sometimes with a white vertical line, but only responses to the green key were reinforced. The question analyzed was how discrimination learning and subsequent generalization of responding to the green stimulus would be influenced by the presence of the previous contextual stimulus only in concurrent conjunction with the green stimulus (S+), only with the vertical stimulus (S−), with both S+ and S−, or with the contextual stimulus totally absent.

The influence of the contextual stimulus appeared in striking fashion: When the contextual stimulus accompanied only the S+, discrimination learning was enhanced; when it accompanied only the S−, discrimination learning was impaired; and when present with both the S+ and S−, the contextual stimulus clearly enhanced responding to the S− (which served to decrease the overall percentage responding to S+ and thus to impair discrimination performance; see Figure 2.2). Furthermore, when the contextual stimulus was presented with either the S+ or the S−, the stimulus control it had acquired was sufficient to retard acquisition of stimulus control by S+: Figure 2.3 shows specifically that

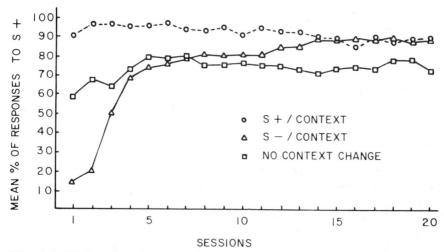

Figure 2.2   This figure shows the accuracy of discrimination performance (percentage responses to S+) when the contextual stimulus previously associated with nondiscriminative, rewarded pecking occurred during discrimination training in conjunction with the S+ or with the S−. When presented in conjunction with the S−, discrimination performance tended to be impaired, but when the contextual stimulus accompanied presentations of the S+, discrimination performance was enhanced. (After Welker et al, 1974. Copyright 1974 by the American Psychological Association. Reprinted by permission.)

when the stimulus that had served as context for initial nondiscriminative VI training accompanied either the S+ or the S− during discrimination training, significant flattening resulted in the generalization gradient. In this gradient, retention of stimulus control is shown by percentage responding to the S+ (555 nm) compared to responding to alternative stimuli. Finally, when the contextual stimulus was completely absent during discrimination training, most subjects failed to respond at all! This strikingly illustrates the control that the contextual stimulus had acquired, because birds without such previous experience readily responded and learned.

Under most circumstances, contextual stimuli have occasion to be differentially associated with reinforcement, implicitly or explicitly. But the experiment by Welker and his associates did not include such circumstances, so their results provide clear support for the notion that contextual stimuli may acquire stimulus control and thus support memory retrieval under a wide spectrum of circumstances.

Aversive conditioning.   Contextual stimuli have been found in other tests to selectively control retrieval of alternative memories following only a minimum of discriminative training. An example is seen when rats are given two kinds of aversive conditioning, each requiring only a few trials given within a single training session. For the first, the rat learns to remain in the start compartment of a two-compartment apparatus and not to enter the alternative compartment ("no-go," or passive avoidance training), and for the second, it learns to do the

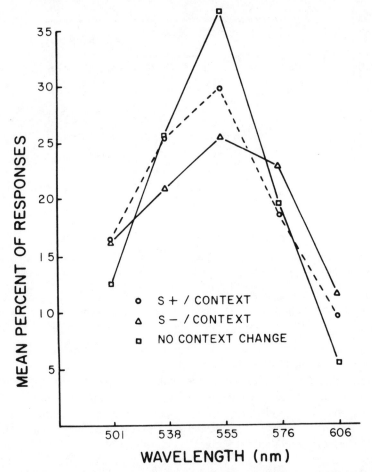

Figure 2.3   This figure indicates, in terms of generalization gradients (S+ was 555 nm.), the effect of presenting the contextual stimulus with either the S+ or S− during discrimination learning. It can be seen that the stimulus control exerted by S+ (reflected by steeper gradients, i.e., relatively more responding to 555 mm than to alternative colors) was impaired when the contextual stimulus had accompanied either the S+ or the S− during discrimination learning. The implication is that the contextual stimulus exerted control over responding during discrimination training.

opposite—to enter rapidly the alternative compartment ("go," or active avoidance training). Following retention intervals of an hour or longer, the rat becomes about equally likely to perform either response. But if a tone is presented throughout "no-go" training and not during "go" training, the probability of a "no-go" response during the retention test is increased substantially if the tone occurs, as illustrated in Figure 2.4 (Spear, 1971).

It should be clear, however, that the significance of any particular context is unlikely to be specifiable with complete accuracy a priori; we may expect variation depending on the species tested, the task being learned, and many circum-

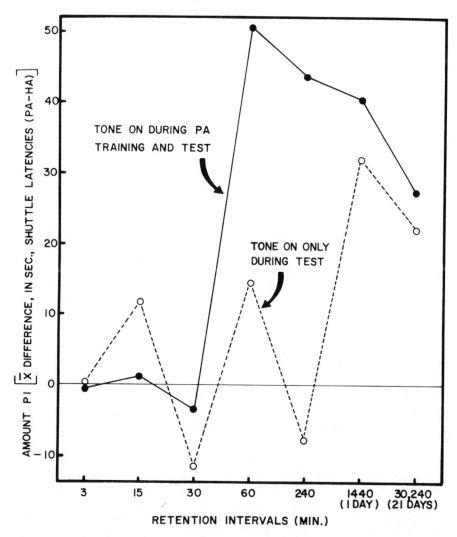

Figure 2.4   This indicates that the influence of passive avoidance training that had preceded active avoidance training was enhanced at a retention test by presenting an aspect of the context (tone) that had occurred with passive avoidance training and with the test (even though the context was redundant to learning of the passive avoidance). Specifically, the index "PI" (proactive interference) is the difference between the test performance of subjects that had learned passive avoidance before active avoidance and those that had not but otherwise were treated the same. The solid line represents data from rats presented with the tone during their prior passive avoidance training and again during the retention test. Rats represented by the dotted line were presented with the tone only during the retention test. The tone was never presented during active avoidance training. The higher the number on the ordinant, the greater the influence of prior passive avoidance training. (After Welker et al, 1974. Copyright 1974 by the American Psychological Association. Reprinted by permission.)

stances of general importance in determining attention. Because of such factors, tests of the potential influence of contextual cues in our laboratory occasionally have yielded negative results. Also, we have found graded effects using the sort of tasks just described. In our laboratory, Robin Timmons and Richard Bryan trained rats in a single session to "no-go" in one experimental room and to "go" in a different experimental room. For some rats, the training always occurred in the same apparatus, which was transported from room to room; for others, these two tasks were learned in a different apparatus (although identical in appearance) in each room. For the most part, the rooms did not differ substantially, although on occasion we have conducted this experiment (intended fundamentally for purposes different from those discussed here) using different rooms in quite different buildings. From the point of view of a human observer, however, the rooms and the apparatuses do not appear very different. But to the rat they apparently do differ, probably on the basis of odor, noise patterns, and other stimuli that humans fail to detect. We have found that when the rat is placed in the start compartment of the apparatus for a retention test, behavior depends very much on precisely what the rat had learned earlier (whether to "go" or to "no-go") in this particular apparatus in this particular room in this particular building. The dissociation is best if the rooms are in different buildings, somewhat less strong if the tasks were learned in different apparatuses in different rooms of the same building, and still less effective if the same apparatus was employed in different rooms in the same building. As mentioned earlier (and to be expanded in Chapter 4), animals trained first to "no-go" and then to "go" in the same apparatus in the same room respond (after a sufficiently long retention interval) as if the memories had interacted completely; that is, the alternative responses become about equally likely.

The results just discussed imply that contextual stimuli acquire stimulus control and, in our terms, acquire the capacity for memory retrieval. Is it not apparent that these events in the external environment function in the same way as instructions to humans, simply telling the animal what to remember? This is not a trivial matter, however. Although we do not know how external contextual stimuli control memory retrieval in animals, we also have yet to determine precisely how instructions control memory retrieval in humans.

Effects on Memory Retrieval in Humans

There is an abundance of anecdotal information indicating that retrieval of particular verbal memories may be impaired when external events are different from those present during storage of the memory, or increased in effectiveness when the circumstances of the environment become more similar to those of storage. An important book by Carr (1925) called attention to such effects, and some studies concerning this idea were mentioned by McGeoch (1942, pp. 501–505). McGeoch (1942) cited evidence that the presence of an audience during memory retrieval impairs retention if memory storage occurred without an audience; that performance appropriate to classroom learning declines when the classroom or the proctor is changed; and that when words are presented for learning against a particular color of background, performance declines if the colors are changed for the retention test. The latter effect is most pronounced when the background color of the *response* items (the items to be recalled) is changed, so it is not simply a matter of misinterpreted stimulus selection.

Extratask contextual stimuli often have been considered to constitute the stimulus to which a set of responses becomes attached, especially under circumstances in which response learning—the immediate accessibility of verbal units—is required for recall. In their initial application of the two-stage model of paired-associate learning, which emphasized the separate stages of response learning and associative learning, Underwood, Runquist, and Schulz (1959) suggested that response learning may consist of associating the list of alternative responses with the external stimulus context. McGovern later introduced a similar explanatory concept in the analysis of the retroactive interference that occurs in the AB–CD paradigm. The AB–CD paradigm employs two paired-associate lists having different responses and different stimulus items. During first-list learning, an association is acquired between the B responses and the stimulus context. Interference in recall of the AB list is attributed to the unlearning of that association during learning of the second list, and the resultant deficit in strength of that contextual association at recall (McGovern, 1964).

More specific suggestions about the role and nature of extratask contextual stimuli have been offered. Underwood (1972) suggests that extratask contextual stimuli may be far greater determinants of free recall than is generally recognized. The set of such stimuli includes not only physical characteristics of the subject's surroundings while learning, but also "all psychological reactions of the subject. It must include his reactions to instructions; it must include any strategy of learning he imposes on himself, or has imposed on him; it must include any affective reactions, including those elicited by the words. All such reactions become a part of the context, and probably the critical part" (Underwood, 1972, p. 14). These psychological cues might be characterized better as internal in nature; we will consider these in a moment.

Bower (1972a) suggests that context is the

background external and introceptive stimulation prevailing during presentation of the phasic experimental stimuli. Included here would be internal factors like posture, temperature, room and apparatus cues, and stray noises, as well as internal physiological stimuli such as a dry throat, pounding heartbeat, stomach gurgles, nausea, and boredom. But more significant than any of these is what the subject is thinking about, what his mental set is, at the time the experimental stimulus intrudes. (p. 93)

Hintzman, Block, and Summers (1973b) similarly have specified contextual cues in their interpretation of how contextual associations influence retention of information concerning serial position of an item presented among a group of other items.

In recent years, several studies testing the effect of nonverbal context on verbal retention have manipulated background color of verbal items, often with the same kinds of results, if not equally strong effects, as those cited by McGeoch (Gottlieb & Lindauer, 1967; Lehr & Duncan, 1970). Simple variation in the background color or shape against which words were presented originally has been found sometimes to disrupt recall (Von Wright, 1959). More gross extra-task changes in external context have been tested since McGeoch's book, and one of the more recent of these (Rand & Wapner, 1967) also may be the most remarkable.

Rand and Wapner had subjects learn a serial list of six nonsense syllables while either standing erect or lying on their backs. Fifteen minutes later, the subjects were asked to relearn the list either in the same postural position as before or in the alternative position. Relearning was more rapid when the posture was the same (3.25 trials) for both learning and relearning than when postures were changed (4.45 trials).

The differences obtained by Rand and Wapner are small, somewhat limited in generality (because not all indexes of retention reflected even this much difference), and as Keppel (1972) has noted, also may be limited to the conditions of considerable proactive interference intrinsic to their experimental design. But on the other hand, the results are remarkable because we rarely consider possible deficits in memory retrieval resulting from the infinite number of postural changes all humans undergo daily. Moreover, Rand and Wapner's effects were statistically significant, and they had taken care in their procedure to minimize contamination by differences in perception that might be caused by differences in posture.

In a somewhat more complicated study, Greenspoon and Ranyard (1957) included conditions in which the posture of some subjects differed while learning a verbal list (sitting down) from their posture during the retention test (standing up); for other subjects, postural position was not changed. Unlike Rand and Wapner, however, Greenspoon and Ranyard added correlated differences in other contextual features (e.g., color and location of experimental room), forming a stimulus compound of extratask context. If one averages across treatment differences that intervened between learning and the retention test, one may conclude that retention was about twice as good when posture and other contextual features were constant during learning and testing as when they were different.

One may prefer to classify postural changes as modifications of organisms' internal stimulus context; indeed, it would be quite reasonable. We now turn to changes in the internal environment which are at least as likely as changes in the external environment to have an effect on memory retrieval.

INTERNAL STIMULUS CONTEXT

Alterations of an organism's physiological system, especially alterations that are traumatic (though not necessarily destructive of tissue), often result in dramatic behavioral changes. In fact, organisms are supplied with a variety of homeostatic-like mechanisms by which they may absorb traumatic events and minimize any long-term consequences. While some sources of trauma, or dramatic physiological change in general, may be relatively "unnatural," other sources, such as being born, growing, sexual maturation, parturition, and menopause, are encountered by all organisms on an ontogenetic basis. In addition, humans have acquired the practice of modifying their internal state by means of chemicals from exogenous sources.

The gross behavioral changes that result from such internal modifications usually are characterized in motivational terms, such as "mood." To what extent might these internal modifications and their accompanying behavioral changes be responsible for changes in the probability of retrieving certain memories? Our hypothesis is that the accessibility of a memory is indeed influenced by an organism's internal state, in humans as well as animals, and to a more pronounced degree than most of us would suspect.

Available evidence does not permit us to determine how general the contextual influence of naturally occurring internal neural and hormonal states might be on memory retrieval by humans. There are, however, suggestions of such an influence. Moreover, we shall see that the breadth of this evidence implies a certain, perhaps surprising, degree of generality. We will consider two separable sources of internal contextual cues, endogenous and exogenous. The endogenously induced sources of interest include chemical events of internal origin; the exogenous sources of interest include drugs that are not normally found in the organism and whose actions do not mimic endogenous chemicals.

Endogenous Sources of Contextual Stimuli

An organism's internal response to any strong stimulus obviously is too complex to be described in detail here. However, we can assert that a hungry, tired, or frightened animal regularly responds with a predictable variety of visceral, hormonal, and neural consequences. Furthermore, we may expect these consequences to recur and induce similar internal states in the animal each time such sieges of hunger, fatigue, or fear recur. Such a set of internal consequences may be regarded as an unusual, distinctive state that may function as a contextual attribute of a particular memory. Subsequent reinstatement of that state may be expected to facilitate retrieval of that memory. Of course, this is a hypothesis, and at present there are not a great deal of supporting data. The results of some experimental tests have encouraged this sort of thinking, however, and we now turn to a sample of those tests.

Hunger as a contextual stimulus. The cue value of the motivational state induced by depriving an animal of his usual ration of food has long been recognized as an important determinant of the effect of hunger. Indeed, convincing theories of motivation have been based exclusively on such cue properties (e.g., Estes, 1958).

Kendler (1946) determined that if rats learn the separate locations of food and water when both hungry and thirsty, they will reliably return to the location that previously held food but not water when they are hungry only; and when made thirsty only, they will return to the place that held water but not food. Kendler raised a theoretical issue that was important for the development of learning theories during the early 1950s; today this issue is just as relevant to the question of when internal contextual cues might be stored in memory and influence subsequent retrieval. The issue is whether an internal state of an animal will serve as an effective cue only when that state is related intrinsically to the reinforcer. For example, is hunger an effective cue only when the animal's response produces food, and not when the response leads to water? Kendler's initial experiment and some of his subsequent ones supported this conclusion. However, this functional restriction on internal states as cues began to be challenged by Amsel (1949).

Amsel taught rats to make a particular choice in a T-maze in order to "reduce their anxiety" about receiving footshock. To establish rapid running to the goal boxes, the rats were given footshock everywhere in the T-maze except in the goal boxes, although no shock was delivered during the critical test trials. During testing, motivational state (hunger or thirst) was the sole cue indicating the correct choice. When the rats were hungry, one choice in the T-maze permitted them to reach a goal box (thus achieving "anxiety reduction") and the alternative choice did not; when the rats were thirsty, the opposite choice led them to a goal box.

Amsel (1949) found that motivational state did function as a cue, but the effect was very small under these circumstances, at most of borderline statistical significance. This cue value was particularly slight in relation to the relatively major influence when the goal box to be entered during hunger included food as well as "anxiety reduction," or, during thirst, held water. Nevertheless, Amsel's evidence was sufficiently convincing to permit a modification of Kendler's original conclusion, encouraging the belief that motivational states might have cue properties whether or not the reinforcer was relevant. That is, the function of an internal state as a contextual cue might be independent of whatever other attributes might accompany that internal state to constitute the acquired memory. Appropriately, Amsel's (1949) conclusion was cautiously qualified: "Irrelevant drive stimuli (of the hunger and thirst type) became connected to rewarded responses with which they are contiguous only as the result of considerable practice" (p. 795).

Still, the stage had been set for further tests of the generality of internal stimuli.

Unfortunately, most of the early studies that investigated the cue value of hunger and thirst are impossible to interpret because of methodological errors stemming from incomplete understanding of hunger and thirst. For example, in those days it was not widely realized that animals deprived of water also inadvertently are made hungry, and vice versa (e.g., Hamilton & Flaherty, 1971, 1973;

Verplanck & Hayes, 1953). Nevertheless, a variety of such experiments began to indicate a general influence of hunger and thirst as contextual cues. Two particularly convincing sets of experiments were portions of doctoral dissertations involving oustanding psychologists whose subsequent contributions to the science of memory are well known. One of these studies was conducted by Seymour Levine under the direction of Howard Kendler; Levine subsequently has produced classic studies on the interrelationships between hormones and behavior, and Kendler, whose work had initiated the immediate controversy, has continued to be a central figure in theories of learning and memory processing. The other study was conducted by Clark Bailey under the direction of the eminent Neal Miller.

Levine (1953) conducted an experiment similar to Amsel's in two major respects. First, the general idea was to see if rats would learn to discriminate right from left when the sole basis of their discrimination was whether they were hungry or thirsty and the consequence of a correct choice was neither food nor water. Specifically, the rat's task was to press a panel located on either the right or the left; when its choice was correct, a bright light was turned off. The albino rat's dislike of bright lights, and preference for mild stimulus change, maintains responding under such circumstances. Second, Levine duplicated Amsel's great patience by giving his animals five training trials each day for 90 days. On a randomly determined half of the days, the rats were hungry, and on the other half they were thirsty. When the rats were hungry, the right panel was correct; when they were thirsty, the left was correct.

The most convincing index of correct responding in Levine's experiment was, of course, the first trial of each day (one can argue that on later trials responding is based on the consequences of that first trial). With this measure, responding to the correct alternative (again determined by whether the rats were hungry or thirsty) was consistently above chance from the seventh day of training on; after about 50 days of training, the probability of a correct response stabilized just above 65%. During the last 12 days of training, about 75% of the first-trial responses were correct. Furthermore, when all trials were considered, 10 of Levine's 11 subjects chose the correct alternative significantly more often than would be expected by chance.

Making two cogent points, Bailey (1955) sought to replicate Levine's results and to obtain further information. First, Bailey noted that one could not conclude safely from the studies of Amsel and Levine that both hunger and thirst were effective cues. Perhaps only one state was effective, while the other "state" simply existed as the null case. Second, Bailey questioned whether the lengthy training sessions required by Amsel and Levine really reflected something unique about internal states as cues. Although their findings were consistent with Hull's (1943, p. 207) earlier supposition concerning "static" cues such as motivational states, neither Amsel nor Levine actually had compared their effects with effects obtained when external contextual stimuli were used to control responding.

Therefore, Bailey added four conditions to Levine's experiment, while maintaining Levine's basic procedures. In addition to Levine's condition in which rats learned to respond on the basis of hunger versus thirst, Bailey added a group of rats trained to respond in a given direction when hungry and in the other direction when not hungry, and another group whose correct choice was determined by whether or not they were thirsty. Bailey also included two groups of rats given the same task except that the correct response was determined by an external stimulus (a tone). The distinction between the latter two conditions is unimportant here, and data for them will be ignored. All animals in the remaining groups acquired the discrimination, and with about equal proficiency. Consistent with Levine's and Amsel's results, Bailey showed that the internal states of hunger and thirst may provide effective contextual cues for the rat, even though the memory does not include reinforcer attributes relevant to these states. An additional experiment in Bailey's dissertation (Bailey & Porter, 1955) established that cats also may employ hunger and thirst as contextual cues.

The evidence mentioned so far in this section concerns conditional discriminations in which the major function of the contextual cues may be discriminitive (cf. Spear, 1976). Hunger also has been established as a contextual cue possibly acting upon memory retrieval: Several experiments have shown that a memory acquired under a particular level of hunger (in terms of hours of food deprivation) is more likely to be manifested at a later retention test if the animal is tested under the same hunger level than if it is tested when more or less hungry. Yamaguchi (1952) trained rats to press a lever for food after they had been deprived of food for 3, 12, 24, 48, or 72 hours. For the retention test, subjects within each of the learning-deprivation groups were deprived of food for 3, 24, 48, or 72 hours; in other words, for each level of hunger in acquisition separate groups of animals were tested under the same level or under one of three alternative levels. The retention test measured the latency with which the animals would move a shutter in order to gain access to the lever. Yamaguchi found generally that the greater the deviation between degree of hunger at training and at testing, the greater the latency of the response (i.e., the poorer the test performance). These differences, albeit rather small, suggest poorer retrieval of the memory for original training the greater the change in level of hunger.

Similar results have been reported by Otis (1957; see John, 1967, p. 70). Rats that had acquired an avoidance response while under one of three levels of hunger later were tested under the same or different levels. Avoidance performance during the retention test always was best when the degree of hunger during testing matched that which prevailed during training.

Finally, there is evidence that memory retrieval in insects similarly may be influenced by changes in the internal consequences of hunger. Schneirla (1934; see Alloway, 1972) placed a complicated maze between an ants' nest and the ants' food source. Following each time the ants traversed the maze to the food source, the maze was removed and they were permitted to return directly to their nest. When the ants finally had become efficient in passing through the maze in this direction, Schneirla reversed it while they were at the food source. This required the ants to traverse the maze along the path they had already learned, but this time following—instead of preceding—their acquisition of food. Schneirla found that the ants showed little or no retention of their previous learning. Even though they had mastered the maze completely when going from the nest to the food source, the ants required about as many trials to learn the maze route back to the nest as they had required during original learning (see also Weiss & Schneirla, 1967). Of course, it is not clear that the failure of the ants to benefit from the prior learning was due to their change in hunger state. What is obvious, however, is that something about the change of stimulus context negated the benefit of prior learning, perhaps owing to a failure of memory retrieval.

Sleep and memory retrieval.   Sleep is an internal contextual state of some distinction. How sleep differs from the waking state has become well known in a variety of dimensions, behavioral, electrophysiological, and biochemical (e.g., Clemente, Purpura, & Mayer, 1972); why sleep occurs is much less clear. It is indeed a paradox that this most obvious and pervasive instance of a homeostatic mechanism should remain the most obscure in purpose. This is not to say that there have been no interesting suggestions regarding what functions sleep might have in absorbing such a large portion of our lives. For example, Stern and Morgane (1974) present data suggesting the importance of sleep for maintaining the critical systems in the brain involving serotonin and catacholamines, on which much of neural transmission is dependent. These systems and neurotransmitters often have been implicated in memory processing. Of particular relevance to memory processing, Stern and Morgane suggest a more general function of sleep, that of promoting the metabolism of protein. Protein synthesis has been suggested as the critical step in the formation of a permanent memory. Furthermore, there is no doubt that sleep is an important determinant of memory processing generally, for either storage or retrieval (e.g., Ekstrand, 1967, 1972; Fishbein, 1970, 1977; Spear & Gordon, 1977).

In addition to whatever direct effect sleep might have on memory processing, the distinctive physiological state associated with it may have an auxiliary effect in the control of memory retrieval. An example may be the low probability of retrieving the memory of a dream while awake. Extreme nightmares, sometimes termed "night terror," which are commonplace in children and often accompanied by screaming and bolting upright in bed, would be maladaptive indeed if they were clearly remembered by the children during their waking hours (they rarely are). Fortunately, most people do not confuse memories representing the content of dreams with memories of more concrete episodes during waking.

There is no direct experimental evidence for the control of memory retrieval by states of sleep. However, the rapid eye movement (REM) sleep stage is a distinctive, extremely important state. When animals are deprived of REM sleep, retrieval of memories acquired before deprivation becomes less probable;

memories acquired during REM deprivation similarly are unlikely to be retrieved when the animal returns to a normal state (e.g., Joy & Prinz, 1969). Animals that are REM deprived are likely to lapse quickly into REM sleep when given the opportunity. It seems likely, therefore, that animals under REM deprivation may have moments of REM sleep even when encountering the learning task. If so, a state of sleep may be simulated during such training but be absent during testing in a normal state, and vice versa, and the difference in context provided by the states present during learning and testing would decrease the probability of retrieval of the memory.

Clearly, a direct test of the function of a sleep state as a retrieval cue will require some creativity; it is no simple matter to instill learning in a sleeping animal, and perhaps more difficult to assess it. A promising step toward such a test has been taken by Berger (1970), who capitalized on the rat's rapid acquisition of conditioned aversions to novel foods. First, Berger established that if ingestion of milk preceded amphetamine injections, the toxic consequences of the amphetamine produced decreased drinking of milk. He next provided a new set of rats with milk for the first time, but anesthetized them before injecting the amphetamine. Although the anesthesia was timed so that the rats still were asleep when they became sick, they incorporated the sickness as part of the memory of drinking milk, as reflected by their subsequent decrease in intake of milk. While other interpretations are possible, these results suggest that such a paradigm might be used to determine whether learning occurs during sleep, and perhaps similar innovative techniques may be used to establish firmly the role of sleep as a contextual cue for memory retrieval.

Time of day (or night) as a contextual stimulus. There are certain regular fluctuations in the physiological processes of all organisms; one of these is the sleep–wake cycle, a special case that occurs within a period of about 24 hours. The temporal regularity of similar cycles of behavior also is well known and is becoming better understood (e.g., Richter, 1967). For example, circadian (from *circa* for "about" and *dies* for "day") cycles of activity can readily be observed in any animal laboratory where the animals are on a regular light–dark cycle. Nocturnal animals, such as the rat, have low levels of activity during the light portion of their cycle; their activity gradually increases near the end of the light portion and continues throughout the dark portion of the cycle, gradually decreasing once again as the time for the light portion approaches. Changes in the circulating level of certain adrenal steroids parallel this course.

We already have seen data by Asratian and his colleagues indicating that if dogs repeat a certain conditioning "problem" during one time of day and a different problem, similar except for the "solution" response acquired and the unconditioned stimulus that elicits it, during another time of day, the dogs are quite capable of using time of training as an internal contextual cue to determine which solution to apply. A study by Holloway and Wansley (1973) indicates further that time of day is an effective contextual cue for the rat as well, and that differences between time of training and time of testing have profound effects on memory retrieval. They gave rats one training trial on an easily learned passive avoidance task, then tested retention after a variety of intervals ranging between 15 minutes and 3 days. For training, the rats were placed into the brighter compartment of a two-compartment box and given a footshock when they entered the darker compartment. With this procedure, a rat placed in the bright compartment for a few minutes shows good evidence of having learned to "passively" avoid the darker compartment by remaining in the bright side. In fact, Holloway and Wansley found that retention of this response was excellent after 15 minutes, 24 hours, 48 hours, and 72 hours, that is, when tests were given at the same time of day as training. However, retention was poorer when the time of day of testing deviated from that of training. The results are shown in Figure 2.5. Holloway and Wansley (1973) confirmed this effect—the dependence of retention on the similarity between time of training and time of testing—with active avoidance learning as well. These experiments also indicated that such effects were independent of the particular time of day at which training occurred (see also Wansley & Holloway, 1975).

In an informative paper, Stroebel (1967) has reported results that lead to the same general conclusion as that of Holloway and Wansley. Several tasks were employed by Stroebel, and he found the clearest circadian effects on learning and retention by using the conditioned emotional response (CER). Although Stroebel eliminated external cyclical cues in his study, the time of day determined by the rat's "clock" apparently was stored as a contextual attribute that subsequently determined memory retrieval.

Stroebel's study is worthy of serious attention for several reasons. With the CER paradigm, Stroebel found a clear deficit in acquisition if animals were not conditioned at the same time each day, but instead were conditioned at randomly determined times. The implication is that consistent circadian cues permit more effective retrieval of memory of the conditioning episode. A related effect of this variable (similarity between time of training and time of testing) was observed in extinction performance: Like acquisition, extinction was slower when tested at randomly determined times rather than at the same time each day; both methods of testing extinction proceeded more slowly if acquisition had occurred at randomly determined, rather than consistent, times. (Time in the circadian cycle as a contextual cue varied during acquisition may be compared with other similarly varied contextual cues critical to extinction, most notably variation in the occurrence and sequence of nonrewarded trials interspersed among rewarded trials; cf. Capaldi, 1971.) This effect was statistically significant for the CER paradigm only, and not for any of five other learning tasks (escape, Sidman avoidance, classical avoidance, punishment, discriminative lever pressing). Stroebel has suggested that this may be attributable to the unavoidable nature of the aversive circumstances in the CER task; perhaps the unique internal consequences of

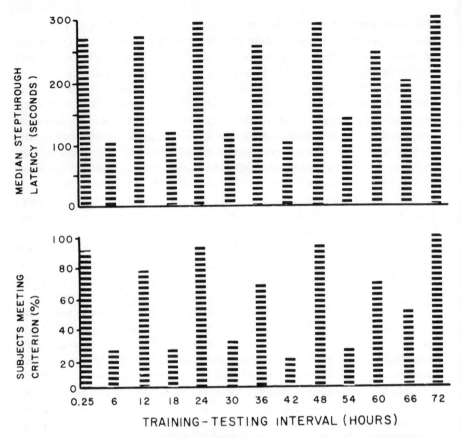

Figure 2.5 The upper and lower figures reflect retention of passive avoidance for tests given at differing intervals following a single passive avoidance training trial. For both figures, the higher the numbers, the better the retention. It can be seen that retention performance is best after retention intervals that are multiples of 24 (or to some extent, multiples of 12). (Adapted from Holloway & Wansley, 1973. Copyright 1973 by the American Association for the Advancement of Science).

unavoidable stress are bound especially by circadian forces. This must remain speculative until more trivial methodological factors are discounted.

Stroebel's other results of interest—relatively ignored so far by other investigators—are those obtained through variation in the number of inversions of the light–dark cycle given rats during the 30–day period between acquisition of a CER and the retention (extinction) test. The number of inversions varied between zero and four. The major aspects of interest is the dramatic forgetting induced by repeated inversions of the light–dark cycle during retention intervals: The greater the number of inversions, the poorer the retention. The magnitude of the forgetting obtained is notable, especially in view of the quantity of data showing little or no forgetting of a CER (when assessed by a single-stimulus test) after comparable intervals when no cycle inversions occur (e.g., Gleitman & Holmes, 1967). The implications of this effect are not yet clear, but the intriguing nature of this apparently powerful source of forgetting presents a problem of potential interest and value to investigators of memory processing.

Internal response to the stress of aversive conditioning as a contextual stimulus. An organism presented with stressful circumstances responds physiologically in very predictable ways that promote two objectives: first, immediate adaptation to the emergency, and second, restoration of spent physiological resources after the trouble has passed. The specific physiological mechanisms involved need not be elaborated here (see deWied & Weijnen, 1970; Ganong & Martini, 1969; Gispen, Griedanns, Bohus, & deWied, 1975; Martini & Ganog, 1966; Selye, 1946). Included among the several immediate neurochemical consequences of stress is hypothalamic activation of the portion of the pituitary that secretes a substance termed ACTH (adrenocorticotropic hormone). ACTH acts within a few minutes of the onset of stress to stimulate the release of steroids from the cortex of the adrenal gland. Some of the specific functions of ACTH and the various adrenal corticoids are well recognized, others barely understood, and probably still others yet to be discovered. What is known, however, is that ACTH itself may act to modify learned behavior and perhaps the learning itself, and that certain corticoids travel through the blood to rest in locations in the brain that have been implicated in the storage and retrieval of memories, such as that of the hippocampus (see deWied & Weijnen, 1970; Gispen et al., 1975).

Given the regularity and distinctive character of the physiological changes that accompany or follow severe stress, the resulting states would seem potential candidates to be contextual attributes of a memory, especially for individuals unaccustomed to such stress. In fact, there is evidence, albeit indirect, that such stress-induced states do become contextual attributes, and thus control retrieval of a memory. This evidence is derived from studies of the Kamin effect, a phenomenon we shall consider in more detail later. For now, it is sufficient to note that the Kamin effect refers to the exaggerated forgetting found after retention intervals of intermediate length (one to six hours) following memory acquisition. Almost exclusively, this effect is found in the context of aversive conditioning, where some external event signals an aversive consequence and the animal can learn to respond following the signal in such a way to avoid the aversive consequence. In contrast to this poor retention after intermediate-length intervals, retention after shorter or longer intervals is relatively good.

The Kamin effect has been explained as an instance of memory retrieval failure (Brush, 1971; Klein & Spear, 1970a; Spear, 1971). This interpretation focuses on the change in internal state that occurs an hour or so after stress but is less severe or absent immediately after stress and 24 hours later. A specific suggestion here is that the animal responds to a new stress differently after the one-hour interval because, essentially, the animal at that time is undergoing the homeostatic process in which its usual internal responses to stress are relatively inhibited. When the retention test is introduced at this time, the animal's modified response to the stress does not simulate the internal state of original acquisition sufficiently to permit effective retrieval of the memory.

If this is an appropriate explanation of the Kamin effect, one would predict that animals acquiring a new memory an hour or so after some stressful experience would retain it less well following recovery than animals that had acquired the same new memory only a few minutes or 24 hours after being stressed. This possibility was tested and confirmed (Spear, Klein, & Riley, 1971; for further discussion of the Kamin effect, see Chapter 4).

A further implication of this interpretation is that the active presence of certain stress-related hormones should result in a sufficiently different internal state (compared to when they are absent) to influence memory retrieval. Two experiments by Pappas and Gray (1971) support this implication. They induced distinct hormonal states by injecting dexamethasone, a drug that simulates the action of certain adrenal corticoids. Dexamethasone specifically acts to inhibit the release of ACTH, with a potency that, in fact, is greater than the potency of naturally produced steroids. In this study, dexamethasone was injected into rats prior to training, prior to testing, prior to both, or prior to neither. When both training and testing were conducted in the presence of dexamethasone, or both were conducted in its absence, retention was better than if the dexamethasone-induced states differed from training to testing. Apparently, when animals trained under the influence of dexamethasone were tested under a normal state, or vice versa, the dissimilar internal stimuli present precluded arousal of the attributes appropriate to the required training, and thus impaired memory retrieval.

Assuming that the effects of the exogenous dexamethasone on internal stimuli are similar to those of endogenously produced corticoids, we may expect similar effects on memory retrieval. In spite of the clarity of Pappas and Gray's results (see also Gray, 1975, for similar effects with exogenous ACTH), some caution is warranted in generalizing from them. Comparisons of the effects of drugs induced endogenously and exogenously can be tricky, particularly the effects of synthetic corticoids and exogenous ACTH, which may influence the adrenal–pituitary system directly or by a variety of reciprocally inhibitory mechanisms. For a wide variety of other exogenously induced drugs, however, there is absolutely no doubt about their capacity to generate internal states that are sufficient distinct to influence memory processing. We turn now to a consideration of these effects.

Exogenously Induced Changes in Internal State as Contextual Stimuli

The plots of two classical silent movies involve forgetting following drug-induced changes in the internal state of key characters. In "The Covered Wagon," the heavily intoxicated old sidekick is given a critical message; sober later, he attempts to deliver the message, but cannot remember it. Fortunately for the heroes, he becomes reintoxicated and promptly recites the saving message. The other movie is "City Lights," in which Charlie Chaplin is befriended by an intoxicated man of considerable wealth. The man invites Charlie to be a guest in his house, but sober the next morning, he fails to recognize Charlie and has him thrown out, then becomes drunk again and invites him in again, and so on.

State-dependent learning conventionally is defined when retention is relatively poor for subjects whose drug-induced state during the retention test differs from the state during original learning. Because this phenomenon is defined in terms of retention scores, we prefer to refer to it as "state-dependent retention," as do others (e.g., Bliss, 1974). The behaviors of the "old sidekick" and of Charlie's erstwhile friend exemplify state-dependent retention.

State-dependent retention in humans.   Relatively few systematic studies have employed human subjects to test state-dependent retention, but there are enough to convince us of the reality of the effect. The initial studies used animal subjects (Girden & Culler, 1937; Lashley, 1917), and use of animal subjects remains the more common practice in such research, for obvious reasons of control and convenience. Very few experiments with humans have been published.

Overton (1972) cites nine studies of human state-dependent retention, several of which are unpublished. The retention tests employed in these experiments usually were for relatively unsophisticated verbal learning tasks with little analytical potential. Still, enough evidence for state-dependent retention has been found using recall or relearning tests of verbal material to suggest that the basic effect is reliable for humans. On the other hand, experiments using recognition tasks have failed to find state-dependent retention, which is of some interest because state-dependent retention in rats seems less likely to occur with simple discrimination tasks than with go–no-go tasks (see Bindra, Nyman, & Wise, 1965; Bindra & Reichert, 1966). Furthermore, studies of incidental-versus-intentional learning of verbal materials indicate that while this distinction (typically induced by orienting instruction) may affect recall substantially, there is relatively little effect on recognition (Craik & Lockhart, 1972; Postman, 1964). It is possible that recognition and discrimination tasks require retrieval of so few memory attributes (perhaps, for example, only a frequency attribute) that contextual stimuli become relatively unimportant (see Underwood, 1971, 1972).

One of the better of the early human state-dependent retention experiments tested habituation to a tone (Powell, Goodwin, Janes, & Hoine, 1971). Following repeated presentations of a 600-Hz tone, the subject's orienting responses, measured in terms of finger pulse volume, heart rate, and galvanic skin response, were assessed on two successive days. During testing, subjects were either in an alcoholic state, defined by prior ingestion of 8 to 10 oz of 80-proof vodka diluted in a soft drink, or in a normal state, defined by ingestion of an equivalent amount of soft drink only. Two groups of eight subjects were tested in the same state on both days, either normal–normal or alcohol–alcohol, and the remaining two groups were trained and tested in different states, either alcohol–normal or normal–alcohol. If we assume that orienting responses to stimuli such as the tone ordinarily would decline with successive experience, but that a shift in state would retard the accumulation of that experience, the two latter groups would be expected to show less decline in responding than the two former groups between training on Day 1 and testing on Day 2.

The differences reported by Powell and his associates were in the expected direction, but did not achieve a satisfactory level of statistical significance, at least not in the limited analyses reported. However, for subjects whose drug state remained the same, physiological indexes on Day 2 generally were significantly correlated in a positive direction with those on Day 1; but for those subjects whose drug state was changed, relative habituation on Day 1 was not correlated with that on Day 2. Unfortunately, the meaning of such correlations is unclear. While they may indicate that individual differences in the orienting response are reordered following a shift in state, the reordering effect may have been on baseline responding rather than on orienting to the tone.

Another of the more thorough, early studies of state-dependent retention in humans also had disappointingly questionable results. Bustamante, Jordon, Vila, Gonzalez, and Insua (1970) intended to study the effect of shifting drug states on retention of geometric figures. Drug states were induced by having subjects ingest pills containing either amphetamine or amobarbitol, or neither (placebos). From an original pool of 787 individuals, they narrowed their sample to 70 subjects capable of performing the task and similar in terms of body weight (to provide better control over dosage). For a variety of reasons, still more subjects were lost as the study progressed, and although the experiment continued for six tests, only the data for the first three are sufficiently free from probable confounding by extreme subject selection.

Bustamante and his associates presented 8 geometric forms on a screen for 3 minutes; then the subjects were given 2 minutes in which to draw all the forms they could remember. From prior testing, these particular subjects were known to be capable of drawing such forms. On subsequent tests, the subjects were asked to draw the 8 critical stimuli, but they were never reexposed to them. The subjects were given the drug in pill form half an hour before each test, and 48 hours elapsed between tests.

Three groups of subjects received the same kind of pill (placebo, amphetamine, or amobarbitol) on each occasion. Four other groups were given a pill different on Day 2 from the pills given on Days 1 and 3. One of these groups was given amphetamines on Days 1 and 3 and a placebo on Day 2; another group was given these drugs in the reverse order. Two corresponding groups similarly received amobarbitol and placebos. The results are shown in Figure 2.6, in which subjects given amphetamine–placebo combinations are grouped together, as are those given amobarbitol–placebo combinations. These are the critical groups

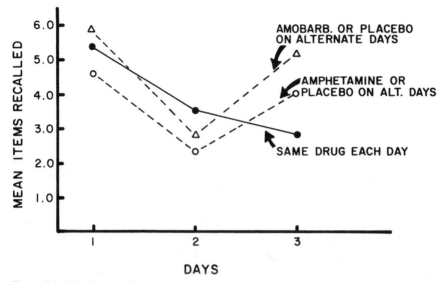

Figure 2.6   This figure indicates the mean number of geometric forms correctly recalled (i.e., redrawn accurately) on Day 1 (i.e. immediately after presentation), Day 2 and Day 3. Subjects indicated by the dotted lines received the same drug during presentation of the forms and the tests on Days 1 and 3, but a different drug on Day 2; those represented by triangles were given amobarbitol on Days 1 and 3 and placebo on Day 2, or vice versa, and those represented by circles were given amphetamine on Days 1 and 3 and placebo on Day 2, or vice versa. Subjects that were given the same drug each day are represented by the solid line.

whose internal state was the same on Days 1 and 3 but differed on Day 2. The third line combines all subjects given the same kind of pill on each occasion. The results support the state-dependent retention notion: A tendency toward greater forgetting on Day 2 can be seen among persons whose state differed from their state during original learning (Day 1), and when the state present during learning was replicated on Day 3, performance improved. However, it is not clear why the improvement on Day 3 was so pronounced as to result in *better* performance than was found for control subjects tested under constant drug conditions throughout the experiment. The difference is substantial and probably is statistically significant (as estimated from within-group variances). But by no set of principles to my knowledge could such an effect occur. One is left not knowing whether to begin searching for processes to account for ultimately better performance among humans given shifts in drug conditions, or to be suspicious of the procedures used. It is notable that Day 3 measures may involve a confounding of context effects and learning effects from testing on Day 2, with Day 3 recall benefiting from the recall of items on Day 2 (Melton, personal communication, 1976).

   Generally, after reviewing the literature on human state-dependent retention, we may reach the same conclusion as Overton: While state-dependent retention almost certainly does occur in humans, there are few thorough and completely convincing experiments, and certainly the analysis of characteristics of this phenomenon in humans has barely begun. A study by Peterson (1974) illustrates the emerging, more analytical experiments that may rapidly advance our knowledge in this area.

Peterson (1974) tested recall of words among subjects who, one day earlier, had learned them while under the influence of alcohol (1.0 ml per Kg of body weight) or while sober (given equivalent amounts of placebo). Half the subjects in each group were tested when in the alcohol-induced state and half when in the sober state. Each subject served in three tasks, two of which involved presenting the subjects explicit categories of words; the other task included words not readily categorized. State-dependent retention occurred when the subjects were required merely to recall the words; but when the category labels were provided, retention was not state dependent. In other words, simple unaided recall was impaired by a change in drug state between learning and testing, but cued recall was not. Such a result may imply a trade-off between external and internal cues, with additional external stimuli compensating as retrieval aids for the absence (change) of internal contextual cues. Peterson's study alone does not permit such a generalization. Clear comparisons among recall conditions are precluded in this study by the correlated use of quite different lists and by possibly peculiar effects of multiple tests. Generally, state-dependent retention experiments have given several different tasks to each subject, which is economical but often unsound methodologically. For example, the influence of proactive or retroactive inference resulting from multiple tests may be sensitive to differences in drug state or change in state, and such sources of variance often have been uncontrolled in studies of state-dependent retention of verbal materials. Nevertheless, the analytical intent of Peterson's experiment is encouraging, and the basic finding of less state-dependent retention with cued than with free recall has been replicated in subsequent studies of a similarly analytical nature (Eich, Weingartner, Stillman, & Gillin, 1975; Keane & Lisman, 1976; Weingartner, Adefris, Eich, & Murphy, 1976).

State-dependent retention in animals.   A complete review of the rapidly growing literature in this area, sometimes referred to as drug dissociation, is quite beyond the scope of our purpose. Insightful descriptions of the history and current issues in this field are provided by John (1967), Bliss (1974), and several papers by Overton (e.g., 1966, 1971, 1972, 1974). Many experiments in this area have used rodents in simple tasks in the "standard" 2×2 factorial design. In this design, drug state during training is varied orthogonally against drug state during testing. For many purposes, these procedures are inadequate (see Overton, 1974).

One of the more striking demonstrations of state-dependent retention in animals was conducted by Bliss (1973) with monkeys in a discrimination task. By selecting the appropriate color of two alternatives (e.g., red correct, green not correct), Bliss' monkeys could acquire their preferred food (peanut or raisin). They learned a particular color discrimination when in one drug-induced state (i.e., following injection of either sodium pentobarbital or saline) and then were tested for retention of that discrimination when in either the same or the alternative state. Retention was measured in terms of either relearning the original discrimination or transfering to the reverse discrimination (both kinds of tests yielded the same conclusion). Providing the proper control conditions in this sort of experiment always is difficult, but Bliss successfully employed an experimental design appropriate for justification of his conclusions about state-dependent retention. Indeed, relative to his complex design, Bliss's results were disarmingly simple: When testing was conducted under the same drug state as training, retention of the original discrimination was nearly perfect; but if testing was conducted under the normal (saline) state when training had been under the drug (sodium pentobarbital) state, or vice versa, retention was almost nil.

A second experiment by Bliss (1973), employing essentially the same experimental design, tested the monkeys with a position rather than a color discrimination. The results were identical in form to those of the first experiment, although the state dependence was less dramatic. Subsequent experiments by Bliss indicate that the latter effect may be attributed to the lesser complexity of the position discrimination task, because with still simpler tasks the monkeys did not show state-dependent retention at all. Bliss also determined an important functional determinant of degree of state-dependent retention, to which we shall refer again because of its potential significance to interpretations of memory retrieval in general: The degree to which monkeys had learned a discrimination determined the extent to which the retention would be state dependent; with better learning of the original problem, retention became less likely to be state dependent.

The "drug discrimination" paradigm developed by Overton (1964, 1966) often is a preferred alternative to the 2 × 2 factorial design for studies in this area because of certain methodological advantages, such as using a subject as its own control (see Overton, 1974). This paradigm is similar to that used by Bliss in that animals are trained to give response A while in one drug state and response B while in the alternative drug state. Typically, several pairings of the drug state and the required response are given. For this reason, and because of the length of time needed for the drug to wear off in order that a new state may be induced, such studies involve a considerable, and sometimes tedious, experimental effort.

For the particular procedure that Overton has perfected, rats learn to turn either right or left in order to escape footshock in a T-maze. The basic task is mastered very rapidly; usually, within five trials the animal learns to choose correctly. To determine whether drugs A and B (or doses A and B of the same drug) are discriminably different to the animal, it is trained to go right when injected with drug A, for example, and the next day it is trained to turn left when injected with drug B. On the third day, the animal again is injected with Drug A and must turn right, and so forth. Thus, the animal's internal state produced by the drug is the principal stimulus in a conditional discrimination. When the animal consistently chooses correctly (that is, in accordance with the drug state's "instructions") on the first trial of each daily session, we may say that the animal has discriminated drugs A and B. The results of such an experiment, in which the animal has learned to turn in one direction after injection with the drug pentobarbital (either 5, 10, 15, or 20 mg/kg) and the other direction after injection with physiological saline, are illustrated in Figure 2.7.

The distinction between state-dependent retention (or drug dissociation) and drug discrimination is a matter of degree, not kind. While drug dissociation may be nominally complete in that training in one drug state may not transfer to another, it would be foolish to conclude that no attributes of the memory acquired with drug A can be retrieved under drug B. As suggested in Chapter 1, many separate indexes of retention should be measured; even if forgetting were complete in terms of each operational measure, it would be unwise still to conclude that memory retrieval failed completely, given available techniques of measurement. Just as drug discrimination varies in degree, so does drug dissociation. However, this does not mean that state-dependent retention must be functionally identical when assessed with different methods of measurement. For example, we already have seen that state dependence may depend on task complexity and

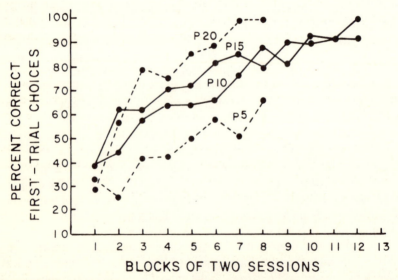

Figure 2.7 Progressive increase in accurate selection of the correct alternative on the first trial of each day is shown for rats given, as their only discriminative stimulus on which to base their choice, prior injections of either saline or a particular dose of pentobarbital. The labels on each line indicate the dose of pentobarbital for that group in mg/kg. It can be seen that the higher the dose of pentobarbital, the better the discrimination between the drug state and the normal (saline) state.

we have further indications that effects of drug dissociation, and perhaps of contextual cues in general, may be quite different when retention is assessed in terms of discrimination performance (recognition) than otherwise.

Overton (1972) summarized a number of principles concerning the influence of drug-induced internal states as contextual stimuli. These are further summarized here:

1. There are a large number of discriminably different states induced by a variety of drugs (e.g., amphetamines, anesthetics, antimuscarinics, nicotinics, etc.). At least a dozen such states have been identified so far.

2. Drugs that more readily pass the blood–brain barrier, and thus have direct effects on the brain as well as the periphery, are discriminated rapidly and, in general, seem to provide the more salient contextual cues as internal states. Generally, such drugs result in more rapid acquisition of differential responding than most external contextual stimuli that have been tested so far.

3. Animals can detect differing doses of the same drug. This is an obvious, but not necessary, extension of the fact that animals can distinguish some-drug from no-drug. Generally, the greater the disparity between drug doses, the better the discrimination.

4. The capacity to acquire such drug discriminations has been found over a wide range of animal species, including rodents, cats, dogs, and monkeys, and over wide range of ages when rats are subjects. In our discussion of the ontogeny of memory processing (Chapter 5), we shall see that very young rats may not have sufficiently mature receptors to be affected by certain drugs. In such cases, age-related differences in drug discrimination may be expected.

5. Drugs that are readily discriminable from the no-drug state also are most likely to be used to excess or otherwise abused; conversely, drugs that are less likely to be detected relative to a no-drug condition are seldom subject to abuse. The potential value of this discovery for applied purposes is obvious (see Overton, 1972).

6. Drugs most likely to result in state-dependent retention (as determined within the 2 × 2 factorial design) also are the most effective in the drug discrimination paradigm. Along the same lines, the principles just presented generally apply to state-dependent retention as tested by either procedure.

Dramatic Changes in Internal State Do Not Inevitably Yield Forgetting

Sometimes, in spite of massive changes in the internal state of an organism, including actual changes in some important neuronal groups where new neurons are formed to replace old ones, forgetting is slight and far from complete. We have already mentioned an example of negligible retention loss in cockroaches beheaded between training and testing. Similarly gross physiological changes occur when insects undergo metamorphosis.

Several studies have indicated that significant postmetamorphosis retention of memories that were acquired prior to metamorphosis is evidenced in the grain beetle, *tenebrio molitor*. Probably the most thorough work on this problem has been conducted by Alloway (1972), who trained grain beetles in larva form to turn a given direction in a T-maze in order to avoid aversive heat and light. After metamorphosis (a total retention interval of about two weeks), he tested the same insects, now in adult form, in the same T-maze. Previously, Alloway had completed extensive work with grain beetles in the same task so that procedural difficulties had been resolved, and he had found, for example, that larvae and adults require about the same number of trials to learn this task.

Alloway found that retention was quite good in spite of the intervening metamorphosis. Beetles trained in the T-maze as larvae required only about half as many trials to relearn the correct turning response as comparable beetles who were untrained in the T-maze but had equivalent experience otherwise. Also, beetles trained as adults to emit the response opposite the one learned as larvae should have inhibited acquisition of this reversal task if prior training is retained. In fact, Alloway found that animals previously trained in the T-maze as larvae did demonstrate retention because they required about twice as many trials to learn the reverse response as animals not trained as larvae.

Alloway took great care to develop this task and use control groups to protect against artifactual transfer caused by nonspecific factors such as sensory adaptation or habituation. Such nonspecific transfer from the larval to the adult stage easily might be mistaken as retention of the memory for the turning response. Alloway's data indicate quite clearly that whatever the extent of the retention loss caused by metamorphosis, the loss is not nearly complete. Tests of retention following metamorphosis from tadpole to frog have yielded a similar conclusion (Miller & Berk, 1977). Accordingly, we may expect that changes in internal contextual stimuli produce few memorial deficits that represent "complete" forgetting. Notably, the retrieval deficits caused by shifts in drug-induced states also are rarely "complete."

Through What Mechanisms Might Drugs Induce State-Dependent Retention?

A variety of explanations have been suggested to interpret the rapid rate, and apparent strength, with which centrally acting drugs develop behavioral control. One explanation implicates perceptual distortion, which occurs when the nature of the organism's perception of the task or of the controlling stimuli differs between training and testing as a result of differing drug states during training and testing. This seems unlikely as the sole explanation, though it may suffice in some instances and may be a component of a more complex explanation in other instances. The inadequacy of this simple perceptual hypothesis is based on a number of facts rather than on a single experiment. As we have seen, modifications of the animal's perceptual world by directly altering the environment, or by drugs that have powerful effects on many parts of the organism's body other than the brain, simply have not proved to be as prepotent as centrally acting drugs. Further, a few experiments have tested the perceptual distortion idea directly and have shown it to be inadequate. For instance, Overton (1968) tested the specific notion that rats see differently when drugged than when normal, consequently learn different things, and so show state-dependent retention. For this, Overton simply blinded rats after they had acquired a discrimination between pentobarbital and saline (no drug). If the discrimination was based on the influence of the drug on the rat's visual perception, destroying the rat's vision should have removed the basis for discriminating the drug states (i.e., if the perceptual system that a drug affects is removed, the drug has nothing to act upon and thus is no different from no-drug). However, Overton found that blinding caused only negligible impairment of the discrimination. Moreover, rats blinded from the beginning of training acquired the drug discrimination almost as rapidly as sighted rats. This implies that if the drug has its effect by altering perception, the perceptual distortion is not within the visual system.

A more general argument against this perceptual interpretation of state-dependent retention is founded on the occurrence of retrograde state-dependent retention, a phenomenon of such importance to interpretations of memory processing in general as to warrant elaboration before further consideration of explanations of state-dependent retention.

Retrograde state-dependent retention.   An issue central to the interpretation of many amnesic phenomena is the extent to which new information about the contingencies of an event is acquired *after* the reinforcer is presented. Suppose, for example, that a thirsty rat regularly has obtained drinking water at a certain spout, but on one occasion when it begins to lick, the spout delivers an electric shock to its tongue and mouth. The rat surely will be somewhat reluctant to lick again at that tube in the near future. But the critical question here is whether the rat will be more reluctant to do so if permitted to remain in the location of that spout than if it or the spout were immediately removed.

Anthropomorphically, the question is whether a few moments of uninterrupted reflection on the preceding assault by the water spout would somehow better affix the rat's memory of the episode and help the rat remember it later. In fact, an early study by Hudson (1950) indicated that something like this may occur. Hudson's procedure was very much like the situation just described. His results indicated that rats remaining in the compartment following shock showed more avoidance of the licking tube on a subsequent test, provided that the physical appearance of the compartment was not altered during the detention.

Generally, there are two distinct ways of interpreting posttrial events that facilitate later retention. The first assumes that the events of the trial, in particular the reinforcing event, initiate some relatively automatic physiological process that will strengthen the memory if allowed to persist uninterrupted. Such a process has been termed "consolidation", and it is a construct of immense importance to understanding memory processing generally. We shall return to "consolidation" often.

An alternative view, less well elaborated so far but perhaps equally potent, is that the immediate postreinforcement period is an important moment of information gathering for the organism: While the organism indeed does consolidate the information it has acquired, this consolidation is more similar to active reorganization than to passive strengthening of the memory. We shall return to this view also, particularly to one version that has undergone careful empirical testing (e.g., Kamin, 1969; Terry & Wagner, 1975; Wagner & Rescorla, 1972; Wagner, Rudy, & Whitlow, 1973). Regardless of which interpretation seems most appropriate, the potential importance of retrograde state-dependent retention should be appreciated.

Wright, Chute, and their colleagues have investigated the effect on retention of inducing a drug state immediately *after* a learning trial. Retention performance in these studies was tested under either the same posttrial drug state or a normal state. Chute and Wright (1973) realized the potential importance of the drug's effect during the first few seconds following the learning trial, so their first study included the relatively laborious technique of injecting the drug directly into the jugular vein through catheters that had been chronically implanted in the rat. Such injections yield almost instantaneous effects.

In the first experiment, rats received a footshock when they stepped from a bright compartment to a darkened one. About 12 seconds later, the animals were injected with a dose of either pentobarbital or an equivalent volume of the vehicle, isotonic saline. The dose of pentobarbitol (15 mg per kg body weight) was known to induce state-dependent retention in other circumstances. Just prior to the retention test 24 hours later, half the rats in each group were injected with pentobarbital and half with saline. The results indicate that animals tested under the same drug state as that induced immediately *following* the training trial showed better avoidance of the darkened compartment than animals tested under a drug state different from that which followed training.

A similar experiment by Wright and Chute (1973) employed a simpler method for immediate posttrial drug infusion: intrathoracic injections. The results of this study support their previous conclusions and are still more impressive statistically. In a third study, Wright, Chute, and McCollum (1973) employed a rapidly learned appetitive discrimination. Again, the conclusion was that memory retrieval is determined by the similarity between the internal state immediately *following* learning and the internal state during the retention test.

As Overton (1974) has indicated, there are subtle methodological problems in testing state-dependent retention with the standard 2 × 2 paradigm, especially when the episode to be stored in memory is one-trial passive avoidance training. However, the use of posttrial injections eliminates most of the problems of interpretation with this paradigm, especially when appetitive conditioning is used. The scientific impact of the retrograde state-dependent retention phenomenon on memory theory will depend on its subsequent replication and elaboration. We shall return to this phenomenon later. For now, we shall consider briefly three of the more important implications of this phenomenon for understanding state-dependent retention.

First, it is clear that the findings concerning retrograde state-dependent retention serve to eliminate interpretations based on drug-induced perceptual distortions during memory storage or memory retrieval, as did Overton's (1968) findings. All animals encountered the training episode under their normal state because the drug state was not initiated until *after* the animals were removed from the training situation.

Second, this phenomenon establishes the importance of the internal context immediately following the learning trial. Because the animals were removed from the experimental situation following the trial, the acquisition of significant new information about the circumstances of training is unlikely. Yet the drug state acquired control over the animal's behavior in accordance with contingencies that had terminated at least 12 seconds *prior* to the onset of the drug state. By what mechanism did this drug state become included in the same "specious present" (cf. James, 1890)—encompassed within the same "psychological moment"—that included contingencies of 12 seconds earlier? How did the drug stimuli and the events of conditioning become attributes of the same memory? The effect may be a result of either of the two processes mentioned earlier: (1) an automatic "consolidation," inevitable barring physiological trauma, that persists for longer than 12 seconds following training and incorporates all contiguous events into a common memory or (2) some relatively self-imposed reorganization of the events of the task stored as memory, perhaps occurring as the organism "scans backward" over the preceding episode because of the surprising event of the injection (cf. Kamin, 1969; Rescorla & Wagner, 1972), and probably sensitive to disruption by nontraumatic environmental events.

Third, to the extent that retrograde state-dependent retention is a general and reliable effect, the conclusions of many memory-processing experiments are suspect. In particular, studies claiming that posttrial injection of certain drugs has caused a deficit in memory *storage* probably are inadequate unless the experimental design included control groups reexposed to the same drugs during the retention test, and this procedure is rare. Among the suspect experiments would be studies of retrograde amnesia induced by electroconvulsive shock (ECS). In fact, ECS effects have been interpreted in terms of state-dependent retention, analogous to the interpretation of Wright and his associates. The importance of this interpretation requires a digression into the potential of ECS for inducing state-dependent retention.

Administration of ECS initiates a variety of changes in general physiological processes, including some that are potentially important for memory processing. These include modifications in the concentration of free fatty acids, protein synthesis, biogenic amines, acetylcholine, and acetylcholinesterases, among others. If these changes persist into the testing period, the state of the animal obviously differs from that prevailing at original training, and the result may be failure in memory retrieval. Some changes are transient, but others may persist for 24 hours—the usual interval between training and testing for the influence of the ECS—and may be maintained for three or four days, gradually subsiding over a period of three to four weeks.

The view that ECS-induced retrograde amnesia may be a special case of state-dependent retention—induced by differences in the physiological state of the animal at training and testing due to the lingering effects of the ECS—has been encouraged by the finding that spontaneous recovery of the acquired memory occurs at a time when many of the ECS-induced changes would have subsided. However, such spontaneous recovery is not always found, and positive and negative instances of its existence are reported about equally often (see Lewis, 1969; Miller & Springer, 1973). Also, while other tests of this particular state-dependent retention hypothesis sometimes have yielded the expected results (e.g., DeVietti & Larson, 1971; Nielson, 1968), a substantial set of experiments have not, or have given other interpretations (e.g., Gardner, Glick, & Jarvik, 1972; Miller, Malinowski, Puk, & Springer, 1972). These inconsistencies suggest that differences between the physiological states induced 24 to 72 hours following ECS and the normal state found prior to ECS are at best only barely sufficient to induce state-dependent retention.

On the other hand, the physiological state occurring immediately after ECS (up to 20 or 30 minutes later) apparently *is* sufficiently different from the normal state to induce state-dependent retention. Retention of a memory acquired shortly after ECS is poorer if testing is conducted in a normal state than if the test also is given shortly after an ECS; conversely, retention of a memory acquired in a normal state is poorer when an ECS is administered just prior to the test than if no such treatment is given (Gardner et al., 1972; Miller et al., 1972). Moreover, a different treatment, which also results in convulsions but is somewhat more subtle and refined than ECS, has been found to induce immediately a state sufficiently different from the normal state to produce state-dependent retention. McIntyre and Reichert (1971) repeatedly stimulated the amygdala of rats (one stimulation every 12 hours) until this resulted fairly regularly in a convulsion. In the more convincing of their two experiments, Experiment 2, rats were trained on a position discrimination to escape footshock. One trial per day was given: Half the animals were trained in a normal state and the other half in the post-ictal state induced by an immediately preceding convulsion. Following acquisition of the position discrimination, the animals were trained on the reverse discrimination while in the state opposite to that under which they had acquired the original discrimination. When reversal learning was complete, retention was tested. The animals were given a series of trials in which the correct alternative was determined by their state: The response learned during the post-ictal state was correct when the animal was tested in that state, and the response learned during the normal state was correct when the animal was tested in the normal state. The results are shown in Figure 2.8. Notice that very little transfer from acquisition training occurred when the animals' state was changed for reversal learning. Also, the animals performed quite accurately during the testing phase, responding in accordance with reinforcement contingencies present under the normal or post-ictal states.

As a whole, results indicate that the post-ictal state following a convulsion (induced by either ECS treatment or stimulation of the amygdala) may differ sufficiently from the normal state to induce state-dependent retention: Memories acquired in the post-ictal state are unlikely to be evidenced during the normal state, and vice versa. Combined with the results of Wright and Chute, this allows for the possibility that posttrial memory processing, like that which occurs during a trial, may be state-dependent if accompanied by a sufficiently profound or

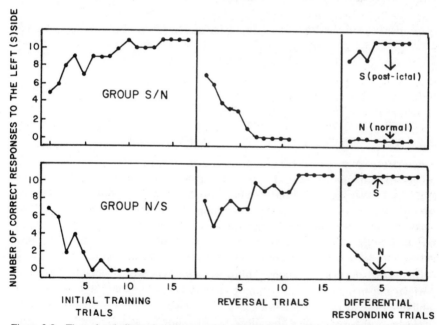

Figure 2.8   These data indicate that rats can solve a discrimination problem using as discriminative stimuli its normal state in comparison to the post-ictal state that follows convulsions induced by direct stimulation of the amygdala. The left panel indicates learning of the discrimination with one trial per day (for subjects in the upper panel this trial is given in the post-ictal state; for subjects in the lower panel these trials are given in the normal state). The response measure on the ordinate is the probability of selecting the side designated as correct when the rat is in the post-ictal state. The center panel indicates acquisition of the reverse discrimination (opposite state, opposite reinforcement contingencies). The third panel indicates the animals' mastery of the discrimination and their consistent correct responding in accord with the physiological state (post-ictal or normal) that accompanied the discrimination trial. (Adapted from McIntyre and Reichert, 1971. © 1971 Pergamon Press Ltd.).

unusual internal condition (as indicated by ECS or barbiturate). The experiments that explain ECS-induced amnesia in terms of state-dependent retention often have been contaminated by reactivation effects, which may be responsible for the positive results (see Miller et al., 1972). We turn next to a brief consideration of these reactivation effects.

Reactivation of memories.   Earlier we suggested the phrase "agents of memory reactivation" to describe contextual cues that enhance retention by their presence at the retention test. The use of such "reactivation" devices—which may be viewed as facilitating memory retrieval—is widespread in our daily lives, perhaps most commonly in the fields of advertising, politics, and public relations. What features of contextual cues make them effective agents of reactivation? What aspects of memories make them more susceptible to reactivation? And how do the characteristics of reactivated memories compare to those of newly acquired memories? Such questions remain unanswered. To understand these "engineering" questions, we first must understand the retrieval process itself. Reviews of studies of reactivation phenomena have appeared together with preliminary suggestions concerning their interpretation (Spear, 1973, 1976). These papers describe how retention deficits arising from differences in age, acquisition of interfering memories, modifications of contextual cues, or subjection to amnesic agents have been shown to be similarly sensitive to the benefits of reactivation treatments. For this reason, we shall often return to this concept of reactivation as we struggle with interpretations of specific sources of forgetting. We shall elaborate on this concept and its supporting evidence in Chapters 7 and 8.

Interpretations of state-dependent retention.   Overton (1971) has suggested that one of several potential explanations might be modeled after Girden's (1940) interpretation of state-dependent retention induced in dogs by curare. The essence of Girden's interpretation is this: First, learning occurs in the cerebral cortex; although subcortical regions have the capacity to control learning, they ordinarily are inhibited from doing so by the cortex. Second, curare effectively decorticates the dogs; thus, learning under the influence of curare occurs in the subcortical regions. Third, when the drug wears off, the dog cannot retrieve the memory of that learning because those regions of the brain are inhibited once again by the cortex.

Girden's theory implies that decorticated animals should not show state-dependent retention. Without a cortex, all learning must proceed subcortically anyway. Girden's experiments yielded precisely this result. At best, however, Girden's interpretation is limited in its generality, as indicated in two exceptionally analytical evaluations of alternative theories of state-dependent retention, one by Bliss (1974) and the other in several papers by Overton (e.g., 1968, 1974). Leiman, Bliss, Powers, and Rosenzweig (1967) found that state-dependent retention of shuttle avoidance in rats was eliminated if the rats were given cortical lesions in the anterior region of the brain. This confirmed Girden's hypothesis. However, Bliss, Sledjeski, and Leiman (1971) found that state-dependent retention of appetitive learning was unimpaired in monkeys given similar lesions. Moreover, Bliss (1974) suggested further indirect evidence unfavorable to Girden's structural hypothesis. First, the implication of this hypothesis is that at least two separable neurostructures exist for each pair of states that together yield state-dependent retention. There are, however, a good many drugs that may be discriminated from, or may induce state-dependent retention together with, the normal state as well as other drug states. For example, states induced by pentobarbital and atropine cause state-dependent retention in conjunction with a normal state and also in conjunction with each other. This implies a multiplicity of independent structures, which is unwieldy and unlikely. Second, the cortical–subcortical hypothesis of Girden is inconsistent with recent studies showing state-dependent retention in goldfish, which lack a neocortex (e.g., Scobie & Bliss, 1974).

Bliss (1974) evaluates several other hypotheses. The "complex-mediating-processes hypothesis" suggests that brain functions employed by an animal to encode adjunctive events of learning, or to represent learning strategies or mediators, may be disrupted selectively by the action of the state-inducing drugs. Consequently, some of the cognitive functions developed in a normal state would be different in the drug state, and so with any change in state (from drugs to normal or vice versa), mediational devices, strategies, or encoding processes would have to be developed anew. Bliss cites evidence that when state-dependent retention occurs EEG patterns associated with the learning undergone by an animal reappear upon inducement of the particular drug state that had accompanied that learning. This provides supportive circumstantial evidence, if we assume that complex mediating processes are represented by a unique EEG pattern. On the other hand, as John (1967) has noted, any hypothesis of state-dependent retention that depends on subtle changes in the central nervous system has the difficult task of explaining why certain of the manipulations that alter excitability in the central nervous system do not result in state-dependent retention—the complex mediating processes hypothesis does not accomplish this (also see Overton, 1971, p. 80). Moreover, this hypothesis is somewhat regressive: To answer the question of why retention is state dependent, this hypothesis breaks down the learning and retention into subprocesses and suggests that each of these is state dependent. Presumably, one could break down each of these subprocesses further. It is not clear that such an explanatory process is helpful.

Two other hypotheses of state-dependent retention receive little support in Bliss' analysis. The "response initiation hypothesis" (see, for example, Bindra & Reichert, 1966) states that the altered drug state disrupts the pathway connecting neural representations of the conditioned or discriminative stimuli with the pertinent neural motivational mechanism. This hypothesis apparently is the only one of major interest that involves a motivational construct in explaining state-dependent retention. The implication is that response initiation is the object of the major effects of state changes and that choice behavior is affected less or not at all. However, there now is clear positive evidence of state-dependent retention in choice behavior (e.g., Bliss, 1973). The "simple–complex hypothesis" (see Sachs, 1967) also suggests that cognitive functioning is impaired, but in such a way as to decrease the animal's scope of perception of irrelevant events surrounding conditioning. The implied consequence is that through this narrowed stimulus selection the animal learns a simpler problem under the drug state than it would under a normal state. In that event, learning should be more rapid under the drug state than under the normal state. However, this occurs only under particular circumstances—the learning of shuttle avoidance—where a quite different interpretation is more readily applicable.

The final hypothesis Bliss evaluates is more an empirical generalization of mechanisms than a theoretical description. In the "drug stimulus hypothesis," the stimulus consequences of a drug are viewed as influencing retention through the same mechanisms of memory retrieval as any other contextual stimulus. I prefer this hypothesis even though it is plagued by three unfortunate problems. First, this hypothesis is not amenable to a critical test because the specific "drug-induced stimuli," whether singly or in constellation, have not been identified, are not predictable by any known principles, and conceivably may be unidentifiable except on an ad hoc basis. Second, with so little direct evidence available concerning this hypothesis, support of it must be based on faith or intuition. Finally, there are several slightly different hypotheses bearing this label, so it is predisposed to misunderstandings. We may compare two versions of this hypothesis, one suggested in Bliss' analysis and the other more consistent with the conceptual framework presented in this chapter.

Bliss (1974) suggests that drug-induced stimuli "become associated with the conditioned stimulus yielding a compound stimulus. This compound stimulus may be expected to differ considerably from the conditioned-stimulus-+-saline condition usually used as the 'normal' state. Changes between states may yield response decrements because of the steep generalization gradients produced by the respective compound stimuli" (p. 1788). This is an entirely reasonable hypothesis. Yet I find three reasons to reject this particular version and consider instead a quite different form of the drug stimulus hypothesis. First, while it is possible that drug-induced stimuli may enter into a compound with the conditioned or discriminative stimuli, the drug-induced stimuli also may be represented as separate, perhaps independent, attributes of the memory. Although neither the drug state stimuli nor the conditioned stimuli are necessary for memory retrieval, either may be sufficient. Second, I find the conventional method of identifying state-dependent retention with simple stimulus generalization decrement to be unnecessary and perhaps misleading, however reasonable it may appear. We earlier mentioned several reasons why stimulus change may produce performance decrement in a retention test: An insufficient number or kind of events similar to those of training are noticed; new events may induce retrieval of competing memories; or new stimuli may elicit disrupting unconditioned responses. For the most part, these factors were not segregated when principles of stimulus generalization were established. Therefore, it is inappropriate to phrase the drug stimulus hypothesis in this way and then argue against it because of inconsistencies between state-dependent retention and the principles of stimulus generalization—the latter principles may have no firmer basis than those of state-dependent retention. Finally, certain data indicate that correlated exteroceptive and drug-induced stimuli indeed may function independently, with both holding the potential for acquiring stimulus control (Connelly, Connelly, & Epps, 1973).

Before further defending the merit of treating the effects of drug stimuli in state-dependent retention as having the same basis as those of any of the contextual stimuli discussed earlier, I must note contrary evidence. This evidence takes two forms and is not dismissed easily. First, the control over responding exerted by drugs (whether assessed in terms of state-dependent retention or in terms of drug discrimination) for the most part has been more powerful than the control exerted by any contextual stimuli that have been tested. Second, while many drugs that induce state-dependent retention have clear peripheral consequences—muscular, neural, hormonal, and in some cases even sensory—these effects alone have not been sufficient; rather, among drugs with such effects in common, only those that pass the blood–brain barrier to influence the brain directly have had strong state-dependent retention effects (see Overton, 1966, 1968, 1971, for evidence bearing on these two areas of contrary evidence).

Why then, do I encourage serious consideration of this hypothesis? Its fundamental advantage, I believe, is that it provides the opportunity for unification of diverse phenomena by using relatively few principles—parsimony, if you will. Moreover, Bliss (1974) has noted a number of functional similarities between the acquisition of a discrimination between drugs and the acquisition of a discrimination between external contextual stimuli. These similarities include the courses of discrimination acquisition, the development of learning sets, and to some extent the associated discriminative sensitivity. Also, note that when differences have been established between these kinds of discriminations they have been largely quantitative. One cannot judge a priori the relative ''salience'' of any stimulus for any given animal under any given circumstances. Many nondrug stimuli of probable importance have not been tested, especially nonneutral events such as odors, tastes, or tactual sensations. It is important to remember that most events conventionally used as conditioned or discriminative stimuli originally were selected precisely because they are neutral, neither attractive nor aversive, neither preferred nor disliked by the animal; this neutrality is unlikely to be the case with drugs, and so their ''salience,'' in any of several meanings of the term, is likely to be greater. It seems premature to conclude that the action of drugs in inducing drug discrimination or state-dependent retention is of a different kind than that exerted by any other contextual stimuli; however, it is equally premature to conclude the converse.

One final note is in order concerning the relationship between drug discrimination and state-dependent retention: We cannot yet be certain that even these are the consequences of common mechanisms. It often has been found, for example, that drug discrimination ultimately occurs after sufficient training, even though there is little evidence for state-dependent retention following the first shift from one state to the other. The conceptual situation in this case is like that in the preceding paragraph: The likelihood of insufficiently sensitive measures of retention, together with other factors, precludes a clear conclusion regarding the presence or absence of state-dependent retention when drug discrimination is observed; and while the case for common processes is stronger than in the preceding paragraph—for example, there is essentially perfect correspondence between drugs that readily induce state-dependent retention and those that are readily discriminated—a firm conclusion in either direction is premature.

SUMMARY AND CONCLUSIONS

This chapter has emphasized the potential importance of contextual stimuli for retention and forgetting. A contextual stimulus is any event noticed by an organism, with the specific exclusion of the features of an episode that are required to define evidence of memory acquisition (i.e., original learning). Contextual stimuli therefore are effectively redundant to the acquisition of a memory for a particular episode, in that the organism need not attend to contextual stimuli in order to be scored as having learned. Within the present conceptual framework, however, if contextual stimuli of an episode are attended to, they will be incorporated as attributes of the memory for the episode. In this role, contextual stimuli are believed to maintain a capacity to effect retrieval of the memory for that episode.

The conceptual framework presented here is based on the ancient principle that a memory will be manifested to the extent that the circumstances at testing match those at training. Hence, manipulations of contextual stimuli are expected to alter manifestation of prior learning, and in our view, through mechanisms responsible for memory retrieval.

Experimental evidence in support of these contentions has fallen into two general classifications: manipulations of contemporary context or prior cueing. Four classes of contextual stimuli were considered, two in relation to the task-(episode)-to-be-learned (intratask and extratask) and two in relation to the learner (internal and external). Several cases of intratask context were shown to influence retention in animals, with conditions of reinforcement a particularly important source. Among humans, semantic context was seen to have corresponding importance for retention. Instances of similar influence by extratask context also were discussed, particularly with respect to experiments involving animal subjects.

The second half of the chapter studied effects of internal stimulus context in animals and humans, the manner in which the memorial influence of such stimuli has been tested, and the principles and theories derived from those tests.

Several points of a more general nature warrant further emphasis at this time, although elaborated in later chapters and elsewhere (e.g., Spear, 1976). The first point concerns the mechanism through which contextual cues may alter retention. Given control of nuisance effects on performance unrelated to retention, contextual stimuli are seen here as possibly altering retention and forgetting through any of three mechanisms. One of these involves the retrieval process: In our terms, the presence at testing of contextual stimuli represented as attributes of a memory will elicit arousal of those attributes if the respective stimuli are noticed, and ultimately retrieval of the target memory may result. Contextual stimuli are thus viewed as promoting accessibility of the target memory.

Contextual stimuli also might alter retention through two other plausible mechanisms, and for neither of these is it necessary to implicate the retrieval process. First, it is possible that all memories are equally accessible and contextual cues merely enhance the individual's *discrimination* of which memory is to be manifested in behavior. The second mechanism also requires the assumption that an assortment of potentially applicable memories are equally accessible, but in this case the contextual stimuli are seen to result in direct inhibition of all accessible memories except the appropriate one. In our view, the difficulty with these nonretrieval explanations is that they fail to provide for the original establishment of the set of accessible memories and do not provide a means through which the "selected" memory becomes manifested in behavior.

This is not to say that contextual stimuli may not have a discriminative function. Indeed, it seems quite clear that for paradigms such as Asratian's "switching" paradigm a major role of the control exerted by contextual stimuli is discriminative. Furthermore, it seems thoroughly reasonable that a memory may consist of discriminative or retrieval attributes or both (Underwood, 1969). Ultimately, we may find that one or the other of these functions is unnecessary. For example, the retrieval process may be found actually to function in terms of a series of conditional discriminations involving only minor elicitation properties. At present, however, it seems most reasonable to view contextual stimuli as having either a retrieval or a discriminative function.

The second general point to be emphasized at this time is an acknowledgment that hard evidence still is sparse concerning the characteristics of the control exerted by contextual stimuli. By our definition, contextual stimuli predict a contingency within a learning episode but are relatively ineffective (compared to conditioned or discriminative stimuli) in predicting the absolute probability of a particular episodic event (such as a reinforcer). Probably the principles governing stimulus control by conditioned or discriminative stimuli (e.g., those concerning stimulus generalization, selection, or compounding) also will apply to control by contextual stimuli, but more direct study of the latter will be necessary before we can be certain.

3
Retention after Short Intervals

OVERVIEW OF SIMPLE RETENTION

Analytical research on memory processing often involves the systematic application of treatments that commonly result in forgetting. One such treatment is to teach the organism competing memories that interfere with retention of the target memory; another is to induce physiological malfunction, especially in the central nervous system. Of central interest in this chapter and the next is "simple retention," the retention that occurs in organisms that have *not* been treated in such a way as to explicitly induce forgetting. We thus minimize consideration of forgetting that results from unusual sources of interference or physiological malfunction, whether purposely administered or accidentally encountered by the organism. Later we shall consider how such events result in retention loss and why this occurs. For now, we are concerned primarily with simple retention, the object of interest when we ask what portion of the words a person has learned will be given correctly by him a few seconds, minutes or hours later. Similarly, simple retention is the issue when we measure the probability that a rat will turn right in a maze one minute or one month after it has learned that food may be obtained on the right side but not on the left, or when we briefly present a symbol to a monkey and test whether it can distinguish it from among others after a 4-minute retention interval.

The most important environmental circumstances for simple retention is length of the retention interval. As mentioned earlier, "retention interval" is defined as any interval longer than that necessary to establish original learning; with multitrial learning, the retention interval must be longer than the intertrial interval. In the study of simple retention, no attempt is made to modify the events that ordinarily would occur during that interval in the organism's life cycle, except that measures are taken to prevent additional practice on the episode to be remembered: Humans should be treated in a manner that would prevent rehearsal during the retention interval, and animals should be housed away from the circumstances of learning.

What sorts of questions have been asked about experimental situations in which the probability of behavioral manifestation of an acquired memory decreases (or increases) the longer the interval since acquisition? Four immediate questions are (1) what is the temporal course of forgetting; (2) how much is forgotten; (3) what is forgotten; and (4) what measures may be taken to prevent forgetting? We turn now to a general consideration of these questions in terms of simple forgetting. Following that, we shall consider phenomena and issues of special relevance to retention after short intervals, often termed *short-term memory* (STM).

Shape of the Function Relating Amount of Retention and Length of the Retention Interval

Traditionally, the retention function has been conceived of as indicating monotonically increasing, negatively accelerated forgetting. In other words, the retention performance has been presumed ordinarily to fall off most rapidly shortly after memory acquisition and then to slow down to a more gradual decrement (see Figure 3.1, from Ebbinghaus, 1913). While it has been conventional to regard Figure 3.1 as an accurate representation of the modal retention function, there is good reason to view it instead as atypical: First, Ebbinghaus employed percentage savings as his index of retention, and this index frequently yields a different function than the indexes used more often today; second, Ebbinghaus' technique entailed maximal proactive interference; and third, his technique also included unspecifiable but strong specific sources of retroactive interference. Furthermore, any attempt to regard such a function as representative of all relationships between retention and retention interval is bound to fail for three additional reasons of general significance.

First, the slope and shape of the retention function depend on the specific species and memory being tested. Perhaps this qualification may be found unnecessary once degree of learning can be equated across tasks and species; however, our technology is far from achieving a solution to the problem of how degree of learning might be controlled for all species tested with any episodes that might be represented as a memory, so this possibility is quite untestable at present.

Second, the slope and shape of the retention function depend on the method used to assess retention. For example, retention in terms of recognition may be dramatically better than in terms of recall, or the converse, depending simply on how subjects are instructed or presented the materials (cf. Tulving & Thomson, 1973; Watkins & Tulving, 1975). Some cases of forgetting may be more apparent measured in terms of latency to respond than when measured in terms of choice (e.g., Hill, Cotton, Spear, & Duncan, 1969). Also, circumstances such as

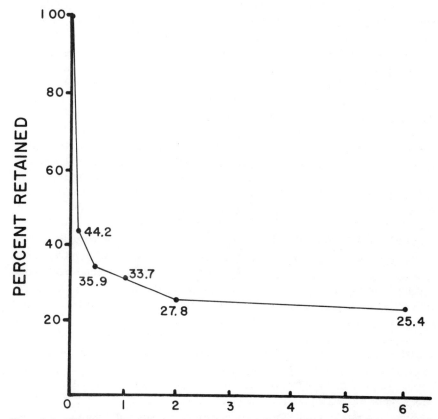

Figure 3.1 This figure represents the conventional conception of negatively accelerated forgetting based on the data derived by Ebbinghaus with his self-testing procedures (adapted from Ebbinhaus, 1913).

the Kamin effect (see Chapter 4) that yield a nonmonotonic retention function with one measure of assessing retention predictably may yield a monotonic function when another measure is used (Spear, 1971, 1973).

Third, a surprisingly large number of retention functions unaccountably have deviated from the classical monotonic decreasing, negatively accelerated form. In fact, many carefully derived retention functions have been neither decreasing nor monotonic but, instead, have been increasing or multiphasic, as we shall see in the next chapter.

What Factors Determine the Magnitude of Forgetting?

From the reasons just discussed, it is obvious that statements concerning the amount and determinants of forgetting cannot have very general applicability. Perhaps the most consistent statements of this sort have been found in the assessment of forgetting of verbal materials by human adults, because it is in this context that the most analytical studies of simple forgetting have taken place. Furthermore, the methods used in this area of study have been more standardized than those used in animal learning.

We can assert with relatively little qualification that a surprisingly small number of factors have seemed to influence the amount of forgetting once methodology is settled. The first factor is proactive or retroactive interference by competing memories that have been previously or subsequently acquired. In simple forgetting, competing memories apparently are acquired extraexperimentally in the course of the individual's natural experiences. Although the mechanisms of such interference effects may be debated continuously, no one who has given serious thought to these problems will deny that competing memories may induce forgetting and clearly do so under specifiable circumstances.

Another factor, tied inextricably to the issue of interference in forgetting, is the nature of the events encountered by the subject between learning and the retention test. While competing memories acquired during this interval may impair retention, simple rehearsal or reexposure to certain stimuli that serve as "reminders" may facilitate retention (i.e., alleviate forgetting). The problem of how a researcher can create a neutral environment during the retention interval is not simple; at present, a solution seems quite beyond the scope of our technology. Certainly a "behavioral vacuum" is not the answer, because suspending an organism's behavior by sensory or response deprivation is known to have dramatic effects of its own. The control of activities during the retention interval is less a problem with animals than with humans, who, though removed from the learning environment, may re-present to themselves through linguistic mediators the materials to be remembered; presumably animals lack these symbolic skills. This human–animal distinction becomes less clear, however, when one considers the mechanisms by which humans evoke memories for rehearsal: Once attention to the to-be-remembered events is terminated, might not these rehearsal-like mechanisms depend on the occurrence of the same sorts of external and internal cues that reactivate memories in animals? Perhaps comprehension of such issues will help us differentiate events that facilitate retention from those that interfere.

The third basic determinant of the magnitude of retention is degree of original learning. In the simplest sense, higher degrees of learning may facilitate retention in either of two ways. In the trivial case, it is obvious that if humans are presented with 12 pairs of words to be remembered, their later retention scores will be better if they give evidence of learning 12 than if they give evidence of learning only 6; similarly, monkeys trained to discriminate symbols will show better retention if their original discrimination performance is 95% accurate rather than 65%. But there is a more significant sense in which degree of learning apparently affects retention: The greater the absolute number or percentage of events of an episode represented (learned) as memory attributes, the more resistant that memory is to sources of forgetting. This statement clearly is theoretical at this time, more a hypothesis than a statement of empirical fact. What we do know is that the rate of forgetting is slowed over time and that amnesia is less likely to be induced the more often an acquired behavior is expressed (practiced). Even when individuals in a group of organisms have learned perfectly (in terms of the measurements used), the members of the group that are given additional practice show better retention. When we speak of degree of learning as affecting retention, reference is to the latter cases. The importance of this variable for retention cannot be overestimated. For instance, Underwood and Keppel (1963a) observe that "speaking now in general of the reliable facts of forgetting, it appears that degree of learning is the only variable involved in a substantial way in retention" (p. 16). On the other hand, degree of learning itself is not well understood. Except for operational distinctions in terms of the accuracy of responding (which may become circular if one is not careful), it is not clear what the components of a "high" degree of learning are that differ from those of "low" degree of learning. We shall return to this issue often.

Conventionally, to say that 75% of what was learned is forgotten is to say one of three things following the retention test: (1) 75% of the subjects failed to behave as if they had acquired the memory; (2) the average subject behaved with only 25% of the efficiency he had shown during original learning; or (3) the average subject behaved as if he had acquired only 25% of the materials he actually had acquired. If we assume a memory to be multidimensional, alternative (3) has clear advantages conceptually, although it rarely is applicable because of the limited number of memory attributes typically measured, especially in the testing of animals. This may change with improved technology (e.g., Springer, 1975). A desirable way to estimate percentage forgetting generally is to consider the entire learning episode as the memory and measure what percent of *all* attributes stored, not just the target attribute, are retrieved. That is, we would ask, Of all possible attributes, what percentage can be produced by the subject? Thus, although a person may be unable to recognize or recall a word previously learned, he or she still may be able to report a number of its characteristics, such as whether it was a long or a short word, to what part of speech it belonged, and features of the experimental room. Animals obviously cannot be interrogated directly, so evidence of such incidental attributes is more difficult to obtain from them, but it is not an impossible task. Generally, however, the influence of degree of learning would become clearer if a thorough assessment of which events are stored as memory attributes originally—before a source of forgetting is introduced—were employed as a baseline for evaluation of the percentage forgotten.

What Is Forgotten?

Determining what is learned has been a controversial topic of learning theory for many years and, of course, is still unsettled. A decision about what is forgotten is no less difficult. There are techniques, however, by which one might arrive at some reasonable judgment. For example, certain stimulus events encountered by an organism between training and the retention test may be more likely than others to facilitate retention. From this we may infer, as a first approximation, that stimuli that act most effectively as agents of reactivation do so by arousing attributes that otherwise would not be retrieved. These attributes then may be identified (at least approximately, in terms of the agents of reactivation) as those that are forgotten in organisms not exposed to reactivation treatments.

Generally, however, "What is forgotten?" is a shallow question; because there is no reason to believe there are any attributes of a memory that would *never* be forgotten, the answer must be "anything, depending." Moreover, to conclude that a particular attribute is never forgotten is to accept the null hypothesis under risky circumstances. What makes the question even less useful is that there appears to be no obvious limit on the number of attributes that conceivably might constitute a memory (but see Underwood, 1972). Nevertheless, different attributes probably are forgotten at different rates (cf. Spear, 1971, 1973), and we can report samplings of memory content that have been investigated in studies of simple retention, such as the following.

1. Conditions of reinforcement, such as reinforcer magnitude (Gleitman & Steinman, 1964; Spear, 1967) and percentage reinforcement (Aiken & Gibson, 1965; Gonzalez, Fernhoff, & David, 1973; Spear & Spitzner, 1967) may be forgotten. As examples, the negative contrast effect that results from shifting between high and low reinforcer magnitudes declines with increasing intervals between the pre- and post-shift stages, and the greater resistance to extinction found after partial reinforcement lessens as the retention interval increases between acquisition and extinction (for further discussion, see Gleitman, 1971; Spear, 1971).

2. Characteristics of the training apparatus, such as the brightness of the walls or more subtle features, may be forgotten. Changes in the brightness of the alley may cause disruption of an animal's established alley-running performance if the changes are made *shortly* after the animal has acquired the running behavior; such a change has relatively little effect if a long retention interval has elapsed since original learning (Perkins & Weyant, 1958; Steinman, 1967). From this we infer that the animal has forgotten the brightness characteristic of the apparatus. Similarly, evidence of fear conditioning in a rat diminishes if the testing apparatus is different from the training apparatus (even when the apparatuses are identical to the human eye). But this occurs only if the test is made relatively soon after training; if a delay of 24 hours or more occurs between training and testing, the shift in the apparatus causes no deterioration in the animal's performance (e.g., McAllister & McAllister, 1971).

3. Habituation of responses to novel stimuli may be forgotten (Parsons, Fagan, & Spear, 1973; Thompson & Spencer, 1966).

4. "Learned helplessness" in dogs, a deficiency in certain instrumental behaviors induced by prior exposure to inescapable punishment, may be forgotten,

quite rapidly under some circumstances (e.g., Overmier & Seligman, 1967; Seligman, Maier, & Solomon, 1971).

5. Classically conditioned drinking may be forgotten (Seligman, Ives, Ames, & Mineka, 1970, Exp. 2).

6. A concept-like behavior acquired by monkeys during the learning of a series of discrimination problems—"learning set"—may be forgotten to a considerable extent after six years (although there may be maximal retention of this concept over six months or so; Stollnitz, 1970).

Intraepisode versus intratrial retention.   By viewing a memory as multidimensional, one can appreciate relatively easily the important distinction between intraepisode, inter trial, and intra trial retention. This concept concerns "what is forgotten" in terms of a memory.

Suppose that the core of a memory to be acquired is a contingency between two events, one a signal (conditioned stimulus, or CS), the other a consequence (unconditioned stimulus, or UCS). It is known that the interval between the signal and the consequence must not be unduly long if an organism is to learn to respond in accordance with the consequence when the signal occurs. In other words, the interval between the CS and the UCS is a critical determinant of conditioning.

The factor of memory processing was not introduced into this learning situation as long as the maximum interval employed for conditioning was on the order of seconds. However, it was discovered that when rats experience a gustatory stimulus as the CS and a visceral consequence as the UCS, significant conditioning still may result in spite of CS–UCS intervals of several hours (Revusky, 1971). This discovery has focused attention on the processes responsible for retention of the CS at the time of presentation of the UCS (i.e., processes of intraepisode retention). Questions concerning the effect of increasing the interval between CS and UCS often have been phrased in terms of the probability of associating a particular response with a particular stimulus, or in terms of the degree of stimulus control exerted by a stimulus over certain classes of responding. It does not change the problem to describe it, as we shall, in terms of the necessary conditions under which attributes become members of a common memory or, more specifically, the necessary conditions under which a CS and a UCS (or UCR) become encoded in memory as a single episode in spite of long intervals between the CS and the UCS. The difference is one of emphasis concerning the factors that influence forgetting of the CS.

We shall have occasion to apply the following distinctions. By the "intraepisode interval" is meant the time elapsed between the occurrence of physically separable events within an episode. By "intratrial interval" is meant the time between the occurrence of a particular event within an episode and the test for the retrieval of the memory that includes a representation of that event. By "intertrial interval" is meant the interval between successive occurrences of an entire episode or successive tests for retention of that episode. These distinctions are useful not only with problems of acquired aversions but also in dealing with the processing of verbal memories for a set of words. Tulving (1964) established the value of such a distinction several years ago in his analysis of multitrial free recall in terms of intratrial retention (between the presentation of a given word in a list and the test for its recall) and intertrial retention (retention between successive tests, that is, the probability of emitting a response given correctly on the immediately preceding trial).

Distinctions such as these have general significance and potential value beyond the labeling of any particular experimental procedure. It is patent that episodes-to-be-remembered are defined by the experimenter. The decision as to which events should constitute the critical episode or precisely how to truncate a sequential set of events for testing one's memory for those events obviously can be quite arbitrary and not necessarily in accord with how the subject views the world. We therefore find it convenient to consider independently intervals between any of the components of the paradigm for studying memory processing—the episode, events within the episode, and the tests for retention. This is reasonable because episodes tested for processing as memories typically include a number of distinctive events separated by intervals that are of importance for theory. In these terms, the intraepisode interval concerns the traditional law of contiguity; the intratrial interval has to do with the short-term memory component of performance and the intertrial interval with the long-term memory component of performance.

We shall apply this distinction in the future chapters, with special use in discussing the basis of acquired aversions (Chapter 5) and the influence of memory content on retention (Chapter 8).

A Minor Classification in the Analysis of Simple Forgetting

General distinctions between tests with humans and animals.   This chapter, like those to follow, is guided by two distinctions: the organisms tested (human or animal) and the memory tested. In considering simple forgetting, we shall continue the practice of discussing human and animal data separately. However, we shall point out conceptual and phenomenal similarities when these arise, in accordance with our belief that some degree of commerce should be maintained between the disciplines of animal and human memory processing. Because it seems inevitable that common memorial processes exist, we shall seek opportunities for integration. But whether or not animals and humans have common memorial processes, we must be aware of the substantial differences in the methods by which memory processing is studied in animals and humans. The following are three such differences:

1. The foremost distinction is in the content of the memories that are tested. Humans usually are tested for *verbal* memories. There have been a few human studies requiring retention of motor skills, pictures, or odors, but for most tasks that are not explicitly verbal, the memory nevertheless may be encoded verbally

via transformations (see Bilodeau, 1966). Humans, except for very young infants, have a vast reservoir of verbal memories and are well practiced at storing, retrieving, and otherwise manipulating these memories. Moreover, some psycholinguists agree with Chomsky in suggesting that humans may be biologically predisposed to the storage and retrieval of verbal memories, perhaps uniquely so (for the opposite opinion, see Gardner & Gardner, 1975). If we are sensitive to the possibility that the characteristics of memory processing may depend on the organism's biological predisposition to notice and incorporate particular attributes within a given memory (cf. Seligman & Hager, 1972), then we must realize that, in this respect, the content of most tasks employed in studies of animal memory processing are on a scale or dimension different from human verbal memories. For example, it has been most convenient to employ aversive conditioning in animal memory studies in order to alleviate a difficult experimental design problem: Appetitive motivational conditions, such as duration of food deprivation, are subject to confounding with length of retention interval. However, it is not at all clear that a rat is predisposed to store and retrieve memories representing the occurrence of footshock-contingent-upon-flashing-light in the same way that humans may be predisposed to manipulate verbal memories. Indeed, the ecological niche in which rats have evolved is especially devoid of lights (flashing or otherwise) during their nocturnal waking hours, and electrical footshock does not occur naturally. Whether we are dealing here with issues relevant to the distinction between semantic and episodic memory (cf. Tulving, 1972) is a matter for future study. Nevertheless, biological dispositions appear to be an important consideration when animal and human memory processing are compared.

2. Another distinction between methods of studying simple forgetting concerns differences between the target memory and other memories acquired by the organism. The components of most tasks used with animals are quite distinct from those of other memories encountered in animals' home environments, whereas there is little distinction between components of humans' verbal memories within and outside the experimental situation. When we discuss the analysis of interference factors in retention, we shall see that discrimination between the target memory and alternative memories is an important determinant of retention.

3. Still another difference in methods concerns the motivational conditions under which animals and humans acquire memories in experimental circumstances. Animals typically are trained under unusually high states of arousal, abnormal degrees of nutritional deprivation, or circumstances in which the danger of severe pain is considerable. It is not clear whether the primary motivation for humans—for example, trying to avoid looking foolish to the experimenter—is comparable in any way to the motivations involved with animals. What is likely, however, is that the internal physiological changes that accompany such experimental motivational states in animals are certainly more drastic than those experienced by humans during their testing.

These are just a few of the procedural differences between studying human and animal memory, and it is important to keep the likelihood of such differences in mind. Toward such realism, we shall continue to consider data from humans and animals separately. Also, we have absolutely no intention of suggesting that the memorial processes of humans and animals are similar just because similar labels have been used.

Distinction between "short-term" and "long-term" memory.   The second classification through which we shall analyze the existing experimental material is the operational distinction between short-term memory and long-term memory. It is convenient to discuss separately experiments in which original learning continues only to a relatively low degree (e.g., the subject views an array of words for 3 seconds) and the retention interval is relatively short (e.g., 10 seconds). These operations define the classification "short-term memory" (STM) and, by exclusion, define its alternative, "long-term memory" (LTM). This operational separation should not be confused with the *conceptual* distinction between short-term memory and long-term memory maintained in some theories, a distinction that now appears to be of limited usefulness, especially in our consideration of the processing that follows acquisition of a memory. Our use of "STM" here is simply to indicate consideration of a memory whose term as a representation of prior events has been relatively short. The remainder of this chapter concerns STM and the next chapter concerns LTM, with emphasis on simple retention in each case.

The origin of the study of retention after short intervals and low degrees of original learning is found in the studies of delayed responding with animals and memory span with humans. Like much of the technology in psychobiological research, both of these methods have been replaced by more effective, more analytical tests of STM; yet both methods continue to be used for clinical diagnosis of physiological or psychological malfunction. These points will become clear as we look at the chronological development of the study of STM.

SHORT-TERM MEMORY IN ANIMALS: DELAYED RESPONSE

In the midst of philosophical argument concerning the role of anthropomorphism in the interpretation of the behavior of animals, the eminent W. S. Hunter (1913) introduced the delayed-response task. This task originally was intended to determine objectively the characteristics of an animal's internal representation of an external stimulus event. Hunter rejected the implications of certain anecdotal evidence for "memories" in animals: For example, because horses reliably can follow the correct path back to their distant stable and behave with apparent anticipation as they grow nearer, it was argued by some that horses therefore possess some "intraorganic cue," like an idea, about the events along the path in relation to the stable. Hunter, however, interpreted this as a lower-level type of cognitive activity, which he referred to as "sensory recognition." He explicitly divorced this concept from that of "memory," conceptualized as possibly including the dating of an event in the past of an organism.

Hunter conducted his research and wrote his paper during the "behaviorist revolution," of which he was a leader. This movement was a critical step in transforming psychology from a branch of philosophy to a scientific enterprise, and it rigorously applied Morgan's canon of not attributing any unnecessary cognitive capacities to animals. Hunter's interpretation of his data was affected accordingly.

What did Hunter mean when he asserted that "sensory recognition," not memory processing, was evidenced when an animal displayed extraordinary persistence toward a stimulus object that previously was associated with food, or when a horse increased its speed as objects closer to home appeared? Winograd (1971) interpreted Hunter's resistance to applying a concept of memory to animals as a typically behavioristic reaction to anthropomorphism, and noted that in doing so Hunter paradoxically assumed the nonbehavioristic view of memory processing as "a mental state involving, it would seem, familiarity, localization in time, and active recall" (p. 261).

Apparently, Hunter allowed the process of "sensory recognition" in an animal because such a process implied neither a "time tag" nor the "spontaneous" production of a memory that was presumed to occur in active recall by humans. In our view, the problem with this is the implicit assumption that *humans* possess the capacity to *spontaneously* produce evidence of a memory: This is misleading and incorrect. All memory retrieval, whether called "active recall," "spontaneous production of memorial evidence," or whatever, is cued by some source. The stimuli that initiate a retrieval process in humans may be internal or external, contextual or simply the instructions to recall; and while the need for such retrieval cues and the need for the retrieval process itself may differ for recognition compared to indexes of memory such as free recall, the distinction between recognition and recall processes still is sufficiently vague to preclude a firm conclusion about the precise dependence on events or cues that stimulate memory retrieval (cf. Tulving & Thomson, 1973; Underwood, 1972; Watkins & Tulving, 1975). It would seem that such a view would fit what we know about human memory better than Hunter's implication that humans have a spontaneous recall process unavailable to animals.

The Hunter experiments.   To test for the existence of symbolic capacities, Hunter applied a "delayed-response" task that had been originated and briefly tested at the University of Chicago by two graduate students, Haugh and Reed, working in association with Carr (see, e.g., Tinklepaugh, 1928). With this task, an animal's selection among alternative stimuli could not be explained in terms of continued responding to a perceptible goal object. To prepare his subjects for the critical "delayed-reaction" or "delayed-response" stage of the task, Hunter first trained the hungry animals to obtain food by entering the only lighted door of three possible doors. After the animal had perfected this discrimination response, Hunter began trials in which the light was shown as before but turned off before the animal was able to complete its response. At first the light was turned off when the animal was en route to its location, then just prior to the animal's initiation of the response; finally, after several hundred shaping trials, delays were introduced between light offset and the opportunity to respond. Because responding was permitted only in the *absence* of the stimulus that signaled the location of the food, reliable correct responding hardly could be caused by sensory recognition. Rather, accurate selecting in the absence of maintained "pointing" or "overt orienting attitudes" in the direction of the correct goal, as a setter might do toward a bird in the field, could perhaps be attributed to control by an internal representational response, or some other form of ideation. Furthermore, Hunter reasoned that the efficiency of ideation could be compared across various species of animals, or even between animals and humans, by increasing the interval between the offset of the light and the opportunity to respond.

Hunter tested rats, dogs, raccoons, and children on this notion. In later studies, Hunter (1917) shifted from his original "indirect" method to a "direct" method in which the light was omitted as a signal for the location of the reward object. With the direct method, the subject simply saw the object through the appropriate door until the retention interval began. Among the subjects tested in this way was Hunter's daughter, Thayer, a toddler who had not yet developed stable language habits when she was tested at 13–16 months of age. Hunter established the longest retention interval that each of his subjects could tolerate before retention no longer was significant. For rats, he estimated this to be about 10 seconds, for raccoons 25 seconds, for dogs 5 minutes, for his 13-month-old daughter about 24 seconds, for 2 1/2-year-old children 50 seconds, and for a 6-year-old child 20 minutes. Hunter denied the use of intraorganic factors by rats simply because for efficient performance after relatively long intervals they were observed to depend on physical orientation toward the appropriate goal compartment. Such physical orientation did not seem necessary for raccoons and children. Hunter entertained the possibility that "sensory thought" might be involved for these subjects. He supposed that when the critical stimulus—the position of the light or the position of the exit holding the rewarded object—was originally shown, it might be represented within the animal as an intraorganic cue, probably of a kinesthetic nature. Hunter suggested that although such cues might "fulfill an ideation function," they probably represented "sensory thought" of an imageless nature rather than higher imaginal thought. Also, he proposed that such intraorganic cues were aroused by the original stimulus, waned during the retention interval, but were rearoused when responding was permitted. Vague as this reasoning sounds, it is both interesting and testable. It is unfortunate, therefore, that this part of Hunter's work essentially was ignored in follow-up research by others.

Hunter's work did generate a good deal of interest. In retrospect, however, much research that followed seems to have been misdirected, as suggested in Chapter 1. This follow-up research concentrated on two questions. First, which animals, if any, have ideation independent of physical orientation, even at the level of Hunter's "sensory thought"? In other words, do animals really have internal mediators (in addition to postural mediators) that they can use? Second, how are species ordered in terms of their capacity for such ideation?

It might seem that the latter question—intriguing, but also unduly seductive of scientific energy—could be answered simply enough by a phylogenetic ordering of mental capacities. But this is not so. The methodology applied to this truly difficult problem so far has been totally inadequate, and essentially no hard principles have evolved from this line of research. The first question also generated experiments that were largely futile in that they offered little understanding of memory processing. If research on the memory *process* had been generated by Hunter's work, as his interpretation of "sensory thought" might well have done under other circumstances, perhaps the history of the psychobiological study of memory processing would have taken a quite different course.

Among the comparative studies of delayed responding, to which we shall return later, there are two classical studies that merit immediate mention because of their interest. One of these studies was conducted by Yerkes, who studied memory in a gorilla belonging to the Ringling Brothers circus; the other was conducted by Tinklepaugh, and it included some creative experiments on memory processing in monkeys.

Yerkes' studies of Congo.   Yerkes contributed a series of papers reporting some behavioral tests of Congo, a young gorilla that at the time was maintained on the estate of John Ringling near the winter quarters of the Ringling and Barnum and Bailey circus, in Florida. These tests, conducted in February and March 1928, became the last of the series because Congo died suddenly in April 1928 from an illness diagnosed as acidosis, probably exacerbated by an inadequate diet (Yerkes, 1928). Yerkes' (1928) paper, entitled "The Mind of a Gorilla," is written in a charming narrative style and includes a great deal of information that is redundant for our purposes. Also included, however, is some instructive information for issues of memory processing.

Prior to these final tests, Congo's quarters had been moved to a different location, so Yerkes had not worked with her for about ten months. Nevertheless, Yerkes believed that Congo showed definite signs of recognizing him. On the other hand, Congo's performance on the previously well-learned "box and pole" task was very poor, indicating considerable forgetting. In this task, Congo could obtain food from a long box only by using a long wooden pole to retrieve the food. Whereas several months earlier she had obtained the food in this manner within 28 seconds of its presentation, on this occasion she failed to obtain the food within a 30-minute interval on each of three daily sessions of testing.

Whether this was due primarily to the drastic change in the environment that accompanied Congo's shift in residence or to some other events occurring in the retention interval is not clear. But obviously the amount of forgetting was considerable.

Subsequently, Yerkes initiated tests of delayed responding. For this task, Congo observed the food being placed in a particular container on a turntable. The food included, for example, "two baked bananas, a large orange and two sweet potatoes" (Yerkes, 1928, p. 36). The turntable, which held empty containers as well, was rotated to prevent Congo from remembering the correct container by physical orientation alone. Under these circumstances, Congo showed efficient retention of the appropriate container after delays of 10 minutes. In a less systematic study, Yerkes found that if Congo was shown food being buried in the ground, she readily could locate it 48 hours later. Substantial memorial capacities thus were established in this famous gorilla, although the underlying processes were left largely unanalyzed.

The Tinklepaugh experiments.   Tinklepaugh (1928) reported a series of creative studies that are more analytical than Yerkes' tests yet are seemingly quaint by comparison with current technology. Tinklepaugh described the dispositions of his four monkeys as "uniform in their original fear and ugliness, showing no signs of former handling" (1928, p. 202). The basic apparatus "consisted of two ordinary 1/2 pint tin drinking cups without handles, an office chair with arms and a board provided with a bracket so that it could be stood up on edge or laid flat on the floor" (p. 203). The general method comprised three steps: First, the monkey was "turned loose in the room" and permitted to explore generally before being "commanded to 'get in the chair'" (p. 204); next, the experimenter placed food (either a banana or lettuce) under one of the cups, "always attempting to secure the animal's attention to the act" (p. 204); and finally, "at the end of the delay period, the animal was commanded to 'come get the food'" (p. 204).

Regardless of the technique, Tinklepaugh's analysis and interpretation of primate memory processing remains important today. For our purposes, the most instructive aspect of Tinklepaugh's work was his use of the "substitution method." The monkey was shown one article of food, such as a banana, being placed under the cup, and when the monkey was not looking a piece of lettuce was substituted for the banana. Ordinarily, Tinkelpaugh's monkeys preferred bananas. Nevertheless, they readily accepted lettuce and consumed it within three or four seconds, provided that they had seen the lettuce placed under the cup originally. But if the monkey had seen a banana placed under the cup and, after solving the problem, found lettuce, the monkey's behavior was quite different. After such a clandestine substitution, the monkey extended her hand to take the food, but then

> her hand dropped to the floor without touching it. She looks at the lettuce, but (unless very hungry) does not touch it. She looks around the cup and behind the board. She stands up and

looks under and around her. She picks the cup up and examines it thoroughly inside and out. She has on occasion turned toward observers present in the room and shrieked at them in apparent anger. After several seconds spent searching, she gives a glance toward the other cup, which she has been taught not to look into, and then walks off to a nearby window. The lettuce is left untouched on the floor. (Tinklepaugh, 1928, pp. 224–225)

In contrast to the 3- or 4-second consumption period that occurred when the monkey "expected" the lettuce, the latency to eat following the substitution episode was between 10 and 33 seconds. The important point that we can make from Tinklepaugh's substitution test is that because the monkey's behavior upon not receiving the originally perceived food differed from their behavior upon receiving it, we may infer that the monkeys had a representation of the food itself as part of the original memory.

Tinklepaugh's data were largely qualitative, to be sure, which may explain their lack of influence on the thinking of most learning theorists during the 1930s. Moreover, even the qualitative differences, if accepted, are subject to alternative explanations. Nevertheless, Tinklepaugh's work does stand as one of the first attempts to identify and study the content of a memory in terms of a particular attribute.

Inferences Concerning Simple Retention Derived from Studies of Delayed Responding

Although studies using the delayed-response technique have begun to decrease in number recently in favor of more sensitive methods, psychological literature over the past 40 to 50 years abounds with this application. Perhaps the most striking aspect of this is the scope of the experimental circumstances in which the delayed-response test has been used. As Fletcher (1965) has noted, "This powerful behavioral assay reveals phylogenetic, ontogenetic, and sex differences; it detects, where other tests fail to detect, the effects of brain lesions, drugs, radiation, and deprivation" (p. 129).

However, because it is not at all clear that the delayed-response test measures memory processing, this technique poses a basic problem that is especially significant to the discussions in this book. In spite of the sensitivity of the delayed-response test to behavioral differences, these differences may have little to do with memory processing.

The concern that the subject's bodily orientation during the retention interval, rather than some internal memorial representation, might be responsible for correct delayed-response performances prompted a number of experiments, as mentioned earlier. To test whether bodily orientation is required for maintaining retention over long delays, a variety of techniques have been employed with dogs, monkeys, cats, and rats. One procedure simply was to remove the animal from the experimental room during the delay (e.g., Beritoff, 1971; MacCorquodale, 1947; Maier, 1929; Tinklepaugh, 1928); another was to rotate the animal in its holding cage during the delay (e.g., MacCorquodale, 1947); another to change the position of the alternative containers during the delay (e.g., Harlow, 1932; Yerkes, 1928); and still another was to simply face the animal away from the alternative containers when it was released following the delay (Yerkes, 1928). In all cases, retention was maintained over sufficiently long intervals to permit the inference that bodily orientation was not a necessary condition for retention, at least not in the simple sense.

However, a related and perhaps more important factor is distractibility. Fletcher (1965) has identified distractibility (during either the initial baiting phase or the retention interval) as a very likely determinant of delayed-response performance. This is especially important because most manipulations of the central nervous system that drastically alter delayed responding also increase general activity or distractibility.

Fletcher (1965) reports data indicating a high correlation between errors in responding following a delay and amount of general activity during the delay. For this test, five adult Rhesus monkeys learned a discrimination with no delay so that they performed perfectly; but after a 5-second delay they made errors on 9% of their choices, and after a 20-second delay they made errors on 16% of their choices. Fletcher measured activity by recording the number of times during the retention interval each monkey interrupted a photo beam across the restraining apparatus, and he found that monkeys with higher activity counts were more likely to choose incorrectly (the rank order correlation was .975).

Of course, one must be cautious about cause-and-effect conclusions. For example, animals may become more active during a retention interval if they have forgotten which container was baited. In addition, there is relatively little effect of general activity during a retention interval on delayed-matching-to-sample (D'Amato, 1973; Jarrard & Moise, 1971). The latter probably is the more analytical test of short-term retention in animals, although such functional differences between this and the delayed-response test also may be due to more interesting factors than merely testing procedure—for example, content of the memory test (typically, position for the delayed-response test, objects for delayed-matching-to-sample). Nevertheless, the fact that such correlations do occur suggests that bodily orientation may be useful to the animal if the opportunity is available. This further emphasizes the limitations of the delayed-response task for analysis of STM.

The delayed-response task also is limited in other respects: There is lack of control over initial memory storage; most techniques intended to ensure attention of the subject to the baiting operation are crude, for example, waiting until the animal "looks at" the appropriate container; and, as Harlow (1951) has noted, with multiple tests the delayed-response task really amounts to successive acquisitions and reversals, which makes the problem a good deal more complex than Hunter initially envisioned. Nevertheless, some principles that may be culled from the work on delayed responding are worth mentioning because they are relevant to the interpretation of tests of STM in animals.

For the purpose of analyzing memory processing, it is useful to consider the variables that have been found to have their effect on delayed responding during one of three separable stages: the "baiting" stage, when the reinforcer is placed in a container, which may involve memory storage; the retention interval; and the choice, or response, stage, which may involve memory retrieval. Fletcher's (1965) summary of the delayed-response literature is ordered in terms of these stages.

Baiting and response stages: storage and retrieval of memory. Not surprisingly, the variables that are particularly important during the initial baiting stage are also known to influence discrimination learning in general. The spatial separation and visual similarity of the alternative containers are such variables. For example, Harrison and Nissen (1941) studied the effects of changing the spatial separation of the alternative containers between the baiting stage and the choice stage. Following baiting, in which the discriminanda were close together for half of the subjects and far apart for the remaining subjects, the animal's view was blocked and the containers moved so that half of the animals in each of the baiting conditions were tested with the discriminanda unchanged and half were tested with the discriminanda in the alternative spatial arrangement, a 2 × 2 factorial design. Harrison and Nissen found that the probability of a correct choice was influenced a good deal more by the spacing during memory storage (or discrimination learning) than by the spacing during testing: Spacing the containers apart rather than close together during training produced more correct responses during testing (80% vs. 65% correct choices), whereas the spacing had almost no effect during testing (71.5% correct choices when containers were spaced during testing, 73.5% correct when they were close together). The more interesting result for our purposes is the apparent detrimental effect that a *change* in the positioning of the discriminanda between training and testing produces: When they were spaced either close together or apart at both baiting and testing, mean responding was 80% accurate; but when they were spaced together during baiting and apart for testing, or vice versa, mean responding was only 64% accurate. This suggests that spatial separation is an important aspect of context that, when not replicated during the test, impedes retrieval of the memory. For the most part, however, factors effective during the choice (response) stage—for example, outcomes of prior responses and distribution of trials—are factors that more readily may be interpreted as influencing performance directly, rather than through effects on memory processing, and spatial separation typically is no exception.

The influence of conditions of reinforcement. One factor that operates during the baiting phase but seems significant for memory processing is reinforcer magnitude. Cowles and Nissen (1937) reported an experiment that localized the effect of reinforcer magnitude as occurring during the baiting (memory storage) stage. Their technique was a simple adaptation of Tinklepaugh's substitution method. Contingent upon a correct choice, all the chimps tested by Cowles and Nissen received the same reinforcer magnitude; but half of the chimps had *seen* that alternative baited with a relatively large magnitude of food, and half had seen it baited with a small magnitude. Retention performance was better for the former group. Perhaps this result was due to more probable attention or enhanced perception of the location of the larger reinforcer. There is reason to believe, however, that the more accurate delayed responding was due to maintained anticipation following baiting with the larger reinforcer. In addition to Tinklepaugh's evidence favoring this interpretation, Medin and Davis (1974) report two supportive experiments showing that speed of responding by monkeys to the correct alternative is faster with a relatively preferred food as the reinforcer. One experiment obtained this result with a 5-second delay after baiting, even though no external cues remained to signal whether the preferred or nonpreferred food was forthcoming.

Other experiments also have shown better delayed-response performance after larger reinforcers (e.g., Meyer & Harlow, 1952). However, in order to replicate and expand the Cowles–Nissen experiment there is need for a systematic study in which reinforcer magnitude is varied independently during both the baiting and the response stages, and orthogonally to length of the delay, in order to identify whether reinforcer magnitude influences storage or retrieval of the memory and to determine whether the extent of this influence depends on factors associated with the delay interval that may induce forgetting of the reinforcer magnitude. We now consider another reason why confirmation of the Cowles and Nissen results is important.

Fletcher (1965) has suggested that correct responding after long delays may be interpreted as a consequence of operant conditioning. With the training procedures used in delayed-responding studies, even those animals as bright as chimpanzees cannot be introduced directly to long retention intervals; rather, they must be introduced gradually to successively longer intervals. Furthermore, retention performance becomes more efficient with successive experiences at tasks such as delayed responding (e.g., D'Amato, 1973). Thus, it may be argued that responding after long delays is developed and maintained by selective reinforcement of whatever the animal is doing during the delays. The suggestion has been that the operant conditioned is the chain of behaviors, however subtle, emitted by the animal during the retention interval.

On the other hand, if it can be shown that conditions of reinforcement following the delay have little influence on retention performance, it would be difficult to maintain that the animal was learning to tolerate long delays by operant conditioning. In this respect, it would be interesting to know whether anything in addition to the original discrimination learning is being controlled by the baiting-phase magnitude of the reinforcer; for example, is the processing of the memory modified (selectively) by the reinforcer magnitude? The magnitude of the reinforcer presented during the baiting stage is important to establish the original discrimination learning. We know from studies of discrimination learning in animals that a position discrimination, as required in the delayed-response task, is acquired more rapidly when more desired reinforcers are available.

A useful test of whether memorial (as opposed to discriminative) processes are affected by reinforcer magnitude would be to employ a retention test for discrimination of objects independent of their spatial location rather than the spatial-position discriminations more frequently used thus far. It is not clear that reinforcer magnitude has any influence on a non-spatial-discrimination task; if there is an influence, it surely is less important than that found for a position discrimination (D'Amato, 1970). Therefore, if memory processes are affected by reinforcer magnitude, the larger reinforcer with an object discrimination may cause improved performance with long delays, but not with zero delays for which a memorial representation is unnecessary.

Retention interval stage.   We have already discussed one factor, general activity, that may operate during the retention interval to affect responding. Another factor of significance, also discussed by Fletcher (1965), is the sequence of retention interval lengths experienced by the primate. This factor also may be considered in relation to a more general question to which we shall return often: How can we maximize retention? Here, original storage of the memory—degree of learning and retention in the absence of the source of forgetting—must be held constant. Given equivalent storage, what procedures can be used to maximize an animal's retention performance after long intervals? One obvious possibility is that the animal may acquire retention skills with practice at delayed responding. We turn now to an examination of some effects of such practice.

Changes in delayed-response accuracy with successive trials.   Accuracy of delayed responding is known to improve with practice. Medin and Davis (1974) cite several studies showing that over several weeks of practicing delayed responding, monkeys typically show an increase of 50% or better in their accuracy following relatively long delays. This phenomenon is important for understanding memory processing for two reasons. First, it is conceivable that quite beyond the established phenomena of "learning to learn" or "learning set" (to be considered later in this chapter), individuals may also "learn to remember." By this we mean that animals and humans may learn to apply mechanisms that alleviate forgetting. For example, certain factors of human verbal behavior, such as the use of mnemonic devices, appear to serve a conservation function by acting in opposition to potential sources of forgetting (see Postman, 1963). Animals, too, may learn functionally similar devices, such as minimizing movement during a retention interval to avoid the acquisition of conflicting memories (for other examples of such mechanisms, see Chapter 8 regarding "mnemonic preparation"). It is assumed that the improved retention is not due to perceptual changes or increases in degree of original learning, but these factors are quite difficult to control, and usually are not controlled, with the delayed-response task. Later we shall see some support for the existence of such mechanisms in monkeys in terms of the delayed-matching-to-sample task, which provides better control of these factors (see D'Amato, 1973).

The second reason for interest in the progressive increase in performance with delayed responding is the possibility that accurate responding depends on the sort of gradual conditioning process mentioned earlier. If this is so—if correct responding after the delay is a consequence of having learned a succession of physical events to bridge the period between baiting and testing—the implication is that the delayed-response task tells us nothing at all about memory retrieval generally. The notion cited earlier is that with successive gradual increases in length of the delay interval (which always terminates in reinforcement contingent upon responding to a particular stimulus), an increasing chain of behavioral links is developed, a chain initiated at the onset of the retention interval and terminated by the correct response. If performance depends on operant conditioning of behavior during the delay, one would expect retention performance to increase with repeated trials at that *same* delay. But two sets of data argue against this position. First, Fletcher (1965) has noted that a gradual increase in length of a retention interval (as contrasted with an abrupt introduction of long intervals) facilitates retention performance at long delays. This is found especially in animals with frontal lesions, and because these lesions cause hyperreactivity it is possible that the animal is able to adapt better to the delayed-response situation with this gradual incrementing technique, independent of memorial processes. Similar phenomena are recognized in other tests of retention with primates (e.g., D'Amato, 1973). Second, instead of the progressive improvement (or at least maintained accuracy) expected from this conditioning viewpoint, gradual *deterioration* of performance may result instead from consecutive trials at the same delay, especially when long delay intervals are used, as illustrated by the following experiments.

Effects of experience with a particular retention interval.   Gleitman, Wilson, Herman, and Rescorla (1963) tested monkeys on delayed responding with either a short (15-second) or a long (4-minute) delay between baiting of the discriminanda and the monkey's opportunity to respond. Four series of 16 trials were presented to each monkey, one series per day. On two of the days, the same retention interval was used throughout—either the short or the long delay. During each of the remaining two days, retention intervals were short on eight of the trials and long on the remaining eight trials; on one of these days, the short-retention-interval trials were given first, followed by the long-interval trials, and the opposite order was presented on the other day.

The results are shown in Figure 3.2. Performance deteriorates throughout the day when all 16 trials in the day had long retention intervals, but no decline occurred when only short retention intervals were used. When the length of the

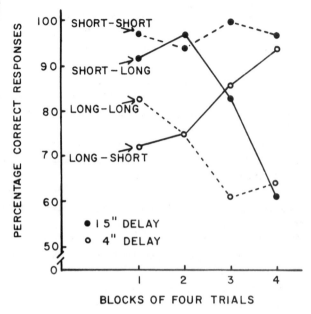

Figure 3.2 Accuracy in delayed responding is shown for monkeys shifted after eight trials from a consistently long delay (15 sec) to a consistently short delay (4 sec), or vice versa, in comparison to performance shown when only short delays or only long delays are experienced throughout the four blocks of four trials each. (Adapted from Gleitman et al., 1963. Copyright 1963 by the American Psychological Association. Reprinted by permission.)

interval was switched midway through the session, the interval presented during the first eight trials seemed to impose some residual effect on performance with the following interval. Animals switched from longer to shorter intervals did not immediately attain the higher level of performance found with short retention intervals alone; furthermore, animals switched from shorter to longer intervals attained initially a level of performance higher than when only long intervals were given. Gleitman and his associates interpret the poorer performance as primarily a consequence of boredom. In other words, given long retention intervals, the monkeys seemed simply to lose interest. The value of a concept such as "boredom", however plausible, is limited without an independent index to measure it (supplementary observations like those of Tinklepaugh would help). Also, trial-by-trial evidence might help us understand the lack of decrement during the second block of "long" trials within the long–short condition. This experiment is suggestive in analytic fashion, nevertheless, and we shall see further evidence for this factor in tests of delayed-matching-to-sample.

Deterioration of retention with successive trials in tests of delayed responding by racoons was reported by Michels and Brown (1959). Ten different retention intervals were included among 50 trials given per day. The intervals ranged between zero and 45 seconds in multiples of 5. Presentation of the different intervals was determined by a Latin Square design; a given interval was presented on five consecutive trials before the next interval was sampled. For all intervals, retention was better the first time that interval was experienced by the animal than in the following four trials (see Figure 3.3). Furthermore, like Gleitman and his associates, Michels and Brown found greater deterioration of performance over trials with longer retention intervals.

Michels and Brown suggest that the *novelty* of a new retention interval somehow facilitates retention performance; as novelty declines with repetitions of an interval, so does performance. But it is difficult to understand how waiting, say, 30 seconds when the organism has just experienced a waiting time of 5 seconds is "novel" in the same way as a stimulus object presented for the first time; some other construct, like "surprise" (cf. Kamin, 1969; Rescorla & Wagner, 1972), might seem more apt. Also, Michels and Brown fail to specify the mechanism through which something like "novelty" might facilitate memory retrieval or any other aspect of memory processing.

Setting aside these difficulties, might we attribute the data of Gleitman and his associates to a facilitating effect of "novelty" when long intervals are preceded by a series of short intervals? Probably not, because Riopelle (1959) indicates that retention is *impaired* rather markedly by the presentation of different reten-

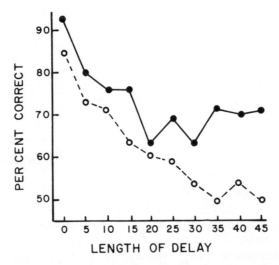

Figure 3.3   Accuracy in delayed responding is shown for raccoons after differing lengths of delay. Each delay occurred for five consecutive trials and a particular delay was equally probably at any point throughout the daily session of 50 delayed-response trials. The point to be made by this figure is that for each delay, retention was better on the first trial of the five-trial block (represented by the closed circles) than for the remaining four trials (the open circles represent average performance for all five trials with a particular delay). (Adapted from Michels and Brown, 1959. Copyright 1959 by the American Psychological Association. Reprinted by permission.)

tion intervals in a random order, although this should maximize the novelty of the retention interval length, at least during the early stages of such a treatment.

Perhaps the results of Gleitman and his associates and Michels and Brown are due to motivational factors, but the "boredom" may be directed toward the consequences of a trial—consistent success with short intervals, frequent failure with long intervals—rather than toward the duration of interval per se. Alternatively, a quite different explanation is found if we look at the effect of intertrial interval (ITI). In another experiment, Gleitman et al. (1963) found that better retention performance occurred after a delay when 20 trials were given at a rate of 2 trials per day than when all 20 trials (each separated by 25 seconds) were massed on one day. This ITI effect also seems amenable to interpretation in terms of "boredom" because the poorer performance occurred late in the 2-trial series, and was primarily a consequence of the deterioration of performance when trials were massed. Notably, however, this and other effects of intertrial or delay intervals also may be explained in terms of differential proactive interference, a topic we shall address shortly.

Data concerning delayed-matching-to-sample also suggest that deterioration of performance with long retention intervals is more apparent with massed than with distributed practice. These data show progressive improvement in retention as monkeys accumulate experience with "long" delays of a few minutes over many weeks of training (see later discussion). In these sorts of tasks, a stimulus to be remembered as "correct" may have been incorrect for the subject on previous trials; the resulting transient interference is especially likely when trials are massed (e.g., Keppel, 1964; Spear, 1971; Underwood & Ekstrand, 1966). Perhaps techniques to combat or compensate for this interference may be acquired with practice (cf. Postman, 1963) or the interference simply may dissipate with relatively long intervals between successive trials. Gleitman and his associates do suggest, moreover, that interaction between competing memories caused by proactive interference also may have contributed to their effects. Therefore, while the basis of the progressive decline in retention with massed trials may well be motivational, as implied by the term *boredom*, there is reason to implicate memorial processes as well.

Further determinants of delayed responding. Three parameters of potential importance to memory processing in the delayed-response task are: (1) the duration of the stimulus that initially indicates the location of the reinforcer; (2) the number of repetitions of this stimulus prior to introduction of the retention interval; and (3) the degree of redundancy of this stimulus.

Studies of the influence of stimulus duration have employed Hunter's original, slightly complicated method of delayed response testing in which, prior to the onset of the delay, a relatively neutral stimulus, such as a light, signals the location of the food (as opposed to the animal's being shown the location of the food directly). If the important stimulus event for the monkey is the *onset* of the stimulus, then further stimulus duration would add to the length of the delay required before responding; thus, we might expect that performance would decline with longer duration of the signaling stimulus. This is precisely what Riopelle (1959) found when he varied duration of the cueing light over a range of 1 to 11 seconds. Perhaps the most important variation in duration of the signaling event occurs in intervals of less then 1 second. Davis (1973) tested this possibility using a refined procedure that has several advantages over the procedure used by Riopelle. Davis found that response accuracy increased with increasing stimulus durations in the range of 8 to 400 milliseconds. Because Davis held delay interval constant at 1 second, the basis of this effect is unclear in terms of memory processing. However, other studies of such effects point, as we shall see later, to the probable conclusion that the influence of stimulus duration in this range is primarily on effectiveness of initial perception or degree of learning because its effect is uniform across different retention intervals.

Davis (1973) also found that delayed responding improves if the signaling stimulus is presented more than once prior to the delay. Later we shall see data suggesting that this effect, like the stimulus duration effect, probably is exerted through perceptual or initial storage processes, at least for short retention intervals following low degrees of learning. In Chapter 8, we shall find generally that the number of repetitions of events to be represented memorially may directly influence retention per se, perhaps mediated by an influence on memory retrieval.

Medin and Davis (1974) present evidence relevant to the parameter of stimulus redundancy. There seems to be no doubt that monkeys are especially flexible in using any of the various sources of information the stimulus situation might provide. Data reported by Harrison and Nissen (1941) indicate that chimpanzees may respond in terms of either relative position of the correct alternative (e.g., the correct object was to the left of the incorrect one) or absolute location, depending on the physical proximity of the alternatives. French (1959) found that squirrel monkeys could respond either by avoiding the incorrect alternative or by approaching the correct alternative. Meyer and Harlow (1952) found that the addition of redundant discriminating features improved delayed responding.

Medin (1969) assessed the effect of stimulus redundancy on memory processing in monkeys by measuring the probability of selecting the correct (baited) cell in a matrix of cells as a function of the location of that cell. Of particular interest is the effect of the number of immediately adjacent alternatives. For example, in a 4 × 4 matrix corner cells have only three adjacent alternatives; cells located on the edge have five; and those in the center have eight (see Figure 3.4). Accuracy of retention was inversely related to the number of adjacent alternatives, as shown in Figure 3.5. Moreover, the effect of redundancy clearly is to modulate forgetting associated with longer retention intervals; when the retention interval is longest, the effect is the most pronounced. The effect is of special interest for theories of memory processing because the differential effect as a function of

CENTER   EDGE   CORNER

DELAY (in seconds)

0

CENTER:

			1
3	90	1	1
	3	1	

EDGE:

			95
			5

CORNER:

89			
9	2		

1

CENTER:

			1
1	1	1	
1	88		
	5	1	1

EDGE:

			7
		6	74
			13

CORNER:

79	4		
17			

2

CENTER:

	10	2	2
8	57	5	
2	4	5	5

EDGE:

			14
		5	68
			13

CORNER:

88			
8	3		
1			

5

CENTER:

	2		
5	13	2	
5	32	8	3
3	20	5	2

EDGE:

		2	25
2	3	54	
		2	12

CORNER:

65	12	1	1
21			

10

CENTER:

			2
8	10	3	2
13	28	11	3
5	15		

EDGE:

		1	14
		1	49
			27
1			7

CORNER:

59	3		5
25	3		
2			
3			

20

CENTER:

4	2	2	13
2	6	6	6
2	11	13	2
11	8	6	6

EDGE:

1		1	27
		2	35
		4	20
1			9

CORNER:

54	3		3
25	5	1	1
3			
3			5

Figure 3.4   Examples of error patterns by monkeys responding to an array of 16 alternatives arranged in a 4 × 4 matrix is shown as a function of delay between presentation and test and as a function of the location of the correct alternative (either in the center of the matrix, edge of the matrix, or corner of the matrix. The numbers indicate the frequency of responding to each cell when a particular (underlined) cell was correct. (Adapted from Medin and Davis, 1974).

length of the retention interval makes this phenomenon one of the few within the entire study of short-term retention in animals that cannot readily be attributed to differences in initial perception or learning. The interpretation of this effect is a matter for further study.

Reactivation treatments to facilitate delayed responding.   An example of a reactivation treatment found effective in delayed responding is cited in the extensive monograph by Beritoff (1971), who studied delayed responding with many species; the example to be cited here concerns retention by dogs. Beritoff's experimental apparatus was an entire room that contained the dog's cage and a number of blinds that masked the location where a food reinforcer might be placed. Ordinarily, the dog remained in its cage during the entire delay interval between the baiting of a blind and the retention test. Beritoff found, however,

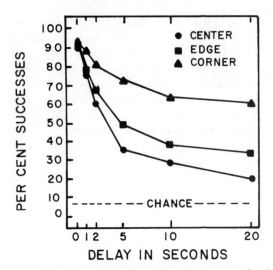

Figure 3.5   Accuracy in delayed responding by monkeys is shown as a function of delay and the particular location of the correct alternative within the 16-cell matrix of alternative locations (the matrix is illustrated in Figure 3.4). (Adapted from Medin 1969. Copyright 1969 by the American Psychological Association. Reprinted by permission.)

that the dog could tolerate longer retention intervals if it was taken out of its cage and walked around the room during the retention interval (presumably without being taken within sight or smell of the food). In other words, given this reactivation treatment, significant retention occurred after longer delay intervals than were otherwise possible. Beritoff interpreted this retention enhancement as due to "movement of the animal about the room (which) can lead to a reinforced production of the image of the location of the food" (1971, p. 13).

SHORT-TERM MEMORY IN ANIMALS: DELAYED MATCHING TO SAMPLE

A technique that is becoming more popular than delayed responding, largely because of technological advances and analytical advantages, is the delayed-matching-to-sample task. This task is by no means new; Mello (1971) points out that it was used by Itard in the eighteenth century in his attempts to teach language to the "wild boy of Aveyron." Because shaping an animal to perform adequately on delayed matching to sample can be a long and tedious task in the absence of sufficient automation, the more easily implemented delayed-response task was preferred until recently.

Delayed matching to sample means precisely what one would expect from the phrase. A subject first is presented a distinctive stimulus as the sample, for example, a vertical line or a green square. The sample is then removed. After a specified retention interval, the sample is presented again (often in a different location than before) along with an alternative stimulus. The subject's task is to select which one of these two stimuli is the item that earlier appeared as a sample.

Communicating the nature of this task to a monkey is not simple: It requires a series of shaping procedures similar to that used by Mello (1971) and shown in Figure 3.6. This figure illustrates the four basic steps required to train the animal before any delays may be introduced between removal of the sample and the matching test. Obviously, this training is a good deal more complicated to instrument than the delayed-response task, in which the monkey must first learn merely to remove food from a container and then select one container over another in accordance with where the food was placed.

Delayed-matching-to-sample offers some analytical advantages over delayed responding, although some of these have been exaggerated. For example, position easily is made an irrelevant cue in the delayed-matching-to-sample task (which eliminates mediation by body orientation during a retention interval), but this also can be accomplished in the delayed-response task. Covert or overt mediation that may be independent of postural orientation is a related type of mediation that is most conveniently controlled by delayed matching to sample,

SEQUENCE OF EVENTS IN A MATCHING TO SAMPLE TRIAL

| 1 | 2 | 3 | 4 | 5 |

Next response starts a trial

Sample key on until
response ratio complete

Delay
interval

Inter-trial
interval

Comparison keys on until
response ratio complete

Figure 3.6   This figure exemplifies the sequence of events with which the monkey must become familiar for tests with the delayed-matching-to-sample procedures. This particular procedure involves four major steps. Throughout the monkey is presented a panel consisting of three round "keys" upon which symbols may be projected. In this case there also is a lamp in the center that may or may not be lighted. At the beginning of a trial (1) the three keys are darkened and the lamp is lighted to indicate that the next response to the sample key (i.e. pressing of the lower key) will initiate a trial. When the monkey presses the sample key, the lamp goes off and the sample stimulus appears on the sample key (2). The monkey may then be required to complete a particular number of presses of the sample key, and when these are accomplished, the delay interval begins (3). The entire panel is darkened during the delay. Following the delay, the two comparison keys become illuminated with alternative symbols (4), one of which is the sample that was lighted before the delay. The monkey's task now is to respond to the key on which the sample is projected. If correct, it is typical that a preferred food (raisin or peanut) is delivered to the monkey, followed by the intertrial interval during which the entire panel is darkened. If incorrect, the intertrial interval begins immediately (Adapted from Mello, 1971. © 1971 Pergamon Press Ltd.).

although it also may be controlled in delayed responding. Blough (1959) discovered a fascinating instance of such mediation when he was testing delayed matching to sample with pigeons.

He presented four pigeons with a sample (either a flickering light or a steady light) through a vertical aperture centered between two circular response keys. Zero, 2, 5, or 10 seconds later, both the flickering and steady lights were presented, one through each key. If the pigeon pecked the key illuminated like the original sample, grain briefly was made available to the hungry bird. Otherwise, no food was presented.

Two of the four birds performed with remarkable accuracy, one choosing correctly on more than 90% of the trials for all retention intervals. Blough noticed that both these birds usually performed certain ritualistic behaviors during the retention interval, depending on which stimulus had served as the sample. Whenever the sample had been the flickering light, one pigeon would step back from the keys and slowly wave its head back and forth; whenever the sample had been the steady light, the same bird would spend the interval pecking at the top of the vertical aperture. The other pigeon spent the retention interval biting at the top of the vertical aperture when the flickering light had been the sample, but pecked directly at the center of this aperture when the steady light had been the sample. It is as if the pigeons had selected one response to represent the flickering light and another to represent the steady light.

Furthermore, Blough found that if these representational responses did not occur, or if they became less distinctive when he attempted to photograph the bird through an open window (and thus modified the stimulus context), performance following the retention interval declined accordingly.

Such overt mediational behavior, while interesting in its own right, must be controlled when the experimenter is interested in measuring memory processing. One way to decrease the probability of such overt representational responses, which might be emitted in any number of subtle forms by the relatively ingenious monkey, is to increase the information load that must be represented. This may be accomplished by increasing the number of possible samples; the more samples there are, the less likely it is that the monkey will develop a reliable peripheral representation of each. Projecting symbols to the monkey in the delayed-matching-to-sample paradigm increases the size of the sample set more conveniently than is possible in most versions of the delayed-response task.

One very clear advantage of the delayed-matching-to-sample task is the control that may be exerted over the actual duration of the sample and over the subjects' actual attention to the sample. The delayed-response task requires the experimenter's subjective judgment as to whether the monkey noticed the placement of the food; but attention in the delayed-matching-to-sample task may be made relatively certain if the monkey is required to make an "observing response" in order to observe the sample and initiate a trial. Thus, Mello's (1971) technique requires the monkey to press the sample key once to turn on the sample and then give 15 additional presses to initiate the retention interval and, ultimately, the comparison stimuli (a similar technique is employed by D'Amato, 1973).

Finally, the use of the computer for automating the delayed-matching-to-sample task has brought with it another advantage, the delay titration procedure, in which the length of the retention interval encountered by a particular animal is determined by that animal's previous accuracy with other retention intervals. The details of the titration procedure vary with various investigators (cf. Jarrard & Moise, 1971; Mello, 1971)—an example will provide an explanation. After the subject (of any species, including human) has learned to match accurately with zero delay between sample and test, the next trial may include a 1-second retention interval. When the subject becomes sufficiently correct with this delay, the next trial will have a 2-second retention interval, and so forth, with successive 1-second increments in retention interval until error rate exceeds a preset value. For example, if one error is made, the next retention interval may become 1 second shorter, and so forth until the subject is given an interval after which it chooses correctly. The size of the increment in retention interval and the criteria for "sufficient accuracy" and "unacceptable error rate" may be varied depending on the capacities and tolerance of the subject. Performance assessed by titration is represented by a distribution of the intervals achieved by the subject, and a single measure of central tendency often is used to characterize retention performance.

The main advantage of the titration procedure should be clear from our previous discussion of the effect of the sequence of retention interval lengths presented animals with the delayed-response task: By having the subject, in effect, select the retention intervals with which she or he will work, the experimenter can minimize the complicating effects of boredom or frustration associated with sequences of intervals that may be too long, short, or irregular.

On the other hand, it may be argued that the titration method underestimates retention capacities. Given the usual preference for more immediate reward attained after shorter retention intervals, the subject may not be inclined to work for longer retention intervals. For this reason, a variety of other procedures have been considered. D'Amato (1973) has used the technique of occasionally interpolating short intervals into a series of long intervals. Using the delayed-response task, Weiskrantz (e.g., 1968) has presented animals with small immediate reinforcers prior to long retention intervals, and Finan (1942) and Beritoff (1971) also permitted their animals to eat during the retention interval in order to maintain attention and responding when tested.

Conditions That Influence Rate of Forgetting in Delayed Matching to Sample

Illumination during the retention interval.   Retention is improved markedly when monkeys spend the retention interval in darkness rather than in normal illumination. This effect has been refined and neatly analyzed by D'Amato and his colleagues (e.g., D'Amato, 1973; D'Amato & O'Neill, 1971; Etkin, 1972).

Although better retention with darkened retention intervals also has been reported in the delayed-response task (Malmo, 1942), the effect appears to be more robust with delayed matching, perhaps because in the latter task there is lower probability of postured orientation as a cue (D'Amato, 1973). A similar effect has been found in tests of very short-term retention with human subjects, restricted perhaps to certain features of iconic memory (see Averback & Sperling, 1961; Kintsch, 1970, p. 150). The basis of this effect in humans and its generality to other cases of short-term retention is unclear.

The magnitude of this effect may account for the wide discrepancy in esti-mated retention capacity of the monkey found by various investigators. Mello (1971) reported that the longest retention interval after which her monkeys regu-larly responded correctly was 232 seconds, 15 times longer than that measured by Jarrard and Moise (1971). A number of procedural differences may have contributed to the better retention found by Mello—slight differences in the titration schedule, type of subject (Mello used Rhesus monkeys; Jarrard & Moise, stump-tail monkeys), and number of alternative stimuli to which the animal was exposed (21 by Mello, 2 by Jarrard & Moise; but see Etkin & D'Amato, 1969)—but the most effective procedural difference probably was Mello's use of darkness during the retention interval.

The basic effect of illumination on delayed matching to sample was discovered first by Etkin (1970). The magnitude of the effect, although not as extensive as implied by our comparison between the results of Mello and those of Jarrard and Moise, is substantial nevertheless. For example, D'Amato and O'Neill (1971) found that after a 120-second delay in darkness all three monkeys performed reliably above chance, but they performed at chance level when normal illumina-tion was maintained during the delay: Darkness during the delay consistently reduced the error rate by about one-third for all four sample stimuli.

In analyzing this illumination effect, D'Amato and O'Neill (1971) tested whether this was a consequence of any special combination of degree of illumina-tion just prior to the appearance of the sample and during the retention interval. They found that so long as the apparatus was dark during the retention interval, less forgetting occurred regardless of the relative illumination prior or subsequent to that interval. Thus, darkness during the retention interval is both necessary and sufficient for improved retention. Etkin (1972) tested the possibility that light might be especially disruptive to retention at certain times during the interval—for example, immediately following presentation of the sample, light might disrupt some aspects of memory storage, such as "consolidation." He found poorer retention after longer durations of light presented during an otherwise dark retention interval, but the point at which light was introduced during the retention interval was of no significant consequence. To test whether the interfering effect of illumination was specific to discrimination using the visual modality, Wor-sham and D'Amato (1973) attempted to train monkeys on an auditory discrimina-tion with the intention of varying illumination during the retention interval.

Interestingly, they were unable to get their monkeys to learn an auditory discrimination, apparently because of the vast amount of experience these monkeys had had with only visual problems in this situation. They did find that filling the retention interval with auditory stimulation (tapes of either white noise or monkeys chattering in the colony room) had no effect on retention of visual samples.

The exact mechanism underlying the effect of illumination has not been determined yet. We may expect the explanation as to why darkness slows forgetting of visual stimuli to be important for understanding memory processing generally; in addition to the robust effect found with monkeys, a similarly important and powerful effect occurs with pigeons (Grant & Roberts, 1976). The results so far seem to indicate that deterioration in retention of a memory that occurs in a particular sensory modality may result from general activity in that sensory system during the retention interval (for further discussion, see D'Amato, 1973). This, however, does not preclude an explanation incorporating a general mechanism of memory processing that is applicable to all sensory systems (see Grant & Roberts, 1976, p. 15).

Repetition of the sample.   Retention in humans clearly is improved by increasing the degree of original learning (Underwood, 1964). One way to vary degree of learning is to vary the number of repetitions of an episode. Jarrard and Moise (1971) present results indicating that delayed matching to sample is more efficient with monkeys after two or four presentations of the sample than after a single presentation. A control experiment indicated that the effect was on memory processing, not simply a consequence of improving the monkey's attention to the sample with repetitions. Unfortunately for our purposes, the effect was not clearly on rate of forgetting: The effect of repetitions was no greater after long delays than after no delay (as indicated by the absence of a significant interaction between length of retention interval and number of repetitions). That repetition of the critical stimulus may have its effect primarily on perception or memory storage rather than susceptibility to forgetting is indicated further by Roberts' (1972) experiments with the pigeon. Like Jarrard and Moise's results, Roberts' data from pigeons indicated that matching of the sample was better with more initial repetitions of the sample, and the benefit was equal across retention intervals. In other words, increasing repetition of the stimulus appears to neither protect against nor counteract sources of forgetting. The experimental method used by Roberts is of some interest, as are his data that indicate forgetting over short intervals in the pigeon.

Roberts conducted three delayed-matching-to-sample experiments bearing upon this issue. His method of varying repetitions of the stimulus (sample) required the bird to respond to that stimulus a certain number of times before it was offered an opportunity to perform the matching response and receive a food reinforcer. Roberts' assumption was that whenever the bird responded to (pecked) the sample, it was noticed and so constituted an effective repetition of the samples. In the first experiment, Roberts required the pigeons to peck the sample 1, 5, or 15 times before delay intervals of 0, 1, 3, or 6 seconds were initiated. The results, shown in Figure 3.7, indicate quite uniform rates of forgetting regardless of the number of repetitions. A second experiment, which compared the relative influence of 1, 2, or 8 repetitions on delayed matching, provided a slight numerical indication of a slower rate of forgetting after more repetitions (see Figure 3.8). This, however, was not the main object of the experiment, and appropriate statistical tests were not reported for this particular comparison. Regardless, when these conditions were compared again in a third experiment, the results (see Figure 3.8) again showed no significant interaction between number of repetitions (2 or 8) and retention interval (0, 2, or 8 seconds), although matching performance was uniformly better with 8 than with 2 repetitions.

It is difficult to escape the conclusion that under these circumstances number of repetitions has little or no effect on forgetting after short intervals. Later we shall examine similar evidence concerning short-term retention of verbal materials by humans.

It may be argued, however, that although the forgetting curves in Figure 3.7 are parallel, percentage forgetting is less with higher numbers of repetitions. In Figure 3.7, for example, if we say that with 15 repetitions responding is 87% correct with no delay and 67% correct with 6 seconds delay, percentage of maximal forgetting possible (with 50% as chance responding) is about 57%. This

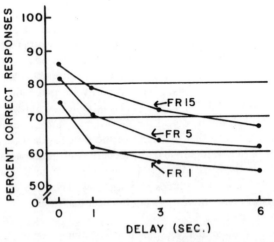

Figure 3.7   Accuracy of responding by pigeons to a previously presented sample following differing delays is shown as a function of the number of times the pigeon was required to peck the sample prior to the onset of the delay. "FR" refers to "fixed ratio", that is, the pigeons were required to peck the sample either 1, 5, or 15 times prior to the onset of the delay. (Adapted from Roberts, 1972. Copyright 1972 by the American Psychological Association. Reprinted by permission.)

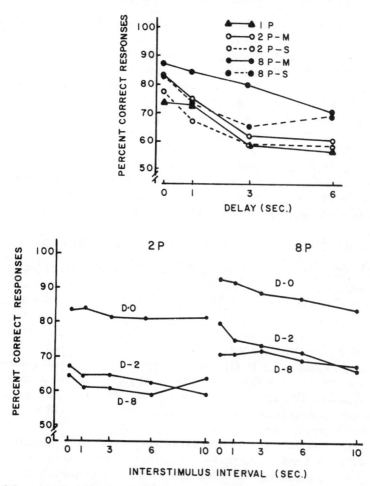

Figure 3.8   Accuracy of delayed responding is shown as a function of the number of experimenter-controlled repetitions of a sample prior to the onset of a delay in the delayed-matching-to-sample paradigm. In this study, the subjects were pigeons. The upper figure shows retention as a function of delay when the delay was preceded by either 1, 2, or 8 presentations of the sample, presented in either massed or spaced fashion. The lower panel indicates relative retention after delays of zero, 2, or 8 seconds (D-0, D-2, D-8) when the sample had been presented on 2 or 8 occasions (2p or 8p). The interval between successive presentations of the sample is represented on the abscissa (Adapted from Roberts, 1972. Copyright 1972 by the American Psychological Association. Reprinted by permission.)

contrasts with the corresponding figures with one repetition, where the decline between 0 and 6 seconds is from about 75% accuracy to 55% accuracy, or 80% loss. With this measure, more repetitions clearly would be said to yield less forgetting.

The problem with this argument is that it compounds the difficulty in the implicit assumption of a linear scale for amount forgotten with that created by initial differences in accuracy (with zero seconds delay). The simple fact is that we cannot know whether different numbers of repetitions would yield that same difference in percentage forgetting if performance with zero seconds delay were equal. If the question for analysis is whether forgetting depends on number of repetitions, it is somewhat unsatisfactory to say that it does, conditionally—provided that performance in the absence of a source of forgetting is unequal. We may find it useful to establish a general principle relating performance (however achieved) in the absence of a source of forgetting to forgetting attributable to that source. If we found that the same relationships prevail regardless of how the initial level of performance is established, such a principle would be important. But we must keep such a principle separate from those of other independent variables (in this case, repetitions).

We conclude, therefore, that forgetting is not altered by number of repetitions of the sort manipulated by Roberts. This is a relatively weak conclusion, as are any based on acceptance of a null hypothesis, but it seems the most appropriate.

Learning to retain.   D'Amato (1973) has presented evidence that monkeys may improve in delayed-matching-to-sample as they accumulate massive amounts of practice—hundreds of sessions—on this task. The nature of this improvement is particularly interesting: It is greater after longer retention intervals and therefore is not merely an increase in degree of original learning or attention, but a genuine increase in retention due to lessened forgetting. Although something like this might be expected in humans who may acquire mechanisms to combat interference with retention, there is no such effect with humans found in the literature. This may be because human subjects have not yet been exposed to thousands of individual retention tests spaced over months or years, as D'Amato's monkeys have.

The reason for such an effect in monkeys is not entirely clear. This effect does follow from D'Amato's interpretation of delayed matching to sample: What is learned and stored in delayed matching to sample is a temporal discrimination between the sample last seen and any one previously seen (D'Amato, 1973). Given the established fact that monkeys improve in discrimination learning after practice with many different kinds of problems, it follows that they also may improve with practice in temporal discriminations and therefore, according to D'Amato's interpretation, in delayed matching to sample.

Other Factors Potentially Important to Delayed Matching to Sample

Stimulus materials: content of the memory.   A variety of manipulations have revealed that stimulus materials have little effect on retention in delayed matching to sample. Mello (1971), for example, found no difference in performance among 21 possible samples that consisted of patterns, colors, and pictures (of monkeys and fruit), with titrated retention intervals maximizing at nearly 4 minutes. Preliminary data by Jarrard and Moise (1971) suggest that colors (red vs. green) might be retained better than patterns (three vertical lines vs. three horizontal lines). However, these monkeys also took more than twice as many trials to *acquire* the pattern discrimination, and because of the preliminary nature of these data it is not clear that the degree of original learning was equated.

Three sets of results by D'Amato and his colleagues agree with Mello (1971), showing that characteristics of the sample and comparison stimuli have little or no effect on retention. Etkin and D'Amato (1969) found no differences in retention when the number of possible samples employed was two, three, or four. This is surprising because we might expect more interference in retention with a smaller sample set. On the other hand, we might also expect a greater probability of subtle, overt mediational mechanisms to represent the samples with a smaller sample set, which conceivably may offset the interference effect.

D'Amato and Worsham (1972; see also D'Amato, 1973) present data indicating that monkeys may form central representations of samples in such a way that it makes little difference how these samples are presented at the retention test. With one procedure, an interval separated the presentation of the sample and a single stimulus, which may or may not match the sample. The monkey's task was to push a button if that stimulus previously had appeared as the sample or to press a lever if that stimulus did not match the sample. Another technique, which D'Amato and Worsham refer to as "conditional matching" and consider a possible analog of recall, was as follows: First, a monkey was trained that a red disk is equal to a triangle and a vertical line is equal to a dot. Next, the monkey was presented the sample (say, the red disk). But instead of including the red disk as one of the alternatives at the test, the triangle was presented as the "correct match." Or the vertical line might be the sample and at the retention test the animal would have to choose between a dot and a triangle. Once shaped to perform these tasks with no retention interval, the monkeys' performance after longer retention intervals was quite good. In fact, D'Amato and Worsham found no convincing evidence that retention is any different with these procedures than with the standard delayed-matching-to-sample methods.

Intertrial interval. We have mentioned that Gleitman and his associates found better delayed responding with wide distribution of practice (a 24-hour interval between blocks of two trials) than with 30 seconds between each trial. So far, variation in distribution of practice has not been as extensive with delayed-matching-to-sample as that of Gleitman and his associates; rather, variation has been on the order of seconds rather than minutes or hours.

When variation in trial distribution with the delayed-response task has included a shorter range (between 8 and 24 seconds—Fletcher & Davis, 1965), no influence of intertrial interval has been found. With delayed-matching-to-sample, however, there is some suggestion that retention may be better with longer intertrial intervals, even within this narrow span.

Jarrard and Moise (1971) used intertrial intervals of 5, 15, 30, or 60 seconds in combination with delay intervals of 0, 5, 15, 30, or 60 seconds. They found better matching performance with intertrial intervals in the 15–60-second range than with 5 seconds. It is not clear from their report whether the effect was greater with a retention interval than with zero delay. This result is notable, however, because studies of delayed-matching-to-sample generally have employed relatively short intertrial intervals (e.g., 8 seconds by Jarrard & Moise, 1970; 10 seconds by Mello, 1971; 15 seconds by Moise, 1970). Moreover, using a technique in which monkeys can initiate a trial at any time after a correct response, thus effectively establishing their own intertrial interval, D'Amato (personal communication, 1973) found that monkeys themselves usually select a relatively short intertrial interval of a few seconds, probably shorter than is optimal for correct performance. Apparently humans are not alone in their ignorance about the most efficient ways to achieve effective learning and remembering.

Additional indication that longer intertrial intervals might yield better delayed matching is provided in a study by Wilson, Kaufman, Zieler, and Lieb (1972). Less interference from previous trials occurred when a 45-second intertrial interval was used than had been found in an earlier study (Kaufman & Wilson, 1970) using an intertrial interval of only 30 seconds.

It is notable that "intertrial interval" has been defined in several ways. In each case it is reasonable to expect length of the intertrial interval to influence retention, although not necessarily for the same reason. In the studies just mentioned, intertrial interval was defined in terms of the interval between different problems, from the test of one problem to the onset of the next problem. Each problem required only one trial and was composed of the presentation of a sample and the matching test. Intertrial interval is defined differently in multiple-trial learning, in which the same problem is repeated on successive trials. In this case, retention after either short or long intervals may benefit enormously from learning with distributed practice. So far, the clearest benefit of this kind has been shown in studies of human verbal learning (e.g., Keppel, 1964; Wickelgren, 1972; see Chapter 8). Also, under certain circumstances of multiple-trial learning one may regard each trial after the first one as a test of retention for information acquired on the previous trial or trials. Such retention depends on the length of the intertrial interval, and this relationship has special importance for certain learning phenomena such as "learning set," as we shall see presently.

Finally, an alternative method of varying intertrial interval within the delayed-matching-to-sample task is notable because of the rather different questions and predictions associated with it. Within a single problem, Roberts (1972) varied the distribution over time of repetitions of the sample while holding constant the number of repetitions. With this procedure, no matching trials were interpolated between repetitions. Roberts found that matching performance decreased about equally across retention intervals as the interval between successive repetitions of the sample increased. He interpreted this as an indication "that removal of the stimulus allows trace strength to decay" (1972, p. 81), an interpretation that is consistent with several effects obtained in this paradigm (see also Grant & Roberts, 1973). It is of interest that very short-term retention of nonverbal stimuli by humans seems to be *facilitated* by moderate spacing of the repeated stimulus (Massaro, 1970) under circumstances where backward masking of the first occurrence may be caused by the repetition.

Probably poststimulus processing is a more important aspect of memory processing for humans than for pigeons, and perhaps the scale of time required for their respective processing of memories is quite different, also.

Duration of sample exposure.   There are two basic ways in which duration of exposure to a stimulus may be varied. One is variation of process time permitted following exposure to a stimulus; this probably is applicable only to humans who can more clearly use such postexposure time to rehearse and organize the materials just presented. The other, more obvious, way of varying duration of exposure to a stimulus is by varying the physical duration of the stimulus.

Massaro (1970) has suggested that the amount of time permitted for perceptual processing of both verbal and nonverbal memories should be a direct determinant of the probability of subsequent retention. For humans, the time permitted for processing immediately following exposure to the stimulus generally is a more potent variable than the duration of actual exposure to the stimulus (e.g., Sperling, 1960, 1963; Aaronson, 1967). There are, however, some exceptions to this. Using relatively complex pictures to be remembered, Shaffer and Shiffrin (1972) found sharp improvement in recognition with increased duration of stimulus presentation (between .125 and 2 seconds). Differences of 1 to 4 seconds of postexposure time had relatively little effect on retention, even when subjects were instructed to rehearse. With a different testing procedure, however, Weaver (1974) has found that the recognition of complex pictures increases with longer postexposure time (2 vs. 6 seconds, in darkness). For simpler pictures that may be distinctly labeled with a word or two, we shall see in Chapter 8 that recognition clearly benefits from postpresentation time for rehearsal, so perhaps the materials used by Weaver were somehow more readily labeled by subjects. A comparable manipulation of "processing time" with monkeys would require either multiple-item samples or unfamiliar and relatively complex stimuli presented as single samples. If postexposure processing time were useful for monkeys, better retention after longer intervals would be expected, but as noted earlier, this result has not been found.

Many delayed-matching studies with monkeys as subjects have permitted the monkeys themselves to control duration of stimulus exposure. However, for the purpose of better evaluating the dramatically efficient retention obtained by their monkeys, D'Amato and Worsham (1972) controlled sample duration, varying it orthogonally to retention interval. Their monkeys were highly practiced with the particular stimuli presented. Nevertheless, it is remarkable that the monkeys' retention performance remained consistently high in spite of durations of the sample averaging only .06 seconds. D'Amato and Worsham concluded that sample duration was of little consequence for retention performance in monkeys. This conclusion is contrary to the facilitation found with delayed responding by monkeys and delayed matching by pigeons (see Davis, 1973; Roberts & Grant, 1974), but the implications of this disagreement are unclear.

Forgetting has seemed unaffected by stimulus duration in the latter experiments (as in D'Amato & Worsham, 1972). A more recent study indicates that with exceptionally well-practiced pigeons who were tested in 15,000–20,000 delayed-matching trials, the pigeon's capacity for correct performance after long intervals may be well beyond that previously estimated if sample duration is sufficiently long: Grant (1976) reported significant retention after a 60-second delay when sample duration was 4 seconds or longer. But here, too, longer durations had equal benefit on immediate (zero delay) tests, implying an effect on original learning rather than on forgetting.

Effect of activities during the retention interval.   Except for the effect of ambient illumination described earlier, retention in delayed-matching-to-sample is surprisingly resistant to nonspecific sources of interference interpolated during the retention interval. By "nonspecific," we mean events that are not formally similar to the episode to be remembered. A striking example is found in an experiment by Moise (1970).

Moise first trained monkeys on a reaction-time task. After extensive training, these monkeys consistently responded to the appearance of a white light with latencies of about 1 second. Thus certain that his animals would not ignore the white light but, in fact, would respond to it rapidly, Moise interpolated presentations of this white light into the retention interval (between the appearance of the sample and the matching test). Moreover, to be sure that the subject had observed the light, he terminated all trials in which the monkey did not respond within 1.25 seconds following the occurrence of the white light. As his major manipulation, Moise varied the number of presentations of the white light (0, 1, or 3) orthogonally to the delay interval (0, 5, 12, 20, or 30 seconds).

Moise found that retention was impaired by these interpolated events, but only slightly. After a 30-second delay, correct responding occurred on 74.5% of the trials without interpolated stimuli, compared to 68.6% and 65.8% of the trials with 1 and 3 interpolated stimuli, respectively. Equally interesting were the results of another experiment by Moise (1970) in which he found that it did not matter at which point in the retention interval the distracting stimuli occurred; presenting three such stimuli at the beginning of a delay period had no greater or less influence on retention than presenting them at the end of the delay period. Again, however, presentation at either point impaired retention somewhat compared to the absence of any distracting stimuli.

Another variation in the physical activities of the monkey during a retention interval was investigated by Jarrard and Moise (1970). Performance of monkeys confined to a chair was compared with that of monkeys free to move about the apparatus during the retention interval. The hypothesis was that attention to the sample, and its subsequent retention, might be facilitated if the animals were restrained from engaging in potentially competing exploratory activities. This manipulation, however, had no noticeable effect on retention performance.

We already have mentioned the experiment by Etkin (1972), who interpolated periods of illumination during an otherwise dark retention interval and found that illumination does impair retention in direct relation to the total duration of illumination, but irrespective of the point during the retention interval at which it was interpolated. Similarly, we have mentioned the study by Worsham and D'Amato (1973) in which interpolated tapes of either general noise or of monkey chatter, to which they almost certainly attended, did not influence delayed-matching-to-sample.

Finally, retention performance has been impaired by interpolating white lights somewhat similar in form to the red or green sample lights to be remembered (Jarrard & Moise, 1971) and by interpolating alternative samples different from the correct one (Jarvik, Goldfarb, & Carley, 1969; Zentall, 1973). Of course, in these cases there is no way for the animal to be "instructed" to match to a stimulus selected by the experimenter; instead, the animal may match with the last stimulus interpolated in the retention interval. For this reason, the proper interpretation of these results is debatable (see Grant & Roberts, 1976, for a fine analysis of this issue). We shall return to these cases in Chapter 4.

AN EXAMPLE OF THE INFLUENCE OF SHORT-TERM RETENTION ON OTHER BEHAVIOR

Retention and forgetting are pervasive aspects of behavior, so it is not surprising to find them applied as explanatory factors throughout the study of behavior. Forgetting, after short intervals in particular, has been considered a determinant of a low-level form of concept formation, "learning set."

Learning set in monkeys is so powerful (and similar versions of this effect are so ubiquitous in many mammals) that every theory of animal learning must deal with it. The definition of learning set may take either a weak or a strong form. In the weak form, learning set is simply the increase in rate of learning that occurs with extensive practice on learning problems of the same type. This is also known as "learning to learn."

Learning set in monkeys more often is used in its strong form—the attainment of a solution after a single trial for discrimination problems of a common type—and it is this version that has been linked to memory processing. Further reference to learning set here will refer to the strong form.

Learning set typically is found when monkeys are given many problems in which they must discriminate between two objects. A food pellet may be obtained if the "correct" object is moved or touched by the monkey, but not when the alternative object is chosen. Each discrimination problem is given for a prescribed number of trials, often six. After many such series of problems, the monkey achieves a learning set such that essentially no errors are made after the first trial. Our question is, How does the monkey accomplish this?

For the casual observer, the answer is simple enough: As the monkey learns that one object is rewarded consistently and the other object is never rewarded within a given problem, all necessary information eventually is seen as given on the first trial. If the object selected is not rewarded, then the alternative will be, and vice versa.

Such an explanation is reasonably descriptive, but it does little to explain the basis of the monkey's behavior. Left unanswered is the fundamental question, How does the monkey come to appreciate, and to apply, the information presented on the first trial? For many years, attempts were made to understand this phenomenon in terms of reinforcement and other principles used in theories of learning (see Harlow, 1959). More recently, a thorough analysis of learning set in terms of memorial processes was made in a Ph.D. dissertation by David Bessemer (1967). Later this work was expanded into a chapter coauthored by Bessemer and Stollnitz (1971).

Conceptual Framework of Bessemer's Thesis

Bessemer based his analysis on three phenomena of memorial behavior. The first is the relationship found between learning rates and subsequent retention when humans learn, in succession, many lists of verbal units such as words. The second is the similar relationship found when monkeys are presented a long series of discrimination problems. Third is a set of relationships observed in studies of learning set that could not be explained by standard theoretical approaches. These three phenomena are elaborated briefly in the following sections.

Retention decrement accompanies learning to learn when humans acquire a series of unrelated lists. Humans typically acquire techniques that enable them to learn more rapidly each of several successive lists of verbal items, even when no specific relationship exists between the lists. At the same time, however, recall of each list after 24 hours or so becomes progressively poorer (even though no additional lists are learned during the interval—Keppel, Postman, & Zavortink, 1968; Underwood, 1945).

Retention decrement and learning set in monkeys. An effect comparable to that just described for humans also occurs in monkeys solving a series of successive discrimination problems. We know, of course, that such problems come to be solved progressively more rapidly. But does successive deterioration in retention also occur? Although we cannot be completely conclusive on this point, evidence suggesting this effect is available. For example, various experiments have shown some progressive loss in retention for solutions to specific problems, although these typically involve long retention intervals that include intervening problems (see Bessemer & Stollnitz, 1971).

One of the more pertinent experiments for our purposes was by Zimmerman (1969). The results of his study include evidence for a negative correlation between proficiency in learning set (confounded, unfortunately, by age) and retention of specific problems. In this experiment, 2-year-old monkeys showed more rapid acquisition of learning set than 6-month-old monkeys. On Trial 2 of each problem, the average performance of the older monkeys was about 20–25% better than that of the younger monkeys. After exposure to 100 problems, the monkeys were reexposed to the same 100 problems, which permits an estimate of retention. Zimmerman found that the older monkeys, which had acquired learning set more effectively, showed more retention loss for specific problems (27%) than the 6-month-old monkeys (10%).

Previous explanations of learning set.   The effects with both humans and monkeys that we have just discussed led Bessemer to suspect that progressively poorer retention of previous problems might be linked to the occurrence of learning set, perhaps causally. But first he dealt with the third issue: How have other theoretical approaches to learning set succeeded in explanation? The answer Bessemer found is, not very well.

Consider, for example, an explanation of learning set in terms of differential reinforcement, in which the basic mechanism is the strengthening of the response to the object rewarded and the weakening of the alternative response that is not rewarded. In this view, learning set is a consequence of the difference in strength produced on the first trial of each problem. This explanation even may be buttressed by additional assumptions that permit enhanced consequences of differential reinforcement with successive problems. Regardless, this basic reinforcement mechanism has been shown to be inadequate; learning set has been demonstrated even when successive problems require a *reversal* of contingencies of Trial 1 for presentation on Trial 2. That is, in some experiments (e.g., McDowell, Gaylord, & Brown, 1965) the object rewarded on Trial 1 of each problem was not rewarded on Trial 2, and vice versa. Yet with successive problems the monkeys eventually learned to choose with consistent accuracy on Trial 2 of each problem, which required a response that had not been rewarded on Trial 1.

Bessemer's Theory and Tests of Some Implications

The theoretical approach that Bessemer prefers has been employed in human concept formation (Levine, 1965). Bessemer suggested that lower primates also may acquire a "hypothesis," which may be stated for the case of typical learning set procedures as "win–stay, lose–shift." We would expect the use of such a hypothesis to be accompanied by the following characteristics of retention:

1. If correct responding is to occur on Trial 2, the subject must retain information concerning the object chosen on Trial 1, whether or not that choice was correct and, thus, rewarded.

2. As more problems are experienced, retention for specific problems need

not continue after long intervals; indeed, such retention is not adaptive because it might interfere with the solution of new problems.

3. On the other hand, we would expect that the hypothesis itself—manifested in behavior by relatively flawless performance on Trial 2 for all similar problems—should be retained over very long intervals.

We see next that all of these characteristics are found in learning set behavior.

For the first characteristic, we would expect that Trial 2 performance should be very sensitive to the interval between Trial 1 and Trial 2 or, more generally, to any manipulation that affects retention of information acquired on Trial 1. As illustrated in Figure 3.9, Deets, Harlow, and Blomquist (1970) have shown that when learning set is well established, Trial 2 performance is significantly poorer after a 20-second retention interval than after a 10-second interval. And Trial 2 performance after a 10-second interval is poorer than after 5 seconds.

Consistent with the second characteristic, Bessemer and Stollnitz (1971, Exp. 5) found very rapid forgetting of specific problems. They gave a series of three-trial problems, then measured retention after 2 to 3 minutes, 1 hour, or 24 hours. What they found was a good deal of retention decrement after 2 to 3 minutes and nearly complete decrement after 1 hour (see Figure 3.10). Note that this does not imply that information acquired about a specific problem is necessarily imper-manent. Memories representing specific problems nevertheless may be perma-

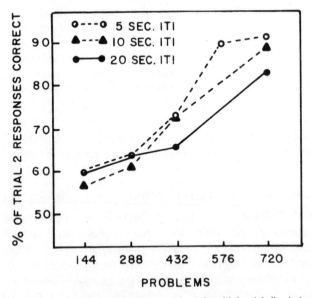

Figure 3.9   This figure shows that after a large number of multiple-trial discrimination problems experienced by monkeys, the percentage of responses correct on Trial 2 of a particular problem becomes inversely proportional to the length of the delay between Trial 1 and Trial 2. For this experiment, the length of this delay (ITI, intertrial interval) was 5, 10 or 20 sec. (Adapted from Deets et al., 1970. Copyright 1970 by the American Psychological Association. Reprinted by permission.)

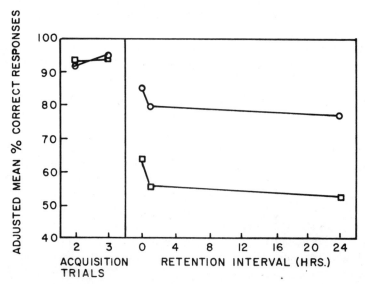

Figure 3.10   This figure shows forgetting of a discrimination between two objects by monkeys that are extraordinarily well experienced with problems of this kind (i.e., "learning-set-sophisticated" monkeys). It can be seen that a great deal of forgetting occurs at the shortest interval tested (2–3 mins.) following presentation of a problem. This forgetting is greatest when the subjects choice on the first trial of a particular problem was not rewarded (lower line); for the upper line, the animals first choice within a particular problem always was correct and was rewarded. (Adapted from Bessemer and Stollnitz, 1971).

nently registered as part of experience. In fact, Bessemer and Stollnitz cite other experiments showing that such information does become, in their terms, "part of long-term memory." The major point here is that as a consequence of information processed about learning set tasks, the monkey does not allow specific contingencies of reinforcement to influence its behavior for long.

The third characteristic is that learning set itself—the "hypothesis" of win-stay, lose–shift—is retained over long periods. Most tests given after intervals of months or a few years have shown essentially no loss in learning set efficiency. After longer periods, however, learning set may be forgotten. Stollnitz (1970) tested monkeys after a six-year interval during which they had experienced only a few discrimination problems. He found a general loss in retention of learning set performance, with an average decline of 23% in accuracy on Trial 2.

The point of this section is to show how the study of retention and forgetting may have value beyond the specific retention phenomena being tested. Bessemer has added insight into an established phenomenon of behavior, learning set, by analyzing the characteristic changes in short-term memory that accompany the development of this phenomenon, and further investigations with other species (blue jays) closely corroborate this analysis (e.g., Kamil & Mauldin, 1975). In doing so, he has added to our understanding of both learning set and short-term retention.

SHORT-TERM RETENTION IN HUMANS

Retention after short intervals has been considered separately from retention after long intervals for nearly a century of psychological investigation. William James (1890) discussed the introspective observation that the use of recently acquired information seems a quite different matter than applying that information at some later time, after it has left consciousness. The latter process, which seems to require retrieval of the information no longer in consciousness, James termed *secondary memory,* and the former, for which the information has been acquired so recently that it has never left consciousness, he termed *primary memory.*

Empirical study of these hypothetically different types of memory processing required, for primary memory, that retention of a small amount of information be tested after short intervals, and for secondary memory, that retention of larger amounts of materials be tested after long intervals. These types of investigations came to be identified in terms of their temporal parameters, as the study of "short-term" or "long-term" memory, though as we shall discuss later, a more useful conceptualization would consider instead whether the memory is in an "active" (primary memory) or "passive" state (secondary memory).

Studies of short-term memory from a biological orientation, using as subjects animals or physiologically impaired humans, have had many concepts and objectives in common with those using normal human subjects, but there have been differences as well. As an example of such a difference, it is not uncommon to find discussions of a hypothetical short-term-memory process within biologically oriented studies to include retention intervals as long as several hours, whereas with normal human subjects reference to short-term memory usually is restricted to intervals of less than a minute. For proper consideration of many issues in retention and forgetting, however, it is necessary to refer to both classes of investigations of short-term retention. It is not necessary to elaborate here about the characteristics of short-term retention with normal human subjects because quite excellent and thorough reviews of this topic may be found elsewhere (Crowder, 1976; Deutsch & Deutsch, 1975; Murdock, 1974). What we shall present at this time is a very brief description of the basic techniques and phenomena in this area for reference later, when this information will be useful with regard to certain general issues of memory processing.

Brief Retention of Sensory Images

To our good fortune, our sensory systems are "wired" to permit us to maintain a sensory impression—an impression that represents the encountered stimuli with faithful integrity—for a brief period after the cessation of direct receptor contact with an environmental event. For humans, this is most useful in the visual system where visual "trace" of an object persists for about 250 milliseconds. This permits us to see, for example, a movie as a continuous stream of events rather than as a sequence of discrete pictures, and the light from a fluorescent bulb as constant when in fact it flickers. Such a maintained visual sensory impression may be termed an *iconic memory* (cf. Neisser, 1967).

Superficially at least, some characteristics of the processing of an iconic memory are similar to those involved in relatively long-term retention. For example, if two similar visual stimuli are presented within 50 milliseconds of each other, humans will report that they did not see the first. This phenomenon is termed *backward masking* and may be likened to retroactive interference measured over much longer intervals of time, as with long-term retention (recall that retroactive interference occurs when the learning of similar materials impairs retention of previously learned materials). The mechanisms responsible for backward masking and retroactive interference probably are quite different, however.

How can we measure retention of information over intervals in the range of milliseconds? An example is provided in a classic experiment by Sperling (1960). In this experiment, humans were presented with two or three rows of letters and numbers, usually with four items per row. Presentation was very brief, about 50 milliseconds for the entire arrangement of letters or numbers. It was known that the most a subject could recall from such a presentation was about four items.

Sperling found that if subjects were signaled properly concerning which row of items they were to concentrate on, they were quite accurate in repeating the items, much more so than was expected if the subjects were not signaled as to which item should be selected for attention. The signals used were tones—a very high tone for the top row, a very low tone for the bottom row, and so forth. By presenting the tones *after* exposure to the items, Sperling could infer how long the subjects "held" the image of all the items while waiting for the signal as to which row they should report. In this way, Sperling could estimate the span of iconic memory for these very familiar items. He found that, in general, the longer the subjects had to "wait" after exposure to the array of items before being signaled which row they should repeat, the less accurate they were. Even with familiar items like numbers and letters, subjects could be reasonably accurate only if signaled within a few hundred milliseconds; the signal was no help at all if presented beyond 1 second after the display.

It is not clear how much "memory" processing is related to retention over intervals in the range between seconds and years, but some interesting possibilities exist. For example, individuals appear to differ rather widely in the processing of sensory representations of this sort, and some children in particular are noted for a capacity to retain intact visual images for a relatively long period, a capacity sometimes termed *eidetic imagery* (for a review, see Gray & Gummerman, 1975). There are now some rather ingenious means for testing such eidetic imagery, essentially by making perception of a new object dependent on a completely faithful representation of a previously perceived object. When children who seem to have excellent eidetic imagery have been tested after long intervals for retention of pictures, however, their performance has been found to be no better than that of children with less capacity for eidetic imagery (Haber & Haber, 1964). On the other hand, Mr. S., the mnemonist studied by Luria (1968), also seemed to have an unusual capacity for such imagery, and of course his long-term retention capacity was superior to that of normal humans, if not unsurpassed. It is therefore unclear whether eidetic imagery, or capacity for processing iconic memories, is related to other aspects of memory processing, except that of course all sensory content of memories must be processed first in this iconic stage.

Retention of Verbal Materials after Short Intervals

If humans are presented a single verbal item and 15 or 20 seconds later are asked to recall it, they almost certainly will do so without error. Accuracy may be impaired by two major factors: a failure in the initial perception of the item or prevention of rehearsal of the item by the subject during the retention interval (see Reitman, 1974). Perception can be assured quite easily, but the control of rehearsal is a problem. Rehearsal by humans (whether or not it is a species-specific behavior found only in humans) is a topic of some interest in terms of how it acts to alleviate forgetting. But in order to test the properties of short-term retention it is necessary first to work under circumstances in which short-term *forgetting* occurs. And for this, rehearsal must be retarded, if not prevented.

There are two general ways in which rehearsal has been retarded in the assessment of short-term retention. One is by employing the "Brown–Peterson paradigm": To prevent rehearsal during the retention interval, subjects are given a distracting task that involves materials not formally similar to those to be remembered. For example, if the item to be recalled is a trigram such as *TRG,* a number such as 873 is presented immediately after the trigram and the subject is asked to count backwards by threes (873, 870, 867 . . .) until the time for recall. Amount of forgetting depends, of course, on the similarity between the materials in the rehearsal prevention task and the item to be recalled (i.e., retroactive interference) and the similarity between materials previously learned in the same context and the item to be recalled (proactive interference).

Rehearsal is retarded in another manner with the "probe" technique of assessing short-term retention. With this technique, items that the subject has been instructed to learn are tested after a certain number of interpolated items of the same kind (and also to be learned) have been presented during the "retention interval." A "probe" or signal is presented to the subject to distinguish which of the previous items he is to recall. A third technique is to consider terminal items in a free-recall list as involving short-term retention and initially presented items as long-term retention. However, it has become apparent that the basis of encoding items falling at the end of a free-recall list (the kind of memory attributes representing these items) may differ from the basis of encoding that accompanies presentation of a single item within the Brown–Peterson or probe techniques. Moreover, the difference is sufficient to yield differing retention phenomena and therefore causes us to question the wisdom of treating these methods in terms of a common process. (Similar functional differences may be found to result from the use of the probe and Brown–Peterson techniques; see Murdock, 1974.)

The study of short-term retention of verbal materials has become voluminous, and it is neither necessary nor desirable to review this information here. Extensive reviews and analysis of the information in this area may be found in books by Murdock (1974), Crowder (1976), and Kintsch (1970, 1974). Again, however, we shall have occasion to refer to this area of information when discussing specific issues of memory processing.

INDIRECT ASSESSMENT OF RETENTION AFTER SHORT INTERVALS

Short-term retention has been studied with another method that is quite different from the direct assessment of retention. Very generally, this method involves two steps. First, treatments intended to alter memory processing are applied shortly after learning. After the side effects of the treatment have dissipated, retention is assessed. Treatments that decrease retention have been applied most often in this context, but some treatments that facilitate retention also have been studied.

We have mentioned how some traumatic events, such as a blow to the head, may impair retention for immediately preceding events. This is called retrograde amnesia—"amnesia" because of the retention loss (although amnesia literally refers to the complete absence of memory) and "retrograde" because the trauma acts on past events. A number of treatments that can cause retrograde amnesia have been identified, and to some extent we know how far backward in time they may be effective.

In principle, we should be able experimentally to manipulate retrograde amnesia to provide inferences about memory processes that occur shortly after learning. By introducing an amnesic treatment at various intervals after learning, we may assess the memory processing that occurred during a particular learning-treatment interval in terms of the extent of amnesia found. Inferences about short-term memory processing would require two simple assumptions: first, that memory processing is halted or otherwise disrupted by amnesic treatment; next, that the memory processing that occurs between learning and the amnesic treatment contributes somehow to later behavior. On this basis, we should be able to assess indirectly the memory processing that occurs between learning and the amnesic treatment, just as we assess such memory processing directly by simply measuring retention after short intervals following learning.

Up to now, however, relatively little experimental manipulation of retrograde amnesia has been directed at understanding short-term memory in any analytical sense. To some extent, this reflects reasonable caution in view of our incomplete knowledge about the amnesic treatments themselves. Instead, analysis of such retrograde amnesic effects more often has been based on two suppositions: An amnesic treatment either negates all processing initiated by the learning experience or impedes expression of this memory processing by altering subsequent memory retrieval.

Memory processing after short intervals may be altered not only by amnesic treatments but also by "hypermnesic" treatments that enhance subsequent retention. Both these effects are important for understanding memory processing from a psychobiological viewpoint, for the information this approach has already produced, and for the above-mentioned potential for understanding short-term retention. In Chapters 6 and 7, we shall consider results and principles derived from the experimental study of amnesic and hypermnesic treatments.

SUMMARY AND CONCLUSIONS

We have discussed the effects on retention of the most commonly acknowledged source of forgetting, the retention interval. Only events within an interval can have explanatory value, not the interval itself, but the analytical and representational importance of "simple forgetting" is evident nevertheless.

Following a discussion of some of the obstacles that may impede the development of general principles, and a consideration of the conceptual boundaries and classification schemes useful in analyzing simple forgetting, the remainder of this chapter emphasized the characteristics of simple retention in animals following short intervals (on the order of seconds, or minutes at most) and with low degrees of original learning. Two methods of studying short-term retention in animals were emphasized, the delayed-response and delayed-matching-to-sample tasks, because these have been most widely applied and most profitable in this area. We omitted discussion of other techniques of potential value because their application has not yet contributed equally significantly to this area, or because they are as yet insufficiently understood. Especially promising techniques, in which the predictive or instrumental value of Signal 2 depends on the nature of a prior Signal 1 and the intersignal interval is varied systematically, have been reported by Honig (1974) and by Terry and Wagner (1975).

The delayed-response task, however ubiquitous in its application during the last 60 years and however useful as a behavioral assay for some reasons, has notable analytical limitations when applied to the study of memory processing. However, appreciation of these limitations has led to refined techniques and to the analysis of questions having considerable importance for memory processing, such as the influence of stimulus redundancy (Medin & Davis, 1974).

A variety of parameters of potential importance to retention after short intervals have been investigated carefully with the delayed-matching-to-sample task. This analysis yielded some surprises. Some variables expected to determine short-term retention do not have much effect on forgetting, for example, factors that might contribute to proactive interference (which we shall study further in the next chapter) and duration and number of repetitions of the stimulus to be remembered. Performance often has been affected by these and other variables, but the effect is uniform across increasingly long retention intervals. This implies an influence on original perception or degree of learning, but precludes clear conclusions about forgetting. On the other hand, degree of ambient illumination during the retention interval has an unexpectedly powerful, and apparently direct, effect on forgetting. If we expose the monkey or pigeon (Maki, Moe & Bierley, 1977) to darkness rather than to light during the retention interval, the length of the interval after which accurate recognition occurs may be several times greater than otherwise.

We discussed a case in which the characteristics of short-term retention were applied toward interpretation of other phenomena of animal behavior. The particular example described was the analysis of learning set in monkeys by Bessemer and Stollnitz (1971). A final brief discussion concerned the analysis of short-term retention in humans, which we shall elaborate upon further in later chapters.

A point worth reemphasizing is the uselessness of basing phylogenetic comparisons, or analyses of individual differences in general, on the "limits" of an individual's capacity for short-term retention. Until the functional determinants of short-term retention are understood better, these limits may shift drastically with changes in testing method. For example, Jarrard and Moise (1971) noted that the retention function of their monkeys tested on delayed matching to sample reached its minimal asymptote (maximal forgetting) with delays of 15 to 20 seconds, similar to the asymptote found in short-term retention by humans tested with the Brown–Peterson paradigm. Subsequently, with a similar task, D'Amato (1973) reported quite different retention functions for monkeys, with the minimal asymptote of accurate responding typically occurring beyond 200 seconds, and up to 500 seconds in some cases. The difference was a simple modification in procedure—degree of ambient illumination (which does not yield a correspondingly dramatic effect in humans). Similarly, while the delayed-matching-to-sample task indicates that pigeons rarely show evidence for retention after intervals longer than 5 seconds, recent procedural modifications have expanded this limit to at least 60 seconds (Grant, 1976). Moreover, a quite different paradigm devised by Honig (1974) has led to consistently accurate responding by pigeons over retention intervals of 30 seconds or more.

4

Analysis of Sources of Forgetting Affecting Long-Term Retention

Now we address a many-faceted question that is perhaps the fundamental problem for the science of memory processing: What is the fate of information acquired by an organism in its more distant past? In other words, how does an "older" memory's potential for influencing behavior differ from that of a more recently acquired memory, and why should such differences occur? Our specific interest here is with memories that were established rather well initially but are not needed for environmental adjustment (i.e., correct performance at the retention test) until several minutes, hours, days, or even years later.

This obviously is an important question for understanding behavior generally, human and animal. Yet, as mentioned earlier, studies of long-term retention in animals historically have been somewhat less than analytic. In retrospect, this paradox is understandable. Initial emphasis in the study of memory processing in animals was on learning or memory storage. This was quite natural for several reasons. First, within the stimulus–response framework employed by most scientists in this area, later manifestation of a well-established memory should depend only on whether the precise stimulus of original training recurred. Second, it was recognized that the *exact* stimulus events of original training could not possibly reappear as such. Thus, the ultimate problem was viewed as one of identifying the effective stimuli (e.g., Guthrie, 1935) or determining how generalized stimuli come to acquire control over behavior. Finally, learning theorists' attention was dominated by the considerable *retention* found, rather than by the little forgetting that occurred (e.g., Skinner, 1950), so it was entirely appropriate that the study of memory processing should concentrate on problems of original learning and subsequent stimulus control.

The fact is, however, that the influence of old memories may be modified drastically by manipulations that do not influence the nominally controlling stimulus in any way whatsoever and that may be quite independent of the conditions of memory storage.

There are four major issues here. The first is the general course of forgetting: Does retention decline with a fairly regular and steady progression over time, or are there sudden dips and rises at various intervals following memory storage? Second is the question of what is forgotten: Are all aspects of an episode forgotten at the same rate and to the same degree, or are certain classes of events especially susceptible or resistant to forgetting? The third issue concerns the sources of forgetting—factors that may explain variations in forgetting or why forgetting occurs at all. Finally, how is long-term retention to be conceptualized? Is it a consequence of one or more stages of processing? Does the memory become more ephemeral as it ages, or does it become progressively "stronger," though perhaps less accessible? And is the aged memory a simple extension of the mode of representation at the time of original learning, or is it qualitatively different? These issues will be emphasized in this and the following chapter.

THE LONG-TERM COURSE OF FORGETTING

The consensus of psychologists and laymen alike is that retention is a monotonically decreasing function of the retention interval: In other words, retention decreases with increasingly longer retention intervals, and older memories are more likely to be forgotten than newer ones. Indeed, this monotonic decline in retention over time is so well engrained in the scientific literature, and in our subjective experience, that its empirical demonstration typically is deemed uninteresting.

A very large number of studies could serve as adequate examples of monotonically decreasing retention. There is no need to illustrate it here because it does not take much imagination to visualize an index of retention that progressively drops as the retention interval represented on the abscissa increases. Typically, the drop in retention is faster in the early stages of the retention interval than later, but this, too, is subjectively reasonable and easy to imagine (see Chapter 3, Figure 3.1). You will recall from our earlier discussion, however, that there is reason to doubt the representative value of this particular "Ebbinghaus" function because of the special procedures with which it was measured.

In recent years, the course of forgetting over time has been tracked more thoroughly than before (which simply means that more retention intervals have been investigated), providing results that are both interesting and counterintuitive. Two reasons may be cited to account for this more thorough investigation. The first is quite elementary. When technical resources were more limited, investigators simply could not afford to train, house, and test the multiple groups of animals needed to cover many different retention intervals. Also, most of the learning tasks employed in earlier years required rather extensive training. Thus, it was economically unfeasible to tap more than two or three retention intervals in a single experiment. The second reason is that there seemed little need to investigate a wide variety of retention intervals, because no theories demanded such a test.

More recently, however, theories of memory have been developed to accommodate multiple stages of memory processing and so require tests after a larger number of retention intervals. Also, a number of learning tasks have been developed that require relatively little training of the animal prior to retention tests. Consequently, it is now quite common to find studies of memory processing in which retention is tested after as many as eight or ten different intervals. The result has been a variety of retention functions. Some of these apparently are

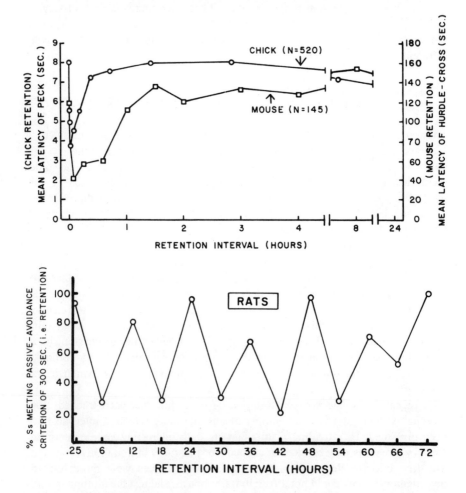

Figure 4.1 Retention as a function of time since passive avoidance training is shown in Figure 4.1a for mice and infant chickens, in Figure 4.1b for rats, in Figure 4.1c for octopus, and in Figure 4.1d for cuttlefish. (4a is adapted from Cherkin, 1971; 4b from Holloway and Wansley, 1973; 4c from Sanders and Barlow, 1971; and 4d from Messenger, 1971).

stable and well analyzed, but others are so improbable and irregular that one is tempted to hope that they do not represent important memory processes because of the complicated theories that would be necessary to explain them.

Multiphasic Retention Functions

To illustrate the variety of retention functions that may be found after brief periods of training, a collection of the results of several experiments is shown in Figure 4.1. The experiments involving mice, rats, or chicks used tasks that have been termed "one-trial passive avoidance," where rats and mice are given a

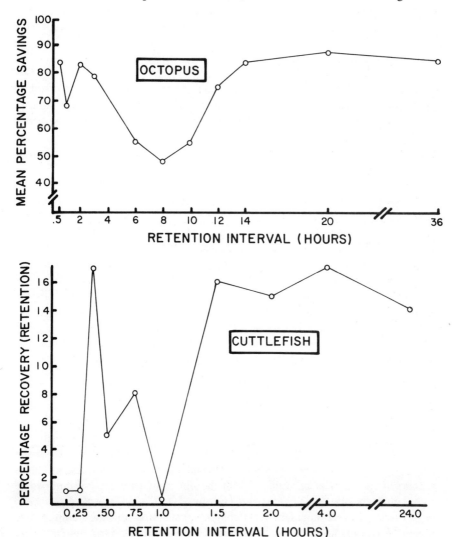

footshock after they step through an enclosure and chicks are given an unpleasant taste after pecking an object. To test retention, the animals are placed back in the training situation and their latency to step through the enclosure or peck the same object is measured. Retention occurs to the extent that the animals delay in responding (stepping through or pecking).

The studies in Figure 4.1 that tested the octopus and the sepia (cuttlefish) involved somewhat more complex tasks and multiple trials. Each octopus was permitted to initiate an attack on a helpless crab. The octopus was punished with an electric shock just prior to the completion of each attack, and the crab was removed. This "passive avoidance" training continued until 1 minute had elapsed in which no attacks occurred. Retention was indexed in terms of the percentage of attacks given during testing, using the 1-minute criterion, relative to the number given during training (Sanders & Barlow, 1971). The cuttlefish were permitted to charge prawns, their usual food, that were enclosed in a glass tube. This response soon attained a criterion of infrequency so that it could be said to be habituated (or was punished sufficiently when the cuttlefish rammed into the invisible glass tube). The tube and the enclosed prawns were removed and then replaced after one of 12 retention intervals in order to measure retention (Messenger, 1971). Like the studies with rats, mice, and chicks, these aquatic studies also may be seen as tests of retention of passive avoidance.

In our view, understanding of these and other multiphasic retention functions must await closer analysis of the behavioral tests employed. Although simple, they are not understood very well. Also, in spite of the temptation to make a great deal out of recurrent inflections in a curve, there are few sound theories that predict multiple inflections solely on the basis of memory processing. There is systematic reason to expect multiple alterations of general activation or perfor-mance effects during a long retention interval, but these are of only methodologi-cal interest here in view of our concern with changes in the accessibility of availability of the memory. For example, it is known that spontaneous activity by rats and mice changes progressively following the particular type of footshock given in these passive avoidance tasks: Activity first increases, then decreases, as time passes since the shock, and investigators such as Ray and Barrett (1969) have shown that the apparent retention increases are highly correlated with these changes in activity.

Some multiple inflections directly relevant to memory processing do seem quite reliable under procedural variation: The circadian-related function derived with rats (top curve in Figure 4.1) has been replicated on several occasions to show independence from shifts in simple performance factors associated with the circadian cycle, and seems readily understandable as a special case of state-dependent retention in accordance with the conceptual framework outlined in earlier chapters (see, e.g., Wansley & Holloway, 1975). Also, it is premature to dismiss some other apparently reliable characteristics of these multiphasic curves. An example is the decrements that have been measured within 1 or 2 minutes following training, obtained with regularity by Cherkin and his colleagues (e.g., Cherkin, 1974), who have tested literally hundreds of fish and chicks. There are, furthermore, other fluctuations that have been measured reliably within the first 24 hours of retention. It is not heresy, therefore, to theorize about retention functions that are not monotonically decreasing.

There are two such functions that warrant further discussion, general reminiscence and the more specific Kamin effect. These functions are known to deviate significantly from the monotonically decreasing shape, and they have a somewhat longer history than those derived only in terms of passive avoidance. "Reminiscence" refers to a retention function that is monotonically increasing starting from the point of original learning up to the time (usually several days or weeks later) that it begins to decrease. The "Kamin effect" is an initial decline in retention followed by recovery within a 24-hour period.

Reminiscence

Reminiscence is an old puzzle in the history of experimental psychology. It is defined when retention is better after long than short intervals, the reverse of forgetting. Reminiscence readily occurs when humans have received massed trials on certain motor learning tasks (apparently regardless of muscular fatigue). After distributed practice, the effect is less clear or does not occur at all. In this context, reminiscence has been explained in terms of dissipation of some hypothetical internal inhibition that builds up on each learning trial. Presumably, this inhibition accumulates during massed trials, but if a sufficiently long interval elapses, the inhibition dissipates and performance improves correspondingly. Another explanation is that relatively weak error tendencies accumulate during massed training, but if a sufficiently long retention interval elapses, these error tendencies may be forgotten in favor of the stronger tendencies toward accurate performance.

These sorts of explanations, in which a negative factor like inhibition impedes the manifestation of a memory after short intervals but not after longer ones, may be contrasted with an alternative view in which the memory is thought actually to increase in "strength" during a retention interval. In many ways, the latter would be the more interesting. Imagine that after struggling with a learning task one need only sit back and rest as learning somehow "continued" and the memory for prior events spontaneously became stronger and stronger. Unfortunately, there is no evidence that this occurs. There are clear indications nevertheless that performance on retention tests may be better after longer retention intervals. It is such effects that have been termed *reminiscence* or, sometimes, *incubation*.

Reminiscence has been established experimentally in two ways. We have already mentioned the first and most dramatic case: Among organisms trained to equivalent levels of performance, better retention is found for those tested after longer intervals of rest. The second case of reminiscence also implies better retention after longer intervals, but this inference is based on a single group of subjects in a "within-subject" test. Subjects are given clusters of massed training trials, each cluster separated by a relatively long interval. For example, five trials may be given with only a few seconds intervening between trials; then five more are given 24 hours later; and so on (e.g., Hill & Spear, 1962; see Figure 4.2). Reminiscence is shown when more improvement in performance occurs between clusters of trials than within. In the Hill and Spear example, in which the index of retention was the speed with which rats ran to a location where they had previously found food, reminiscence was defined by greater improvement between trials separated by 24 hours (for example, between Trials 15 and 16) than between trials separated by only a few seconds (for example, between Trials 14 and 15 or between Trials 16 and 17. In addition to the groups given massed (M) trials with a few seconds intervening within days, Figure 4.2 also depicts the lesser reminiscence over a 24-hour period when several minutes elapsed between trials within each day [spaced or S trials; for further consideration of this effect of trial spacing and reinforcer magnitude (1 vs. 4 pellets in Figure 4.2), see Hill, Erlebacher, & Spear, 1965].

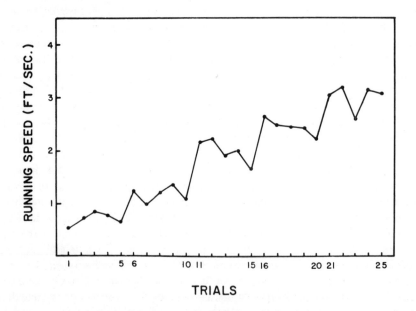

Figure 4.2   This figure illustrates that under certain conditions retention following a 24 hour interval (e.g. performance on Trial 11, or on Trial 16, or on Trial 21) is greater than that found following the 15 sec interval ("massed" trials) between trials within a day (e.g. performance on Trials 10, 15, and 20). (Adapted from Hill and Spear, 1962. Copyright 1962 by the American Psychological Association. Reprinted by permission.)

Reminiscence in humans.   We have mentioned that reminiscence in humans occurs readily in certain tasks involving acquisition of perceptual motor skills (e.g., Huang & Payne, 1975). Similar evidence has been reported for certain tests of verbal memory. However, as Underwood (1966) has noted, the latter is largely a "pre-World War II" trend in that its frequent appearance in the literature prior to 1940 did not continue after 1950. Presumably, the increasing precision of more modern methodology accounts for this, together with analytical splitting of the phenomenon into separate concerns.

In part because of the critical analysis of McGeoch (1935), it became clear that reminiscence should be defined independently of two potentially contaminating, though interesting, factors. One of these factors is rehearsal, which may occur during the retention interval to increase retention in later tests. More recently, Erdelyi and his colleagues have focused on this factor as an important determinant of the reminiscence that may be found using relatively complex pictures as stimuli (Erdelyi & Becker, 1974; Erdelyi & Kleinbard, 1976).

The second factor contributing to some early demonstrations of reminiscence, but now receiving separate study, is the influence of multiple retention tests. If subjects are given interpolated retention tests that include information as to the correct responses (e.g., the anticipation technique), it is quite clear that the basic index of reminiscence is contaminated by new learning and the results are uninteresting in terms of retention and forgetting. And even if feedback concerning correct responding were not given during interpolated retention tests, the occurrence of these interpolated tests would not satisfy the basic conditions for testing reminiscence in the sense intended by McGeoch (1935) and Ward (1937); as part of the original episode to be learned, materials presented for an interpolated retention test may serve as reactivation treatments to alleviate forgetting, a topic we shall address in Chapter 8.

Another phenomenon, different from the more conventional "reminiscence" of concern here but still classified by some as reminiscence, has been tested by investigators concerned with the determinants of retrieval (e.g., Buschke, 1975). These tests concern the retrieval at a later period of episodic events not retrieved at an earlier test. In other words, after observing a long list of words, subjects may be unable to recall certain items in the list at time x although able to do so at time $x + y$, even though there has been no additional practice. This finding has clear importance for understanding memory retrieval. If, however, the net percentage of words recalled at time $x + y$ is no greater than that recalled at time x, one may choose not to incorporate this as an instance of reminiscence (note that all items recalled at time x are not necessarily also recalled at time $x + y$).

Concerning the retention of verbal units, it generally is conceded that three solid demonstrations of reminiscence may be found in the literature, represented by Keppel and Underwood (1967), Peterson (1966), and Ward (1937). These cases of reminiscence occurred over very short intervals, 2 minutes in the case of the Ward study and several seconds for the others. It may be noted that a series of experiments by Scheirer and Voss (1969) isolated the source of reminiscence for single items presented in the Brown–Peterson paradigm (Keppel & Underwood, 1967; Peterson, 1966) as differential proactive interference attributable to differences in the interval between successive items-to-be-remembered. Nevertheless, the robustness of these cases of reminiscence—an initially rapid decline in retention followed by later recovery—is illustrated in its occurrence with a variety of materials, high- and low-frequency words, high and low meaningful trigrams of the consonant–vowel–consonant (CVC) form, and trigrams of the consonant–consonant–consonant (CCC) form.

Reminiscence in animals.   Like the human studies, research on reminiscence in animals occurred mainly prior to 1940. However, as we shall soon see, the phenomenon itself has been given considerable attention more recently under a new name, *incubation*.

Also like the earlier studies of reminiscence in human verbal memory, tests with animals sometimes had clear methodological deficiencies by today's standards. For example, Magdsick (1936) conducted a quite extensive study of the relative retention of maze learning with different delays by rats of different ages. Her idea was to test a suggestion from some previous studies that reminiscence might be stronger in younger subjects, an intriguing notion. Magdsick did report "reminiscence," but this effect was due entirely to the relatively poor performance of subjects given the shortest retention interval (which amounted to continuous practice on the water maze task). This condition also differed from all longer retention intervals in that the animals were not returned to their home cage between training and testing. Because the rat had to swim to safety in the task employed, the animals in this immediate-retention test group also differed in terms of how wet they were when the first retention trial occurred and also undoubtedly in terms of their temperature regulation during that trial.

A similar example is an experiment by Anderson (1940). Anderson's experiment was simply designed and involved only four different conditions: separate groups of rats were tested after retention intervals of 0, 1, 5, or 10 days following several days of practice on a complex maze given at the rate of 5 trials per day. The study was an admirable effort nevertheless, with 36 rats per group and requiring three years for completion. When Anderson compared retention scores for the first day of the retention test, he found a trend toward reminiscence: Animals given the longer retention intervals made fewer errors. We can see in Figure 4.3 that Anderson's reminiscence effect was due entirely to differences that occurred on the first retention trial.

Anderson's results after the longer intervals are understandable in relation to the performance deficit during the last trials in a daily session and on the immediate retention test. Throughout learning and the retention test, reminiscence occurred within subjects in that fewer errors occurred on the first trial of a daily session than on later trials. But why should the rats tested immediately after

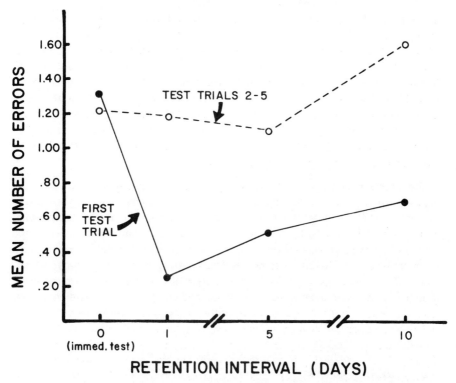

Figure 4.3   Retention of learned performance on a complex maze is shown for tests given immediately (0), or after 1, 5, or 10 days following training (the lower the score on the ordinant, the better the retention). It can be seen that in terms of the score on the first test trial, retention is better following a one day interval than on the immediate test, thus defining reminisence. The magnitude of the effect is small, however, and is not seen on subsequent test trials. (Adapted from Anderson, 1940. Copyright 1940 by the American Psychological Association. Reproduced by permission.)

learning have made so many more errors (on what amounted to Trial 6, the first "retention" trial) in comparison to Trial 5 (last "learning" trial)? Procedurally, Trial 6 was no more different from Trial 5 than Trial 5 was from Trial 4. Anderson suggests that because these animals had been accustomed to receiving five trials per day throughout training, the introduction of a sixth trial has "in some way disconcerted the animals. They seemed excited and jumpy..." (1940, p. 403). It was as if the rats had learned to count to five! Moreover, following this "sixth" trial, the number of errors declined in the remaining five test trials for this "immediate" group.

We learn two things from Anderson's data. The first is that animals may become quite sensitive to a change in contextual stimuli as subtle as the cumulative number or duration of runs through the maze. Thus, we must be wary of procedures in which contextual change may be the likely cause of a decrement in the expected performance of groups tested after very short intervals. It is quite a different thing to say that reminiscence is a result of better performance after longer intervals than to say that it is a result of artificially depressed performance after short intervals. Second, Anderson has shown a clear case of reminiscence using the within-subject design—greater gain between days (i.e., after a 24-hour rest) than within days. Similar effects were found and analyzed in terms of running speeds in a straight alley by Hill and his colleagues (Hill & Spear, 1962; Hill, Erlebacher, & Spear, 1965). In each case, the reminiscence seems more parsimoniously viewed as due to factors depressing performance before the retention interval rather than facilitation of memory processing during the retention interval.

The Deutsch theory.   A more contemporary instance of reminiscence may be found among data obtained by Deutsch and his colleagues in testing his theory of the role of neurotransmitters in memory processing. We shall return to this theory later (Chapter 7), but will mention at this point that it predicts reminiscence as a regular feature of retention functions. Some indirect support of this prediction may be found in terms of pharmacological manipulations, which confirm expectations of the theory, but the reminiscence predicted among non-drugged control animals has been verified, so far, in only one experiment to my knowledge (Deutsch, 1973, has reviewed this work). If verified, this experiment would be perhaps the clearest instance of reminiscence attributable to features of memory processing.

Incubation

The term *incubation* has been applied almost exclusively within studies involving fear conditioning. Often there has been particular reference to a hypothetical increase in the emotional response of fear as time passes following a fearful episode. Otherwise, incubation is defined exactly like reminiscence.

We shall speak of "incubation" because it is applied so widely in the existing literature, but it is a most unfortunate choice of terms. The connotation of incubation most often is of some active growth process, which implies that, following a painful episode, the "seed" of fear is planted in the organism and somehow expands spontaneously over time to influence behavior increasingly. As such, "incubation" tends to fall into use as an explanatory concept when in fact there is no empirical evidence that such a growth process exists. At best, this term should only *describe* organisms' better retention of aversive events measured after long intervals than after short intervals. The more rigorous theorists have restricted themselves to this descriptive usage (e.g., McAllister & McAllister, 1967; Spevack & Suboski, 1969). The review by McAllister and McAllister (1967) is a particularly fine critique of this area of study and still warrants close reading (also see McAllister & McAllister, 1971).

Incubation in humans.   The earliest study of incubation used human subjects (Diven, 1937; McAllister & McAllister have since dismissed this study as methodologically inadequate). Subsequently, incubation has been reported often in humans, primarily in terms of a progressive increase in autonomic indexes of emotion following an aversive event. The most frequently used autonomic indexes of emotion are the galvanic skin response (GSR) and heart rate.

For example, Bindra and Cameron (1953) presented subjects with either of two letters, B or V. Fifteen seconds later, a buzzer sounded and, if the letter V had been presented, the subject received a light shock to his fingers. After eight such presentations, the subject was allowed to rest for 10 minutes before being presented these events once more. Bindra and Cameron found that the GSRs of these subjects increased significantly during the rest interval; and it did not matter very much which letter appeared, as the GSR increased when either B or V appeared. This surprising generalization between these letters is a finding of some importance for later explanations of the incubation effect.

In a study similar to that of Bindra and Cameron, Golin (1961) presented subjects with a series of words. Two of these words were followed 15 seconds later by a shock, and another (the control word) was followed 15 seconds later by a light. Compared to the GSR measured immediately after presentation of the series, GSR to the previously shocked words was significantly increased after a 30-minute rest, and this increase was greater than that found for the control words.

An example of incubation measured in terms of heart rate is found in a study by Breznitz (1967). Subjects were told that they would receive an electric shock after a certain interval, either 3, 6, or 12 minutes later (actually, they were never shocked). When this threatening statement was made, subjects' heart rates increased rather suddenly. Soon afterward, however, their heart rates decreased. At a point about midway to the point in time at which the subjects had been told they would be shocked, heart rate began to increase again, to a new level that was greatest for the subjects with the longest interval.

Incubation in animals.   Incubation has been measured in animals following various tasks of aversive conditioning. We already have seen some indication of incubation after one-trial passive avoidance in the examples of multiphasic retention functions. Other examples of increasing avoidance performance with increasing time following training may be seen in Figure 4.4. The top portion of this figure shows retention performance of rats that have been shocked after stepping from one compartment through an opening into another compartment, and the bottom portion shows retention performance of mice given a similar treatment.

Another notable example of incubation in animals is that reported by Gabriel (1967) following active avoidance conditioning in the rabbit. In these studies (also see Gabriel, 1972), the rabbits were presented a tone for 5 seconds (the CS) followed by an aversive shock (the UCS). Each rabbit could avoid the shock by rotating a wheel slightly, as long as this response occurred during the CS. Once a rabbit attained the learning criterion, extinction trials were given. Figure 4.5

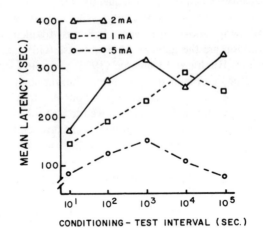

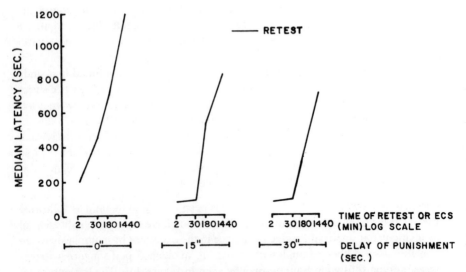

Figure 4.4   Retention of passive avoidance in rats is shown to indicate incubation (better retention the longer the interval) under some conditions. These figures suggest that under those conditions in which passive avoidance training is most effective (higher intensity of punishing footshock in the upper figure and shorter delay of punishment between a step-through response and footshock shown in the lower figure) incubation seems more apparent. This principle seems to have limited usefulness for our purposes, however, because it is unclear that such cases of incubation have anything to do with memory processing. (Upper figure is adapted from Zammit-Montebello, et al., 1969. Copyright 1969 by the American Psychological Association. Reprinted by permission. Lower figure is adapted from Geller and Jarvik, 1970).

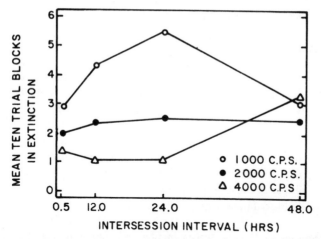

Figure 4.5   This figure shows indications of incubation in rabbits in terms of the retention of learned active avoidance. This figure indicates still another factor that seemed to influence incubation, in this case the particular frequency of the tone used as the conditioned stimulus during testing (adapted from Gabriel, 1967).

indicates the number of 10-trial blocks given during extinction until the rabbits failed to give an avoidance response on at least 9 of the 10 extinction trials within a given block. The progressive increase in the tendency to make avoidance responses following the 24-hour rest period (most marked for the 1000 c.p.s. condition) defines incubation.

Explaining incubation.   On the basis of the literature, we can suggest some answers to why incubation occurs. In spite of the proverb that after falling off a horse one should jump back on immediately to avoid developing a fear of horses, it seems quite unlikely that the emotional response to aversive events really increases spontaneously over time. For humans, verbal mediation and rehearsal probably are important determinants of the increase in autonomic indexes of fear. For animals, an autonomic index of fear (similar to the GSR) actually *decreases* progressively following an aversive event, in spite of the increase in the instrumental index of fear (Pinel, Malsbury, & Corcoran, 1971).

Why, then, does the increase in instrumental responding occur? There appear to be three reasons for incubation, all a good deal less mysterious and perhaps less exciting than the prospect of a spontaneous increase in fear, but also more plausible.

The first two reasons apply primarily to the incubation that has been measured after one-trial passive avoidance training. First, Miller (1961) has suggested that the stimulus context of a test given 24 hours after training is a good bit more similar to the context associated with learning than is the context immediately after training. For example, the animal still may be suffering the aftereffects of footshock immediately after training, which creates a stimulus context different from that prevailing during most of the original training; but these aftereffects would dissipate 24 hours later, making the context at testing more similar to that existing prior to original training. There are fewer cues soon after training that correspond to the events leading up to learning (and so, fewer cues consistent with the attributes of that memory), and there is, therefore, less evidence of the learning at that point. The second reason is that, at least for rats and mice, the experience of footshock often results in hyperactivity that gradually dissipates over a 24-hour interval. Thus, whether or not the shock received by a rat or mouse was contingent upon its stepping into another compartment, the animal would be more likely to step through soon after receiving the shock, and less likely later on, simply because of the activity level changes. Indeed, Geller and Jarvik (1970) present data showing precisely this effect on step-through latencies, even though the footshock was received in a distinctly different apparatus prior to retention interval. This "mock incubation" function is shown in Figure 4.6.

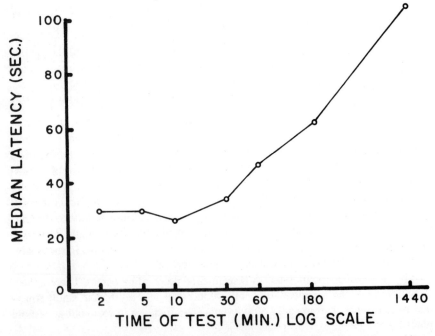

Figure 4.6   This figure illustrates the increase in the tendency toward appropriate passive avoidance performance (i.e. withholding a stepthrough response) as the interval increases between a footshock delivered outside the avoidance apparatus and the retention test. The point is that this "incubation" function occurs even though the circumstances of the retention test may have no relationship to those of the footshock, and so the function seems attributable to relatively trivial performance factors rather than the processing of memories concerning the contingencies surrounding the footshock (adapted from Geller and Jarvik, 1970).

The third explanation of incubation applies to a wider variety of circumstances, including much of the human data. The core of this explanation is that incubation is a consequence of *poorer*, not better, retention of the circumstances of the aversive episode. In particular, it is fear of the stimuli *associated* with the critical predictor stimulus (the CS) of the aversive event that increases over time, but fear of the CS itself does not increase. To say it another way, fear of generalized stimuli may increase with time, although fear of the original stimulus probably does not. This explanation has been applied successfully to human data by Saltz and Asdourian (1963) and by McAllister and McAllister (1967). Gabriel (1972) has applied a special version of this explanation to his data, producing a history sufficiently interesting to outline here.

Incubation reflects increasing generalization. In introducing the argument based on increased generalization of fear over time, Saltz and Asdourian noted that earlier experiments showing incubation in humans had employed an extraordinarily long interval between the CS and the UCS (e.g., 12 or 15 seconds). This probably permitted partial conditioning to a variety of contextual stimuli other than the nominal CS. Whether by chance or by design, a large percentage of the investigations of incubation with one-trial passive avoidance in animals have used an analogous procedure. Typically, a long delay of several seconds has occurred between the time the animal steps into the critical compartment and the delivery of shock to that animal.

The precise role of such a delay in the incubation effect is unclear. This delay was varied in an experiment by Geller, Jarvik, and Robustelli (1970). In this study, a clear incubation effect was found with a 30-second delay between the step-through response and the footshock, but a much weaker and shorter incubation function occurred with a 240-second delay. It is not clear whether delays shorter than 30 seconds also would have produced less of an incubation effect, although it seems probable. In the author's laboratory, for example, incubation is not found with this task in the absence of a delay. However, it is clear that such a long delay between the response and the aversive stimulus is not always a necessary condition of incubation. The most elaborate study of incubation in which such a delay is not used is that of Gabriel (e.g., 1972) and his colleagues.

In Gabriel's procedure, the UCS follows the onset of the CS by 4 seconds. In Gabriel's explanation of incubation, responses that occur between successive occurrences of the CS—intertrial responses—play an important role. These intertrial responses also increase with increasingly long retention intervals, accompanying the increase in responding that occurs with the CS.

Gabriel attributes the increase in intertrial responses to the progressive loss of discrimination between the CS and other aspects of the apparatus. The implication is that the increasing number of responses occurring to the CS after longer intervals (characteristic of incubation) is a result of responding to these other stimuli in addition to responding to the CS. Thus, Gabriel attributes incubation to stimulus compounding.

Gabriel and his colleagues have gathered one of the most complete and analytical sets of data concerning incubation. They have shown, for example, that exposure to the apparatus during the retention interval, which acts to extinguish generalized responding to the apparatus, reduces responding to the CS after a long retention interval. Unfortunately, they have not proceeded to show that this manipulation would have less effect after a short interval than after a long one. So, though it is suggestive, it is not clear that this factor accounts for the increasing trend in retention over time.

Gabriel (1968) has noted that if incubation is a consequence of stimulus generalization, then less incubation should occur after higher degrees of conditioning because less stimulus generalization is known to occur after higher degrees of learning. Support for this argument is somewhat tenuous, however, as shown in the data presented in Figure 4.7. For these data, separate groups of

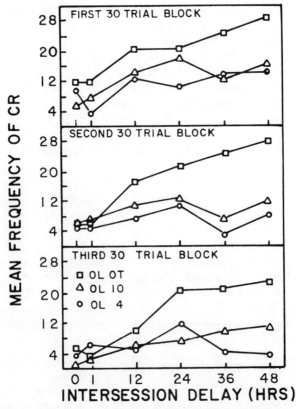

Figure 4.7 Retention of active avoidance is shown in terms of the frequency of a conditioned response after differing intervals following training. The tendency toward incubation is strongest for those animals given the highest degree of original training: Group OLOT received 150 trials of overtraining following achievement of the avoidance criterion; Group OL 10 merely had achieved that criterion and group OL4 had achieved a lower criterion of original training (adapted from Gabriel, 1968. Copyright 1968 by the American Psychological Association. Reprinted by permission.)

animals were trained by Gabriel (1968) to 4 consecutive avoidances, 10 consecutive avoidances, or 10 consecutive avoidances plus 150 trials of overtraining.
Retention was tested after either 7 minutes, 1 hour, 12 hours, 24 hours, 36 hours,
or 48 hours. The retention test was 90 extinction trials. The extinction data are
plotted in Figure 4.7 in three blocks of 30 trials each. As can be seen, incubation
tended to be stronger with higher degrees of learning, exactly opposite to Gabriel's prediction. Notably, similar results were obtained by Zammit-Montebello,
Black, Marquis, and Suboski (1969), if we make the reasonable assumption that
higher degrees of learning accompany more severe footshock in one-trial passive
avoidance.

Finally, to test this theory further, Gabriel and Vogt (1972) manipulated
changes in the stimulus context orthogonal to retention interval. Again, however,
Gabriel's interpretation in terms of stimulus generalization alone seems less than
compelling, albeit still plausible. The data from Gabriel and Vogt are replotted in
Figure 4.8. When the data are replotted in this way, it would appear that (1) some
increase in indiscriminate responding indeed does occur as Gabriel predicted; (2)
the maximum increase occurs sooner in time if no stimuli have been changed;

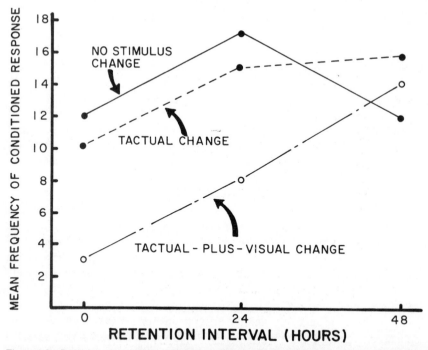

Figure 4.8   Retention of avoidance conditioning is shown as a function of the extent of the change in
contextual stimuli between training and testing. There is a tendency toward greater incubation the
greater the stimulus change. A similar functional relationship has been summarized by McAllister &
McAllister (1971) with respect to a quite different data base. This effect apparently is due to the
decrement that accompanies contextual change following a short retention interval rather than to an
increase in retention following a long retention interval. (adapted from Gabriel and Vogt, 1972).

and (3) stimulus control by the CS is disrupted by contextual change on the immediate test but recovers over longer retention intervals.

The basic incubation effect may result from impairment of memory retrieval in the immediate test where stimulus conditions differ from those of training (especially during extinction), in spite of the experimenter's efforts to maintain the same nominal stimuli. The consequences of a series of conditioning trials leave the subject in a quite different state for a short-term test than when conditioning began. Further, this different state, or impairment, should be greater after more trials (though it is countered by the extra strength of conditioning). Thus, we would expect more incubation after overtraining, as Gabriel's results indicate.

In addition, there is some indication from Frey and Gavin's (1975) work with Pavlovian aversive conditioning in rabbits that, for at least a short period (20 minutes) after training, the rabbits may be deficient in *any* aversive conditioning task. By further deflating immediate retention performance, this general effect would add to the decrement caused by the change in contextual stimuli (from those of training), resulting in still poorer performance immediately after training relative to that found after a longer retention interval.

The Kamin Effect

The Kamin effect is the special case of a nonmonotonic function that has received more attention than any other. This effect is defined by unusually poor retention found an hour or so after learning, in contrast to relatively good retention soon after learning or 24 hours later. Of course, retention declines again after several days or weeks have passed, but this is to be expected.

What was not expected is the exaggerated forgetting that occurs after intervals of intermediate length, usually between 1 and 6 hours after training. Kamin (1957) was the first to establish and emphasize the nonmonotonic nature of this retention function. His original experiment involved avoidance conditioning, as have most subsequent analyses. Because the effect does not occur readily following simple appetitive conditioning, it probably is restricted to learning situations that are particularly stressful, if not limited entirely to aversive conditioning.

The importance of the Kamin effect may be traced to three factors. First, the effect reliably occurs in a variety of circumstances and cannot readily be attributed to simple artifacts, such as activity changes directly induced by the aversive reinforcer. Second, the point in time of exaggerated forgetting has been linked to physiological processes of major importance. Third, certain aspects of the Kamin effect—the environmental and task variables that affect it, the behavioral measures most likely to reveal it, and the implications for understanding avoidance responding in general under conditions of emotional turbulence—have attracted the attention of theorists concerned with motivation, learning, and memory processing. We shall examine each of these factors in turn.

Establishing the Kamin effect. The Kamin effect has been measured in rodents with a wide variety of learning tasks and procedures. The literature in this area, up to about 1970, has been summmarized and analyzed exhaustively by Brush (1971). The reader is referred to Brush's chapter for details.

The Kamin effect has been studied in terms of two-way shuttle avoidance, one-way active avoidance, signaled escape training, Pavlovian fear conditioning, and discriminated escape. This effect also has occurred in certain kinds of passive avoidance tasks, although as indicated earlier (pages 161–163), the precise shape of the retention function following one-trial passive conditioning is not clear, and because one-trial passive avoidance results are subject to a variety of artifacts, they are somewhat difficult to interpret. For example, Brush (1971) has concluded that fear conditioning is a necessary and sufficient condition for the Kamin effect; with one-trial passive avoidance, it is not always clear whether fear in fact is conditioned, nor to what aspect of the training circumstances fear might be conditioned.

What is important, however, is that the Kamin effect has been well established following passive avoidance training, especially with multiple trials. This eliminates the possibility that the poorer retention after intermediate-length retention intervals may be attributed simply and directly to a decrement in general activity at that point. Poorer retention in active avoidance easily can be confused with decreased activity levels. But poorer passive avoidance retention would be indicated by *increased* responding, and this is obviously not a result of decreased general activity. The Kamin effect following passive avoidance learning has been studied in a number of experiments and so far has been found to have the same characteristics as the Kamin effect following active avoidance learning (Klein & Spear, 1970a, b; Klein, 1972; Singh, Sakellaris, & Brush, 1971; Spear, Klein, & Riley, 1971).

This is not to say that changes in general activity or reactivity following aversive conditioning may not contribute some variance to the retention function. It is quite possible that *stimulus* consequences of activity or reactivity decrements may play some indirect role in the Kamin effect, especially activity decrements that may occur after intervals of intermediate length. We shall return to this point presently.

Physiological processes associated with the Kamin effect.   We have known for some time that certain physiological consequences of a stress source, such as aversive conditioning, continue in a regular temporal course after the source of the stress has terminated. This temporal course reflects the animal's homeostatic struggle to readjust following stress, and it bears at least a superficial similarity to the temporal course of retention following stress. The latter, of course, is represented by the Kamin effect.

Aspects of an animal's adaptation to stress (such as the temporal course of this adaptation) were analyzed in 1946 in an influential paper by Hans Selye. One of the unique features of Selye's idea was that the physiological changes that occur are not specific to the particular source of the stress. Instead, these physiological effects will follow regularly from any of a variety of "stress" sources that may inflict pain, tissue damage, or, it now appears, conditioned fear. Following an initial alarm reaction to stress by its sympathetic nervous system, the animal shows a "general adaptation syndrome." This serves to counter the initial depletion of certain physiological stores that occurs immediately following stress, and to prepare the animal for its renewal of normal biological processes. For example, markedly enhanced activity of the adrenal–pituitary system is one of the initial responses to stress. This includes the almost immediate release of ACTH from the adenohypophysis that, in turn, increases the production and release of various corticoids from the adrenal cortex. Catecholamines are released from the adrenal medulla, leading to consequential drastic shifts in cardiovascular and renal functions, and carbohydrate metabolism is dramatically altered.

The particularly important observation by Selye that is related to the Kamin effect is the occurrence of a refractory period following the response to stress during which the system is relatively unable to respond to further stress. This period begins about an hour after initial stress and persists for a few hours thereafter. Selye suggested two reasons for this refractory period. First, the organism is then deficient of certain substances such as ACTH and glucose, through which it ordinarily would respond to immediate stress. Second, there seemed to be an excess of other substances, specifically histamine adenosin derivatives, acetylcholine, and salt-active corticoids. It was presumed necessary for homeostasis to be reestablished in the organism before it could respond (internally) in a "normal" fashion to new stress.

Knowledge of physiology (especially endocrinology) relevant to the Kamin effect has become much more sophisticated in the years since Selye published his review. Even so, Selye's suggestion for the general pattern of an organism's internal response to stress is still recognized as characteristic of the physiological consequences of stress. So far, analyses of the Kamin effect have focused on two particular physiological systems that persist in activity when the activity is initiated by stress. One is the adrenal-pituitary system, and the other is "parasympathetic rebound," which has been linked to both peripheral and central catecholamines and also to central cholinergic activity.

The first, based on changes in adrenal–pituitary activity, has emphasized the importance of the decrement in ACTH release that occurs within approximately an hour after stress. Because ACTH has been shown to have direct effects on avoidance learning and its extinction, and these effects are apparently independent of the corticotropic influence of ACTH on the adrenals, ACTH is a natural focus of attention for psychologists concerned with retention of avoidance conditioning. Reviews of the influence of this hormone on avoidance learning may be found in papers by DeWied (e.g., 1974), Levine (1968), and DiGiusto, Cairncross, and King (1971; see also Brush, 1971).

"Parasympathetic rebound" refers to the possibility that the homeostatic response to severe sympathetic activity may result in an exaggerated parasympathetic reaction centrally that may be manifested as general response suppression (for a review, see Anisman, 1975). This is applicable to the Kamin effect primarily for cases in which decreased general activity is observed. As we soon shall see, however, there is a more plausible way in which this mechanism may apply indirectly to an explanation of the Kamin effect.

Characteristics of the Kamin Effect

There are four especially significant characteristics of the Kamin effect that may lead to its explanation. We will consider each in turn.

Content of the memory.   The Kamin effect probably is restricted to retention of learning that is singularly stressful, perhaps only to learning involving fear conditioning. Brush, Myer, and Palmer (1963) have shown that not only is fear conditioning a sufficient condition for the Kamin effect, but it may be necessary. Brush and his associates found that unsignaled escape learning (in which no stimulus specifically predicts the occurrence of an aversive stimulus) did not result in a Kamin effect.

No published studies have convincingly established a Kamin effect with appetitive conditioning. It is claimed that such an effect was found in retention of a visual discrimination by rats trained with food as the reinforcer (Tribhowan, Rucker, & McDiarmid, 1971). Unfortunately, this experiment appears to have been analyzed incorrectly. These investigators used a covariance analysis that assumed that reversal learning would be related directly to rate of original learning (i.e., positive transfer), but their conclusion was based on the assumption of *negative* transfer between original learning and reversal. Moreover, although covariance is acceptable under some circumstances, its use was inappropriate in this study because the condition defining the Kamin effect (animals given a 4-hour retention interval) included the most deviant acquisition scores and yet the covariance analysis was directed primarily toward this critical condition. While one may still argue that these results are suggestive, it would seem risky to conclude on the basis of this single, somewhat questionable experiment that the Kamin effect occurs in appetitive conditioning. Moreover, in several of our own experiments we have failed to obtain a Kamin effect following simple appetitive conditioning in the straight runway. (See Spear, 1971, pp. 50–52, regarding control groups used as a baseline for evaluating the interactions between memories of differing magnitudes of the reinforcer.)

Point of poorest retention.   Although the point of minimum retention within a 24-hour period fluctuates from study to study, this fluctuation is lawful. Brush (1971) has established an empirical generalization that states that the interval of minimal retention is inversely related to the original degree of fear conditioning. In other words, the higher the degree of original fear conditioning, the earlier the point of minimal retention occurs.

Brush conceptualizes avoidance learning as occurring in two stages. The first is Pavlovian conditioning of fear to the stimulus (the CS) that predicts the aversive event. The second is instrumental learning, which enables the animal to escape the CS and thus avoid the primary aversive stimulus. Brush concludes that it is the degree of the Pavlovian conditioning that is the primary determinant of the shape of the Kamin function, and he marshalls impressive support for this conclusion (Brush, 1971, pp. 438–443).

Measurement. The Kamin effect seems to appear most robustly when the measure of retention is the number of trials required to attain some relatively rigorous criterion of performance. In contrast, when only the first one or two trials from the retention test are scored, monotonically decreasing retention is found instead of the Kamin effect.

Kamin (1963) noted this relationship and suggested that warm-up factors dominate during the early trials of a retention test. This appeal to warm-up provides a heuristic aid, although little in the way of explanation. We suggest later and elsewhere (Spear, 1971, 1973) one possible reason why multitrial measurement of the Kamin effect may be so critical. But note that there are some circumstances under which a Kamin effect does show in performance on the first retention trial (e.g., Singh et al., 1971). Still, among over 20 experiments that my colleagues and I have published as positive instances of the Kamin effect in terms of trials to criterion, none of these showed a Kamin effect on the first retention trial (e.g., Bryan & Spear, 1976; Klein, 1972; Klein & Spear, 1970a, b).

Eliminating the Kamin effect through reactivation treatments. A variety of reactivation treatments preceding the retention test may alleviate the Kamin effect. These include confinement in the learning apparatus for a period of time (e.g., Bintz, 1972), injections of ACTH either intraperitoneally or centrally (Klein, 1972; Levine & Brush, 1967; Singh et al., 1971), electrical stimulation of the hypothalamus in a location that yields release of ACTH (Klein, 1972), and pretest stress in the form of either unavoidable, inescapable footshocks or forced swimming (Klein, 1972; Klein & Spear, 1970b). The possible significance of this characteristic and the others are discussed later.

Explanations of the Kamin Effect

The first explanations of the Kamin effect assumed that the strength of conditioned fear increased in some regular temporal course following training. Some investigators suggested that the fear becomes maximal after intervals of intermediate length and that this has the effect of making the animal immobile ("freezing") and less able to perform the instrumental response; others suggested instead that fear is weak and relatively ineffective in motivating behavior after intermediate intervals compared with 24 hours later.

Later, Brush, Myer, and Palmer (1963) emphasized the internal imbalance between the sympathetic and parasympathetic systems, which is maximal after intervals of intermediate length. They suggest that this imbalance has the effect of hindering the animal's capacity to cope with avoidance conditioning.

Grossman (1967) suggests that transfer between the short-term and long-term storage systems during memory processing may occur at intermediate intervals following training and that during this transfer manifestation of a memory may be hindered. More recent explanations have become increasingly specific and fall into two categories—motivational and memorial.

Motivational explanations.   There are two levels of explanation within the theme of motivation. The simplest possibility is that after an intermediate interval following training, the animal is generally debilitated, slow to move, or inactive on a broad scale. Such an explanation obviously is inadequate to account for the facts. As noted earlier, the application of certain experimental paradigms is not due simply to uncontrolled differences in general activity level. While animals may be somewhat less active at this point than at shorter or longer intervals after training, this activity difference in itself is not sufficient to account for the Kamin effect. We noted earlier, for instance, that the Kamin effect has been found to occur both with passive and active avoidance training and an explanation in terms of inactivity cannot account for both of these at once.

A more plausible explanation also emphasizes motivational deficits after an intermediate interval but in a more complex sense. The animals are viewed as either less emotional about the danger or less able to cope with the requirements of the task. These deficits are a result of imbalanced neurochemistry of the organism that provides the sources of activity, for example, mobilizing glucose reserves, an increasing general arousal needed for the emergency. Such an imbalance might result from the sort of parasympathetic overreaction suggested by Brush, Myer, and Palmer (1963) and others (e.g., Anisman, 1975; Barrett, Leith, & Ray, 1971), or from any number of systems implied originally by Selye (1946).

A memorial explanation.   The exaggerated forgetting after intermediate intervals has been attributed by some investigators to failure in memory retrieval (e.g., Klein & Spear, 1970a; Spear, 1971, 1973). The basic idea is that certain of the cues present after an intermediate interval are assumed to deviate unusually from the cues present during learning, more so than the cues present shortly after learning or 24 hours later. Internal cues are suspected to be the primary source of the deviation. Deviation in these cues may be attributed to any of the several sources of neurochemical imbalance mentioned previously, or to the behavioral consequences of such imbalance, such as proprioceptive stimuli ensuing from a generally decreased activity level.

Deviation between internal cues present during learning and during the intermediate retention test is believed to be especially important in terms of the animal's altered response to new stress. When sources of pain or conditioned fear are encountered an hour or so after aversive conditioning, the animal's internal neurochemical response is, for a limited period, quite different from both the neurochemical response elicited by the original conditioning and that found a few minutes after conditioning (or 24 hours later, when the animal is largely recovered). This particular suggestion is consistent with two characteristics of the Kamin effect listed earlier. These are, first, that the Kamin effect usually is not apparent until after the first one or two relearning (shocked) trials, and second, that treatments that partially correct the neurochemical imbalance prior to the intermediate interval test act to decrease the retention loss at that time.

This memory retrieval explanation, consistent also with other characteristics of the Kamin effect, was developed in essentially three steps.

First, it was established that rats were not necessarily less proficient in coping with the general requirements of an aversive conditioning task after an intermediate retention interval relative to coping after shorter or longer intervals. Aversive conditioning after an interval of intermediate length was found sometimes to proceed more slowly but at other times to proceed more rapidly than after shorter or longer intervals, depending on the extent to which retrieval of the memory of original learning interfered with responding in the aversive conditioning task used for testing. The previously uniform findings of poorer retention after intermediate intervals were due to the use of a relearning (*positive* transfer) test in the same task to assess retention. It was established further that the activity requirements of the task were irrelevant to the occurrence of the Kamin effect. The same relationship holds whether the avoidance task requires the animal to emit a particular response quickly (active avoidance) or to refrain from a particular response (passive avoidance) in order to complete a successful avoidance. These points were established by the appropriate selection of parameters for two nominally conflicting tasks, active avoidance and passive avoidance, to ensure negative transfer from the learning of one task to the learning of the other. Under these circumstances, the negative transfer observed a few minutes after learning the first task, and 24 hours later, is not found after an intermediate-length interval, regardless of whether the first task has been active avoidance and the second passive avoidance or vice versa. In fact, as can be seen in Figure 4.9, after intermediate intervals animals performed no differently than naive animals. It was as if the memory of original learning had no influence on their behavior after an intermediate interval (Klein, 1972; Klein & Spear, 1970a, b; Spear, 1971). A further set of several experiments by Bryan and Spear (1976) has confirmed the basic findings of these negative-transfer tests in terms of retention of discrimination learning. These experiments further preclude an explanation of the Kamin effect in terms of the direct consequences of an activity or reactivity decrement after intermediate intervals, because the response measure (choice behavior) is known to be unaffected by such decrements.

The second step was to pursue further an implication of this memory retrieval explanation. The explanation states, in effect, that after an intermediate interval animals tend not to retrieve the memory because their internal state (especially their physiological response to new stress) differs from that of original learning. Animals at the more extreme intervals, whose internal state more closely approx-

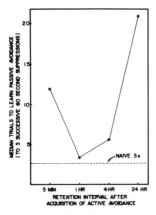 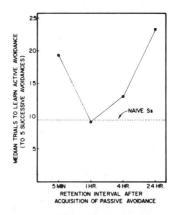

Figure 4.9 The Kamin effect is illustrated in terms of two experiments that employed as a retention task that yielded negative transfer from original learning. In the left figure, animals were tested on a conflicting passive avoidance task at different intervals after learning of active avoidance, and for the right figure, animals were tested on an active avoidance task at different intervals after learning of passive avoidance. In each case, parameters were arranged to ensure negative transfer on an immediate test. These figures illustrate that poor avoidance performance at intermediate intervals following training is not inevitable; in these cases, avoidance performance appropriate to the test actually is better after intervals of intermediate length than after shorter or longer intervals. These figures also illustrate that the same functions occur regardless of the level of general activity required of the animal; in the left figure good performance is associated with low levels of activity, and in the right figure good performance is associated with high levels of activity. (adapted from Klein and Spear, 1970a. Copyright 1970 by the American Psychological Association. Reprinted by permission.)

imated that of original learning, are more likely to retrieve the memory. In other words, this is a case of state-dependent retention in which the animal's "normal" state during original learning differs from the corresponding state that occurs after an interval of intermediate length. If this is an accurate assessment, it should be possible to show a deficit in memory retrieval when an animal later is tested in a "normal" state, if the animal had learned the task originally under an "intermediate-interval state." The latter could be induced by stressing the animal under training-like circumstances an hour or so before learning. Precisely these results were obtained (Spear, Klein, & Riley, 1971). Together with the previous studies, these results form a symmetrical case of state-dependent retention.

The third step was to identify more precisely the internal cues that are so modified after an intermediate-length retention interval that memory retrieval is impaired. The experimental strategy was to modify the animal's internal state just prior to the retention test so that its state after an intermediate-length interval would approximate more closely the internal state associated with original learning. This should alleviate the deficit in memory retrieval if this explanation is correct. The physiological events influenced by such pretest treatment then could

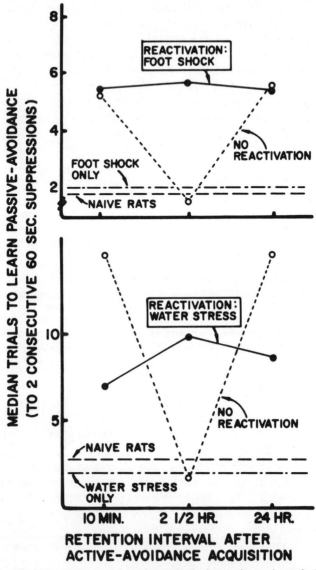

Figure 4.10 Alleviation of the poor forgetting typically found after an interval of intermediate length (i.e., Kamin Effect) is illustrated with two reactivation treatments. In the upper figure the reactivation treatment consisted of five footshocks presented in a neutral chamber 5 min. before testing, and in the lower figure the reactivation treatment was 2 min. of forced swimming in room temperature water presented 5 min. before testing. A negative transfer passive-avoidance test assessed the retention of active avoidance learning (see Figure 4.9). (Adapted from Spear, 1973).

be assumed to represent the specific retrieval cues that are altered more after an intermediate interval than after shorter or longer intervals.

The initial hypothesis was that the critical cues would be some aspect of Selye's general-adaptation syndrome. More specifically, adrenal–pituitary activity was suspected first. Indeed, it was found initially that the critical aspect of the pretest (reactivation) treatment was that it be some source of general stress. The Kamin effect was eliminated not only by pretest presentation of footshocks like those given during original learning but also by forcing the animal to swim in a bucket of water for 2 minutes prior to testing. These results are shown in Figure 4.10.

Next, Klein (1972) began to test the more specific hypothesis that the critical agent of retrieval was ACTH activation. As a reactivation treatment, Klein stimulated the hypothalamus in the region of the median eminence in such a way as to induce release of ACTH; by improving retention after an intermediate retention interval, this, too, eliminated the Kamin effect. Also, Klein determined that the Kamin effect could be eliminated in an analogous fashion by implanting crystals of ACTH directly into this region of the hypothalamus. In contrast, stimulation of another area of the brain that does not activate release of ACTH (the ventral hippocampus) did not influence the Kamin effect. The results of these experiments are shown in Figure 4.11.

Further comments on the Kamin effect.   Probably it is premature to assert that the Kamin effect is entirely a consequence of the type of memory retrieval

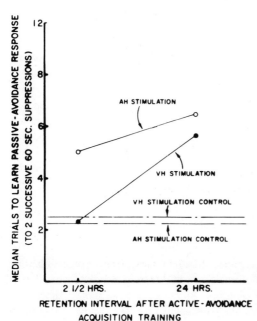

Figure 4.11 Alleviation of forgetting typically found 2 1/2 hrs. after avoidance training is shown for animals given electrical stimulation in the anterior hypothalamus just prior to the retention test. Stimulation in this area of the hypothalamus results in the release of ACTH from the pituitary, whereas stimulation in the ventral hypocampus (VH) does not. Because forgetting was alleviated with the former stimulation and not the latter, pituitary-adrenal activity is implicated as a possible factor in the forgetting that typically occurs 2 1/2 hours after avoidance training. The stimulation-control animals received only the brain stimulation prior to testing but no original training (adapted from Klein, 1972. Copyright 1972 by the American Psychological Association. Reprinted by permission.)

deficit outlined here. We can be certain that the Kamin effect is something more than a curious anomaly in animal memory. Rather, it provides a vehicle for analyzing animal memory processes that may have considerable generality (see Spear, 1973). Moreover, through the work of Brush and Levine and of Klein, this phenomenon has been useful in showing another instance of the importance of the hormone ACTH for animal learning and memory.

It is notable, however, that while adrenal–pituitary activity may be a sufficient determinant of the Kamin effect, it is not necessary. Several studies have indicated that the Kamin effect may occur in either hypophysectomized or adrenalectomized rats. Apparently, any of a variety of parallel systems, such as parasympathetic rebound, may provide the physiological changes following stress that mediate failure in memory retrieval after intervals of intermediate length.

DETERMINANTS OF FORGETTING OVER LONG INTERVALS

As with the parallel issue in animals, of primary interest here are the determinants of how much and how rapidly forgetting occurs in humans, and why. We shall address these issues later. For now, a few general statements will suffice concerning simple forgetting of verbal events.

It will be no surprise to learn that simple retention by humans apparently is a monotonically decreasing function of the length of the retention interval. Other functions, such as the nonmonotonic functions found in retention by animals and the reminiscence effects found with humans, as discussed earlier, simply have not appeared with sufficient reliability to become theoretical issues. This may be due to the verbal content of memories tested in humans; reminiscence over an interval of 5 minutes may be found in retention of pictures but not words (Shapiro & Erdelyi, 1974). Perhaps, also, the absence from the literature of such multiphasic retention functions in human verbal retention is simply due to the fact that they have not been tested yet. Because humans are not the captive population that animals are, the retention intervals tested in humans have been restricted, for convenience, to either less than an hour or multiples of 24 hours.

Forgetting is caused by interference. There is no doubt about this, but the major task is to determine under what circumstances, and through what mechanisms, this occurs. Later we shall consider instances in which retention by humans *may* be found to depend on certain other factors: the nature of the task [e.g., free recall often yields more forgetting than paired-associate or recognition tasks (in which more of the verbal context of learning is presented at the test)]; the content of the events being represented in memory (e.g., forgetting may differ for words and pictures or for verbal units of differing meaningfulness); and the subject's behavior during memory storage, which might determine "mnemonic preparation" for retrieval. But aside from the direct and indirect contributions of interference (and degree of learning) to forgetting, the striking aspect of human forgetting of verbal materials is its invariance. Underwood (1964, 1966a,1972) has presented this point most effectively. Subjects who have learned a single set of paired verbal items in the laboratory context consistently forget about 20% after one day and about 50% after one week, and even factors such as individual differences in learning rate make surprisingly little difference.

The real issues, then, center on aspects of the dependency between forgetting and interference: the acquisition of competing memories, the circumstances of that acquisition relative to the acquisition of the critical memory, and the interaction between the critical and competing memories up to and including the point at which retrieval of the critical memory is required. These issues are most effectively considered within the context of "sources of forgetting" generally.

Before examining some specific sources of forgetting, we should first consider the question in its most general sense: Assuming that dominant features of behavior have evolved because of their adaptive value, why does forgetting occur? Sometimes a well-learned set of events, representations, or responses seems readily available "on demand." At other times, perhaps even with the same memories, the learning seems to have been in vain; the memory cannot be retrieved and cannot be applied to contemporary behavior. Forgetting of crucial information at crucial times frequently costs its victims fortunes and even lives. One wonders how God and Darwin could have been so thoughtless as to permit this exasperating characteristic to have developed throughout the evolution of animals (and perhaps plants as well), to reach its apex with humans.

On the other hand, forgetting is more a blessing than a curse. We would be in a sorry state indeed if our awareness were bombarded by all the telephone numbers we had ever learned each time we used the telephone, or by the name of every person we had ever met each time we approached a friend on the street.

The joy of forgetting is well illustrated by the individual who has experienced some traumatic event in childhood or more recently, but over time is able to forget it. We are delighted to be done with such memories. Perhaps the best illustration of our good fortune in having normally imperfect retention can be found in the difficulties in adjustment encountered by the mnemonist described by Luria (1968). This unfortunate man had great difficulty forgetting and found it necessary to devise mechanisms to do so in order to keep his mind relatively uncluttered.

We need not elaborate further on the existence or value of the phenomenon of forgetting, because both are widely appreciated. What is at issue here is how we may account for it. We reviewed some prescientific suggestions in Chapter 1. If we are not nearer the truth now, we do seem closer to a working understanding of what causes forgetting. At least we are able to manipulate forgetting and to predict roughly when it will occur and how much to expect. We turn next to a consideration of the theoretical concepts that have been used to analyze scientifically the sources of forgetting.

Decay

Decay is perhaps the most poorly defined "source" of forgetting that we will consider. One could say quite fairly that decay is a useless construct. If this statement seems too strong, it is warranted at least in relation to the frequency with which decay has been used inappropriately for "explaining" forgetting.

Historically, "decay" has had two uses. One is simply descriptive of the decline in learned performance as time passes since learning; certainly this is appropriate. But there is danger in the tendency to slip into using decay in an explanatory sense when forgetting cannot be understood otherwise. McGeoch's (1932) eloquent exposition of the value of interference principles for explaining forgetting reduced the use of decay for explanatory purposes. Decay, McGeoch noted, can be useful scientifically only to the extent that it refers to identifiable events that occur during the retention interval, because time alone explains nothing.

We now may be approaching a period in which, with the accurate identification of previously unobservable or undetected physiological events, a concept like decay again might be useful. If, for example, the biological substrate of a memory (which is still unidentified, of course) is shown to be subject to progressive disintegration through some metabolic process, then decay might be used in an explanatory sense. Perhaps it is this sort of reasoning that has prompted a recurrence of the use of decay for theoretical purposes (e.g., Cherkin, 1969; Gleitman, 1971; Wickelgren, 1972, 1975a,b).

However, we still must be cautious. Obviously, even observed deterioration of a physiological substrate of a memory would not automatically mean that memorial behavior is affected correspondingly. For example, perhaps memories are represented with such redundancy physiologically that degradation of the physiological substrate of a memory might influence the overt memorial behavior only when the degradation is so pronounced and widespread that the organism is dead. Furthermore, physiological modification of such a substrate does not automatically imply forgetting, as Dawkins (1971) has suggested and as the results of Rosenzweig, Mollgaard, Diamond, and Bennett (1972) have implied. Empirically, the death or modification of structures in a memory substrate may imply new learning, not new forgetting. As Dawkins points out, a computer need not be constructed by selectively forming only the connections that are needed among its various components for the intricate circuits; it also could be constructed by first making all possible connections and then selectively removing the undesired ones.

Interference

Few will deny that something like interference contributes to forgetting. But here, too, we must be cautious, because interference has been conceptualized broadly in at least two ways. The traditional and more widely applied conception of interference in retention includes a set of specific identifiable mechanisms.

Through these mechanisms, similar but incompatible behavioral tendencies develop prior to or subsequent to learning and act to reduce later retention. A second conception of interference is as nonspecific noise in the organism's information-processing system. In this view (e.g., Weiskrantz, 1966), interference has a neurophysiological source, is a basic biological characteristic of animals and humans, and may be increased or decreased by intense physiological trauma, especially abnormal trauma.

The latter view of interference is rather like the view taken of decay in its biological inevitability, although interference is believed more often to act on memory retrieval rather than memory storage. Also like decay, this conception of interference is rather intractable scientifically because it has not been tied to observable events or manipulations, biological or environmental. As such, this "interference" tends to be tautological in that it can neither be proved nor disproved, and like decay, it is susceptible to casual use as a makeshift explanation. On the other hand, Weiskrantz (1966) has used this conception to advantage, and perhaps in the future this kind of interference will be measurable directly or conceptualized more concretely in other respects; but for now it is a relatively useless concept, or at least less useful than the more traditional former view of "interference," to which we now turn.

Interference Theory

The development of interference theory (e.g., McGeoch, 1942; Postman & Underwood, 1973; Underwood & Postman, 1960) has taken an approach toward the understanding of human memory processing that sets it apart from most other theories in this area. The value lies in its specification of empirically observable mechanisms that collectively make up the interfering action in retention. The historical development of this theory and description of these mechanisms have been reviewed thoroughly elsewhere (e.g., Postman, 1971; Postman & Underwood, 1973), but it is useful nevertheless to describe briefly the basic parameter and principal mechanisms currently applied.

Similarity: the fundamental parameter. In a general sense, it is similarity between the material to be retained and the interfering material that determines retention. Complexity arises when we attempt to determine the critical dimensions of similarity. Clearly, learning to punt a football properly is unlikely to interfere with retention of the words to "The Star-Spangled Banner," but what about the interference of punting on remembering how to kick field goals, or the interference of learning a new song on remembering another song? And if one remembers a long list of words like *pear, lion,* and *match,* will the subsequent learning of a list like *perch, line,* and *mask* be more likely to cause forgetting than a list like *apple, tiger,* and *lighter*? That is, is acoustical similarity more important than semantic similarity? If a rat must remember to turn left to obtain a reinforcer in one maze, will more interference be caused by learning to turn right in another maze that smells the same, one that looks the same, or one that feels the same? That is, is olfactory, visual, or tactual similarity the more important determinant of interference?

Obviously, the dimensions of similarity are numerous and the critical "similarity" may rest as much in the context of the learning as in the content. Nevertheless, within interference theory one may say generally that if the content of two memories is not at all similar, there is no reason to expect that the learning of one will influence the retention of the other.

Basic mechanisms of interference.   Two sets of mechanisms are employed by interference theory. The first is to account for the fact that organisms get mixed up regarding which memory an environmental event belongs to. The second concerns the organism's failure to respond at all in terms of some attributes of a memory after an intervening memory has been acquired. This mechanism must be capable of accounting for either of two sources of interference—proactive and retroactive. The source of proactive interference rests among memories acquired prior to the critical, to-be-tested memory, and that of retroactive interference includes memories acquired between acquisition of the critical memory and the test for retention.

The first set of mechanisms include *response competition* and *list differentiation. Response competition* (or "reproductive inhibition," as it was sometimes conceptualized) was the primary factor proposed by McGeoch in the 1930s to account for both negative transfer and retroactive interference. His ideas were based specifically on cases in which two lists of verbal paired associates were learned and the responses in the two lists differed but the stimuli were the same. In such a setting, the operation of response competition is obvious. If only one response may be given to a stimulus but two are available, and the incorrect response happens to be the more dominant (for whatever reason), then we can expect negative transfer and retroactive interference in retention. Theoretically, the advantage of this concept is that it can actually be *observed* when the incorrect response, rather than the correct response, is emitted by the subject. Unfortunately, when errors are made, subjects most often give no response at all, and intrusions indicating response competition are rare. This circumstance ultimately led to the introduction of a second set of mechanisms, which will be discussed shortly.

First, let us review the other "confusion factor," list differentiation, which was studied by Underwood (1945). In this classic study, subjects learned several paired-associate lists having the same stimuli but different responses. The idea was that when the learning of one list interferes with retention of another, one source of the deficit may be the subject's inability to identify which list a particular item appeared in. It was believed that under these circumstances subjects were most likely to give overt intrusion errors. The concept of list differentiation supplies the needed explanatory power to account for certain phenomena of proactive interference and has the advantage of being directly testable (e.g., Winograd, 1968) so that its characteristics may be assessed directly. List differentiation clearly influences the occurrence of intrusions, and probably forgetting as well, through its action on specific response competition. We shall see that it may also determine the impact of another, more recently devised factor, "generalized competition" or "response set interference."

A second set of interference mechanisms became apparent through a study by Melton and Irwin (1940). They found that increments in the degree of interfering learning increased the amount of retroactive interference in retention a good deal more consistently than it increased the number of intrusion errors. It was obvious that some factor other than response competition was responsible, because response competition was related conceptually to overt intrusions. Further, list differentiation could not account for the entire effect (Thune & Underwood, 1943). This mysterious "factor X," with which Melton and Irwin explained their data, soon became known as *unlearning*.

Unlearning has been shown to be a factor in retroactive interference when, following acquisition of the second, interfering list, retention of the first list is assessed in the absence of response competition or list differentiation. These conditions can be approximated by permitting subjects to give the responses to *both* lists and by giving them a long period in which to respond. Under these circumstances, subjects are quite unable to remember about half of the responses of the first list even though they had learned to recite the entire list perfectly just minutes before. (For a review of studies concerning unlearning, see Kausler, 1974; Keppel, 1968; Postman, 1971; Postman & Underwood, 1973; Spear, 1970.)

While unlearning presumably operates at the level of an individual item within a list of words, a similar mechanism, *generalized competition,* operates on the entire list of responses as a whole. When tested on a list that they have just studied, humans have a strong tendency to restrict their overt responses to items that actually appeared in the list. It is as if subjects learn very rapidly to recognize items not on the list and to reject them at recall in favor of items that were on the list. This tendency has been attributed to a hypothetical "selector mechanism" and has been applied to interference theory under the heading "response set interference" (see Postman, Stark, & Fraser, 1968; Underwood & Shulz, 1960). In a retroactive interference situation, this momentary tendency for subjects to restrict their responses to the most recent list learned obviously will be manifested as increased interference in retention of the first list.

Shortly we shall return to the characteristics of these mechanisms of interference and consider alternative interpretations of how interference causes forgetting. First we must consider how generally in the processing of verbal memory we might apply the principle of interference.

Generality of interference theory.   It should be obvious that interference theory developed within the context of human verbal learning and has been restricted largely to the learning of lists of verbal units. How generally might interference theory be applied to account for forgetting? This question is beyond the scope of our present concern, and in any case the appropriate tests simply have not been generated. However, interference concepts have been applied in the analysis of some other cases of forgetting, including the area of animal memory.

While interference concepts have been applied with some success to forgetting of motor learning by humans that would seem to involve little linguistic mediation (Bilodeau, 1966), extrapolation of these concepts to memory processing by animals is more complex. This complexity can be attributed to three general sources. The first concerns the obvious fact that humans can be instructed what to remember while animals cannot. When organisms have learned on successive occasions to give different responses to the same stimuli, it is one thing to test interference effects when subjects are instructed to give responses from the last set learned; it is quite a different matter to test subjects without any instructions at all aboat what it is they are to remember. Yet the latter is the necessary case with lower animals. Thus, with animals we may expect that, in addition to depending on the interference mechanisms proposed by interference theory, retention also depends on both the animals' general disposition to do the last thing learned and the contextual similarity between the learning of either conflicting task and the retention test.

A second complication in the application of interference theory to memory processing by animals is equally obvious: The content of experimentally induced memories differs in animals and humans. For example, we have mentioned that the theoretical mechanisms of interference theory were evolved primarily to account for interference in memories consisting of lists of verbal items. Most tasks used for testing animals, however, have involved a single, discrete response signaled by a single stimulus. Because constructs like the selector mechanism and response set interference deal exclusively with an ensemble of responses, and because interference theory has perhaps its greatest difficulty accounting for the fate of a single response within a list (see Postman & Underwood, 1973), it should not be surprising that there is difficulty in applying interference theory concepts to memory processing by animals.

Nevertheless, there can be no doubt that the acquisition of conflicting memories may enhance forgetting in animals. Reviews of most relevant experiments and issues in this area may be found elsewhere and need not be elaborated here (see Gleitman, 1971; Medin & Davis, 1974; Spear, 1967, 1971, 1973; Winograd, 1971).

Generally, we know what to expect from an animal immediately after it has acquired two or more conflicting memories: Unless the context of testing is altered drastically, the last memory acquired will be manifested. This means, of course, that retroactive interference (RI) is very strong at first, although it becomes progressively weaker as the retention interval lengthens. A problem arises with proactive interference (PI): As the retention interval increases, is forgetting of the most recently acquired memory made increasingly greater by interference from previously acquired conflicting memories? Discrimination learning, involving a choice of responses by the animal, has been used frequently to test this possibility, with prior learning of the reverse discrimination as the source of the PI. This instance of the PI effect seems to depend on the complexity of the memory that is acquired, although it is not yet clear what the dimensions of complexity are. Nevertheless, with the simple position discrimination, as when an animal learns to make the same turn to the same location for reward while the alternative turn and location are not rewarded, PI is rarely seen. PI occurs more frequently when the animal must learn to respond to the same, specific stimulus (e.g., the brighter of two stimuli) for a reward, even though this sometimes requires one response and sometimes another (Burr & Thomas, 1972; Gleitman, 1971; Spear, 1971). Finally, unpublished data gathered in our laboratory by my colleague, Norman Richter, indicates that with a still more complex task, such as the Lashley Maze III, this effect of PI on retention is perhaps more robust than in either of the preceding cases. To solve the Lashley Maze III, the animal must learn to make different responses at each of several choice points in order to receive a reward. If rats previously have learned the opposite set of responses, we found that forgetting of the more recently acquired set after a 4-week interval is enhanced significantly.

There is, however, a case of simple responding by animals that appears to be subject to PI. This case also might be described as an increase in mutual interference between conflicting memories as the interval following either response increases. Such is the case when "go" (active avoidance) and "no-go" (passive avoidance) responses are acquired under the same circumstances. If, for example, a rat first is trained not to enter a black compartment, then is trained to enter it rapidly, subsequent forgetting of the latter response is enhanced markedly by the prior acquisition of the conflicting no-go memory (see Figure 4.12).

A third complexity in translating interference theory mechanisms to animal memory is perhaps the most significant. Whereas the theoretical mechanisms of interference for human verbal learning have been observed independently of the forgetting and are well understood, this cannot be said for the interference mechanisms applied to understanding memory processing by animals.

On the other hand, another aspect of interference, the influence of context, is becoming understood better with animals than with humans. Perhaps context is more important for retention in animals than in humans. Context to animals is like instructions to humans: If the context is unchanged, the animal can "assume" that the same response is required; but if the context changes it may mean that the requirements about what response is to be made have also changed. Of course, context is much more than this and probably influences human memory processing a good deal more than generally is recognized. Nevertheless, its influence in showing the interaction between conflicting memories with animals, especially under circumstances such as the go-no-go tasks just mentioned, is especially profound. We proceed next to a closer examination of interference

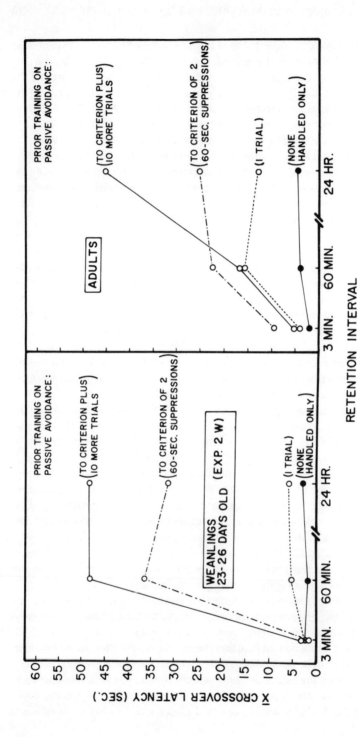

Figure 4.12 This figure shows that with increasing lengths of retention interval following active avoidance learning, the impairment to retention of active avoidance caused by prior passive avoidance training increases. Furthermore, the ultimate impairment to active avoidance retention is greater the higher the degree of the prior passive avoidance training. (The higher the cross-over latency, the greater the tendency toward appropriate passive avoidance performance and the less the tendency toward active avoidance performance.) (adapted from Spear et al., 1971).

as a source of forgetting, with emphasis first on experiments with animals, then on those with human subjects.

INTERFERENCE AND FORGETTING IN ANIMALS

We may consider first the basic issues as they pertain in particular to nonverbal organisms. My selection of "important" issues is influenced by two prejudices: Interference and retention are more fundamental than extinction and spontaneous recovery, and contextual changes between training and testing are the basic source of many phenomena associated with interference (RI and PI).

I find it useful to consider the process of extinction as involving primarily the acquisition of a conflicting memory that has most of its attributes in common with those of the critical memory, but with important differences in key attributes such as those representing the conditions of reinforcement and the response. Moreover, I believe that for most experimental extinction procedures there is no need to consider influences from any other source (such as inhibitory processes).

One immediate implication of the first prejudice is that earlier attempts to interpret the time-related changes in RI and PI as consequences of "spontaneous recovery" following an "extinction-like unlearning process" were 180 degrees out of phase. Instead, extinction and spontaneous recovery should be viewed as special cases of interference and forgetting. Perhaps this view (see, e.g., Estes, 1955, 1959; Razran, 1939) might have developed had McGeoch, Melton, and Underwood preceded Pavlov historically.

Among the advantages of viewing RI and PI as more basic than extinction and spontaneous recovery is the fact that greater generality is possible: Conceptually, extinction concerns only the declining contingencies of reinforcement for a learned response, but RI and PI deal simultaneously with an increase in contingencies associated with the one response and a decrease in contingencies associated with an alternative response, which probably is representative of a greater variety of circumstances (cf. Bower, 1972a; Estes, 1955, 1959, 1970; Spear, 1971). Also, there is now a greater variety of analytical evidence pertaining to retention subjected to RI and PI than to spontaneous recovery following extinction operations. Certainly theorizing on the former has far outstripped theorizing concerning the latter.

My second prejudice is that many phenomena associated with RI and PI may be reduced to special cases of changes in the contextual stimuli noticed at testing compared to those noticed during learning. For example, in the cases of both RI and PI test stimuli corresponding to attributes of the most recent learning are more likely to be present and noticed on an immediate test, although this may change, depending on the length of the retention interval. We shall not elaborate on this view here (see Spear, 1971), but the following discussion may be more acceptable now that these biases are out in the open.

An important issue concerning RI and PI is the extent to which these treatments interact with other sources of forgetting. If the influence of interference is tempered by the presence of another source of forgetting (for example, a long retention interval or a brain concussion), there exists the possibility that these constructs simply represent special cases of one common source of forgetting. It is well known that length of the retention interval determines the impact of conflicting memories on retention. It is notable also that other nominal sources of forgetting, such as aging and certain kinds of brain damage, modify the impact of conflicting memories on retention: Interference effects often are greater in brain-damaged, very young, or very old individuals (e.g., Iversen, 1973; Kay, 1959; Spear, Gordon, & Chiszar, 1972; Warrington & Weiskrantz, 1973). Hence, it is of interest to consider changes over time in the effect of RI and PI on retention. Forgetting typically decreases in the former and apparently increases in the latter case, until a sufficiently long retention interval has elapsed so that the distinction between RI and PI becomes insignificant.

The fundamental parameter controlling both sources of interference is similarity, as we have mentioned, so a continuing issue is how "similarity" is determined. A related question is whether interference in retention might occur even though there may be no attributes in common between the memory being tested and the memory acquired retroactively or proactively to it. In other words, does new learning with no conceivable relationship to another memory ever disrupt retention of the latter? We shall discuss this issue later with respect to RI.

For the most part, RI in animals has been of little interest, probably for two reasons. First, as long as the animal is given no indication ("instructions") that the retention test requires the prior memory rather than the more recent one, RI is quite unremarkable. With maximal RI, the animal responds solely in accordance with its latest learning; but this is what the animal typically has been taught anyway with multiple-trial training. It is conceivable that animals may be biologically predisposed for this because of the survival value of behaving in accordance with more recent experience. In this sense, RI is verified in each of the thousands of experiments that have included extinction or discrimination reversal or, more generally, any shifts in the conditions or contingencies of reinforcement.

By presenting the animal with some sort of "instructional signal" regarding which of two sequentially acquired memories should be retrieved, we should be able to draw relevant theoretical inferences about RI and PI in humans. This has not been accomplished often, so typically there is little point in maintaining a distinction between RI and PI in tests with animals (Spear, 1971). For theoretical considerations, therefore, one may refer more generally to interaction between conflicting memories. For experimental considerations, on the other hand, the problem and procedural paradigms often are discussed more comfortably by referring separately to RI and PI.

One final general note. The technical distinction between RI and PI is in the temporal ordering of acquisition of the memory to be retrieved and the interfering memory: If the interfering memory is acquired first, we test for PI; if it is acquired second, we test for RI. Animals in the control condition for either effect acquire only the memory to be retrieved. To illustrate, Table 4.1 presents experimental paradigms that assess PI under circumstances historically quite common in the study of learning and motivation. In our laboratory, animals tested with these paradigms soon after learning behave in accordance with that learning. But as the retention interval increases, animals behave more in accordance with prior learning, which, in this experimentally restricted case, is the only alternative. This result becomes interesting because the forgetting of most recent learning is more marked under the PI condition than under the control condition (but we must emphasize that this does not always occur, as will be discussed shortly). The important point here is that greater forgetting in the PI condition may be simply a consequence of the animal's forgetting the *temporal ordering* of the learning episode. Responding in accordance with the latest learning is less likely, the less the accuracy of discrimination between latest and prior learning.

We now may consider interaction between conflicting memories under the nominal classifications of proactive interference and retroactive interference.

Issues in the Understanding of Proactive Interference in Animals

Of basic interest is what determines retention of latest learning. The greater forgetting of latest learning that accompanies longer retention intervals does *not*

TABLE 4.1
Experimental Paradigms Yielding More Rapid Forgetting Because of
Prior Conflicting Learning—PI in Retention by Animals[a]

Paradigm	Condition[b]	Prior learning	Most recent learning	Retention test
1.	PI	Traverse runway (rapidly) for food	Traverse runway (slowly) for no food (i.e., extinction)	Retention test trial (soon after most recent learning or later)
	C	None (but equivalent handling)		
2.	PI	Traverse runway (rapidly) for large palatable food reinforcer	Traverse runway (slowly) for unpalatable or small food reinforcer	Retention test trial (soon, or later)
	C	None (but equivalent handling)		
3.	PI	Traverse runway (rapidly) for food	Traverse runway (slowly), punished (shocked) in goal box	Retention test trial (soon, or later)
	C	None (but equivalent handling)		

[a]From Spear, 1971.
[b]PI, proactive interference; C, control.

necessarily imply better retention of prior learning: It is quite possible for the previously acquired conflicting memory to interfere increasingly with retention of latest learning without becoming more accessible for retrieval itself. Appropriate tests of this possibility, and analysis of when it may or may not be expected, have not been feasible with most experimental preparations for testing PI. To do so requires that the alternative memories be indexed in such a way that their retrieval is not mutually exclusive. For example, if a rat that can turn only left or right learns first to do one and then to do the other, forgetting to turn left is always accompanied by an increased frequency of turning right, but this does not necessarily imply better access to the memory involving a right turn; to determine whether accessibility of the latter memory has changed, the rat must be permitted at least three alternatives. Better approximations of such tests are available in the human verbal memory-processing area (Barnes & Underwood, 1959), but these too have their limitations (see Postman, 1971).

The search for an experimental preparation that regularly yields increasing PI with longer retention intervals (a requirement for PI if one assumes equivalent learning, with and without the source of interference, prior to the retention interval) has been a problem. As reviews of this area of study indicate, this basic PI effect has not been found in very simple discrimination tasks involving spatial discriminations, although it has been found fairly regularly in the forgetting of visual discriminations (Burr & Thomas, 1972; Gleitman, 1971; Spear, 1971). In view of the apparently regular occurrence of this effect with complex mazes (see earlier discussion), this may imply that single-choice position discriminations are immune to PI because of their "simplicity," although we shall discuss some alternative interpretations presently.

For many purposes, the analysis of interference effects in animals has proceeded most effectively with tests of retention after very short intervals. These tests are similar to those discussed in Chapter 3 but are discussed here because of their value for understanding the role of interference in forgetting by animals.

PI in delayed matching and delayed responding by primates. It is notable that some relatively complex position discriminations in tests of delayed responding with monkeys have failed to implicate PI as an important determinant of forgetting in this task. Like retention of verbal discrimination learning in humans—that is, recognition memory for which of two words is "correct" (see Underwood, Zimmerman & Freund, 1971)—retention by primates in delayed-responding or delayed-matching tasks has appeared to be strikingly resistant to effects of PI. This fact has great significance for theory. We saw in Chapter 3 that substantial forgetting does occur in delayed responding and delayed matching. If this forgetting cannot be attributed to PI, then we must look beyond *specific* interference factors for the forgetting source (no specific source of RI is present in such tasks).

Medin and Davis (1974) discuss evidence concerning PI in delayed responding by primates and present several sets of data that indicate, at the very least, more resistance to PI than is conventionally expected. First, evidence is taken from a study by Medin (1969) in which monkeys were given 48 trials per day for 15 days on a delayed-response task. The task (see Chapter 3) was to select the appropriate cell among 16 cells arranged in a 4 × 4 matrix. Trials within each daily session included delays of 0, 1, 2, 5, 10, or 20 seconds between baiting and the retention test, with the occurrence of a particular delay determined randomly. If PI were accumulating within a daily session, one would expect that rate of forgetting would increase progressively. This did not occur, however, as can be seen in Figure 4.13. Instead, forgetting rates were fairly constant throughout a daily session of 48 test trials. These data did include evidence that prior trials influence test behavior: More errors than normally expected were due to the repetition of behavior appropriate to the just-preceding trial. But as mentioned earlier, this does not constitute evidence for PI in retention. A similar state of affairs has occurred in the study of discrimination retention by rats, in which PI did not increase forgetting in spite of evidence from intrusions that the prior learning otherwise affected test behavior (see Spear, 1971).

Medin and Davis conclude that two other predictions from considerations of PI also failed to be confirmed, the first deriving from a manipulation of intertrial interval and the second concerning the possibility of release from PI by a shift in the class of the stimulus used to cue the correct response. To this we might add the surprising indifference to sources of PI found with monkeys tested in delayed matching (e.g., Etkin & D'Amato, 1969). There are, furthermore, a variety of

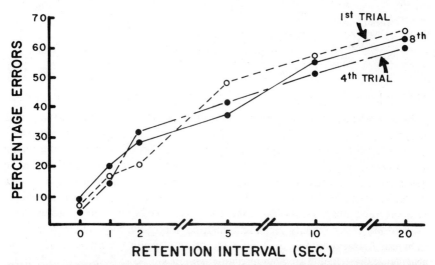

Figure 4.13   This figure illustrates that in a delayed response task with monkeys as subjects, when several different delayed response trials are given within a day, interference from preceding trials has relatively little influence on forgetting in later trials. The forgetting found over intervals up to 20 sec (the higher the percentage errors, the greater the forgetting) is no greater on the eighth trial of a day than on the first trial. (adapted from Medin and Davis, 1974).

data indicating that primates may be quite resistant to the influence of cumulative PI (e.g., Zimmerman, 1969; see Medin & Davis, 1974), although it is difficult to determine whether the positive features of the cumulative practice on a common type of retention test might not override the deleterious effects of cumulative PI. We have seen that retention by primates in the delayed-response and delayed-matching tasks does improve with practice.

It does not appear, however, that primates' retention of discrimination learning generally is immune to PI influence (see, e.g., Connor & Meyer, 1971). It should be clear that the absence of PI discussed here has arisen with the context of short-term retention, and may or may not apply to other instances of retention by monkeys. We have noted also how the rapid forgetting that occurs under conditions conducive to PI—in particular, during acquisition of a long series of successively presented discrimination problems—may be used to advantage by monkeys in acquiring learning sets (see Chapter 3 regarding Bessemer & Stollnitz, 1971).

PI in delayed matching by pigeons.   The influence of PI on short-term retention in pigeons has been tested systematically, but the circumstances of testing are somewhat different from those concerning monkeys. Generally, instead of testing PI from intertrial or interproblem sources, most PI tests with pigeons have manipulated interference within an individual delayed-matching trial. Zentall and Hogan (1974), for instance, presented two successive sample stimuli to a pigeon and tested the efficiency with which the bird responded in accordance with the most recently presented stimulus. This study is rather unusual in that it employed only one pigeon, which was tested repeatedly in three different experiments. While this certainly cannot be faulted on economic grounds, one might worry about how widely these results can be generalized. Otherwise, these experiments were carefully conducted and the results were interesting.

In each of the first two experiments by Zentall and Hogan, the pigeon was presented with a particular sample color (red, blue, or green) and had to peck that sample five times (which ensured attention) in order to initiate the retention test (presentation of the matching stimuli—the sample and an alternative) and possible reinforcement. The matching stimuli followed the five pecks with a delay of either 0 or 5 seconds. In addition, on some trials the sample was preceded immediately by a different stimulus color, to which the pigeon also had to respond five times. The question, of course, was whether presenting the stimulus prior to the sample would increase forgetting during the 5-second period.

In the first experiment, the prior stimulus was always different from the alternative presented during the matching test. PI did occur during the early trials of testing: Forgetting was greater after 5 seconds when the sample had been preceded by a different stimulus than without the prior stimulus. Zentall and Hogan's (1974) second experiment was conducted under the reasonable notion that the "32 experimental sessions in Experiment 1 can be thought of as training with the instruction, 'respond to the stimulus last seen' '' (p. 110). For this second experiment, the prior stimulus always was presented as the alternative to the correct sample during the matching test. The question then became, in practical terms, whether the bird could respond after a delay in accordance with the stimulus most recently presented. In other words, could the pigeon remember as well after 5 seconds as after zero seconds which of the two alternative stimuli had been presented last? The answer is that the pigeon could not, and this PI effect persisted over 34 daily sessions of testing. This PI effect then was examined over several delay intervals ranging between 0 and 6 seconds (Experiment 3), with the result of PI in retention as shown in Figure 4.14.

With somewhat different procedures, Grant and Roberts (1973) analyzed short-term retention in the pigeon under circumstances involving potential intra-trial interference much like that employed by Zentall and Hogan. In spite of thorough testing, Grant and Roberts obtained no evidence that their intratrial source of PI enhanced forgetting, which indicates limitations on the generality of this source of PI. Subsequently, however, Grant (1975) found that *inter*trial PI, in which a delayed-matching trial was preceded by another complete, but con-flicting, delayed-matching trial, did result in more rapid forgetting with the source of PI than without it. Grant analyzed this effect in detail. To test the basic PI effect, he presented pigeons with two successive delayed-matching trials that involved the same two stimuli, but the alternative that was correct during the first

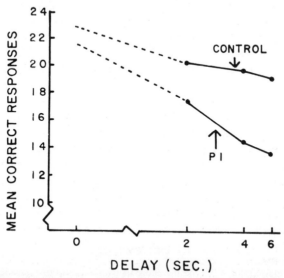

Figure 4.14   This figure illustrates that for pigeons given a delayed matching to sample task, forgetting may increase somewhat more rapidly with a source of proactive interference (PI) than without (control). (Adapted from Zentall and Hogan, 1974; for further analysis of this particular effect, see Zentall and Hogan, 1977).

trial was incorrect during the second, and so forth. Compared with the forgetting on trials in which the sample was not immediately preceded by a conflicting matching trial, forgetting (over a 6-second interval) was increased significantly by the source of PI (see Figure 4.15).

Grant also hypothesized that the enhanced forgetting caused by a prior, conflicting matching trial depends on the length of the interval between that conflicting trial and the presentation of the critical sample. This prediction is consistent with evidence from avoidance learning by rats and verbal learning by humans that PI depends on the interval between acquisition of the prior conflicting memory and acquisition of the critical memory that is tested (Gordon & Spear, 1973; Spear, 1971; Underwood & Freund, 1968). Grant compared the effect on delayed matching (after intervals of 0, 2, 6, or 10 seconds) of preceding the sample by a conflicting matching trial, which had been completed 2, 20, or 40 seconds previously. PI was reduced drastically with an intertask interval of 20 or 40 seconds compared to a 2-second intertask interval (see Figure 4.16).

Over longer intervals (24 hours), PI also has been found to inflate forgetting by pigeons of a relatively well-learned visual discrimination. Burr and Thomas (1972), in a thorough experiment employing generalization gradients to assess

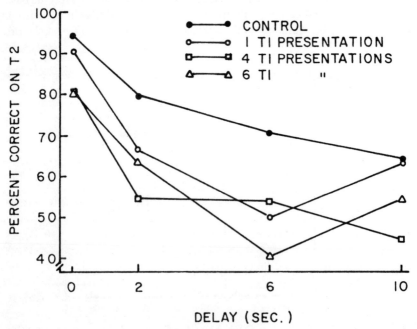

Figure 4.15 For pigeons in a delayed matching to sample task, this figure illustrates that greater forgetting over a 6 sec interval occurs among animals previously given conflicting delayed-matching-to-sample trials (TI presentations) than when such conflicting trials were not given previously within the same day (control). (Adapted from Grant, 1975. Copyright 1975 the American Psychological Association. Reprinted by permission.)

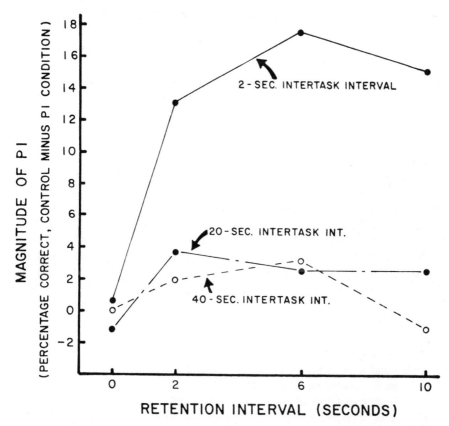

Figure 4.16   For pigeons in a delayed matching to sample task, this figure illustrates that the magnitude of proactive interference from a prior conflicting trial may be decreased if a sufficiently long interval (20 sec or 40 sec) intervenes between the conflicting task and the critical stimulus to be remembered.

retention, found that birds that previously had acquired the reverse discrimination had greater increase in forgetting of a discrimination over 24 hours than birds that had no prior conflicting learning. They found, furthermore, that this PI was greater for subjects that had acquired the critical discrimination under massed practice than for those that had acquired it under the same widely distributed practice conditions as were given for prior conflicting learning. This effect is similar in form to that obtained by Keppel (1964) in tests of retention of verbal items in humans. Keppel found that under conditions conducive to PI, retention of verbal units acquired under massed practice is a great deal poorer than when acquisition occurs under widely distributed practice. In such cases, the differential distributions of practice in prior learning and latest learning serves to decrease markedly the forgetting caused by PI (also see Underwood & Ekstrand, 1966, 1967). We shall discuss this factor again in Chapter 8.

Further analysis of the determinants of PI in retention by animals.   We now may consider the few remaining features of PI that might lead to the sorts of principles needed for understanding its role in forgetting. The first factor to be emphasized (actually, reemphasized) is the remarkable tendency for certain animals to perform in accordance with the most recent reinforcement contingencies. Because the influence of PI is likely to be transient, typically dissipating after only a few test trials, this countertendency to perform in accordance with the most recent reinforcement contingencies is most evident under the circumstances of relearning or over extended test sessions, as shown in the following example.

Calhoun and Handley (1973) gave rats one discrimination reversal per day for 32 consecutive days, then introduced a retention interval of 32 days. To test retention, half the animals were given a 300-trial test session where all the discriminations were identical to the one on their last session 32 days earlier; the remaining animals were given a similar test on the reverse discrimination. To the extent that the animals behaved in accordance with the most recent contingencies of reinforcement (i.e., that of 32 days earlier) rather than in accordance with the alternative contingencies (which they had experienced for half of the previous 32 sessions), we would expect fewer errors in animals tested with the same reinforcement contingencies as the last training session than in those tested with the reverse contingencies. This was the case. The unchanged group on the average made only about half as many errors as the reversed group. There are potential alternative interpretations. For example, the better retention performance conceivably may have been a consequence of *17* daily sessions under the more recent contingencies (including acquisition on Day 1) and only 16 sessions under the others. Such remote possibilities aside, this provides a dramatic example of the tendency of animals to respond in accordance with the last things they have learned. By definition, a source of PI disrupts this tendency. It is of some interest, therefore, to ask under what conditions this tendency will be maintained—which simply phrases the PI problem somewhat differently than ordinarily.

Apparently, humans also have a disposition to recall events most recently learned, even in spite of instructions to do otherwise. We referred earlier to this powerful characteristic of human memory processing, the "selector mechanism," and shall do so again because of its general significance. The selector mechanism was introduced by Underwood and Schulz (1960) to account for the impressive efficiency with which humans suppress responding with "extralist intrusions," verbal items that do not appear among a list of items subjects are instructed to learn. When subjects learn a second list of verbal items intended to interfere retroactively with a previously acquired first list, the selector mechanism is said to cause "activation of the newly prescribed responses and the inhibition or suppression of the earlier ones" (Postman & Underwood, 1973, p. 23). The important characteristic of the selector mechanism for our present interest is its inertia. The test for RI requires that the subject respond with items from the first list of verbal items, but suppression of these items initiated in learning the second list continues for a period on the order of 20 or 30 minutes thereafter. This, of course, contributes to the RI measured within this time span after learning the two lists.

The effect of the selector mechanism may be stated in another way. It is as if there is a 20- or 30-minute "protection interval" following learning, such that items in the last list are relatively immune from the forgetting otherwise caused by mechanisms such as failure in list differentiation. The generality with which sets, or lists, of acquired verbal units are protected from forgetting from other sources during this brief interval is unclear. However, an effect that may be said to be analogous has been studied with animals under circumstances in which the source of forgetting involved must be classified separately from list differentiation. Discussion of this protection interval (also see Spear, 1971) requires some introductory remarks.

We have alluded to studies of PI in animals that implicate impaired discrimination of the temporal ordering of prior events as one of the underlying mechanisms of this interference (see also D'Amato, 1973; Gleitman, 1971; Spear, 1971). Other underlying mechanisms also have been indicated in a paradigm involving the acquisition of two successive, conflicting avoidance tasks (Spear, 1971).

In this PI paradigm, the rat acquires two conflicting avoidance response tendencies, first no-go, then go (the alternative ordering also yields increasing PI with longer retention intervals; see Spear, Gordon, & Martin, 1973). The circumstances under which the conflicting response tendencies are acquired are identical except for the reinforcement contingencies. Initially, the rat learns to avoid receiving footshock in the second compartment of a two-compartment apparatus by "passively" remaining in the first compartment. Then the reinforcement contingencies are shifted so that the rat learns to actively avoid footshock in the first compartment by running rapidly into the second. When a "neutral" retention test is given later (neutral in that no footshock whatsoever is employed), these animals forget their more recent active avoidance learning more rapidly than animals that had learned only the active avoidance; this is consistent with the paradigmatic case defining PI (see Figure 4.13). Through proper selection of the training parameters, both the rate of acquisition of the critical memory (active avoidance) and the extent of retention after a short interval can be made equal for animals with and without the prior conflicting learning. With this task, it is found that PI decreases the longer the interval separating acquisition of the conflicting memories (analogous to the results cited earlier concerning short-term retention in the pigeon and in human verbal memory processing). Also, it has been determined that PI is greater the higher the degree of prior learning and the lower the degree of latest learning. But to illustrate the incomplete nature of this particular analysis of PI, we may note that it is not yet certain whether the critical determinant of this relationship might be the ratio of degree of prior learning to degree of most recent learning, rather than their absolute values. Similar circumstances exist for distribution of practice: Wider distribution of practice of most recent learning results in resistance to PI, but, analogous to the results just cited, it is unclear whether this effect depends on the relative distributions of the practice given for prior and most recent learning or on the absolute distribution of most recent learning.

Among a variety of potential interpretations of this instance of PI is the possibility that the tendency to respond in accordance with the conflicting prior learning is inhibited actively during acquisition of the most recent task. During the retention interval, the inhibition gradually weakens, permitting the prior learning to interfere with retention. The inhibition may weaken because it dissipates automatically; or perhaps disinhibition is caused by some strong stimulus, the occurrence of which becomes more probable the longer the retention interval; or perhaps the inhibition is of a cognitive sort, which somehow is diminished as a result of a shift in the memories being processed after the animal has been removed from the context of the prior and most recent learning. Such an interpretation in terms of inhibition now seems unlikely, at least as the sole determinant of interference in retention. A drastic reduction in PI occurs as a consequence of increasing the intertask interval, a manipulation that would not seem to influence the development of inhibition of previously acquired response tendencies during the more recent task (e.g., Gordon & Spear, 1973; Spear, 1971). Also, the probability of retrieving either of the conflicting memories seems readily manipulable by treatments that are known to reactivate either the first or the second of the acquired memories. It is of some interest, however, that reactivation of the previously acquired memory, in some cases at least, appears to be less likely to occur relatively soon after recent memory acquisition. In other words, it is as if some 'minimal "protection interval" exists following most recent learning, so that retrieval of that memory not only is especially probable but also is "shielded" from interference that might be caused by retrieval of competing or conflicting memories (Spear, 1971; Spear, Bryan, Gordon, Chiszar, & Timmons, 1977).

Finally, what is referred to here as an interaction between conflicting *memories* in determination of PI may be just that, as opposed to a time-dependent modification of *response tendencies* per se. Gordon and Spear (1973) found that whereas PI effects did not occur when a 24-hour interval intervened between the prior and the most recent learning, enhanced forgetting of the latter nevertheless could be obtained if the memory of the prior learning was "reactivated" just prior to most recent learning. Operationally, to "reactivate" simply means to reexpose the animal to the experimental apparatus in a manner similar to that of prior learning (see Gordon, 1973, for a thorough replication and extension of this result). This implies that a necessary condition of PI is simultaneous activation of the two conflicting memories rather than the contiguous occurrence of the two opposing responses per se (for further discussion of these and related issues, see Spear, 1971).

Retroactive Interference (RI) in Retention by Animals

Because of the disposition of animals to perform the response most recently practiced or most recently reinforced—due perhaps to the absence of instructions to do otherwise, or because in the course of acquiring a memory for a laboratory task an animal typically is required to perform in accordance with the most recently reinforced response—RI has seemed to be a relatively uninteresting problem. Responding in accordance with most recent learning inevitably would appear as a deficit in the measure of retention of original learning, provided that conflicting tasks are involved (as would be so in the study of RI). In this setting, RI seems trivial.

The study of RI with animals becomes more interesting for understanding forgetting under two circumstances that have undergone recent study. The first is when forgetting is caused by interpolation of an event that, though clearly perceived by the animal, does not require a response contrary to those that occurred during original learning. The second case is when interpolated events interfere with retention of prior learning even though there is no apparent similarity between the prior learning and the interpolated events. These cases have occurred together in two studies of RI in pigeons tested over very short retention intervals, one by Zentall (1973) and the other by Grant and Roberts (1973).

Zentall (1973) tested pigeons on a delayed-matching-to-sample task. The stimuli were two colors, red and green; a 5-second interval always elapsed between presentation of the sample (either red or green) and the matching test (choice between red and green). After the birds had learned to match the sample with an accuracy of nearly 85% correct choices, daily sessions of 96 trials were introduced to test RI. During these tests, one of three stimuli occurred on the sample key during the 5-second retention interval: For one-third of the trials, the sample key was dark; for another third, a vertical white line appeared on the key; for the remaining third, the key was yellow. With the dark-key condition as the baseline of minimal interference, Zentall found that interpolation of the yellow stimulus resulted in poorer retention. The vertical line also tended to interfere with retention relative to the dark-key condition, especially during the first daily testing session. These results suggested that RI could be caused by the interpolation of stimuli with relatively little formal similarity to the critical stimulus of original learning, although a "similarity" interpretation should not be ruled out.

A subsequent analysis by Grant and Roberts (1973) suggested that similarity was not an important determinant of this case of RI. The Grant–Roberts experiments were designed to distinguish among the alternative interpretations of Zentall for his results of greater RI with the yellow stimulus than with the vertical line. Zentall had suggested that the yellow stimulus may have been either more similar to the samples (red or green) or more salient than the other RI source, the vertical line. *Salience* is a term that has come to have several meanings (cf. Wagner & Rescorla, 1972). For our present purposes, it refers to the probability of attracting attention or preventing distraction by alternative attention. In fact, Grant and Roberts' data indicated greater salience of colors than of patterns of dots. Subjects required about three times as many daily sessions to master simultaneous matching-to-sample for the dots than for the colors (though this may also be interpreted in associative rather than attentional terms; see Rescorla & Wagner, 1972; Wagner & Rescorla, 1972).

Grant and Roberts (1973) varied the nature of the interpolated stimuli intended to create RI. In a completely balanced design, the interfering stimuli were either more or less salient (colors or patterns of dots) and were either familiar to the animal or novel. Interpolated stimuli were presented during the 5-second delay between the presentation of the sample and the matching test. The results indicated substantial RI within each of the classes of interpolated stimuli. However, there was no consistent trend for colors to cause more RI than dot patterns; furthermore, there was no consistent trend for novel stimuli to cause more RI than familiar stimuli. One particular pattern consistently produced more RI than another, and one color consistently produced more RI than the other, but the dimensions underlying these effects are unclear.

Because the critical dimension underlying RI seemed to be neither similarity to the sample, nor salience, nor familiarity of the interfering stimulus, Grant and Roberts (1973) suggested alternative dimensions that might have governed interference in their experimental situation. However, neither figure complexity nor the total surface area of the stimulus-emitting light seemed to account completely for the effects. It is notable that within the color dimension similarity between the interpolated stimulus and the sample is important: The closer the wavelengths (color) of the interpolated stimulus and the sample, the poorer the retention. But in this case an interpretive problem arises in the same fashion as in an earlier experiment by Jarvik, Goldfarb, and Carley (1969). Jarvik and his associates found that delayed matching by monkeys could be disrupted considerably by interpolating, between the presentation of the sample and the matching task, the sole alternative stimulus (against which the sample was to be compared at the test). But in such a situation the animal may simply be following "instructions." Having been taught for many weeks to respond in accordance with the last stimulus seen prior to the matching test, the monkey reasonably would be expected to respond in accordance with the interpolated stimulus rather than with the sample. When interpolated stimuli more similar to the sample than to the test alternative cause less RI, it is as if the subject were responding to an "extra" generalized presentation of the sample itself just prior to the retention test. Selection among these and other interpretations awaits investigation of a fairly broad continuum of stimuli within classes (e.g., more than two colors) and the establishment of a clearer baseline to represent zero RI.

We conclude from the studies of Grant and Roberts and of Zentall that in spite of their creativity and general value, the basic source of RI in these experiments remains unclear, at least in the sense that the dimension determining the relative amount of interference of an interpolated stimulus is as yet unsettled. At this time, and with reference only to these cases of short-term retention, the dimension does not appear to be purely a matter of formal similarity between the interfering stimulus and either the stimulus to be remembered or the alternative stimulus presented at the retention test. The better answer, derived from a series of careful experiments by Grant and Roberts (1976), is that illumination from any source during the retention interval can account for much of the RI believed in earlier studies (such as that of Zentall, 1973) to be caused by specific interpolated stimuli. We therefore will consider *non*specific sources of RI, for which we may cite more evidence.

Nonspecific RI in Animals

Although it is unclear that "voluntary" or spontaneous activity initiated by animals during a retention interval is itself a direct cause of RI over short intervals (in terms of delayed responding or delayed matching; see Chapter 3), there are indications that activities structured and demanded by the experimenter during the retention interval may result in forgetting in delayed matching. Moise (1970) found that requiring the monkey to perform a signal detection task during the retention interval impaired delayed-matching performance in proportion to the number of detection trials imposed, though it did not matter whether these detection trials were imposed early or late in the retention interval.

Evidence for nonspecific sources of RI also may be found following relatively high degrees of learning and long retention intervals. Parsons and Spear (1972) found increased forgetting of acquired avoidance behavior among rats exposed to an enriched environment during a 28-day retention interval. Honig (1974) found impairment of an acquired discrimination following a retention interval during which pigeons responded to stimuli of a different dimension than those of the prior discrimination, under conditions in which each of the stimuli resulted in equal probability of reinforcement. In Honig's experiments, RI was caused, in effect, by training the animal *not* to respond differentially to alternative stimuli of a particular dimension.

A particularly elegant case of nonspecific RI has been reported by Wickens (1973; Wickens, Tuber, Nield, & Wickens, 1977). Wickens' basic experimental paradigm, to which we shall have occasion to return later (Chapter 8), constitutes perhaps the best animal preparation yet devised for testing transfer and RI and is comparable to the tests in paired-associate verbal learning that have been so successful in analyzing these phenomena. Wickens classically conditioned cats under circumstances where either of two conditioned stimuli (light or tone) could be paired with footshock to either forepaw. With two independent stimuli and two apparently independent responses, it was possible first to condition animals on one stimulus–response combination and then to transfer to another combination. For example, after training with Stimulus A (e.g., light) and Response B (e.g., withdrawal of the left forepaw induced by a mild shock), a cat was given a transfer task (which also constituted interpolated learning in the test of RI). Considering the initial task as A–B, this subsequent task took either of three forms: A–D (same stimulus with a different response—withdrawal of right forepaw induced by shock); C–D (a different stimulus, e.g., tone, and the different response—withdrawal of right forepaw); or C–B (the different stimulus paired with the same response—withdrawal of left forepaw). RI was measured by presenting these cats with the original Stimulus A and comparing the retention results with those of animals given only the A–B training and no interpolated task.

Wickens' RI tests suggested that nonspecific sources quite effectively produce RI. Cats given the A–B, C–D sequence of conditioning were much less likely to respond with B when presented Stimulus A than cats previously given the A–B, A–D sequence. Even though the latter condition included the same stimuli during original learning and interpolated learning and thus potentially provided specific interference (in terms of the similarity between these two conflicting memories), RI was greater for animals for which no specific components of the interpolated and original tasks were the same. The RI, assessed in terms of the relative rates of relearning the original A–B pairing, yielded the same pattern of results: Cats given the interpolated C–D conditioning required about twice as many trials to relearn A–B as cats given the interpolated A–D conditioning.

A final type of evidence that implicates nonspecific sources of RI is indirect and is based on the alleviation of forgetting when the forgetting presumably is caused by nonspecific sources of RI. We shall see in Chapter 8 that RI may be counteracted by experimentally induced events interpolated prior to testing; similarly, RI from "natural" sources may be reduced if an individual is prevented from becoming exposed to such sources of RI between learning and testing. For example, Mishkin, Dunkel, and Rosveld (1959) fitted a monkey with translucent contact occluders that completely impaired the animal's visual acuity; specific visual patterns apparently could not be detected or differentiated during the nine consecutive months in which these occluders were worn. The monkey had been trained on a "fairly difficult discrimination between two visual patterns" (Mishkin et al., 1958, p. 1220) prior to the application of the occluders. When the occluders were removed nine months later the monkey was described as having "complete retention of the visual habit" (p. 1220). Assuming that the monkey would have forgotten more if the occluders had not been worn, the benefit to retention provided by the occluders may be attributed to the absence of relatively nonspecific sources of RI that ordinarily might accompany normal visual perception. In a similar vein, Hicks, McDaniel, and Hensley (1973) trained isopods on a position discrimination. Both groups of animals were permitted a long retention interval of exposure to the apparatus. The isopods employed in this experiment are of the type commonly referred to as "pill bugs" because they roll into a "pill" and remain immobilized under certain conditions. Prior to the retention test, half of the subjects were immobilized and half were permitted opportunity for typical activity. The immobilized animals showed better retention than the active animals. While neither of these experiments has much analytical value, they do provide examples of the sorts of evidence that might indicate the action of nonspecific sources of RI.

INTERFERENCE AND FORGETTING IN HUMANS

The basic characteristics of the most common scientific treatment of interference, which we term *interference theory,* were described earlier in general terms. The general form of the empirical basis and principles associated with interference theory has evolved relatively unchanged from McGeoch to Underwood and Postman, although the substance of the empirical basis has grown considerably and the principles have been modified accordingly.

The beauty of interference theory is its isolation of only a few factors—really only two—to account for a very great deal of what is known about transfer and about forgetting caused by PI and RI. Furthermore, these factors themselves are subject to independent measurement and study, as we have mentioned. So much for the beauty. A major difficulty of this interpretative scheme is its shortcoming in accounting for extraexperimental sources of forgetting, the events in a human's experience outside the laboratory that cause a subject to forget what has been acquired, and tested for, in the laboratory. When both the interfering material and the material to be recalled have been acquired and tested in the laboratory, interference theory has done quite well in explanation. Even here, however, difficulties have arisen. For example, it now appears likely that PI cannot be explained solely on the basis of the same two factors that explain RI (Hasher & Johnson, 1975; Postman, Stark, & Burns, 1974; For elaboration, see pp. 213–215). Certainly it will come as no surprise that interference theory has been challenged, but the origin of the challenge is interesting: For the most part, it comes from scientists whose academic ancestry leads back to McGeoch (Greeno, James, & DaPolito, 1971; Martin, 1971; Runquist, 1975). The history of interference theory and the issues under challenge have been discussed thoroughly and eloquently elsewhere (Postman, 1971; Postman & Underwood, 1973). Our discussion will be limited to a brief outline of the current principles of interference theory and brief reference to some alternative interpretations. (Empirical support and elaboration of the topics discussed may be found in the references just given, especially the papers by Postman.)

Mechanisms Responsible for RI

The two basic factors of interference theory are unlearning and response competition. These factors combine to produce forgetting attributable to RI, but may be assessed separately with proper measurement techniques. The most common of these techniques, and perhaps the most important historically, is the "modified modified free recall" or "MMFR" procedure, which, in principle, eliminates response competition by permitting the subject to respond with all responses—those to be recalled and those interfering—in the absence of time pressure. We may now consider the mechanisms that are most likely to be responsible for RI.

Unlearning. Unlearning occurs as the subject acquires the interpolated task. It is reflected in a reduction in the accessibility of the responses represented in the memory of the critical task and, to a lesser extent, in the accessibility of the associations between stimuli and those responses. Unlearning operates at the time of interpolated learning, not during the retention test, but acquisition of interpolated learning does not *require* unlearning of the responses and associations of the previous episode. We have noted that long-term retention in humans typically has been assessed in terms of multiple sets of verbal units. Accordingly, unlearning may occur for only a portion of the list episode (i.e., the list of verbal items and the events accompanying its presentation for learning), and in fact, unlearning rarely affects more than an average of 50% of the items in an episode. The magnitude of unlearning may be enhanced by increasing the degree of learning of the interpolated task, or by any of a variety of manipulations that increase the likelihood that subjects will respond (covertly or overtly) during interpolated learning with a response appropriate to original learning. If the interpolated learning involves the same stimuli as the original learning but paired with different responses, unlearning has a clearly detrimental, though small, effect on the originally acquired associations (see Petrich, 1974). Unlearning also may operate on individual responses, but its clearest effect is on the entire group of responses acquired during original learning. The latter effect has been referred to as "generalized competition," but more recently, and more often, it has been described as "response set interference" (there is good reason for this terminology but it is irrelevant to our present purpose).

Response set interference. The most thorough analysis of response set interference stemmed from a study by Postman, Stark, and Fraser (1968), and its further analysis is attributable largely to Postman and his colleagues. This analysis began with acknowledgment of the powerful selector mechanism (mentioned previously in reference to the effectiveness with which humans categorize sets of responses) in separating the responses to be excluded from those to be learned, even before learning the latter.

In the case of RI following presentation of an interpolated list episode, the selector mechanism serves to activate the new responses and suppress the old ones associated with original learning: This is "response set interference." Response set interference is strong and persists for 20 or 30 minutes following interpolated learning; it dissipates thereafter, and this leads to an absolute rise in the accessibility of responses of the original list. At this point, this accessibility is immediately reversible if a new set of responses is presented to the subject to be learned. Response set interference is treated separately from unlearning because it acts only on the responses and not on associations between these responses and specific stimuli. This is evidenced by the presence of absolute recovery from response set interference after 30 minutes, as long as conflicting responses are present in the original and interpolated lists but regardless of whether conflicting *associations* exist between common stimuli in the original and interpolated lists. Also, RI may occur if stimuli and responses from the first list are paired again in different combinations to form the second list; but without differences in the sets of responses, there is no evidence of recovery from this RI over a 30-minute period.

It has been clear for some time that when the original and interpolated tasks require different responses, most of RI can be attributed to a decrease in the accessibility of the original responses. However, this loss in response accessibility formerly was attributed to unlearning of the association between each separate response item and the "experimental context." Response set interference has become the preferred interpretation for a variety of reasons, including the general tendency for humans to group sets of responses together, the relatively transitory unlearning found for associations between the responses and specific stimuli, and the difficulty in identifying what is meant by "experimental context." When this last difficulty is solved, our conception of how responses decrease in accessibility during RI might be changed. Until then, response set interference seems to be the most useful interpretation.

Response competition.   The second major factor in RI is specific competition. Like McGeoch's reproductive inhibition, it is a process that acts to block the production of alternative responses, whether correct or incorrect, at recall. Specific competition is a particularly active contributor to RI when list differentiation is low and the subject has difficulty determining whether a particular response "belongs" to the memory being tested or to that acquired during interpolated learning.

Interference Factors in PI

It is obvious that PI will not depend on factors such as unlearning and response set interference that decrease the accessibility of responses and associations of prior learning. Indeed, response set interference may serve to *reduce* PI temporarily by protecting responses from potential sources of PI for a period of 20–30 minutes following learning (see Wickens & Dalezman, 1974). Thus, only one of the two basic factors of interference theory, response competition, need be considered to explain PI. It has become obvious, however, that this factor alone is inadequate for explaining PI, so we must search beyond the two basic factors of interference theory.

Response competition.   There can be no doubt that response competition does contribute heavily to PI. Between prior and latest learning, response competition clearly appears to increase to the extent that subjects fail to differentiate lists. Underwood and his colleagues have shown that retention by subjects exposed to a source of PI may be increased greatly—approximately doubled in some cases—and PI similarily reduced if the prior and latest learning are presented in such a way as to yield differentiation between them at the time of the retention test (Underwood & Ekstrand, 1966, 1967; Underwood & Freund, 1968). At one time, it appeared that PI might be restricted primarily to conditions under which response competition is particularly apparent, as when the subject is placed under time pressure during the retention test, but it now appears quite clear that substantial PI may occur whether recall is paced or not. Moreover, PI occurs quite readily under testing procedures that ostensibly eliminate response competition, for example, under the "MMFR" procedure mentioned earlier, in which subjects are free to recall all responses from any lists they have learned. It does not help to argue that this procedure therefore does not eliminate response competition, because this merely begs the question, as Postman, Stark, and Burns (1974) have noted. The specific deficit in retention attributable to PI also appears to be identifiable in terms of both decrements in the associations between stimulus and response items, and decrements in the simple probability of emitting the appropriate response items (Postman et al., 1974).

Finally, and in some respects most troublesome of all, a considerable number of thorough tests of PI in retention of verbal items have failed to find an increase in the influence of a source of PI after a long, compared to a short, retention interval, as very often has been the case in studies of PI with animals (Spear, 1971). This allows the possibility that a good deal of the variance attributed to PI in retention is, in fact, due to PI in *learning*, that is, that degree of learning has not been controlled properly or that prior learning alters the nature of the learning of verbal items (e.g., Hasher & Johnson, 1975). Taken together, these facts have led to consideration of factors other than response competition in the analysis of PI.

Alternative interpretations of PI.   An interpretation by Keppel (1968) implies that verbal items subject to a source of PI may be acquired (learned) in a manner that is different, qualitatively or quantitively, from the manner in which items are acquired in the absence of interference. However, this interpretation is couched in terms of the original two factors of interference theory: Items subject to a source of PI are viewed as more susceptible to extraexperimental sources of RI during the retention interval that produce greater unlearning of the items (see also Houston, 1969, 1971).

A specific interpretation of the poorer learning of items subject to PI has been tested and substantiated, at least indirectly, in experiments by Hasher and Johnson (1975) and by Postman and his associates (1974, Exp. 2). The notion investigated in both studies was that when common stimuli appear in the first and second lists, the subject uses the more effective mediators to associate the stimuli with the responses in the first list. In order to combat negative transfer while learning the second list, the subject must use different mediators that turn out to be "second-rate" and result in learning that is less stable. The experiment by

Hasher and Johnson (Experiment 1) showed that when the mediators that subjects reported using to learn the second of two lists were employed by different subjects to learn a single list of words, more forgetting occurred than if they had employed mediators previously applied to items not subject to the source of PI. Postman and his associates found a reduction in PI in retention when the prior learning was unlikely to use up the best mediators and so left them for use during later learning.

A final alternative mechanism of PI suggested by Postman and Hasher (1972) is worth mentioning in view of the evidence that the influence of PI on retention may operate on response accessibility per se. These authors suggested that following the dissipation of response set interference (interference from the second set of responses acting on the first), the simultaneous accessibility of both sets of responses may result in "output interference" (see Chapter 8), a general decrease in the probability of recalling a particular item in a set as the set increases, which then is apt to decrease the accessibility of the more recent responses.

SUMMARY AND CONCLUSIONS

This chapter has considered two basic issues of long-term retention—the course and source of forgetting. We first discussed retention functions, which are viewed as aberrant because, unlike the classical Ebbinghaus function (which, we have noted, may not be representative), these do not decrease monotonically. Two such functions, incubation and the Kamin effect, were considered in detail as models of how analysis and explanation might proceed for other cases.

Incubation, the monotonic increase in anxiety-related performance over time, was discussed as an instance in which forgetting of specific features of an episode leads to flattening of the generalization function. With this flattening, increased responding of an indiscriminate nature occurs that, with certain measurement techniques, is mistaken for a genuine facilitation of retention.

The Kamin effect, characterized by exaggerated forgetting of aversive conditioning following intervals of 1–6 hours, was discussed as an instance in which time-dependent physiological changes largely peripheral to neurophysiological representations of a memory have significant influence on the retention function. Our analysis of the Kamin effect indicated that beyond the time-dependent changes in activity or reactivity caused by the stress of prior aversive conditioning, evidence has identified the stimulus consequences of these time-dependent physiological changes and the resultant deficit in memory retrieval as the basis for the Kamin effect.

The second half of the chapter focused on interference as a primary source of forgetting. By interference is meant, generally, a deterrent to the manifestation of an acquired memory due to having acquired similar but conflicting memories. Interference also might be viewed as a biologically inevitable source of forgetting, a result of "noise" from normal neurophysiological activity that impairs memory processing. This latter concept, however, like decay, lacks analytical potential, at least in view of our present knowledge of physiology.

Greater analytical potential has been found in the more functionalistic view of interference as a behavioral conflict in manifesting one of two or more conflicting memories that are similar but not identical in content. This view was elaborated initially in the context of humans' retention of discrete verbal units and has progressively expanded its scope during the past half-century. A theoretical framework, "interference theory," was developed, tightly, through constructs tied closely to the facts of human learning.

There is some difficulty in translating the constructs of interference theory for use in psychobiological research with animals, but analogous principles still appear useful. Analysis of interference effects is proceeding with animals in terms of short-term as well as long-term retention, but it is too early to determine the value of new principles emerging from this work. Generally, however, there is no doubt that previously acquired conflicting memories produce proactive interference and subsequently acquired conflicting memories produce retroactive interference, and both induce forgetting over a broad spectrum of species and circumstances.

5
Further Sources of Forgetting and Related Issues

This chapter continues our discussion of major sources of forgetting in long-term retention. As in the preceding chapter, discussion focuses on general issues that can be addressed in the study of a particular source of forgetting, rather than on that source itself. Beyond the intrinsic interest in identification of the particular events that may alter retention, there are special insights into memory processing in general that may be achieved through investigation of these events.

Within this orientation, the sources of forgetting of interest in this chapter concern ontogenetic influences on forgetting, warm-up decrement, intraepisodic retention, and abnormal sources of forgetting. For introductory purposes, we may illustrate this orientation with examples: Aging, in the broad ontogenetic sense, is an important source of forgetting because it may provide a model of forgetting that may arise from progressive physiological and behavioral change induced by any number of circumstances; warm-up decrement is important because its omnipotence marks it as a possible model for the general influence of a retention interval and because of its probable interaction with other sources of forgetting; intraepisodic retention (retention for the occurrence, within an episode, of a prior event such as the CS, at the time of a separable event such as the UCS) is important because its characteristics should help us identify how a sequence of events becomes conceptualized as an episode and encapsulated as such in memorial representation; and abnormal sources of forgetting are important because their study permits us to assess which of the many behavioral and physiological correlates of memory processing actually are necessary or sufficient for retention and forgetting. It will require no more than a moment to realize several additional reasons for the study of each of these sources of forgetting. We shall encounter many such reasons in the following discussion, beginning with ontogenetic change as a source of forgetting.

AGING AND THE PROCESSING OF MEMORIES

Ontogeny of the Capacity for Retention: General Issues

It is intriguing to ask at what age or level of maturation animals and humans acquire a capacity to retrieve acquired memories, but a simple answer is unlikely. Certainly it is feasible to ask at what age one may find a significant level of retention an hour, or a day, or a month after learning is established. However, it is a great leap between this, which is essentially an empirical question to be answered in terms of specific organism–episode combinations, and the desire for a general formula specifying the relationship between maturation and the capacity for retention. Moreover, an answer to the specific empirical question is precluded by methodological difficulties, and construction of a general formula is precluded by limitations on generalization once the empirical question is answered. It is necessary to consider these factors to appreciate existing facts and interpretations concerning the ontogeny of memory processing.

Methodological issues.   Comparison of retention among animals of different ages involves the "comparative" problem, which also is inherent in the study of several classes of subject variables such as species differences, sex differences, and so forth. Often the physical requirements of the tasks effectively differ for animals of different ages, especially if motor or sensory capacities are correlated with age. For example, if a rat is required to jump a hurdle to obtain a reinforcer, a hurdle of a height easily stepped over by an adult may provide an impossible leap for an infant or weanling rat. Furthermore, the precise response emitted by the subject to solve an instrumental learning task often varies from subject to subject. A rat may traverse a maze by running, crawling, or walking; a lever may be depressed with one paw, two paws, or the head; and so on. Not only must we be cautious in comparing retention for learning acquired at different ages and with correspondingly different responses, but we must also be cautious in comparing retention acquired with specific responses that may differ from those employed by the same animals in testing after they have matured. The general comparative problem has been discussed thoroughly, especially within the context of species differences (Bitterman, 1960; Hodos & Campbell, 1969), so we will not elaborate on the similar problems that arise in terms of age differences. One pervasive problem requires discussion, however. This is the need to isolate learning and motivational effects in the analysis of retention differences. The former are notably sensitive to age differences and, as we have seen, easily confused with effects of retention.

Distinguishing learning and motivational effects from retention differences.   We shall soon discuss differences in retention and forgetting by animals of different ages. The clearer ontogenetic effects of this sort customarily are studied under the heading "long-term retention" and concern changes in retention taking place over days, weeks, or months rather than seconds or minutes. The reason these particular retention effects are clearer is because they have been separated from the effects of learning and motivation. The basic phenomena and the potential explanations may apply equally in the case of short-term retention, but existing data that might be useful for analyzing short-term retention necessarily have involved lower degrees of original learning, and the experimental designs simply do not permit extrication of learning differences. This illustrates the problem in a general sense; soon we will become more specific. First, however, we will consider briefly how this problem has evolved within the context of ontogenetic research.

Campbell (1967) has reviewed the history of attempts to relate the efficiency of subsequent retention to the ontogenetic level of the organism at the time of original learning. The several ambitious studies of this problem that appeared prior to 1960 were united in their failure to eliminate the confounding of age differences with real or probable differences in motivation and degree of original learning. Earlier we saw (p. 34) that Underwood demonstrated for verbal tasks how it is dangerous to assume that equivalent levels of learning follow either an equal number of learning trials or attainment of a common performance criterion. We note also, however, that it is unclear whether the same underlying relationship between degree of learning ("number of reinforcements," cf. Underwood, 1964) and retention holds for animals and humans, particularly when animals are tested in tasks like avoidance learning in which the reinforcer may be ambiguous. Also, for some animal learning tasks requiring a large number of training trials and a gradual approach to criterion performance, the problem of equivalent learning may be less important. As Campbell (1967) has shown, however, the failure to even appreciate this as a problem for some tasks has negated the usefulness of early studies relating age and retention.

An additional source of uncontrolled variance cited by Campbell is the differential effects of motivational conditions on animals of different ages, particularly with appetitive motivation. However, a solution to this problem has been found: Certain sources of electric shock yield detection and aversion thresholds that are invariant among rats from the age of weaning through maturity. Moreover, several learning tasks that involve aversive conditioning yield equivalent learning by immature and mature animals when equivalence is indexed by both the amount of training required to achieve a given criterion of performance and by more subtle characteristics of the learning. Under these conditions, subsequent decrement in retention between a test given one day after learning and a test given several days or several weeks later is dramatically greater for animals that are physiologically immature during learning.

Another way to approach the problem of separating learning and retention differences in immature and mature animals is to arrange experimental conditions so that the degree of original learning is clearly greater for the younger animals. If we assume that greater learning results in correspondingly better retention among animals of the same age, then if retention by immature animals with a high degree of original learning still is poorer than that by mature animals with a lower degree of learning, the most parsimonious conclusion is poorer retention by younger organisms. Such experiments have been completed, with the conclusion that young animals do retain more poorly than older animals.

Finally, it has been shown that under conditions that yield a greater decrement in retention over a long retention interval for immature rats than for adults, an orthogonal variable, intensity of the aversive stimulus, does not influence changes in retention, although shock intensity causes significant differences in the number of trials required to achieve the learning criterion (a measure not influenced by the age difference). Thus, under these conditions at least, learning differences are not sufficient to explain the occurrence of retention differences. So even if "real" age differences in learning were undetected by the measuring instrument, it does not follow that the retention effects were due to learning and not age differences. (For a review of these effects, see Campbell & Spear, 1972.)

Limits on generalizations about the ontogeny of retention.   Simple generalizations about individual differences and psychological capacities have long been both the temptation and the bane of experimental psychologists. Particularly enticing have been generalizations about the characteristics of cognitive processes such as those that constitute retention capacity. Since the publication of Hunter's (1913) monograph, questions of species differences in retention often have been raised. In response to questions such as "Can the pigeon tolerate as long a retention interval as the monkey?" researchers have attempted to set limits in absolute terms: Following a single presentation of a stimulus, it was assumed that a pigeon can tolerate an interval of little more than 5 seconds before evidence for retention of that stimulus diminishes, while a monkey's accuracy under similar circumstances is maintained for intervals of as long as 15 seconds (or is it 4 minutes, or 9 minutes? See D'Amato, 1973). It should be quite clear that such statements are premature even today (see Chapter 3). Just as rats or any other animals may be trained to perform the most amazing feats given enough patience by the trainer, conditions can be arranged following a single presentation of a stimulus so that pigeons exceed their "typical retention capacity," stretching it to 30 seconds or more under some circumstances (Grant, personal communication, 1975; Honig, 1974). Similarly, in view of the wide range over which memory processing may be manifested, absolute statements about the age at which retention capacity achieves a certain level are equally doomed. Such statements must be qualified heavily according to the procedures and tasks involved in the testing of retention. A clear illustration is provided by Volokhov (1970).

Volokhov shows that relationships between age and efficiency in memory processing are not stated readily in general terms even within a given species. In the dog, for example, learning of stimuli detected by differing sensory systems may differ widely as a function of the ages at which the dog first gives a primitive orienting response, a more mature investigatory response, and later, habituation to that stimulus (see Table 5.1). Volokhov cites evidence from the Russian literature indicating that appetitive conditioning in the dog may be found at 1 day of age if the conditioned stimulus involves olfaction and taste, 7 to 9 days of age if the conditioned stimulus is tactile temperature, 10 to 12 days of age if it is vestibular, and 15 to 16 days if it is auditory, and if the conditioned stimulus is visual, conditioning may not occur until the dog is 22 to 25 days of age (see Table 5.2).

In noting some disagreement within the Russian literature regarding the ontogenetic development of the dog's susceptibility to conditioning, Volokhov cites evidence that the relationship observed may depend on the requirements of the task: If a delay occurs between presentation of the conditioned and unconditioned stimuli, conditioning in very young dogs may proceed a good deal more slowly than in older animals, even though conditioning may be equally rapid in dogs of diverse ages in the absence of delay.

Volokhov cites additional evidence indicating that the relationship between conditioning and age of the animal may depend on the specific nature of the conditioned response; for example, special deficits in the conditioning of young animals occur whenever withholding of a response is required.

Lastly, Volokhov indicates that the age at which conditioning becomes effective also depends on the reinforcer and on phylogenetic status: Appetitive conditioning typically may occur prior to the age at which aversive conditioning is found, and "with highly organized animals (cat, dog, monkey) born immature [there is] a definite tendency for the formation of conditioned reflexes to occur at a later time period than in lower organized vertebrates (pigeon, rat, rabbit)" (1970, p. 599).

The evidence cited by Volokhov illustrates quite nicely the infeasibility of any general statement concerning the age at which an aspect of memory processing first becomes effective. While the ontogenetic relationships established in Vol-

TABLE 5.1[a]
Periods of Appearance, Development, and Extinction of the Orienting Reaction from the Different Sensory Systems in the Developing Dog

	Age when different stages appear (in days)		
Sensory system	Primitive reaction	Investigating reaction	Extinction reaction
Olfactory	1	1	38–48
Somesthetic	1	15–16	40–45
Auditory	9–15	16–24	40–45
Visual	15–19	20–28	52–68

[a]From Volokhov, 1970.

TABLE 5.2[a]
Appearance of the Alimentary Motor Conditioned Reflexes in the Dog
and Rabbit During Ontogeny (Days after Birth)

	Dog		Rabbit	
	(Troshikhin 1957)		(Ivanitsky 1958)	
Analyzer	Conditioned stimulus	Days after birth	Conditioned stimulus	Days after birth
Olfaction and taste	aromatic oils	1	Camphor oil	1
Tactile temperature	fan with hot air	7–9	fan with hot air	10–11
Vestibular	swinging	10–12	—	—
Auditory	bell tone 800 cps	15–16	tone 500 cps	11–13
Visual	lamp 40 W	22–25	lamp 40 W	13–15

[a]From Volokhov, 1970.

okhov's review appear to be accountable more directly to sensory or motor deficiencies than to fundamental changes in the processing of memories, the difficulties and complexities in achieving general conclusions about the latter are clearly evident. This does not preclude relatively circumscribed statements. For example, one may attain conclusions about the ontogeny of memory processing for a particular species and a definite set of events to be represented as a memory. Understanding this, we now may consider related questions under two separate headings: At what age does the capacity for retention begin to function, and at what age does such a capacity improve? In considering these questions, we shall refer most frequently to the ontogeny of learning and retention in rats and mice. The bulk of relevant data has been gathered in this context, and for good reason. A very great deal is known about the precise neurophysiological changes that occur in the growing rat and mouse, and environmental influences on these animals may be tightly regulated; it is inevitable that one or both of these factors is linked to the ontogenetic changes that occur in memory processing.

At What Age Does Capacity for Retention Begin to Function?

In recent years, a good deal of attention has been directed to the rate of behavioral development in rats, mice, and other animals classed as altricial (i.e., so immature and relatively helpless at birth that considerable parental care is required afterwards; the opposite class is "precocial"), and the factors that influence these rates of development. Included in this interest have been studies concerning memory processing. Caldwell and Werboff (1962) presented evidence that classical conditioning may occur within 1 to 8 hours after birth in the rat (also see, e.g., Fuller & Christake, 1959; Fuller, Easler, & Banks, 1950). Instrumental conditioning has been somewhat more difficult to study, but ingenious procedures have been devised to show such learning in the dog within the first few days of life (Bacon & Stanley, 1970; Stanley, 1970).

It has been customary to assume that a particular level of neural maturation must be achieved for learning to occur. Thus, the onset of learning often is taken as an important index of development (e.g., Scott & Fuller, 1965). Increasingly, however, scientists have become more sensitive to the interrelationships among phylogenetically and ontogenetically determined capacities for certain behaviors and to the many intricacies in the measurement of learning. As a consequence of these developments, it has become increasingly clear that "onset of learning" is unlikely to be identified in such general terms, and without further qualifications as to the nature of the learning, "onset" is unlikely to be useful as a developmental index.

Given the apparent capacity for learning in the simplest of organisms (probably even in single-cell animals), and given the capacity for conditioning of a single neuron within a larger system of neurons, we should not be surprised to find that increasingly sensitive measures of behavioral plasticity will show a given species of animal to be capable of learning at increasingly younger ages. The importance of measurement technique is exemplified in the insightful studies of Rosenblatt (e.g., 1972) showing that within the first postnatal hours kittens acquire subtle discriminations, not only tactile in nature but olfactory and thermal as well, in order to become efficient in acquiring nourishment from a particular nipple.

The point is that beyond the identification of initial capacities for memory storage and learning soon after birth even in altricial animals, we may anticipate that with properly sensitive measuring instruments, the capacities to learn, and perhaps the manifestation of this learning as well, will be found in early prenatal stages. Approached from this perspective, studies of the ontogeny of learning may be no less important, but they do take on a different character than has been attributed to them in the past.

We are concerned here not with the onset of learning but with the onset of retention. Investigations of this issue are plagued with many of the same difficulties associated with determining the onset of learning. These investigations, however, have the advantage of beginning with an established preparation known to index learning (and so retention as well) at a particular age. Thus, for example, the difficulty in isolating the onset of memory-processing capacities from those of sensory–motor capacities is avoided. Also, when studying retention the question to be asked when manipulating the age variable is in a form perhaps best suited for the investigation of such a subject variable: The question concerns the *interaction* between age and an experimenter-controlled environmental variable, presence-versus-absence of a source of forgetting. For the most part, the "source of forgetting" manipulated in the studies we shall discuss is an interval between learning and testing. Within this orientation, rather than providing an answer to the question "At what stage of ontogenetic development does the capacity for retention commence?" we are limited to asking, "At what age does a source of forgetting have less influence than at an earlier age?"

Even in this restricted form, however, ontogenetic investigations are subject to a number of methodological and interpretive difficulties, and we do not wish to minimize these. For example, a memory acquired in early infancy may be manifested later in terms of a different behavior more appropriate to that later stage of development (e.g., Rosenblatt, 1971), and this presents clear problems in measurement of retention when an interval is the source of forgetting. Throughout our discussion, we shall consider methodological problems such as these. For now, we turn to a set of experiments that have investigated the question of the onset of the capacity for retention.

The Misanin-Nagy studies. The most thorough set of studies treating the ontogenetic emergence of both learning and retention has been conducted by Misanin, Nagy, and their colleagues, testing aversive conditioning in the neonatal rat and mouse (e.g., Misanin, Nagy, Keiser, & Bowen, 1971; Nagy, Misanin, Newman, Olsen, & Hinderliter, 1972). We now turn our attention to these studies.

The procedure employed by Misanin and Nagy includes training of neonatal rats and mice to perform an instrumental response in order to escape a mild shock delivered through a grid floor. The task initially employed was a straight runway in which learning apparently was manifested over successive training trials by a progressive decrease in competing behavior (where "competing behavior" is a turn by the animal that does not enhance its progress toward shock termination in the goal at the opposite end of the runway). With this task, mice of a certain genetic strain (C_3H) exhibited learning by the age of 3 days, and relatively mixed-strain mice (Swiss-Webster) and rats (Wistar) showed learning at about 5 days of age. Significant savings in retention tests were obtained only for animals 9 days of age and older. A large number of control conditions were needed to establish these relationships, but even though these were adequate, some interpretive difficulties resulted from indexing learning in terms of competing behavior.

In the Misanin-Nagy studies, several functional relationships were established in terms of the competing-response index of escape learning. For example, mice trained at 8 days of age exhibit significant retention in terms of a relearning test given after 1 hour, less retention after 6 hours, and no evidence of retention after 24 hours. In mice trained at 10 days of age, significant retention is found at each of these intervals (Nagy, Misanin, & Westel, 1973). On the same task with rats as subjects, retention after 24 hours is significant for animals trained when 9 days old but not for those trained when 7 days old. Furthermore, rats trained at 9 days of age and rendered amnesic by hypothermia (rapid cooling of the animal soon after training) showed an effect that is well established with adult animals: The amnesic effect is greater the sooner hypothermia follows training (Misanin et al.,

1971). Misanin and his associates interpret the latter effect as indicating the development at 9 days of age of adult-like processes for long-term retention.

Degree of learning and retention by neonates.   Nagy and Mueller (1973) investigated the possibility that in 9-day-old mice the apparent onset of the capacity for retention after 24 hours is attributable to a higher degree of learning by these animals compared to younger mice, rather than to processes more directly responsible for retention. Groups of mice trained at either 7 or 9 days of age received 0, 10, 25, or 40 trials of massed practice in the straight-alley escape task. When the mice were tested 24 hours later, significant retention was found for all groups of the 9-day-old mice but for none of the 7-day-old mice, including the 7-day-olds that had received 40 training trials. Even the 9-day-olds given only 10 trials showed significant retention. But although the acquisition performance of 7-day-old mice given 40 training trials was quite similar to that of 9-day-olds given 25 training trials, retention by the 7-day-olds was nonsignificant after all levels of training.

These results tend to support the view that the inferior retention by the younger animals is indeed due to characteristics of ontogenetic development other than degree of original learning. This interpretation is supported further by data based on retention of a discrimination: Nagy, Pagano, and Gable (1976) could find no evidence of savings 24 hours after T-maze (position) training of 9-day-old mice, whether 12, 24, or 40 training trials had been given, although 11-day-old mice showed better retention with more training trials. Variation in shock intensity also has not altered the ontogenetic relationships found in terms of retention (Nagy, 1976). While caution is still appropriate and more studies of this sort would be helpful, we may tentatively conclude that these ontogenetic effects on retention are not due to simple confounding of age by differences in degree of learning or, in the case of the discrimination measure, differences in effective shock intensity.

Interpretive problems and improved procedures.   Two problems arose in the interpretation of results obtained with the particular competing-response measure employed by Misanin and Nagy, problems that threatened to impede the progress of this valuable series of studies. First, risk is always present in using a response measure that requires a subjective judgment on the part of the experimenter (in terms of what is and what is not a competing response). However, the definitions used by these investigators (a 180° turn constituted a competing response) and the many replications by various experimenters within their laboratories indicate that this is less of a problem than ordinarily might be the case. A more difficult problem concerns lack of auxiliary evidence of learning, especially for the youngest neonates. With the straight-alley escape task, 5-day-old rats and mice progressively decreased the number of competing responses exhibited during training, but their *speeds* of escaping did not improve. This puzzle caused some theorists to dismiss the data of Misanin, Nagy, and their coworkers for learning in rodents under 13 days of age (Campbell, Riccio, & Rohrbaugh, 1971). In combination, these problems encouraged the view that the studies of Misanin and Nagy reflected ontogenetic changes in reactivity to shock, rather than learning.

Aware of these difficulties, Misanin, Nagy, and their colleagues analyzed their straight-alley escape task more closely with a variety of response measures. In addition, they began to employ discriminative escape learning, in which neonates not only were required to move from one location to another but also had to select the alternative path that led to escape rather than the other path, which led to further shock. Without considering the details of this analysis (see Misanin, Haigh, Hinderliter, & Nagy, 1973), several conclusions are justified. When tested on the discriminative escape task, a T-maze position discrimination, neither rats nor mice 9 days of age or younger were likely to solve the discrimination, although it could readily be solved by mice a day or two older. Older animals also exhibited retention of this acquired discrimination over a 24-hour period (Misanin et al., 1973; Nagy & Sandmann, 1973). The relationship between age and acquisition of the position discrimination is depicted in Figure 5.1.

Misanin and his associates (1973) further determined that rats as young as 7 days of age increase their speed of escape with training, but this does not occur for 5-day-olds. For 5-day-old rats, moreover, reduction in competing behavior was as likely to develop in animals given noncontingent shock as in those given shock that terminated when the escape response occurred. However, many of the behavioral consequences of the escape training that occurred in the trained rats did *not* occur in 5-day-old control animals given only noncontingent shock. This convinced Misanin and his associates that animals of this age indeed do have the capacity for instrumental learning in this situation. Noting that the typical escape learning task, even in a straight alley, requires an animal to learn not only to move but also to move in a particular direction, Misanin, Chubb, Quinn, and Schweikert (1974) devised a nondirectional escape task. In this task, the rat could escape by climbing, in *any* direction, out of a small, well-like depression in the floor of the apparatus. With this task, rats both 5 and 7 days of age increased their speed of escaping over 25 training trials.

Misanin and Nagy's major contribution to this area is in expanding and elaborating the evidence to indicate that the ontogeny of retention capacity is not isomorphic to the ontogeny of learning capacity. This has been shown by other investigators (see Campbell & Spear, 1972), but with animals a good bit more mature neurophysiologically than those tested by Misanin and Nagy. This suggests that in order to understand the ontogeny of retention capacity, we may need to consider neurophysiological and behavioral changes occurring at the young ages dealt with by Misanin and Nagy in the same way that we consider these changes occurring with the older, though still immature, animals.

We now may consider what is known about the latter cases. In doing so, the questions posed no longer are those concerning the emergence of retention capac-

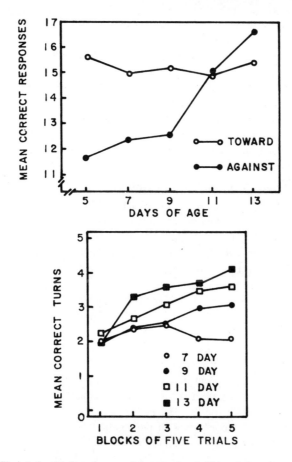

Figure 5.1   The relationship between age of the animal and efficacy in learning a spatial discrimination to escape footshock is shown for rats (upper figure) and mice (lower figure). The upper figure indicates that this relationship is clearest when the animals are trained against their initial turning preference. The lower figure shows the differential course of acquisition of the discrimination across blocks of five trials for mice of different ages (the upper figure is adapted from Misanin et al., 1973. Copyright 1973 by the American Psychological Association. Reproduced by permission. The lower figure from Nagy and Murphy, 1974.)

ity; instead, the question is, At what age does the capacity for retention become adult-like?

At What Age Does the Capacity for Retention Improve?: Infantile Amnesia

Aging appears to induce at least two significant changes in retention capacity. The first is that information acquired by very young organisms, however rapidly acquired and readily accessible for retrieval in infancy or early childhood, suffers extraordinary forgetting when the organism becomes an adult. Second, information acquired by unusually old adults also may be subject to extraordinary forgetting. Both effects have a wealth of anecdotal support, but both are extremely difficult problems to deal with experimentally. A good bit more is known about the former effect, which we call infantile amnesia, than about the latter, senile amnesia, both in terms of the nature of the effect and in terms of the physiological and psychological factors that might be used to explain it. Therefore, most of this section will deal with infantile amnesia. This topic initially received attention within the context of human memory processing, so it is this aspect that we will consider first.

Infantile amnesia in humans. In spite of a keen capacity for memory processing in infants and toddlers, often astonishing even to their delighted parents, there is an equally clear *failure* in retention of events encountered during this period once adolescence and adulthood are reached. The questions we shall consider are whether this effect has the status of a general biological phenomenon and, if so, how it might be explained. First, however, we shall appraise some early investigations of this effect.

Assuming that past experience is responsible for one's psychological adjustment, it is obvious that personality theorists and psychoanalysts would be interested in infantile amnesia. Freud believed that the early experiences of childhood were forgotten in the process of repressing infantile sexuality. It is interesting to note Freud's implication that such an effect might represent a general biological function, independent of cultural education. Thus, we would expect the effect to appear widely, perhaps among animals as well as humans (Freud, 1935; see Schachtel, 1947, pp. 2, 3).

Within this context of concern with personality development, a number of intriguing and encompassing explanations for infantile amnesia have been suggested, largely in the absence of systematic data. Allport (1937) summarized the following as prevalent interpretations: Unlike adult experiences, the experiences of an infant are not represented verbally, so they are unavailable for conscious conceptualization; the context of early experience is viewed so differently by young children and adults that recall of events within that context cannot occur in adulthood; events that occurred during an infant's hedonistic existence are repressed when the "reality principle" is encountered; and finally (in terms of the limited knowledge of the central nervous system at that time) lack of myelinization in the areas of the brain that ordinarily would store memories prevents maintenance of "traces" of the infant's experience. Schachtel (1947) suggested a combination of the verbalization and context interpretations mentioned by Allport: "The categories (or schemata) of adult memory are not suitable receptacles for early childhood experiences and therefore not fit to preserve these experiences and enable their recall" (p. 4). Noting the importance, in a child's world, of smells, tastes, and affective states for which linguistic representation is inadequate (even for adults), Schachtel implied that as adults we simply may lose the mechanisms by which events previously were represented. Said Schachtel, "The adult is usually not capable of experiencing what the child experiences; more often than not he is not even capable of imagining what the child experiences" (1947, p. 4).

Endless, and thoughtful, speculation on the basis of infantile amnesia exists in the literature. But, like the discussions of mnemonics by ancient philosophers, there is an absence of substance in terms of empirical evidence. We must turn to a more systematic consideration of data collected from clinical, anecdotal, and questionnaire sources, which will carry us closer to substantial evidence.

Preliminary empirical sketches of infantile amnesia in humans. Evidence concerning retention of the events of early childhood has been obtained simply by asking people to describe their earliest memories. A surprising number of studies of this sort have been conducted (for reviews, see Dudycha & Dudycha, 1941; Waldfogel, 1948). The techniques of asking about early memories have varied from mailed questionnaires to personal interviews and introspections carried to a reasonable degree of thoroughness. The validity of the events individuals report to have occurred in childhood sometimes has been checked fairly carefully (Dudycha & Dudycha, 1933), but probably more often this validity check—a critical issue in such research—has not been made. Most of the data are based on reports by university students, but faculty members, nonuniversity adults, adolescents, and children as young as 6 or 7 years old also have served as subjects.

Throughout all methods of study, there is fairly general agreement that very few specific events that occurred prior to the third or fourth year of life can be recalled, but for succeeding years the number of such events recalled increases sharply. Dudycha and Dudycha (1941) cite five substantial studies that report the average age of the earliest reported memory as 3.0, 3.0, 3.5, 3.7, and 3.8 years. Mare (1935) found that from among 270 autobiographies only three authors reported experiences that occurred before the age of 2, and only 13 before the age of 3. While there are occasional reports of memories occurring in the first year of life (and at least one subject claimed to have remembered being born), Dudycha and Dudycha (1933) found that only 4% of the valid memories they recorded fell in the first year.

When subjects were asked to report their earliest memories of fearful experiences, Means (1936) found that only 9% reported such memories as registered before the age of 6, and Jersild and Holmes (1935) found that 21% reported fearful memories registered before the age of 5. Although some emotional content usually is included in the earliest memories of childhood, there is disagreement over whether pleasant or unpleasant memories are more likely to be recalled.

Dudycha and Dudycha (1941) consider some interesting breakdowns of the data. Females seem to recall earlier memories than males, although the differences are rather small. More substantial differences are found in the content of earliest memories; women seem more likely than men to report minor details and memories involving "joy," but males are more likely to report memories involving "fear." Most of the reported memories were in the visual modality, in agreement with the results of an experiment by Lindquist (1945) that suggested that "a child's visual memory appears at a considerably earlier age than its auditory memory" (p. 595).

These relationships may be taken merely as entertainment or as a source of ideas for experiments or pretheoretical concepts. They should not be taken as factual relationships concerning retention. Controlled experimental tests are needed to establish the credibility of the basic phenomenon of relatively poor retention of specific early experiences after a very long interval.

Preliminary experimental tests of infantile amnesia in humans. Until recent years, it was very rare for behavioral experiments to be conducted on young children or infants except where the child happened to be the offspring of an experimental psychologist. Even today, rarely can one arrange experimental circumstances such that long-term retention can be tested with such young subjects. One suitable example, however, is an experiment by Lindquist (1945). This experiment is lacking in methodological rigor, to be sure, and is somewhat "folksy" in its approach, but it is valuable nevertheless. Linquist was concerned with how accurate young children would be in recognizing their mothers after they have been separated for varying lengths of time. He conducted these tests on children who had been confined to the hospital and, for various reasons, were not visited by their mothers for some period of time.

The ages of the children varied between 6 and 36 months. Just before the child was ready to leave the hospital, Linquist recorded whether the child recognized its mother and how this recognition was accomplished. The measurement technique was rather crude. At first the mother stood behind a screen so that the child could not see her, and spoke a few words without saying the child's name. If the child did not indicate recognition, the mother then stood a few yards away from the child and smiled, but did not speak. If there still were no signs of recognition, the mother was permitted to go very near the child and speak to it. Lindquist's method of scoring recognition also was crude, admittedly so, but says Lindquist: "As a rule the child lights up in a quite special way, looks steadily at its mother in spite of other persons being present, laughs in most cases, moves its legs and breathes more rapidly. Older children begin to cry and, if they are able to talk, to call for 'mother' " (1945, p. 595).

In all, 85 children were tested for recognition after periods of separation from their mothers of 2 to 54 days. Among the 6 children tested at 6 months of age, only 1 recognition was registered after an interval of 5 days, and none following longer intervals. Lindquist presented his data graphically in terms of responding by individual subjects and was appropriately cautious concerning its interpretive value. As an approximation, however, these data may be summarized as follows:

Between the ages of 6 and 9 months where retention intervals ranged from 4 to 54 days, mothers were recognized on 24% of the occasions. Recognition increased markedly thereafter: For ages 6 to 12 (inclusive), 13 to 24, and 25 to 36 months, recognition was 48%, 67%, and 92%, respectively. For these ages, the longest intervals that accompanied a recognition were 22, 23, and 35 days. It is of some interest that none of the 51 infants younger than 16 months of age were scored as having recognized their mother's *voice,* regardless of the retention interval.

In an experiment with some similarities to Lindquist's, Levy (1960) investigated how well infants remember the aversive circumstances of receiving an inoculation. He found generally that up until the age of 6 months, infants who had been inoculated previously were indistinguishable from infants who had not been injected. Thereafter, retention of a previous inoculation gradually increased with age.

Toward better techniques for assessing memory processing by human infants.   While the studies by Lindquist and Levy did not depend on introspections by the subject to assess retention, measurement was still largely qualitative and based essentially on the judgment of the principal investigator. In recent years, much more has been learned about the behavior of infants and how to quantify the products of memory processing.

One technique that has become used widely employs measurement of habituation to more or less novel stimuli as the index of information processing by the infant. Habituation typically has been measured in terms of either duration of eye fixation or heart rate. Both of these measures are influenced markedly by presenting the infant with novel stimuli. The study of attention processes in particular has employed this procedure (e.g., Kagan & Lewis, 1965), and its extrapolation to other processes (whether warranted or not) has been rapid. For example, Kagan (1972) has used such data as the basis of his suggestion that the age of 8 to 9 months "marks the maturational frontier when infants begin to generate hypotheses" (p. 81).

Some investigators have asked how long information may be held by very young infants; that is, what is their capacity for retention? Pancratz and Cohen (1970) tested 16 male and 16 female infants 4 to 5 months old. Subjects were presented a simple stimulus to which habituation was known to be rapid (a green circle, blue triangle, red square, or yellow rod). Each infant was given ten 15-second presentations with .1 second between each presentation. During successive presentations, eye fixations by the male subjects progressively declined while fixations by the female subjects did not. For our purposes, we shall ignore this interesting sex difference and concentrate on the retention shown by the male subjects.

A retention test was given either immediately or 5 minutes after the initial 10 presentations. This test consisted of exposure to the previous stimulus, presented exactly as before except that novel stimuli were interpolated between presentations. The purpose of the novel stimuli was to separate fatigue and habituation effects; to the extent that the subjects fixated on the novel stimuli, decline in responding to the familiar stimuli could not be attributed to fatigue.

On the immediate test, retention of the habituation to the familiar stimulus was clearly evident; eye fixations on the familiar stimulus were only about one-third the duration of the fixations on the novel stimulus. After a 5-minute retention interval, however, fixation duration to the familiar and novel stimuli did not differ, indicating complete forgetting of the habituation over this interval.

As a matter of interest, we may note that immature rats, like human infants, habituate more slowly than their adult counterparts, and also may forget habituation a good deal more rapidly than older animals (e.g., Feigley, Parsons, Hamilton, & Spear, 1972; Parsons, Fagan, & Spear 1973; Williams, Hamilton, & Carlton, 1975). While such forgetting has not been tested directly in humans of different ages, the Pancratz and Cohen results imply that infants may forget habituation more rapidly than older children.

As techinques improve, we may expect to learn more about such forgetting in immature humans. For example, it has already been suggested by Fagan (1970, 1971) that the technique employed by Pancratz and Cohen may have underestimated retention capacity in infants. Fagan found that when the retention tests consisted of simultaneous presentation of a familiar and a novel stimulus, retention of habituation was maintained over intervals as long as 7 minutes. In the future, we can expect to learn much more about the ontogeny of retention from such studies (for a review of this work, see Cohen & Gelber, 1975).

At best, such data relate only tangentially to infantile amnesia. These studies do show that in spite of considerable learning capacity in human infants, and even neonates, retention capacity appears relatively transitory. So far, however, nothing has been determined about whether these apparent differences between infants and older children really reflect differences in retention or are only a consequence of differing degrees of original learning. More important perhaps, the retention intervals tested have been on the order of seconds, minutes, or at most days, and have not approached the intervals of several years that constitute the commonly observed infantile amnesia effects.

It is here that research on lower animals makes a major contribution. Biomedical research long has depended on the use of animal subjects when humans cannot be employed for one reason or another.

Infantile amnesia in animals.   We mentioned earlier that the development of tasks that could be learned equally rapidly by immature and mature animals and psychophysical studies by Campbell (1967) led to experiments with evidence that there is a deficiency in long-term retention for memories acquired prior to neurophysiological maturity. We have briefly cited some of the techniques employed to ensure that the retention differences found were due to the animal's age and not to age-related differences in degree of learning or motivation (see also Campbell & Spear, 1972). Retention typically is compared between rats within the age range of 15 to 24 days and adult rats 80 days of age or older. After intervals of a few weeks following learning, retention is poorer for the younger animals, although rates of acquisition, resistance to extinction, and short-term retention may have been equivalent; in some cases, retention has been poorer for the younger animals even though their degree of original learning was greater.

Among several sets of experiments indicating infantile amnesia in animals, three are of particular interest. Figure 5.2 shows retention of active avoidance behavior after 1 or 28 days for animals that had mastered the one-way avoidance task to a criterion of 5 consecutive avoidances prior to the retention interval. These previously unpublished data were gathered by Norman Richter in our laboratory at the onset of our work on this problem. The effect clearly is greater forgetting for animals younger at the time of training. Feigley and Spear (1970) compared retention of weanling and adult animals on the same active avoidance task, with orthogonal variation in intensity of the footshock, the UCS. The results (see Figure 5.3) indicated that over all levels of shock intensity, forgetting over 28 days was greater in the younger animals.

Feigley and Spear (1970) also trained animals on a passive avoidance task when either weanlings or adults (see Figure 5.4). Separate groups of animals were

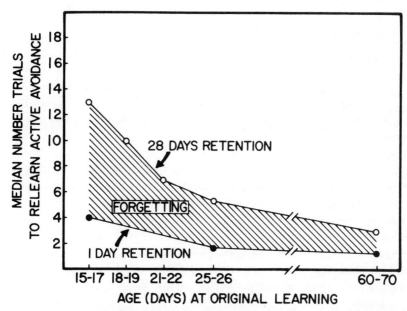

Figure 5.2   Amount of forgetting of one-way active avoidance by rats over a 28 day retention interval is shown for animals that learned active avoidance originally at different ages. The lower line indicates the relearning of one set of animals tested one day after attainment of the active avoidance criterion of five consecutive avoidances and the upper line indicates the relearning of another set of animals tested 28 days after learning, to this same criterion. (Unpublished data: Richter, N.G. & Spear, N.E. 1968).

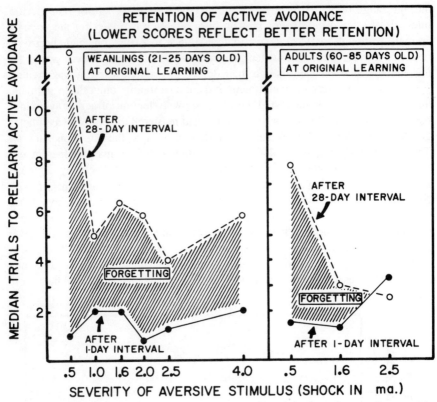

Figure 5.3   Forgetting of one-way active avoidance by animals trained as either weanlings or adults is shown as a function of the intensity of the footshock employed as the UCS (the same intensity was employed during acquisition and the retention test). Adapted from Feigley & Spear, 1970. Copyright 1970 by the American Psychological Association. Reproduced by permission.

trained under different intensities and durations of punishment (footshock) for stepping from one compartment to another. Each animal was trained to a criterion of three consecutive passive avoidances. Retention after 28 days obviously was poorer for the younger animals in all conditions of footshock intensity and duration.

Figure 5.5 shows retention of a position discrimination acquired by rats between the ages of 15 and 35 days and tested after intervals of 1, 7, or 14 days. This figure indicates more rapid forgetting the younger the animal, a relationship that is not predictable on the basis of either rate of acquiring the position discrimination or terminal acquisition performance prior to the retention interval.

We have not exhausted the applicable data indicating infantile amnesia in animals. Furthermore, other data suggesting such an effect in a variety of indexes of a memory, including classical fear conditioning (Campbell & Campbell, 1962; Spear & Parsons, 1976) and the conditioned emotional response (CER; Coulter,

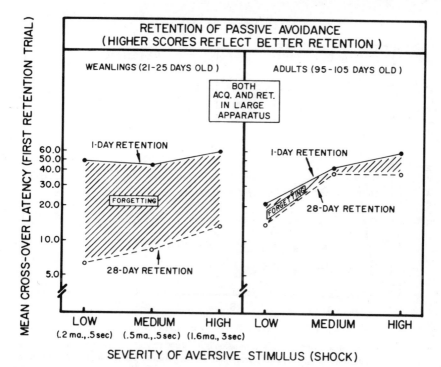

Figure 5.4   Forgetting of passive avoidance over a 28 day retention interval is shown for rats that had learned passive avoidance either as weanlings or as adults. The groups differed in the intensity and duration of the footshock used as punishment for failing to passively avoid. The higher the latency on the ordinate, the better the retention (Adapted from Feigley & Spear, 1970).

Collier, & Campbell, 1976), cannot be admitted as applicable evidence because there is uncertainty about differences in degree of original learning. Even in these cases, however, it seems unlikely that degree of learning can account for all of the differential retention obtained; much of this variance probably is due to age differences. When immature animals have not shown more rapid forgetting than adults, this seems to be attributable to the relatively advanced age of the youngest animals at the conclusion of acquisition training (e.g., Doty, 1966), or to procedures expected to minimize the influence of the age differences on retention (e.g., Thompson, Koenigsberg, & Tennison, 1965; see also Campbell & Spear, 1972).

Campbell and Spear (1972) have suggested several potential explanations for infantile amnesia in animals, including explanations based primarily on experiential factors or primarily on aspects of neurophysiological maturation. Without reiterating the content of these suggestions, we will consider briefly some examples of experiential factors and neurophysiological maturation in rats, and how these may enter into explanations for infantile amnesia.

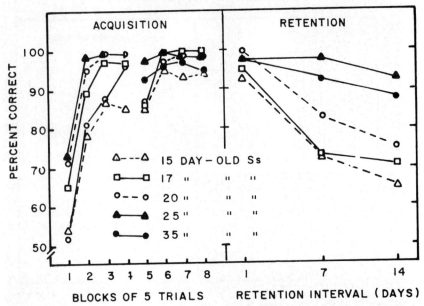

Figure 5.5   Performance on a spatial discrimination is indicated for rats that acquired the discrimination when 15 to 35 days of age. The left panel indicates acquisition performance completed at the ages indicated and the right panel indicates retention performance 1, 7, or 14 days after acquisition (adapted from Campbell et al., 1974. Copyright 1974 by the American Psychological Association. Reprinted by permission.)

Selected Details of Physiological and Behavioral Development in the Rat

The newborn rat is a distinctly unattractive, hairless creature with an almost reptilian appearance (see Figure 5.6). This altricial mammal has no known cognitive abilities at birth, unlike the precocial guinea pig, which readily can learn to press a lever to obtain nourishment within an hour after it is born. There is some evidence that by 2 days of age the rat may give some weak signs of response to the odor of its mother, but response to distinctive odors is not certain until about the seventh or eighth day after birth. In most other respects as well, it is several days after birth before the neonatal rat behaves with any apparent concern for its environment beyond the source of its milk.

Fortunately for the rat population, this period of helplessness is accompanied by an amazing capacity for resisting destruction. The newborn rat can tolerate anoxia for almost an hour, whereas an adult rat under similar conditions is rendered unconscious within seconds; the neonatal rat is essentially poikilothermic and can survive a temporary body temperature as low as 1°C, while adult rats die if their temperature lowers to 15°C.

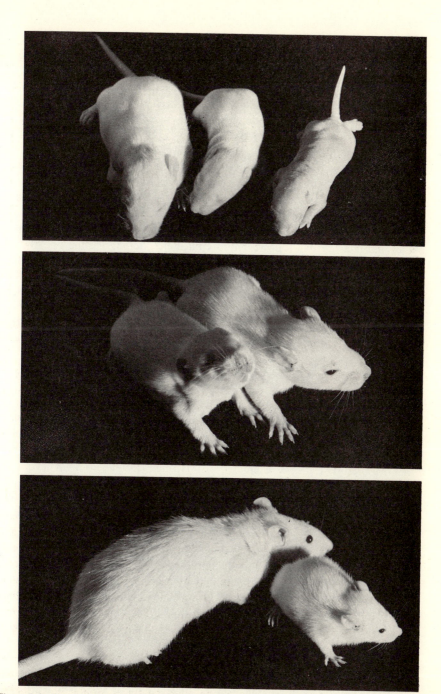

Figure 5.6 Rats of differing ages are shown to illustrate physical changes during growth. Figure 5.6a shows rats of the ages 3, 5 and 7 days (shown right to left); Figure 5.6b shows an 11 day old rat on the left (eyes not yet open) next to a 15 day old rat; Figure 5.6c shows a 60 day old rat (sexually mature) with a 21 day old rat (age of weaning in most laboratories).

Two weeks after birth, the infant rat will have developed into an attractive, toy-like animal (see Figure 5.6), soft and furry and increasingly mobile. Its capacity for learning about its environment is evident; for instance, rats at this age readily discriminate some odors: For otherwise identical environments, they prefer the one that has the odor of their home nest (Gregory & Pfaff, 1971). This capacity also may be responsible for the 2-week-old rat's apparent emotional response to separation from its mother. One immediate consequence of separation is a loss of about 3°C in body temperature (Hofer, 1973). But even if body temperatures are maintained at the same level as in the nest, striking behavioral and physiological changes occur when these animals are in a novel environment. Their mobility increases. They increase the number of times they raise their bodies and their heads. Their respiratory rates are altered, and their heart rates drop drastically and persevere at these lower levels for some time. While 2-week-old rat pups placed in the same sort of novel environment *with* their mothers also may have a somewhat slowed heart rate, this persists for only about 2 minutes (Hofer, 1973).

These effects are stronger and more regular for 14–15-day-old rats than for younger ones. Also, of course, these effects differ for older rats. One week later, these pups quite readily will leave their nest area and will not be discouraged from doing so by their mother, whose milk will have declined in quality and who will retrieve the pups less often when they stray from the nest. In the interim, further dramatic physiological and behavioral changes occur.

The rat's eyes begin to open between 13 and 15 days of age. Shortly thereafter, its patterns of mobility become adult-like, shifting from a low crawl to more discrete stepping. At 15 days of age, spontaneous activity peaks in isolated rats (e.g., Moorcroft, Lytle, & Campbell, 1971), then declines to adult levels between the ages of 25 and 30 days. Next there begins a series of changes in the central nervous system (CNS) that appear particularly likely to be relevant to the ontogeny of memory processing. Most of these changes, which we shall discuss shortly, are monotonic and reach asymptote in adulthood. However, some, like spontaneous activity, may be nonmonotonic. Such nonmonotonic changes with age are not well understood, but are intriguing. For example, Essman (1973) presents data suggesting that the 17-day-old mouse, in comparison with *either* younger or older mice of the same kind, has higher endogenous rates of protein synthesis in areas of the CNS linked to memory processing, including the cerebral cortex, basal ganglia, and diencephalon and midbrain. Protein synthesis is viewed by some as essential to memory storage (see Chapter 6); do 17-day-old mice have a special need for memory storage?

As our knowledge concerning neurophysiological systems important to memory processing grows in parallel with the increasingly detailed ontogenetic description of these neurophysiological systems and other related behaviors, we can begin to piece together hypotheses about how the ontogeny of memory processing is related to neurophysiological development. What is known about neurophysiological development has become increasingly coordinated (see

Gottlieb, 1974; Himwich, 1970; Riesen, 1975; Rosenzweig & Bennett, 1976; Sterman, McGinty, & Adinolfi, 1971), and Campbell and Spear (1972) have suggested possible relationships between the development of specific aspects of neurophysiology and the development of retention capacity. Following is a brief review of this and related material.

Ontogeny of the endocrine system. The importance of hormones in the development, maintenance, and performance of animals is widely recognized. Furthermore, a deficit or excess of any of several hormones may influence not only the animal's later appearance and behavior in general but perhaps in learning capacity as well. While the latter is still somewhat questionable, relevant supportive data are growing rapidly. For instance, Schapiro (1968, 1971), Davenport (e.g., Davenport, Gonzalez, Hennies, & Hagquist, 1976), and others (Murphy & Nagy, 1976; Rego, 1976; Stone & Greenough, 1975) have marshaled evidence to argue that varying quantities of thyroxin in the neonatal rat may influence later learning and retention over short intervals. The relationship of such effects to the development of long-term retention is not yet apparent, however.

At present, the hormone that has been linked most often to learning and retention is the adrenocorticotrophic hormone (ACTH) secreted by the anterior pituitary (and probably by the posterior pituitary as well). This hormone long has been recognized for its action in the release of steroids from the adrenal cortex. A good deal is known about how ACTH and these corticosteroids reciprocally control each other's activations by servomechanisms. Both substances are suspected, however, of having additional functions. For example, ACTH has been hypothesized to have a general excitatory effect, and some corticosteroids have a net depressive or inhibitory effect (McEwen & Weiss, 1970). At the level of individual neurons in certain subcortical brain areas, corticosteroids (or their artificial stimulator, dexamethasone) seem typically to be inhibitory and only seldom are excitatory, while ACTH activates many of these neurons (Steiner, 1970). Several studies have indicated that if the polypeptide ACTH is fragmented such that the amino acids responsible for its effect on the adrenals are eliminated, there nevertheless is an effect of the substance on instrumental conditioning and extinction, which may reflect an influence on the learning process (e.g., DeWied & Weijnan, 1970; Gold & Van Buskirk, 1976; J. A. Gray, personal communication, 1974). In other words, regardless of the effect of ACTH on the adrenals, which is conventionally believed to be its primary or only function, it may nevertheless influence learning. Furthermore, some retention phenomena have been shown to be sensitive to manipulations of endogenous ACTH (Klein, 1972). For this reason, some mention of the ontogeny of adrenal pituitary activity is relevant here.

The most dramatic aspect of the development of the adrenal–pituitary system is that it appears to be nearly nonfunctional for several days after birth in the rat. Analysis of the blood of the newborn rat often indicates adrenal–pituitary activity. In part, this probably is due to interaction with the mother. Although such activity is found with adrenalectomized mothers, it could possibly be due to action on the fetal adrenals by the mother's ACTH, which may (or may not) pass through the placental barrier. What is clear is that adrenal–pituitary response to stress is damped if not shut off in the newborn. If the fetus does indeed show an appropriate adrenal–pituitary response to stress, as some literature suggests, a massive refractory period must be caused by birth: A wide variety of stressors, all of which result in the release of ACTH within a few minutes in adults, have been found to have little or no influence on the release of ACTH for rat pups between the ages of about 1 and 10 days. There is some variation across studies, but it does appear that ACTH secretion is unlikely to be provoked in the rat before at least the fifth day postpartum, while nearly all stressors do so after the fourteenth day. The reason for this "stress-nonresponsive" ("stress-underresponsive" is more accurate) period is somewhat mysterious. It cannot be due to ineffectiveness of the ACTH existing in the pituitary of the neonatal rat. The amount of ACTH activity possible in the 1-day-old rat is quite sufficient to stimulate corticoid release from the adrenals if that ACTH were released in the circulation (Schapiro, 1968). The implication is that the stress-nonresponsive period in neonates is due to a deficiency in the signal that ordinarily is responsible for the release of ACTH from the pituitary upon the occurrence of stress. The anterior pituitary has a vascular, though not a neuronal, connection with the hypothalamus, and it is likely that the hypothalamus is responsible to some extent for controlling the release of ACTH. During this period, the hypothalamus seems to be immature in a number of neurological ways, and probably functionally as well (e.g., Lytle, Moorecraft, & Campbell, 1971). There are other possible sources of this nonresponse period. For example, it has been hypothesized that through the action of secretory cells in the median eminence region of the hypothalamus, a so-far-unidentified substance termed the corticotrophin releasing factor (CRF) is secreted and carried through the hypophyseal portal vascular system to the pituitary, where it effects ACTH release. Schapiro (1968) has noted that during the first week of the rat's life there is no detectable CRF activity in the hypothalamus. Furthermore, the hypophyseal portal vascular system itself is not established until about five days after birth. Another substance suspected to be responsible for the activation of ACTH, vasopressin (a hormone released from the posterior pituitary) also is deficient in these neonatal rats.

There are a variety of other respects in which the adrenal–pituitary response to stress is immature in the neonate. For example, infant rats metabolize corticoids a good deal more slowly than adults. Shapiro and his colleagues have recorded the half-life of the dominant adrenal steroid in the rat, corticosterone, as about 100 minutes in the 2-day-old rat; it is about 25 minutes in the adult. Because circulating corticosterone has the effect of inhibiting further release of ACTH, this may be viewed as another factor potentially relevant to the ontogeny of memory processing. Although the relationship between maturation of the pituitary-adrenal system and memory processing remains speculative, recent evidence implicating the hormonal activity of this system in memory processing suggests such a relationship may be important.

Ontogeny of neuronal morphology.   Sphingomyelin is a lipid found in all neuronal membranes and is a major component of myelin, the white fatty substance that surrounds and insulates neurons. Myelin originates from the membrane of glial cells that repeatedly wrap themselves around the axon of a neuron. Because it is detected easily, myelin was one of the first elements in the CNS suspected to be important for behavior. To some, myelin seemed all the more important because it was so sparse in neonatal altricial animals (including humans), and perhaps also because the rough analogy with insulated electrical wiring was so congenial. We have mentioned already that Allport (1937) suggested the lack of myelinization in the infant as one basis for infantile amnesia. We know also that individuals in whom myelin does not develop suffer a mental retardation, which has been termed the Spielmyer–Vogt syndrome. In rats and humans, the maturation of myelinization in the brain is roughly correlated with the appearance of adult-like capacities for long-term retention.

The development of myelin in the brain proceeds, like other neurophysiological characteristics, in a generally caudal–rostral direction. Myelin begins to appear in the brain of the rat at the age of about 10 days and continues to be added in some areas until well beyond the point of sexual maturity. In the thalamus, for example, myelination begins on about the tenth to twelfth day after birth and continues until about the fortieth to fiftieth day. The cortex is the last to be myelinated, beginning around the twenty-first day and continuing until about the sixtieth day.

In many species, some structures in the cerebellum and brain stem are myelinated at birth (those of the rat are not), but myelinization in the CNS areas most often linked with higher cognitive functions begins a good deal later and continues for some time thereafter. The 3-month-old human has only traces of myelin in the association areas of the cortex; the growth of myelin there continues at least beyond the age of 10 years, with some evidence suggesting that it continues until about age 40. More than half of the myelin that develops in the frontal lobes does so after the first years of life.

It is unlikely that myelinization plays a direct role in memory processing, but there are several ways in which its influence might be exerted indirectly (cf. Campbell & Spear, 1972). For example, the length of the neural refractory period seems to be inversely related to the amount of myelin present. Consequently, an immature animal deficient in myelinization relative to adults will be correspondingly deficient in the amount of information that may be processed per unit of time (see Scherrer, 1967). It seems reasonable to expect that retention might be positively related to the amount of redundancy in the information stored. If so, the limits imposed on the immature animal in terms of amount of information processed may be expected to lead to relatively deficient retention. A similar limitation on information processing may be caused by the low velocity of neural conduction in unmyelinated fibers. Speed of neural conduction increases as myelinization increases in a number of animals, including man. For example, in the kitten there is a twentyfold increase in the velocity of neural conduction between about 20 days of age and adulthood. It seems plausible that the animal's perception of the events of a learning situation might depend on speed of neural conduction—including rapidity of stimulus detection, proprioceptive feedback, and so forth—and that when tested after the conduction speed has increased, the animal may show forgetting because proprioceptive feedback and perception of the events of testing deviate from the animal's original encoding of these events.

For the purpose of memory processing, synaptogenesis probably is more important than myelinization as an ontogenetic event of neuronal morphology. As the rat ages from 15 days to 30 days, at which point long-term retention seems adult-like, the number of synapses in the animal's cerebral cortex increases tenfold, or more. A corresponding rate of synaptogenesis may be found in the human between birth and two or three years of age. The relationship of synaptogenesis to the ontogeny of memory processing has been discussed elsewhere (Campbell & Spear, 1972; Campbell & Coulter, 1976). It is worth mentioning here in order to emphasize two plausible hypotheses of infantile amnesia that make use of this relationship. The first emphasizes the importance of a large number of synapses during memory storage: Perhaps the larger number of synapses available in the adult brain permit a certain redundancy in storage that facilitates later retrieval; the immature rat without this advantage of redundancy in storage is left with a disadvantage at the time of retrieval. The second hypothesis is that the increase in synaptogenesis, and the corresponding increase in the complexity of processing information, may act to impede access to memories acquired in infancy, even though memory storage originally was quite adequate.

Ontogeny of arousal and inhibitory functions. Several dramatic developments occur in the rat's behavior around the age of 15 days. The most obvious are opening of the eyes and the onset of more adult-like mobility patterns. It is also at about this age that the rat, and similar altricial mammals such as the hamster, peak in terms of the spontaneous activity exhibited during isolation from the mother and littermates. In comparison with younger and older animals, the 15-day-old displays a good deal more activity moving from place to place in a relatively novel cage, rearing, climbing, grooming, and sniffing. Moreover, the 15-day-old is less likely than older animals to cease relatively fruitless unrewarded responding, and less likely to be dissuaded from responding by punishment. This developmental phenomenon has been the subject of an admirable series of studies by Campbell and his associates, and has potential importance for the ontogeny of memory processing. We turn now to a brief description of the rationale and discoveries of Campbell and his associates.

They began with the generalization that neurophysiological development proceeds in a caudal-to-rostral manner, suggested many years ago by Hughlings Jackson. This generalization implied that general arousal functions controlled by the reticular formation in the caudal portion of the CNS should develop prior to the inhibitory control functions, which seemed likely to lie more rostrally in the telencephalon and frontal cortex. Evidence existing at the time indicated that in the adult animal stimulation in these areas, especially the hippocampus and the telencephalon, resulted in the inhibition of reticular activity. One of the first studies (Campbell, Lytle, & Fibiger, 1969) tested the hypothesis that two systems in the brain were controlled by different transmitter substances. One system was excitatory and included catecholamines as neurotransmitters; the other system was suggested to be inhibitory in nature, antagonistic to behavioral arousal, and involved acetylcholine and serotonin as the neurotransmitters. Furthermore, it was known that acetylcholine is concentrated in the more rostral portions of the brain. This implied that the cholinergic system would mature relatively late. Furthermore, at about the time this study was published, independent research by others was beginning to establish that for the neonatal rat catecholamine concentration was two or three times as great in the caudal as in the rostral portions of the brain, with the more widely distributed adult concentration developing gradually by the age of about 30 days.

Campbell and his colleagues tested the effect of three drugs, scopolamine, amphetamine, and parachlorophenylalanine (PCPA), on the spontaneous activity of rats whose ages were 10, 15, 20, 25, or 100 days. These drugs were known to increase activity in adults, but probably for different reasons. The action of scopolamine is anticholinergic, disrupting the transmission function of acetylcholine and thus increasing activity by removing the inhibitory influence otherwise present. PCPA is a drug that blocks synthesis of serotonin and would thus be expected to increase activity by removing an inhibitory influence. Amphetamine enhances adrenergic activity and directly increases general arousal. Campbell and his associates reasoned that if the adrenergic system developed before the cholinergic and serotonergic systems, there should be a point in the young rats' life when amphetamine influenced their activity but scopolamine and PCPA did not. This is precisely what they found. Spontaneous activity was enhanced at the earliest age they tested (10 days after birth). Scopolamine, however, had no effect on rats younger than 20 days of age, while PCPA did not influence activity until postnatal day 15. This developmental sequence in which spontaneous activity may be controlled by drugs influencing the adrenergic, serotonergic, and cholinergic systems has been confirmed in several experiments (Fibiger, Lytle, & Campbell, 1970; also see Campbell & Mabry, 1973, and Mabry & Campbell, 1975). A particularly thorough and informative review of the ontogeny of these neurotransmitters is found in a scholarly chapter by Lanier, Dunn, and VanHartesveldt (1976).

Further support for the view that developing systems in the caudal portion of the brain come to inhibit spontaneous activity has been gathered in Campbell's laboratory by Moorcraft (1971), who found that for rats 20 days of age or older, lesions in the frontal neocortex or the hippocampus resulted in potentiation of activity during food deprivation. Similar lesions on animals younger than 20 days of age, however, had no influence on activity whether the animals were food deprived or not.

This work by Campbell and his associates has been verified and expanded by others. Relative to rats older than 20 days of age, rats between the ages of 15 and 20 days are deficient in terms of passive avoidance performance (e.g., Feigley, 1974; Riccio, Rohrbaugh, & Hodges, 1968), suppression of instrumental behavior following punishment (Riccio & Marrazo, 1972), spontaneous alternation (e.g., Egger, Livesey, & Dawson, 1973), and habituation (Brunner, Roth, & Rossi, 1970; Wilson & Riccio, 1973). These deficiencies result from the infant rat's relative ineffectiveness in ceasing ongoing behavior such as stepping from one compartment into another, jumping a small hurdle, active avoidance performance previously learned but not punished, turning in a particular direction in a T-maze, poking its nose into a hole, and licking.

In addition to the data of Campbell and his associates, there is evidence that prior to the age of 20 days the inhibitory deficit in the rat is linked with the development of the serotonergic and cholinergic nervous systems. For example, for passive avoidance learning (Feigley, 1974) and alternation behavior (Egger, Livesey, & Dawson, 1973), scopolamine, an anticholinergic drug, influences behavior after the age of 20 days but not before. This is to be expected if the cholinergic nervous system is so immature and ineffective prior to the age of 20 days that its disruption has little behavioral consequence.

In some cases, however, it is clear that the inhibitory deficit has not ended when the rat reaches 20 days of age, particularly in the case of passive avoidance learning (Feigley & Spear, 1970) and certain behavior in a position discrimination task (Bronstein & Spear, 1972). But of course one could hardly expect to find a complete transition from no inhibition to full inhibition at the age of 20 days. For example, one sort of inhibitory behavior—cessation of activity in response to the mother's odors—may appear in rat pups as young as 2 days of age, although some measures of this behavior indicate that it begins to occur most strongly after about 6 or 7 days (Schapiro & Salas, 1970). Perhaps this particular case of inhibitory behavior is mediated by systems controlling olfaction that are more primitive than the cholinergic system. Similarly, the apparent inhibitory deficits sometimes found in adolescent animals older than 20 days of age may be due to a variety of mechanisms other than a still only partially mature cholinergic system.

There is reason to believe that this pattern of developing inhibitory capacity is general across a variety of altricial species. Campbell and Mabry (1972) have found a pattern in the ontogeny of spontaneous activity assessed by several different response measures that is the same in the hamster as in the rat (but absent in the precocial guinea pig). Furthermore, inhibitory deficiencies in infant humans assessed primarily with habituation measures are well known (e.g., Cohen and Gelber, 1975).

What are the implications of this developing inhibitory capacity for the ontogeny of retention? One possible consequence might be greater interference in retention for immature organisms, which have a deficiency in inhibition processes, than in mature organisms without this deficiency. First, if stimulus selection depends on some sort of inhibitory process (Richardson, 1976; Rudy, 1974), we may expect that immature organisms deficient in this respect often would fail to select the stimulus characteristics of an episode that might best serve to discriminate the memory of that episode from conflicting memories (cf. Hale & Taweel, 1974a, b). This implies differences between immature and mature organisms in the quality of memory storage, but this would not be surprising and need not be accompanied by differences in quantitative aspects of original learning. Subsequent to memory storage, a general deficiency in inhibitory processes might lead to inappropriate retrieval of memories, causing the latter to interact with conflicting memories and, hence, enhanced forgetting (e.g., Gordon & Spear, 1973). Finally, if retention is tested in immature animals or humans prior to the full development of inhibitory processing, we may find an excess of "false positives" in recognizing, and perhaps in retrieving, the appropriate target attributes of a memory.

Comment on physiological and behavioral development as determinants of the ontogeny of retention. The preceding suggestions concerning how developmental influences might influence retention must be regarded as speculative (Campbell & Spear, 1972). However, also as suggested by Campbell and Spear, these speculations are testable in view of the known potential for experimentally manipulating the endocrine system, neurophysiology, and processes such as inhibition. A more difficult task is isolating the relative contributions of physiological and behavioral changes in retention capacity; in the truest sense, this probably never can be accomplished, certainly not with precision. Yet we may achieve some weighting of these factors through comparisons of altricial and prococial animals, which have similar exposure to environmental factors but differ markedly in the rate of physiological change following birth (recognizing that environmental exposure itself will depend on a certain degree of physiological development). For example, Campbell, Misanin, White, & Lytle (1974) found relatively little retention deficit attributable to the age at which (precocial) guinea pigs were trained, whereas the reverse clearly occurred for (altricial) rats. This comparative approach is difficult analytically, but it nevertheless may provide general guidance concerning which class of variables—primarily experiential or primarily physiological—is more likely to lead to the general principles we seek for understanding the ontogeny of retention.

Further Ontogenetic Changes of Possible Relevance to Retention

A variety of predictions may be generated concerning the long-term retention of verbal materials in children compared to adults (e.g., Corsini, 1971; Goulet, 1968; Hagen, 1971; Keppel, 1964). One obvious prediction concerns age and potentially interfering extraexperimental verbal learning. This source of inter-ference should be greater in older subjects with more verbal experience; thus, better retention by children than by adults would be predicted. This effect would be contrary to infantile amnesia, of course. There is at least one confirmation of this prediction (Walen, 1970), although this effect was limited to only one of several response measures. On the other hand, a study by Hasher and Thomas (1973), which included sufficiently long retention intervals and care in equating degree of original learning has indicated no differences in retention between children and adults. For the most part, however, there are few adequate tests of how long-term retention of verbal materials compares for children and adults. This may be attributed in part to the difficulty of obtaining sufficiently young subjects, testing them after appropriately long intervals, and equating degree of learning across varying ages, and in part to simple methodological deficiencies such as the absence of control conditions to evaluate simple performance changes due to maturation between learning and the retention test (e.g., Adams, 1973).

With the increase in knowledge about memory processing in young humans, we may expect the evolution of interesting predictions concerning ontogenetic factors in long-term retention. For example, if is known that children as young as 3 years of age have quite well-developed associative networks among verbal items, and that their difficulty may be not so much in producing adequate verbal associates as in inhibiting an inappropriate one (Hall & Halperin, 1972). Yet when the task is free recall of a list of common words, one can readily find progressive increases in the number of items recalled between 3 or 4 years of age and adulthood (e.g., Jablonski, 1974). While this may be due in part to dif-ferences in an idealized "memory span"—the amount of information that can be held momentarily at different ages—we know also that learning devices "mnemonic preparation"; see Chapter 8) become more prevalent with age. It is quite clear that the use of rehearsal strategies in free recall differs as the child grows older (see Hagen, 1971; Haith, 1971; Ornstein & Liberty, 1973). It is known, furthermore, that the deficiencies in younger subjects may be reduced if they are provided with devices of mnemonic preparation, for example, mediators for paired-associate learning (Rohrer, 1973), and strategies for organization (Liberty & Ornstein, 1973) like those used by older subjects. On the other hand, there are indications that the duration of iconic memory may differ with age, with the duration of sensory images being perhaps better for younger humans (Brown, 1965; Gummerman & Gray, 1972). This sort of information may lead to predic-tions concerning differential retention in young and old humans, but there is little point in speculating here about what these predictions will be.

For more general cases of the ontogeny of retention, we may elaborate briefly on some of the more likely factors that may contribute to poorer retention for memories acquired during immaturity compared to maturity. For example, be-cause of the fewer dendritic (synaptic) connections in the immature rat, memories may be stored with less redundancy than in the mature rat. This in itself may limit the effectiveness of subsequent retrieval of these memories. Furthermore, subsequent addition of new synaptic connections may make earlier memorial representations less accessible; hence, these early memories are retrieved less effectively by adults. Such synaptogenesis is of course found in human children as well as other altricial animals. In like fashion, emerging species-specific behaviors or conflicting memories acquired in childhood may interfere extraordinarily with early memories. Maturation-induced changes in information processing, such as in perception, similarly may impair retrieval of these early memories or their translation into contemporary behavior. Resolution of these and other alternative explanations of this effect should help us understand not only infantile amnesia but also memory processing and behavioral development in general.

Several sources have suggested that the inverse relationship obtained between age and rate of forgetting (reported, e.g., by Campbell & Campbell, 1962) was a direct consequence of the greater generalization decrement in the younger rats between training and later testing. Perkins (1965) expressed this belief: "The stimulus situation to which fear was learned may be altered so much by stimulus changes resulting from growth that there is nearly complete generalization decrement resulting from maturation induced stimulus changes" (pp. 46–47).

There appear to be three general sources of growth-induced "generalization decrement" for immature rats during a retention interval. These may be categorized as dissociation factors, perceptual changes, and response changes.

Dissociation factors.   Overton (e.g., 1964, 1966, 1972) has reported his own and other work showing that learning acquired under the influence of drugs may not be apparent in a subsequent test when the organism is not drugged, and vice versa (see Chapter 2). Investigation of this phenomenon has become increasingly refined, and there are some particularly striking examples (e.g., Bliss, 1973). There is reason to expect that a comparable effect may occur between training in infancy and testing in adulthood as a result of background level and composition of hormones (see preceding discussion regarding adrenal–pituitary maturation; then see Gray, 1975).

In addition to this general case, there are suggestions that hormones that are specifically implicated in certain learning tasks undergo important changes with increasing age. As one example, the hormone corticosterone has been implicated as an important determinant of performance in an avoidance learning task (e.g., Brush & Levine, 1966; Weiss, McEwan, Silva, & Kalkut, 1969), and it is known that production of this steroid hormone in response to stress produced by an electric shock increases considerably with age (Levine & Mullins, 1968). Also, greater forgetting of avoidance learning occurs in rats trained when sexually immature and tested when sexually mature than in rats both trained and tested when sexually mature (though this clearly is not the only change occurring during these ages, and perhaps not the most important). That physiological changes accompanying sexual maturity are important for avoidance learning has been determined by two kinds of evidence. As an example of the first, Feigley and Spear (1970) found that sexually mature female rats (over 60 days of age) acquired a one-way avoidance response more rapidly than sexually mature males, while there was no difference between sexually immature males and sexually immature females (21–25 days old) in avoidance learning. The second kind of evidence is exemplified in the finding of Hirsch (1969) that females ovariectomized at 25 days of age did not show avoidance learning superiority over males when tested at 60 days of age, although sham-operated females did. A possible implication, then, is that infant or weanling rats (either females or males, or perhaps both) learn an avoidance task in the absence of stimulus-producing hormonal responses that accompany the same learning once the rat attains maturity; the resulting stimulus change between learning and the long-term retention test may be sufficient to result in retention loss.

Changes in perception of the unconditioned stimulus (UCS) or reinforcer. An extensive consideration of developmental changes in perception of the UCS is presented by Campbell (1967). Most of his discussion concerned detection, aversion, and tetanization thresholds for footshock as a function of age. One learning task used appetitive reinforcers, however, and Campbell reports that a 20-mg Noyes food pellet has approximately the same reinforcing value for an infant rat as a 45-mg Noyes pellet has for an adult (see also Campbell & Jaynes, 1969).

Generally, detection and aversion thresholds are identical for footshock, and for certain shock sources these thresholds do not differ among rats older than the typical age of weaning. Although Campbell did not systematically test the aversion thresholds of unweaned rats, it is known that escape latencies for a given intensity of shock decrease between 15 and 25 days of age (e.g., Klein & Spear, 1969). These differences do not seem to be attributable to simple developmental changes in mobility, since comparable latency differences were not found when the animals avoided the shock. Therefore, it is plausible to attribute these escape differences to increasing aversion thresholds in rats younger than 25 days. It is also possible, particularly with high shock intensity, that these escape latency differences may have been due to fractional episodes of tetanization occurring with greater strength in the younger animals. Campbell reported that while neither detection nor aversion thresholds differed for rats above 21 days of age, younger rats did have a tendency to tetanize at lower shock levels than older rats.

Changes in perception of conditioned stimuli. Although there are few directly applicable data, there seem to be three potential sources of change in the perception of conditioned or discriminative stimuli with increasing age. The most fundamental of these sources is change in the psychophysical functions relating detection or discrimination thresholds to intensity of the stimulus. A second probable change is attentional: In the simplest case, we would expect that the stimuli to which the rat attends should change as the rat grows, simply because an infant rat may not be in a physical position for sensory reception of certain stimuli that are obvious to more fully grown rats. For example, the brightness or textural characteristics of a ledge 2 1/2 inches high may go unnoticed by the infant too short to see the top of the ledge, whereas it may be attended to and employed as a discriminative or contextual cue by the more mature rat. Finally, there is the possibility of perceptual and attentional changes induced by perceptual learning (e.g., Epstein, 1967). To the extent that the infant rat experiences perceptual learning during a retention interval, its perception of stimulus elements associated with the experimental test will be modified and accompanied by retention loss.

Changes in the unconditioned response (UCR).   One aspect of the ontogeny of learning that historically has received minimal attention is the UCR. It seems likely that infant rats, especially preweanling rats, may have underdeveloped or different UCRs to shock than older ones. Of course, this characteristic may be quite independent of differences in perceptual thresholds for shock, or in mobility.

There are two fundamental means by which growth-induced changes in the UCR could produce poor retention scores: Changes in response-produced stimuli may produce dissociation, some special cases of which were suggested earlier; or physical disorientation might result, particularly if the unconditioned and instrumental responses combine additively.

Summary

This section has emphasized maturation-induced changes in the efficacy of memory processing, in terms of age-related differences in retention. These issues present a classical instance of the "comparative problem"—experimental analysis of individual differences in behavior—and the accompanying limits on general conclusions in this area were discussed through examples.

Experimental evidence was examined concerning the emergence of retention capacity in neonatal altricial rodents. Methodological and technological problems have limited research in this area, with special problems being associated with measurement of instrumental responding. This area of study has determined, however, that a capacity for learning does not imply capacity for retention. Also, this work has focused attention on a particular set of neurophysiological mechanisms that may be responsible for this rudimentary learning and its retention in neonates but may differ from later-maturing mechanisms that may determine learning and retention in older animals.

Questions concerning the achievement of adult-like levels of retention capacity have rearoused interest in the phenomenon of infantile amnesia. In spite of a good deal of evidence for this phenomenon in humans, its experimental analysis has been largely nonexistent because of immense practical problems. However, experimental preparations for testing this phenomenon with animals have been developed. Potential explanations of infantile amnesia were discussed through consideration of ontogenetic changes in neurophysiology and ancillary behavioral changes.

WARM-UP DECREMENT

When subjects leave a partially or fully learned task and return 24 hours later to continue practicing it, it is virtually inevitable that their initial performance will be poor relative to that of 24 hours earlier. Quite rapidly, though, the individual's performance will return to the level expected on the basis of prior achievement. While such a decrement is simply our operational definition of forgetting, it is common to attribute at least a portion of this forgetting to a lack of "warm-up." Applying the term *warm-up* gains nothing in explanatory power unless one can determine that the process responsible for it is different from other processes underlying retention and forgetting. To consider this question, we must first analyze the previous conceptions of the nature of "warm-up." (For a review of earlier work on warm-up and further consideration of the relationship between warm-up and forgetting, see Adams, 1961.)

Warm-up decrement, the deficit in performance that is attributed to lack of warm-up, has been studied through the application of certain warm-up treatments that alleviate the decrement. In practical terms, there can be no doubt about the importance of warm-up for tasks involving large-muscle activity. Every good baseball manager knows how many pitches each of his relief pitchers requires to "warm up" sufficiently to enter a game. Every football coach knows that if he is planning to switch quarterbacks, the replacement must first "warm up" by handling the ball and throwing it on the sidelines. Accordingly, warm-up effects of this sort have been studied extensively in the area of human motor learning.

While such gross warm-up activities may have some relevance to the retention of specific memories, of more interest to us here are tasks involving more "cognitive" activities involving memories with relatively little relation to muscular activities. Warm-up is also a concern in cognitive tasks, for reasons analogous to those regarding muscular skills.

The critical question of warm-up is this: To what extent is there really a general cognitive warm-up factor, distinct from the specific stimulus (informational) effects of a warm-up activity, that may facilitate retrieval of relevant memories? To benefit retention performance in human motor learning, the content of the warm-up experience must be fairly specific to the task at hand, at least in terms of the general mode of activity, though not necessarily in terms of the specific muscles used (e.g., Schmidt & Nacson, 1971). Similarly, it appears that for warm-up decrement to be alleviated significantly in human verbal learning, the warm-up experience must include the same class of materials as in the current task (e.g., Postman, 1971). This restriction is somewhat less important for subjects who have had a great deal of experience learning verbal tasks in the laboratory. Otherwise, except for some trivial effects such as posturing oneself for maximal perception and attention, warm-up has seemed to have relatively little effect. Even the limited effect found following exposure to certain verbal items may be due to a "cueing" effect of similar or associated items in the testing material. So it seems likely that *general* cognitive warming up in certain areas of knowledge—a general warming up analogous to that of a bullpen pitcher, but different from general arousal or specific muscular activity—is not a significant factor in most memorial behavior.

A comparable general conclusion about warm-up in animals is unlikely at the moment, perhaps because warm-up decrement is a stronger and more widespread phenomenon in animals than in humans. The potency of this effect is particularly evident in certain tasks, especially those involving free-operant responding to avoid or escape aversive stimuli. The Sidman avoidance procedure is a typical example. In this procedure, an animal can learn to postpone footshocks for a short time by pressing a lever, but another footshock will be delivered shortly unless the lever is pressed again within a certain time span, and so on. So much warm-up decrement occurs with this procedure, and occurs so persistently over literally weeks and months of daily training sessions, that investigators typically discard the first 25% or so of the daily record of an animal's behavior. Such dramatically recurrent forgetting may or may not involve the same processes as less dramatic cases of forgetting after a 24-hour interval following only one or two training sessions. For our present purposes, we shall tentatively consider these cases together in our analysis of warm-up decrement as a source of forgetting in animals.

Analysis of Warm-up Decrement in Animals

Although *warm-up* is a term frequently used in studies of animal learning, paradoxically, it has been neglected to a great extent in theories of memory processing (cf. Adams, 1961). Typically, "warm-up decrement" is defined operationally as poor performance on the initial trials of a daily training session relative to both the terminal trials of the immediately preceding session and the subsequent trials of that current session. Events that alleviate warm-up decrement are termed *warm-up treatments*. Warm-up decrement has been identified frequently in both aversive (e.g., Nakamura & Anderson, 1962) and appetitive (e.g., Logan, 1960) conditioning, with perhaps more consistency and magnitude in the former case (cf. Hill, Erlebacher, & Spear, 1965).

Understanding warm-up effects in lower animals requires attention to two issues. The first is whether facilitation of retention by a warm-up treatment concerns primarily motor skill and hence requires muscular activation of the specific instrumental response. For humans, retention of motor skills is enhanced more clearly by warm-up treatments than retention of cognitive skills such as retention of verbal materials, as noted earlier (cf. Adams, 1961; Lazar, 1967). Moreover, motor activity may provide extraordinarily important memory attributes for lower animals, so practice of the learned response may be a necessary component of an effective warm-up treatment regardless of the importance of favorable bodily attitudes for manifesting the target attribute of the memory. Just as warm-up treatment in human verbal retention apparently is more effective when the stimuli comprising the treatment are represented as attributes of the original memory (Postman, 1969), so alleviation of warm-up decrement in animals may require motor activity that has been represented as attributes of the original memory.

More important for our purposes is the second issue: whether treatments that alleviate warm-up decrement do so only by heightening motivation or arousal, or by directly facilitating memory retrieval. We favor the latter view: Warm-up decrement occurs because a sufficient number of retrieval cues are absent or not noticed during the early stages of a retraining or testing session. With increasing exposure to stimuli associated with prior training, the probability that a rat will notice an effective retrieval cue presumably increases also, thus increasing the probability of retrieving the target attribute of the memory. We now consider an example of warm-up decrement preliminary to examining evidence toward a decision about the basis of warm-up decrement and the effect of warm-up treatments (see also Spear, 1973; Spear, Gordon, & Martin, 1973).

An interesting illustration of warm-up decrement may be found in a study by DiCara and Miller (1968) in which the conditioning episode given rats took place under circumstances that undoubtedly constituted a unique experience in the life of each animal. Placed under the influence of the paralytic agent curare, with respiration maintained by confinement in a sort of miniature iron lung, the rats learned to change their heart rate to avoid punishment. Half the animals avoided punishment by increasing their heart rate (from an initial average of 405 to an average of 461 beats per minute), and the other half avoided punishment by decreasing their heart rate (from an initial average of 418 to an average of 347 beats per minute). All the rats then were left alone in their home cages for three months before a retention test was given. These animals had been given a 30-minute adaptation period in the apparatus prior to the commencement of conditioning trials, and a similar 30-minute period, during which neither CS nor UCS occurred, was given prior to the retention test. Heart rates were measured during the latter adaptation period, and it is these data that are of interest. During the initial portion of this period, heart rates were about the same for all rats regardless of prior conditioning, so "forgetting" was defined operationally. Soon, however, heart rates did begin to change in precisely the direction in which the animals had been trained previously; progressively throughout this 30-minute adaptation period, the animals previously trained to have rapid heart rates increased their rates and those previously trained to have slow heart rates decreased their rates. These changes are attributed to the control the contextual features of the apparatus had acquired over heart rate. In our terms, the subjects had represented these contextual (environmental) features as attributes of the memory for the learning episode. Perhaps with increasing time in the apparatus, the probability increased that the animal would notice the contextual stimuli, leading ultimately to the arousal of the target attribute of heart rate.

Determinants of warm-up decrement.   We have mentioned the prevalence of warm-up decrement in free-operant avoidance conditioning tasks. Warm-up decrement has also been obtained in conditioned escape learning (Dinsmoor, 1962), discriminated avoidance (e.g., Hoffman, Fleshler, & Chorny, 1961), shuttle avoidance (e.g., Nakamura & Anderson, 1962), avoidance requiring a wheel-turn response (Reynierse, Zerbolio, & Denny, 1964), and conditioned aggression (Lyon & Ozolins, 1970). The ubiquitousness of warm-up decrement in such aversive conditioning tasks is illustrated (as noted earlier), by the common practice for investigators simply to discount data from the early portions of a day's training session as unrepresentative (e.g., Sidman, 1953, reported only the final hour of each of several 3-hour daily training sessions).

The extent of warm-up decrement in appetitive conditioning is greater with wider spacing of trials within sessions and with lower reinforcer magnitude (e.g., Hill & Spear, 1962; Hill et al., 1965). With aversive conditioning in rats, warm-up decrement may be reduced by employing greater intensity of the aversive stimulus (usually shock; see Azrin, Holz, & Hake, 1963; but see Hoffman et al., 1961; Powell, 1970), the presence of shock prior to the retention test (Hoffman et al., 1961), larger numbers of shocks received during the early portion of a testing period (Dinsmoor, 1962), and the presence of a warning signal in conjunction with Sidman avoidance (Ulrich, Holz, & Azrin, 1964; but see Foree & LoLordo, 1970). The magnitude of warm-up decrement may vary with species (Powell & Peck, 1969; Powell, 1972), but the laboratory rat and pigeon generally are quite susceptible to warm-up decrement.

The extent of muscular practice (Powell & Peck, 1969) does not appear to be an important determinant of warm-up decrement in rats, nor does sensory adaptation (Azrin et al., 1963).

Hoffman, Fleshler, and Chorny (1961) tested the widely held notion that warm-up decrement is due to relatively low motivation early in a daily training session. This study investigated a variety of factors that Hoffman and his associates suspected might control warm-up, including the possibility that warm-up decrement in discriminated avoidance performance might be eliminated by a series of shocks presented immediately prior to a training session. They found that this treatment did alleviate warm-up decrement and, moreover, that the shocks were sufficient; it did not matter whether they were preceded by the discriminative stimulus or whether the lever was present to permit response practice. Moreover, simply confining the rat in the experimental apparatus for a period prior to a training session did not reduce the warm-up decrement. Still, it was not entirely clear that motivation induced by shock is the necessary determinant of warm-up—the warm-up effect was not influenced by increasing shock intensity. Nevertheless, Hoffman and his associates (1961) suggested that

> The detailed explanation of warm-up will probably be found in processes which are induced by aversive stimulation. Although we cannot specify the detailed characteristics of these processes at present, they probably are motivational in nature and involve the gradual development of emotionality in one form or another, and the warm-up itself probably reflects this development. (p. 315; see also Dinsmoor, 1962; Nakamura & Anderson, 1962)

It is notable that Hoffman and his associates re-presented the original reinforcer (footshock) to alleviate warm-up decrement. Similarly, when appetitive conditioning is studied, performance decrements attributable to either the retention interval, extinction, or counterconditioning are known to disappear with remarkable rapidity if the organism is re-presented with the specific reinforcer used with original learning, whether or not the reoccurrence of the appetitive reinforcer is response contingent (e.g., Reid, 1958; Spear, 1967).

The reinforcer's function in alleviating warm-up decrement might be as a contextual stimulus that, when noticed by an organism, acts as a retrieval cue to facilitate access to the target memory attribute or the entire memory; this effect of the reinforcer need not be mediated solely by the *energizing* characteristics of motivation. In support of this notion are data suggesting that alleviation of warm-up decrement through presentation of the reinforcer is not simply a consequence of reestablishing a sufficient level of motivational energy. For example, Carter and Bruno (1968) used the procedure of differential reinforcement of low rates of responding (DRL) and found that extinguished DRL behavior was reacquired rapidly following a reinforced response but not following a nonreinforced response. Efficient DRL performance requires low levels of responding, probably the antithesis of highly energized behavior, so it would be difficult to argue that the reinforcer alleviated warm-up decrements through its simple energizing effects. Moreover, this rapid reacquisition occurred even though, prior to the reinforcement, extinction was so thorough that the animal had not responded until nearly 2 hours into the reacquisition session.

Other results equally opposed to a motivation interpretation of warm-up decrement indicate that motivation induced by the reinforcer or unconditioned stimulus (UCS) is not necessary for the alleviation of warm-up decrement. For example, while agreeing in general with the motivational interpretation of Hoffman and his associates, Nakamura and Anderson (1962) noted also that this probably was not a complete explanation, because their experiment revealed that a warm-up decrement occurred and then progressively was alleviated with further testing during *extinction* as well as acquisition, and shock was never presented during their extinction procedure. Deficiency in UCS-induced motivation is an incomplete explanation of warm-up decrement if recovery from the decrement occurs in the absence of unconditioned aversive stimulation. Bullock (1960) obtained results in agreement with those of Nakamura and Anderson. With rats pressing levers in free-operant avoidance, rather than running in shuttle box avoidance, Bullock, too, found within-session recovery from warm-up decrement during a shock-free extinction treatment. Azrin and his associates (1963) found, similarly, that warm-up decrement in a punishment paradigm persisted even after punishment was discontinued.

A second set of results suggests that motivational enhancement is not sufficient to alleviate warm-up decrement: The occurrence of shock alone may not alter warm-up decrement without the reappearance of other events associated with original learning. Hake and Azrin (1965) found differential warm-up decrement among pigeons even though the birds were equated in terms of the presentation of shock. Lyon and Ozolins (1970) found that 50 inescapable shocks presented prior to a daily session did not alleviate warm-up decrement unless a particular inter-shock interval, 64 seconds, was used.

Finally, data gathered by Sidman (1962) also argue against a simple motivational explanation of warm-up decrement. The rats in his study were presented two concurrent operant avoidance problems, one associated with each of two levers. At the beginning of each session, one rat consistently responded to one of the levers at a high rate while showing a distinct warm-up decrement on the alternative lever. Assuming that motivational changes would be unlikely to affect similar responses differentially within the same rat, these results imply that this warm-up effect was attributable to other causes, perhaps memorial.

It would appear that following a rest period (e.g., of 24 hours), the absence of UCS-induced motivation early in a training session can account for at most only a small portion of warm-up decrement, which might itself be mediated by the cue properties of motivation rather than by the arousal or emotional aspects of motivation.

We now submit the following interpretation of warm-up decrement in terms of memory retrieval: The appropriate memory attributes are not aroused early in a training session because the corresponding retrieval cues are not present, or are not noticed by the animal at that time. A portion of these missing retrieval cues may be the hormonal and neurophysiological events in the animal that determine a particular level of its "fear," but other critical retrieval cues may be missing also. This interpretation implies that an increase in fear should be neither sufficient nor necessary to eliminate warm-up decrement, because if enough alternative retrieval cues are available to arouse associated attributes, memory retrieval may proceed in spite of a relatively low fear level.

Spear, Gordon, and Martin (1973) have completed a series of experiments that suggest a deficit in memory retrieval, rather than in motivation, as the primary source of warm-up decrement. First, we assumed that a deficit in motivation such as fear would impair performance on *any* aversive conditioning task, while a deficit in memory processing would be specific to the task previously learned. Second, we studied the influence of a warm-up treatment 24 hours after active avoidance had been learned; but instead of employing relearning of this task for the retention test, we gave a passive avoidance task in which successful avoidance was contingent upon withholding the previously acquired active avoidance response. With the training parameters we applied, performance on this passive avoidance task is inversely related to the amount of previous active avoidance training, which permits the inference that passive avoidance would be poorest when the memory of prior active avoidance training was most accessible, and vice versa.

The active avoidance task was a signaled Sidman avoidance procedure with a 20-second response–shock interval, a 5-second CS (flashing light plus white noise), and a 3-second shock–shock interval. A "response" required that the rat poke its nose into a hole in the wall of the avoidance chamber. This version of Sidman avoidance is learned rapidly, and most rats acquire the performance criterion of 4-minutes-without-shock within 30 to 50 minutes of training. However, a sizable warm-up decrement occurs 24 hours later.

For the warm-up treatment administered just prior to the retention test, the rat was confined in the avoidance apparatus for 5 minutes and presented with 15 pairings of the 5-second CS and the 1-second footshock. During this warm-up treatment, the hole was blocked off, prohibiting the avoidance response. Such CS–UCS pairings are known to facilitate avoidance learning under some circumstances, although we expected such an effect to be small relative to its warm-up effect because the CS was not necessary for learning in this case. This expectation was confirmed: This particular "warm-up treatment" did not significantly improve retention performance when given instead as "overtraining" immediately after original learning, indicating that this treatment did not add significantly to the avoidance learning that had occurred originally. Nevertheless, in two experiments we found that when this treatment immediately *preceded* the retention test (passive avoidance), the number of (punished) responses more than doubled (see Figure 5.7). If the effect of the treatment had been simply to increase fear or some other motivational aspect, passive avoidance performance should have been improved (i.e., the number of responses at the retention test should have been decreased by this treatment). Instead, the warm-up treatment increased responding, as would have been expected had the accessibility of the active avoidance memory been increased.

Using a completely different set of active and passive avoidance tasks (one-way avoidance, involving hurdle jumping rather than nose poking), the same phenomenon was replicated in two further experiments that yielded additional results indicating that the treatment-induced alleviation of warm-up decrement was due to neither enhanced motivation nor additional learning (Spear et al., 1973, Exp. 4 and 5). Therefore, we conclude that the effect of these treatments was to enhance memory retrieval.

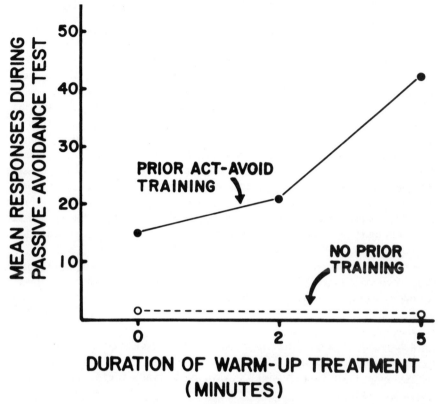

DURATION OF WARM-UP TREATMENT (MINUTES)

Figure 5.7   Retention of a modified free-operant active-avoidance task is shown for rats given differing durations of a warm-up treatment just prior to the retention test. The retention test was a passive avoidance task that yielded negative transfer from the active avoidance learning, such that the higher the number of responses on the ordinant, the better the retention of active avoidance. Animals represented by the dotted line had not previously learned the active avoidance task; their performance indicates that the warm-up treatment itself, in the absence of the acquired memory of active avoidance, had no influence on this response measure (adapted from Spear et al., 1973).

INTRAEPISODIC RETENTION: LONG-DELAY CONDITIONING

Systematic analysis of the dramatically effective conditioning that accompanies food poisoning has had a profound effect on theoretical approaches to learning and conditioning. The circumstances governing acquisition of an aversion to a gustatory stimulus followed by a noxious visceral consequence, for example, seem so different from those governing other instances of conditioning that some theorists have questioned whether there can be general principles of learning. Perhaps, these theorists suggest, the generality of "laws of learning" may be severely curtailed by a need to consider different laws that depend on what is being learned and who is learning (e.g., Garcia, McGowan, & Green, 1972; Seligman, 1970; for the opposing view, see Krane & Wagner, 1975).

This debatable issue is beside the point of this chapter and will not be addressed directly. It requires some mention, though, because one possibly singular characteristic of acquired taste aversions concerns forgetting and retention. This relationship will become clear in terms of the conventional paradigm for studying long-delay conditioning: After the rat tastes a novel substance such as saccharin, it is injected with a toxic substance such as lithium chloride. Even under the most rapid handling of these operations, the onset of the sickness does not occur until several minutes have elapsed since drinking the saccharin. Yet upon subsequent opportunities the rat will drink little or no saccharin, even though this ordinarily is a preferred substance (in the concentrations used for these experiments). Furthermore, even if injections of the toxic substance are delayed for as long as several minutes or even a few hours following the animal's last taste of saccharin, future intake of saccharin is reduced.

In our general terms, we may consider this taste aversion paradigm to represent "intraepisodic retention," in which one event of an episode becomes incorporated with a later event within the same memory. When this occurs, we may infer retention of the first event at the time the second occurs and ask what factors promote or impede this retention. Intraepisodic retention has not occurred with most conventional tests of learning, when events-to-be-associated are separated by more than a few seconds. Therefore, when intraepisodic retention appears in terms of acquired taste aversions even when the interval between separate events is as long as a few hours, it is of considerable interest to determine what specifically is promoting this retention.

It was essentially through this route that Revusky (1971) developed a theory of long-delay conditioning. The purpose of this portion of the chapter is to consider intraepisodic retention (long-delay conditioning) within the context of the Revusky theory.

Long-Delay Conditioning in Perspective

Long-delay conditioning is not a trivial effect. Its broad generality has long been recognized by ethologists with respect to the rapidly acquired aversions to poisonous substances that occur in spite of a delay in the toxic effect of the poison. Long-delay conditioning is sufficiently robust, for example, so that the practice of "teaching" acquired aversions for simulated "lambs" to coyotes is under serious consideration by the Federal Department of Agriculture as a relatively innocuous means for decreasing sheep killing by coyotes. The coyotes are given access to meat wrapped in lamb's wool that has been treated to induce a nonfatal illness when eaten. An aversion to such a package is rapidly acquired and seems to generalize to real lambs.

Interpretation of long-delay conditioning must go beyond simple peripheral mediation by stimulus aftereffects of the ingested substance that serves as the CS (the illness is the UCS). Remote possibilities such as regurgitation from the gut of previously ingested CS, which might bridge the gap between CS and UCS, have been discounted also. A convincing argument has been made that whatever mediation occurs must be in the central nervous system (Revusky & Garcia, 1970).

If long-delay learning is such a robust and important effect, why was its study neglected for so long? Familiar answers have attributed this neglect to theoretical bias and general methodological rigidity, and these probably apply to some extent. But there is in addition an aspect of methodological convenience that probably prevented someone from stumbling upon such effects much earlier; this is the previous conventional use of a "neutral" CS, a CS that by itself does not noticeably alter the animal's behavior. The value of using a neutral CS was that it theoretically enhanced the generality of obtained relationships and limited the need to worry about unconditioned effects of the CS (even though appropriate control groups often were included in conditioning studies as a matter of course). In contrast, it was through the use of CSs to which animals rarely respond neutrally—preferred tastes, for example—that delayed conditioning was discovered.

Nonneutral CSs have an immediate advantage because the animal's attention to them is essentially guaranteed (although, as Revusky shows, the effects of long-delay conditioning are not typically explainable as simple attentional effects). Moreover, it is possible that memory attributes representing nonneutral CSs are more readily acquired than neutral CSs. Our major concern here, however, is whether nonneutral CSs might be especially resistant to sources of forgetting. Staddon (1974), for instance, has found it useful to simply assume that the occurrence of food pellets is "more memorable" than the occurrence of a visual stimulus shown on a pigeon key, which is viewed as more neutral biologically. The general question of the influence of nonneutral CSs in conditioning has begun to be analyzed (e.g., Henderson, 1973; Morrison & Collyer, 1974), but the influence of the property of "neutrality" on long-delay conditioning is far from clear.

Revusky's Interference Theory of Long-Delay Conditioning

Revusky (1971) suggests that long-delay conditioning depends on two general factors: retention of the CS at the time the UCS is presented and mutual "relevance" in the relationships among the CS, the UCS, and the stimulus context. Retention of the CS and its association with the UCS may be impaired by interference, but in principle, retention of the CS is long-lasting and not subject to decrement through some decay-like process. Revusky's theory is a general theory of the association between two events of any kind, and is not restricted to Pavlovian conditioning.

Sources of interference in long-delay conditioning may be either proactive or retroactive and may operate on either the CS or the UCS. Of primary interest here is retention of the CS. Proactive interference in retention of the CS may occur if prior learning has involved similar CSs or the identical CS, and retroactive interference may occur owing to new learning involving a similar CS during the CS–UCS interval. Revusky provides a detailed discussion of how the influence of interference in his system is viewed, including some interesting implications of this view, such as the role of (apparently paradoxical) secondary reinforcement effects. A review of some of these points is useful here.

In Revusky's theory, mechanisms of interference in retention and transfer may be applied in three ways to account for variance in long-delay learning. First, proactive and retroactive interference may influence retention of the CS prior to the occurrence of the UCS. Second, these sources of interference may contribute to negative transfer in associating the CS and the UCS. Third, the same sorts of competing assocations that are responsible for this interference may be applied to account for "relevance."

Revusky suggests that the concept of "relevance" may be applied to either the stimulus, the situation (i.e., context), or the response. Because our concern here is limited, we need not consider this concept in depth. Suffice it to say that "relevance" is used to describe how it is that if we consume 12 éclairs and have a stomachache a few hours later, we are more likely to attribute the stomachache to the éclairs than to any water consumed, television programs watched, or books read in the interim. In terms of the experimental paradigm generally applied, a rat made ill a few hours after ingesting a novel substance is more likely to associate the illness with the novel substance than with intervening events such as the familiar odor of the female rat at the other end of the vivarium or ingestion of food pellets of the sort eaten since birth.

Revusky cites several conditions necessary for the "relevance" needed to yield long-delay conditioning. With perhaps some loss of information, these may be paraphrased briefly as two conditions. The first is that the animal should be predisposed to associate this particular CS and UCS. Second, this predisposition for association must be greater than that for association between either of these members and other events occurring in the general proximity.

This is the gist of the theory, with some details and a few general factors omitted. Our primary interest is whether a concept such as "relevance" is necessary and what implications "relevance" (or "biological preparedness"; see Seligman & Hager, 1972) may have for retention.

Three classes of evidence for the role of relevance in long-delay conditioning may be considered. The first concerns the neurophysiological substrate that mediates memory processing. Garcia and Ervin (1968) have noted certain anatomical features of the brain that suggest that separate systems mediate the processing of memories associated with internal events (e.g., gustatory stimuli and visceral consequences) and those associated with external events (e.g., visual or auditory stimuli and cutaneous consequences). Garcia and his colleagues have continued to gather evidence for this possibility (e.g., Garcia, et al., 1972). The second class of evidence is ethological in nature and assumptive rather than empirical: A certain adaptive value has been seen in the tendency for animals to associate, within a common memory, the gustatory characteristics of ingested substances and internal physiological consequences that may not occur until several minutes or a few hours later. The phenomenal referent here is an animal's learning of which (poisonous) substances it should not eat and which (nonpoisonous) substances it should if appropriate metabolic regulation is to be maintained. The third class of evidence concerns the apparent relationship between the content of the episode and intraepisodic retention. Initial studies indicated that internal events such as the taste of unusually flavored water and subsequent illness are associated even though they are separated by a few hours, while external events (auditory or visual signals paired with food or footshock) are not associated if they are separated by more than a few seconds. Furthermore, an association involving a taste and a footshock has seemed unlikely to be acquired at all, as has the association between a visual–auditory signal and toxicosis (but see Krane & Wagner, 1975, for contrary evidence).

Now in a general sense, how can the phenomena and theory of long-delay conditioning help us understand retention and forgetting related to the intraepisodic interval? Although an empirical distinction within long-delay conditioning has not been drawn between effects on acquisition of an event and effects on its retention, at least not in terms of available data, there is reason to believe that we are dealing, at least in part, with retention effects. The Revusky theory is notably similar in form to the original Underwood–Postman theory (1960). The important mechanisms include proactive and retroactive interference in retention of the first event (CS), as determined by acquired competing associations. In view of the complexities and modifications of interference theory that have arisen since presentation of the original Underwood–Postman theory, the Revusky theory might be viewed as naive. We shall see, however, that this aspect of the Revusky theory has received compelling empirical support.

The concept of "relevance" also leads to considerations of retention in terms of the determinants of memory retrieval. If it is required that an animal be predisposed to associate a particular UCS with a particular CS, then perfect retention of the CS at the time of the UCS apparently is not sufficient for conditioning. However, just as retrieved cues are implicitly presented by a retention test, presentation of the UCS may be viewed as a potential cue for retrieval of the memory attribute representing the CS. The notion is this: To say that a CS is predisposed to become associated with a UCS is to say that the CS and UCS are attributes of a common memory. It should not matter in principle whether the CS and UCS were acquired as attributes of a common memory sometime in the animal's history—perhaps ingestion and toxicosis become associated in a general sense early in life through mechanisms such as aftertaste and regurgitation, and thus contiguity or contingency, although such mechanisms are not necessary later—or as biological dispositions attributable to how the central nervous system is "wired." The critical feature is that presentation of the UCS facilitates retrieval of the CS because they are, in effect, attributes of a common memory.

This reasoning, in combination with the facts of long-delay conditioning, imply to us that intratrial retention depends, in part at least, on the sorts of proactive and retroactive interference implied by Revusky. Insofar as identifying the specific source and mechanisms of this interference is concerned, the same testing problems exist as in the Underwood–Postman theory. For example, if the major source of the interference is to be attributable to conflicting memories acquired outside of the experimental situation, might not the context of the experimental and extraexperimental situations be too different and, hence, transfer between extraexperimental and experimental episodes too weak to account for the forgetting that exists? The following experiments, nevertheless, have begun to support Revusky's view that long-delay conditioning depends on the extent of interference in retention of the CS.

The Lett Experiments on Delay of Reinforcement

A series of experiments by Lett (1973, 1974, 1975) has provided the principal support for Revusky's theory. Lett assumed that Revusky's theory of long-delay learning can, in principle, apply to the association between any intraepisodic events. The association Lett tested was between a correct choice and the reinforcer for that choice. Her question was whether the conventional failure to find long-delay learning with exteroceptive stimuli is caused by interfering associations acquired by the animal between presentation of the CS and presentation of the UCS. In demonstrations of long-delay conditioning involving gustatory stimuli and visceral consequences, the animal typically spends the duration of the CS–UCS interval in its home cage, where there is little opportunity for interference with retention of the gustatory stimulus. In contrast, the typical procedure with exteroceptive stimuli is to leave the animal in the testing situation between the CS and the UCS, which may promote more interference in retention of the CS. For Lett's purpose, therefore, the contextual difference between the experimental and extraexperimental environments is not ignored, nor does it create theoretical problems; indeed, it has an explicit place in her tests. The proper tests can be accomplished with relative convenience in long-delay conditioning with animals because, unlike the *extraexperimental* forgetting to be explained by the Underwood–Postman theory, the forgetting that is of concern in long-delay learning occurs within the experimental situation.

Initial procedure.   Food reward was given to each rat at differing times following a correct discrimination. The delays that elapsed between the correct response and the reward were extraordinarily long in relation to previous experiments of this kind. Lett's first study involved learning of a T-maze position discrimination. Among the three experiments in this study, rats were given a huge food reward (25–30 gm of wet mash) after delays of .5, 1, 2, 4, 5, or 8 minutes following the correct choice. In previous studies, in which the animal remained in the experimental apparatus during the delay interval between a response and presentation of the reward, learning was unlikely whenever delays increased beyond about 5 seconds; the *shortest* delay used by Lett was six times longer.

In addition to the confinement of the animal during the delay, other procedures used by Lett were unusual. On each day of training, the rat received trials until a correct response was made (half the animals were correct when they turned left into a small white compartment, and half were correct when they turned right into a large black compartment). Immediately after a correct response, the animal was returned to its home cage, where it spent the entire delay interval. At the end of that interval, the animal was placed back into the start box compartment, where it was fed the 25–30-gram reward, its entire daily ration of food. Thus, the reward for the correct response was presented in a location completely removed from the discriminanda.

This obviously was a very tedious set of experiments to conduct. Because several trials might elapse before a reward was given, the animals often were reluctant even to leave the start compartment and make a choice of any kind. Eventually, however, after 20 or 30 days of training, the rats began to choose the correct alternative more often than one would expect simply on the basis of chance; in other words, learning occurred.

Following 70 days of training, at which time the rats were choosing with better than 80% accuracy, reversal training was begun. For reversal training, the originally correct side no longer was followed by reward, but the previously incorrect response was. Within 40 to 50 trials of reversal training, this new response was chosen on about 80% of the trials. Somewhat surprisingly, learning did not depend on the duration of delay; correct responding was about equally likely within the range of .5 minute and 8 minutes' delay. If Lett's procedures were indeed successful in completely eliminating all retroactive or proactive interference in retention of the most recent choice at the time of reward, one would expect just these results. In terms of Revusky's theory, if all sources of interference were removed, delay should make no difference.

Because a particular turning response determined a correct choice in Lett's experiment, it was possible that proprioceptive aftereffects lingered throughout the delay interval and became asociated with the occurrence of the reward. The consequence would have been generalized reinforcement of the correct response through peripheral mediation. This would remove the need to consider memory processing during the delay. In fact, an earlier study by Perkins (1947) that had found learning over unusually long delays (2 min) was explained in precisely this way. This peripheral mediation explanation evolved when a subsequent experiment (Grice, 1948) used a visual discrimination for which proprioceptive cues were irrelevant and found no learning when delays of more than 5 seconds elapsed between the correct response and the reward.

Visual discrimination. To ensure that her results could not be accounted for in terms of proprioceptive mediation during the delay interval, Lett (1974) tested rats on a visual discrimination task. The basic procedures, however, remained similar to those of her previous experiment.

For this study, Lett employed a 1-minute delay between the correct response and the reward. As before, the rats were given continued trials each day until a correct response was made, and after each trial the animal spent a 1-minute delay in the home cage. For half of the animals the correct response was choice of the black alternative, and for the other half the white alternative was correct. After a correct response and the animal's subsequent 1-minute period in the home cage, the rat was returned to the start box, where it found a container holding 2.5 milliliters of 25% sucrose solution, which is a preferred delicacy for rats. After the sucrose solution was consumed, the animal was returned to its home cage until the next day's training.

The rats were trained for 100 days. As illustrated in Figure 5.8, learning occurred in spite of the 1-minute delay between responding and presentation of the reward.

A third set of experiments by Lett (1975) dramatically extended the length of the delay between the response and reward and included a direct test of Revusky's interference interpretation. This study tested learning of a position discrimination (as in Lett, 1973) but employed sucrose solution as the reward (as in Lett, 1974).

With procedures essentially the same as previously, the first two experiments included groups given delays of 1, 20, or 60 minutes between a correct response and presentation of a reward in the start box. Learning occurred, and duration of the delay made no difference (see Figure 5.9).

For the third experiment, Lett (1975) varied the proportion of the delay between the correct response and the reward during which the rat was confined in its chosen alternative of the T-maze relative to that spent in the home cage. The procedures were like those used previously, except that all rats were given a 2-minute delay between each response and return to the start box. Thus, a 2-minute "delay of reinforcement" occurred for all rats between the correct response and return to the start box for reward. One group of rats spent the entire 2-minute delay period in their home cage; a second group spent the first 15 seconds in the chosen alternative and the remaining time in their home cage; the third group spent the first minute in the chosen alternative and the remaining minute in the home cage. If the critical determinant of learning is retention of the most recent response when the reward is presented, and if this retention is decreased by interfering associations acquired during confinement in the apparatus, then one would expect to find poorer learning of the discrimination for animals spending a longer portion of their delay interval in the apparatus. That is precisely what Lett found, as shown in Figure 5.10.

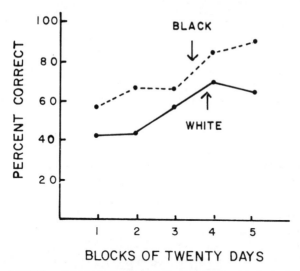

Figure 5.8   Acquisition of a brightness discrimination by rats, in spite of a 1 min. delay between the correct response and delivery of the reward, is indicated throughout 100 days of training. For animals represented by the dotted lines the black alternative of the T-maze was correct, and for animals represented by the solid line the white alternative was correct (adapted from Lett, 1974).

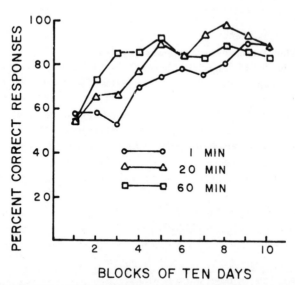

Figure 5.9   Acquisition of a spatial discrimination by rats, in spite of delays of either 1, 20, or 60 min. between the correct response and delivery of the reward, is shown during the course of 100 days of training (adapted from Lett, 1975).

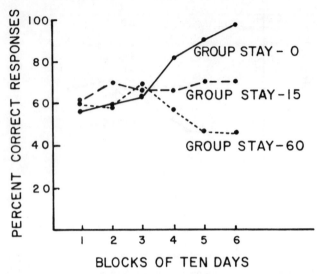

Figure 5.10   Acquisition of a spatial discrimination by rats is shown for animals given a 2 min. delay between a correct response and delivery of the reward. The groups differed in the portion of their 2 min. delay during which they remained in the chosen alternative: rats in Group Stay-60 remained in the chosen alternative for 60 sec. before being returned to their home cages for the remainder of the delay; rats in Group Stay-15 remained in the chosen alternative for 15 sec. before being returned to their home cages; rats in Group Stay-0 were removed from the chosen alternative immediately after a choice and placed into their home cages. (adapted from Lett, 1975).

Two important points are accomplished by this series of experiments by Lett. First, the generality of long-delay learning is established beyond the original cases involving only interoceptive events. Results with a similar paradigm by Revusky (1974) also may tend to enhance this generalization (as do further studies, some of which will be discussed with reference to content of memory in Chapter 8). Second, Lett confirmed the contention that long-delay learning depends on the absence, during the delay, of interference, which otherwise serves to impair retention of prior events.

Potential Problems in the Interpretation of Long-Delay Learning

Evidence has begun to question the need for a concept such as "relevance." There appear to be limits to the generalization that long-delay learning occurs only when interoceptive events such as gustatory stimuli and visceral consequences are to be associated, but not with exteroceptive events or any combination of exteroceptive and interoceptive events. Lett's experiments, for example, question the need for "relevance" by showing that long-delay learning can be a general feature of memory processing, regardless of the events to be represented in memory. Further tests raise further questions about the generalization just presented. The following examples may be cited:

1. Revusky and Garcia (1970, pp. 26–31) note that with extended training, conditioning may occur even when it involves associations between exteroceptive stimuli and relatively immediate visceral consequences, as well as when gustatory stimuli (flavors) are to be associated with an exteroceptive consequence (electrical shock). These studies have not involved long delays between the CS and the UCS, and perhaps the extended training serves to decrease negative transfer from prior association and interference in retention of the CS when the UCS occurs. Nevertheless, these results limit the concept of relevance.

2. Krane and Wagner (1975) tested the idea that while different classes of stimuli may differ in terms of their conditionability as CSs, the conditionability may depend on the temporal relationship between the CS and the UCS instead of on the nature of the UCS. They suggest in particular that an auditory–visual CS is more effective than a gustatory CS when the UCS occurs in close temporal contiguity, but that the opposite is true with a delay between the CS and the UCS. To some extent, this hypothesis is consistent with the Revusky–Garcia evidence just cited, but a direct test was warranted nevertheless.

The experiment by Krane and Wagner included three groups of rats given a particular exteroceptive CS (flashing light plus a tone) whenever they licked from a spout. Three other groups were given an interoceptive CS (taste of saccharin) whenever they licked from a spout. The UCS was a footshock that occurred for different groups either 5, 30, or 210 seconds after the CS. Conditioning involving the light–tone and the footshock was poorer the longer the CS–UCS interval, as usual. The interesting finding was that when the taste of saccharin was the CS, conditioning was *better* at 30 seconds and 210 seconds than with the 5-second CS–UCS interval. While these data do not establish that this relationship is independent of the nature of the UCS, they do tend to confirm the original idea of Krane and Wagner. And regardless, the surprising "reminiscence" (better retention of the CS at the time of the UCS, the longer the interval) is not easily explained and seems to add complexity to the concept of relevance.

3. Morrison and Collyer (1974) presented rats with a novel taste simultaneous with the occurrence of a light. Each such pairing was followed a few minutes later by toxicosis induced by lithium chloride. This sequence was presented on three occasions. Subsequently, the rats demonstrated an acquired aversion to the light (in terms of conditioned suppression). It is not clear whether mediation by the taste was necessary, although presumably it was. This is nevertheless a clear case of long-delay conditioning involving an exteroceptive CS and a noxious visceral (interoceptive) consequence. The place of such mediation within the concept of relevance has not been pursued.

4. It is well known that rats will behave in such a way as to obtain a balanced diet. Further, malnourished rats that normally have access to only an unbalanced

diet acquire a preference for stimuli paired with needed nutrients. Simson and Booth found that contiguous presentation of an odorized, imbalanced (protein-free) diet and a substance for correcting the imbalance (a variety of amino acids) resulted in a conditioned preference for the odor. However, long-delay conditioning with these two interoceptive events did not occur: If the UCS (amino acids) was not presented until 1 hour after the CS (odorized food), the conditioned preference for the odor did not develop. It is unclear as yet whether this represents a general difference in the potential for long-delay conditioning of preference compared to aversions.

Further comments on Lett's tests of the Revusky theory. Alternative interpretations of Lett's results are inevitable, however tight and reasonable Revusky's theory may seem. The history of experimental psychology consistently has shown an ingenuity for fresh views. A particularly clever and plausible new interpretation of the Lett data was suggested by M. R. Denny in his presidential address to the Midwestern Psychological Association (1974).

Studying Lett's procedure, Denny noted that following an incorrect response in the T-maze the rat ultimately was replaced to the "start" location in which, on earlier occasions (after correct responses), it had found a very large quantity of food reward or a very palatable bit of sucrose solution. Once the expectation for this reward develops, says Denny, the animal should be frustrated upon its absence. This frustration may be presumed to be aversive. The animal's tendency then would be to escape this start location. Because of a general tendency of rats to spontaneously alternate, the rat should "escape" to the alternative opposite from that just selected. The alternative just selected (prior to being placed in the nonrewarded "start" location) was, of course, the incorrect side. In escaping frustration, therefore, the animal would go to the "correct" side. The result, Denny hypothesizes, is an increasing probability that the rat will choose this "correct" side when returned to the start location. The mechanism underlying this learning may be in accordance with elicitation theory or simple contiguity, or due to reinforcement by escape from frustration.

According to Denny, therefore, whenever the rat encountered the empty start location, as on the first trial of each day (which is the trial of importance in Lett's data), the conditioned response would occur. This conditioned response happens to be the "correct" response, to the experimenter. The result will be an *apparent* acquisition of the discrimination, apparent only because this "acquired discrimination" does not require the formation of an association between the correct response and the experimenter-defined appetitive reward. It is this association that is of primary importance to the interpretation by Lett and Revusky.

This creative alternative interpretation is presented as an illustration of theories that may deal with apparently retention-forgetting phenomena without invoking memory processing beyond initial storage. In a preliminary test conducted by Denny himself, his hypothesis was not supported. However, the basic results obtained by Lett were replicated by Denny. The latter is notable because for at least one further study modeled after that of Lett, the replication of Lett's basic effect was debatable (Roberts, 1976; also see Lett, 1977).

The Generality of Intraepisodic Retention

Implicit in the preceding discussion is the assumption that intraepisodic and intertrial retention are determined by common processes. This may be an incorrect assumption. The determinants of tolerance for long delays between a conditioned and an unconditioned stimulus or between an instrumental response and a reinforcer may be different from those controlling an organism's capacity for the retention of the episode encompassing these environmental contingencies. A hint of such a difference may be found in the work of D'Amato and Cox (1976).

Depending on factors such as the prior laboratory experience of the monkeys, D'Amato and Cox found that monkeys capable of exhibiting excellent retention over intervals of several minutes in a delayed-matching-to-sample task initially had great difficulty maintaining correct responding or learning a new discrimination when a delay of reinforcement followed a discriminative response, even though this delay was only a few seconds in length.

Is it possible that factors such as "anticipation" or "foresight" might contribute a different source of variance, possibly emotional in nature, in the case of intratrial retention than is found in intertrial retention? Could the former case of retention represent a more "active" maintenance of a memory while in the latter case some more "passive" form of maintenance is typical? For now, there is little hard evidence available for addressing these interesting possibilities.

PHYSIOLOGICAL TRAUMA

This well-known source of forgetting caused by an unusual physiological event from an exogenous source must be classified as "abnormal" because it occurs relatively infrequently in nature. It is often imposed experimentally because disruption of the norm is an effective technique for understanding a process. In Chapters 6 and 7, we shall consider related cases of both clinical and experimental instances of amnesia in more detail, but as a general source of forgetting trauma warrants brief mention here.

Two aspects of forgetting induced by physiological disruption are of interest in this section because they specifically concern long-term retention. The first concerns whether this source can affect memories that were stored for a long period prior to physiological insult. There is no doubt that there is a temporal gradient of retrograde amnesia. We shall discuss this in more detail later, but generally, this gradient reflects the fact that memories acquired just prior to physiological insult are subject to more disruption than the "old" memories acquired in the more distant past. What is not clear, however, is whether "old" memories, those of interest in this chapter, are affected at all.

The fact is that this question has rarely been studied experimentally. There are a very large number of experiments showing that physiological disruption ordinarily does not influence relatively old memories but may if a "reactivation" treatment precedes the disruption (see Chapter 7 and 8), and there are also a number of studies showing that certain brain lesions may disrupt memories acquired several days before (see Iversen, 1973). However, few brain lesion experiments have varied the interval between training and the lesion (see McGaugh & Herz, 1972). Such experiments are difficult and expensive. Furthermore, they would concern issues of localization of function, another aspect that we shall discuss shortly. It is useful, therefore, to consider an experimental test of old memories in brain-damaged humans.

Warrington and her colleagues (Sanders & Warrington, 1971; Warrington & Sanders, 1971; Warrington & Weiskrantz, 1973) devised some questionnaire tests for recall or multiple-choice recognition of well-known events to which their subjects had been exposed. The items in these questions were ordered chronologically and concerned labels and descriptions of events or pictures of individuals in the news during the period from the 1930s to the 1970s. Warrington and her colleagues sought to determine whether amnesics, including those with relatively recently acquired brain damage, were any better in retention of old memories than in retention of newer ones. They concluded that the memory deficits in these amnesic patients are not so temporally bound as conventionally is believed. Instead, the deficiency for old memories was as great as that for more recent memories. (Later, we shall discuss the results of a similar, but improved, test employed more recently by Squire and his colleagues to investigate a similar loss of "old" memories in humans following electroshock therapy.)

The second point in this section concerns the specific locus in the brain in which physiological disruption, especially lesions, occurs. The classical question, as we have seen previously, is whether there is any particular portion of the brain in which all memories are stored. Of course, it has been known for centuries that localization of function does exist in the brain in the gross sense that certain portions of the brain control the motor activity of particular parts of the body and others control particular sensory modalities. But the classical answer concerning a general storehouse of memories has been offered by Lashley (e.g., 1950), who concluded that such a discrete storehouse does not exist, at least not in the CNS cortex. This generalization is no longer useful, however. It now appears that certain previously acquired memories may be disrupted by lesions in some areas but not in others, and that this occurs independently of sensory disruption (see, e.g., Gross, 1973; Iversen, 1973). Perhaps the simplest and most obvious case may be found in humans: Typically, a lesion in certain parts of the left hemisphere severely impairs verbal capacities while lesions in the right hemisphere do not. Given some reasonable assumptions, one may infer that verbal memories are disrupted selectively.

ARE THERE DIFFERENT KINDS OR STAGES OF MEMORY PROCESSING?

By this time, it should be apparent that no one can really be sure precisely what constitutes memory processing. Indeed, the domain of biological processes might best be considered under the heading "memory processing" cannot yet be defined clearly and remains an intriguing mystery. For example, we know that organisms may be treated to produce physiological immunization, so that for varying periods of time the organism will be resistant to assault or general biological interaction from other, usually smaller, organisms. Treatment that induces this immunization may or may not be understood in terms of the chain of biological activities through which it acts. The duration of the effect may depend on the nature of the treatment, the intensity or quality of the treatment, or the extent to which the organism is exposed to events that would counter the treatment. This duration may not be readily predictable. Analogies with memory are clear, which prompts us to ask whether immunization is a special case of memory processing, or vice versa.

Other time-dependent processes also may be viewed as analogous to, or special cases of, memory processing. One familiar example is the circadian rhythms that all organisms, including humans, seem to possess. We know that many behaviors function on a 24-hour basis when the organism is exposed to the usual stimuli that defines a day, such as differences in light and temperature. But we also know that when these external stimuli are removed the organism continues to behave in a cyclical way, as if the stimuli were still there. When this occurs, are the processes that maintain the organism's behavioral activity, general arousal, and internal hormonal activity "on schedule" the same as, similar to, or only analogous to the processes that act on memories? The same question may be asked of a variety of rhythmic biological processes, from the metabolically timed, multifaceted mechanisms of Selye's (1946) general adaptation syndrome to the simple heartbeat. Perhaps when the physiological basis of memory is understood better we may understand the relationships among these processes.

Given these biological processes, which conceivably could be viewed as kinds of memory processing, it is only natural that within the domain of psychobiological events to which we have been referring, the question would be raised concerning how many kinds of memory processing there are. We have already used one classification of memorial phenomena based on operational distinctions. Here, *short-term retention* refers to tests of retention within seconds or minutes after a relatively low degree of learning, and *long-term retention*, by mutual exclusion, refers to longer retention intervals with higher degrees of learning. Many theorists have gone a bit further than this, of course, and have viewed these operationally distinct phenomena as reflecting qualitatively different types of memory processing, conventionally termed *short-term memory* and *long-term memory*. We shall continue to prefer the operationally based terminology, *short-*

term retention and *long-term retention*. Let us briefly consider the evidence for and against such a conception. (For a more thorough consideration of these issues, see Clayton, 1974; Melton, 1963; Murdock, 1972, 1974; Squire, 1975; Wickelgren, 1973, 1975a,b).

Issues in the Theoretical Distinction between Short-Term and Long-Term Retention

Short-term retention in a theoretical sense must concern only time-dependent processes. Thus, the fact that most studies of short-term retention have used low degrees of learning, for example, should be entirely coincidental for theoretical purposes. Processes presumed to be unique to short-term retention processes must be those that occur soon after training, while processes presumed to be unique to long-term retention occur later—it is as simple as that. Our question is whether these processes in fact are different, in form or in effect.

The most common conceptual distinction between these two processes may be illustrated by Hebb's (1949) general conception, which serves more as a metaphor than as a description of the fact. Hebb suggested that an assembly of cells becomes interconnected as a consequence of learning and that, for a while, neural impulses will reverberate around this circuit. In this labile state of reverberation, the memorial representation of learning is particularly susceptible to disruption, including general disruption from neurological assault such as that produced by electroconvulsive shock. Without a sufficient number of learning trials (excitations), this reverberation will gradually die away, and no memorial representation will remain. However, if the reverberation can be maintained by sufficient repetitions, then the interconnections among the cell assembly (and eventually among the more complex representations, the "phase sequences") become permanent. This is the stage of long-term retention in which the memorial representation presumably is resistant or not susceptible to destruction by temporary physiological aberration in the brain. Of two classes of physiological insult relevant to this section, dynamic (e.g., electroconvulsive shock) or static (e.g., removal of brain tissue), reference here is to the former.

This sort of conceptualization was readily and widely accepted because it agreed both with intuition and with some dramatic clinical observations. Whereas an intense conversation may result in our forgetting the name of an individual to whom we were introduced a few minutes earlier, we may readily recall the names of childhood friends we have not seen for several years (for an interesting study of the latter phenomenon, see Bahrick, Bahrick, & Wittlinger, 1975). This implies that we can hold information in an apparently transitory, ephemeral state for a brief period; but without sufficient repetition to transfer it to a more permanent state, certain time-related processes will operate on the memory store to remove it from our potential use.

Clinical evidence.   The notion of distinct, time-related processes agrees with two remarkable effects on memory processing that have been documented clinically. The first involves physiological insult from severe brain concussion or electroconvulsive shock, and the second involves certain memory deficits that result from brain damage. We have already mentioned the well-known clinical reports (e.g., Russell & Nathan, 1946; see also Chapter 6) indicating that memories acquired just prior to acute brain insult involving concussion or seizure seem more likely to suffer subsequent retention deficit than memories for more remote events. This has been taken as evidence that in the early stages of a memory's existence the structure of a memory is more susceptible to destruction than later. Hence the distinction between an early, ephemeral process underlying short-term retention and the more robust and resistant process underlying long-term retention.

The second effect of clinical origin concerns certain forms of amnesia, including, in particular, amnesia associated with damage to the temporal regions of the brain and, to some extent, amnesia associated with the Korsakoff syndrome or senility. The effects of these afflications have been characterized as deficiencies in attaining a normal level of long-term retention, and the locus of these afflictions as associated with some process required for long-term retention of new information. For example, such patients seem unable to retain information for longer than a few minutes after their attention has been distracted from the task at hand, although they are seemingly unimpaired in their capacity to repeat information just presented to them or to retrieve memories acquired prior to the disease or brain damage. Depending on the pretheoretical disposition of the particular investigator, such memory defects have been interpreted as a deficiency in transfer from a short-term to a long-term processing system or simply as a deficiency in the long-term system.

For a number of years, this basically anecdotal, clinical evidence was deeply ingrained into the folklore of psychologists and biologists concerned with memory processing. Indeed, such effects do suggest intriguing differences between processes underlying short-term and long-term retention. Our concern is with how firmly these suggestions have withstood tough scientific scrutiny. The answer, in our opinion, is that the grain of truth in these suggestions was magnified beyond proportion to its analytical importance, probably misleadingly so.

Contrary evidence. In the following two chapters, we shall consider a large body of literature concerning the experimental analysis of the selective destruction of more recently acquired memories through brain insult. For now, we may restrict our attention to two characteristics of these analyses that illustrate their failure to provide a distinction between processes underlying short-term and long-term retention.

First, it is questionable whether any memorial representation of an event really is destroyed by brain insult of a dynamic nature, regardless of the temporal relationship between the insult and the events to be remembered. We now know that for a variety of types of brain insult the forgetting that occurs is characterized better as due to failure in memory retrieval rather than as due to disruption of memory storage. With appropriate treatment (such as the reactivation treatments mentioned earlier), maintenance of the memory may be established. One of the most dramatic examples of such an effect is reported by Bickford, Mulder, Dodge, Svien, and Rome (1958). These investigators electrically stimulated the human brain by means of electrodes implanted deeply into the brain and tested the effect on retention of verbal materials presented just prior to the stimulation. In tests given relatively soon after this treatment, the amount of retention was found to be controlled precisely by variation in the intensity or duration of the stimulation (poorer retention the greater the intensity or duration of stimulation). However, in spite of the initial retention deficit, ultimate evidence for retention after longer intervals was strong regardless of the characteristics of the stimulation.

Second, one may question the experimental strategy that has been applied to studying short-term retention through brain insult. Weiskrantz (1970) made the following cogent argument: Experiments directed at these problems concentrated on establishing a stable length for the interval between memory acquisition and brain insult after which the latter does not influence retention. (We shall see that this has not been successful.) Weiskrantz notes, however, that this interval is not really the most important for theory. The more important interval is that which establishes how long after learning a brain insult can be applied and result in *no* retention, for brain insult applied at that point or for all shorter intervals. When this interval has been examined closely, it appears that it is so short (on the order of milliseconds) as to be uninteresting in terms of memory processing (as opposed, for example, to sensory registration and perception).

The clinical data that have seemed to support a distinction between short- and long-term memory processing also are now suspect. The characteristics of amnesia in humans have been shown to have been misunderstood. We shall discuss this in more detail in the following chapter, but two general points are useful here. First, it is generally true for these patients, even the often-tested HM studied by Milner (e.g., 1966), and others that new learning can be established for long-term retention. The nature of the task that is being learned is very important. For example, the permanent acquisition of new motor skills has been demonstrated by HM. Furthermore, the relative efficiency in retention by amnesics, as compared to normals, may be altered drastically by variations in the nature of the retention test.

The second point established by Weiskrantz, Warrington, and others is that it now seems quite unlikely that processes responsible for short-term retention must necessarily precede those underlying long-term retention. Several brain-damaged patients have been found to have severe deficits as measured by a variety of short-term retention tests, but essentially normal capacity in tests of long-term retention (Warrington & Weiskrantz, 1973; Weiskrantz, 1970; also, Weiskrantz & Warrington, personal communication, 1973). This effect has prompted Weiskrantz (1970) to suggest that when information is acquired it immediately enters a long-term memory state. He suggests also that what is meant by a ''short-term memory process'' may be simply rehearsal activities entered into by humans to accommodate an overload of information destined for the "long-term memory store." If the unique process underlying short-term retention is rehearsal, then it is certainly important for understanding memory in humans; but if it is no more, this process may apply only to human verbal behavior and consequently have little generality.

Comparison of functional relationships.   One way to determine whether hypothetical processes differ in kind is to ask whether independent variables affect them in the same way. To what extent are there such functional differences between short-term retention and long-term retention? Clayton (1974) has presented a most instructive analysis of the study of human verbal retention (see also Wickelgren, 1973a,1975b).

First, Clayton notes that some variables seem to have the same effect: The facilitating effect of natural language mediators and higher degrees of original learning, and the impairment caused by retroactive or proactive interference, have been equivalent whether short-term or long-term retention is measured. On the other hand, a much larger number of variables have been found to have differing effects, influencing measures of short-term retention in one way and long-term retention in the other, or affecting one measure more than the other. The nature of these functional differences, however, is such that it would be quite plausible to accommodate these facts in one theory without requiring the assumption of two different kinds of memory processing.

Even a brief reference to these functional differences requires that we mention how, within a single experiment, short-term retention and long-term retention may be assessed. One method is through a variation in the Brown–Peterson paradigm mentioned in Chapter 3. In this paradigm, presentation of some verbal material to be retained is followed by a brief retention interval during which the subject is occupied with a distractor task intended to minimize rehearsal. If an effect obtained after a few seconds deviates from that found after longer intervals, we may infer that the short-term processes act differently than long-term processes. A second means is through presentation of a list of verbal items for immediate free recall by the subject. In these cases, the items presented at the end of the list are sometimes said to be controlled by short-term processes and those at the beginning of the list by long-term processes.

Clayton's review indicates that two variables having a strong effect on short-term retention—mode with which the items are presented (visually or auditorily) and degree of auditory confusion (between items to be remembered and interfering material)—rarely influence long-term retention. The former sometimes affects long-term retention in the sense of the first few items presented in a free-recall list. When it does occur, however, this effect is opposite that found for items near the end of such a list (short-term retention): Retention for items at the beginning of the list is better with visual presentation, and retention for those at the end is better with auditory presentation. Clayton suggests that these effects may be explained by what has been termed *echoic memory*, a more persistant aftereffect of auditory stimuli compared to visual stimuli.

In the case of auditory similarity between critical and interfering items, such auditory encoding is not a property of the objective similarity between those items. We really should not view "echoic memory" as a separate kind of memory processing; it is sensory specific, and thus cannot be a general property of memory processing, so perhaps it is more properly viewed as a property of sensation and perception (the distinction here admittedly is very fuzzy).

A large number of other variables seem to have more effect on long-term than on short-term retention, which in practice generally means more effect on the initial items of a free-recall task than on later items. According to Clayton's review, these variables include intelligence and age of subjects, characteristics of items to be remembered (including their frequency, meaningfulness, imagery, and associate structure), difficulty of concurrent tasks, and presentation rate. Because of the clear importance of rehearsal for retention, it is reasonable to expect that deficits in retention of items given in the initial part of a free-recall list (i.e., long-term retention) can be attributed to rehearsal deficiency. Indeed, poorer long-term retention by very old or very young subjects (cf. Ornstein & Liberty, 1973), by subjects with low IQs, when presentation is rapid, or when concurrent tasks are difficult may be attributed directly to the lower amount or poorer quality of rehearsal that occurs for these kinds of subjects and in these kinds of tasks. To account for the effects of frequency, meaningfulness, imagery, and associative structure—variables known to have an especially profound influence on rate of learning over successive trials—it seems natural to expect that rehearsals of items low in these characteristics will be less effective in the same way that successive practice trials are less effective with these items.

Thus, as Weiskrantz suggested within a different context, we are in a position in which differences attributed by some theorists to differing processes underlying short-term and long-term retention may be attributed more parsimoniously to differences in the effectiveness of a particular amount of rehearsal activity. This makes rehearsal no less interesting, indeed more interesting, as a problem concerning memory processing, as we shall see in a later chapter. But rehearsal is a good deal more constrained in its generality than a process underlying all cases of short-term retention would be. The same lack of generality may be applied to iconic or echoic memory as separate memory processes, particularly when it is noted that results related to modality differences may also be interpreted in terms of the differential availability of retrieval cues for different modalities.

Further evidence.   Another line of investigation also tests the hypothesis that memories undergo a different, more ephemeral and transitory sort of processing for a short period following training than is required for long-term retention. This asks to what extent the modification of a memory shortly after learning is achieved more readily than the modification of a memory that presumably is well established (in long-term memory) but has recently been retrieved or reactivated. We shall treat this issue when we consider abnormal memory processing. However, for now it is notable that similar effects with amnesic or hypermnesic agents have been found following the reactivation of old, well-established memories as have been found following acquisition of a new memory (see Gordon, 1973; Lewis, 1969; Meyer, 1972; Spear, 1976).

Nontemporal Distinctions May Identify Kinds of Memory Processing

The theoretical distinction between "short-term memory" and "long-term memory," as conventionally conceived in terms of the temporal parameter, no longer seems useful and seems also to have dwindling empirical support. This definitely does not eliminate the need to consider separate stages, phases, or kinds of memory processing; however, what seem likely to emerge in place of the temporally based distinctions are distinctions based on the accessibility of a stored memory.

As knowledge increases about iconic and echoic memory and about the consolidation process, some version of temporally based distinctions between kinds of memory processing seems inevitable, although with reference to far shorter intervals than has typically been identified with "short-term" memory. Unique characteristics of processing within the first milliseconds after sensory detection seem likely to serve as a basis for identifying possibly unique memory processes (Crowder, 1976; Deutsch & Deutsch, 1975). Beyond this, the most useful distinctions made among aspects of memory processing will probably concern whether the memory is in an "active" state (and, hence, relatively accessible) or in a "passive" state (and not accessible without additional information and special processing). These dimensions may not provide the only basis for identifying distinctive kinds of memory processing, but they seem to be the most evident at this time. We shall have further occasion to consider the concept of "active" and "passive" memory states in subsequent chapters.

SUMMARY AND CONCLUSIONS

Like the previous chapter, this chapter considered basic sources of forgetting in long-term retention. Also addressed was the value, for theory, of distinguishing separate memory processes on a temporal basis in terms of the duration of processing time available following initial perception—"short-term memory" and "long-term memory."

The first source of forgetting discussed was aging. In this context, "aging" refers to the set of behavioral and physiological changes that constitute maturation. It has seemed appropriate to infer that these changes are a source of forgetting, because long-term retention among organisms learning when they are immature is poorer than that of organisms that learn after maturity is reached. This phenomenon is termed *infantile amnesia*. The particular maturation-induced changes responsible for infantile amnesia have yet to be identified. In light of this, the physiological and behavioral changes discussed were those viewed hypothetically as plausible specific sources of forgetting. The ontogeny of retention capacity was discussed in conjunction with infantile amnesia and the methodological impediments to analysis of these phenomena.

The second source of forgetting considered was as *warm-up decrement*. This generic term represents the simple tendency for lesser retention following an interval of nonpractice than immediately after learning. This effect was considered separately from the general influence of retention intervals on forgetting because warm-up decrement often persists over a very large number of training sessions and hence to some extent seems independent of degree of training, and because warm-up decrement dissipates so rapidly with practice early in a retraining session. Through consideration of a variety of empirical characteristics of warm-up decrement and experiments showing that warm-up decrement may be modified by presenting certain events just prior to a retraining session, it was concluded that a likely cause of many instances of warm-up decrement is a deficit in memory processing, in particular, a deficit in memory retrieval.

The third potential source of forgetting concerned a specific aspect of intraepisodic retention, the influence of long delays between one event (a signal or CS) and another (a consequence or UCS). The referent phenomenon was acquired taste aversion. It is now well known that if a novel taste such as saccharin is followed by illness, an aversion to saccharin develops even when the intraepisodic interval between the taste and the illness is several minutes or hours in length. Within the view that the taste (CS) must be remembered at the time of the illness (UCS) for the conditioned aversion to take place, the question is, Why is the CS not forgotten during the interval? This question arises from the common failure to show conditioning between an exteroceptive CS and UCS when they are separated by more than a few seconds. A theory put forward by Revusky (1971) has addressed this question, and several experiments by Lett and others have tested it under circumstances other than the taste aversion paradigm. The general conclusion emerging from these studies is that long-delay conditioning is not unique to taste aversion and that the conditions governing this phenomenon are consistent with the expectations of Revusky's theory.

The final source of forgetting, physiological trauma, was discussed quite briefly, serving primarily as an introduction to the more detailed discussion to be found in Chapters 6 and 7. Two points were presented. First, the "age" of a memory is an important determinant of its susceptibility to the detrimental effects of physiological trauma, but old memories are not inevitably spared in favor of new ones. Second, physiological trauma directed at certain areas of the brain may be more detrimental to particular memories than trauma directed at other brain areas.

The final section of the chapter considered the possibility of different kinds, stages, or phases of memory processing. Evidence from a number of sources was addressed in considering whether the most prevalent distinction, short-term *versus* long-term memory, has merit. The conclusion was that when based entirely on a temporal distinction, separate consideration of these "kinds of memory processing" has restricted value. It was suggested that a more useful distinction could be made in terms of accessibility of a particular memory, specifically, whether a memory is in an active or a passive state. The value of this distinction should become apparent in subsequent chapters.

6

The Abnormal Processing of Memories

Memory processing may occur under "abnormal" circumstances that result from specifiable pathological conditions. More generally, these circumstances result from disruption of the normal physiological status of an organism by neural damage or other sources of interference with the action of the central nervous system (CNS). Our first concern in this chapter will be clinical cases of human subjects suffering from disease or trauma of the brain that yields exaggerated forgetting. We shall also consider briefly abnormal circumstances that appear to accelerate forgetting, but have no obvious link to physiological misfunction. Thereafter, we shall examine methods that have been applied in the experimental analysis of the abnormal processing of memories, including a variety of physiological manipulations employed in the study of memory processing in animals. It will be of value to discuss the characteristics of these physiological manipulations (principally, electrical or chemical disruption of the CNS) and to describe their basic behavioral consequences together with the rationale underlying their application.

ABNORMAL PROCESSING OF MEMORIES BY HUMANS

Tests of how effectively human patients process memories have long been a principal diagnostic tool of psychologists and neurologists. These clinical tests typically have limited potential for analysis, but the nature of the disruption to memory processing can take so many different forms that these rough tests may provide at least some diagnostic decisions by casting a broad, though imprecise, net. In discussing sources of abnormality (in this case, deficiency) in memory processing, Whitty and Lishman (1966) note that

> The range of memory defect is considerable. It may be a partial loss of registration, appearing simply as exaggerated forgetfulness; a severe inability to recall or record all current events,

with preservation of more distant memories; a limited but complete amnesia for a sharply defined period; repeated episodes of such amnesia; or a period of partial amnesia with hazy and inaccurate recollection. (pp. 72–73)

In view of the potential scope of amnesic effects, we must place some limits on our discussion here. These limits are set in terms of the nature of the memory processing being studied and the analytical potential of the source of the abnormality. We shall restrict our discussion to consideration of what Tulving (1972) has termed *episodic memories*. Such a memory is an individual's representation of an episode or set of events that may be dated temporally. For example, a particular discussion with one's physician, the location of a new house to which one has recently moved, or the name of the current president of the United States would be considered to be represented as episodic memories. Through this restriction, we exclude conditions such as apraxia (inability to apply a particular object for its proper use, even though the individual may be able to say the name and describe the uses), agnosia (inability to recognize objects through certain sensory modalities in spite of adequate capacity for detection through that modality), and aphasia (a disturbance in verbal communication, such as an inability to say the name of a common object). While disruption of the processing of episodic memories may contribute to these afflictions, this contribution is not obvious.

As the second restriction, we shall concentrate on amnesia that has arisen in humans from one of three sources—damage to the temporal regions of the brain, alcoholism advanced to the stages of the Korsakoff syndrome, or electroconvulsive shock applied for therapeutic reasons. These sources cause the products of memory processing to be dramatically abnormal, but are accompanied by circumstances that make them especially advantageous for analytical purposes. Except for the exaggerated forgetting that accompanies these sources, the patients tested are otherwise generally normal in terms of cognitive functioning. Also, the memory processing assessed in these cases can usually be evaluated purely in terms of the exaggerated forgetting that occurs, because perception and initial learning may be established independently. Finally, the same three sources of abnormal memory processing in humans may be applied in analogous fashion to animals, so their effects can be examined experimentally under the most carefully controlled conditions.

Amnesia in Humans Caused by Brain Damage

Massive cellular damage to the brain has produced cases of abnormal memory processing that may be the most interesting and useful cases of abnormality for the purpose of formulating general theories of memory processing. A motorcyclist may be thrown from his vehicle and strike the side of his head against the curb; a child may fall from a swing and land with the side of her head on a rock; to treat certain cases of epilepsy, a neurologist may consider it useful to surgically remove specific portions of the brain. In each of these cases, millions of brain cells will be lost or killed by direct puncture or exposure to blood. We should not be surprised, therefore, to find dramatic changes in behavior.

However, certain cases exist in which most forms of perceptual and cognitive behaviors, as well as motor skills and general emotional balance, have remained normal, but the processing of memories by these individuals is quite abnormal. Such cases are relatively rare; soon we shall review the experimental studies that have analyzed memory processing in such cases, and the number of human amnesics actually tested rarely is more than five or six per study. The accumulation of even this small number typically is achieved only at great expense and effort on the part of the experimenter.

The well-known group of patients given bilateral surgical removal of the temporal lobes of the brain by the neurosurgeon Scoville were tested psychologically by Milner (e.g., Scoville & Milner, 1957). Cases like these have particular analytical potential because of the relative control over the location of the lesions. However, of several such patients, only four suffered clear impairment to memory processing of the type that is of interest to us here, and three of these had so many other problems that either they were untestable or their data were uninterpretable.

The analytical difficulties inherent in this area may be illustrated in terms of the latter three cases. One of these was a physician diagnosed as paranoiac and characterized by a history of violent aggressive behavior, including a homicidal attack on his wife. As a consequence of surgery, aggression was reduced, as was his capacity for memory processing, but the man's general behavior was still characterized as quite paranoid. The other two cases exhibited behavioral disorders that not only made testing and interpretation of the results difficult but also were so severe that their memory-processing defects were not noticeable immediately. One woman, diagnosed as manic–depressive, displayed normal memory processing when questioned casually, but exhibited generally disruptive behaviors of an irritable and anxious nature; the third case suffered from a psychotic condition that was not alleviated by the surgery and was so severe that it was quite a long time before any memory deficit was detected (see also Isaacson, 1972). The remaining patient, HM, has been presented as a paradigmatic case of human amnesia and studied so widely that some detail about his history and behavior is of interest.

At about the age of 10, HM began to exhibit minor epileptic seizures, possibly attributable to a bicycle accident that had produced brief periods of unconsciousness a year or so earlier (although this was not clearly established as the cause). By the time HM was 16, the seizures had increased substantially in their intensity and duration and continued to do so thereafter. Although he graduated from high school and worked for a while building electrical motors, the increased severity of the seizures soon forced him to leave this job. At the age of 27, HM agreed to an operation by Scoville that involved removal of the internal part of the temporal lobe of both hemispheres of the brain, a large portion of the hippocampus, and a portion of the amygdala, but left relatively untouched the temporal neocortex.

After the operation, tests revealed that HM's IQ was unimpaired and that his linguistic behavior remained generally normal. He suffered retrograde amnesia for the period of a year or two prior to the operation, but otherwise seemed normal in his capacity to recall earlier memories.

HM's problem was in retention of new information over intervals longer than several seconds, or at most minutes—events of his contemporary life came to have little or no influence on his behavior. Shortly after the operation, his family moved to a new house; they moved again a few years later, but HM did not learn the new address or the location of the new house and often mistakenly returned to the one where he had lived prior to the operation (following the second move, HM did indicate some awareness of having moved but was not able to remember where). He regularly cared for the lawn, but each time he had to ask where the lawnmower was kept; he treated his neighbors as strangers, never learning their names; he reworked the same puzzles each day without apparent boredom or awareness of having seen them before; he had to be reminded to shave and even to eat each day, although he performed both activities with normal efficiency. On the other hand, there were some indications of rudiments of new learning: HM showed some knowledge of the assassination of John F. Kennedy and the death of Pope John, recognized the name of one astronaut, and could recognize his own house from a distance (Milner, Corkin, & Teuber, 1968).

Generally, then, the behavior associated with this affliction (henceforth referred to simply as human amnesia) is characterized as relatively normal in intelligence, perceptual–sensory capacity, and personality, but deficient in processing information in order to incorporate it as a relatively permanent memory (i.e., representation). We must realize that amnesics (like victims of similar afflictions such as aphasia) may function with apparent normality if they can be provided with appropriate reminders such as explicit notes indicating their address, phone number, what to do at what time, and so forth. They may be able to carry on a "small-talk" conversation flawlessly by employing the heavily overlearned comments typically employed by all of us in such instances. Yet this amnesia may preclude many normal activities and prevent many forms of employment. For example, one patient with whom I have had personal contact no longer could enjoy reading, not even the simplest of novels or magazine articles; every page and paragraph appeared in isolation because the patient failed to remember any of the previous content. For analogous reasons, even television shows of the usual 30- or 60-minute length could not be enjoyed, with the exception of certain sporting events and, in this particular case, Tom and Jerry cartoons. These limitations are especially striking when one realizes that this patient, in spite of his amnesia, has a measured IQ probably higher than that of most of the persons treating him, including his psychiatrists.

Limitations and general considerations in the analysis of amnesia.   A major limitation in the analysis of abnormal memory processing in humans is the need to cope with a subject variable (i.e., different classes of human subjects) as

the major independent variable. Like the difficulty of comparing memory processing in rats and monkeys, we find that the difference between amnesics and
normals is in terms of so many different dimensions that the simple discovery of
better retention by one class of subjects is of relatively little analytical use.

The characteristics that uniquely define an amnesic (as opposed to a normal)
often cannot be specified. For instance, although neurological or behavioral tests
may indicate that some portion of the brain is not functioning properly, it often
cannot be determined whether the malfunctioning is due to a tumor or a lesion,
and the precise location cannot be determined until the patient is dead. Thus, for
practical purposes, the precise source of the amnesic syndrome typically is unspecifiable.

While a diagnostician may recommend that Patients A and B be treated together as amnesics because of their general behavior and because both are known
to have suffered damage to the temporal regions of the brain, the differences in
the locations of these lesions may be so great as to preclude a common understanding of the difficulties. The analytical problem may be compared to the
problem of seeking a common understanding of the behavioral effects in Patient
C, who has lost an arm, and in Patient D, who has lost a leg, although both may
be classified as having lost a limb. This somewhat grim analogy aside, we should
be aware that a pool of subjects labeled ''amnesics'' may be considered together
on the basis of where the brain is presumed to be malfunctioning, or what portion
a surgeon intended to remove, even though the particular normal and abnormal
portions of the brain may differ as much among the amnesics as between amnesics and normals. While the sites of brain damage in humans may be identified
to some extent by techniques such as angiography (where contrast material
injected into the bloodstream is detected in the blood vessels of the brain by
X-ray photography), these are dangerous methods frequently associated with
morbidity and occasionally with mortality. Better and safer techniques are available, although the accuracy of histology for identifying lesion sites is not yet
achievable in living patients. A particularly promising technique is computerized
axial tomography, introduced to the U.S.A. in 1972 but not applied widely until
four or five years later. This technique transforms numerous X-ray images of the
head, taken from many angles, into a three-dimensional representation constructed by computer.

The primary means by which amnesics are identified, of course, is in terms of
their gross behavior and the products of their memory processing, in their responding to general questions or discussion with their physicians, or in unusual
behavior such as inability to find their way home from work. Such an individual
may be identified as an amnesic even in the absence of the sort of structural
damage that is known to cause amnesic behavior in other individuals. Therefore,
conclusions derived from tests comparing the behaviors of normals with those of
amnesics are limited to statements in the form of response–response laws (see
Spence, 1944). In other words, regardless of how cleverly the researcher initiates

memory-processing comparisons between persons termed amnesics (on the basis just presented) and persons termed normals, differences can lead no further than conclusions of this type: Persons classified together because they respond in a particular way under certain conditions (e.g., amnesics) predictably yield response pattern X under other conditions (the experimental conditions at hand), while another class of persons known to respond differently than the amnesics under the first conditions (e.g., the normals) may predictably emit response Y under the experimental conditions. We must recognize that such a conclusion is quite different in nature than "a lesion in Area 17 of the brain changes behaviors from the (Y) type to the (X) type," and of course, a response–response relationship holds a good deal less analytical potential.

For purposes of analysis, persons diagnosed as suffering the Korsakoff syndrome may be grouped together with other persons labeled amnesic, even though the etiology of the Korsakoff syndrome (advanced alcoholism, including nutritional deficiency) is quite different from that of epilepsy or accidental brain damage. This practice of grouping different types of amnesics has been justified by scientists in this area on the basis of the striking similarity between the forgetting shown by Korsakoff patients and the classical amnesic syndrome in persons with damage to the hippocampal regions of the brain. This, of course, is quite appropriate for the construction of response–response laws. Moreover, autopsies on persons classified as having the Korsakoff syndrome consistently have indicated relatively localized damage to the mamillary bodies and the medial thalamus, areas intimately connected with the hippocampus. Unfortunately for analytical purposes, advanced alcoholism is often accompanied by a deficiency of the Vitamin B group, especially thiamine; some cases of amnesia have been attributed entirely to such nutritional deficiencies (see Whitty & Lishman, 1966). So it is usually impossible to determine the precise relationship between the lesions found in Korsakoff victims and their deficits in memory processing. Also, as behavioral analysis has become more sophisticated important differences in memory processing have begun to be detected for persons with different etiologies of similar malfunctions of the brain, so grouping Korsakoff and temporal-damaged patients together as "amnesics" seems increasingly inappropriate (Butters & Cermak, 1975).

We must deal, therefore, with interpretations of a class of apparently abnormal behaviors (amnesia) that have not been tied firmly to clear, physically defined operations. That is, while the dependent variable (the measure of memory processing) typically is tied to clear operations of measurement, the independent variable (whatever it is that causes amnesics to be different from normals) is less stable and usually unclear. We are in fact not really sure how to arrive at a uniform definition of this affliction independent of the behavior measured. To me, this would ordinarily be an unconscionable scientific circumstance for the purpose of experimental design. In this case, however, two factors permit us to take seriously experiments analyzing the amnesic syndrome. First, we can arrive at a rough, independent physical description of the presumed common basis of amnesia—damage to the limbic system of the brain, probably specifically to the hippocampus and its immediate efferents and afferents—that offers a promise of a firm distinction between amnesics and normals independent of their behavior. Second, the characteristics of the amnesic syndrome are so dramatically singular, so obviously detectable, and so pervasive in behavior that they promise at least some solid response–response relationships.

The experimental analysis of human amnesia has been hampered by practical problems and the elementary difficulties and expense required to reach and test the few amnesic patients who otherwise are relatively normal. For the most part, these are outpatients who do not require the constant care and protection of a hospital, so they are unlikely to be concentrated in any particular locale. Like any other persons engaged in day-to-day existence, these patients may be less than pleased about being hounded by psychologists interested in testing their capacity for learning and retention. The associated problems of arranging a time and location for testing them are obvious.

Another factor that has tended to limit the progress of investigators in this area concerns the restricted expertise of the scientists interested in such patients. The special knowledge and skills of these scientists have tended to fall short of what is necessary for a complete examination of memory processing. Interest in am- nesic patients, and accessibility to them as experimental subjects, has arisen primarily among psychiatrists, clinical psychologists, and neurologists. Al- though these specialists may be expert in the diagnosis and treatment of abnormal behaviors generally, they typically have lacked sophistication in testing verbal memory processing and awareness of the understanding gained throughout 50 years of studying normals on such tasks. There are, however, some notable exceptions to this general analytical weakness (e.g., Baddeley & Warrington, 1970, 1973; Cermak, Butters, & Gerrein, 1973; Shallice & Warrington, 1970).

Diseases in the brain often accompany amnesia in humans, and this presents an additional problem in the analysis of memory processing. Isaacson (1972) has discussed this problem, noting that "the majority of patients in whom a distur- bance of recent memories has been reported were suffering from an epileptic disorder so severe as to eliminate normal activities and to justify the surgery" (p. 53). Among the several patients operated on by Scoville, the only nonepileptics who became amnesic previously had been diagnosed as psychotic and had been exposed to insulin and ECS treatment, which undoubtedly caused seizures in the brain similar to those suffered by epileptics.

Perhaps the major problem that impedes a clear understanding of human amnesia is a vexing inconsistency between the behavioral characteristics of this syndrome in humans and the behavioral characteristics of animals that have suffered lesions in the brain in precise correspondence with the location of lesions found in human amnesics. Briefly, the drastic forgetting found in human amnesics simply has not been found in lesioned animal subjects. In later sections, we shall consider one likely reconciliation of this paradox by Weiskrantz and his associates. Here we may mention two further considerations that may be relevant to such a paradox. First, it is possible that different classes of memorial content are processed in discretely separable portions of the brain. For example, memories involving aversive stimuli may be processed in one portion, those involving visual discriminations leading to appetitive rewards in another, those involving relatively abstract generalizations or rudimentary concepts in another, and so forth. Isaacson (1972) has commented on this possibility, as have Carlton and Markiewicz (1973). The implication is that memory processing following a particular lesion in animals may become more like that found in humans as the content of the events represented in the area of the lesion become more similar. Such considerations of specific locations in the brain as responsible for specific memory content become reasonable in view of the conclusion that Lashley's laws of equipotentiality and mass action simply are no longer viable (e.g., Barbizet, 1970; Iversen, 1973).

As our final consideration in the general analysis of human amnesia, it is important to realize that a significant discrepancy may exist between what an amnesic says he remembers and the extent to which that memory influences his behavior. For example, Talland (1965) cites two cases in which the behavior of amnesic patients clearly was influenced by past events, yet these patients professed no knowledge of these events upon questioning. One case is the classic example reported by Claparede (1911) in which he hid a pin between his fingers and shook hands with the patient, jabbing her in the process. Thereafter, the patient was reluctant to shake hands with him again—indeed, she refused to do so—although she was unable to describe why she behaved in this way. When questioned only a few minutes after the jabbing, she reported no memory of the incident, yet her behavior indicated that memory attributes representing some portion of that episode had been permanently acquired. A second example reported by Talland concerned a patient whose brother had been killed in an automobile accident a few months earlier. During one interview, this patient responded with quite accurate answers concerning the circumstances of his brother's death and also provided accurate information concerning details of the wedding plans of a surviving brother. Yet this patient had asserted only a few days before that a letter he had just received from his surviving brother was in fact from his deceased brother, and a few days after the interview the patient could not be convinced that he had recalled any information concerning the current activities of either of his brothers.

A report by Sidman, Stoddard, and Mohr (1968) similarly includes evidence that HM exhibited some dissociation between what he remembered and what he said he remembered. Following a series of trials on which HM exhibited significant learning of a discrimination between a circle and various elipses, he was interrupted in this task, engaged in discussion, and then questioned about the nature of the task he had just been doing. HM could not recall that the alternative stimuli were elipses and a circle (he suggested that they might be crosses). Yet when given further trials on the same discrimination task HM continued at the level he had achieved prior to the interruption, showing no impairment of the acquired discrimination. Starr and Phillips (1970) studied an amnesic patient who learned to play a new tune on the piano. When questioned on the following day, this patient did not remember having learned the new tune, but when presented the first few notes of the tune he proceeded to play it in its entirety.

These cases emphasize a point that recurs often in this book: Methods of assessing retention (verbal reports compared to sensory–motor responses, in these cases) may differ in sensitivity of measurement as well as in the retrieval cues they provide.

The amnesic syndrome.   We have seen examples of how the amnesic syndrome *appears*: After intervals of a few seconds, there apparently is no marked deficiency in short-term retention, as evidenced by the amnesic's normal capacity for casual conversation; except for a failure to recall events that occurred during a period just prior to brain damage (extending backward in time sometimes as much as a year or more), retention for memories acquired long before brain damage seems relatively normal; and the deficit has been characterized as an impairment in the permanent accumulation of new information (as evidenced by impairment in new learning or in new long-term retention) or, more theoretically, an impairment of the "long-term memory process." The formulation of the characteristics of this syndrome appears to be consistent with typical encounters with these patients; for example, physicians and psychologists regularly visit such a patient and engage in normal conversation, only to have the patient show no signs of ever having met them minutes following any particular visit. This formulation led to theoretical decisions about the nature of memory processing, in particular to the widely accepted decision to consider at least two separate memory processes, one for short-term retention and one for long-term retention, and the further decision that information is transfered from one of these processes (or "stores") to the other (e.g., Milner, 1966; Wickelgren, 1973). We may now examine some results of the experimental investigations of memory processing in amnesics to determine how this original formulation of the amnesic syndrome has fared.

Short-term retention in amnesics and normals.   Drachman and Arbit (1966) were among the first to consider the theoretical distinction between short-term retention and long-term retention in an empirical investigation with amnesics. They concluded that amnesics performed at a normal level on short-term tests. These tests were of the classical memory span type, in which retention of a series of digits is measured immediately after their presentation. Amnesics in this study appeared to be deficient in tasks requiring permanent accumulation of new information. This study is subject to criticism on a variety of grounds, including the constitution of the control groups, but perhaps more important, it does not answer the question of how amnesics perform in short-term retention tasks that include distraction between presentation of the material and its recall.

It had been conventional to view retention by amnesics as dependent on continuous rehearsal from the moment of presentation and to expect that any distraction from this rehearsal would lead to drastic retention deficits (Milner, 1966). It was soon discovered, however, that retention by amnesics could be essentially normal after intervals up to a minute in length, even though verbal rehearsal could not possibly aid retention, or if the subject were distracted from rehearsing.

Wickelgren (1968) tested HM for the recognition of tones at various delays after their presentation, a task in which verbal mediation is unlikely and probably impossible. It was found that HM forgot at a rate no different from that of nonamnesic subjects. Similarly, Warrington and Baddeley (1974) employed a task with visual stimuli in which rehearsal was precluded effectively. Amnesics and matched control subjects were presented a sheet of white paper on which a single dot had been placed; the subject's task was to reproduce the location of the dot after intervals of 0, 5, 10, 30, or 60 seconds, during which the subject's attention was occupied by another task. Retention performance by the amnesics did not differ from that of their controls at any delay interval. Baddeley and Warrington (1970) had obtained similar results in a different task using verbal stimuli. Using the Brown–Peterson paradigm, in which rehearsal is reduced or prevented by a distractor task (see Chapter 3), short-term retention by amnesics was compared with that of matched control subjects. All subjects were shown sets of three words and asked to recall them after intervals ranging between 0 and 60 seconds. Rate of forgetting was almost indistinguishable between amnesics and normals (see Figure 6.1). From among the six experiments reported by Baddeley and Warrington, equivalent short-term retention by amnesics and normals was indicated by these further results: Retention of the terminal items in a free-recall list did not differ for amnesics and controls when a 30-second delay and an interpolated task occurred between presentation of the lists and the test; with the Brown–Peterson technique, amnesics were no more susceptible than were controls to the buildup of proactive interference (previously identified by Keppel & Underwood, 1962, as a major contributor to forgetting in this task); amnesics were no different from controls in recalling one of four previously presented paired-associate items (the task was based on the probe technique of assessing short-term retention; see Chapter 3); and amnesics did not differ from normals in their immediate recall of sets of digits ranging in number from five to eight.

While these data would appear to establish that amnesics show normal retention over intervals less than a minute in length, the generality of this conclusion is not yet firmly established. Tests of Korsakoff patients by Butters, Cermak, and their colleagues, in a series of experiments equal in proficiency to those of Baddeley and Warrington (e.g., Butters, Lewis, Cermak, & Goodglass, 1973;

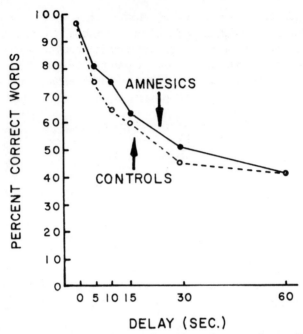

Figure 6.1 Relative rate of forgetting by amnesic patients and nonamnesic control patients tested with the Brown-Peterson paradigm over intervals up to 60 seconds in length (adapted from Baddeley and Warrington, 1970).

Cermak, Butters, & Gerrein, 1973; Cermak, Butters, & Goodglass, 1971), consistently found these amnesics to be deficient in short-term retention measured after intervals of a minute or less. The evidence gathered by these investigators is substantial and robust. They have noted, furthermore, that Korsakoff patients appear to have subtle visual deficits ordinarily missed when retention·is measured with a 0-second interval using the Brown–Peterson task. Their evidence also indicates that while proactive interference in short-term retention may affect amnesic Korsakoff patients and normals equally, under some circumstances cumulative proactive interference builds up a good deal more rapidly among the amnesics, in opposition to the results obtained by Baddeley and Warrington and cited earlier (Butters & Cermak, 1975). Later we shall mention other differences in the results obtained by the Butters–Cermak and Weiskrantz–Warrington groups.

These discrepancies are difficult to reconcile, not because there are mysteriously few differences between the conditions of these sets of experiments but because there are so many (see Butters & Cermak, 1974). The most obvious difference is in the subject populations, those of the Butters–Cermak group being alcoholics advanced to the stages of the Korsakoff syndrome and those of Weiskrantz–Warrington and their colleagues being primarily victims of brain damage from other sources. There also are procedural differences, such as the nature of the distractor tasks interpolated during the retention intervals. The latter difference might be understandable in terms of the effects different distractor tasks may have on how the subjects process the materials mnemonically. There is evidence to indicate that the nature and effectiveness of such processing is different in amnesics and normals, and certain distractor tasks may enhance this difference. We shall return to this point shortly.

Retrograde effects.   Although amnesics characteristically are impaired in terms of retention for events during a period of several days or several months preceding the onset of their illness, their retention for earlier years and for childhood conventionally has been considered to be normal. This conclusion is questioned by the results of a study by Sanders and Warrington (1971). As a test of long-term retention in patients suffering amnesia attributable to brain damage, these investigators constructed a questionnaire concerning events of the past 40 years. The test required subjects to recall or recognize (from among several alternatives) the correct answer to items concerning either past events or the identification of famous persons. The results of this test given to five amnesic patients and 200 normal control subjects of about the same age are shown in Figure 6.2. The results indicate clearly that there is a retention deficit for past

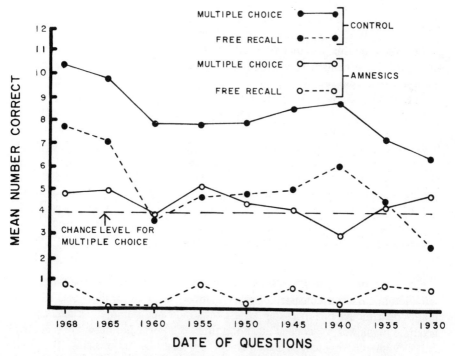

Figure 6.2   Relative accuracy by amnesic patients and nonamnesic control patients in response to questionnaire items (either free recall or multiple choice) associated historically with specific years during the patients' lives (adapted from Sanders and Warrington, 1971).

events that matches the deficit for recent events. The implication is that, at least for items that are not heavily overlearned, amnesics suffer deficits in retention for memories acquired prior to their illness as well as for those acquired subsequently.

Deficiency in the acquisition and retention of new information.   We have seen that amnesics may suffer some deficit in retention measured after a minute or so and in retention for memories acquired prior to their illness, but these are not their primary deficiencies and certainly not the most obvious. Retention involving memories acquired since the patient was diagnosed as amnesic is the major deficiency associated with this illness. We will now consider the characteristics and analysis of this deficiency.

There never has been any doubt that retention deficits after long intervals exist for amnesic patients: This fact is encountered in virtually all the experiments to be discussed (reviews of general evidence for this deficit have been reported by Talland, 1965, and Milner, 1966). While equivalent original learning by amnesics and control subjects has rarely been established, the differences in retention typically are too great to be accounted for on that basis alone. What is in doubt is the magnitude and generality of this retention deficit. If the deficit were absolute and complete regardless of the nature of the task, then we might conclude that behavioral investigations could do little toward understanding amnesia and, conversely, that the behavior of amnesics could tell us little about memory processing in normals; rather, it would then appear that some neural or pharmacological mechanism necessary for long-term retention simply is absent in amnesics. We shall see that this definitely is not the case. This simple solution is precluded by three facts: Amnesics do acquire memories with a degree of permanence sufficient to yield significant long-term retention; the extent of their long-term retention depends on the conditions of the particular task; and, in strictly behavioral terms, amnesics appear to process new information differently than normals. These facts are taken into consideration in the following discussion. We shall first discuss the evolution of evidence that this long-term retention deficit is not absolute, then take a brief look at evidence for "processing deficiencies" in amnesics, and finally review a series of experiments by Weiskrantz and Warrington that show that retention by amnesics may be drastically influenced by the conditions of the task, in particular by the conditions that influence memory retrieval.

Evidence of long-term retention in amnesics.   Initial tests of long-term retention in amnesics consisted of tasks relatively difficult for them or uncongenial to their modes of processing. These tests indicated minimal permanence of acquired memories, or none at all. For a time, this served to mask the scattered but accumulating evidence for permanent new learning in amnesics. This evidence arose first, and for a while most frequently, in terms of perceptual–motor skills. Milner (1962) found that the amnesic patient HM progressively improved his performance on a mirror-drawing task over a three-day sequence of practice. Milner, Corkin, and Teuber (1968) later reported significant savings in HM's retention scores after an interval of six days had elapsed since he had practiced a particular visual maze. Corkin (1968) found evidence of relatively permanent improvement in HM's performance as a consequence of practicing on three motor learning tasks, including substantial retention on one of these tasks after a delay of four days. In tests with another amnesic patient, Starr and Phillips (1970) found similar evidence of permanent acquisition of new information, primarily in performance on motor tasks. They reported significant savings scores for this patient after an interval of two weeks following original practice. However, this patient showed less evidence of permanent acquisition of verbal materials, although it clearly existed to some extent, as indexed by intrusions during learning from verbal items previously presented. (This is the patient mentioned earlier who was able to play a recently learned piece on the piano but could not recall having learned it.)

There is increasing evidence that amnesics may acquire verbal materials with some permanence. For example, Baddeley and Warrington (1973) tested amnesics on the task of long-term retention introduced by Hebb (1961). In this task, several series of verbal items (in this case, digits) are presented to the subject for recall. One (or more) of these same series of items is repeated from time to time while the remainder are not. To the extent that permanent acquisition of new information accumulates as a function of practice, recall of the repeated series of items should be better than that of nonrepeated series. Baddeley and Warrington found that amnesics, like normals, benefited in their recall from repetition of the series. The most extensively studied instances of long-term retention of verbal materials by amnesics are those found in the series of experiments by Weiskrantz and Warrington, which we shall discuss shortly.

The point I wish to emphasize in this section is that the evidence for a capacity for long-term retention in amnesics may vary depending on the testing procedure. Certain tasks provide clear evidence for long-term retention that reflects permanent acquisition of new information. This is not to imply that the retention deficit in amnesics can be eliminated just by selecting the proper task; for most of these instances, retention by the amnesics, though clearly present, was inferior to that shown by nonamnesic control subjects. However, because it is now clear that the memory-processing deficit of amnesics is not absolute, we may ask how the amnesics differ from normals in terms of information processing for long-term retention.

Amnesics may process information differently than normals.   Experimental manipulations of the content of the memories tested, of the task requirements, and of potential aids to retention have provided information to pinpoint specific deficiencies in memory processing by amnesics. Baddeley and Warrington (1973; see also Jones, 1974) presented amnesics and normals with groups of four words that could be combined to provide a basis for a visual image. The experimenter presented a group of four words in such a way as to describe the image for each subject; the subject was given 11 seconds to "form" the image; and then other sets of words were given with the same general procedure, except that the image instruction was not given in each case. Control subjects had better recall of lists given with imagery instructions than of those given without instructions; amnesics did not show differences in list recall, even though they reported that they did form the images. These results suggest that amnesic subjects may be less able to utilize opportunities for "mnemonic preparation" (see Chapter 8) than normals. This suggestion may be limited to memory processing involving imagery, however, because in some other instances that might be described as mnemonic preparation—for example, organizational devices such as clustering—amnesics appear not to be deficient relative to normals (Baddeley & Warrington, 1973).

Amnesic subjects may benefit more than normals from certain cues for recall provided during the retention test, a point especially pertinent to our later discussion of the Weiskrantz–Warrington analysis. Cermak, Butters, and Gerrein (1973) presented a list of words to subjects (Korsakoff patients and normals) and tested their retention of the list either immediately or after a 1-minute interval filled with a distractor task. When the retention test was accompanied by cues that were either the names of categories of items that had appeared in the list or associates of the items, the Korsakoff patients tended to benefit more than the normal subjects. This conclusion applies, however, only for subjects given a 1-minute delay between presentation of the items and the retention test. With immediate recall, the opposite relationship appeared and Korsakoff patients tended to benefit less from cueing than alcoholic controls. The basis of this intriguing interaction is not clear (see Butters & Cermak, 1975; Cermak & Butters, 1972; Weiskrantz & Warrington, 1975). The interaction occurs in terms of absolute number of items recalled and does not appear to be artifactually influenced by ceiling or basement effects of measurement. Furthermore, the apparently special benefit of cueing for Korsakoff patients is consistent with earlier results of Warrington and Weiskrantz (1971), who also had used a 1-minute interval between presentation and test.

Considerable evidence indicates that amnesic subjects have more difficulty withholding incorrect responses during a retention test than normals. Gardner, Boller, Moreines, and Butters (1973) found that Korsakoff patients given a series of word lists for free recall were more likely to respond inappropriately with items from previous lists than either nonamnesic subjects given the same tasks or nonamnesic subjects who had not been given any prior lists. Weiskrantz, Warrington, and their colleagues have accumulated a large number of studies with a variety of materials all indicating that for transfer tasks in which a different response is required to a particular stimulus than previously, amnesic subjects suffer a good deal more negative transfer than normals (Warrington & Weiskrantz, 1974; Winocur & Weiskrantz, 1976). Cermak and his associates (1973) found that Korsakoff patients tested on a continuous recognition task (see

Underwood, 1965) gave more false recognitions of two particular types— homonym and associative errors—than control subjects.

Experiments by Cermak and his associates (1973) indicate less responding by amnesic Korsakoff patients to semantic features of verbal material than is found in normals. Two experiments tested the effectiveness of Korsakoff patients in benefitting from different classes of cues (rhyming, associative, and category cues), and a third experiment involved a continuous recognition task. The results indicated that relative to alcoholic controls, Korsakoff amnesics were less influenced by semantic features of words but about equally affected by their acoustic or associative features. The lesser effect among Korsakoff patients of the semantic dimension of words is further illustrated in a study by Cermak, Butters, and Moreines (1974). This study tested release from cumulative proactive interference in the Brown–Peterson paradigm upon a shift in the kinds of materials the subject is to remember. This technique has been used as a means for identifying differences in the conceptual encoding normal subjects apply to different words. It is known that a shift in the conceptual grouping of successively presented items releases the proactive interference exerted by previous items. Cermak and his associates found that Korsakoff patients exhibited a substantial release from proactive interference when the materials to be remembered were changed from sets of three consonants to sets of three digits, but there was essentially no release following a taxonomic shift (e.g., from the category "vegetables" to the category "animals"). Such a taxonomic shift is accompanied by substantial release among normal subjects. (As an aside, an intriguing feature of these data is why proactive interference should have built up at all among Korsakoff patients when a series of categorically similar words were presented; this cumulation of interference from previous items would seem to imply relatively permanent acquisition of new information).

Collectively, these results of Cermak and his colleagues indicate a deficit in semantic encoding among Korsakoff patients. They do not, however, assess directly the nature of this semantic deficit. In this respect, the inference of Butters and Cermak (1975) seems quite reasonable. They suggest that Korsakoff patients are quite capable of encoding along semantic as well as acoustic and associative dimensions. Left to their own devices, however, Korsakoff amnesics are relatively unlikely to employ semantic encoding compared to acoustic or associative encoding. A related alternative is that Korsakoff patients are less likely to attend to semantic dimensions initially (Oscar-Berman, 1973).

Each of these apparent differences in processing by amnesics has been amplified and extended in a coherent series of experiments by Weiskrantz and Warrington, to which we now turn.

Circumstances of the task determine the extent of the amnesic's deficiencies: the Weiskrantz–Warrington experiments.   Based largely on the behavior of the epileptic patients on whom Scoville had performed brain surgery, but also in accordance with contemporary literature dealing with consolidation in animal subjects and short-term retention in human subjects, Milner (1966) suggested that the basic deficiency of amnesic subjects resided in the transfer of information from the hypothetical "short-term memory store" to permanence in the "long-term memory store." This was deduced from the evidence available at that time, which indicated that the difficulty of amnesics was not in short-term retention (hence, it could not be localized in terms of *entry* into the short-term store) nor in retrograde deficits for events prior to the onset of the amnesic illness (hence, the problem was not in retrieval from the long-term store). Because the locus of the brain damage in amnesics is in the region of the hippocampus, Milner proposed that it was this structure that was responsible for the transfer of information from the short-term store to the long-term store.

Given the once-common assumption amplified by Hebb's (1949) theory—that information from a short-term memory store feeds serially into a long-term memory store, thus progressing from a transient to a more permanent state in storage—and given the identification of the hippocampal structure as the portion of the brain most likely to be defective in amnesics, the Milner theory became widely accepted. Nevertheless, this interpretation seemed to Weiskrantz (1970) to be both dramatic and surprising:

> It is dramatic because one knows so little about the physiological foundations of LTM (long-term memory) that any lead as to where to concentrate one's efforts is welcome. It is surprising because the past efforts to locate the "engram" have merely confirmed its elusiveness; if it is so difficult to locate the engram, it is surprising that one can so easily locate the gate that controls entry into it. (p. 22)

The skepticism reflected in Weiskrantz's comments was prompted in part by a paradox that baffled many psychobiologists at that time. To understand the behavior and specific deficits in the memory processing of humans with lesions in the temporal portions of the brain, the scientific strategy that has most often led to the solution of medical puzzles—experimental analysis of the effect with animals—was employed. The paradox arose because this strategy appeared to be unsuccessful; comparable lesions in animals did not cause memory deficits like those reported clinically in humans.

Weiskrantz and Warrington conducted a series of studies yielding two influential conclusions that we shall summarize prior to describing their empirical evolution. These conclusions altered the course of research and the nature of theorizing concerning memory processing, both in amnesics and in normals. First, contrary not only to the assumptions of the Milner theory but also to those of some principal models of memory processing at that time (e.g., Atkinson & Shiffrin, 1968), evidence obtained by Weiskrantz and Warrington indicated that the serial progression of information from a short-term to a long-term store was neither likely nor necessary. This led Weiskrantz and others to view the hypothetical short-term store as a good deal simpler and of less general importance than was conventionally believed (Weiskrantz, 1970; Wickelgren, 1975a). We shall treat this conclusion as secondary, however, and shall postpone discussion of it for a moment. The second conclusion may have been more important, if only for its indirect effect on scientific strategies: This was that damage to the hippocampal region of the brain indeed does affect humans and animals in similar ways. The previous misunderstanding (I continue to anticipate the following discussion) was traced to an incorrect behavioral analysis of amnesia in man. In fact, the basic psychological consequences (of the temporal lesions) had been revealed more accurately in the experiments with animals than in the clinical observations with man.

In their initial studies, Warrington and Weiskrantz (1968) had wanted to compare the retention of amnesic patients and normals after intervals of up to 15 minutes. Retention was difficult to evaluate, however; with the conventional method of presenting a list of ten stimulus words for various numbers of trials, the amnesic patients were not able to reach a level of learning sufficiently close to that of the controls for meaningful comparison of retention.

Warrington and Weiskrantz then looked for a task that would not be learned too rapidly by control subjects but still could be learned to perfection by amnesics. They found that such a task had been reported in a paper concerning visual recognition in children (Gollon, 1960). The materials to be learned in this task are pictures or words presented in fragmented form. The fragmented form looks as if the word or picture has been drawn in pencil and then a thin eraser has been run through it; here, degrees of fragmentation would be graded in terms of how many times the "eraser" had passed through the picture or word in random directions. Examples of this material are shown in Figure 6.3.

To illustrate how learning is assessed with this method, it is convenient to describe the specific procedure employed in one of the more enlightening experiments of this series (Warrington & Weiskrantz, 1970). Subjects were presented a list of nine high-frequency words. Two fragmented versions of each word were prepared, as shown in Figure 6.3. Each time a word was presented, it appeared first in its more fragmented form; then it appeared in its less fragmented form; and finally the whole word was shown. A word was scored as correct when it was identified appropriately in its more fragmented form; an error was counted each time either of the fragmented words was identified incorrectly.

This procedure has two advantages. First, it provides the amnesics with a task that they can learn completely in a relatively short time. Second, it serendipitously provided a task in which errors were unlikely to take the form of errors of commission; rather, the errors that occur with this task are of omission, the "I-don't-know-the-answer" variety. Of importance to conclusions about memory processing is the fact that the practice effects were specific to the items presented rather than to general perceptual learning, as we shall see.

A result of major significance obtained by Weiskrantz and Warrington (1970a) was that significant long-term retention was shown by the amnesics, not only after a 24-hour interval between learning and retention but also after a 72-hour interval. Moreover, the amnesics' retention after 72 hours did not differ statisti-

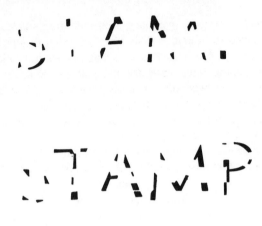

Figure 6.3   This exemplifies the degrees of fragmentation of words or pictures to be learned by amnesics in the fragmented-form procedure employed by Weiskrantz and Warrington (adapted from Weiskrantz and Warrington, 1970).

cally from that shown by the normal control subjects for the same delay. It remained possible, however, that this "retention" by the amnesics was only perceptual learning or accommodation, a modification of the perceptual process that enabled the amnesics to "solve" fragmented pictures better. To show that this was not the case, Weiskrantz and Warrington (1970b) replicated the basic phenomena with a different kind of material. Rather than using fragmented forms of the entire word as before, only the first two letters of five-letter words were presented initially, then the first three letters, and finally all five letters.

The experimenters found that the advantage of this method of presentation for the amnesic subjects was not that it permitted more efficient storage of the memory but that it permitted more effective retrieval. This important point was established by comparing the results of two separate experiments, each of which assessed retention by the same three methods. In the first experiment, the subjects learned the words with the fragmented-word procedure; in the second, they were presented the list of words in intact form and asked to read them aloud. For both experiments, each subject then was presented three lists. Retention of one list was measured by free recall; the subjects simply spoke as many words from the list as they could remember. For another list, recognition of the critical words from among alternative words was measured. For the third list, the words were presented in fragmented form and were to be identified, the same procedure as that used during the original learning trials in the first experiment.

The results, presented in Figure 6.4, indicate that the retention deficit of the amnesic subjects may be decreased (in this case, completely eliminated) if retention is tested by the fragmented-word technique. If the test is by free recall or recognition procedures, the difference between normals and amnesics is maintained. More to the point, it does not matter so much how the materials are presented during original learning as how they are tested. Finally, because the effect was found both with fragmented words and when the initial letters of the words provided the cueing information, generality was enhanced and the perceptual learning argument could be eliminated.

These findings must be taken cautiously because they require direct comparisons across different experiments. They tend, however, to support the inference that the critical source of the amnesic's mnemonic impairment is in the act of memory retrieval. Furthermore, this deficit may be alleviated by the availability of partial information, which serves as additional retrieval cues when memory retrieval is required. Warrington and Weiskrantz suggest that without additional retrieval cues, amnesic individuals are less effective than normals in preventing the retrieval and expression of inappropriate information. In other words, the amnesic patients tested in these studies were not deficient primarily in the transfer of information from the short-term to the long-term "memory store," nor did they suffer inadequate "memory consolidation." Rather, they reflect a deficit in the processes ordinarily employed to reject or inhibit inaccurate information.

The viability of this interpretation was demonstrated further in a series of five experiments (Warrington & Weiskrantz, 1974). The first two experiments tested the relative effect in amnesic and control subjects of cueing the recall of words by presenting the first three letters of each word. Consistent with their earlier results, they found in the first experiment that the recall scores of the amnesics and normals did not differ when subjects were provided cues for recall, although the amnesics were markedly deficient on a recognition task (accuracy in recognition was only about one-third that of the control subjects). In accordance with their interpretation, we may conclude that the information provided by cueing in the recall test restricted the pool from which the subject might select alternative responses, hence assisting amnesics in withholding expression of alternative (incorrect) responses. With the recognition test, in which alternative responses must be provided by the experimenter and hence are equally available, the amnesics' deficiencies are apparent. Through this reasoning, we also expect that the benefit of cueing to amnesics would lessen as the number of possible words appropriate to the cue increases (in this case, the number of possible words having the same first three letters as those provided by the cue). This prediction was verified in Experiment 2, although with only borderline statistical significance.

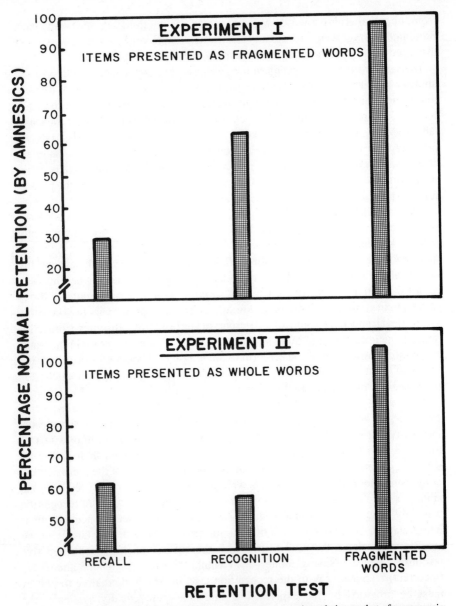

Figure 6.4   This figure shows the percentage retention by amnesics relative to that of nonamnesic control subjects for items learned either with the fragmented word technique (upper panel) or with the more conventional, whole word technique (lower panel). This retention is shown to be a function of the type of retention test (either conventional recall or recognition procedures, or relearning with the same fragmented-word technique used during original learning). (adapted from Weiskrantz and Warrington, 1970b.)

Experiments 3, 4, and 5 directly pursued the implication that amnesic patients should be more susceptible than normals to the detrimental effects of interfering learning on recall. Generally, the results of these experiments indicated that amnesic patients were impaired more than control subjects by the interfering effects of previously learned words that were associated with the same recall cues (the same first three letters or the same category) as items currently tested. As well as supporting the Weiskrantz–Warrington interpretation, the fact that amnesics suffer any interference whatsoever from prior learning, acquired 10 minutes earlier or more in some cases, provides clear evidence that amnesics are capable of permanent new learning under the proper circumstances.

The Weiskrantz–Warrington interference hypothesis of human amnesia has been considered by Weiskrantz and Warrington (1975) in the light of experimental evidence and alternative hypotheses. Their arguments are persuasive in describing advantages of the interference hypothesis relative to the encoding hypothesis (that amnesia is traceable to the patient's deficiency in semantic encoding), the familiarity hypothesis (that amnesics are deficient primarily in recognizing what is familiar; see Gaffan, 1976), and the associative learning hypothesis (that amnesics are deficient in "time tagging" of episodic memories, in the use of spatial attributes for constructing appropriate "cognitive maps," or in the employment of contextual cues for memory processing). Perhaps more persuasive is the empirical evidence reviewed by Weiskrantz and Warrington for the greater susceptibility to interference effects among amnesic subjects, and the further evidence that "the more effectively interference phenomena are constrained the more nearly normal is the long-term memory of the patient..." (1975a, p. 425).

The Weiskrantz–Warrington interference interpretation of amnesia may account for several other characteristics of human amnesia. It is consistent with the considerable number of intrusions from prior learning that appear in the retention protocols of amnesic patients (Baddeley & Warrington, 1970; Starr & Phillips, 1970; Warrington & Weiskrantz, 1968). It is consistent with the fact that the other task in which amnesic patients have shown significant learning and effective retention over long intervals is motor learning, which is particularly resistant to interference from prior, conflicting learning (Adams, 1967; Duncan & Underwood, 1953; see Weiskrantz, 1971). It is consistent with the finding that recognition by amnesics appears to be more inferior to that of normals than their recall (if one assumes that simply replying "yes" or "no" incorrectly, as in recognition, presents a more difficult "withholding" or inhibitory problem than emission of an incorrect word). It is consistent with the facts that persons with amnesia benefit from certain mnemonic techniques of categorizing in the same way that normals do, and that orthographic or semantic cueing prior to recall may in fact benefit amnesic patients more than controls. Although not specifically analyzed in the experiment by Warrington and Weiskrantz (1971), percentage normal recall by amnesic individuals was about twice as great with semantic cueing as without. (This statement requires qualification, however, in that it is based on a percentage index that is prone to distortion by ceiling or basement effects in measurement and the generality of the effect is limited, as shown in our discussion of the studies by Cermak and Butters, 1972, and Cermak et al., 1973). And finally, it is consistent with the general collection of behaviors measured in rats and monkeys that have been subjected to hippocampal or general temporal lesions. The dominant characteristics of these animals are an inability to inhibit inappropriate responses and an enhanced susceptibility to interference-induced forgetting (e.g., Gross, 1973; Iversen, 1973; Jarrard, 1975; Weiskrantz, 1971).

If Weiskrantz and Warrington are correct in viewing amnesia as symptomatic of a deficiency in controlling interfering memories, it is easy to understand how amnesic patients, unable to sort out correct from incorrect representations of specific events, might resort to the kinds of confabulations that are reported (see Talland, 1965) and, eventually, to the easier response that they "simply do not remember." Similar affective behaviors not directly related to memory processing may account for at least some of the dramatic deficits in short-term retention that are reported. For example, you may recall the classic case mentioned previously, in which the psychiatrist pricked a patient with a pin hidden in his hand as they shook hands. Later the patient was reluctant to shake hands again, although she would not (or perhaps could not) report why. It is not difficult to imagine that an institutionalized person, especially one experiencing difficulty in keeping different events separate and well classified, would be somewhat reluctant to suggest that such a preposterous event as being stuck with a pin by her doctor actually could have occurred.

A possible modification of the Weiskrantz–Warrington view.   In considering how amnesics may differ from normals in their memory processing, we should keep in mind the alternative view that the fundamental source of human amnesia may be no different in its effects than sources of forgetting common to normal subjects. It seems clear that amnesics process memories differently than normals during original encoding (Butters & Cermak, 1975) and when rehearsing (Cermak, Naus & Reale, 1976). Still, the retrieval processing of memories exhibited by amnesics under conventional testing conditions may be no different from the processing exhibited by normals exposed to an explicit source of forgetting, such as a long retention interval. A preliminary test of this idea is found in an experiment conducted by Woods and Piercy (1974). They tested only normal subjects, using procedures analogous to those of Warrington and Weiskrantz (1970; though different in possibly critical respects—see Weiskrantz & Warrington, 1975b). These subjects were tested either 1 minute or 1 week following original learning. Just as the cueing by Warrington and Weiskrantz benefited the amnesic subjects more than their controls, these cueing procedures benefited the normal subjects tested after a 1-week interval more than subjects tested after a 1-minute interval. These results indicate that, while these cueing procedures do alleviate forgetting, they may act on forgetting by normal subjects in the same way that they act on forgetting by amnesic subjects. Perhaps it may generally be the case that cueing procedures are more effective the greater the forgetting among a variety of (nominally distinct) sources of the forgetting. (For an analogous result found when a subject variable, age, was manipulated in cueing experiments with animals, see Spear & Parsons, 1976).

Another implication of these results may be suggested. Suppose it is indeed the case that normals gain more benefit from cueing the more they have forgotten, while amnesics benefit from cueing at short intervals (one minute) where there is little benefit for normals. These relationships may not be due to differences in retrieval per se but may instead be due to the amnesics' deficiency in storing redundant contextual cues. Within the conceptual framework of this book (see Chapters 1 and 2), retention should depend on the degree of correspondence between the events noticed at testing and those stored as attributes of the memory. I have been intrigued for some time by the notion that many characteristics of abnormal memory processing might be explained by the simple assumption that inadequate numbers of redundant contextual cues are acquired when the central nervous system is less than optimal in its functioning. Perhaps in the case under discussion it is the continued presence of contextual events and their corresponding (redundant) memory attributes that makes it possible for normals to recall without cueing by target components after short intervals, but not after long intervals when the more evanescent contextual cues have been lost or reused for conflicting memories. Then the need for target-related semantic cues among amnesics might mean that they had not stored the redundant contextual cues. Present data do not permit a full argument in defense of such a storage interpretation, neither will they allow much confidence in my notion concerning insufficient contextual cue utilization in abnormal memory processing generally. The point is, however, that even if cueing does yield retention among amnesics equivalent to that of normals, interpretations in terms of the retrieval process should be cautious through consideration of alternative interpretations based on storage differences.

Does "long-term memory" depend on prior "short-term memory" processing?   A remarkable case of memory-processing impairment, studied initially by Warrington and Shallice (1969) and discussed briefly in Chapter 5, has altered assumptions about the hypothetical relationship between a short-term and a long-term memory process. Like evidence gathered in the Weiskrantz–Warrington studies, this case was not consistent with Milner's interpretation of amnesia as a deficit in the transfer of information from a short-term to a long-term memory store. There can be no doubt of some functional differences between short-term and long-term retention, at least insofar as these two have been identified here. Differences in phenomena and influential variables associated with retention after short and long intervals have been identified in both normal subjects (e.g., Bjork, 1976; Glanzer, 1972) and amnesic patients, as we have just described. If these differences truly reflect separate memory processes, how are these processes related? Must information pass through the "short-term memory store" before it can become relatively permanently stored in a "long-term memory store"? Alternatively, perhaps these are relatively independent systems. We shall see that the latter interpretation has led to the view that the "short-term memory process" may be a relatively unimportant aspect of information processing (at least as a memory process per se) representing a much simpler determinant of performance.

The patient studied by Warrington and Shallice suffered brain damage as a consequence of a motorcycle accident. Specifically, a lesion occurred in the left posterior cortex. The unusual deficit in this patient [though not unique (Warrington, E. K., personal communication, 1974); see also Warrington & Weiskrantz, 1973] included a striking deficiency in short-term retention for acoustically presented materials. This subject, KF (since deceased) had an auditory memory span inferior to his visual memory span, which probably is opposite to the situation in most normals. Warrington and Shallice determined that KF's deficit was not attributable to deficient auditory *perception*, because he could rapidly identify acoustically presented stimuli; nor was it due to ineffective speech production, because his performance did not improve when the verbal requirements was eliminated from the retention test. Furthermore, when numbers, letters, or words were spoken to KF for immediate recall, he nearly always was correct if only one item was presented. But if two items were spoken to him, KF's accuracy dropped nearly 40%, and it continued to decline when three or four items were to be remembered. Generally, regardless of the length of the series of items, KF could rarely recall more than one or two from that series.

The amazing point about KF is that his verbal learning, as indexed by his capacity to acquire representations of the presented material over repeated trials and later recall the material, was essentially normal. When KF was presented a list of items for free recall, for example, his retention of items in the early and middle portions of the list, his "long-term memory component" (Glanzer, 1972), was quite good, easily at normal levels. For KF (and similar cases subsequently identified by Warrington), information clearly entered the "long-term memory store" without being held and processed for any significant period in the "short-term store." Although this might not be the normal mode of memory processing, it does imply that information *need* not be held in a "short-term store" to become permanently represented in a "long-term store." Hence, the interpretation of amnesia by Milner (1966) is called into question.

It could be that long- and short-term memory processes are independent and function in parallel as equally important processes of memory. An interesting alternative interpretation suggested by Weiskrantz (1970), mentioned also in Chapter 5, is that information enters the long-term memory system directly from perception and perceptual aftereffects. When, however, the transfer to the long-

term memory system becomes overtaxed by too much information, human subjects employ an overload emergency system, that is, rehearsal. Such a view
requires that short-term memory be dependent especially on linguistic capacity
(for rehearsal), and as such, "we may never find an analogue of this type of
short-term (memory) in non-linguistic animals" (Weiskrantz, 1970, p. 72).

This view thus classifies a short-term memory process differently than has
usually been suggested. In the hierarchy of higher mental processes, short-term
memory as a rehearsal process would be relegated to a lower position rather like a
diligence or persistence aspect of performance. From this reasoning, Weiskrantz
(1970) concludes

> that the nervous system may, in fact, be less complex than some experimental psychologists
> have considered in the past, in that if something *can* enter a permanent store it will do so pretty
> smartly without having to pass through buffers and filters and feed-back loops of varying
> degrees of complexity, although such complexities may appear when entry into a long-term
> memory system is made difficult. (pp. 72–73)

Summary.   The experimental analysis of amnesia—deficits in new learning
or retention not obviously attributable to defective perception, simple performance factors, extremes in temperament and other personality defects, or generally inferior intelligence—has progressed rapidly since the pioneering work by
Milner and others (e.g., Talland, 1965). The early generalizations were that
amnesics are relatively normal in terms of retention assessed after intervals of a
few seconds and for events that occurred prior to the onset of their illness, but are
incapable of permanent acquisition of new information. Each of these three
aspects requires modification in view of subsequent research: Evidence for normal short-term retention in amnesics has been countered by instances of poorer
retention by similar patients (especially Korsakoff cases) over intervals of less
than 1 minute in length; tests of the questionnaire type have indicated that
amnesics show poorer retention for events that occurred prior to their illness than
nonamnesic control subjects; and given the proper circumstances of learning and
testing, amnesics may acquire new information permanently. These results indicate in part that amnesics should not be characterized merely as less effective in
their processing of memories; rather, they may differ from normals in *how* they
process memories, or they may be ineffective in only one aspect of memory
processing (such as encoding or retrieval) while relatively normal in other aspects.

This new information, together with the analysis of cases of brain damage
resulting in poor short-term retention but unaffected long-term retention, has
tended to decrease the plausibility of Milner's original interpretation of amnesia.
It now seems unlikely that the primary deficit of amnesics is in the transfer of
information from a short-term to a long-term "memory store"; there is evidence
of a basic deficiency in memory retrieval among amnesics, a deficiency assessed
long after the supposed time at which information transfers out of a short-term
store. Also, it is now clear that the processing of a memory does not *require* its

serial transfer to a long-term "store" following extensive processing in a short-term "store," as Milner assumed when formulating her theory. New theories of human anterograde amnesia have arisen, including principally the interference, encoding, familiarity, and associative-learning hypothesis (Weiskrantz & Warrington, 1975; see also Baddeley, 1975).

Retrograde Amnesia in Humans Following Acute Brain Trauma

A blow to the head sufficient to cause severe concussion is likely to induce forgetting. When the forgetting is of immediately preceding events, it is typically termed *retrograde amnesia*; when it is for subsequent events, it is typically termed *anterograde amnesia*. These cases of amnesia do not accompany all instances of brain trauma. For example, neither type of amnesia is typical following certain types of gunshot wounds of the head (Russell & Nathan, 1946). We use the general term *brain trauma*, however, because gross disturbances of the brain other than concussion may have similar effects on forgetting. The most common source of such disturbance is electroconvulsive therapy administered to mentally disturbed patients, which we shall discuss shortly.

Amnesia induced by concussion of the brain.   Blows to the head, accidental or purposeful, are not uncommon consequences of the rough-and-tumble play of children and young adults. Many of us have experienced concussion and the accompanying retention deficits. Lynch and Yarnell (1973) interviewed football players at differing times after injuries had been received by the players during a game. Brief neurological examinations accompanied each interview, and of 18 players questioned, 6 were determined to have suffered brain concussion. Eight of the players had significant injuries excluding concussion (e.g., broken nose), and 4 were not injured at all. All players were interviewed within 30 seconds of their injury, then again 3 to 5 minutes later, and again on other occasions during the game, at intervals of 5 to 20 minutes. When interviewed 3 to 5 minutes or later following injury, none of the concussed players could recall events that had occurred just prior to the initial interview (i.e., events leading to their injury), while all of the other players could recall them. This is retrograde amnesia.

Two other characteristics of Lynch and Yarnell's results are of interest, and we shall return to them in our later discussion of better-controlled, laboratory experiments. First, some concussed players were found later to have recovered from their retention deficits and could describe the previously forgotten events. Second, all of the concussed players (like all of the others) showed accurate retention of events leading to their injury when interviewed 30 seconds after the injury, although they gave no evidence of this retention a few minutes later. Both of these phenomena, extrapolated to the results of controlled laboratory experiments with animals, have been important for shaping theories of memory processing in general (e.g., McGaugh & Dawson, 1971), and we shall see further examples of them, both in studies with human subjects and in studies using animals.

The most extensive study of the sort conducted by Lynch and Yarnell is that of Russell and Nathan (1946), mentioned briefly in Chapter 1. This paper described several consequences of brain trauma, including retrograde amnesia (and its reduction with the passage of time), anterograde amnesia, and the subject's general confusion following such trauma. For example, Russell and Nathan describe the case of a young man involved in a motorcycle accident who suffered a bruise on one portion of his head and slight bleeding from the ear, but no fracture:

> A week after the accident he was able to converse sensibly, and the nursing staff considered that he had fully recovered consciousness. When questioned, however, he said that the date was in February, 1922, and that he was a schoolboy. He had no recollection of five years spent in Australia, and two years in this country [England] working on a golf course. Two weeks after the injury he remembered the five years spent in Australia, and remembered returning to this country; the past two years were, however, a complete blank as far as memory was concerned. Three weeks after the injury he returned to the village where he had been working for two years. Everything looked strange, and he had no recollection of ever having been there before. He lost his way on more than one occasion. Still feeling a stranger to the district he returned to work; he was able to do his work satisfactorily, but had difficulty in remembering what he had actually done during the day. About ten weeks after the accident the events of the past two years were gradually recollected and finally he was able to remember everything up to within a few minutes of the accident. (Gross & Zeigler, 1969, p. 17)

The preceding case illustrates the typical general confusion and extensive retrograde amnesia that may result from a brain trauma. Also typical is the gradual shrinking (to an apparently irreducible amount) of the period of time over which the amnesic cannot remember events. Again, each of these is a common feature that will be discussed in reference to other studies, and it is important to keep them in mind in the critical analysis of analogous experimental data.

Russell and Nathan analyzed over 1,000 cases of persons who had suffered general concussion to the brain. More than 80% of these could recall nothing of the events that had occurred during the 30-minute period immediately preceding their brain trauma; yet most of these individuals (4 out of every 5) could recall events just prior to this 30-minute period. This suggests that an important portion of the processing of a memory of an event continues for a brief period beyond the initial sensation and perception of that event. Cases of accidental brain trauma, however, are an inconvenient vehicle for analyzing this aspect of memory processing. Obviously, one cannot conduct experiments in which randomly specified groups of humans are administered severe brain trauma. Rather, animal subjects offer the best potential for the experimental analysis of traumatic amnesia. However, the clinical application of electroconvulsive therapy to humans has provided an opportunity for relatively systematic investigation of how this kind of brain trauma might affect the processing of memories.

The influence of electroconvulsive shock on memory processing.   In the late 1930s, following centuries of misguided and often horrible treatments prescribed by physicians for mentally ill persons, attention centered on the apparent therapeutic benefit of induced convulsions. The initial application of convulsions for this purpose may have arisen from the observation that some symptoms of psychosis are alleviated following extreme fever (which itself may be accompanied by minor convulsions). Fink et al (1974) notes the obscure reasons given in defense of this practice: "Convulsions were introduced in the belief that epilepsy was a rare diagnosis among schizophrenic patients, as if seizures 'protected' the epileptic from psychosis" (p. 2). Nevertheless, the practice continued. First electricity was the source of the convulsions, later drugs were used for the same purpose, and still later there was a return to electricity as it became apparent that this was the more effective method. Fink cites several studies indicating relative success for electroconvulsive therapy (ECT), especially for depressive illnesses, compared to the lesser therapeutic value of using certain drugs to induce convulsions. However, the method of inducing seizures appears to be less important than the total number of seizures and their frequency per unit of time. The application of electroconvulsive therapy continues to be common nevertheless, and a more substantial body of literature exists concerning the influence of this treatment on memory processing than concerning the other convulsants, which provides a reason for limiting our discussion to this source of brain trauma.

Deficits in memory processing are obvious in persons subjected to ECT. Opposing views consider this deficit as either instrumental for or coincidental to alleviation of the symptoms of mental illness. As an example of the former, Rodnick (1942) linked the therapeutic effect of ECT to the weakening of retention for more recently acquired behavioral patterns. Because the most recent behaviors of mental patients (Rodnick was concerned particularly with schizophrenia) are likely to be abnormal, in contrast to their less recent, normal behavior that preceded their illness, Rodnick believed the effect of the retention deficit was to weaken abnormal habits and permit normal behavior to become dominant again. More contemporary scientists also have suggested a distinct relationship between the therapeutic and memorial consequences of convulsions induced by ECT (e.g., Meyer, 1972). An alternative view is that the therapeutic effects of an electrically induced convulsion are independent of their adverse effects on memory processing, or that at most, any relationship is weak. This view, which probably is the more prevalent (especially in relation to treatment of depressive patients), is supported by evidence for a functional dissociation between the therapeutic and memorial effects. For example, unilateral application of ECT in the dominant hemisphere of the brain (i.e., passing electrical current through only one side of the head and brain, usually the left side in right-handed persons) is more detrimental to most cases of human memory processing than unilateral ECT to the nondominant hemisphere, but it makes little or no difference in the therapeutic value (d'Elia, 1970, 1974). Also, while the therapeutic effectiveness of ECT appears to depend on the extent of the resultant seizure activity (as monitored by the EEG), the consequences for memory processing in humans seem relatively independent of this index (Ottosson, 1960).

When we evaluate the influence of ECT on memory processing, we should bear in mind that there have been no published studies (and, it is hoped, none conducted) in which ECT has been used purely as a research tool. Rather, the primary intention of its use is therapeutic, and the systematic attainment of knowledge concerning its influence on memory processing has been secondary. Scientists seeking the latter information thus have been restricted enormously in terms of experimental design.

The following four general problems exemplify the difficulties one faces in interpreting results of such studies. First, it is difficult to generalize beyond the sample of subjects actually tested in these experiments because the subjects obviously are not randomly selected. Generalizing to normal populations is precluded by the nature of the extreme illnesses of the subjects involved (e.g., consider the low motivation level that characterizes the depressed patient), and it is no simple matter to separate the effects of the various drugs that typically accompany the administration of ECT (although more recently drug-only control subjects have been included in experimental designs). A second difficulty is the frequent failure to specify the exact nature of the electrical current (e.g., wave form, duration, and intensity) and to take into account the number of previous treatments of this sort experienced by the patients. Third, because the experimental analysis of memory processing is a secondary matter in these cases, precise control over the temporal intervals between learning and the ECT is difficult to establish. And fourth, as mentioned earlier regarding other cases of human amnesia, the scientists who are most sophisticated in assessing human memory processing typically have not been involved in these studies. This is not to suggest that all this work has been fruitless, however; useful information has been derived from a few fine studies, most notably those by Cronholm and his associates (see Cronholm, 1969).

A large number of studies have shown that ECT drastically accelerates forgetting of events that occurred up to an hour prior to its administration (for reviews, see Cronholm, 1969; Dornbush & Williams, 1974; Williams, 1969). While no studies have reported thorough investigation of temporal gradients of retrograde amnesia throughout this period, Cronholm and Lagergren (1959) measured such a gradient over relatively short intervals. In this experiment, patients were simply presented a number between 1 and 15 (excluding 13), which they were asked to remember. The number was presented 60, 15, or 5 seconds prior to the administration of ECT; the 60-second group included 50 subjects, and the 15- and 5-second groups included 64 subjects each, a sizable sample. Beginning 10 minutes after the ECT, subjects were asked to recall the number. If the subjects failed in their recall, they were repeatedly asked to try again after various intervals extending up to 36 hours later, although nearly all subjects who did recall correctly did so within 2 to 3 hours of the therapy. The results indicated that recall was more likely to be correct (and to occur sooner following therapy) the longer the interval between presentation of the number and the ECT (see Figure

6.5). We shall see further examples of retrograde amnesia gradients when we discuss analogous effects in animals.

In view of the common complaints of patients regarding retention deficits associated with intervals of several hours or days preceding therapy, it is unfortunate that retrograde gradients for these longer intervals have not been studied more systematically. However, evidence of retrograde amnesia has been recorded for events that preceded ECT by quite long intervals. Squire and his associates have investigated the amnesic effects of ECT for periods extending several years prior to treatment. These investigators, like Sanders and Warrington (1971), discussed earlier, constructed questionnaires to test retention of events to which a subject presumably was exposed several years earlier, such as television shows or American racehorses, that may be identified uniquely with a particular year. With this technique, Squire (1974) found that after patients had been exposed to five ECTs their retention for events occurring during the previous three decades was significantly impaired relative not only to control subjects but also to patients who had been exposed to only one ECT. In a subsequent experiment, Squire, Slater, and Chace (1975) employed a within-subject test in which subjects were given two different, but equivalent, forms of the test, one prior to their first ECT and the other after their fifth treatment. Here the ECT was found to have significantly enhanced forgetting for events that had occurred one to three years earlier but not for events that had occurred before that (the authors measured up to 17 years prior to the treatment). In neither of these studies was IQ significantly influenced by the ECT. Collectively, these results indicate that retrograde amnesia from ECT may extend back several years, though not indefi-

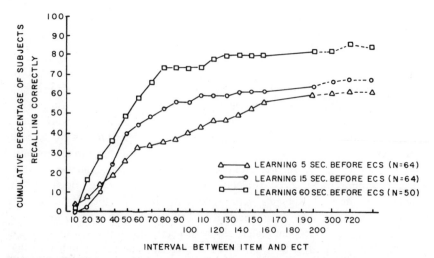

Figure 6.5   Cumulative percentage of patients recalling correctly a number that had been presented before the administration of electroconvulsive shock therapy is shown as a function of time after the therapy. (from Cronholm, 1969).

nitely, and that the extent of this amnesia may depend on the number of occasions on which a given patient has received ECT.

Finally, experimental evidence has tended to support patients' subjective reports of anterograde amnesia in the form of deficits in retention of materials learned following ECT. There are indications that this effect may be fairly persistant, and that as a patient receives more ECT treatments this anterograde amnesia increases. As we shall discuss shortly, the analysis of anterograde amnesia is more complicated than that of retrograde amnesia because of the possibility of impaired perceptual or initial learning processes, but some admirably thorough studies on this topic have been reported (Cronholm & Molander, 1957; Squire & Miller, 1974). We may expect to see an increase in systematic investigations of anterograde amnesia in the future, both with humans and with animals.

Summary.   Clinical evidence indicates that persons suffering severe brain trauma may be impaired in their retention of events that immediately preceded the trauma. Generally, retention for prior events is more likely to be impaired the closer in time the prior events are to the trauma. Characteristically, this retention deficit subsides over time, and although there may remain "islands" of preceding events for which retention is never observed, in particular the events that immediately preceded the trauma, these persisting deficits become significant only if one can be certain that they would not have occurred otherwise, that is, without the trauma. It is difficult, perhaps impossible, to ascertain the latter for cases of accidental brain trauma, but an opportunity for more careful analysis of this effect in humans is provided by mentally ill persons exposed to ECT. This form of therapy is accompanied by the same side effects as accidental brain concussion—retrograde and anterograde amnesia and temporary general confusion.

Experiments investigating the retrograde amnesia that accompanies ECT have confirmed that a greater retention deficit occurs for prior events more closely related temporally to the ECT, although significant retention deficits may be found for events in the patient's more remote past as well. The relationship between the therapeutic effect of ECS and its influence on memory processing is unclear, but there are growing indications that these may be largely independent consequences. The several methodological problems in this research imply a continuing need for more analytical procedures using animals as subjects.

Retrograde Amnesia in Humans Attributable to External Environmental Events

If in learning a list of words a subject finds one of the words in a list to be singular in some way, that item is likely to be recalled with exceptional effectiveness (often termed the *Von Restorff effect*; see Wallace, 1965). In addition, however, unusually *poor* recall may occur for words that immediately precede the singular word (retrograde amnesia) and for words that just follow it (anterograde amnesia). For example, suppose subjects in the experimental group are given a single opportunity to study the following list for recall: *baby, surface, pony, ankle, minute, Plato, sickness, dragon, cattle, license, menace, temper.* A control group is given a similar list with a word such as *railroad* in place of *Plato.* Retrograde amnesia in the experimental group would be defined by their poorer recall of *minute,* and perhaps also of *ankle,* which immediately preceded *Plato*; anterograde amnesia for the experimental group would be shown by their poorer recall of *sickness,* which immediately followed *Plato*; and the Von Restorff effect would be shown by better recall of the word *Plato* than of *railroad.*

Our particular interest centers on the retrograde amnesia effect. It should be clear that this effect easily could be termed *retroactive interference* because it shares characteristics of phenomena labeled with this term (see Chapter 4). Presumably, the original reason for calling the present effect retrograde amnesia was its gross similarity to clinical cases of retrograde amnesia in terms of the dependence of the effect on the temporal relationship between the item to be learned and the subsequent interfering event. Although such forgetting had been suggested in a number of studies of the Von Restorff effect, the retrograde amnesia effect was first demonstrated dramatically in an experiment by Tulving (1969). Tulving gave his subjects a list like the one in the preceding paragraph, warning them in advance that a famous name would appear and that they should take special pains to remember it. The retrograde amnesia effect obtained by Tulving was much greater than had been found in previous studies investigating the Von Restorff effect, perhaps because most previous studies had based their results on repeated presentations and recalls of a list, and the retrograde amnesia effect tends to decline with repeated exposure to a list (see Detterman, 1975a).

Tulving's special instructions warning subjects of the singular item and encouraging them to remember it have been shown to be unnecessary for the retrograde amnesia effect (Saufley & Winograd, 1970). Moreover, the effect is sufficiently robust to be studied in paradigms other than the free-recall situation, as exemplified in the study by Landauer (1974) that employed repeated presentations of a paired-associate list. Finally, it is notable that this amnesic effect occurs with a variety of forms of the critical (surprising) item, including photographs of nudes or merely an unusually loud vocal occurrence of any word (Detterman, 1975a, b; Detterman & Ellis, 1972).

The obvious explanation of this retrograde amnesia effect assumes that the occurrence of an especially notable item distracts the subjects from rehearsal of the immediately preceding items. Assuming that recall is dependent on simple rote rehearsal, recall of the immediately preceding items should be lessened. Several tests have indicated that this simple-rehearsal explanation is unsatisfactory. Detterman and Ellis (1972) instructed their subjects not to rehearse, which apparently was effective in view of the resultant decrement in recall of items occurring early in the list, but this did not influence the retrograde amnesia effect. These investigators also conducted a more indirect test, varying the rates of item presentation and the duration of exposure to the critical (singular, surprising) item. Because faster rates of presentation should reduce rehearsal of all items, the simple-rehearsal hypothesis would predict that retention of the items immediately preceding the surprising item should show relatively less decrement when all items were presented more rapidly, but this did not occur (however, they did find that the longer the duration of the surprising item, the greater the retrograde amnesia).

As an alternative to the simple-rehearsal explanation, which depends on quantity of rote repetition, retrograde amnesia might be attributed instead to a deficit in the quality of rehearsal. In a preliminary test of this alternative, Detterman (1975a) specifically informed subjects of the possible difficulty in recalling the items that immediately preceded the surprising (in this case, extra-loud) item. His intent was to encourage the subjects to devise rehearsal strategies to circumvent this difficulty. However, this detracted only slightly, if at all, from the retrograde amnesia effect. It is notable that although the retrograde amnesia effect occurred in this experiment, the Von Restorff effect (enhanced recall of the surprising, extra-loud item) did not. This result tends to preclude still another plausible alternative explanation of the retrograde amnesia effect that would be based on enhanced retroactive interference of the immediately preceding items through overlearning (the Von Restorff effect) of the surprising item.

While it probably is premature to discount the possibility that this kind of retrograde amnesia is mediated by an effect on rehearsal processes, the locus of the deficit more likely may be in the process of retrieval rather than in the storage (i.e., degree of original learning) of the items that precede the surprising item. Detterman (1975a) has shown that this retrograde amnesia dissipates if a sufficiently long interval (120 seconds) elapses between presentation of the list and the retention test. This implies that the original deficit was not solely in terms of storage of the items. A similar implication may be drawn from the results of Detterman (1975b), which also indicate that variation in the conditions of the retention test may influence the extent of retrograde amnesia. In this experiment, retrograde amnesia for items immediately preceding the surprising (extra-loud) word was eliminated when subjects were presented recall cues (the first two letters of each word in the list) after an initial recall attempt. Like the result reported by Detterman (1975a), this result implies that this retrograde amnesia effect may reside in the retrieval process.

It is obvious that this case of retrograde amnesia may have little in common, in terms of etiology, with instances of abnormal memory processing in humans that are directly traceable to traumatic physiological disturbances. However, these "retrograde amnesias" are considered together for two reasons beyond their common labels. First, we shall soon discuss parallel studies with animals in which psychologically surprising events act retroactively to impair retention, with effects somewhat similar to those caused by traumatic physiological disturbances. Second, it is useful to be aware that a major source of forgetting in humans may be abnormal memory processing induced by unusual circumstances that appear to be definable only in environmental or behavioral terms, rather than in terms of physiological defects. This source of forgetting is sometimes considered under the headings "hysterical amnesia" or "psychogenic loss of memory" (Stengel, 1966). Less extreme forms of these cases have played an important role in the development of Freudian psychoanalysis but have received virtually no attention in experimental analysis. This may be attributable in part to the failure of scientists to develop a model of this affliction suitable for research with animals, and in part to a predisposition of medical personnel to assume that all abnormal processing must be accompanied by abnormal functioning of the central nervous system. According to this attitude, other origins of such afflictions may be dismissed pending "more accurate" diagnosis of the neural defect.

The following is an example described by Barbizet (1970) under the heading "hysterical amnesia":

> Irene, 32 years of age, left for her holidays in Spain with her father and husband. She had a "nervous attack" on the road. Seen by a doctor who attributed the trouble to a heat stroke, she was taken to a hospital. Here her behavior continued to be strange; she seemed to be confused and constantly repeated that she did not know where she was. She was brought back to France ten days later, where she saw Doctor Fabiani, who found her in excellent physical condition, replying easily to questions, but declaring that she remembered nothing of the journey to Spain, although her memory of the events prior to the voyage and those after the return trip, which took place the preceding day, was normal. He discovered that this young woman, who was very attached to her father, was in her third marriage, and that the "attack" came on after a dispute had taken place between her husband and her father. These facts, the sudden and total character of the memory lacuna and the absence of signs of organic disturbance, led to a faradic (electroconvulsive) therapy, which very quickly brought about the return (!) of her memory and a perfectly organized account of her voyage. A psychotherapy was then undertaken, which revealed a hysterical personality and the persistence of an infantile fixation to her father. (pp. 139–140)

It is difficult to suppress the speculation that such severe, and quite genuine, deficits in memory retrieval may be produced psychologically through mechanisms of mnemonic processing (see Chapter 8) that may commonly be at work in less obvious and less dramatic instances of selective forgetting.

Summary. Instances of human amnesia unaccompanied by abnormal physiological events were discussed, with emphasis on an apparently exaggerated retention deficit found for words that are presented just prior to an especially notable or distinctive word. This "retrograde amnesia" has been found under circumstances in which the characteristic "notable" is defined in terms of an unusual visual or auditory characteristic of the word, or in terms of words that represent something particularly significant to the subjects. The deficit does not seem attributable to a reduction in rote rehearsal of the preceding items, although the quality of the rehearsal of these items may prove to be an important determinant of this effect. However, the amnesia apparently is not completely permanent, and this dependence on the conditions of the retention test may imply involvement of the memory retrieval process in determining this amnesic effect.

SOURCES OF RETROGRADE AMNESIA IN
EXPERIMENTS WITH ANIMAL SUBJECTS

This section has two purposes. The first is to describe how various amnesic agents have been studied in experiments using animal subjects. The second is to consider the issues that arise when one moves from experimental observations to interpretation in terms of memory processing. We will find it convenient to refer repeatedly to certain interpretations of the effects of some amnesic agents. This is useful for understanding the investigators' reasons for conducting their studies. However, we shall not attempt to evaluate these interpretations until later, so be aware that the interpretations described in this section may not necessarily be the most widely accepted nor even the most reasonable.

Importance of Retrograde Effects

The effect of independent variables on memory processing, especially memory retrieval, is assessed most clearly when the variation is imposed long after acquisition of the memory. But the most dramatic effects of amnesic or hypermnesic treatments are obtained when they are applied just prior to, or *immediately* following, the events-to-be-remembered. Experiments of this kind are likely to be relatively uninteresting for understanding memory processing, however. For example, amnesic treatments prior to training or very shortly thereafter (say, 500 msec or less) may impair perceptual processes. To take an extreme case, it would be trivial to show that amnesia results when electroconvulsive shock (ECS) is administered to an animal just prior to a training trial, because we know that little or none of the environment is perceived just after an ECS. We also know that "backward masking" of perception may occur. "Backward masking" is defined when events that follow very soon after a stimulus alter or prevent perception of that stimulus. Less obvious, but no less real, are other effects on perception that may result from presentation of amnesic agents.

Therefore, amnesia may be understood best through *retrograde* amnesia, and the clearest interpretation of all may be obtained when a retrograde amnesia gradient is measured. A retrograde amnesia gradient, for our purposes, is the function that indicates that an amnesic agent is more effective the sooner it follows training. An idealized representation is given in Figure 6.1 (page 290).

A gradient of retrograde amnesia implies characteristics of an amnesic agent that are particularly important. First, by showing that an effect caused soon after training is not produced by a later application of the treatment, one can be reasonably certain the amnesia is not a trivial consequence of a permanent impairment to the animal's capacity to perform. To take an extreme example, a low retention score would be measured if the animal's head were cut off just after training; but the same low retention score would be obtained if the animal's head were cut off still later, so the critical gradient would not occur. However ridiculous this example may appear, there are amnesic agents that have effects nearly as severe as those of beheading, though usually more temporary, often less well understood, and much less conspicuous.

Second, most amnesic agents do affect perceptual processes for a short time. But a retrograde gradient shows that the treatment with the greatest effect is the one separated from the retention test by the longest interval. Therefore, we safely can assert that the amnesic treatment's effects on perception at the retention test were not responsible for the retention differences.

A third analytical advantage offered by a retrograde amnesia gradient concerns memory processing that may occur following training. If we could identify the point soon after training at which amnesic agents completely obliterate retention (called *t min* by Weiskrantz, 1970) and the precise interval after which an amnesic agent has no effect at all (*t max*), then the exact temporal course of posttraining processing could be mapped.

Theoretical Basis of Retrograde Effects

Posttraining memorial processes are very important theoretically. Briefly, most studies of retrograde amnesia have been directed toward understanding processes of memory storage. It has been assumed that memory storage requires a "consolidation" process. It is inevitable that some process like this accounts for the manner in which an internal representation of external events is established in the central nervous system. What is not inevitable is that such a process may extent beyond termination of the perceptual process. Nevertheless, this is a reasonable assumption, and it has been a primary object of study when retrograde amnesia gradients have been measured.

In addition to a consolidation process for initial storage of a memory, other posttraining processes may be important for reinforcement (which may or may not be separable from consolidation; see Landauer, 1969; Wagner & Rescorla, 1972; Wagner, Rudy, & Whitlow, 1973) or for further elaboration of the memory (which may or may not be different from consolidation; see Lewis, 1969). Also of interest is memory processing that may occur for a short period following any activation of a memory, whether original acquisition or subsequent retrieval of the memory. We shall consider all these issues eventually, but first we turn to a description of some amnesic agents, their side effects, and how they have been used to study memory processing.

Electrical Stimulation of the Central Nervous System: Electroconvulsive Shock and Directed Stimulation of the Brain

Because of the electrochemical nature of neural transmission, it is not surprising that most amnesic agents have been either electrical stimulation or chemicals applied to the central nervous system. We shall see, however, that other amnesic agents that are not electrical or chemical in nature also may profoundly affect the electrical and chemical activity of the central nervous system.

Two classes of electrical stimulation have been used, one with diffuse, relatively unbounded electrical effects, the other with more discrete electrical direction and neurological consequences. The former is electroconvulsive shock (ECS); we will term the latter "directed electrical stimulation of the brain" (DESB).

Operationally, ECS is applied by passing a strong electrical current through the head of the subject by means of two electrodes attached externally to the brain. For rats and mice, the most conventional procedure is to attach one electrode to each ear (transpinnate) or to touch one electrode to each eye (transcorneal); for humans, the electrodes are taped to the side of the head. The particular mode of application is significant because some disparate results seem to be correlated with different kinds of ECS application. These differences in results can probably be traced to a common basic source: differences in the intensity and localization of the current that actually passes through the brain. The particular pathway an electrical current takes through the brain is an especially important determinant of amnesia; by using screws surgically implanted into the skull as electrodes, some control may be obtained over the current pathway, even with ECS. The intensity of the current used for ECS is sufficient to produce a convlusion (motor seizure) and usually requires at least 30 milliamperes for rats given the transpinnate application, although less current intensity is needed if ECS is delivered transcorneally or through skull-screw electrodes.

Our primary concern here is with the retrograde amnesia that results from ECS, and in particular with its experimental analysis through studies of animal behavior. Duncan (1949) published the first influential, systematic instance of a retrograde amnesia gradient caused by posttrial application of ECS. This was by no means the first experimental test of the memorial consequences of ECS. As mentioned earlier, Duncan himself published two previous papers concerning investigation of a retrograde amnesia gradient (Duncan, 1945, 1948), but his 1949 study is a landmark in this area because his method was so thorough and the results so orderly.

The importance of Duncan's study lies in the clear gradient of retrograde amnesia that resulted, even though his particular technique later was realized to be inadequate for a memory consolidation interpretation of the gradient. Duncan trained nine groups of rats on a shuttle-box avoidance task. In this task, the rat was required to leave one compartment and enter the alternative one within 10 seconds of the onset of a light in order to avoid footshock. All the rats received one training trial per day for 18 days. The length of the interval between completion of a trial and application of ECS was varied systematically between 20 seconds and 14 hours for eight of the groups. The ninth group did not receive ECS. As shown in Figure 6.6, the avoidance response was performed with increasingly less efficiency the sooner ECS followed each trial.

In subsequent years, experiments in this area modified and refined the procedures of such studies. The major change was the development of tasks that could show substantial learning after one trial in order to permit a more precise estimate

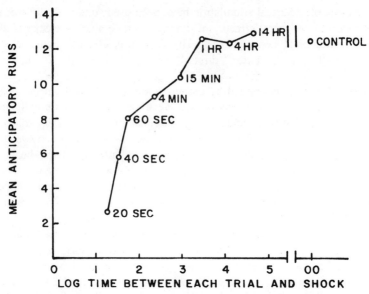

Figure 6.6   The mean number of active avoidances during testing is shown for rats as a function of the time between a daily training trial and subsequent administration of an electroconvulsive shock (adapted from Duncan, 1949. Copyright 1949 by the American Psychological Association. Reproduction.)

of when the external conditions necessary for memory storage had ceased. With this innovation, the time course of posttraining internal (neural and hormonal) processes could be mapped more clearly. Also, additional modifications in procedure and design were included to control some of the side effects of ECS, such as its possible punishing effects.

Probably because of its convenience and economy, ECS continued to be the most commonly used amnesic agent through tests of a variety of theories. Clearly, ECS can produce massive retrograde amnesia for a variety of tasks and animal species. What is not so clear is the basis of its effect on memory processing. We turn next to a brief review of some of the many effects of ECS that, in some cases, may explain its consequences for the processing of memories.

Side effects of ECS.   The administration of ECS is accompanied by innumerable behavioral and physiological changes in the organism, in addition to its effect on retention. There are three particularly common behavioral side effects of ECS. One of these is the punishing effects of ECS after multiple presentations, although the effects typically are relatively negligible if only a single ECS is given (but see Kesner, 1973; Misanin, Smith, & Miller, 1971). On the other hand, human patients seldom report pain as a consequence of multiple treatments that are properly administered, even in the absence of a variety of drugs currently applied with ECS. However, a single ECS has been shown to produce lower operant levels of lever pressing, less open-field activity, and longer latencies of stepping down from a platform, in addition to weight loss and modification of heart rate (e.g., Routtenberg & Kay, 1965). Other behavioral effects of ECS are decreased aversion thresholds to footshock (Pryor, Peache, & Scott, 1972) and decreased intake of food and water (Layden & Birch, 1969).

The biochemical consequences of ECS are common to most convulsive agents and have been summarized in a number of sources (e.g., Fink, Kety, McGaugh, & Williams, 1974). One of the more important of these sources is Essman (1972, 1974), who notes the following five consequences of ECS, some of which seem to be likely candidates for the basis of the amnesic properties of ECS, in view of recent theories of the physiological basis of memory. There is an increase in the permeability of the blood–brain barrier; depletion of energy reserves such as the concentration of glycogen, glucose, and ATP in the brain; reduction of 20–25% of the total RNA in certain portions of the brain; general decrement of protein synthesis; and modification in the concentration and action of important neural transmitters—adrenergic, cholinergic, and serotonergic—and their chemical precursors. A consequence of ECS that also seems to be an important correlate of amnesia (and perhaps a consequence of the preceding biochemical effects) is the altered electrical activity occurring in various portions of the brain. We shall return to this point later when we discuss potassium chloride, which has the effect of depressing such electrical activity.

Direct electrical stimulation of the brain (DESB).   Retrograde amnesia may also result from localized DESB. This procedure has analytical advantages not only because amnesia may be studied in relation to the anatomical sites where electrical stimulation is applied but also because localized DESB usually is not accompanied by the behavioral convulsions that cause many of the side effects found with ECS.

Studies vary in terms of the extent to which the locus of the critical neural disruption has been identified clearly in terms of neuroanatomical structures. Experimental procedures involve either relatively gross cortical stimulation or stimulation to specific subcortical structures.

The technique of cortical DESB with relatively localized action requires the implantation of screws in the skull to serve as electrodes. In a representative case (Gold, Macri, & McGaugh, 1973), four screws are implanted, the tips of which may touch the dura but presumably do not pass through it into the cortex. Two screws are implanted in the anterior portion of the skull, each 1 to 2 millimeters on opposite sides of the skull's midline separating the two brain hemispheres. Two other screw-electrodes are attached in the posterior portion of the skull, equidistant from the midline and about 3 to 4 millimeters apart.

Of course, current could pass between any two of these four electrodes. However, the relative effects of current between the two anterior electrodes and between the two posterior electrodes are particularly interesting. For example, Gold, Macri, and McGaugh (1973) found that retrograde amnesia gradients obtained from stimulation of the posterior electrodes have shallower slopes than those obtained from the frontal cortex. Over the posterior cortex, a stimulation of

5 milliamperes for .5 second could be delayed for 1 hour and amnesia for passive avoidance training still was obtained. In contrast, the longest delay found for corresponding conditions in the frontal cortex was 30 minutes. For both locations of stimulation, the gradients were less steep with higher-intensity current. Note that because of the more efficient and effective current pathway, retrograde amnesia may be obtained with current levels of less than 10 milliamperes, a good deal lower than is required with ECS.

The second general technique is to stimulate discrete subcortical structures through depth electrodes, using current in the microamp range. Generally, these studies have found that stimulation of the hippocampus or amygdala often results in amnesia (e.g., Goddard, 1964; Lidsky & Slotnick, 1971). Because of current spread, it is sometimes unclear whether the amnesia is a consequence of stimulation only at the locus of the electrode indicated by histology. Also, because of interconnections among subcortical structures like the amygdala and hippocampus, it is not always clear which is the more critical in the production of amnesia.

However, some experiments have been admirably analytical in localizing the site of the effect (e.g., Kesner & Doty, 1968). Bresnahan and Routtenberg (1972) identified electrical stimulation of the medial nucleus of the amygdala as a source of amnesia for passive avoidance training. They also worked to eliminate any contaminating effects the stimulation may have had on perceptual or motivational processes, a criticism frequently directed toward such studies of amnesia. Bresnahan and Routtenberg applied stimulation *during* each learning trial. However, by using multiple-trial learning they were able to suggest strongly from their data that rate and final degree of learning were unaffected by the ESB. They did find that subsequent retention was impaired. This experiment in fact measured anterograde, rather than retrograde, amnesia, and this effect actually may represent an instance of state-dependent retention.

It is of interest that retrograde amnesia has been found from localized electrical stimulation via depth electrodes in humans, although the amnesia produced was of a relatively transient nature (Bickford, Mulder, Dodge, Svien, & Rome, 1958).

Other Environmental Sources of Retrograde Amnesia

Before we describe pharmacological treatments that induce amnesia, there are three environmental manipulations that warrant brief mention. Two of these, modification of body temperature and reduction in oxygen, have been studied for several years and were mentioned in the important review by Glickman (1961). The other manipulation, more recently developed and less thoroughly studied, seems to produce processes associated with psychological surprise (Wagner, Rudy, & Whitlow, 1973).

Hypothermia and hyperthermia.   Both very hot and very cold environments have been investigated as determinants of retention. However, it is only with rapid cooling of the animal to produce hypothermia that clear retrograde amnesia gradients have been found (e.g., Riccio, Hodges, & Randall, 1968; see Figure 6.7). Some retention decrement has been reported following hyperthermia, but the heating treatment had been applied over relatively long periods during the retention interval in these studies. Also, while these consequences of increasing body temperature may have important theoretical implications (e.g., Gleitman, 1971), the studies are addressed to a somewhat different issue than our present concern, so we will return to these data later.

Riccio and his colleagues have applied hypothermia in order to replicate and extend many of the basic phenomena of retrograde amnesia. The basic technique is admirably simple. Rats are given passive avoidance training in which footshock is delivered when the rat crosses from a white compartment into the adjoining black compartment. Hypothermia is then induced by immersing the restrained rat in water up to its neck for 10 to 11 minutes. The water temperature is maintained at 35° to 40° F and body temperature is lowered to a mean of 68.5° (measured by a colonic thermometer).

As can be seen in Figure 6.7, the interval between passive avoidance training and application of hypothermia is critical. For independent groups of rats immersed in the water 20 seconds, 5 minutes, 15 minutes, or 60 minutes after the training trial, retention was poorer the sooner the animals were immersed. A subsequent experiment (Riccio, Gaebelein, & Cohen, 1968) indicated that hypothermia was not punishing and did not exert its primary effect through a generalized conditioned emotional response. Rather, the hypothermia acted

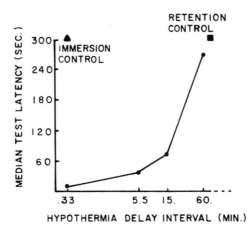

Figure 6.7 Retention of passive avoidance as shown for rats as a function of the delay between the passive avoidance training trial and the introduction of hypothermia (solid line). Rats in the immersion-control condition were given passive avoidance training then immersed in body-temperature water, and those in the retention-control condition were given the passive avoidance training trial but no further treatment prior to testing. The higher the number on the ordinate, the better the retention (adapted from Riccio et al., 1968. Copyright 1968 by the American Psychological Association. Reprinted by permission.)

mainly on the memory representing the contingencies of the avoidance task and the context of its occurrence.

Hypoxia. Retrograde amnesia may be caused by hypoxia (sometimes termed *anoxia*). Hypoxia refers generally to any decrease in the organism's oxygen supply below that ordinarily needed by physiological functions, and it may result from any number of treatments. For example, one technique, used in Giurgea's laboratory in Belgium (e.g., Giurgea, LeFevre, Lescrenier, & David-Remacle, 1971; Sara & LeFevre, 1972), is to place the rat in an airtight cage and mix pure nitrogen with the atmosphere until the final oxygen content is about 3 1/2 percent. The amnesic treatment is defined as 10 minutes of exposure in this mixture. An alternative technique, used by Paolino, Quartermain, and Miller (1966), is to increase the proportion of carbon dioxide (CO_2) in the atmosphere by means of dry ice. The rat is placed on a wire grid floor 4 inches above dry ice in an enclosed cylinder. If the rat remains in the cylinder for 25 seconds, maximum anesthesia occurs, as characterized by the absence of a standing posture, a drop in blood pressure, and a temporary absence of respiration.

Hypoxia induced shortly after a single passive avoidance training trial produces retrograde amnesia in rats and mice. The gradient relating retention of passive avoidance to the interval between training and the hypoxia treatment is shown in Figure 6.8. Like ECS and hypothermia, hypoxia has a wide variety of physiological and neurochemical effects, so the precise mechanism by which retrograde amnesia occurs is not clear at this point.

Some experiments have failed to find retrograde amnesia as a consequence of hypoxia (e.g., Vacher, King, & Miller, 1968). Careful comparison of the proce-

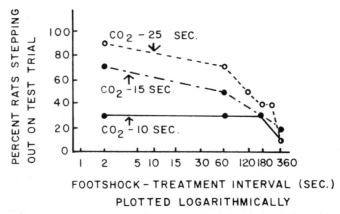

Figure 6.8 The relationship between retention of passive avoidance (the higher the number on the ordinate, the better the retention) and the interval between passive avoidance training and the administration of hypoxia is shown for animals given either of three intensities of the hypoxia treatment: A duration of either 25 sec., 15 sec., or 10 sec. exposure to carbon dioxide (adapted from Paolino, Quartermain and Miller, 1966).

dures used when conflicting results are obtained should help us understand why retrograde amnesia is sometimes caused by hypoxia and sometimes not. In this respect, it is notable that Giurgea and his associates (1971), who produced amnesic effects by inducing hypoxia immediately after each of several daily sessions of discriminated avoidance training, were able to eliminate this amnesia by injecting the drug "piracetam" (or UCB 6215). This drug seems to have a particular anticonvulsant activity directed at the cerebral cortex. We shall see that seizures in the brain are an important, perhaps necessary, precursor to retrograde amnesia.

Incongruity of stimulus events. A posttraining treatment that may be termed *psychological incongruity* and linked to the surprise arising from unexpected events has been studied by Wagner, Rudy, and Whitlow (1973) for its effects on memory processing. As we shall see, Wagner and his associates found that this treatment impaired retention more the sooner it followed a training trial.

Of all the events that we are terming *amnesic agents,* incongruity is the most innocuous physiologically. We are concerned here with incongruity in terms of Pavlovian conditioning. For example, if a clicking noise always occurs just before an electrical shock is delivered to a rabbit in the vicinity of its eye, enough pairings of this kind will result in a reliable eyelid response following the clicking noise. An incongruous event would be defined by the clicking noise presented *without* a subsequent shock, or perhaps followed by a squirt of sugar water in the mouth instead, or by presenting the eye shock following some congenial stimulus like stroking of the rabbit's fur.

Wagner and his colleagues took three ingenious, but relatively simple, steps prior to establishing that posttrial incongruity may disrupt memory processes. First, Wagner and Rescorla developed a theory of learning based on the concept that variation in reinforcement may arise depending upon the subject's expectations about the events that follow the CS (Rescorla & Wagner, 1972; Wagner, 1971; Wagner & Rescorla, 1972). Fundamentally, the notion is that the change in associative strength developed between the CS and the UCS in Pavlovian conditioning is not constant; instead, reinforcement depends on the extent to which the UCS is "unexpected" or "surprising." This principle was evaluated thoroughly and supported in a series of careful experiments. It provides a useful alternative to viewing phenomena like "stimulus selection" and "blocking" in terms of attentional processes. In its strongest form, this principle asserts that "learning occurs only to the degree that the UCS, or its absence, is 'unexpected' or 'surprising' " (Wagner et al., 1973, p. 308).

The second step taken by Wagner and his colleagues was to examine the effects that led to the above principle. They reasoned that perhaps the unexpected character of a UCS is critical to learning because only such events will initiate a "scanning backward" over the memories representing antecedent events. Further, perhaps such a rehearsal-like process is necessary, or at least facilitating, for the animal's learning about the relationship between the CS and the UCS. This step emphasizes the importance of processes that occur following a learning trial.

The third step (Wagner, 1971) was the reasonable assumption of a finite capacity for such "rehearsal": If an animal is occupied by scanning backward over one set of antecedent stimuli, then it should be unable to search its memory simultaneously for a different episode, or at least should do so less efficiently. This final step constitutes a testable idea, and it is the ensuing tests that are reported by Wagner and his associates.

We shall return to the matter of interpretation later. For now, note that concepts like "scanning backward" and "limited rehearsal capacity" merely provide the framework of a model that can be tested. They do not necessarily imply that a rabbit is "rehearsing" in any way similar to the way humans may rehearse verbal materials.

The actual experiments conducted by Wagner and his associates are characteristically careful and thoroughly controlled, and the details of procedure are correspondingly complex. For our purposes, we need consider only the general experimental strategy and basic results. The experimenters exposed rabbits to one of three CSs. One CS was a clicking noise, another a flashing light, and the third a vibration on the animal's chest. The first step in the procedure was to pair one CS with occurrence of shock and another CS with absence of shock. This established that an incongruent episode would be defined if the CS that predicted shock were followed by the absence of shock, or if the CS that predicted the absence of shock were followed by shock. Then the basic test was to present pairings of the third CS with shock followed immediately by either incongruent or congruent events and to assess learning of the third CS–UCS contingency.

The results quite clearly showed relatively impaired Pavlovian conditioning when pairings of the third CS and UCS were followed soon afterward by an incongruent episode as compared with a congruent episode. Moreover, the gradient obtained (see Figure 6.9) indicated that the sooner an incongruent episode ("PTE" in Figure 6.9) followed a pairing ("trial" in Figure 6.9), the slower the learning.

This is a different type of gradient than we saw in most of the cases discussed earlier because it is not based on single retention tests. Rather, each point represents the amount of learning accomplished after a number of trials (like the gradient produced originally by Duncan, 1949). This is a subtle matter that we shall treat again in Chapter 7, when we consider interpretations of amnesic effects.

Pharmacological Sources of Retrograde Amnesia

Many drugs may be injected in an animal prior to training in order to produce impaired performance on a retention test. Such a procedure is particularly inadequate for determining the effect of a drug on memory; in fact, such a proce-

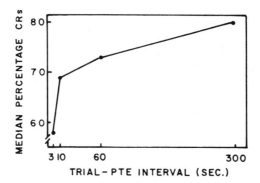

Figure 6.9   Mean percentage of conditioned responses is seen to be an increasing function of the time between the conditioning trial and the introduction of an incongruous, post-trial event (PTE) (adapted from Wagner et al., 1973. Copyright 1973 by the American Psychological Association. Reproduced by permission.)

dure by itself is worthless for understanding the effect of that chemical on behavior. This may be emphasized further by noting Jarvik's (1972) remark:

> After surveying the psychopharmacological literature of the last century, one gets the distinct impression that learning and memory are psychological functions which are not very sensitive to drugs. At least, no drugs have been found which specifically affect either learning or memory without also influencing or being capable of influencing psychological processes such as motivation, arousal, attention, sleep, and motor activity. Only posttrial drug administration eliminates the possibility of an action upon acquisition, but few studies have successfully demonstrated posttrial drug effects. (p. 468)

The biological literature is replete with studies purporting to test the influence of drugs on memory, and the number of such drugs is approaching infinity. We shall restrict our attention here to three representative drugs or classes of drugs selected for their theoretical importance, and studies that have been designed to eliminate contamination of memorial effects that might occur through the drug's modification of simple performance capacity or of perceptual or motivational processes.

Based on what we now know about neurophysiology, the following four classes of drug-induced effects logically seem apt to impair memory: (1) damping of electrical activity in certain regions of the brain; (2) decrement in general arousal that might impair neural recruitment or otherwise impede posttraining memory processes or memory retrieval processes; (3) interference with the chemical substances that apparently serve as neurotransmitters in the brain, like acetylcholine, serotonin, dopamine, and norepinephrine; and (4) interference with the synthesis of macromolecules such as proteins, which many scientists suspect serve a vital function in the physiological basis of memory storage. Examples of drugs that may produce these effects are, respectively, potassium chloride (KCl), anesthetics (e.g., ether), agents that oppose neurotransmitter activity (e.g., anticholinergics such as scopolamine that act in opposition to acetylcholine), and antibiotics (e.g., cycloheximide).

Localized Damping of Endogenous Electrical Activity ("Spreading Depression")

Simple electrolytic lesioning of neural tissue following learning has often been applied toward identifying the function of that tissue for memory storage. However, the technique of simple lesioning constrains experimental design and may limit the conclusions one can make. For example, a simple lesion induced prior to training may impair subsequent retention by its effect on perception, memory storage, information processing during the retention interval, or memory retrieval. If the lesion were reversible and tissue could be made to cease functioning and then later restored to normal functioning, the role of that tissue in memory processing could be determined more precisely. Spreading depression induced by KCl is a candidate for the technique for producing reversible lesions long sought by psychobiologists.

Applied directly to the brain, potassium chloride (KCl) causes depression of cerebral electrical activity. This depression spreads out beyond the point of application, but the functional consequence for neural structures is that it produces a "reversible lesion."

General method for inducing spreading depression.   The application of KCl to produce cortical spreading depression is a simple matter technically. Typically, filter paper soaked in a solution of 25% KCl is applied through a hole in the skull to the dura, the permeable covering over the cortex. The hole in the skull is typically round, 3 to 4 millimeters in diameter. Following the operation, the hole is protected from temperature changes and foreign matter by suturing the scalp over it, by attaching a plastic lid, or by implating a covered cannula through which the KCl can be delivered later. If spreading depression is to be directed at a subcortical structure, the cannula is implanted through the cortex into the subcortex. For precise control of dosage, the electrical consequences of KCl must be monitored by an EEG (further technical details are described by Bures & Buresova, 1972; Schneider, 1973).

Physiological effects of potassium chloride.   The basic objective of applying KCl is to create, in the extreme, electrical silence. More generally, spreading depression alters the electrical activity of neural tissue. Upon application of KCl, the depression effect actually spreads, persistently so, across the cortex. The rate of the spread is on the order of 2 to 6 millimeters per minute, and EEG activity may be suppressed or altered for as long as 3 hours or more. Twenty-four hours after application of KCl, the EEG is back to normal. But the EEG is, after all, a gross measuring instrument; subtle, more or less permanent effects may be undetected.

Generally, the parameter values just listed for the length of EEG suppression are rough approximation; the exact values applied in any given experiment will vary depending on the circumstances. As Bures and Buresova (1972) have noted, "It is obvious that the relationship between contact area, CSD (cortical spreading depression) threshold, concentration and volume of the drug and duration of behavioral impairment is not simple" (p. 329).

A wide variety of side effects from cortically applied KCl accompany the changes in electrical activity. The spread is diffuse and not always confined to the cortex (e.g., Schneider, 1973), so subcortical structures important to learning and memory may also be depressed. These subcortical areas include the hypothalamus, amygdala, caudate nucleus, and reticular formation. On the cortex, the depression originally was thought to be restricted to the hemisphere on which KCl was applied. But it is notable that in anesthesized animals, at least, the alternative hemisphere also may suffer some minor depression effects (however, in normally functioning animals the cortices of the hemispheres do seem to be mutually isolated). Finally, it is interesting that the hippocampus, the subcortical structure identified most often with memory processing, seems to be isolated from the effects of cortical depression (for further discussion of these issues, see Bures & Buresova, 1972; Schneider, 1973).

Nonelectrical effects that may contribute to retention deficits.   There are a variety of side effects that result from the application of KCl to the brain. The major effects are a reduction in protein synthesis and some tissue damage. However, the former is very small compared to the level of reduction in protein synthesis necessary for obstruction of memory processes. Concerning tissue damage, Carlton and Markiewicz (1973) have reported that the effect of KCl on memory processing is unrelated to the size of the lesion that occurs. Further, rats made amnesic by KCl are retrainable quite readily, so the lesions do not affect the animal's capacity to perform. Carlton and Markiewicz also discounted other side effects of KCl as possible contaminants of retention effects. These include the slowed rate of recovery from anesthesia caused by KCl and the possibilities that KCl might influence appetitive behavior or cause a general disinhibitory effect (which otherwise might be mistaken for forgetting of inhibitory conditioning).

Obvious sensory–motor effects result when KCl is applied to the cortex, and these are so numerous and reliable that Bures and Buresova (1972, pp. 331, 333) list several simple motor tests that may be used to determine whether the spreading depression is effective. For example, postural behaviors quite clearly are affected.

Memorial effects of applying potassium chloride to the cortex.   We have referred to spreading depression from KCl as a "reversible lesion," and the effects on memory processing are very much what one would expect from a lesion. Spreading depression applied to the cortex has two particularly analytical uses in attempts to understand memory processing. One use is to study the extent to which memories are stored separately in the cerebral hemispheres and the requirements for transfer of memories from one hemisphere to the other. The second use is to investigate certain time-dependent processes that may influence retention.

To study hemispheric localization of memories, Bures and Buresova (1960) trained rats on either a one-way avoidance task or a discrimination problem for avoiding footshock. They based their reasoning on previous studies by Sperry (e.g., Sperry, Stamm, & Miner, 1956), which showed that an animal with surgically divided cerebral hemispheres may be trained, given the necessary sensory control, to behave as if it had two separate, independent brains. Bures and Buresova trained animals with one hemisphere depressed and found no evidence that it had "learned" when it was depressed, in spite of independent evidence of excellent retention by the other hemisphere. The interesting part of this demonstration is that neither hemisphere was depressed *between* training and testing: The hemisphere tested was depressed essentially only during training, and the alternative hemisphere only during testing. So in spite of approximately 20 hours during which the hemispheres may have "communicated" about what was stored in the hemisphere not depressed during training, no evidence was found later for such storage in the hemisphere that *was* depressed during training.

If a memory is stored in only one hemisphere during training because of unilateral spreading depression in the other, can it ever be transfered to the alternative hemisphere (or must the latter always be trained completely)? The answer is yes, such transfer can occur, and the conditions for establishing it are as intriguing as the absence of transfer initially. The basic condition necessary for transfer is that both hemispheres be functional during at least one training trial. There are also some temporal requirements regarding the duration of simultaneous cerebral function. Ray and Emley (1964) found that a period of 15 seconds of simultaneous functioning after such a training trial was insufficient for transfer, but if depression was not reintroduced for 10 minutes, transfer did occur. Subsequently, Albert (1966) analyzed these temporal characteristics in a more detailed set of experiments. Among the many experiments he conducted, we are concerned only with those that dealt with spreading depression.

Albert first trained rats to perform an active avoidance task while one hemisphere was depressed. After the depressive effects had dissipated, he gave a single active avoidance trial. For animals that were not treated further, transfer occurred to the previously depressed hemisphere, as expected from previous results like those of Ray and Emley (1964). For the experimental groups, Albert was interested in two relationships. First, how much time is required for information to be transfered from the undepressed to the previously depressed hemisphere? Second, after transfer, how much processing ("consolidation") time in the previously depressed hemisphere is required to establish a stable memorial representation there?

To deal with the first question, Albert introduced spreading depression (by means of KCl) in the previously *un*depressed hemisphere at different intervals after the transfer trial. If the KCl treatment was applied 30 seconds later, amnesia, albeit incomplete, occurred. But if a delay of 3 minutes elapsed before the KCl was administered, no amnesia was measured. Processing time in the previously depressed hemisphere appeared to take a good deal longer. If this "receiving" hemisphere was depressed within 2 hours after the transfer trial, retention measured on the subsequent test was negligible.

In the preceding discussion, we found it convenient to refer to "unilateral memory storage" when one hemisphere was depressed during training. Similarly, we spoke of subsequent transfer to the relatively ignorant hemisphere as "establishing memory storage" in that hemisphere, with the temporal requirements of that storage reflecting "rates of memory consolidation." While this language and interpretation makes intuitive sense and is quite reasonable within certain theoretical views, it is notable that alternative explanations have been derived using quite different language and concepts, and emphasizing the stimulus consequences of the KCl treatment (see Schneider, 1967, 1973).

Retrograde amnesia effects of potassium chloride applied cortically or subcortically.   For our purposes, perhaps the most interesting effect of KCl is its influence as an agent of retrograde amnesia. Bures and Buresova (1963) and Pearlman (1966) found that retrograde amnesia results if bilateral depression is given following training. The former study found that some amnesia occurred as long as the spreading depression was applied within 2 hours after training, but the latter study found that the depression had to be applied within 10 minutes if amnesia was to occur. As Schneider (1973) has pointed out, this discrepancy is probably due to differences in the duration of the depression.

Schneider, Advokat, Kapp, and Sherman (1969) depressed a single hemisphere following training and found amnesia if the depression occurred within 3 minutes, but not if it occurred 15 minutes or longer following training.

Retrograde amnesia caused by KCl-induced electrical depression in the hippocampus has been studied by Carlton and his colleagues (see Carlton & Markiewicz, 1973). Carlton's typical procedure is to inject KCl through a cannula into the hippocampus 24 hours after training, and to test after the animals have recovered. While the KCl is injected, Carlton and his colleagues regularly monitor the electrical consequences to determine the extent of the electrical silence that occurs. When a test is given 4 days later, amnesia is found to be in direct proportion to the duration of the electrical silence induced.

There are two particularly notable features of the data reported by Carlton and his colleagues. First, the memory that is tested for disruption represents an episode of classical conditioning, the effect of which is measured by conditioned suppression. This is notable because this is the only task for which Carlton has found retrograde amnesia from spreading depression in the hippocampus. Using precisely the same techniques of applying KCl, no amnesia has been found for complex discrimination learning or operant lever pressing, tested with a variety of schedules of reinforcement. The more obvious explanations of this anomaly have been covered by Carlton and Markiewicz (1973), so the reader is referred to that paper for further discussion. For example, it is not that the conditioned suppression technique simply is more sensitive to detection of the relatively low degree of learning that may have resulted from some procedures applied by Carlton and his associates, because increasing the number of pairings of the CS and UCS (up to 40) does not reduce the amnesia caused by the spreading depression.

The other notable feature of this instance of retrograde amnesia is that it is transient. Hughes (1969) found that in spite of evidence for essentially no retention 4 days after the amnesic treatment, a test given 21 days later showed excellent retention, indicating that the memory had "recovered."

The basis of the amnesia produced by hippocampal spreading depression is unclear. The data seem consistent with Carlton's explanation that the effect is simply that of a recoverable lesion. However, two processes may be operating here. Kapp and Schneider (1971) replicated Hughes' (1969) results when KCl was injected 1 day after training; but if KCl was injected 10 seconds after training, no evidence of retention was found even after 21 days. Apparently, the permanence of this amnesic effect (like others to be discussed in Chapters 7 and 8) is proportional to the interval between training and administration of the amnesic agent.

Alterations in General Arousal: Anesthetics and Barbiturates

Anesthetics whose action is primarily on the central nervous system (ether is a common example) have been shown to induce amnesia. Certain barbiturates having other effects in common with ether, such as decreased arousal, also have appeared to have amnesic effects.

Obviously, if these drugs were administered *prior* to learning, it would be difficult or impossible to separate analgesic and general performance effects from their effects on memory processing. Therefore, only studies of retrograde amnesia, in which the drug is not administered until after training is complete, are of interest to us here.

Ether has been found to induce retrograde amnesia in a variety of circumstances. Pearlman, Sharpless, and Jarvik (1961) were intrigued by conflicting reports that memory processing in humans seems to be impaired at some stages of ether anesthesia, yet under other circumstances it is improved. These investigators trained thirsty rats to press a bar for water, then electrified the bar, which resulted in a rapid cessation of pressing. Ten seconds, 5 minutes, or 10 minutes following the shock, rats were confined with ether fumes and became anesthetized within 35 seconds to a level that would be sufficiently deep for surgery. Twenty-four hours later, the rats returned to pressing the bar (i.e., forgot the shock) if they had been exposed to ether within 10 seconds or 5 minutes following training, but not if the delay was 10 minutes or if they had not been anesthetized at all.

In subsequent studies, ether has been found to induce retrograde amnesia following appetitive training (Herz, 1969) with mice as well as rats (Essman & Jarvik, 1961), and with infant chickens when imprinting was the "learning task" (Gutekunst & Youniss, 1963). However, the critical posttraining time of administering the ether—the slope of the retrograde amnesia gradient—has varied greatly. In some cases, amnesia occurred even though exposure to ether was delayed as long as 24 hours after training (Alpern & Kimble, 1967); in other instances, retrograde amnesia has not been obtained even when ether was administered as soon as 40 seconds after training (e.g., McGaugh & Zornetzer, 1970). One factor clearly responsible for this variance is ambient temperature. Cherkin (1968), a biochemist prominent in the behavioral study of amnesia, has noted that the effective concentration of the ether is related directly to temperature. Thus, with warm temperature (38°C), Alpern and Kimble produced amnesia in spite of a long delay between training and etherization, but under cooler conditions (24°C) they were unable to produce amnesia with the same procedures. We shall see later that Cherkin and others have shown that the effect of the interval between training and application of the amnesic agent depends importantly on the effective intensity (or concentration, in this case) of the amnesic agent.

Pearlman and his associates (1961) also found that the barbiturate pentobarbitol induced significant amnesia even when administered as long as 10 minutes after training. It is notable that the pentobarbitol was injected directly into the jugular vein through chronically implanted catheters and was sufficiently strong (30 mg/kg) so that surgical levels of anesthesia occurred within 10 seconds after the injection and continued for about an hour. Previously, Leukel (1957) had found a similar amnesic effect following a high dose of pentobarbitol (44 mg/kg) when administered within 1 minute after each of several daily training trials on a complex maze in which the rats learned to swim to safety.

As a preliminary point of interpretation, we should note that a more recent experiment by Chute and Wright (1973), similar to that of Pearlman and his associates in its use of passive avoidance training and injection shortly thereafter of pentobarbitol directly into the jugular vein, obtained the same "amnesic" effect. However, while Pearlman and his associates interpreted the effect as being caused by impairment of the consolidation process of memory storage, Chute and Wright concluded that the impairment was better conceptualized as a case of state-dependent retention. The effect discovered by Chute and Wright has not been studied thoroughly, but if substantiated, it would indicate that barbiturate-induced amnesia may be due to mechanisms responsible for state dependent retention (e.g., impaired memory retrieval) rather than simply impaired storage.

Drugs That Affect Cholinergic Neural Transmission

Obstruction of the cholinergic nervous system in the brain seems a likely technique, on clinical, empirical, and theoretical grounds, for influencing memory processing. Scopolamine, an agent that blocks cholinergic transmission, is used commonly as a substitute for anesthesia during childbirth. Ostensibly, there is some benefit from this. This benefit is often reported by physicians as "subsequent forgetting of the traumatic experience," although some subjective reports indicate that its action may be more like that of a barbiturate or a frontal lobotomy in that the pain is perceived clearly but is less annoying. Empirically, there is increasingly clear evidence that cholinergic transmission is critical for habituation (e.g., Carlton, 1963, 1969; Feigley & Hamilton, 1971), simple learning such as passive avoidance (e.g., Feigley, 1974), and perhaps retention of relatively complex learning as well (Deutsch, 1972). Theoretically, cholinergic transmission has been linked to inhibitory processes in general, and such processes may be critical to certain stages of memory processing (cf. Carlton, 1963, 1969).

For our present interest in memory processing following information input, the most interesting theoretical and empirical effort concerning cholinergic transmission is that of Deutsch and his colleagues (e.g., Deutsch, 1969, 1972). Deutsch's theory is based on these three principles: Learning is a consequence of an increase in postsynaptic sensitivity to the transmitter, acetylcholine, and subsequent retention depends on the level of this sensitivity; following learning, this sensitivity fluctuates in a regular but nonmonotonic manner, first increasing for intervals on the order of several days, then decreasing; and the decrease in sensitivity can be counteracted by an appropriate dose of an anticholinesterase such as DFP or physostigmine, while the increase in sensitivity can be counteracted by an anticholinergic agent such as scopolamine.

It is well established that an anticholinesterase, by interfering with the chemical breakdown of acetylcholine, may facilitate cholinergic transmission under some limited conditions, and that an anticholinergic, by occupying the postsynaptic sites that ordinarily take up acetylcholine, may block cholinergic transmission. Deutsch's theory is somewhat controversial; data in support of the first two principles just given are not prevalent, and while such a theory based on the action of neurotransmitters is needed and potentially critical for understanding memory processing, not all psychobiologists agree on the viability of those particular principles. For now, however, we are concerned with the amnesic effects that have been shown in tests of this theory.

Deutsch (1972) reports experiments in which rats were injected with an anticholinesterase (DFP in some experiments, physostigmine in others) at different intervals after learning. The learning task was a brightness discrimination. Training trials were presented in relatively massed fashion until each rat attained a fairly strict criterion of performance. All animals were tested 24 hours after their injection. Amnesia was shown for rats that had been injected 30 minutes after their last training trial or 14 days after training. In similar experiments, the anticholinergic scopolamine was injected under the same conditions but no effects were found for animals injected 40 minutes or 14 days after training, although those injected 1 or 3 days after training showed significant amnesia. Using a different task (passive avoidance) and species (mice), Glick and Zimmerberg (1972) also found that scopolamine induced amnesia if injected very soon after training.

Disruption of Protein Synthesis: Antibiotics

To say that protein synthesis is important to an animal is the grandest of understatements. Every organ in an animal's body depends on protein that the animal itself has synthesized, because protein is one substance that an animal cannot replace directly by eating something or someone else; there simply is no general means through which proteins from other organisms can be incorporated into the cells of the consumer. Moreover, for many of the more vital organs such as the brain, over half of the weight (excluding water) is protein. The critical status of protein in all of the permanent structures of an organism, together with some other less obvious biological facts and hypotheses, inspired the learned guess during the early 1950s that protein might be the basis for the relatively permanent representation of events involving the learning process. The weak form of this general hypothesis is that protein is necessary for the establishment of a memory in storage; in its strong form, a memory is stored as protein (e.g., Gerard, 1953; Halstead, 1951; see Gaito and Bonnet, 1971).

The exact mechanisms suggested as the instrument for registering memories in the brain have taken a number of forms. These include morphological growth at the synapse and changes in the properties or probabilities of electrochemical transmission of neural energy. Irrespective of the specifics, essentially all such mechanisms in some way implicate a change in protein synthesis that permits the creation of new protein.

There are, however, alternative means (other than the production of new protein) by which memory storage could be effected. Booth (1973) has described a few of these in a very instructive chapter. He has also opposed arguments about two other characteristics that have led to theories citing the formation of new protein as the basis of memorial representation in the brain. One of these is the argument that because cellular requirements in the brain could be satisfied easily with a much lower rate of protein synthesis than actually exists, the "extra" activity of protein synthesis must be devoted to memory processing. The other argument is that macromolecules such as proteins are particularly suited for storing information because of their sequential structure. Booth's explanation against these points need not be repeated here except to note that he argues effectively that memory is not necessarily coded in protein structure.

Nevertheless, it is fashionable to suppose that memory is coded as protein; there has been little empirical evidence so far to suggest that it is not. The reasons for supposing it in the first place are sensibly informed, and they well may be correct. Moreover, if we assume a protein basis of memory storage, there are a number of tests that may be applied immediately because a good deal is understood at present about how protein synthesis can be controlled. The basic rationale has been that if protein synthesis is reduced drastically, memory storage should not occur; it is this source of ''amnesia'' that we shall discuss next. Our discussion of the converse sort of investigation, based on the rationale that if memory storage occurs, then protein synthesis should have increased, will be brief because it is controversial and more tangential than relevant to our purpose.

Throughout this discussion, it should be clear that we are talking about *quantitative* variations in protein synthesis. There are a large number of different species of protein in the brain, and it is not at all clear which, if any, is critical to memory storage (for a review, see Gaito & Bonnet, 1971).

If storage in long-term memory depends on protein or RNA, then variation in retention should correspond to variation in the rate at which these molecules are synthesized. There are a variety of means by which protein or RNA synthesis may be varied. Generally, these include modification of either the external or the internal environment of the organism, which, in turn, requires some adaptive sorts of activities by the organism. Gaito and Bonnet have described some of the variations in sensory stimulation or forced motor activity that result in changes in protein or RNA synthesis. The general result has been that moderate stimulation or organismic activity produces an increase in such synthesis, while more severe or intense treatments result in a decrease in protein synthesis.

A pertinent example of a source of intense stimulation that decreases RNA synthesis is electroconvulsive shock (ECS). Within one minute following the convulsion, RNA synthesis is reduced 10–30% in all areas of the brain analyzed, with the greatest decrements occurring in areas believed to be critical for memory storage, such as the frontal and temporal cortices and the hippocampus. Convulsions induced by metrazol result in a similar reduction in RNA synthesis.

Perhaps the most efficient means of varying rates of RNA and protein synthesis is by introducing chemicals into the organism. There are chemicals available that increase the rate of RNA synthesis, such as tricyanoaminopropene (TCP) and magnesium pemoline, both of which have been tested in memory experiments for possible hypermnesic effects, but so far with equivocal results. However, the most extensive work on the role of RNA and protein synthesis in memory processing tested the effects of antibiotic drugs, which drastically reduce the rate of synthesis. To reduce RNA synthesis, the drug actinomycin-D has often been applied. To reduce protein synthesis, the drug puromycin was used in some of the more important early studies, and more recently the glutarimide derivatives cycloheximide and acetoxycycloheximide have been employed. As Gaito and Bonnet (1971) point out, however, all of the drugs that reduce protein synthesis have, to some extent, another common effect, a reduction in the amount of messenger RNA that reaches the cytoplasm.

Nature of the memory deficit in memory processing.   That injection of antibiotics produces retention decrement is indisputable. The basic effect has been shown not only with rats and mice but also with goldfish (e.g., Agranoff, 1971), chickens (Mark & Watts, 1971), and toads (Titus & Costanzo, 1972), for both appetitive and aversive conditioning, and when the content of the memory acquired includes instrumental avoidance or discrimination.

There are several restrictions on these effects, however. For amnesia to occur, the application of the antibiotic, which is usually intracerebral and directed at the temporal regions of the brain, including the cortex and the area of the hippocampus, must either precede training by a short interval or follow it by a short interval. Usually the pretraining interval is timed so that inhibition of protein synthesis (or, in relatively few tests, RNA synthesis, e.g., Barondes & Jarvik, 1964) is maximal at the time of training. Injections following training are usually ineffective unless they occur within a few minutes, although with goldfish the posttraining injection may be delayed for a longer period (Agranoff, 1971) and even with mice there is at least one experiment indicating that injection of an antibiotic (acetoxycycloheximide) may be delayed for as long as 18 hours after passive avoidance training and still yield a small amnesic effect (Swanson, McGaugh, & Cotman, 1969).

The time of testing also is important in an interesting way. No amnesia is found if animals treated with an antibiotic are tested within a few hours after training. Typically, this interval of "protection" against amnesia is about 3 hours (although Quinton, 1971, did find amnesia as soon as 1 1/2 hours after training). However, tests given 6 or 24 hours later show unmistakable retention deficits. It is not clear whether this interval is controlled by drug dosage, which in any case must be sufficient to impair protein synthesis by about 90% or more if amnesia is to occur.

The amnesia that occurs is quite sensitive to degree of original learning and is not seen when high levels of original learning have been achieved. Perhaps the effect of the high degree of original training may be counteracted by higher levels of synthesis inhibition, although this has not been established, and anyway, much higher levels of inhibition would probably result in the death of still more animals (antibiotics sometimes kill their recipients in these experiments, presenting a problem that we shall discuss shortly).

These are the empirical facts; reference to the basic experiments may be found in a variety of sources (e.g., Agranoff, 1971; Barondes, 1975; McGaugh &

Herz, 1972). Interpretation of these results is quite another matter. It is useful to consider briefly interpretive issues specific to antibiotics as amnesia-inducing agents; these issues will be considered in further detail in Chapter 7.

How are these effects of antibiotics on memory to be interpreted? Because of the obvious importance of protein synthesis to the animal's biological maintenance, and because antibiotics act generally on many systems, not only on memory processing, we may presume that the side effects of these agents are severe. And indeed they are. The obvious effect is the production of a very sick animal suffering from anorexia and diarrhea. In most of these experiments, 10–15% of the animals die. Typically, then, an animal acquires a memory when it is very sick and then is tested for retrieval when it is well, or at least less sick. This obvious point has caused investigators to employ a number of rather ingeniously derived controls in addition to the implicit controls provided by the basic temporal effects. Such controls seem to have eliminated the influence of potentially contaminating factors such as state-dependent retention (e.g., Daniels, 1971) and effects on general activity (e.g., Segal, Squire, & Barondes, 1971) that might alter the interpretation of at least some characteristics of the antibiotic-induced amnesia. A more dramatic challenge to the conventional interpretation of these effects has been made by Reinis (1969), who suggests that puromycin does indeed block the expression of memory, but that the basis of this action is not its inhibition of protein synthesis but rather "the formation of pathological products which are able to change the activity of nerve cells" (p. 44).

Probably the most important data that will serve to alter the interpretation of the effects of antibiotics on memory are those showing that the amnesia produced is not permanent. An increasing number of studies have found alleviation of the amnesia, thus implicating memory retrieval, by one of three methods. First, there is an intriguing series of studies by Flexner and his associates that has implicated, first, hormonal activity of the adrenal–pituitary system (e.g., Flexner & Flexner, 1970), and later, the action of norepinephrine in the adrenergic nervous system (e.g., Serota, Roberts, & Flexner, 1972; see also Nakajima, 1975) as important for initial suppression and eventual recovery of a memory. A second method for inducing recovery from the amnesic effects of an inhibitor of protein synthesis is to present the subject, just before the retention test, with the footshock associated with the prior learning or with any of several drugs (e.g., Quartermain & Botwinick, 1975; Quartermain, McEwen, & Azmitia, 1970). Finally, a large number of investigators have found that animals left alone will recover "spontaneously" from the amnesic effects of these agents after a relatively long interval. Barondes and Squire (1972) review these data and suggest some physiological mechanisms through which this recovery might be mediated.

The major effect of this widespread evidence that amnesia induced by inhibiting protein synthesis is not permanent is to argue against a simple conception of permanent memory as represented in protein form. Apparently, either a more complex (e.g., Barondes & Squire, 1972) or a different (e.g., Booth, 1973) explanation is needed. In this respect, an intriguing suggestion is introduced in a chapter by Booth and Pilcher (1973).

Booth and Pilcher first cite evidence that rats readily acquire a conditioned aversion to an odor when that specific odor is present at the time the rats are injected with cycloheximide, and that similar aversions to specific places and visually cued situations may also be conditioned if similarly paired with poisoning of the animal. They then advance this novel suggestion: Animals that have been injected with an antibiotic and then learn to avoid shock by entering a particular location, by responding to a particular visual cue, or by remaining in a particular location (passive avoidance) later may appear to exhibit amnesia by failing to avoid shock as effectively as before. But this does not reflect amnesia for the contingencies of footshock; rather, it shows retention of the conditioned aversion for that particular location in the maze (or visual cue or portion of the passive avoidance apparatus) associated with the noxious consequences of the antibiotic. "Thus, the failure to perform correctly during long-term retest may not be because the animal has forgotten what is correct. It may be rather that the animal is in conflict between, for example, avoiding electric shocks and avoiding antibiotic-induced sickness" (Booth & Pilcher, 1973, p. 108). In other words, arrival at the rewarded location has always been accompanied by sickness; when the animal is tested, failure to return there need not mean forgetting about shock but could mean remembering about the sickness.

It is not clear how Booth and Pilcher's explanation can account for recovery from antibiotic-induced amnesia. However, the time-course of retention of either of two conflicting memories is a complex matter (see, e.g., Spear, 1971; see also Chapter 4). Perhaps the recovery data may eventually be accommodated within Booth and Pilcher's interpretation. Notably, suggestions similar to that of Booth and Pilcher have also been made in reports by Titus and Costanzo (1972) with respect to the effects of antibiotics, by Berger (1972) with respect to a variety of other "psychoactive" drugs, and more recently by Nakajima (1973, 1975) regarding the antibiotic cycloheximide. On the other hand, certain data seem quite inconsistent with the Booth–Pilcher explanation (Quartermain & Botwinick, 1975; see especially Exp. 1B). A resolution of these discrepencies awaits further information.

Summary

We have discussed the importance of analyzing the effects of retrograde amnesia in animals, with particular reference to the importance of the temporal gradient of retrograde amnesia. A variety of experimental preparations for its study were described. These typically include exposure of an animal to conditions known to induce learning, followed by exposure to an amnesic agent and finally assessment of the animal's retention. The great majority of amnesic agents that have been tested thoroughly may be described as physiologically traumatic. The several side effects of such treatments were described, and we noted the analytical burden on the investigator to extract the influence of these agents on memory processing from their influence on other aspects of behavior. The technical advances in this area have been substantial, however, and a good deal has been learned about the precise influence of these traumatic amnesic agents on memory processing. Several amnesic agents were considered, including electroconvulsive shock, directed stimulation of the brain, a variety of drugs, and one treatment (psychological surprise) that apparently is physiologically innocuous.

SUMMARY AND CONCLUSIONS

This chapter concerned abnormal circumstances that seem to promote abnormal memory processing. The discussion was limited to instances of exaggerated forgetting. We shall have occasion in Chapter 7 to consider the opposite situation—exaggerated retention.

This chapter was intended primarily to describe major phenomena associated with abnormal processing of memories and to consider how they may be analyzed. For humans, the major phenomena are anterograde amnesia caused by brain damage or disease and retrograde amnesia caused by neurophysiological trauma such as electroconvulsive therapy or by psychological trauma of varying degrees, including relatively innocuous "surprise." For animals, the major phenomena concern experimentally induced retrograde amnesia created by a variety of traumatic environmental or chemical treatments. Probably it need not be added that through analysis of abnormal memory processing the basis of normal memory processing can be determined. Following this introduction to the abnormal processing of memories, Chapter 7 concerns its further analysis.

Perhaps the most carefully analyzed instance of abnormal memory processing in humans is the anterograde amnesia that results from brain damage to the temporal area of the brain, in the region of the hippocampus, or from alcoholism advanced to the stage identified as the Korsakoff syndrome. Although they are etiologically different, these afflictions have in common damage of related areas in the brain. Also, the amnesic consequences of these afflictions are similar. Analysis of this class of abnormal memory processing is limited methodologically to the determination of response–response relationships. With the aid of increasingly sophisticated techniques for assessing human memory processing, however, and through ancillary investigations of experimentally induced brain damage in animals, knowledge in this area has become increasingly refined. One consequence is the development of several testable and relatively sophisticated theories of human amnesia to replace the previously dominant formulation of Milner (1966). Milner's theory had assumed that amnesics are basically deficient in the transfer of information from a short-term to a long-term memory store.

Extensive empirical investigations by two research groups, led by Weiskrantz and Warrington in England and by Butters and Cermak in the United States, have led to consideration of several theories. Four of the more prominent are the interference, encoding, familiarity, and associative learning hypotheses.

The understanding of human retrograde amnesia induced by physiological trauma has been impeded by basic methodological difficulties. The analysis of retrograde amnesia for words followed by a surprising event has progressed further, but is still incomplete. These instances of retrograde amnesia have the common feature of subsequent recovery from the amnesia. Also, it has seemed likely that the basis of both may be found in terms of ineffective memory retrieval processes or deficient mnemonic preparation (e.g., type of rehearsal; see Chapter 8). It is not yet possible, though, to determine whether these cases of amnesia are related in more fundamental respects.

The experimental analysis of retrograde amnesia has proceeded most effectively in experiments with animal subjects. A good deal is known about the characteristics of amnesia produced by a variety of traumatic treatments. Perhaps most important for analytical purposes is the retrograde amnesia gradient. This gradient represents the fact that, for most of the treatments discussed, the amnesic effect is greater the sooner the treatment follows original training. Yet even though retrograde amnesia may be put under rigorous experimental control with precise manipulations of the amnesic treatments, analysis is made difficult by the multiple effects of all traumatic amnesic treatments. The necessary and sufficient effects responsible for amnesia have not been isolated. At present, three consequences associated with most treatments—brain seizures of various types, disruption of neurotransmitter activity, and impairment of protein synthesis—seem likely candidates.

7
Experimental Analysis of Amnesia and Hypermnesia

Having discussed how exaggerated forgetting may be induced by a variety of abnormal physiological or behavioral circumstances, we may now analyze this forgetting through experiments that have placed the abnormal circumstances under precise experimental control. The analytical advantages of this are obvious, and there are two general goals of this approach. Of relatively less concern has been the goal of simulating the circumstances leading to clinical cases of deficient memory processing, which might be useful in understanding the basis of applied diagnostic and medical approaches. This is the minor goal because it seems premature until we have a better understanding of how memories are processed. The major interest, therefore, is to analyze memory processing experimentally under abnormal circumstances in order to understand it under normal circumstances, a widely applied scientific strategy.

The plan of this chapter is to examine amnesia and hypermnesia, two classes of abnormal memory processing that have been analyzed extensively. We will emphasize the former simply because it has received more attention and is understood better.

Following our discussion of the analytical importance of the gradient of retrograde anmesia, we shall discuss five general determinants of retrograde amnesia and its accompanying gradient. These five determinants, selected for their general importance to theories of memory processing, are (1) conditions of training that probably have their effect through an influence on the degree of original learning; (2) type and intensity of the amnesic agent; (3) content of the memory being processed prior to administration of the amnesic agent; (4) length of the retention interval; and (5) structure of the retention interval in terms of the events that take place between learning and the retention test. The final section of this chapter will consider hypermnesia (facilitated retention) in animals and man resulting from agents that act to modify the organism in a physiological or in a psychological sense.

GRADIENT OF RETROGRADE AMNESIA

From the start, the most intriguing aspect of amnesia has been its retrograde action. Certainly, there are interesting cases of anterograde amnesia that have been analyzed both clinically and experimentally. We discussed some examples earlier, and shall return to instances of anterograde amnesia of the sort likely to attract increasing experimental attention. But at present retrograde effects remain more useful analytically, and more interesting, for the following two reasons.

First, it is not surprising that a physiologically traumatic event might result in failure to register and retain memories representing subsequent events, as occurs with anterograde amnesia. The reason it is not surprising is that such an effect could be accounted for by defects in any number of psychological processes, such as sensory detection and perception. But retrograde amnesia occurs even when the trauma follows a to-be-remembered event by an interval sufficiently long to ensure the completion of sensory–perceptual processes. Thus, we may infer more assuredly that a defect in *memory* processing caused the amnesia.

Second, a basic problem in the history of learning theory has been understanding how a reinforcing event like a food pellet or footshock presented *after* a response could act retroactively to alter the subsequent probability of that response. In the positivistic analysis of learning, for example, it did not help to introduce a concept like "memory" or "memory processing," because there seemed to be no means for measuring such entities. Retrograde amnesia, however, appeared to provide a somewhat more amenable case, methodologically, in which events affected the preceding psychological process of learning, that is, storage. The simplest explanation seemed to be that the memory storage process in fact had *not* been completed prior to the trauma; in spite of the completion of the sensory–perception stages, the event was not permanently registered in memory. The storage process must take more time than perception, it was reasoned, because amnesia resulted when the trauma halted memory processing before its completion.

Here was an exceptional opportunity to measure the duration of the storage process: Simply present organisms with information that ordinarily would be stored in memory, then introduce a traumatic treatment to the CNS after varying intervals following the information. The time required for completion of the memory storage process would be indicated by the interval between training and traumatic treatment after which *some* evidence of the training appears on the retention test. In other words, until the memory storage process is completed, disruption by traumatic treatment should result in no subsequent evidence that learning has occurred; but the minimum interval (t min) following training at which a traumatic treatment does *not* completely obliterate evidence of a memory theoretically would define the duration of the memory storage process. It is notable that this interval, t min, prior to which a treatment obliterates all evidence of a memory, has not received much experimental attention relative to the interval, t max, after which a trauma produces no decrement in the evidence for a permanent memory. This paradoxical and unfortunate state of affairs has also been considered by Weiskrantz (1970).

As we have mentioned, a persisting process of memory storage had been suggested around the turn of the century by Müller and Pilzecker. This has been termed a *consolidation* process. To account for retroactive interference, Müller and Pilzecker suggested that subsequent learning disrupted this process. This initial application to human learning and retention was unsuccessful because it failed to incorporate the profound effect of similarity on retroactive interference (see McGeoch, 1932). Perhaps ultimately this application was doomed to fail in tests with humans anyway, simply because humans process information into memory storage so rapidly. Subjectively, we can agree that such processing can be quite rapid indeed, but there is better evidence. For instance, Sperling (1967) has estimated that even when humans *explicitly* rehearse, they may rehearse a set of 6 letters in 1.0 second; and from a visual display exposed for only .05 seconds, humans can maintain for a short period as many as 18 unrelated letters. Similarly, commenting on clinical cases of retrograde amnesia, Russell (1948) suggests that memory storage in humans is probably complete in 1 or 2 seconds. While analysis of such rapid "memory storage" by humans would have strained existing technology (and still does), the presumably slower processing by lower animals might provide a ready estimate of how much time is required for storage of a memory.

This lengthy introduction is intended to emphasize the importance of the retrograde amnesia gradient. The gradient shows how subsequent retention performance is related to the interval between the occurrence of events presumed to be critical to formation of the memory and delivery of the traumatic treatment (amnesic agent).

An idealized retrograde amnesia gradient is shown in Figure 7.1. In actual practice, of course, retention must be assessed against a baseline of unconditioned performance, and a variety of additional, rather esoteric, controls are required to achieve empirically proper gradients.

The sharp point of inflection turning upward from "no retention" to "some retention" ideally would define *t min,* and that from "some" to "complete retention" would define *t max.* The inevitable difference between *t min* and *t max* is one feature that has precluded a sharp, clear estimate of the duration of the storage process, or the rate of "consolidation." Perhaps unfortunately, the term *consolidation* may tend to elicit an image of a small pool of liquid gelatin located somewhere in the brain—the events of training have provided the appropriate mixture but the gelatin is not really usable for an interval until it "solidifies." Such an image has tended to obscure the facts.

An interesting possibility, however, was that the period of time required for the gelatin to solidify—for "consolidation"—might be a constant, restricted only by species. In retrospect, this sort of conceptualization is overly optimistic; it is now recognized to be premature or even inappropriate, simply because

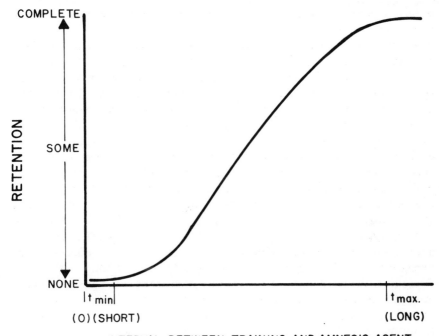

Figure 7.1   Idealized gradient of retrograde amnesia.

"consolidation time," the shape of the gradient, is too variable. It soon became clear that the gradient of retrograde amnesia depends on several aspects of conditions of learning and testing, as well as the amnesic agent itself.

CONDITIONS OF LEARNING DETERMINE AMNESIA

Degree of Learning Prior to Amnesic Treatment

That degree of original learning affects susceptibility to amnesia has become quite clear through many experiments. The relationship appears simple; an amnesic agent typically is less likely to be effective the greater the degree of original training. By degree of learning is meant, as before, retention in the absence of the source of forgetting; in this case, it is retention in the absence of the amnesic treatment. This operational definition poses no problem, although conceptualizing what is meant by degree of learning at a theoretical level is a difficult and uncertain matter that will be addressed later.

The interpretation of this effect of degree of learning may depend on how that degree of learning was achieved (and circumstances of the amnesic agent). For example, if training requires many widely spaced trials and the agent is not delivered until after training ends, the retrograde action might be expected to influence only the information gained in the last trial. This is especially obvious if one takes the view that an amnesic agent is effective only if administered prior to the completion of consolidation. If so, one would expect that with sufficiently spaced training trials, consolidation for each trial would be complete prior to the next; the amnesic agent would influence only information acquired in the last trial; and the previously consolidated information would perhaps cumulate toward a relationship of less amnesic effect with more training trials. But even without assuming a consolidation theory, the manner in which a particular degree of learning is achieved may be considered important for retention. We shall return to this issue in Chapter 8.

Generally, however, while the implications of a consolidation view should be kept in mind, the fact is that the influence of degree of learning on amnesia is so general as to go beyond this view. Whether degree of learning is manipulated by variables other than number or spacing of training trials, and whether the amnesic agent actually is administered prior to training (with its major effect assumed during training, as in the case of most antibiotics) or after training, the general relationship that has emerged is less forgetting (amnesia) with a higher degree of original learning.

This relationship appeared first in studies of amnesia caused by antibiotics that drastically inhibit protein synthesis in the brain. Mice trained to a criterion of nine correct discriminations in ten consecutive trials had little retention loss a day later even though protein synthesis at the time of learning had been greatly impaired by acetoxycycloheximide. By comparison, mice originally trained to a less stringent criterion (say, six correct responses in seven trials) showed marked forgetting under the same conditions (e.g., Barondes & Cohen, 1967; Cohen & Barondes, 1968; Flexner, Flexner, & Roberts, 1966). A similar relationship has been found for retention of visual discrimination learning by the quail and retention of avoidance learning by the goldfish, with puromycin as the amnesic agent (Agranoff & Klinger, 1964; Mayor, 1973). Flood, Bennett, Rosenzweig, and Orme (1972) found that it was not always possible to compensate for high degrees of learning by increasing dosage; amnesia failed to occur under some conditions of training even though near-lethal dosages of cycloheximide were given.

A thorough analysis of the relationship between degree of learning and amnesia induced by cycloheximide has been conducted by Quartermain and Botwinick (1975) as a practical step toward establishing the optimal conditions for amnesia. This information was important for the proper exploitation of an experimental preparation these investigators had devised for special analytical purposes. Hungry mice are trained on a position discrimination in a T-maze (e.g., a left turn is rewarded with food) and then are trained on the reverse discrimination (a right turn is rewarded). The critical memory subjected to amnesia by cycloheximide is that of the reverse discrimination. These investigators found the extent of the amnesia for reversal to be quite sensitive to the degree of training given on both the original and the reverse discrimination: When degree of original training was held constant, reversal training to either a high or a low criterion of discrimination performance resulted in less amnesic effect of cycloheximide than with an intermediate degree of reversal training. In terms of specific parameter values, amnesia occurred with greatest effect when 20 training trials had been given on the original discrimination (which yielded a mean of about 11 correct responses) and when reversal training was continued until 17 correct responses were given (which required a mean of 28.5 trials); less, but still significant, amnesia for reversal was found when either 9 or 35 correct reversal discriminations had been given. This complication implies that we are not likely to find simple answers to the question of how protein synthesis influences memory processing, especially until we understand better the precise environmental determinants and behavioral consequences of variation in the relative numbers of training trials associated with two successively acquired, conflicting memories. Studies of experimentally induced amnesia that do not attend to these points of behavioral analysis (unlike the extensive study by Quartermain & Botwinick, which is exceptionally complete in most respects) are unlikely to advance our knowledge.

Generally, increases in degree of training appear to protect memories from the adverse effects of a variety of amnesic agents. For example, Buresova and Bures (1969) applied potassium chloride to the cortex of rats to cause an extended period of spreading depression following training. They found that this resulted in retrograde amnesia if the rats had been given only 3 days of training on a T-maze discrimination task, but not if 12 days of training had been given.

Because most studies of induced amnesia use tasks learned in one trial, degree of training in terms of number of trials is not always a suitable parameter. Under these circumstances, degree of learning may be assumed to increase with increases in performance determinants (such as intensity or duration of punishment in avoidance learning). It is clear that amnesia induced by peripherally applied ECS is less likely to occur the greater the intensity of the shock used in aversive conditioning (Flood et al., 1972; Ray & Bivens, 1968). With hypoxia as the amnesic agent, Sara (1975) reports a similar relationship: If training conditions produce certain (high) levels of retention in the control conditions, animals administered the amnesic agent show no amnesia.

Finally, there is evidence that with humans, well-overlearned, skilled sensory–motor acts may be resistant to a variety of drug effects (Heimann, 1968).

The reason for this effect is unclear, which is not surprising since neither the basic determinants and processes that underlie "degree of original learning" nor the critical effects of the amnesic agents are completely clear. However, a thorough study of this relationship by Flood and his associates (1972) has indicated a variety of behavioral parameters that may be important. This study indicates that amnesia may still occur following high degrees of original learning if retention tests are given after sufficiently long retention intervals. This could reflect either of two conditions: The measure of retention used in this study merely is insensitive to differences in behavior soon after training; or (a more important alternative) the amnesic agent acts in concert with other sources of forgetting, such as those that lead to less accessibility of a memory following a long retention interval.

In a speculative vein concerning the latter alternative, we may consider some extraordinary results by Howard, Glendenning, and Meyer (1974). These results could enrich our understanding of the effect of degree of learning on the influence of an amnesic agent. We will omit details of how these and previous results in this series were gathered (see Meyer, 1972). Briefly, the method was to present rats with a series of learning problems, some of which had common motivational requirements (i.e., for some problems the animal was hungry and rewarded with food upon reaching a solution; for other problems the solution permitted the animal to avoid or escape painful footshock). The experiments by Howard and his associates, like others in this series, showed that if the solution of the last three problems was followed immediately by an ECS, amnesia occurred for the first problem learned (if the motivational requirements of the first and third problems were the same); but amnesia did not occur for the third problem learned. This is contrary to the typical retrograde amnesia gradient because solution to the last problem is temporally closest to the ECS (although these multiple-trial problems may involve processes different from those represented by a retrograde amnesia gradient for one-trial learning). Also in opposition to the retrograde amnesia gradient—and this is the point of primary interest here— Howard and his associates found that amnesia for the third problem could be induced by increasing the delay interval between solution of the problem and administration of ECS. Specifically, if the animals were given a retention interval of 3 days after solving the three problems, then were given a single trial on the third problem followed by an ECS, amnesia occurred for that problem. Howard and his colleagues emphasize that this effect was not large, but it was significant statistically and was replicated in two separate experiments. Probably it is safe to assume that if no "reminder" trial had been given, amnesia would not have occurred. But because this is uncertain, the interpretation of interest here will be incomplete, as we shall see in a moment.

Lewis (1976) suggests that the earlier failure of Howard and his associates to obtain amnesia for the third problem was because the memory for this problem was too "salient" when ECS was administered immediately following solution of the problem. He claims (1969, 1976) that amnesia is more likely to be induced for a memory that is "in transition" from an active to an inactive state, or vice versa. In other words (if we assume that it is appropriate to substitute the terms *accessible* or *retrievable* for *salient*), an amnesic agent is relatively unlikely to influence subsequent retention scores under two conditions: if the agent is administered so long after acquisition that the memory is inaccessible, or if it is administered too soon following an extraordinarily large amount of acquisition training. In the latter case, the memory is presumed to be especially accessible or retrievable, or is presumed perhaps to include a "strength" attribute that we do not understand yet.

A case could be made that the third problem learned by the rats in the paradigm of Howard and his associates may be extraordinarily well learned and especially accessible soon after training as a result of overlearning of the contextual cues common to all three problems. We could argue further that overlearning of the specific elements of the third problem must occur if the animal is to be protected from pervasive proactive interference caused by the conflicting prior learning. The problem with this reasoning is that it is not yet clear how we might best conceptualize "degree of learning." For example, should we subscribe to a relatively global term like *salience* of a memory, or would we benefit more from separate consideration of the momentary accessibility of the memory and some strength attribute of the memory? The further problem in interpreting the experiment by Howard and his colleagues that is, as mentioned earlier, we cannot be sure whether their prior reminder trial was necessary for the ECS to cause amnesia for the third problem or if the particular combination of degree of learning and the retention interval were sufficient. Independent variation in degree of learning, retention interval, and presence of a reminder trial in this study might have provided an empirical distinction between memory "salience" (degree of learning) and memory accessibility (enhanced retention probability due to the reminder trial).

While it seems especially plausible that some common "strength of memory" dimension may be fundamental to these and other effects discussed in this section, no principles currently exist to tell us what "strength of memory" might mean. For now, we are limited to speculation concerning which of several alternatives provides the best concept of "degree of learning."

The conceptualization of degree of learning is of further importance because of other experiential factors that influence amnesia. If an animal is exposed to the circumstances of training and permitted to explore them prior to the introduction of reinforcement contingencies, the effectiveness of a subsequent amnesic agent is lessened ("familiarization effect"). In a similar fashion, prior exposure to specific elements of training and to the amnesic agent itself attenuates subsequent amnesic effects. We turn now to a brief review and analysis of these consequences of experience.

The Familiarization Effect

Lewis, Miller, and Misanin (1968) found that if rats were permitted free exploration of the apparatus in which they were to be trained, amnesia of passive avoidance learning was not likely to be induced by ECS. Later, the same authors

(1969) showed that prior familiarization protected rats from amnesia even when the ECS was delivered as soon as .5 seconds following the learning trial. This represents a drastic shortening of the previously estimated gradient of retrograde amnesia. Miller (1970) also found this dramatically shortened gradient along with a variety of other results concerning the circumstances that control the power of the familiarization effect. For example, his data suggest that the influence of familiarization may be greater the more complex the learning environment.

Familiarization prior to training has also been found to attenuate the amnesic effects of hypothermia on retention of a conditioned emotional response (CER) involving a learning task quite different from that used by Lewis and his colleagues (Jensen & Riccio, 1970). Experiments by Adams and Calhoun (1972) similarly show that the amnesic effects of ECS may be decreased if the animal previously has explored the training environment.

The interpretation by Lewis and his associates (1968, 1969) of the familiarization effect is interesting. They suggested that the function of familiarization was to prepare a memorial framework into which representations of the events of learning might be incorporated or "elaborated" more readily (see also Lewis, 1969). However, the empirically drawn picture of the familiarization effect soon became more complex, and somewhat hazy.

Some conflicting evidence.   Dawson and McGaugh (1973) did not find that familiarization attenuated the amnesic effects of ECS. Their procedures were different from those of Lewis and his colleagues, and two of these procedural differences appear especially important.

First, the passive avoidance task used by Dawson and McGaugh required mice to "step through" an opening between two compartments prior to delivery of the footshock; in both studies by Lewis and his associates, shock was delivered when rats "stepped down" from a platform onto a grid floor. Complete details of these tasks are unimportant for our purposes, but we shall see in a moment why this particular procedural difference may be critical.

The second difference was in the method of delivering ECS. Dawson and McGaugh used the transcorneal technique, whereas Lewis and his colleagues (1968, 1969) applied ECS through the ears (transpinnate). It was this difference that Dawson and McGaugh regarded as critical. They suggested that with the transpinnate application the electrode clips attached to the rat's ears have extra punishing effects. This punishing effect may summate with the footshock to reduce the amnesia caused by the ECS (recall that the probability of amnesia is related inversely to the severity of the aversive stimulus).

However, it would appear that the familiarization effect of Lewis and his associates is too robust (see Miller, 1970) to be accounted for by such a relatively small increase in the severity of the aversive stimulus. Moreover, familiarization prior to training clearly affects retention through at least one mechanism other than its punishing effects; this must be so, because Dawson and McGaugh found that familiarization tended to *enhance* the amnesic effects of ECS (see also Miller, 1970).

Toward resolution. Fortunately, a fairly simple answer may resolve this dilemma. Familiarization probably indirectly influences susceptibility to amnesia through its effect on degree of original learning.

It is quite clear that under some circumstances familiarization may facilitate degree of learning markedly, as evidenced by the enhancement of retention in animals not exposed to amnesic treatments. Moreover, this facilitation clearly is obtained with at least one task (the step-through task; see King & Glasser, 1973). A similar facilitation in degree of learning has seemed to occur also with the step-down task, for example, in data reported by Galosy & Thompson (1971). Unfortunately, this effect was not analyzed statistically by these authors for animals given passive avoidance training and no subsequent ECS. However, the average increase in step-down latency following passive avoidance training was about twice as great among animals given some degree of prior familiarization as among animals given no prior familiarization. The increased degree of learning from familiarization may be manifested in the special form of increased discrimination and not necessarily in changes in vigor (i.e., latency; see Miller, 1970, for absence of the latter effect).

Under certain circumstances, however, prior familiarization seems to retard original learning. Like Dawson and McGaugh (1969), Sara and Lefevre (1973) found that familiarization enhanced retrograde amnesia. Indeed, her effects were a good deal stronger than those of Dawson and McGaugh and were replicated for amnesia caused by either ECS or hypoxia. Most important, and in agreement with the findings of Dawson and McGaugh (1969, Exp. 1), Sara's procedure for familiarization clearly *impaired* passive avoidance learning.

The implication is that familiarization will enhance amnesia to the same extent that it impairs degree of original learning; but familiarization will attenuate amnesia to the extent that original learning is facilitated by this treatment. Unfortunately, it is not clear from the work by Lewis and his colleagues that familiarization in fact did enhance degree of learning. Their attempts to demonstrate such enhancement were hampered by limitations (i.e., ceiling effects) on their response measure, but probably the enhanced learning could be shown with different techniques of measurement.

Another explanation of the familiarization effect is possible if we assume that its action is primarily on the probability of memory retrieval rather than the degree of learning. This also assumes that the effect of ECS itself is to influence memory retrieval rather than (or in addition to) disrupting or preventing its storage. Although no studies have tested directly the influence of the ECS on the animal's use of information acquired during familiarization, it is known that the sorts of information probably acquired during familiarization may also be subject to memory impairment caused by ECS (Barrett & Ray, 1969). In other words, under some circumstances the ECS might cause amnesia for the familiarization experience as well as for the avoidance training. Perhaps these experiments differ in the extent to which application of this familiarization information is impaired (or not impaired) by the amnesic treatment and thus is available for application at the time of memory retrieval.

Generally, however, it is not at all surprising that prior familiarization might sometimes facilitate later retention and might impair it under other circumstances. In all of these tasks, the rat's tendency to go somewhere, to step down or to step through, is decreased by passive avoidance training through which it learns not-to-go. Following the sequential acquisition of two conflicting memories, go and no-go, a variety of factors may operate to determine at the retention test whether the tendency to go (perhaps partially acquired during familiarization) or the tendency to no-go will dominate (Spear, 1971; Spear, Gordon, & Martin, 1973).

Broad familiarization with the context of the subsequent reinforcement contingencies is by no means the only instance of prior experience that influences susceptibility to retrograde amnesia. We turn now to a set of such experiences that have this common effect. We must consider the entire set in order to have the proper perspective on the experiential determinants of amnesia.

Attenuation of Amnesia by a Prior Sequence of Training and Amnesic Treatment

If an amnesic treatment prevents consolidation and hence prevents the existence of a memory, one would expect that with retraining the animal must begin anew, "from scratch," to develop a memorial representation of the events of that training. If this is the case, and if this retraining is also followed by an amnesic treatment, we would expect the animal to return again to a state of naiveté concerning the events of training. But this does not occur: The amnesic agent is not effective in impairing the effects of retraining.

Initial tests of the phenomenon.   In 1969, three sets of investigators studied this problem, each with a different amnesic agent, and thus enhanced the generality of their common conclusion. Riccio and Stikes (1969) applied hypothermia following both training and retraining; in analogous tests, Kesner, McDonough, and Doty (1970) used ECS, and Nachman and Meinecke (1969) applied both hypoxia and ECS. The common result may be described simply. The first sequence of training followed by the amnesic agent resulted in the usual extensive amnesia; but after the second sequence the animals behaved almost as if they had not received the amnesic treatment at all.

Many of the more obvious explanations for this finding may be discounted rather quickly. It might seem, for example, that the animals are somehow adapting to the effects of the amnesic treatment so that the second one has no effect. Such a possibility was tested by Jensen & Riccio (1970) in an experiment with hypothermia as the amnesic agent. Following initial training, but prior to a retraining-treatment (hypothermia) sequence given to all animals, these investigators introduced an extinction treatment for some subjects, which reduced their performance to the same level as that produced by hypothermia. Because hypothermia was not given, adaptation to it as an amnesic treatment must be discounted for these subjects as a factor that might attenuate the effects of the posttraining hypothermia treatment. Nevertheless, the latter treatment did not cause amnesia in these trained-but-extinguished subjects: Retention after retraining was unaffected by hypothermia. Although subject to other interpretations, these data suggest that the general phenomenon of resistance to amnesia is not merely a result of prior adaptation to the amnesic treatment.

A test of two theories. According to Hinderliter, Smith, and Misanin (1973), this phenomenon provides an opportunity to test the opposing predictions of two theoretical frameworks, described as "consolidation" and "elaboration" (the latter is used by Lewis, 1969, in reference to continuing posttrial processing of memories). Hinderliter and his associates interpreted these theoretical frameworks as providing the following accounts of this phenomenon. According to the consolidation view, "the initial amnesic treatments did not produce a full amnesia and, thus, there is less to consolidate, and possibly, more rapid consolidation, following the second learning trial." For the elaboration view, "memory for the second event is incorporated into a previously structured memory system and hence retrieval is facilitated" (Hinderliter et al., 1973, p. 671).

Hinderliter and his associates deduced that the elaboration view would predict a similar attenuation of amnesia following retraining if the animals previously experienced only a few of the separable events of training, because in this view these events apparently are believed to contribute independently to the animal's memorial representation of the learning episode. In contrast, the consolidation position would predict such an effect only if the prior experience included a complete training trial.

Hinderliter and his colleagues (1973) then completed two thorough experiments testing these alternative views. Operationally, the experiments asked whether prior experience with only the aversive stimulus to be used for training (footshock) or with only the amnesic treatment (ECS) would attenuate amnesia. They found that attenuation of amnesia did occur in both cases. Control conditions ensured that experience with either the ECS or footshock had no significant unconditioned effects, that is, no influence on performance by untrained animals. Their results may be seen in Figures 7.2 and 7.3. In both figures, longer step-down latencies indicate better retention of passive avoidance. In Figure 7.2 the influence of prior experience with only the ECS (electroshock or E) is shown, and in Figure 7.3 the influence of prior footshock (FS) is shown. The primary locus of the effects of prior experience was with the basic experimental groups (FS–E). These groups had been given ECS immediately after the training trial. The clear effect in each case (prior ECS, Figure 7.2; prior footshock, Figure 7.3) was to drastically reduce the amnesic effect of ECS (i.e., to increase latency and, hence, retention).

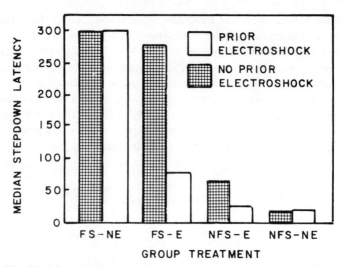

Figure 7.2   The influence of prior experience with an electroconvulsive shock ("electroshock") is shown for rats that differed in the treatment associated with their passive avoidance training. For designation of treatment in this figure, FS refers to the delivery of footshock during passive avoidance training, E refers to the delivery of electroconvulsive shock following passive avoidance training, and an N preceding these designations refers to the absence of the treatment (adapted from Hinderliter et al., 1973. © 1973 Pergamon Press Ltd.)

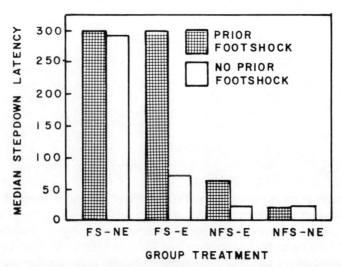

Figure 7.3   The influence of experience with footshock prior to passive avoidance training is indicated for the four different treatments associated with passive avoidance training. As in Figure 7.2, FS refers to footshock, E to electroconvulsive shock and N to the absence of the treatment (adapted from Hinderliter et al., 1973. © 1973 Pergamon Press Ltd.)

These results appear to dispute the argument that in studies of this phenomenon some consolidation (though incomplete) occurs following the first amnesic treatment and combines with the partial consolidation of subsequent training to make the memory trace impervious to further amnesic treatment. In doing so, the data of Hinderliter and his associates also tend to support the elaboration hypothesis by showing that familiarity with certain individual components of training is sufficient to retard amnesic effects. However, there appear to remain at least two ways in which a consolidation view could account for these results.

First, by maintaining a rather different position than most previous theorists, one could view consolidation of each memory attribute (e.g., the footshock) as a separate event. Although not inconsistent with the conceptual framework of this book, this view by itself leaves unanswered the question of how the entire ensemble of previously consolidated attributes becomes consolidated.

The second potential interpretation from a consolidation theory perhaps is more likely. Bloch (1970; see also Bloch, Deweer, & Hennevin, 1970) has shown that increased arousal, produced in the central nervous system through stimulation of the reticular formation, may decrease the effects of an amnesic agent. Others have shown this with analeptic drugs (see McGaugh & Herz, 1972). There are additional indications that general arousal may be increased in an animal given ECS 24 hours earlier (Misanin, 1970; Misanin & Lewis, 1970), and perhaps also by a footshock delivered in a manner similar to that of Hinderliter and his associates (Banker, Hunt, & Pagano, 1969). Accordingly, the attenuation of amnesia in the Hinderliter study may conceivably be attributed to an increase in rate of consolidation caused by the arousal effects of the ECS or footshocks. Thus (such an interpretation would continue), rate of consolidation was enhanced by the arousal and the process was completed before the onset of the amnesic agent.

The plausibility of this second interpretation depends on the extent to which arousal caused by a footshock or ECS is maintained over the 24 hours that elapsed between treatment and training in the Hinderliter study. Further, we must suppose that whatever arousal remains after 24 hours must speed the rate of consolidation to a completion simultaneous with the offset of footshock, because ECS was delivered within a few milliseconds after footshock in the Hinderliter study. Because such events are unlikely, an alternative interpretation such as the elaboration view of Hinderliter and his associates would seem the more reasonable.

Prior experience as an aid to discrimination among the reinforcer-contingent events of training.   A surprising breadth has been found in the spectrum of prior experiences that may subsequently serve to protect animals from retention deficits due to amnesic agents. Jensen, Riccio, and Gehres (1975) found that the amnesic effects of hypothermia following passive avoidance training were prevented in rats that previously had been exposed to other avoidance tasks. In one experiment, prior training on a different kind of passive avoidance task prevented amnesia, as did prior training on one-way active avoidance in another experiment. In the latter, moreover, control animals given only footshock—without the actual contingencies of active avoidance—also became relatively immune from the subsequent amnesic effects of hypothermia on retention of the passive avoidance training.

Under some circumstances, the extent to which prior experience acts to protect animals against subsequent amnesic effects seems to depend on the degree of similarity between the stimuli present during prior experience and those present during training (Miller, 1970). This would appear to be a likely principle, although in some cases the precise stimulus dimension involved is difficult to identify. Lefevre, David-Remacle, and Sara (1975) found that rats raised in a generally enriched environment were significantly more resistant to the amnesic effects of ECS than rats raised in typical laboratory cages, and David-Remacle (1973) found that the amnesic effects of hypoxia could be prevented by a single injection of distilled water 35 minutes before training.

Riccio and his colleagues (Riccio, 1975; Jensen et al., 1975) note that the fragility of amnesic effects among animals exposed to any of this wide variety of early experiences stands in sharp contrast to the general robustness of these amnesic effects. They suggest that prior experience enables the animal to distinguish more clearly the events of training from those of the amnesic treatment. Otherwise—that is, under ordinary circumstances, without the prior experience—the amnesic treatment becomes incorporated as an attribute of the same memory (which encompasses representations of the treatment together with those of training), and retrieval of the target attribute at the retention test is impaired in the absence of representation of the amnesic treatment. Riccio and his colleagues have obtained significant experimental support for this position (Hinderliter, Webster, & Riccio, 1975). No matter how this interesting interpretation fares when subjected to further testing, it does emphasize a plausible way in which an animal's prior experiences, through their enhancement of degree of learning, may offer protection against amnesia. If the enhanced learning aids some aspect of discrimination (between, for example, the events of training and those of the amnesic treatment), then the effect of this enhanced learning is unlikely to appear in the test behavior of control animals not given the amnesic agent. In other words, prior experience with a task may aid animals given the amnesic agent in determining that the amnesic agent is not a part of the task, but this advantage of prior learning will not show up in the behavior of animals not given the amnesic agent. However, this should not detract from the application of this common intervening variable, degree of learning, to account for the influence of the conditions of learning (including prior experience) on amnesia.

Summary and Comments

The extent of the retention decrement produced by amnesic agents depends on a variety of experiential and environmental conditions that precede training. If animals are familiarized with either the specific circumstances of training or experiences that might be related otherwise to the requirements of training, an amnesic agent may have little or no retrograde effect. This may be viewed as a consequence of specific or nonspecific transfer of training, with the primary effect of the prior experiences being the enhancement of degree of learning preceding the amnesic treatment. Other experiments show that other manipulations that conceivably might alter degree of learning—number of training trials, stringency of the performance criterion before cessation of training, or intensity of the aversive stimulus in one-trial passive avoidance learning—also act to decrease retrograde amnesia.

As an alternative to invoking the concept of degree of learning, we might account for the influence of certain of these variables in a different manner, by emphasizing the effectiveness of the amnesic treatment rather than the effectiveness of the training. We shall soon examine evidence that the degree of retrograde amnesia produced by an amnesic agent depends on the intensity or extent of the trauma induced in the CNS by that agent. It is well known that a physiological system's resistance to insult may fluctuate depending on the condition of that system. Thus, it is possible that conditions of training, such as the intensity of a reinforcer, may serve to determine the susceptibility of the individual's system to the effects of the amnesic treatment. For example, an animal's physiological reactions to being in an unfamiliar location (e.g., if only a few training trials were given) may lower the animal's "resistance" (e.g., brain-seizure threshold) to subsequent ECS, and thereby increase the effective intensity of ECS (Brennan, 1975b,has developed and tested this idea). This appears to be a promising approach toward understanding how the conditions of training determine retrograde amnesia.

CHARACTERISTICS OF THE AMNESIC AGENT DETERMINE AMNESIA

It should be clear at this point that retrograde amnesia is not really "all-or-none." In fact, it is rarely, if ever, complete. So we may speak interchangeably of "probability of amnesia" and "degree of amnesia" when we refer to the extent of retention decrement, so long as we have a reasonably continuous index of behavior as our retention measure.

One of the clearest factors determining amnesia is intensity of the amnesic treatment: Probability of retrograde amnesia is a monotonic increasing function of this factor. Electroshock is the amnesic agent that is varied in intensity most conveniently, so most studies of this parameter have used some form of ECS. However, the intensity of other amnesic agents, such as hypothermia, also predicts degree of amnesia. Indeed, one of the most thorough studies in this area is that by Cherkin (1969, 1974), using a vaporized form of the convulsant flurothyl. Cherkin found that degree of amnesia in chicks was a monotonically increasing function of his indexes of both intensity and duration of the flurothyl treatment given following training with a single passive avoidance trial. Similar results have been found by Paolino, Quartermain, and Miller (1966) concerning the amnesic effects of carbon dioxide.

Our discussion will concern primarily the amnesic consequences of differing intensities of electroshock because of the more complete story available with this agent. At one level, the basic relationship is quite simple. But complexities arise when one raises the ultimate question of what the underlying neural mechanism might be that controls this relationship.

Amnesic Consequences of Differing Intensities of Electroshock

As experimental work with ECS became increasingly widespread, the probability of retrograde amnesia was observed to depend not only on the nominal intensity of the current but also on how it was administered (transcorneal, transpinnate, or through screws attached directly to the skull), and on other apparently trivial aspects, such as whether the animals were deprived of food (even when the task did not involve food reward). It soon was discovered that the critical factor in "whole-brain" stimulation (i.e., stimulation through transpinnate or transcorneal application) is primarily the amount of current that ultimately reaches the brain. The effects of differing modes of delivery, anatomically differing current pathways, and whether the rats are fat or lean are apparently simple reflections of associated differences in electrical resistance in the circuit in the brain and in nonneural shunts around the brain (Ray & Barrett, 1969; Miller & Spear, 1969).

How do we know that it is simple variation in resistance that determines total current reaching the brain? We infer this from the more frequent occurrence of behavioral seizures and retrograde amnesia when the electrical resistance between the electrodes and the brain is relatively low. Perhaps, then, the intensity of the current reaching the brain is important only to the extent that it produces a behavioral seizure (i.e., a convulsion). Are behavioral seizures actually the fundamental and necessary determinant of amnesia? The answer is no, because although the occurrence of a behavioral seizure is correlated with the occurrence of amnesia, the correlation is not at all perfect. That behavioral seizures are not necessary for retrograde amnesia has been shown in three ways.

First, there are an increasing number of studies indicating that retrograde amnesia may result from low-intensity current applied directly to discrete areas of the subcortical limbic system, and behavioral convulsions do not usually accompany such stimulation (e.g., Peeke & Herz, 1971; Vardaris & Schwartz, 1971; Wilburn & Kesner, 1972; Wyers & Deadwyler, 1971). Second, as McGaugh and Herz (1972) have pointed out, a variety of studies have found the current thresholds for retrograde amnesia to be lower than those for the tonic phase of the behavioral convulsion.

The third and most thorough source of evidence that behavioral convulsions are not necessary for amnesia is a series of analytical studies by Zornetzer, McGaugh, and their colleagues. These investigators directly manipulated the probability of a behavioral seizure across a variety of levels of current applied to the brain. To prevent the occurrence of a behavioral convulsion, they exposed some animals to an anticonvulsant drug, such as ether, just prior to applying electroshock to the brain. Following initial experiments showing that amnesia would occur even when behavioral seizures were prevented in this way (e.g., McGaugh & Alpern, 1966), a more extensive test was applied by Zornetzer and McGaugh (1971).

As the first step in this study, Zornetzer and McGaugh carefully determined the probability and type of behavioral seizures (convulsions) for mice for each of 20 levels of transcorneally applied electroshock (see Figure 7.4). For their purposes, they defined clonic convulsions as ''jerky movements of the jaws, forepaws and hindlimbs and sometimes tonic flexion of the hindlimbs'' and clonic–tonic convulsions as ''a brief period of clonic hindlimb flexion followed by a longer period of whole body tonic extension'' (Zornetzer & McGaugh, 1971, p. 402).

The major experiment assessed the probability of retrograde amnesia among mice treated like those represented in Figure 7.4. The amnesia found for the mice that were susceptible to convulsions was compared with that found for mice

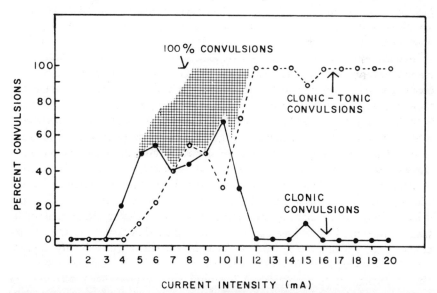

Figure 7.4   This figure indicates the percentage of mice having clonic or clonic-tonic convulsions following transcorneal electroshock. The darkened area indicates the combined percentage of the two convulsion patterns at each intensity (adapted from Zornetzer and McGaugh, 1971).

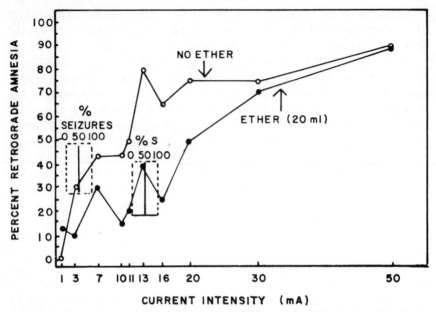

Figure 7.5   Degree of retrograde amnesia is shown for mice given different intensities of electroshock following passive avoidance training. The range of brain seizure threshold is shown for mice
treated with ether (and hence showing no behavioral convulsions) and those not treated with ether
prior to the delivery of the transcorneal electroshock (adapted from Zornetzer and McGaugh, 1971).

made resistant to such convulsions. The anticonvulsant treatment was to expose
the mice to ether for 30 seconds prior to the amnesic treatment; this treatment
prevented behavioral convulsions entirely. The results of this experiment are
shown in Figure 7.5. We should note that the percentage of seizures referred to in
Figure 7.5 refers to seizures in the brain. Brain seizures clearly are not correlated
with behavioral seizures among animals exposed to ether (excluding, of course,
conditions in which ether itself might cause amnesia), and behavioral seizures
alone do not determine amnesia.

Figure 7.5 illustrates several important points. First, as the intensity of the
stimulus current is increased, the probability of amnesia rises for both groups,
that is, for etherized mice that do not convulse and nonetherized mice that do.
Thus, behavioral convulsions apparently are not a primary determinant of amnesia. Second, Figure 7.5 illustrates that amnesia *is* related importantly to brain
seizures. The threshold for brain seizures was raised by preceding the transcorneal shock with etherization: A 2.8-milliampere current was sufficient to
produce brain seizures in at least 50% of the untreated mice, while a 13.2-
milliampere current was needed for a comparable effect in etherized mice. If the
curves in Figure 7.5 are transposed such that the abscissa represents deviation of
current away from the level of current defining the threshold of brain seizures for

each group of mice, these curves overlap rather neatly (see Figure 7.6). Figure 7.6 thus lends support to the notion that the main determinant of amnesia may be the extent to which current intensity is above or below the brain seizure threshold. The third point illustrated in Figure 7.5 is that the mere occurrence of a brain seizure is not the only determinant of amnesia. The probability of retrograde amnesia continues to increase well beyond the point at which all animals had brain seizures. This important point demands further consideration.

While it is possible that amount of current per se determines the increase in amnesia that continues beyond the threshold of brain seizures, the more probable source is some relatively subtle aspect of the abnormal brain activity caused by high levels of current. Accordingly, Zornetzer and McGaugh (1972) examined two types of electrical activity in the brain that occur following stimulation of the frontal cortex in rats; there is a primary after-discharge, "a hypersynchronous iterative spiking activity," and a secondary after-discharge, "a monophasic discharge which increases in amplitude with successive waves and abruptly terminates shortly after reaching peak amplitude" (p. 233).

First, Zornetzer and McGaugh systematically verified the relationship between these two after-discharges and the intensity of frontal stimulation. Next, they trained rats to press a lever to obtain drinking water, and then punished them for doing so by administering a painful electric shock contingent upon a lever press.

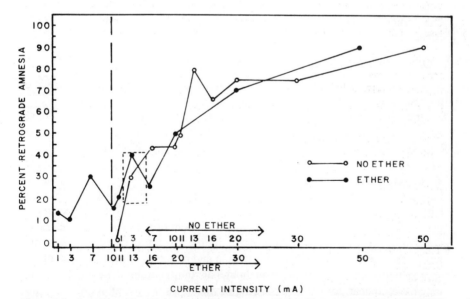

CURRENT INTENSITY (mA)

Figure 7.6 Superimposition of the range of brain seizure threshold among animals treated or not treated with ether prior to the amnesic treatment is shown. (These are the same data depicted in Figure 7.5). It can be seen that when the threshold for brain seizure is held constant, a common relationship appears between percent retrograde amnesia and intensity of the amnesic treatment. (adapted from Zornetzer and McGaugh, 1971).

Finally, these subjects were given one of several possible quantities of stimulation (0–6 ma) to the frontal cortex, and retention of the punishing event was assessed. The results reveal a direct relationship between degree of amnesia and intensity of frontal stimulation. Furthermore, ad hoc analyses of these data suggest that with current intensity held constant, amnesia is more powerful for animals that had a primary after-discharge than for those that had none and for animals that had both a primary and a secondary after-discharge than for those having only the primary after-discharge.

The importance of the secondary after-discharge is substantiated in another experiment by Zornetzer (1972), in which the amnesic agent was electrical stimulation of the midbrain. However, the precise significance of this factor remains unsettled. Using a somewhat different learning task, a subsequent study from the same laboratory (Gold & McGaugh, 1973) found no relationship between degree of retrograde amnesia and characteristics of the primary or secondary after-discharges. What remains at present, therefore, is the relatively weak conclusion that current intensity per se may be a more fundamental determinant of amnesia than any of the physiological correlates identified so far.

Another brain activity that apparently predicts retrograde amnesia is the theta rhythm (Landfield, 1972; Landfield, McGaugh, & Tusa, 1972). Understanding this activity may also help us understand how the intensity of the amnesic treatment determines amnesia. However, the controversy over the significance of this particular neural response is beyond the scope of our present concern (see Black, 1972).

Other Characteristics of the Amnesic Agent

Among several potential candidates, two additional general characteristics of amnesic agents seem particularly important.

First, there is increasing evidence that the characteristics of amnesic consequences of an agent may be determined in part by the particular neuroanatomical location of the agent-induced stimulation (or other physiological insult) within, as well as between, generally recognized structures in the brain. For example, Zornetzer and his colleagues have found different characteristics of amnesia depending on which portion of the hippocampus is stimulated (Zornetzer & Chronister, 1973; Zornetzer, Chronister, & Ross, 1973). Anatomical location of neural disruption may also interact with the content of the memory to determine the characteristics of amnesia. For example, the disruption of a particular structure in the brain may impair the acquisition and retention of memories involving approach to appetitive stimuli, even though disruption of the same brain structure may have no bearing on the processing of memories involving aversive stimuli, or vice versa (e.g., Carlton & Markiewicz, 1973; Zornetzer & Chronister, 1973). Later we shall see how the anatomical location of physiological disruption may also interact with conditions of the retention test to determine the characteristics of amnesia (Kesner & Conner, 1974).

The second general characteristic of amnesic agents is that the neurophysiological basis of action may differ, even though they result in similar amnesic effects on behavior. For example, Cherkin (1974) has suggested that acute hypoxia may induce retrograde amnesia by causing permanent damage to brain regions concerned with memory storage or retrieval. Carlton and Markiewicz (1973) have presented a similar suggestion for the amnesic consequences of the localized application of potassium chloride. For other agents such as electroshock or drugs, it is generally assumed that permanent damage does not occur.

AMNESIA MAY DEPEND ON THE CONTENT OF THE MEMORY TO BE PROCESSED

We saw earlier how parameters controlling the conditions of learning and the severity of the amnesic treatments may determine the extent to which animals treated with an amnesic agent differ in retention from untreated animals. An important implication here is that amnesia appears in gradations: Treatments that induce amnesia rarely, if ever, are completely effective. Gradations of amnesia exist within, as well as between, memories; while certain attributes may be forgotten owing to an amnesic agent, others are spared, as reflected by different response measures.

Selective Amnesia

Differing degrees of amnesia accompanying different indexes of retention have been reported by Carew (1970). In this study, rats given ECS were easily identified as amnesic for the footshock they had received upon stepping off a platform or through a doorway, because they were not especially hesitant about stepping off or through when tested. However, the same rats reliably avoided the specific *location* where they previously had received the footshock. This implies that the memory attribute representing location, or the attribute permitting *discrimination* among alternative locations, is spared the amnesic effect. Similar results have been reported by Banker, Hunt, and Pagano (1969). Unlike these experiments of Carew and Banker and his associates, most studies of amnesia have depended on a single index of retention. Of interest here are the few studies that have included supplementary indexes of retention, typically autonomic correlates of conditioning.

One obvious (and obviously crude) autonomic index of aversive conditioning is defecation. For many years, psychologists have noticed that although amnesia is clearly indicated when a rat given an amnesic agent plunges ahead to perform a previously punished act, retention of some aversive aspect of the situation is often evidenced by an exaggerated amount of defecation by the rat (e.g., Chorover & Schiller, 1965). Defecation has continued to be measured as a more or less incidental index of retention (e.g., Mendoza & Adams, 1969; Yaginuma

& Iwahara, 1971), but more tractable measures of emotion, such as changes in heart rate, have become more common. The rat's unconditioned response to footshock and other aversive events is tachycardia (increase in heart rate). When re-presented specific stimuli previously paired with aversive events during conditioning, stimuli that might be said to evoke "fear," rats that had been given an amnesic treatment following conditioning show a decline in heart rate or less tachycardia than rats not given the amnesic treatment. Although it is an obviously complex measure, this conditioned alteration in heart rate has become an important index of acquired memories (see Obrist, Black, Brener, & DiCara, 1974).

It is with the heart rate index of fear that a clear case of selective amnesia has been observed. When ECS has been administered following Pavlovian conditioning in rats and sheep, amnesia has clearly occurred for skeletal indexes of conditioning, but the heart rate response has been found to be unaffected (Mendoza & Adams, 1969; Naitoh, 1971). Similar effects have been found with rats in terms of instrumental passive avoidance responding (Hine & Paolino, 1970). Also, injection of puromycin apparently impairs retention of instrumental avoidance behavior by goldfish while having little effect on their retention of heart rate responses (Schoel & Agranoff, 1972).

Does Amnesia Occur for Autonomic Responding?

Are the representations of changes in the motor or skeletal system the only memory attributes affected by amnesic treatments? This does not appear to be the case.

Avis (1969) found that posttraining injections of potassium chloride into a rat's hippocampus eliminated not only conditioned suppression of licking but also the changes in heart rate that otherwise accompany the conditioned stimulus. Auerbach and Carlton (1971) found that similar posttraining injections of potassium chloride also eliminated the increase in plasma corticosterone that otherwise accompanies the conditioned stimulus. Davis and Holmes (1971), using an ingenious technique to classically condition the respiratory (bronchial pump) movements in cataleptic goldfish, found that subsequent ECS clearly induced amnesia for this autonomic response. Further studies have also indicated that ECS results in amnesia in rats for both the heart rate and skeletal indexes of retention (Caul & Barrett, 1972; DeVietti & Kallioinen, 1972). Clearly, conventional amnesic agents are capable of influencing autonomic conditioning, in spite of the contrary evidence reported in the studies cited earlier.

Springer's Systematic Comparison of Amnesia for Autonomic and Skeletal Responding

Fortunately, the preceding set of apparently discrepant facts has been put into good order by a study conducted by Springer (1973, 1975). Springer presented rats with white noise paired with a footshock. Some of these rats were given ECS following the footshock. Afterward, Springer measured the extent to which the white noise suppressed drinking and altered the heart rate. In addition to his careful analysis of certain parameters, Springer introduced a very important refinement: For each animal, he measured heart rate at precisely the same time that he measured rate of drinking. A variety of esoteric control groups appear to have eliminated the many potential artifacts in such a study.

Springer's initial steps were to establish (for his procedures) the parameters that result in clear conditioned suppression of licking and to assess the minimal intensity of ECS needed to induce amnesia in terms of lick suppression. Next, an ECS of either 45 milliamperes (the minimum needed to produce amnesia for lick suppression) or 100 milliamperes was given following conditioning, and Springer compared amnesia measured in changes in heart rate, defecation, and lick suppression. When a current of 45 milliamperes was used, only lick suppression indicated amnesia; but when a current of 100 milliamperes was used, all three indexes of retention showed some degree of amnesia, though apparently less amnesia occurred in terms of the autonomic measures than for lick suppression. Springer noted that the previous experiments showing amnesia for both skeletal and autonomic responding had used higher levels of ECS than those that failed to find amnesia in terms of autonomic measures. His data confirm this.

Springer's major experiment compared the retrograde amnesia gradients found in terms of lick suppression, defecation, and heart rate. The single pairing of the conditioned stimulus and footshock was followed by a 170-milliampere ECS after a delay of either 0, 3.5, 8, 15, or 60 seconds. The main result was the discovery that a steeper gradient occurred for the autonomic measures than for the skeletal index. Amnesia for lick suppression was found when ECS was delayed as long as 15 seconds following pairing of the conditioned and unconditioned stimuli, but not thereafter. In contrast, no amnesia occurred in terms of defecation if ECS was delayed longer than 3.5 seconds, and amnesia in terms of heart rate occurred only for the animals that received ECS immediately (i.e., within as few milliseconds after conditioning as the programming equipment permitted).

These results establish that both skeletal and autonomic responses are subject to amnesia, given the appropriate conditions. However, it is also apparent that autonomic responding is more resistant to amnesia than skeletal responding. Perhaps this applies only to amnesia induced by ECS. Nevertheless, the basis of the effect is as enticingly suggestive as it is uncertain. Little would be added to any explanation by simply suggesting that attributes representing autonomic responses consolidate at unusually rapid rates. Rather, this appears to be a genuine opportunity for a neurologically based theory. Perhaps it is the case, as Springer suggests, that skeletal responses are more "complex" in the sense that they require activity among a larger number of neurons or among a broader set of structures in the brain, and therefore require longer processing times. This quite appropriately might be termed a longer consolidation time, but the explanatory value of such a view would be enhanced by considering the underlying neurological mechanisms in detail.

LENGTH OF RETENTION INTERVAL DETERMINES AMNESIA

Tests of retention to assess the effect of an amnesic treatment conventionally have been administered 24 hours after training. This interval is most convenient in that it is sufficiently long to permit the dissipation of the more obvious aftereffects of most amnesic agents, yet is easily arranged.

Clinical cases of traumatic amnesia in humans long have indicated a "shrink-age" of amnesia as time passes since the traumatic event; most patients gradually improve over time in their recall of memories for which they had been made amnesic retroactively. This important fact was incorporated into a theory of retrograde amnesia by Weiskrantz (1966). This theory inspired consideration of memory retrieval failure, rather than storage failure, as the proposed source of amnesia.

For our present purposes, we shall assume that the interval between training and administration of the amnesic agent is relatively negligible, so the retention interval here refers to the interval between training (and administration of the amnesic agent) and the retention test. Variation in this interval has yielded two sets of results, one applying to intervals of less than 24 hours, the other to longer intervals. In retrospect, this division suggests that the use of 24 hours·as the most often selected interval was a fortunate accident, because the data indicate that amnesia often is maximal at that point. Less amnesia occurs when intervals shorter than 24 hours are employed, and, at least sometimes, less amnesia also occurs when intervals greater than 24 hours are employed.

"Growth" of Amnesia up to 24 Hours Following the Amnesic Treatment

Evidence when ECS is the amnesic agent.   When ECS is applied to induce amnesia following passive avoidance training, the effects of the retention interval may be stated quite simply. Animals tested soon after the ECS show significant retention, but unusually rapid forgetting occurs thereafter; hence, considerable amnesia is measured 24 hours later.

This relationship has been established under conditions where any artifactual effects that the amnesic agent might have on performance have been controlled very well. To take an extreme example of such an artifact, if the amnesic treatment were to render the animal unconscious for a few hours, its performance would indicate excellent "retention" of passive avoidance for this period. But 24 hours later, after the animal recovered consciousness, it might be measured as having forgotten passive avoidance. Such a demonstration, even in more subtle forms, clearly is less than satisfactory.

Geller and Jarvik (1968) and McGaugh and Landfield (1970) have shown that mice given ECS 20 seconds after a passive avoidance training trial do not appear amnesic when tested 1 hour later although they do when tested 24 hours later.

Moreover, these studies did not find similar changes in the behavior of untrained animals given the same amnesic treatment, which indicates absence of contamination by systemic effects of the extreme sort exemplified in the preceding paragraph.

In a similar experiment with rats, Miller and Springer (1971) tested their animals 15, 30, 60, or 120 minutes after a training–ECS sequence. They had found previously that rats recover normal posture within 15 minutes after the ECS. Other potential systemic effects of this amnesic agent were avoided by using carefully devised control conditions. In two experiments, Miller and Springer determined that animals tested 15 minutes after the amnesic treatment were significantly less amnesic than those tested 30, 60, or 120 minutes later.

This phenomenon is not yet well understood. It is notable, therefore, that McGaugh and Landfield found relatively little amnesia shortly after the amnesic treatment only when they used a relatively long interval (20 seconds) between training and ECS. When this interval was shorter (8 seconds), amnesia was increased disproportionately in terms of the test given 1 hour later, when retention was no better than that found after 24 hours. An analogous result has been found by Lee-Teng, Magnus, Kanner, and Hochman (1970), who tested day-old chickens using the passive avoidance task devised by Cherkin (e.g., 1969). Following training, transcranial current was delivered through bitemporally attached electrodes. Lee-Teng and her associates found that the effect of the interval between amnesic treatment and the test depends on the previous interval between training and the amnesic treatment (which, in turn, probably determines the basic amnesic effect). But unlike McGaugh and Landfield's results, the specific relationship found by Lee-Teng and her associates indicated *more* "growth" of amnesia over 24 hours when the amnesic treatment immediately followed the training trial than when some delay ensued. The reason for the opposing relationship is unclear. Perhaps it is not mere coincidence that the effect of retention interval in both studies depended on the interval between training and the amnesic treatment, however. We shall see later that the effects of retention intervals longer than 24 hours also depend, at least in part, on the absolute effectiveness of the amnesic treatment, which, in turn, depends on the training–treatment interval.

Evidence with discrete subcortical stimulation as the amnesic agent.   Growth of amnesia in the 24-hour interval following the amnesic treatment has also been found with direct stimulation of discrete structures in the brain. Experiments by Kesner and Conner (1972, 1974) exemplify this effect with clear results that are potentially profound in their implications.

Kesner and Conner trained hungry rats to press a lever for sugar water. When a stable pressing rate was obtained, bar pressing was punished with a single, very severe footshock. Four seconds later, the rats received low-intensity current through electrodes implanted in their brains—in the hippocampus for some rats, the midbrain reticular formation for others, and the amygdala for still others. One minute or 24 hours later, the animals were given the opportunity to press the lever for sugar water. The extent to which lever pressing was suppressed as a consequence of the prior footshock—the measure of retention—is shown in Figure 7.7.

Rats stimulated in the hippocampus show amnesia when tested 24 hours after the amnesic treatment, but not when tested after only 1 minute. Thus, localized hippocampal stimulation yields amnesia that "grows" with the passage of time. In a subsequent experiment, Kesner and Conner showed that this growth of amnesia is significant after about 4 minutes have passed since stimulation. Because of the difference in time course, similarities with the changes in amnesia found with other amnesic agents may be only coincidental.

Nevertheless, the potential significance of the Kesner and Conner study lies primarily in the fact that animals stimulated in either the midbrain reticular formation or the amygdala are also rendered amnesic, but with different time

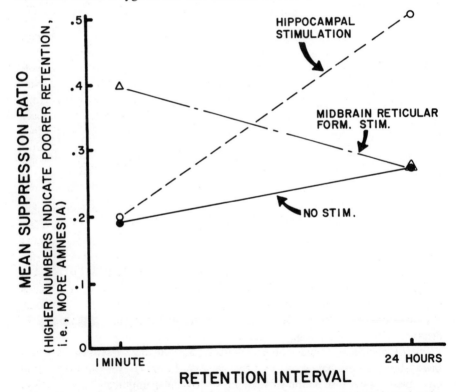

Figure 7.7 This figure shows that when discretely located stimulation in the brain is used as the amnesic treatment, the change in retention over a 24 hour period may differ in form. In this case the amnesia produced by stimulation of the midbrain reticular formation seems to decrease while the amnesia due to hippocampal stimulation seems to increase over the same 24 hour period (adapted from Kesner and Connor, 1972. Copyright 1972 by the American Association for the Advancement of Science.)

courses. In fact, stimulation of the midbrain reticular formation produced precisely the opposite change in retention to that found after hippocampal stimulation: Retention tested 1 minute after reticular stimulation indicates more amnesia than is found either 4 minutes or 24 hours later. Following stimulation of the amygdala, amnesia occurs equally after 4 minutes and 24 hours. Interpretation of this particular disjunction in the effects of different amnesic agents is difficult. The time-dependent effect of the reticular stimulation is especially hard to decipher without knowing the simple perceptual-motor effects of such stimulation on test performance 1 minute later. One clear implication of these data, though, is that the "growth-of-amnesia effect" is far from understood and may be a good deal more complex, and important, than was suspected originally.

Evidence with antibiotics as the amnesic agent.   Growth of amnesia over time has been found perhaps most frequently with the glutarimide derivatives, acetoxycycloheximide and cycloheximide, as amnesic agents. If animals are trained while these agents are producing maximal inhibition of protein synthesis in the brain, no amnesia is measured in tests given shortly after training, but considerable amnesia is found at later tests (e.g., after 24 hours).

This problem has been studied most extensively by Barondes and his colleagues (e.g., Barondes & Cohen, 1968; Barondes & Squire, 1972). In these tests, learning has usually involved the acquisition of a position or brightness discrimination by mice. However, the basic phenomenon has been replicated in many laboratories using similar procedures (e.g., Daniels, 1971) or with various other tasks, including passive avoidance training (e.g., Swanson, McGaugh, & Cotman, 1969), and a variety of different species, including rats (e.g., Quartermain et al., 1972), goldfish (e.g., Agranoff, 1971), and chickens (e.g., Watts & Mark, 1971).

It is useful to begin by dismissing some obvious potential explanations that could easily account for both the basic amnesic effect of antibiotics and the effect of retention interval. For example, perhaps this is a case of state-dependent learning: Because these drugs induce fairly rapid illness, one might expect the animals to show good retention a few hours after training when they are still sick, but poorer retention 24 hours later when they are less sick. Such explanations have been tested and dismissed in several studies (e.g., Daniels, 1971; Quartermain & Botwinick, 1975). Different or at least more complex explanations are needed.

Initially, the time course seemed quite clear: Retention was found up to 3 hours after training, but not after 6 hours or longer. Soon, however, it was found that retention was sometimes impaired sooner after training (e.g., Quinton, 1971) or even during training if it continued longer than 40 minutes after injection of cycloheximide (Squire, Smith, & Barondes, 1973), while under other conditions retention was relatively unimpaired until 24 hours after training. The precise time course appears to depend on a number of factors, including magnitude of the reinforcer, level of performance achieved during training, and type of task (see, e.g., Barondes & Squire, 1972; Quartermain & McEwen, 1970). The time course also seems quite different for fish than for rats or mice and, moreover, may depend on the strain of mouse (Agranoff, 1971; Randt, Barnett, McEwen, & Quartermain, 1971).

These difficulties notwithstanding, it is clear that amnesia from antibiotics increases for some time following administration of the amnesic agent, and this increase occurs, paradoxically, at the same time that the most direct biological effects of the agent are declining.

Evidence with several other amnesic agents.   To further illustrate the robustness of the effect under discussion, we may note still more conditions under which it has occurred. Retrograde amnesia has been found to increase during the first 24 hours when hypoxia has been used as the amnesic agent following passive avoidance training (Sara, 1974) and when hypothermia has been applied to very young rats following escape learning (Misanin, Nagy, Keiser, & Bowen, 1971). A similar effect occurs when the analeptic drug Metrazol is given to mice following passive avoidance training (Palfai & Kurtz, 1973). Using newly hatched chicks trained on Cherkin's passive avoidance task, Benowitz and Sperry (1973) found that after administration of intracranial injections of lithium chloride, amnesia was slight or absent following short intervals of about 20 minutes, but clearly present 24 hours later.

Finally, it is notable that a similar growth in hypermnesia (to which we shall turn shortly) has been found following administration of the convulsant flurothyl to goldfish shortly after passive avoidance training (Riege & Cherkin, 1973). In this experiment, flurothyl acted to enhance retention measured 16, 64, or 256 hours later, but not when the goldfish were tested only 1 hour following training.

Empirical extension to "normal" forgetting.   A possible explanation for the progressive increase in amnesia over time is that these amnesic agents simply serve to accelerate the processes normally responsible for forgetting. For example, suppose that memories normally are protected from forgetting by a certain redundancy of representation in the CNS, and that the result of these amnesic agents is to limit this redundancy. In other words, perhaps the number of neurological representations of the memory may be limited by the amnesic agent. As time passes and the treated animal becomes subjected to the normally increasing difficulties in retention (caused by factors such as interference from competing memories), the redundant representations of the memory that normally protect these animals against retrieval failure are either not available or not usable because of the amnesic agent.

Changes in Amnesia over Periods Longer Than 24 Hours

Following the initial growth of amnesia, there may be a gradual recession of the amnesia effects. We have discussed such recovery in terms of human memory processing (Chapter 6). After intervals of several days or weeks, animals exposed to an amnesic treatment may show no difference in retention from animals that have not been exposed. With certain amnesic agents, such as potassium chloride or inhibitors of protein synthesis (specifically, the heximides), eventual "spontaneous" recovery from amnesia is well established, and the conditions under which it occurs are relatively clear (e.g., Barondes & Squire, 1972; Carlton & Markiewicz, 1973). A number of studies have found such recovery when ECS is the amnesic treatment, but a majority have not found recovery; on occasion, amnesia has even been found to increase over a period of several weeks.

The issues of the generality of such recovery following ECS and what conditions might control it are of obvious theoretical importance, but specific evidence will not be discussed here for two reasons. First, these data have been reviewed in other sources (e.g., Lewis, 1969; McGaugh & Herz, 1972; Miller & Springer, 1973). Second, it is practically certain that any recovery from amnesia is not "spontaneous"; rather, it is contingent upon the activation of some aspect of memory processing involving the release, activation, or development of biological systems and is controlled by external or internal stimulation. Thus, clearer analysis of this phenomenon may be found when recovery is manipulated by systematic variation in such stimulation. Such stimulus-induced recovery, or reactivation of a memory, has implications of broad theoretical importance that we shall discuss in the next section.

Nevertheless, on the basis of existing data we may make some relatively educated guesses concerning the factors conducive to "spontaneous" recovery from amnesia.

First, it appears that such recovery is more likely to be found when subjects previously tested are retested later. Indeed, the first experimental instance of such recovery (Zinken & Miller, 1967) used precisely this procedure. Comparisons between this technique and a more appropriate procedure, testing independent groups only once after different retention intervals, show more recovery with the technique of repeated testing (King & Glasser, 1970; but see Hughes et al., 1970). The procedure of retesting the same subjects is inappropriate for demonstrating recovery because the effect of the retention interval is confounded by that of the experience (differing numbers of prior tests) of the subjects. More to the point, the testing experience provides the animal with stimuli that may serve to reactivate the memory for which the animal had been rendered amnesic. Such stimulus-induced reactivation is a very real effect to which we shall return.

A second point, also somewhat methodological in nature, is that "recovery" may be measured after long intervals either because the amnesia of the treated animals is alleviated and their retention improves over time on an absolute basis, or because animals in the control condition suffer forgetting from some other source and retention of the treated animals "improves" relative to these controls. In other words, even if the treated group has no change in retention over the same period, a decrease in amnesia is recorded whenever they show less forgetting than the controls. At present, it is not possible to argue logically that the former case is "real" amnesia and the latter is not, because no absolute estimate of amnesia is possible; that is, amnesia cannot be indicated beyond the relative retention of the treated and untreated animals.

Finally, it probably is possible to say that recovery from amnesia generally is more likely to occur when amnesic treatments are relatively ephemeral in their effects, for example, when amnesic treatment is less intense or when there is a longer interval between training and the amnesic treatment (e.g., Miller, 1968).

STRUCTURE OF THE RETENTION INTERVAL DETERMINES AMNESIA

"Structure" of the retention interval refers to the nature and temporal arrangement of the events that occur during the interval. We shall see that the extent of the retrograde amnesia caused by an amnesic agent depends on the events to which an animal is exposed between the amnesic agent and the retention test— what the animal perceives, where it perceives it, and how it responds to it. As in the previous section, when we speak of "retention interval" we refer primarily to the interval between administration of the amnesic agent and the retention test, and assume that the interval between training and the amnesic agent is relatively negligible. Later in this section, and again in Chapter 8, we shall have occasion to refer to the influence of the structure of the interval between training and administration of the amnesic agent in determining later amnesia (cf. "implicit reactivation").

For purposes of classification, we should consider two general amnesic phenomena caused by events occurring during the retention interval. Classification is based on when these events take place: throughout the retention interval or on a single occasion, involving a relatively modest portion of the retention interval, usually occurring near the end.

Influence of the Subject's Environment During the Retention Interval

Peters, Calhoun, and Adams (1973) took the view that ECS is a special case of cerebral trauma, generally similar to other traumas such as cortical ablation. They noted that in certain studies of cortical ablation retention deficits decreased if the animal was housed in dark isolation between the surgical operation and the retention test. On this basis, Peters and his associates varied the manner in which rats were housed following administration of an ECS after training on a one-trial appetitive task. During the retention interval, animals were housed either in a darkened ("light-tight") isolation chamber or in their quarters in the illuminated colony room. The basic finding was that forgetting attributable to the ECS was significantly less severe for animals housed in the isolation chamber.

In a later study, Calhoun, Prewett, Peters, and Adams (1975) replicated the basic finding of Peters and his associates and extended it. First, they determined that dark isolation of their rats during the retention interval decreased the amnesic effect of ECS on retention of passive avoidance training, as it had with appetitive training. Next, Calhoun and her associates returned to the appetitive conditioning paradigm to test the specific effect of illumination during the retention interval. Again, half of the animals tested spent the retention interval in the isolation chambers and half in the colony room, but this time the isolation chambers were illuminated for half of the animals and darkened for the others, while the colony room also was illuminated for half of the animals and darkened for the others. Again they found that alleviation of the amnesic consequences of ECS occurred for subjects in dark isolation chambers. However, no such alleviation was measured for subjects in illuminated isolation. Similarly, animals housed in the darkened colony room during the retention interval also tended to show better retention following ECS than animals housed in the lighted colony room, although this difference was not statistically significant in terms of the analyses applied by Calhoun and her associates. (It is interesting to note that animals not given ECS showed a tendency toward the opposite relationship).

From these studies, we make the general conclusion that retrograde amnesia may be affected by stimulus conditions present during the retention interval. More specifically, it appears that under at least some conditions amnesia is reduced if the animals are housed in total darkness during the retention interval. We saw earlier (Chapter 3) that ambient darkness tends to alleviate forgetting under other circumstances as well. However, we should consider a further study by Adams and his colleagues that indicates that these similar results probably are not due to the same processes.

With different circumstances of training and testing, isolation in darkness during the retention interval has been found to have a quite different effect on the influence of ECS. Adams, Calhoun, Davis, and Peters (1974) noted that the alleviation of amnesia found by Peters and his associates (and Calhoun et al.) was precisely opposite to an earlier result—further impairment in retention—found for isolated animals previously given cortical ablation (e.g., Meyer, Isaac, & Maher, 1958). Making the assumption that the precise nature of the brain trauma may be insignificant, Adams and his associates tested the hypothesis that the critical difference between these studies was in the nature of the learning task. Peters and his colleagues (and Calhoun et al.) had tested animals on a simple one-trial learning task, while Meyer and his associates had employed a relatively complex discrimination task that required multiple training trials. Therefore, Adams and his associates employed a multiple-trial task, training rats on a one-way active avoidance task to a criterion of 9 avoidances among 10 trials, which required an average of about 25 training trials. Following training, half of the animals were administered ECS and half were not, and half of each of these groups were housed in dark isolation and half in the illuminated colony room. As

Adams and his colleagues had predicted (and precisely opposite the results of Peters et al. and Calhoun et al.), animals housed in dark isolation during the retention interval had an *augmented* amnesic effect of ECS. In other words, Adams and his associates found more retrograde amnesia for animals housed in dark isolation than for animals housed in the illuminated colony room.

It should be noted that these studies are of a preliminary nature and that it is not yet certain that the different effects of dark isolation can be attributed to the difference in the number of training trials required in these tasks. But if this does become certain, an important functional difference would be established in terms of the consequences of an amnesic agent following single-trial, as compared to multiple-trial, learning. In accordance with the consolidation hypothesis, the locus of the effect of post-training ECS on memory processing may differ in these two instances, with a deficit in memory storage being more likely with a single-training trial and a deficit in some other aspect, such as retrieval, more likely with multitrial training. This, of course, has been the working hypothesis within a consolidation framework and is the rationale for using a one-trial learning task; but because of the lack of functional differences apparent between the characteristics of retention under these two circumstances, this reasoning has had little empirical support.

In the studies by Peters and Adams and their associates, the animals were kept under a fixed housing condition for the entire length of the retention. The effect of the housing conditions, however, did not depend on the length of the retention interval (hence we did not mention the latter variable). This implies that the total duration of dark isolation (which, for subjects with this housing condition, would co-vary with length of the retention interval) may be less important than the temporal location of this experience during the retention interval. This further permits the possibility that dark isolation has its major effect if initiated very soon after the amnesic agent. Furthering the likelihood of the latter, Hinderliter, Smith, and Misanin (1976) have shown that by confining rats for 1 hour in isolation like that employed by Adams and his colleagues, ECS-induced amnesia may be alleviated significantly. The interpretation offered by Hinderliter and his associates, linked to earlier results and explanations of Misanin and his colleagues concerning sensory-isolation effects on amnesia, potentially has general significance.

Other environmental manipulations known to alter amnesic effects, in particular, continued confinement in the training apparatus (e.g., Robustelli, Geller, & Jarvik, 1968; see Spear, 1973, for a review of such studies) have also appeared to be more effective if administered soon after training. Mah and Albert (1974) found that if the animal is reexposed to the training apparatus during the retention interval, the amnesic effects of ECS may be reduced (see also Adams, 1966), but only if the 15-minute period of reexposure is initiated immediately following the amnesic treatment, and not if reexposure is postponed until 15 minutes later.

Like the experiment by Mah and Albert, a number of other studies also have found that certain treatments may alleviate retrograde amnesia if administered at a point in the retention interval better described as "prior to the retention test" rather than "just subsequent to the amnesic treatment." The distinction sought here will become clear in the following section.

Specific Treatments That Alleviate Amnesia When Administered Prior to the Retention Test

We may now consider a variety of stimuli, both drugs and external environmental events, that are applied during the retention interval and prevent the retention deficit normally caused by an amnesic agent. Typically, these stimuli are presented nearer in time to the retention test than to the amnesic agent, although this particular temporal arrangement may not be critical in all cases. The spectrum of conditions under which such "direct reactivation of memory" has been found is extraordinarily broad, as we shall see.

The most general implication of the effects discussed here is that whenever direct reactivation treatments are successful in reducing amnesic effects, the action of the amnesic agent has not been to prevent the formation of the stored memory or to destroy it. As we have stated before, this is not to imply that failure in memory storage or destruction of a stored memory may not occur sometimes. But given the reality of direct reactivation effects and the ubiquity of the potential for direct reactivation following amnesic treatments, assertions concerning the action of these agents on memory storage must be limited to the hypothetical case because they are impossible to verify. These points and reviews of specific instances of direct reactivation treatments that reduce amnesia have been published previously (e.g., Lewis, 1969, 1976; Miller & Springer, 1973, 1974; Spear, 1973, 1976). Therefore, our review will be limited to the few cases needed to illustrate the specific points and principles we wish to establish.

We shall consider two general cases in which the effects of amnesic agents are reduced, often to the point of complete elimination (in operational terms) of amnesia. The first case involves the administration of drugs; the second, the administration of particular external stimuli, usually events that accompanied original learning. It is quite possible that the critical internal consequence of these two cases is common; that is, the external events may initiate the same sorts of physiological activity in the peripheral or central nervous system as the exogenous chemicals (i.e., drugs). It does seem likely that the ultimate consequences of action on the processing of the memory would be common for these two cases and presumably affect some aspect of memory retrieval, although this is yet to be determined. As we consider examples of these cases, these points will be reintroduced, although sometimes only indirectly. In addition, we shall return in Chapter 8 to a general consideration of events that precede or accompany the retention test and serve to reduce deficits in retention arising from a variety of sources of forgetting.

Alleviation of amnesia by drugs related to hormonal activity.   The class of drugs affecting the pituitary–adrenal system may have its action of alleviating amnesia mediated by both peripheral and central nervous system mechanisms.

Peripheral systems are especially likely to be involved when the particular amnesic agent is physiologically diffuse, such as when an antibiotic is injected peripherally rather than directly into the brain (see Nakajima, 1973). Pituitary–adrenal action on memory processing may also be directed centrally. It is now known that adrenal corticoids may occupy binding sites in the brain and thereby directly influence its action (see DeWied & Weijnen, 1970). While it is not clear that ACTH (the pituitary hormone that acts to release adrenal corticoids for their entry into the bloodstream) directly enters the brain, there is good reason to believe that its action on memory processing goes beyond its action on the adrenals and perhaps is focused somehow on the brain, as we shall see.

The involvement of the pituitary–adrenal system in amnesia induced by antibiotics became apparent in a series of experiments conducted by L. B. Flexner, J. B. Flexner, and their associates. In these studies, amnesia was induced in mice by bilateral cerebral injection of a dose of puromycin sufficient to inhibit drastically the synthesis of protein. Flexner and Flexner (1970) found that removal of both adrenals prior to training prevented the amnesic effect of puromycin. Because ACTH has been implicated in memory processing on a variety of grounds, Flexner and Flexner suggested that the effect they observed may have been due to the greater quantity of ACTH released in their adrenalectomized animals (corticoids from the adrenals ordinarily would act within a negative-feedback system to limit the output of further ACTH from the pituitary). To test this idea, Flexner and Flexner (1971) injected mice with ACTH in a gelatin form that remains in the system a relatively long time, and then tested the amnesic effects of puromycin in these mice. They found that with the appropriate dosage of ACTH amnesia could be decreased by an injection given as early as 3 days prior to training or as late as 16 hours after training. In a subsequent study, Quinton (1972; reported by Rigter & Van Riezen, 1975) found that injections of ACTH in mice also reduced the amnesic effects of cycloheximide. The precise mechanism of action through which ACTH alleviated amnesia is unclear from these experiments, although Flexner and Flexner provide empirical reason to believe that it is not due to enhanced original learning or to motivational effects.

It is conceivable that the lessened amnesia reported by Flexner and Flexner and by Quinton may have been due to some action of adrenal corticoids released through the injected ACTH. Further experiments, however, have indicated that ACTH has a capacity for reactivation of memories that is independent of its action on the adrenals. Chemical techniques have permitted the manufacture of a fractionated form of ACTH, termed ACTH 4-10, in which the amino acids primarily responsible for stimulation of the adrenals effectively have been removed. In other words, injection of this form of ACTH into a hypophysectomized animal having no endogenous source of ACTH releases few, if any, adrenal steroids. Rigter, Van Riezen, and De Wied (1974) found that if ACTH 4-10 was injected into an animal 1 hour before its retention test, amnesia induced by hypoxia was decreased. Subsequently, Rigter and Van Riezen (1975) found that retrograde amnesia induced by ECS similarly could be reduced if ACTH

4-10 was injected 1 hour prior to the retention test. As Rigter and Van Riezen note, the robustness of this reactivation effect of ACTH has been demonstrated through its occurrence with four different amnesic agents following either aversive or appetitive conditioning. Finally, both the study by Rigter and Van Riezen and that by Rigter and his associates found this reactivation effect only if ACTH was injected 1 hour before testing but not if it was injected 1 hour before training. These authors suggest that ACTH therefore may promote retrieval of memories that otherwise would be subject to amnesia.

While the preceding results show that alleviation of amnesia may be caused by ACTH independent of the latter's effect on adrenal steroids, there also is evidence that these steroids themselves may act to alleviate amnesia. Nakajima (1975) found that if corticosterone (i.e., the major adrenal steroid of the mouse and rat) was administered immediately or 30 minutes after training, animals subjected to inhibition of protein synthesis by cycloheximide showed less amnesia when tested 7 days later than otherwise would have been expected. However, corticosterone did not decrease the amnesic effects of cycloheximide if injected 3 or 24 hours after training. Barondes and Cohen (1968) also reported that injections of corticosterone soon after training decreased the amnesic effects of an antibiotic. It is possible that this reactivation effect of corticosterone may be unique to antibiotic amnesic agents. This would be in accordance with Nakajima's theory, which emphasizes the peripheral effects of antibiotics on the adrenals. Nakajima (1975, Exps. 2 and 3) has shown that action of the antibiotic cycloheximide on the central nervous system is not a necessary condition for its amnesic effect; with Nakajima's procedures, the action of cycloheximide on the adrenals apparently is sufficient to produce amnesia.

The role of central catecholamines in alleviating amnesia. The last drugs of interest for their action in alleviating amnesia are those whose effect apparently is mediated by action on the adrenergic nervous system. A variety of experiments have shown that the retention deficit induced by antibiotics may be lessened by injections of drugs such as *d*-amphetamine and imipramine, which stimulate action of the neurons for which the major neurotransmitter is the catecholamine norephinephrine (e.g., Barondes & Cohen, 1968; Roberts, Flexner, & Flexner, 1970; Serota, Roberts, & Flexner, 1972). On the basis of these and other data, Quartermain and his colleagues have suggested that the basis of the amnesia caused by antibiotics may be impairment of the action of central catecholamines. In support of this reasoning, they have shown that various drugs that act to raise norepinephrine levels in the brain have the common effect of alleviating amnesia induced by cycloheximide, although they function through quite different mechanisms. Furthermore, any of several drugs that act to deplete catecholamines in the brain serve also to induce amnesia in mice in a manner quite similar to that of cycloheximide (Quartermain & Botwinick, 1975).

The reactivation effects of some of the drugs just mentioned—those relevant to the action of the pituitary–adrenal system and those that influence central catecholamines—may be limited in their generality beyond amnesia induced by antibiotics. This particular case of amnesia has several characteristics that differ from amnesias induced by other sources of brain trauma. For example, retention is more likely to improve with the mere passage of time following an amnesic dose of an antibiotic than after other sources of amnesia. In the Quartermain and Botwinick study, as a specific instance, the amnesic effects were alleviated for all animals two days after training, whether or not drugs were introduced as reactivation treatments. Undoubtedly, many of the drugs mentioned earlier may also have reactivation effects under other circumstances as well (see, e.g., Klein, 1972).

Alleviation of amnesia in terms of state-dependent retention. As we have used the term here, *amnesia* may be applied to instances of state-dependent retention induced by drugs: Both amnesia and state-dependent retention imply forgetting (operationally defined) resulting from relatively abnormal sources. A reasonable interpretation of many reactivation treatments that alleviate amnesia or forgetting in general is that such treatments serve to increase the similarity between events noticed at the retention test and events of learning that have been represented as attributes of the stored memory. State-dependent retention may also be interpreted in this way, although not necessarily (Bliss, 1974; Spear, 1976; see also Chapter 2).

State-dependent retention offers a potential explanation of retention deficits arising from certain amnesic agents, although such a view is not accepted widely. Two general hypotheses concerning the role of state-dependent retention yield somewhat different predictions as to how amnesia is alleviated by reactivation treatment. To appreciate these hypotheses, it is useful to know that the amnesic agent involved in testing these views has been ECS and to recall the variety of physiological consequences of an ECS (see Chapter 6). Note also that some physiological consequences of probable importance for memory processing, such as alterations in neurotransmitters in the brain, are fairly persistent and have sizable effects lasting up to 4 days or more following ECS.

One hypothesis focuses primarily on the persisting aftereffects of an ECS, holding that the physiological state of the organism at the time of training (prior to the ECS) must be reestablished at the time of the retention test or a deficit in retention will be measured. Therefore, whenever retention tests are given before normal dissipation of the aftereffects of ECS, amnesia will occur unless the animal is treated somehow to alleviate these aftereffects. On this basis, tests administered after the dissipation of these aftereffects should not show amnesia. The second hypothesis depends on the assumption that memory processing persists following training. The state of the animal during this posttraining memory processing is assumed to be critical; retention at a later test depends on the recurrence of this posttraining state. In other words, a drastically novel physiological state induced by the amnesic agent prevails during this critical posttraining period of memory processing (i.e., consolidation or whatever), and as this state dissipates and the normal state is reestablished prior to the retention test, a deficit in retention occurs.

The first hypothesis was tested initially by Nielson (1968) and DeVietti and Larson (1971) and the second by Thompson and Neely (1970). There seems to be no doubt that ECS is capable of inducing state-dependent retention under a variety of circumstances, and both hypotheses have been useful for explaining certain amnesic effects of ECS over an impressively wide variety of learning circumstances (DeVietti & Hopfer,1974a; DeVietti, Mayse, & Morris, 1974; Thompson & Grossman, 1972). Yet neither hypothesis is completely convincing. The first explicitly predicts inevitable spontaneous recovery from amnesia with the passage of time, a phenomenon that remains to be established. The second assumes that state-dependent retention will occur even though the critical state is not induced until after training has ceased. Although support for the latter effect exists (Chute & Wright, 1973), it is limited support, and the effect is not firmly established. Furthermore, the second hypothesis has acquired its support from instances of alleviated amnesia that may readily be interpreted otherwise (see Miller, Malinowski, Puk, & Springer, 1972). From a broad perspective, however, the data generated in testing these two hypotheses provide further instances in which the effects of retrograde amnesia may be reduced.

This topic is of interest at this point because of potential implications of the second state-dependent hypothesis for understanding the action of certain drugs in inducing retrograde amnesia. If the physiological state present during post-training processing must also be present at the time of the retention test in order to avoid a retention deficit, then retrograde amnesia induced by any drug is subject to the same interpretation and to the possibility that it might be alleviated if that drug were injected again prior to the retention test. Such a possibility always exists when drugs are injected prior to training; hence, posttraining injections have been used in part to preclude interpretation in terms of state-dependent retention. To the extent that the second hypothesis concerning posttraining processing is substantiated, however, a large number of cases of drug-induced retrograde amnesia may need to be reevaluated in terms of state-dependent retention.

Direct Reactivation: Alleviation of Amnesia Induced by Nondrug Stimuli

Amnesia following administration of an amnesic agent (usually ECS or another neural convulsant) is reduced if events similar to those encountered during training are presented to the subject during the retention interval. This effect—we prefer the term *direct reactivation*—has been replicated often; there is no doubt about its reliability. What is in doubt is the interpretation of this effect and the nature of the dimension defining the similarity between the events of training and the events of the reactivation treatment (and, to some extent, whether it is necessary that they be similar at all). A related issue concerns the generality of the effect, that is, whether it is unique to amnesia caused by brain trauma.

Evidence that helps describe the direct-reactivation phenomenon has been reviewed in several sources (Lewis, 1969, 1976; McGaugh & Herz, 1972; Miller & Springer, 1973, 1974; Spear, 1973, 1976) and is applicable to analysis of the effect. Briefly, the evidence indicates that direct reactivation has the following four characteristics: First, events effective as agents of direct reactivation include noncontingent reexposure to the reinforcer (e.g., the footshock, if original learning involves avoidance or escape of footshock), reexposure to portions of the apparatus in which instrumental learning occurred, or reexposure to the CS in the case of classical (Pavlovian) conditioning. Second, there is some suggestion that the agent of reactivation need not be identical to an external event of training. For example, Springer and Miller (1972) found that amnesia for passive avoidance (withholding a response that had led to being plunged into cold water) could be reduced by a reactivation treatment consisting of a noncontingent footshock. Bounds on this generality have appeared, however. For example, Miller, Ott, Berk, and Springer (1974) found that reexposure to the appetitive stimulus alleviated amnesia for appetitive conditioning, but administration of a noncontingent footshock did not. Third, reduction in amnesia following reactivation treatment is relatively permanent (e.g., Miller & Springer, 1972), although it is not yet clear how this permanence compares with permanence of original training in the absence of an amnesic agent. Finally, the consequences of reactivation treatment are greater the less severe the amnesia, whether the variation in degree of amnesia results from differences in strength of original learning, in intensity of the amnesic agent, or in the interval permitted to elapse between training and administration of the amnesic agent (see Cherkin, 1972; Gold & King, 1974; Kesner & Conner, 1974; Miller & Springer, 1974).

This last characteristic of direct reactivation has led to some disagreement concerning the interpretation and implications of the basic phenomenon. The core of the argument is presented in papers by Miller and Springer (1974) and Gold and King (1974). Briefly, Gold and King argue that reactivation treatments add new learning sufficiently consistent with that of original learning to produce summation of the two learning experiences. The result is increased retention scores, but only, Gold and King maintain, if amnesia was incomplete and some storage of memory occurred. Miller and Springer argue that new learning is not likely to be responsible for the effects obtained; rather, the alleviated amnesia that occurs is consistent with the view that this amnesia results from failure of memory retrieval rather than of memory storage. These papers and their general arguments are instructive, and they discuss additional points that seem to lead to the following conclusions.

The viability of a consolidation theory does not depend on the interpretation of how events may alleviate amnesia. Some version of consolidation theory inevitably will be true. Just as stored memories may increase or decrease in their accessibility and manifestation in behavior, so potential representations of external events may become relatively permanent memories or characteristics of individuals' dispositions (i.e., through consolidation). What we may learn from circumstances that alleviate amnesia, and what is important about the interpretations of reactivation treatments, is the boundaries that circumscribe the useful application of consolidation as an explanation.

Reactivation treatments and other variables used to modify amnesic effects have revealed that there are several circumstances under which amnesic agents appear neither to destroy nor to retard the development of an individual's representation (memory) of events concerning reinforcement contingencies unless the amnesic agent is delivered nearly simultaneously with the occurrence of those events. Perhaps circumstances do exist in which the storage or maintenance of the memory following an amnesic agent indeed depends on a consolidation period that extends well beyond sensory registration and perception. It now appears that one way to test this most effectively is to use reactivation treatments to estimate the probability of reduction in amnesia. Confirmation of the null hypothesis (i.e., no reduction in amnesia; hence, storage failure) will remain a problem unless the evidence becomes so overwhelming as to make the assumption of ultimate retrieval less admissible than that of the absence of the memory. The application of such reactivation tests at least may provide an alternative means of operationally defining "severity of amnesia." We noted earlier that it is hardly surprising to find that the more severe the amnesia (or forgetting in general), the more difficult its alleviation. While this relationship is somewhat less than a conceptual breakthrough, it nevertheless may add to our understanding as an operational identification.

Finally, it remains possible that the phenomenon under discussion may lead to empirical generalizations that are of value for understanding memory processing beyond the limitations of traumatic amnesia. The determinants and characteristics of the alleviated amnesia discussed here are similar to those of alleviated forgetting generally, over a variety of sources of forgetting (Spear, 1973, 1976; see Chapter 8). This does not permit the conclusion that the retention deficits from these sources have a common basis. For example, we have cautioned in this chapter that the mechanisms responsible for amnesia induced by antibiotics may be different from mechanisms for other cases of amnesia. Nevertheless, the possibility of such a generalization, whatever its boundaries, could lead to principles of memory processing having wide applicability.

ANTEROGRADE AMNESIA

We have seen in previous chapters that a relatively small number of factors have been found to affect the forgetting associated with the passage of time, once equivalence of perception and original learning is established. Of the factors that do alter such forgetting, most depend on events occurring between the time of learning and the time of the retention test. This may appear to be reasonable intuitively: Would we not expect events following learning to determine its later manifestation more fully than events simultaneous with or prior to it? In fact, however, there is little a priori basis for this expectation, and its apparent empirical support may be merely a consequence of experimental convenience. Treatments prior to or simultaneous with training are likely to differentially influence perception or degree of original learning, and so additional control conditions (often involving numerous additional groups of subjects or entire experiments) are required to permit conclusions about forgetting independent of effects on perception or learning. These difficulties may be circumvented when experimental treatments follow original training, as occurs in the study of retrograde amnesia. Thus, the greater number of posttraining than pretraining events found to influence retention may be due in part to the greater ease in establishing the former as determinants of retention.

There is sound historical precedent, however, for expecting that pretraining events might influence forgetting in important respects. The most obvious is the general case of proactive interference in human verbal memory processing, which was emphasized by Underwood (1945). It led to basic readjustments in estimates of simple forgetting (Underwood, 1957) and to the formulation of important theories of forgetting (Underwood & Postman, 1960).

Abnormal events that precede training and may influence forgetting also have potential importance for understanding memory processing in general. A special case of such anterograde amnesia—chronic amnesia suffered by humans having damage to the temporal regions of their brain—was discussed at length in Chapter 6, and the importance of these cases to theories of memory processing were documented. We now will consider other potential advances found through examination of experimentally induced anterograde amnesia.

Again we must consider methodological limitations in our selection of analytically acceptable instances of anterograde amnesia. We have mentioned the general difficulty encountered in holding perception and degree of original learning constant when physiologically traumatic events are introduced prior to training. A related difficulty exists in that the training procedures used most often to study retrograde amnesia simply are not applicable to the study of anterograde amnesia. For example, the commonly used passive avoidance tasks that involve only one training trial often yield avoidance performance among normal subjects that exceeds the limits of measurement; these subjects simply avoid as long as is possible and thus have a "ceiling" imposed on the index of their behavior. This does not permit the close monitoring of degree of original learning required for studies of anterograde amnesia. What is needed for such monitoring is training that involves several trials on which performance may be measured concurrently (see Underwood, 1964). The following two studies provide examples that illustrate the interest in and potential analytical value of understanding anterograde amnesia.

Pretraining Inferotemporal Lesions and Retention in Monkeys

We mentioned earlier that the exaggerated forgetting shown by humans suffering temporal lesions to the brain has not been duplicated closely in experimental studies with animals. However, Gross (1973; see also Iversen, 1973) has reviewed evidence to suggest that, when induced prior to training, "inferotemporal lesions [in the monkey] seem to interfere with some mnemonic or associative function" (p. 93). The evidence includes suggestions that this mnemonic interference may be measured in terms of a retention test, although it is not always apparent during original learning. Taken to a common, but not overly stringent, criterion of visual discrimination learning, animals with inferotemporal lesions later show retention inferior to that of normals (Gross, 1973). This is suggestive but not convincing evidence for anterograde amnesia because the acquisition of a common criterion of learning does not guarantee equal degrees of learning (Underwood, 1954). However, an additional characteristic of retention in monkeys with inferotemporal lesions suggests a mechanism that might contribute to anterograde amnesia in these animals: Gross, Cowey, and Manning (1971) obtained evidence suggesting that animals with these lesions may be more susceptible to retroactive interference than normals. Compared with either normal monkeys or monkeys with lesions elsewhere, those given inferotemporal lesions had a greater deficit in retention of prior learning following the acquisition of a conflicting memory (for a parallel effect with rats, see Jarrard, 1975). Because retrograde interference, like the effect of a retention interval, depends on degree of original learning, and because we cannot be certain that original learning was equal for lesioned and nonlesioned animals, we cannot be completely confident that temporally lesioned monkeys are more susceptible to interference than normals. But this interpretation is intriguing because it matches the Weiskrantz–Warrington interpretation of the anterograde amnesia in humans with temporal brain damage. Also, in accordance with our related discussion in Chapter 6, we might speculate that this deficiency is a consequence of the lesser capacity of the monkeys with inferotemporal lesions to incorporate, into the alternative memories, contextual cues ordinarily used by normal monkeys to aid in discriminating alternative memories when retrieval of one is required. Data gathered by Manning (1971) suggest that monkeys with inferotemporal lesions learn less than normals do about "background cues" (Gross, 1973, p. 96).

Anterograde Amnesia Induced by Conventional Amnesic Agents

It is well known that in addition to their deficiencies in remembering events that preceded the treatment, humans administered ECS subsequently complain of difficulties in remembering events that they learned soon after the treatment.

Increasing experimental data suggest that such anterograde effects are systematic: Learning that more closely follows an amnesic agent is more likely to suffer a deficit in retention than learning that follows the amnesic agent by a longer interval. Kopp, Bohdanecky, and Jarvik (1968) and Zerbolio (1969) reported a subsequent retention deficit in mice given ECS before one-trial passive avoidance training, provided that the amnesic agent did not precede training by too long an interval. We just mentioned, however, that under such circumstances it is not possible to know whether ECS had influenced original learning or retention. An experiment by Springer, Schoel, Klinger, and Agranoff (1975) provides evidence of anterograde amnesia effects resulting from both ECS and the antibiotic puromycin under circumstances in which the influence of these agents on perception and original leaning was controlled better.

Springer and his associates tested goldfish on a shuttle avoidance task that has been employed for several years by Agranoff and his colleagues. This task requires several training trials, on each of which improvement in performance may be measured. Springer and his associates found that neither prior ECS nor prior injections of puromycin influenced the learning scores of their goldfish; this permits a clear test of the influence of these prior treatments on subsequent retention. When ECS was administered to the fish 30 minutes prior to training, retention was impaired when measured after intervals of 2, 6, 24, or 72 hours following training. When ECS was administered 1.5, 2.5, or 4.0 hours prior to training, retention after relatively short intervals was not impaired, but retention was impaired 72 hours after training. Control experiments by Springer and his associates (Exp. 2) indicated that this anterograde amnesia is not a reflection of state-dependent retention. Finally, it was also determined that if puromycin is injected 24, 16, 8, or 4 hours prior to training, retention measured 8 days later is impaired significantly. This impairment is not a consequence of permanent neurophysiological disruption caused by the puromycin, however, because goldfish injected with this drug 48 hours prior to training do not exhibit a subsequent retention deficit.

This study nicely illustrates the phenomenon of anterograde amnesia and, in addition, presents examples of how such data may be useful analytically. For example, it was found in this study that pretraining injections of puromycin caused no greater retention deficit than posttraining injections, which dismisses the possibility that the interfering action of puromycin is mediated by some consequential, time-dependent accumulation of toxic products or depletion of existing proteins. Furthermore, because ECS administered an hour or so before training impairs long-term retention without impairing the original learning, its primary action does not appear to be transient destruction of a memory before it can be stored in some permanent form; rather, these data imply that ECS induces persistent effects, perhaps a biochemical nature, that may influence the processing of a memory for a long period following its administration.

HYPERMNESIA

The contribution from clinical cases of amnesia to the surge in its experimental analysis may be appreciated readily. Examples emphasized earlier—the many cases of traumatic amnesia caused by World War II and summarized in the influential report of Russell and Nathan (1946)—provided a clear impetus to research using abnormal treatments such as ECS or drugs toward understanding normal memory. What may not be appreciated is that prior to World War II there also was a good deal of attention given to clinical cases in which abnormal conditions resulted in *better* retention than otherwise would have been expected.

Stratton (1919) analyzed several cases of "retroactive hypermnesia," instances of unusually good recall of events that occurred during the period of several hours preceding intense emotional excitement. Russell (1948) commented on the extremely clear retention many amnesic patients show for events preceding brain trauma (except, of course, for the one or two seconds that immediately preceded this trauma). McGeoch (1942) considered hypermnesias that may "occur in manias, in moments of danger, while going under an anaesthetic, and in emotional excitement," or as a consequence of hypnosis, to be sufficiently important to warrant discussion in his well-respected and influential discussion of human retention (see pp. 330–332). However, there was limited scientific interest in hypermnesia during and shortly after World War II. This is illustrated by the fact that this portion of McGeoch's book was unchanged in the revision published ten years later (McGeoch & Irion, 1952).

What Is Meant by Hypermnesia?

Hypermnesia generally refers to extraordinarily effective memory processing; for medical purposes, the term is most commonly used in reference to the manifestation of memories induced (apparently) through physiological trauma or therapeutic treatment such as hypnosis. Our use of this term is consistent with these meanings: We define hypermnesia as enhanced retention independent of the external, nonorganismic conditions of training, with restrictions as follows.

We must be explicit in distinguishing hypermnesia from *reminiscence* or *incubation* (Chapter 4). These two terms refer to enhanced retention for subjects exposed to a longer retention interval than others. In keeping with the general sense of hypermnesia as reflecting more effective processing of memory within a given period, our use of this term will exclude the effects of a retention interval as incorporated within the constructs "reminiscence" and "incubation."

With this operational definition, it is understood that hypermnesia is also to be distinguished from instances of improved retention mediated by reactivation treatments (see Chapter 8) or by modifications of contemporary context (see Chapter 2). Both refer to events that may alleviate forgetting among subjects undergoing normal processing of memories.

Our use of the term *hypermnesia* is in reference to memory processing that occurs under abnormal circumstances and is unusually effective: Operationally, hypermnesia is enhanced retention associated with an unusual physiological state. For this assessment, we must be sensitive to the question of whether the memory processing itself has been influenced by a hypermnesic treatment or whether performance factors have been altered. Equally difficult to ascertain when hypermnesic treatments occur between training and the retention test is the extent to which these treatments may act as reactivation treatments by providing stimuli similar to those of training. These conceptual distinctions are not easily drawn empirically. Accordingly, we must be aware that it is somewhat presumptuous to discuss the characteristics of hypermnesia because it is not entirely clear that it exists. However, I am not convinced by the argument that abnormal physiological events may yield impaired processing of memories but not improved processing, so hypermnesia seems well worth considering at least as a potential phenomenon.

Our use of *hypermnesia* may be illustrated by exclusion, in terms of examples that do not fit our definition. Shapiro and Erdelyi (1974) used *hypermnesia* in reference to their results suggesting improved retention with increasing length of the retention interval. In this study, human subjects were presented with a list of 60 simple sketches of discrete objects (e.g., football, table, fish) or with the labels of these objects. Either 30 seconds or 5 minutes following their presentation, the subjects wrote the names of as many of these items as they could remember. For subjects originally presented the pictures, recall was 12% better after the long interval than after the short one (subjects given words showed very little change—actually, a slight decline—over the same interval). The former difference is of only borderline statistical significance, although it is in general agreement with a possibly analogous effect gathered earlier by Erdelyi and Becker (1974). The apparent phenomenon reported by Shapiro and Erdelyi does not qualify as hypermnesia for our purposes because their effect was a consequence of manipulating retention interval and a nonorganismic aspect of training (content of the memory). As another example, Kleinsmith and Kaplan (1963, 1964) found increasing retention with increases in retention interval when certain "arousing" words were tested for recall. To the extent that this enhanced retention could be attributed to degree of arousal per se, rather than to the nature of the materials to be learned (a distinction that was not possible with the method applied in these cases), our concept of hypermnesia could apply. Our intention is to restrict consideration of hypermnesia to the behaviors apparently referred to by Stratton, Russell, and McGeoch in the references mentioned earlier.

A final, somewhat esoteric clarification and cautionary note is needed here: Hypermnesia must refer only to facilitation of normal retention caused by a hypermnesic treatment (i.e., in comparison to that of untreated normal animals); it should not refer to facilitation of retention to normal levels or below among subjects suffering abnormally impaired memory processing. In our view, the latter case of facilitation can rarely be distinguished from the effects of reactivation treatments that alleviate memory impairment. Therefore, our definition of hypermnesia requires a baseline of normal memory processing, and we shall reserve our use of the term *hypermnesia* to cases in which retention is facilitated relative to that of normals. This issue is particularly relevant in considering, say, the "facilitating" effects of direct electrical stimulation of the brain when electrodes implanted in preparation for the stimulation have resulted in abnormal physiological functioning before administration of the hypermnesic treatment.

There is a very good reason why hypermnesia has not been studied experimentally with human subjects: The emotional excitement that may be required would be difficult to provide, and perhaps unethical, in an experimental situation. An exception is the "induced hypermnesia" of experimental hypnosis, which we shall discuss later.

With animals as subjects, however, it is relatively convenient to study a variety of abnormal physiological conditions that might result in abnormal retention. Since the mid-1960s, the possibility of such memory facilitation has been investigated at length with animal subjects, through the direct application of electrical stimulation or drugs into the brain. In addition to the obvious advantages to which such studies might lead (consider the possibility of a synthesized "memory pill"), these investigations have also been applied toward the theoretical analysis of memory processing.

Chemical Facilitation of Memory: Drug-Induced Hypermnesia

General background.   Scientists tend to be split rather dichotomously in terms of their attitude toward the state of knowledge in this area. This split is exemplified by the contrasting contents of two sets of analytical reviews of this area, one by Calhoun (1971), the other by McGaugh and his colleagues (Dawson & McGaugh, 1973; McGaugh, 1973; McGaugh & Herz, 1972). Calhoun critically analyzes a large number of specific experiments, including those reporting facilitation of memory processing by certain drugs and those reporting failure to find such facilitation with the same drugs. He concludes that it is premature to assert that any of the drugs in question clearly exert a facilitating effect on memory processing. On the other hand, McGaugh and his associates conclude that memory processing indeed is influenced by certain drugs, and that the action of these drugs is to facilitate the storage process in particular. The discussion by McGaugh and his associates continues beyond this basic conclusion to include consideration of the neurophysiological mechanisms that might be responsible for such cases of drug-induced hypermnesia.

This difference of opinion, certainly not restricted to these specific authors, may be traceable to a variety of factors, perhaps including differences among scientists in the extent of evidence needed to be convincing and the historical reluctance of psychologists to believe that memory processing can be facilitated by factors unrelated to learning. But for the most part the split in opinion can be attributed to these specific facts: The pharmacological and physiological actions of the drugs are not understood well; many of the experiments have been found to have subtle methodological flaws that tend to negate interpretations of positive results; and the effects that have been found apparently are sensitive to a large number of special parameters, so replication of previous results has not always been achieved. Our position is to accept the weight of the data as evidence that certain treatments may result in facilitation of memory processing.

In this section, we are concerned particularly with the action of a certain class of drugs termed *analeptic*. Chemically, these drugs are a surprisingly diverse group, but they have in common the action of neurophysiological arousal (not necessarily reflected in overt behavior), which is the medical definition of analeptic. The sense in which *analeptic* is used here is defined in *Stedman's Medical Dictionary* (1972) as "strengthening; stimulating; invigorating," with specific usage as "central nervous system stimulant." It is useful to note that although the term *CNS stimulant* has come to be used clinically in a manner synonymous with *antidepressant,* this is a quite inaccurate characterization of analeptics. In fact, CNS stimulants such as amphetamine often induce in humans many of the symptoms characteristic of clinical depression.

The analeptic agents that have been tested most frequently for their facilitating effect on memory include the convulsants strychnine, diazadamantan (1757 IS), picrotoxin, metrazol (pentylenetetrazol), the xanthines, including especially caffeine, and magnesium pemoline, an analeptic without severe convulsant action.

The latter three drugs are of singular interest because each has been tested often with humans. The histories of their application have been rather different, however. Metrazol has been used with geriatric patients suffering from senility or cerebral arteriosclerosis. These patients are given subconvulsive doses, and the action of this drug is not only as a cerebral stimulant but also as a vasodilator to increase blood flow in the brain. Reportedly, metrazol seems to provide real improvements in general "mental alertness," and in some cases provides apparent alleviation of the memorial difficulties generally characterized as "forgetfulness." Caffeine has been tested often because it is so common and easily administered. The third drug, magnesium pemoline, has known biochemical effects on RNA in the brain, so it has attracted particular interest in view of the often-hypothesized role of RNA in memory storage.

A number of systematic experiments involving human memory have been conducted with these three drugs, but so far it has not been possible to draw any clear conclusion from this very complex research. In contrast, some strikingly impressive data from research with animals have been collected in systematic studies, especially with certain of the other analeptics. There is no need to review these data in detail, there being a sufficient number of reviews already available (see earlier discussion). Instead, we will restrict ourselves to citing a few exemplary studies for purposes of illustration.

Hypermnesia in animals induced by analeptic drugs.   Analeptic drugs are known to affect a variety of behaviors, but our interest here is with their effects on memory processing only. The likelihood of such effects became particularly evident through a rigorous set of studies completed by McGaugh and Krivanek (1970; see also Krivanek & McGaugh, 1968, 1969). These experiments demonstrated facilitation in the rate at which mice acquire a visual discrimination for food reward when each daily session of three trials was followed after certain intervals by certain doses of analeptic drugs. (As with amnesic agents, injection prior to training may confound the effects of analeptics on performance during that training session with their effects on memory processing; hence the need for posttrial injection and variation in posttrial delay of injection.) In general, the locus of the facilitation may have been in initial storage of the information received just prior to the drug or in processes related to retention but not original learning.

When injection immediately follows a daily session, attainment of a criteria of 9 correct responses out of 10 is more rapid the higher the dose of pentylenetetrazol (metrazol), up to 20 mg/kg (see Figure 7.8). With strychnine, the dose-response relationship is somewhat more complex: Optimum facilitation occurs at about .1 mg/kg and at about 1.0 mg/kg; facilitation is reduced or absent with doses in the intermediate range. With higher doses, there is the risk that convulsions will be induced, particularly if the animal is placed into a novel or otherwise very stimulating environment following the injection. Similarly, with doses of pentylenetetrazol higher than those used by McGaugh and Krivaneck, convulsions are induced that are known to impair, rather than facilitate, memory processing (e.g., Palfai & Chillag, 1971).

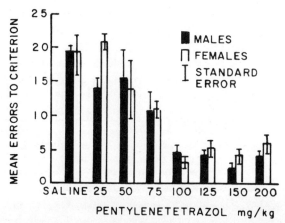

Figure 7.8   The mean number of errors needed before acquisition of a brightness discrimination by mice is shown for animals that differed in the dose of pentylenetetrazol administered following each daily session of trials on the discrimination task (adapted from Krivanek and McGaugh, 1968).

A general feature of analeptic agents is that at higher dosages they may very likely induce amnesia instead of hypermnesia. For example, Cherkin, Meinecke, and Garman (1975) found that posttraining administration of a relatively strong dose of the convulsant flurothyl induced retrograde amnesia, while a lesser dose administered under the same circumstances induced retrograde hypermnesia. Such a dose-dependent reversal of retrograde effects has also been found with other types of agents. For example, posttraining administration of ether, mentioned earlier as a potential amnesic agent, may result in retrograde hypermnesia under some circumstances (Wimer & Huston, 1974).

The relationship between degree of facilitation and time of drug injection preceding or following training—the retrograde hypermnesia gradient—potentially is as important analytically as the gradient of retrograde amnesia. For strychnine sulfate (.1 mg/kg), this relationship is shown in Figure 7.9; for pentylenetetrazol (15 mg/kg), this relationship is shown in Figure 7.10. It is quite clear that, with either drug, the more remote in time the injection is from training, the less influence the drug has on learning the discrimination. However, strychnine remained effective (in these studies) when injected as long as 1 hour after the training trial, while pentylenetetrazol influenced learning rate only if injected 15 minutes or sooner following training. Unfortunately, these particular intervals have little generality beyond this experiment. In fact, the slope of this

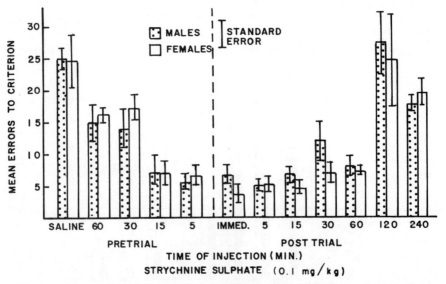

Figure 7.9   The mean number of errors required before learning a brightness discrimination is shown for mice that differed in when they were administered strychnine in relation to the time of the daily session of training trials. The vertical line indicates the time of training, so animals represented by bars to the left of that line received injections prior to training and those to the right received injections following training. The closer the temporal proximity of training and the injection, the more rapid the learning (adapted from McGaugh and Krivanek, 1970. © 1970 Pergamon Press Ltd.).

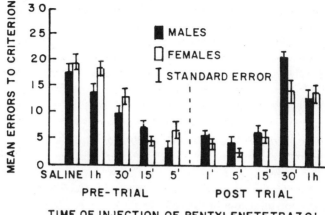

Figure 7.10   The mean number of errors required to learn a brightness discrimination is shown for mice that differed in when they were administered pentylene-tetrazol in relation to the time of the daily training trials. The vertical dotted line represents the time of training, so animals represented by bars to the left of that line were injected prior to training and those represented by bars to the right were injected following training (adapted from Krivanek and McGaugh, 1968).

gradient fluctuates with variations in a variety of experimental parameters, and there may be many not yet determined.

Nevertheless, some generality can be found for the basic fact of facilitation of memory processing by analeptics over a wide variety of drugs and tasks. Moreover, this facilitation does not require a cumulative effect of the analeptic over a long series of daily training-and-drug sessions. Rather, a single injection of strychnine following a single training session has been found to produce significantly superior retention of rapidly learned tasks such as passive avoidance (Franchina & Moore, 1968; Gordon & Spear, 1973).

The precise anatomical location of the hypermnesic action of analeptic drugs has also been examined. In all the studies mentioned earlier, drugs were injected intraperitoneally (IP) and therefore had undetermined loci of action (except for the gross distinction sometimes made between drugs that are likely to enter the brain and those that are not). The pharmacological action of analeptics is presumed to be partially on the reticular formation. Accordingly, Alpern (1968) implanted relatively long-lasting crystals of strychnine into the reticular formation. As expected, facilitation of memory processing occurred, as measured by improved retention. In another location of the brain, the hippocampus, Grossman (1969) injected small quantities of pentylenetetrazol through implanted cannulae and tested the effect of this treatment on subsequent discrimination learning. Grossman's training procedures were similar to those of McGaugh and Krivanek. When pentylenetetrazol was injected into the hippocampus 5 minutes before a training session, rate of learning was facilitated in comparison to that of animals that also had cannulae in the hippocampus but were not injected with the analeptic. However, animals injected with pentylenetetrazol were no better than unimplanted (and therefore undrugged) normal animals not subject to the brain damage caused by the operation and insertion of the cannulae. This set of results presents a problem of interpretation, mentioned earlier, to which we shall return when we discuss the facilitating effects of brain stimulation on memory processing.

Hypermnesia in animals induced by hormones.   Gold and VanBuskirk (1975) trained thirsty rats to lick in a particular location, then punished the licking with footshock. The footshock was followed immediately by treatments intended to modify the retention of this punishment: injection of either saline or one of several possible doses of epinephrine (the hormone secreted by the adrenal medulla, also known as adrenaline).

In previous studies of the effect of epinephrine on learning and retention, injection of this substance was given prior to training with inconclusive results: sometimes facilitation, sometimes disruption, and sometimes no effect at all. Gold and VanBuskirk, however, found a hypermnesic effect of epinephrine with doses of .01, .05, or .1 mg/kg (epinephrine doses of .001 or .5 mg/kg had no effect). Subjects given intermediate dosages of epinephrine had mean latencies to lick that were two to three times as great as those of animals injected with only saline. In a second experiment, Gold and VanBuskirk found that this hypermnesic effect depends on injection of the epinephrine soon after training: The effect occurs if the injection is given within 10 minutes after the punishment, but not if it is given 30 minutes or longer following punishment. This time dependency precludes the possibility that epinephrine may alleviate forgetting through action similar to that of reactivation treatments administered prior to the retention test.

Subsequently, Gold and VanBuskirk (1976) tested the hypermnesic effects of a variety of hormones. Using the same procedures as before, they found that appropriate doses each of epinephrine, norepinephrine (the other product of the adrenal medulla), and ACTH (from the pituitary) result in hypermnesia if injected immediately after training. The same substances have no effect if delayed until 2 hours after training. Various doses of corticosterone or vasopressin also have no effect on subsequent retention, even when injected immediately after training.

Gold and VanBuskirk (1976) suggest that the action of the substances that induce hypermnesia is not necessarily to alter characteristics of the consolidation process but, rather, to provide an event that aids the animal in evaluating the extent to which prior events should be stored as a memory. The implication is that the reinforcement effect of the punishment is enhanced. Whether this is due to enhancement of the effective intensity of the punishment (as represented memorially by the rat) or to prolonged processing of the events of training or to some other mechanism is a matter for further investigation. This interpretation is of interest in that it appears more similar to the posttraining processing considered by Wagner, Rudy, and Whitlow (1973) and others (e.g., Kamin, 1969) than to the earlier conceptualizations of the consolidation process as a relatively inevitable physiological event.

Hypermnesia in animals induced by cholinergic drugs.   The theory of Deutsch (1969, 1972) implies that the injection of an anticholinesterase (such as physostigmine) should induce hypermnesia. Deutsch's theory specifically predicts a facilitating effect of physostigmine injected after either very short or very long intervals following training. The purpose here is not to evaluate either the theory or the generality of the hypermnesic effect of anticholinesterases on animals but, rather, to produce an illustration of such an effect. One such illustration is provided nicely in an experiment by Alpern and Marriott (1973).

The study by Alpern and Marriott employed an effective, easily adaptable test of short-term retention in mice. Briefly, following a series of successive reversals on a position discrimination task in a T-maze, learning set was established such that following a single reversal trial animals would perform accurately thereafter on immediately successive trials. However, in the absence of immediately successive trials, rapid forgetting of the reversal occurred during the first 30 minutes following the first reversal trial. Alpern and Marriott found that this rapid forgetting could be slowed if mice were given injections of physostigmine (2.0 mg/kg) 30 minutes prior to administration of their critical "information" trial (the single reversal trial): Forgetting after a 25-minute interval was decreased, although forgetting after a shorter interval (15 minutes) was not (see Figure 7.11). Potential interpretive problems are present in this experiment because the injections were administered prior to training and so might possibly have modified motivational or perceptual processes, and because there is confounding between length of the retention interval and length of the interval since injection. Alpern and Marriott argued effectively that these were not important factors, however. This illustration provides a further example of a potentially interesting source of hypermnesia, though like other examples, it does not provide clear information whether the locus of the effect is in initial storage or later processing of the memory.

It is notable that this review does not exhaust the list of specific drugs that, on the basis of empirical evidence, seem to be likely candidates as hypermnesic agents. Further drugs of this type have been discussed by McGaugh (1973).

Issues of Significance for Interpretation

Having introduced sufficient examples to establish that hypermnesia in animals is a genuine phenomenon, we now consider issues of special importance to the interpretation of research in this area. Among several aspects of methodology

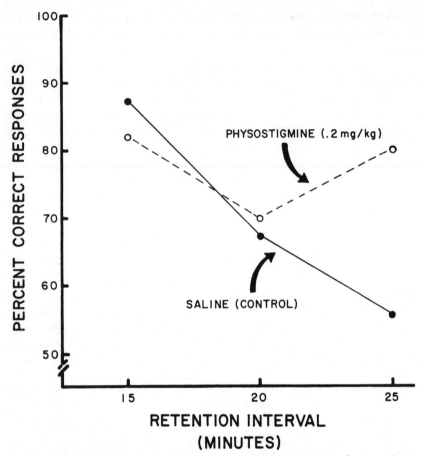

Figure 7.11   This figure shows that under circumstances of heavy proactive interference and consequential rapid forgetting in mice, prior injections of physostigmine may retard forgetting (adapted
from Alpern and Marriott, 1973. © 1973 Pergamon Press Ltd.).

that are recognized as critical for conducting and evaluating experiments of this
kind, the following seem sufficiently important to warrant independent review.

Further considerations of posttrial administration of the drug.   A truism
concerning drugs is that their effects are multiple, and even with the most
familiar drugs, many effects simply are unknown. Analeptic drugs in particular
have been shown to have distinct effects on a variety of factors important for
performance in learning tasks (see Calhoun, 1971). Injected prior to training,
these drugs very well might induce differences in motivational, perceptual, and
general attentional processes, and in sensitization or general activity levels.
These effects obviously are very difficult to separate from effects on memory

processing. It was for this reason that in 1959 McGaugh implemented posttraining administration of these drugs for his analysis of their effect on memory processing.

Even so, Calhoun (1971) has pointed to two limitations of posttraining administration. First, it does not make "theoretical sense" to employ such a procedure unless one maintains a belief in some form of consolidation process or, more generally, in the possibility that memories are labile and subject to strengthening following training for a period significantly longer than the interval needed for perception. Second, only drugs that act rapidly enough to exert their action prior to the halting of memory processing can be expected to be effective. Thus, the effect of any drug that has delayed action (because of, for example, slow absorption rate) will not be apparent if administration is subsequent to training.

Dose-response curves.   Aside from the simple advantage of maximizing information, there are two analytical reasons for testing a variety of drug doses in any experiment. The first is simply that the validity of negative results is increased. If many different doses are applied with no effect, we can base decisions on this null finding with relatively little concern that a "proper" dose might have been effective if tested.

Of course, if an effect is found, one dose is sufficient when the question is only "Does the drug have any effect?" With a variety of dosages of some drugs, however, we may make a useful distinction between moderate doses that may have "physiologic" effects—neurochemical consequences that are quite within the limits of normal physiological functioning—and heavier doses that result in "pharmacological aberrations"—chemical effects that clearly are physiologically abnormal. This distinction is significant psychologically and may be detected through dose–response relationships, the second reason for such tests.

Tests of retention should be free of nonmemorial effects of the drug.   The test for retention should be given after an interval sufficiently long to permit normal metabolic dissipation of the specific, direct effects of the drug, and also to permit dissipation of any secondary effects on other processes that the drug might have.

We implied earlier that because some drugs may have cumulative effects, the fewer injections given an animal, the better. Thus, tasks acquired in a single session of training are especially useful. Furthermore, it may be questioned for some drugs (such as strychnine) whether the effects of even a single injection dissipate as rapidly as has been assumed. Cooper and Krass (1963) found that strychnine injected in rats 72 hours or 24 hours prior to testing influenced the number of errors on a Hebb–Williams maze problem. Because most studies have tested the effects of analeptic drugs within 24 hours after the final application, the results of Cooper and Krass indicate that these drugs could influence performance at the retention test quite apart from their effect on memory storage.

It is notable that such proactive effects of strychnine and other analeptics have not been confirmed in experiments by Greenough and McGaugh (1965) or by Crabbe and Alpern (1973). Also, a proactive effect on test performance apparently is not a serious limitation on the general assessment of the hypermnesic action of analeptics for the following reason: The retrograde gradients shown earlier (see Figures 7.8, 7.9, and 7.10) indicate that if an injection of strychnine follows training by longer than 1 hour, it has no effect on test performance. Holding constant the interval between training and testing, longer intervals between training and the posttrial injection imply shorter intervals between the injection and the test. Therefore, one should expect the opposite results—greater effect at 1 hour or more—if the important effect of strychnine were proactive (i.e., if the strychnine were acting directly on test performance rather than enhancing training effects). Moreover, recent experiments have included control groups injected with strychnine but not trained prior to a "test." Their results show that under circumstances in which strychnine does facilitate retention, strychnine alone (i.e., without prior training) does not influence test performance relative to saline alone (Crabbe & Alpern, 1973; Gordon & Spear, 1973).

Importance of the environment following administration of the analeptic drug.   Scientists injecting strychnine into intact animals are well aware that these animals are likely to convulse if exposed to an especially stimulating environment (see Calhoun, 1971). More subtle environmental effects may also influence the conclusions of studies of memory processing with these drugs. For example, Papsdorf, Snyder, and Cholewiak (1968) administered strychnine to rabbits following classical conditioning of the nictitating membrane and found facilitation of this response (which in fact may have been a performance effect rather than a memory-processing effect; see Cholewiak, Hammond, Siegler, & Papsdorf, 1968). Nevertheless, the facilitation occurred only if the animals were maintained in an experimental chamber between training and testing, and not if they were maintained in their home cages.

More lengthy environmental treatments also alter certain effects of strychnine: An interaction has been found between the effects of a long series of daily injections of strychnine and the degree of environmental enrichment to which rats are exposed during this period (LeBoeuf & Peeke, 1969; Peeke, LeBoeuf, & Herz, 1971). For the animals living in an enriched environment, strychnine enhanced rates of learning a complex maze; but for those that had lived in an impoverished environment, there was a tendency for strychnine to impair maze learning. These studies should be viewed in relation to one conducted by Calhoun (1966), who found that posttrial administration of strychnine facilitated discrimination learning for animals housed in a quiet environment following the injection but not for animals housed in a highly stimulating environment (in fact, learning was impaired for the latter). It should be noted, however, that the stimulation provided by the enriched environment in the former set of experiments was less severe and probably more pleasant for rats than the stimulating environment of Calhoun's experiment. If both sets of results reflect the summation of neural stimulation provided by each of three sources—the environment, the drug, and the organism's internal hormonal reactions to these stimuli—it is possible that the internal stress created by isolation potentiated the effect of strychnine to the level that produced convulsions and resulted in amnesic effects. This reasoning requires the uncertain assumption that the enriched environment used by Peeke and his associates potentiated the effects of strychnine to a level that aided memory processing, but not high enough to cause seizures.

Moderate or low doses of strychnine might also require interaction with environmental stimulation to produce a hypermnesic effect because of mechanisms quite different from those just cited. For example, suppose we assume that one mechanism of the action of analeptic drugs is to modify the impact of extraexperimental interference on retention. Analeptics such as strychnine are known to decrease activity levels, which, in turn, could result in a reduction of opportunity for acquiring interfering, competing memories during a retention interval spent in an enriched environment (cf. Parsons & Spear, 1972). But rather than such speculation, what is really needed is experimental tests of alternative mechanisms for the facilitating effect of analeptics, because as yet there has been very little research directed to this question.

Further difficulties in interpretation.   In spite of the several convincing and thorough experiments that have shown facilitation of memory processing by analeptic drugs, the parameters controlling these effects are far from clear, even when the preceding methodological problems have been resolved. For example, thorough studies have been published in which analeptics have failed to influence memory processing (e.g., Kulkarni, 1972; Prien, Wayner, & Kahan, 1963; Stein & Kimble, 1966). Moreover, the finding of some clear effects of strychnine on maze *performance,* as opposed to maze *learning* (e.g., Dusewicz, 1972), is sufficient to make one constantly wary. The complexity and the unsettled nature of the controlling parameters may be illustrated further in a thorough study conducted by Krivanek (1971), who collaborated with McGaugh on the earlier demonstrations of analeptic-induced facilitation of retention. In testing the effects of pentylenetetrazol on aversive conditioning, Krivanek found facilitation of retention scores under certain circumstances, but in other cases he found either no effect or disruption of memory processing. The particular effect depended on the dose of the drug in combination with task complexity, degree of food deprivation, intensity of the aversive stimulus, and to some extent, the sex of the mice.

A final question of importance for theory is whether analeptics administered following training have their effect on a short-term consolidation-like process or on some other aspect of memory processing. From the retrograde hypermnesia gradients presented earlier (see Figure 7.9), it appears that a single posttraining injection of strychnine does not induce hypermnesia unless it is presented within about an hour following training. However, several experiments have found a facilitating effect on retention, apparently uncontaminated by performance differences, even though strychnine was not administered to the animals until a few days after training was completed (Alpern & Crabbe, 1973; Crabbe & Alpern, 1973; Gordon, 1973; Gordon & Spear, 1973).

Alpern and Crabbe (1972) gave mice a small amount of training on a multiple-choice visual discrimination task, then tested retention several days later. Different numbers of strychnine injections were administered during the retention interval, but none until at least 24 hours after initial training. With multiple injections spread throughout the retention interval, hypermnesic effects were obtained. This general result was replicated by Crabbe and Alpern (1973), with the additional finding of a similar hypermnesic effect using metrazol, but neither caffeine nor nicotine influenced retention, and similar administration of d-amphetamine tended to impair retention. When original training was not given, these drugs had no effect on test scores in either study; apparently, no proactive effects of these drugs artifactually influenced retention performance or acquisition of the memory (the retention test was a reacquisition test). The striking aspect of these studies by Alpern and Crabbe is that their results are so unexpected in view of the conventional retroactive hypermnesic effect strychnine and metrazol that previously had seemed limited to training–injection intervals of about an hour or less.

The results of the Alpern–Crabbe studies suggest that rather than facilitation in memory storage, hypermnesia caused by strychnine may be a consequence of alleviation of forgetting, perhaps due to temporarily enhanced accessibility of stored memories. Gordon and Spear obtained more evidence consistent with this interpretation. These investigators found that hypermnesia could be induced by a single injection of strychnine given up to 72 hours following training, depending on the particular events that immediately precede the injection. Hypermnesia occurred in these experiments if, immediately preceding the strychnine injection, rats previously given passive avoidance training were also given a treatment intended to reactivate the memory of this training. Under these circumstances, Gordon (1973) later found a surprising similarity between two empirically generated retrograde hypermnesia gradients, one gradient relating retention performance to the interval between a *reactivation treatment* and the strychnine injection, and the other relating retention to the interval between *original training* and the strychnine injection.

Perhaps in the studies by Alpern and Crabbe strychnine was effective long after training because the handling of the animals just prior to injection served to reactivate the memory of training, enhancing its susceptibility to the strychnine effects (for evidence that handling may be effective reactivation treatment in tasks similar to that used by Alpern & Crabbe, see Lewis, Bregman, & Mahan, 1972). However, efforts to test this notion have so far been hampered by an inability to replicate the basic findings of Alpern and Crabbe (Gordon, Brennan, & Rose, 1975).

Hypermnesia in Animals Induced by Extreme Ambient Temperatures

Earlier we discussed the amnesic effect of hypothermia in rats. It is notable that in poikilotherms such as fish, whose body and brain temperatures depend on ambient environmental temperature, hypermnesia has been found to result from a shift from very cold to warm water temperatures (Riege & Cherkin, 1973). Moreover, this hypermnesia was retrograde in its action and also time dependent. A similar facilitation in retention, perhaps identifiable as hypermnesia, has been reported for grain beetles maintained in cold ambient temperatures (Werber, 1974).

Facilitation of Memory Processing by Direct Electrical Stimulation of the Brain

We have discussed the studies by Alpern (1968) and Grossman (1969) that attempted to localize the site of drug action for hypermnesia by means of discrete applications of the drugs within the brain. In a similar fashion, several investigators have attempted to facilitate memory processing by passing low levels of electrical current through implanted electrodes in discrete areas of the brain.

Because degree of arousal has long been viewed as a critical determinant of memory processing (see Bloch, 1970), it is reasonable that electrical stimulation has most frequently been applied to the region associated with the control of arousal—the reticular formation. Several experiments have also stimulated the hippocampus (Erickson & Patel, 1969; Landfield, McGaugh, & Tusa, in McGaugh & Herz, 1972; Stein & Chorover, 1968). Increased general arousal probably is not the sole consequence of this stimulation. Aspects of memory processing per se may also be influenced by stimulation in this area, through mechanisms such as selective neuronal recruitment of the neurological representation of critical memory attributes.

Stimulation in either the dorsal hippocampus or the mesencephalic reticular formation has resulted in facilitated rates of learning, whereas stimulation in some other areas, such as the cortex, has not. But this "facilitated learning" requires a special interpretation. Our interpretation of these facilitating effects must be guarded—although stimulated animals have been observed to learn more rapidly than unstimulated animals having identically implanted electrodes, performance by the stimulated animals has not surpassed that of normal unimplanted animals (in fact, learning by stimulated animals is usually poorer relative to the latter animals).

The implication is similar to that of the experiment by Grossman described earlier. Apparently, the implanted electrode itself causes neurological dysfunction by creating a lesion-like effect. To some extent, stimulation in these areas apparently can compensate for the resulting impairment of learning. A clear effect of this sort is reported in the following experiment by Denti, McGaugh, Landfield, and Shinkman (1970).

Denti and her associates (1970) compared three groups of rats in terms of how rapidly they learned a modified (unsignaled) shuttle avoidance task. Animals in two of these groups had electrodes implanted into the limbic system of the brain (with the tips of the electrodes located in the mesencephalic reticular formation), and the third group served as an unoperated control condition. In order to ensure that the effect of the electrical stimulation was purely retroactive, these animals received only one training trial per day. Stimulation was presented over a period of 90 seconds immediately following each daily trial and consisted of 6 consecutive seconds of .1-millisecond phasic pulses (presented at a rate of 300 Hz) alternated with 3 consecutive seconds of no stimulation.

The results (see Figure 7.12) show quite clearly that learning was facilitated for stimulated animals in comparison with animals that received no stimulation through their electrodes, but that both were inferior to normals. A subsequent experiment of a similar nature by Landfield and his associates (described by McGaugh & Herz, 1972) showed that a similar procedure of stimulation was ineffective if given 5 minutes, rather than immediately, after a training trial. This establishes the retroactive nature of the effect for both this and the Denti study, and demonstrates that the stimulation was not exercising its influence on the subsequent trial. Nevertheless, Denti and her associates found that animals implanted with electrodes (whether stimulated or not) are inferior to unoperated controls in terms of learning rates. The stimulation serves to alleviate this learning deficit but does not induce hypermnesia relative to unoperated control subjects.

McGaugh and Herz (1972), however, cite studies indicating that the effects of stimulation like that under discussion may be absolute instead of only compen-

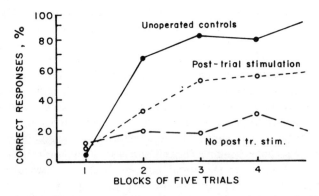

Figure 7.12 Learning of active avoidance is shown for rats having implanted electrodes in the mesencephalic reticular formation but no electrical stimulation in that area (lower dotted line), similarly implanted rats given electrical stimulation through their electrodes following each daily training trial (upper dotted line), and rats with no implanted electrodes (solid line). While the electrical stimulation improved learning among animals implanted with electrodes, there was no improvement relative to animals without implanted electrodes. (adapted from Denti et al., 1970. © 1970 Pergamon Press Ltd.).

satory for a lesion effect. Unfortunately, a report of these studies included in a lecture by Bloch given at Oxford University includes little methodological detail. The interesting report by Bloch (1970) warrants one comment. Generally, Bloch implicates arousal mediated by the reticular formation as particularly critical for the memory storage process and further suggests (p. 570) that such arousal probably is relatively unimportant for the retrieval process. In a test of retention 5 days after learning, Bloch found no effect when the reticular formation was stimulated preceding the retention test. Although these results are indirectly supportive of the conclusion by McGaugh and Herz that it is the storage phase of memory processing that is facilitated in these experiments, it should be clear that the matter is not yet settled. Negative results are particularly unlikely to permit firm conclusions, particularly in this case, where too much arousal probably has interfering effects that might mask any benefit to retrieval and yield the same null effect as too little arousal.

Facilitation of Memory Processing by Means of Hypnotism

Hypnotists have long claimed that a person's ability to retrieve certain classes of memories can be collectively increased or decreased through suggestions given to him or her under a hypnotic or somnambulant trance. Because we are interested in any abnormal treatments that might facilitate memory retrieval, controlled empirical cases of such an effect are of interest.

A limited amount of experimental support exists for hypnotically induced facilitation in retention over a short period or for periods as long as a year (e.g., Stalnaker & Riddle, 1932). The extent to which this benefit to retrieval can be attributed to the hypnotic trance or simply to the request (suggestion) that retention occur typically was not analyzed in these early experiments.

An example of such evidence (and its typically limited nature) is provided in a report by Blum, Graef, Hauenstein, and Passini (1971). On the basis of the dramatic accuracy with which one of their subjects had recalled a hypnotic dream that occurred two years earlier, Blum and his associates hypothesized that this excellent retention was due to the "distinctive mental context" induced by the hypnotic procedures (this context having been present both when the critical memory was acquired and when it was to be recalled). To test this hypothesis, a few persons were hypnotized, provided with verbal suggestions to create an appropriately distinctive mental state, and then told of a particular episode. Unknown to the subjects, this episode would later be tested for recall. In some cases the episode was complex and bizarre, in others simple and rational; but each episode was accompanied by a distinctive mental state.

A specific instance of a context-and-episode combination is useful for illustration. To create the distinctive mental state, the subject was "hypnotized" and told to imagine he was floating two feet above the couch on which he was lying, was surrounded by a "beautiful blue mist," and could "feel a light breeze blowing." A lengthy, bizarre episode was then described to the subject. In essence, the subject was to imagine President Lyndon Johnson (the date was spring 1967) in cowboy hat and boots, but with the face of Sammy Davis, Jr., leading a peace march in Hanoi.

After an interval of 143 days, Blum and his associates had this subject return to the laboratory, but gave no indication that he would be tested for recall. The subject was hypnotized as before and permitted to hear a tape recording of the instructions presented to him 143 days earlier, asking him to imagine floating in a blue mist, feeling a light breeze, and so forth. At this point, the subject was asked to describe that episode. Blum and his associates report that the subject, with halting speech and a frequently incredulous tone to his voice, proceeded to describe President Johnson, in a cowboy hat and looking like Sammy Davis, Jr., giving a speech against the war in Viet Nam.

Illustrations and anecdotes similar to those of Blum and his colleagues, interesting but not rigorous, have inspired a few more systematic investigations of this topic. We now turn to an example of an experimental study of hypermnesia induced through techniques of suggestion and hypnotism.

Memory retrieval and hypnotically induced age regression. Throughout the psychological literature, there are some dramatic consequences of hypnotic age regression. For example, Gidro-Frank and Bowersbuch (1948) hypnotically regressed three adult subjects to infancy. When the suggested hypnotic age was less than 6 months, a dorsiflexion of the great toe was induced by plantar stimulation; this Babinski reflex ordinarily occurs in infancy but disappears rapidly by toddlerhood. Moreover, Gidro-Frank and Bowersbuch observed a gradual development of this infantile reflex as they "rejuvenated" their subjects month by month with hypnotic suggestion. Similar results are reported by True and Stephenson (1951).

Reiff and Scheerer's study of age regression. In one of the more thorough attempts at demonstration and preliminary analysis of hypnotically induced hypermnesia, Reiff and Scheerer (1959) tried to facilitate the retrieval of childhood memories by inducing age regression in adults through hypnosis. This extension of the Ph.D. dissertation completed by Reiff under the direction of Scheerer represents a relatively careful experimental study of this aspect of behavior, which too often has been approached through mysticism rather than science. Their work holds additional interest for its relationship to the problem of "infantile amnesia," discussed in Chapter 5.

Reiff and Scheerer were concerned with the retrieval of memories having perhaps more "cognitive" content than the Babinski reflex. They hypothesized a particular memory mechanism that acts to facilitate retrieval through hypnotic age regression. They proposed that the critical condition of memory retrieval was neither suggestion nor the hypnotic state per se but, rather, "the revival of functional schemata . . . consistent with the age at which the [to-be-remembered] event was experienced" (Reiff & Scheerer, 1959, p. 212).

The term *schema* or *schemata* was introduced by the great British psychologist Henry Head early in the twentieth century. Later the term was employed in a somewhat revised form in the influential book by Bartlett (1932), and it is popularized today by Piaget and his followers. *Schemata* has traditionally been a rather fuzzy concept not amenable to clear definition either in operational terms or as an intervening variable. It may be regarded generally as a way of thinking, a manner of organizing and classifying environmental events. Reiff and Scheerer viewed alterations in the schemata of their subjects as a major objective of their research. For their purposes, the "schemata" were considered to include three processes: (1) the cognitive aspects of behavior, including perception and thinking; (2) emotional aspects; and (3) "the cognitive–emotional aspects of action such as crawling, grasping, manipulation, etc." (Reiff & Scheerer, 1959, p. 57).

The basic experimental strategy of Reiff and Scheerer included two sets of studies. In the first, subjects who had been regressed to a particular age were tested on tasks appropriate for children of that age. Their performance was compared to the performance of control subjects who were not hypnotized but were asked to try to simulate their behavior at this particular age of childhood. The tasks included tests for children similar to those introduced by Piaget for testing stages of development, as well as other tests devised by Reiff and Scheerer (such as asking the subjects to recite and write the pledge of allegiance to the U.S. flag). The second set of experiments included tests for recall of specific events that had occurred at the age to which subjects were regressed.

The first set of experiments was intended to determine how the subjects generally behaved at a particular age (specifically, age 7 or 10). From a variety of statistical tests of these data, the authors concluded that the regressed subjects indeed did behave in accordance with the age to which they were regressed, and did so more consistently than unhypnotized subjects merely asked to simulate this behavior. It was concluded further that when deviations from the intended age occurred, the regressed subjects tended to act younger than was intended, whereas the simulating subjects tended to act older.

In the second set of studies, subjects responded to questionnaires and interviews testing the recall of specific events at ages 7 or 10: Where do you live? Where did you live when you were 4 years old? What school do you go to? What is the name of your teacher? Where do you sit in your classroom? Regressed subjects showed significantly greater recall (relative to their adulthood waking state) than the simulating controls. The latter subjects did not differ in their responses when tested before and after being asked to simulate childhood. In these initial experiments, the memories could not be verified (an inevitable problem in any study of childhood memories). Subsequently, however, verification from some of the subjects' school records tended to substantiate the validity of some of Reiff and Scheerer's results. In addition, Reiff and Scheerer report the results of more general questioning, which include some individual cases of remarkable facilitation in retrieval of memories representing specific events in their subjects' past, for which validity was verified.

Critique of the Reiff–Scheerer study.   We do not wish to present the results of Reiff and Scheerer (1959) as irrefutable evidence for hypnotically induced hypermnesia. Neither is it our purpose to present a methodological critique of this work, which in fact has been accomplished rather well by the authors themselves (see also O'Connell, Shor, & Orne, 1970). Instead, our objective is to call attention to one experimental approach to the study of hypermnesia that, when properly refined, may help us understand how memories are processed generally and how their ultimate retrieval is determined. Note, however, that evidence obtained subsequently to the Reiff–Scheerer studies has not been encouraging in this respect. In the paper that includes a comprehensive review and critique of this work, O'Connell and his associates (1970) report a thorough study of their own replicating and extending that of Reiff and Scheerer; their results failed to confirm the existence of hypermnesia with these procedures.

SUMMARY AND CONCLUSIONS

The analysis of three instances of abnormal memory processing is particularly pertinent to the purpose of this book. These instances are retrograde amnesia, anterograde amnesia, and hypermnesia.

A large number of studies of retrograde amnesia with animal subjects permit us to state initial principles as to what governs this instance of abnormal memory processing. The most important principle is that the degree of amnesia is inversely related to the interval between the occurrence of the episode to be remembered and the subsequent amnesic agent. In other words, the shorter the interval between the episode and the treatment, the greater the amnesia for the episode. This relationship is conventionally described in terms of a gradient of retrograde amnesia, and this gradient has had a profound impact on theories of memory processing.

A related principle is that the gradient of retrograde amnesia is variable; it is not constant within a particular species nor even for a particular task or amnesic agent. This, too, has had a profound impact on theories of memory processing, because it shows that instead of a direct reflection of an underlying time-dependent consolidation process, this gradient is more properly viewed as an empirical statement of the time-dependent interference created by an amnesic agent with perhaps many aspects of memory processing.

Five general circumstances were identified as major determinants of retrograde amnesia. These are (1) conditions of learning; (2) characteristics of the amnesic agent; (3) the content of the episode to be processed as a memory; (4) the length of the retention interval; and (5) the structure of the retention interval. The related principles may tentatively be stated as follows: (1) A variety of operations that influence amnesia would seem to be best viewed as converging upon the intervening variable, degree of learning, such that the greater the degree of learning, the less the amnesia. (2) Retrograde amnesia is greater with higher intensities of the amnesic agent, which seems most conveniently dimensionalized in terms of electroshock; the anatomical locus of the action of an amnesic agent also is undeniably important, but in a complex fashion. (3) Memories indexed primarily by autonomic responding seem more resistant to retrograde amnesia than those indexed by skeletal responding, although the basis of this is far from clear. (4) As the retention interval increases between an episode–amnesic treatment combination and the test for retention, amnesia seems first to increase (for about one day) and then may or may not decrease; the evidence for the former relationship is much more substantial than for the latter. (5) Finally, amnesia depends very importantly on the events that occur between the administration of the amnesic agent and the retention test; for a variety of amnesic agents and a variety of circumstances of training and testing, it is known that amnesia may be alleviated by administering substances that alter hormonal or neurotransmitter activity or by reexposing the subjects to events associated with the original episode. There would appear to be great promise for understanding memory processing in general through further comprehension of these principles and characteristics of retrograde amnesia.

Anterograde amnesia among humans suffering brain damage or Korsakoff's syndrome was considered at some length in Chapter 6. In terms of experimental manipulations of anterograde amnesia, however, progress has been limited by methodological difficulties. For anterograde amnesia, the amnesic agent must be presented prior to or simultaneously with the episode to be remembered, and we do not yet have the proper techniques for ensuring equal perception and learning of the episode among subjects given and not given amnesic treatments under these circumstances. To the extent that this difficulty is solved, we may expect increasingly profitable study of anterograde amnesia. The few examples discussed indicated important new insights about memory processing that may evolve in terms of this phenomenon.

Hypermnesia (exaggerated retention), considered for many years within clinical settings, has been brought under experimental control in experiments with animals. In spite of many methodological impediments, instances of hypermnesia in animals have been established and studied through the administration of analeptic drugs. Further such instances appear likely from the administration of certain hormones, chemicals that alter neurotransmitters, extreme ambient temperatures, and direct electrical stimulation of the brain, although these cases have been studied less thoroughly than those using analeptic agents. Finally, hypermnesia in humans has received increasing experimental attention through techniques involving hypnotism and general suggestion. It is not yet clear how useful these techniques will be, and certainly an established body of knowledge is not available in this area. We can expect, however, that this research will usefully be integrated with other aspects of abnormal memory processing in humans to further enlighten us about memory processing in general.

8
Three Major Issues

We turn now to three major issues I find important, which have potentially general application and are testable experimentally, and for which a good deal of evidence already has been gathered. The resolution of these issues will have critical and broad consequences for understanding the processing of memories. It is toward their resolution that I present a brief review and some interpretations of each.

MAJOR ISSUE: WHAT GOVERNS RETRIEVAL OF A MEMORY?

Arising from the notion that an available memory is only sometimes accessible for manifestation in behavior, an important issue is what determines accessibility and ultimate retrieval of a memory.

We may assume that a memory is totally accessible immediately after learning and that thereafter sources of forgetting, sometimes explicit but in other instances unspecified, serve to reduce the accessibility and retrieval probability of the memory. The question is, What are the events that may return the memory to its earlier state of accessibility following a source of forgetting, and how do these events function to have this effect?

The experimental paradigm for addressing this question is straightforward: Holding constant the conditions of memory storage and the source of forgetting, certain events are presented to subjects after exposure to the source of forgetting but before assessment of their retention. If forgetting is thereby alleviated—and to establish this we must be certain that effects on retention performance are not due directly to new learning arising from these interpolated events or to nonmemorial effects (perceptual, motivational, etc.)—we may then conclude that the interpolated events acted either on the retrieval process or on its effectiveness.

Conceptually, we would expect that facilitation of the retrieval *process* would be nonspecific in nature, acting diffusely to enhance whatever neurophysiologic mechanisms are required to accomplish retrieval of any memory. A potential example might be arousal-inducing events that facilitate mechanisms such as neural recruitment and sharpened discrimination. But even when the retrieval process is functioning in an optimal manner, retrieval *effectiveness* may be enhanced further by the occurrence of events corresponding to attributes of the particular memory to be retrieved. Again, arousal (accessibility) of memory attributes is believed to be an essentially direct consequence of the subject's notice of events sufficiently similar to those represented by the attributes; retrieval of the remaining attributes of the memory may depend on the number, proportion, or kind of attributes aroused directly.

Events that alleviate forgetting by enhancing the effectiveness of retrieval may take either of the two forms discussed earlier, "contemporary context" or "prior cueing" (see Chapter 2; also see Spear, 1976). Manipulation of contemporary context involves events present throughout the retention test. With prior cueing, the critical events occur and terminate before the onset of testing. Tests with these manipulations have addressed a variety of issues important to theories of memory processing. We turn now to further empirical examples of manipulations of contemporary context (see also Chapter 2), with particular reference to the theoretical issues associated with these manipulations. We shall have occasion also to refer to cases of prior cueing, which has received less attention to date.

Contemporary Context Affects Processing of Verbal Memories

Major theoretical alternatives for understanding recognition and recall have been tested through empirical manipulations of contemporary context. We may summarize briefly the theoretical setting of these empirical tests.

A fundamental disagreement exists among theorists in how they view the processes of recognition and recall of verbal materials. Some theorists believe that the processing of memories is fundamentally the same whether recognition or recall is required, while others believe quite different processing is involved. Those taking the former position expect retrieval to be an important aspect of both recognition and recall, so both measures should be affected by the similarity between the semantic context of training and that of testing. Theorists holding the latter position expect recognition to be affected relatively little by manipulations of semantic context and assume that the retrieval process is of little importance for recognition. At the same time, the latter position views recall as sensitive to the semantic context of testing, but with less regard for the orthographic similarity between context at recall and that of original learning.

Given this overview, we may now examine theories and theoretical issues concerning the influence of contemporary context on retention, with emphasis on semantic context and the processing of verbal materials.

Issues relevant to effects of cueing by semantic context.   In answering the questions of how recognition and recall are accomplished, why they are imperfect, and how they might be improved in terms of the circumstances of the retention test, we may distinguish two alternative approaches: "encoding specificity theory" and "tagging theory." [The intended distinction is that described by Watkins and Tulving, 1975, with reference to "episodic" theory vs. tagging theory; "encoding specificity" is the preferred label here to avoid confusion with Tulving's (1972) distinction between episodic and semantic memory.] Although these alternatives hold some similar views of the processing of verbal memories, and although differences between them easily may be exaggerated in light of trends toward their integration, these alternatives provide a convenient setting to consider issues of broad significance for memory processing. (For further elaboration of these views, see Anderson & Bower, 1974; Kintsch, 1970; Martin, 1975; Reder, Anderson, & Bjork, 1974; Underwood, 1972; Watkins & Tulving, 1975.)

Encoding specificity theory is easier to characterize than the alternative, which really represents the opinions of several rather diverse theorists and hence presents a less monolithic viewpoint.

Encoding specificity theory assumes that whenever an event (such as a word) is perceived, the representation of that event is stored together with the representation of accompanying events; that is, all perceived events of an episode are stored together as a conglomerate entity. If a given word is to be recalled on a retention test, its retrieval therefore depends on the presence of test events that sufficiently match those of the original episode. Within this theory, recognition is also viewed as dependent on a similar retrieval process. Recognition of a particular word therefore is not assumed to occur simultaneously with its perception at the retention test (i.e., "automatic access" is not assumed) and should be sensitive to the contextual features of the retention test. This follows from the view that a particular word is represented memorially in multiple fashion in association with each of the many episodes within which it has been perceived. The alternative ("tagging") view is that a single representation of a word is tapped for each episode in the human's experience. This alternative view thus assumes "transsituational identity," while encoding specificity theory does not. When a previously presented word appears on the recognition test, its failure to be recognized is viewed by encoding specificity theory as less a matter of the final decision mechanism and more a failure to retrieve that item owing to insufficient contextual support that matches that of the original episode.

Within this framework of encoding specificity theory, therefore, a word previously presented at learning may not be recognized in relative isolation from the context that accompanied that learning, yet that word would be both recognized and recalled if that context (such as a semantic cue) were present at the retention test. This leads to the expectation that not only will semantic context influence recognition, but under certain circumstances unrecognizable words may be recallable if the proper aspects of the episode are presented.

Finally, encoding specificity theory incorporates the encoding specificity principle. This principle states that words presented as cues to aid retention will be effective only if they had appeared in the list of words learned initially as part of the original episode, or in other words, "What is stored is determined by what is perceived and how it is encoded, and what is stored determines what retrieval cues are effective in providing access to what is stored" (Tulving & Thomson, 1973, p. 353). On this basis, we would expect that words presented as cues at the retention test would be unlikely to facilitate recall of list items if they had not also appeared in the original list, even if the cue words were strong associates of the list items. But extralist cue words of this type have been found to facilitate recall under some circumstances. This fact has led to controversy, as we shall see.

The set of alternative views, somewhat diverse and perhaps incompatibly grouped as tagging theory, yields alternative predictions. Among this group of theorists are those who contend (though perhaps not all for the same reasons) that semantic context should have little or no influence on recognition; that inevitably, a particular word will have greater probability of being recognized than recalled; and that extralist associates of list words may aid in their recall if presented as part of the context of the retention test (e.g., Anderson & Bower, 1972; Kintsch, 1970; Underwood, 1971, 1972, 1974). We may now examine the evidence.

Effect of semantic context on recognition. While certain alterations in semantic context clearly may impair recognition, I must first emphasize that a considerable portion of recognition and its associated phenomena may be explained without reference to semantic context and memory retrieval. Frequency theory, developed by Underwood and his students to account for many instances of recognition, provides the example. This successful theory is based entirely on a few simple principles concerning frequency discriminations and has little regard for changes in context between learning and testing, implying little or no influence of such changes on recognition (for reviews, see Ekert & Kanek, 1974; Kausler, 1974; Underwood, 1971; Wallace, 1972). With the establishment of boundary conditions to this theory, however, certain effects of semantic context on recognition appear inevitable (cf. Underwood, 1974).

When semantic context is changed between learning and testing, recognition may be impaired through either of the two mechanisms identified in Chapter 2: interference caused by the subject's notice of new contextual stimuli that arouse conflicting memories, or ineffectual retrieval due to insufficient numbers or kinds of contextual stimuli in common with those present during learning.

Another potential source of recognition decrement is the nonsemantic (e.g., orthographic) changes in context (see Chapter 2). Still another might be the effects of semantic or nonsemantic contextual change on decision factors in retention such as an individual's criterion for response evocation. Murdock (1974) has discussed some effects of such decision factors on retention, but little is known as to how contextual change might affect them, so we shall not discuss this aspect further.

The interference-linked source of the recognition deficit apparently is manifested when change in semantic context alters the meaning of a homograph. Suppose that persons are presented the items *blueberry* JAM and *baseball* PITCHER and later are tested for recognition of the capitalized words when presented in the form *traffic* JAM and *water* PITCHER. Failure to recognize the capitalized words in their new context may be due to the arousal of memories involving the alternative meanings of the items. Because words generally fall along a continuum of the homographic characteristic, such a mechanism often may be responsible for recognition deficits upon shifts in semantic context (Martin, 1975).

Evidence that recognition may be impaired upon a change in semantic context is now common. The classical reference experiment was conducted by Light and Carter-Sobell (1970). These investigators found that subjects presented critical words as part of a simple sentence (*The catcher signaled the relief* PITCHER) suffered a 25% decrement in recognition of the capitalized word when the semantic context was altered (*The catcher drank from the water* PITCHER). Further, a 10% recognition decrement was found when the context was changed but the meaning of the critical word was not (*The baseball manager named his starting* PITCHER). The latter case—in which changes in the meaning of the word are not the entire source of the recognition decrement—has been replicated frequently. For example, if subjects initially are presented pairs of words and then are tested for recognition of one of them presented alone or presented with a different word than before, recognition errors may be 40–50% greater than when the same item is presented for testing with its original partner word (DaPolito, Barker, & Wiant, 1972; Underwood, 1974, Exp. 4). It is clear that contemporary context can have an important influence on recognition. At the same time, it is notable that the strong effects of semantic context found by Light and Carter-Sobell have not always been obtained (e.g., when entire sentences do not accompany the critical items; Hunt & Ellis, 1974).

The influence of semantic context on recall.   By presenting certain words as cues during testing, recall may be improved. This is a restricted effect with clear boundaries. The characteristics of this effect are of interest for general consideration of memory retrieval, however.

The value of semantic context for aiding recall has long been recognized by therapists working with aphasic patients. Eisenson (1973) notes the common assumption of aphasiologists that their task is to aid the patient in providing appropriate semantic context "to help him retrieve what he knows more readily than if he were left to his own devices" (p. 134). Among normal humans, the appearance of cue words has had an especially beneficial effect on recall of lists of categorized words, and it is in this setting that the effect has been most thoroughly analyzed experimentally.

A typical procedure has been to present subjects a list of about 20 categorized words, including exemplars such as *France, England, Spain,* and *Germany* together with *cabbage, bean, carrots,* and *lettuce,* and so forth. Recall of list items may be increased as much as 50–100% by presenting the category names (country, vegetable) during testing, especially if these category names had themselves appeared in the original list to be learned. The extra benefit of the latter circumstance is consistent with the encoding specificity principle, mentioned earlier with respect to the episodic theory of Tulving and his associates. This is by no means the only circumstance under which semantic cueing aids recall, however. Recall of a similar list of words may also be aided by presenting strong associates of the list items (e.g., Bahrick, 1970) or even by presenting to the subject a few of the items that had appeared in the list (e.g., Wood, 1972), although the latter treatment is perhaps more likely to result in impaired recall, a point to which we shall return shortly.

The benefit of semantic cueing is not limited to the recall of single lists of individual words. When sentences are presented for recall, the presence of one portion of the sentence may facilitate recall of the remainder (D'Agostino & DeRemer, 1973). Similarly, when pairs of words are presented to be learned and recall of only the right-hand member of each pair is requested, the presence of the left-hand member profoundly benefits recall (Tulving & Osler, 1968; Tulving & Thomson, 1973). Finally, when two consecutive lists are presented for learning and mutual interference in their recall is to be expected, semantic cueing has been found to alleviate both retroactive interference (Blake & Okada, 1973; Tulving & Psotka, 1971) and proactive interference (Gardiner, Craik, & Birtwistle, 1972; Wickens & Dalezman, 1974, Exp. 2).

The benefit of semantic context for recall has been shown in especially striking fashion by this demonstration: Under certain circumstances following presentation of several pairs of stimulus and response words, the latter may be recalled with far greater accuracy when provided the stimulus word than when it must be recognized from among a set of alternative items (Tulving & Thomson, 1973; Watkins & Tulving, 1975; Wiseman & Tulving, 1976). The recall of unrecognizable words is a very significant discovery for theories of memory processing. This result has also aroused critical questions regarding the methodology and procedure on which the finding is based (Light, Kimble, & Pellegrino, 1975;

Santa & Lamwers, 1974, 1976). There is no doubt, however, that the recall produced by semantic cueing can consistently exceed the product of certain recognition tests (Tulving & Wiseman, 1975) and therefore may serve as a convincing example of the retention benefits from cueing by semantic context.

The evidence just presented tells us that by presenting semantic cues that increase the similarity between the contexts of testing and original learning, recall can be facilitated under diverse circumstances. It is of some interest, therefore, that similar manipulations may actually impair recall.

Although they are somewhat paradoxical intuitively, negative effects of cueing began to be suspected through tests conducted by Slamecka (1968, 1969). Slamecka completed several thorough experiments to test the influence of presenting portions of a learned list as cues for recall of the remaining items. In contrast to the predictions of several theories, presenting part of the list during testing did not benefit recall of the remaining items; in fact, this procedure tended to impair that recall.

Following a short period of skepticism concerning the significance of Slamecka's findings, similar negative effects of cueing by list items began to be analyzed systematically. One line of analysis viewed presentation of a portion of a list at testing as precluding recall of those items by the subject during the test. Accordingly, it was determined that whenever recall was restricted by requiring subjects to confine their responses to one portion of a list before recalling the remainder—for example, requiring recall of the first half of the list before recalling the second half—poorer recall was found for the remainder of the items than if no restrictions were imposed. The implication is that the production of certain items in a list (or perhaps only their appearance) inhibits recall of the remaining items. The same principle is exhibited when one or more list items are presented along with category names as cues for the recall of a categorized list. The typical benefit of presenting the category names is reduced when other list items appear with them, and this detriment to recall increases the greater the number of other list items presented (for reviews of this and similar evidence, see Roediger, 1973, 1974).

Introspectively, a perhaps similar effect may commonly be observed if we try to recall as many members as we can of a particularly large conceptual category, such as all the vegetables we can think of or all the states in the United States. Following a burst of responses and the emission of a few trailing items with increasing interitem interval, we may attribute the failure to exhaust our knowledge of these categories to inhibition of the weaker items upon response with the stronger items (cf. Roediger, 1974). This kind of notion has been applied in terms of the concept "output interference" to explain certain negative effects of cueing and recall on subsequent recall, although this view seems less viable than an explanation in terms of "cue overload" (which we will not elaborate at this time; see Watkins & Watkins, 1975). The general point to be made is that cueing through manipulations of contemporary context may have some rather counterintuitive negative effects that nevertheless may reflect fundamental properties of the processing of memories.

Context, Cueing, and Retention of Basic Conditioning

After the interpolation of a source of forgetting, retrieval of the memory representing a conditioning episode may be facilitated by presenting to the subject some component of the conditioning situation (for the most part, we are now referring to animals as subjects). We infer retrieval of the memory when behavior corresponds to that expected as an immediate consequence of training, that is, behavior expected without the forgetting source. In Chapters 2 and 7, we considered examples of such facilitated retrieval within our general theoretical framework, viewing memory retrieval as some function of the number or kind of memory attributes aroused when the subject notices stimuli sufficiently similar to those represented in storage of the conditioning episode. This framework implies an apparent paradox: How can presentation of some portions of the conditioning situation—in particular, the conditioned or discriminative stimulus—be expected to enhance manifestation of the learned behavior when we know that this very operation is used for extinction, to decrease manifestation of learned behavior? We must briefly consider this issue before continuing our discussion of the characteristics and scope of circumstances that may enhance memory retrieval.

Evidence implying a reactivation effect of the conditioned or discriminative stimulus. It seems inevitable that presentation of the conditioned or discriminative stimulus must have the potential to activate a memory. Yet it is equally inevitable that if unaccompanied by the previous reinforcement contingencies, presentations of the CS will result in extinction (i.e., incorporation of the CS within a new conflicting memory having different reinforcement contingencies than earlier). Therefore, pretest presentation of only the CS or only the discriminative stimulus may alleviate forgetting, but only under the circumstances that would minimize the countereffects of extinction. Instances of such an effect are rare in the literature, but a few can be found.

Intrinsic to the psychotherapy techniques of implosive therapy and flooding is the assumption that by presenting to phobics the "CS" (object of their fear) within a clinical setting—where no adverse consequences could possibly accompany it—extinction will ultimately occur, thus alleviating the phobia. The initial effect of presenting this CS is to generate the subject's usual fearful response, which presumably accompanies retrieval of the memories that have included that feared object as an attribute. Whenever such therapy is applied, therefore, it is assumed implicitly that presentation of the CS has reactivation consequences in addition to extinction effects. In experiments with both animals and humans, there is further scattered evidence that manifestation of a memory may increase in probability following a short-duration presentation of the CS, even though with a longer duration of CS presentation this probability is lowered and extinction occurs (Eysenck, 1967; Miller & Levis, 1971; Rohrbaugh & Riccio, 1970).

Additional cases of apparent reactivation effects induced by the CS are notable. An example may be found in the tests of retroactive interference by Wickens (1973, as discussed in Chapter 4; see also Wickens et al., 1977; see Bruce & Weaver, 1973, for an apparently similar effect). Employing a Pavlovian conditioning paradigm with cats as subjects, Wickens compared the retroactive interference produced in an AB–AD paradigm with that in an AB–CD paradigm. To accomplish this, Wickens first presented pairings of a light and a shock to the left paw until the cats consistently withdrew that paw in response to the light. Next he introduced a second task, either light paired with shock to the right paw (AD) or tone paired with shock to the right paw (CD). In terms of either a recall or a relearning measure of retention of AB, performance was markedly better following interpolated AD conditioning than following interpolated CD conditioning. This suggests that when the stimulus "A" of original learning was presented as part of the interpolated task, it served to reactivate, or to maintain or perhaps even strengthen, the memory of original learning. The implication may be that reactivation of the original memory was accomplished during interpolated learning. Hints of a similar effect, though by no means certain, may be found in studies by Ho (1928) and Waters and Vitale (1945; see also Spear, 1976).

Further suggestions of reactivation effects.   Behavior appropriate to original learning declines following a decrement in magnitude of an appetitive reinforcer (including its elimination, i.e., the procedure for extinction). If subjects later are presented certain events associated with original learning, however, the learned behavior has frequently been found to reappear rapidly, as if the memory of original learning had been reactivated. For example, after rats were exposed to an extinction treatment for 47 days, Homzie (1974) found a return to acquisition behaviors when they were provided a particular sequence of events (response, followed shortly by a nonrewarded trial) unique to acquisition. Also, following extinction or a decrease in the magnitude of the reinforcer, consumption of the particular reinforcer associated with acquisition has been shown to yield acquisition-like behaviors (e.g., Campbell, Phillips, Fixsen, & Crumbaugh, 1968; Spear, 1967).

In terms of aversive conditioning as well, there is ample evidence that extinguished behavior may recover with dramatic rapidity following noncontingent presentation of the aversive stimulus of original learning. Following extinction of conditioned suppression previously learned by pigeons through the application of electrical shocks, Hoffman (1969) presented a few brief electrical shocks of the same type to his subjects. The result was a return of the conditioned suppression. Moreover, the behavior exhibited was quite specific to the stimulus of original conditioning. Wilson (1971) trained rats to perform a passive avoidance, then initiated extinction procedures that had the effect of eliminating the passive avoidance performance. Thereafter, the animals were administered noncontingent footshock in a different apparatus. This treatment resulted in dramatic recovery of the animals' earlier conditioned avoidance behavior. This recovery could not be accounted for in terms of new learning during administration of the noncontingent footshock or in terms of conditioned consequences of the shock itself. Similar results have been obtained by Rescorla and Heth (1975).

Alleviation of forgetting by reactivation treatment.   Forgetting due to any of a number of sources has been found to be reduced by reactivation treatments that precede the retention test. These cases differ in a significant manner from the examples of alleviated forgetting with human subjects: Whereas the cueing treatments applied in studies with humans have conventionally been presented simultaneously with the retention test and so may be termed manipulations of contemporary context, the corresponding treatments with animals have often preceded testing and so typically constitute instances of prior cueing.

Deficits in retention found after relatively short intervals are often attributed to "warm-up decrement." Warm-up decrement was discussed in Chapter 4 regarding whether motivational or memory retrieval factors provide better explanations of this retention decrement; I concluded that the evidence favors the latter. Tests concerning this question have employed reactivation treatments and thus provide examples of alleviated forgetting. When the source of forgetting is an interval considerably longer than that typically used to define warm-up decrement, similar alleviation has been found by treatments that precede the test, though not immediately preceding. A simple example has been reported by Spear and Parsons (1976). Rats were exposed to a particular version of Pavlovian fear conditioning that is accompanied by considerable forgetting over a 4-week interval. One day prior to the end of this interval, each animal in the reactivation condition was administered a footshock with the same characteristics as the UCS of original conditioning (but in a neutral apparatus) and then returned to its home cage and not tested until 24 hours later. A large number of experiments have indicated that this procedure results in marked alleviation of the forgetting that is otherwise found at the retention test. The magnitude of this alleviation is shown in Figure 8.1. In this figure, better retention is indicated by higher reciprocal latencies and by more rapidly increasing reciprocal latencies over blocks of trials. Several control experiments have ensured that the effect cannot be explained either on the basis of significant new learning or in terms of enhanced general activity caused by the reactivation treatment.

Similar alleviation (or possible prevention) of forgetting has been caused by re-presenting components of the conditioning situation on a number of occasions distributed throughout the retention interval (often termed the *reinstatement paradigm*). Certain instances of this effect may be explained in part in terms of the significant new learning that may occur when particular reactivation treatments are used (e.g., Campbell & Jaynes, 1966, 1969; Campbell, Jaynes, & Misanin, 1968), although a complete account of these effects in terms of new learning would be possible only if very complex and unlikely assumptions were

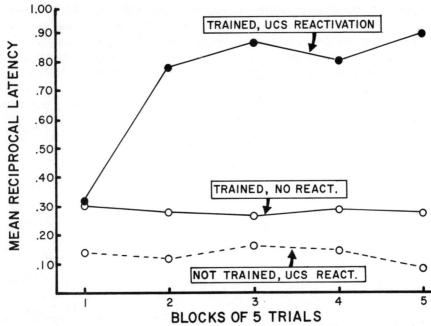

Figure 8.1   This figure summarizes data from several similar experiments to illustrate the influence of a reactivation treatment on retention assessed 28 days after original conditioning. Evidence of conditioning in this task is shown by relatively high reciprocal latencies and acceleration in these speeds over blocks of trials. This figure shows the three basic conditions that have been replicated among a large number of experiments in our laboratory. Animals represented by the solid lines were tested for retention 28 days after their conditioning trials. The conditioned animals depicted by the closed circles were given the reactivation treatment 24 hours prior to their retention test; those shown by the open circles were not. The lower line, dotted with open circles, illustrates the data of one basic control condition, rats not given original conditioning but presented the reactivation treatment 24 hours prior to a "retention test". For some experiments animals in this control condition are given noncontingent footshocks under the same circumstances as would have been included in original conditioning, and the point of this control condition is to illustrate that the reactivation treatment is not sufficient in itself to yield a high level of retention performance. (from Medin, 1976).

made. In other cases, the alleviated forgetting attributable to such multiple reactivation treatments seems inexplainable in terms of new learning (e.g., Silvestri, Rohrbaugh, & Riccio, 1970; Spear & Parsons, 1976).

Forgetting attributable to retroactive or proactive interference has also been alleviated by manipulations of either contemporary context or prior cueing. Cases concerned with contemporary context were dicussed earlier (Chapter 2), but warrant quick mention. Briefly, animals exposed successively to circumstances that yield conflicting memories—paradigmatically, similar discriminative or conditioned stimuli but opposing responses, such as go *versus* no-go, turn right *versus* turn left, and so forth—subsequently show much greater forgetting than if only one of the alternative memories had been acquired. However, forgetting may be decreased by presenting a distinctive contextual stimulus associated uniquely with the memory being tested. Contextual stimuli that have reduced the retroactive or proactive interference arising from conflicting memories have included features of the apparatus, the reinforcer, extraapparatus circumstances, and internal drug state (e.g., Spear, 1967, 1971, 1976; Spear, Bryan, Gordon, Chiszar, & Timmins, manuscript in preparation; Zentall, 1970). Although less frequently tested, reactivation treatments presented prior to the retention test have also been found to alleviate retroactive or proactive interference, presumably through their action of selectively enhancing retrieval of one of the alternative conflicting memories (Spear et al., 1973).

Experimentally induced amnesia may be alleviated if, prior to the retention test, the subject is administered the reinforcer associated with original learning. Typically, this reactivation treatment is administered 24 hours prior to testing. Similar effects have occurred whether the reinforcer is appetitive or aversive in nature. In Chapter 7, I mentioned that forgetting due to several specific sources of amnesia has been found to be alleviated in similar fashion. Most frequently, the analysis of these effects has proceeded in terms of traumatic amnesic treatments (electroconvulsive shock, hypoxia, hypothermia), but the amnesic effects of certain drugs that modify the action of neurotransmitters may also be alleviated by these reactivation treatments (Hamberg & Fulton, 1972; Wiener & Messer, 1973).

Aging is another source of forgetting that may be susceptible to alleviation by reactivation treatments (by *aging,* I am referring primarily to maturation of a neurophysiological or behavioral character that occurs from birth to adulthood, although these comments might possibly apply to the aging process generally). We might expect, therefore, that reactivation treatments would be more effective in alleviating the forgetting of immature than mature animals. Preliminary tests have not supported this possibility (Spear & Parsons, 1976). This may imply a functional difference between forgetting caused by aging and that arising from other sources.

Finally, forgetting that seems to be attributable to internal neurochemical changes between learning and testing—the Kamin effect, exaggerated forgetting found 1 to 6 hours after aversive conditioning—has been shown to be alleviated if the retention test is preceded by any of several reactivation treatments (Klein, 1972; Klein & Spear, 1970; Singh, Sakellaris, & Brush, 1971).

Issues in the Interpretation of Reactivation Effects

In principle, the explanation of how manipulations of contemporary context or prior cueing alleviate forgetting seems simple and straightforward: Because such reactivation effects apparently certify that forgetting found in the absence of the reactivation treatment is due to a failure in memory retrieval rather than to loss or dilution of the memory from storage, we may interpret such effects as facilitation in the effectiveness or in the process of memory retrieval. Accordingly, we might apply the general conceptual framework presented earlier. But the apparent simplicity is misleading. Localizing the problem as one of memory retrieval adds only a small amount of explanatory power. The vague form of the earlier conceptual framework limits its explanatory and predictive value, and although I believe this framework is not strictly tautological, it could be if misused. The great danger is that interpretations in terms of memory retrieval may often be selected because of the biases of the theorist rather than because it is demanded by the data. Thus, in addition to our consideration of mechanisms through which specific forms of reactivation effects are manifested, we should discuss issues fundamental to the interpretation of reactivation effects generally.

Cueing effects in the processing of verbal memories.   A variety of mechanisms underlying the effects of semantic cueing have been discussed by Tulving and Thompson (1973) and by Underwood (1972). In spite of the valuable guidance provided by the encoding specificity principle, it is not sufficient to explain all cueing effects, particularly extralist cueing.

In my view, a necessary component of a complete explanation of semantic cueing may be the action of the implicit associative response (IAR). There is sound evidence that whenever a human sees, hears, or says a word, associates to that word (IARs) are likely to be elicited (or perhaps emitted covertly by the subject; Underwood, 1965, 1972). One general possibility therefore is that a cue word may elicit a required list item simply because it is an IAR. This begs the question, however: What sort of discriminative processing might be responsible for the final product's being the list item rather than some other IAR of the cue word?

Because such a limited class of cue words seems effective, it might be suggested that only the "strongest" IAR will be elicited and that the benefit to recall occurs because each list word is stored together with its strongest IAR, such as its category name. Opposing this possibility, Underwood (1972) has noted that such a practice of storing a cue word together with each list item would be unreasonable; the memory load would then be doubled and additional discriminative demands would automatically be imposed when recall of the list words alone is requested. This practice might be less maladaptive and the additional processing demands might be reduced if the potential cue word stored with each list item were always a superordinate, such as the name of the category to which the item belongs. Without further assumptions, however, this would severely limit the generality of such semantic cueing effects. A similar limitation would hold if extralist cueing were primarily a relatively trivial phenomenon of guessing combined with some discriminative processing.

Does this then lead us to the conclusion that reactivation of memories in humans is an unlikely or unimportant process? I believe the answer to this is no, because the bulk of the events that may serve to reactivate memories in humans are not necessarily semantic. We have addressed elsewhere the potential for alleviation of forgetting by nonsemantic cues (see Chapter 2; Spear, 1976), and it is notable that both Underwood (1972) and Bower (1972a) have emphasized a similar possibility.

General issues in the study of memory retrieval through reactivation treatments.   It is fundamental that present techniques do not permit a clear estimate of memory storage independent of memory retrieval. The inferences that we may draw from tests of retention and forgetting are limited by this factor. If retention is measured, we can say that some retrieval has occurred and memory storage did not fail; the measurement of forgetting tells us only that the target memory was not retrieved, but it does not address the state of the storage of that target memory. If we knew the optimal conditions for memory retrieval, the occurrence of forgetting might lead to inferences concerning memory storage, but we do not know them. In combination with the difficulty in conceptualizing "failure in memory storage"—for example, does this include cases in which potential retrieval cues failed to be incorporated in that storage?—the conclusion emerging is that a great deal of explanatory power cannot be expected from a simple distinction between storage failure and retrieval failure. My preference is to assume that once established, memory storage is maintained, and to test the retrieval process together with the characteristics of active and passive memories. But this is not the only approach, and it may not be the best.

An important issue is whether reactivation treatments alter retention performance through their action on the process or effectiveness of retrieval, or whether new information acquired from the reactivation treatments can account for the entire effect. I am convinced of the merit of three general objections to the latter, "new-learning," interpretation. First, it is conventional to assess reactivation effects in comparison with the influence of the same reactivation treatment given to animals treated identically except for acquisition of the memory being tested. By itself, therefore, new learning derived from the reactivation treatment could not be a sufficient condition for explanation. Second, because many reactivation treatments meet the procedural requirements for the occurrence of extinction, any absolute effects of these treatments would be expected to yield extinction and so detract rather than add to retention performance. Third, the consequences of presenting reactivation treatments often are not consistent with the fundamental characteristics of learning; for instance, for a task in which performance is known to improve with increasing numbers of training trials, presentation of multiple reactivation treatments has no greater effect than presentation of a single reactivation treatment (Spear & Parsons, 1976). In addition to these general objections, a variety of additional criticisms may be addressed to specific applications of the new-learning explanation (Miller & Springer, 1974). Therefore, while it is obvious that each experiment must be judged on its own merits, the bulk of the evidence insists that a new-learning interpretation of reactivation treatments hardly ever is applicable and even more rarely is sufficient.

Another question of analytical importance also concerns the necessary and sufficient conditions for alleviating forgetting. The question is whether a reactivation treatment acts primarily to modify the general level of arousal of the organism or whether it is instead stimulus specific. The latter seems the more likely explanation to date, because stimuli that have similar arousal effects have not been equally effective for alleviating forgetting, whereas stimuli more similar to the components of original learning have been more likely to alleviate forgetting even though their arousal value may be less or greater than the alternative (e.g., Miller, Ott, Berk, & Springer, 1974; Spear, N.S. & Bryan, R.G., manuscript in preparation; Springer & Miller, 1972). On the other hand, it would be surprising if manipulations of general arousal per se did not alter retrieval of a memory on some occasions, although the determinants of such an effect have not been studied systematically.

Finally, it would appear that manipulations of reactivation treatments in terms of contemporary context or prior cueing can provide a useful tool for studying the characteristics of an "active" or "working" state of a memory, a concept that seems inevitable, though often in different terms (e.g., "accessible" vs. "available" memories; we have discussed this feature previously—see Spear, 1976; also see Baddeley & Hitch, 1974, for a somewhat different viewpoint). In studying the characteristics of an active memory, a basic issue is to determine the mechanisms through which a memory arrives at that state. Presumably, these would be the mechanisms responsible for alleviation of forgetting through reactivation treatments. On several occasions in this book, I have mentioned my preferred hypothesis: that the elicitation and retrieval of the target attribute of a memory depend on the arousal of a sufficient number or kind of the remaining attributes of that memory. At least two alternative mechanisms seem plausible, however. One alternative is to assume that a number of potentially appropriate memories are equally accessible prior to manipulations of contemporary context or prior cueing and that the effect of these manipulations is to enhance the individual's discrimination of which memory is to be manifested in behavior. The second alternative also would assume equal accessibility of an assortment of potentially applicable memories, but would suppose that manipulations of contemporary context or prior cueing result in the direct inhibition of all accessible memories except the appropriate one. In my view, the difficulty with both of these alternatives is that they fail to address the question of how the set of memories become established as accessible and how the "selected" memory becomes manifested in behavior (for further discussion, see Spear, 1976).

MAJOR ISSUE: MNEMONIC PREPARATION

There is abundant evidence that organisms perform operations collectively termed *mnemonic preparation* that may alter the forgetting and retention of information. Many circumstances of retention and forgetting are beyond the control of the subject. For instance, the content of what is to be remembered and the conditions under which the information is to be manifested in behavior (i.e., the conditions of contemporary context or prior cueing that may aid or impede retrieval) typically are set; there is not much an individual can do to modify these. But there is a set of devices applied by humans and animals that may either retard or enhance forgetting. This set may be viewed in terms of a continuum of "cognitive demand," with sheer frequency of exposure to acquired information at one extreme and elaborate symbolic transformations of the information at the other.

It is conventional to assume that when mnemonic preparation involves sufficient cognitive demand of a symbolic nature we must be dealing with behavior that is uniquely human. But this is not certain, and one cannot specify at precisely which point on the continuum of cognitive demand we no longer need concern ourselves with data derived from lower animals. In reality, however, there is little evidence of any kind that bears upon the issue of how mnemonic preparation is used or might be used by animals to alter their forgetting. So the bulk of our considerations with this topic concern human behavior.

We shall proceed by considering a brief review of the evidence for each of several selected classes of mnemonic preparation, including an evaluation of their effectiveness, examples of how these instances of mnemonic preparation have been conceptualized in terms of theory, and their historical relationship with earlier approaches to the study of learning and forgetting.

In terms of the last item, historical relationship, perhaps the most potent determinant of retention and forgetting throughout a century of systematic study has been degree of original learning. This variable qualifies as an instance of mnemonic preparation because a most fundamental way to increase one's degree of original learning of an episode is to engage in repetitions of that episode—in other words, practice, practice, practice. The frequency with which one is exposed to a particular set of events does not in itself guarantee better learning or retention, and factors such as the distribution and form of such repetitions may have a profound influence on their ultimate effect. But otherwise, frequency ordinarily is such an important determinant of degree of learning that we tend to use these terms interchangeably. Therefore, before discussing in more general terms the influence of degree of learning on forgetting, we shall consider briefly how frequency of repetition may influence the processing of memories.

Frequency of Repetition

In this book and elsewhere, I have taken the view that a memory consists of separable, probably independent, attributes. One of several attributes that might constitute a memory for an episode is the number of repetitions of that episode (the "frequency" attribute; see Underwood, 1969). An alternative to the multiple-component view of a memory is "strength theory." Here, the fundamental dimension of a memory is taken to be its strength, and strength is assumed to increase in cumulative fashion upon repetition of the event represented by the memory. Because of the summation feature, this view assumes that even when repetitions of the particular event may be distinguished by different contextual features, information about these features will be lost and so will the identity of each individual repetition.

This last feature of strength theory is inconsistent with a good deal of hard evidence. Certainly when a subject is given the task of learning a set of verbal items many features of the items other than their strengths can subsequently be identified by these subjects. Subjects do very well in reporting a number of orthographic and semantic characteristics of such items and can report accurately whether they had been seen or heard, and if heard, whether spoken by a man or woman. Of particular relevance to the effect of repetition, we shall see that subjects are also singularly effective in judging precisely how many repetitions had occurred for a particular verbal item (Hintzman & Block, 1971).

The appeal of strength theory has been its simplicity and the possibility that other characteristics of a memory might be derived from it. Particularly intriguing was the possibility that by comparing the relative strengths of a memory subjects might derive information as to when the events represented by that memory actually had occurred. In other words, relative recency might be derived from relative frequency. This seemed feasible under the assumption that the strength of a memory progressively wanes in regular fashion as time passes following its acquisition. This notion has not been supported, however, largely because the effects of frequency and recency have so often been found to be independent.

For example, Hintzman and Block (1971) found that subjects presented two consecutive lists in which some words were repeated on two or five occasions had no difficulty in judging quite accurately the relative frequency of items in each list and the relative recency of the items as well. Furthermore, there was no tendency to judge items in the more recent list as relatively more frequent or the more frequent items as relatively more recent. Also opposed to strength theory is this common finding in free recall: Although the initial items in a list typically have the greatest probability of being recalled correctly, much higher than for items occurring in the middle of the list, the latter are regularly judged as having occurred more recently (e.g., Underwood, 1969).

The evidence therefore suggests that strength theory, at least in this basic form, is unlikely to provide a profitable conceptualization of the effects of repetition (although a notion such as strength ultimately might be incorporated usefully within a multiple-attribute approach to conceptualizing memory). It seems appropriate, therefore, to consider the characteristics of a frequency attribute in our discussion of the fundamental influence of frequency of repetition on processing of a memory.

It may safely be concluded that subjects presented a set of verbal items will subsequently show better recall or recognition the more frequently an item is presented. It is not so clear, however, that frequency of repetition has a special effect on forgetting distinct from initial learning. The proper empirical test for this question requires comparison of the influence of repetition with and without a source of forgetting; a further requirement is to arrange for equal performance without the source of forgetting (i.e., equal degrees of learning) in spite of differing repetitions, and this is a difficult but not insurmountable problem.

There are indications that frequency of repetition may influence recognition more than recall, but this question is not amenable to direct testing until equivalent tests of recognition and recall have been achieved (cf. Light, Kimble, & Pellegrino, 1975).

Repetition and retention.   The ubiquity of the benefit from repetition of words presented for recall is reflected in this statement by Underwood, Zimmerman, and Freund (1971): "That recall will be a direct function of the number of presentations (i.e., frequency of occurrence) is taken for granted" (p. 160). This relationship applies consistently when the number of words presented exceed the memory span and immediate recall is requested. The effect is so general that we need not elaborate on it, although we shall discuss it again when considering the important influence of the distribution of such repetitions.

The benefit of repetitions is not inevitable, however, and the source of the benefit is not always so clear. The following three cases illustrate this point:

1. Within the Brown–Peterson paradigm for testing short-term retention, the more frequent the repetition of items prior to the retention interval, the better the retention performance, whether the items are trigrams or units of three words or units of five words. Nevertheless, it remains unclear whether the effect of the repetitions is different with a source of forgetting than without or, in other words, whether repetitions affect forgetting or only original learning (Fuchs & Melton, 1974; Hellyer, 1962; Underwood, 1964). The statement also applies to short-term retention in terms of recognition of numbers (Wickelgren & Norman, 1971).

2. When a sequence of units is presented for later recall or recognition and certain items are repeated, the benefit from the repetition seems to be greater when it occurs earlier in the sequence. Again, however, it is unclear whether this benefit is in retention or original learning (Deutsch, 1975; Lewis & Bartz, 1970).

3. Finally, there is some indication that repetition can be harmful to retention under certain circumstances. Hall and Pierce (1974) found that when subjects were instructed explicitly to repeat items in a free-recall list, forgetting by children over a 90-minute period was increased (forgetting by adults was unaffected by this instruction). This is consistent with the impairment in recall (but not in recognition) often found when adult subjects are required to fill the interitem intervals with experimenter-prescribed forms of repetition of items (Glanzer, 1972; Glanzer & Meinzer, 1967). The effect on forgetting may be unique to subject-generated repetitions; with variation in the number of repetitions of words presented in a long list, percentage forgetting 1 day later (relative to

immediately after presentation) is less for items more frequently repeated (Underwood, Zimmerman, & Freund, 1971; this effect has not been maintained over a 7-day retention interval).

Finally, because frequency of repetition may aid in discriminating among memories (more theoretically: may provide a useful discriminative attribute), it is of interest to determine the characteristics of the retention of such frequency information following a source of forgetting. Underwood and his associates (1971) found that judgments of how frequently a particular word had been repeated declined in accuracy over a 7-day interval: As the retention interval lengthened, frequency estimates were decreased for words repeated often and were increased for words seldom or never repeated. The discriminative value of a frequency attribute therefore may be expected to decrease following an interpolated retention interval.

The conclusion that emerges is that simple, physical repetition may improve retention under some circumstances, but this is not an inevitable relationship. The limitations of repetition for this purpose will be reemphasized in our later discussion of rehearsal and levels of processing.

Degree of learning.   Across a broad range of circumstances, it has been verified that the higher the degree of learning of verbal materials, the less the forgetting. In other words, the better the retention in the absence of a source of forgetting, the less the decrement caused by the source of forgetting. This generalization holds when the source of forgetting is a retention interval, probably also holds when the source of forgetting is retroactive or proactive interference, and may be applicable as well when the source of forgetting is abnormal physiological functioning (e.g., a brain concussion). This relationship is well established and needs no further elaboration (see Spear, 1970; Underwood, 1964, 1966a, 1972; Underwood & Keppel, 1963). Although it is less clear in terms of basic conditioning with animals, there is substantial evidence that sources of forgetting such as amnesic treatments are less effective the higher the original degree of learning (see Chapter 6).

Evidence of this sort implies that degree of learning may provide an index of how resistant a memory will be to forgetting. In view of the sensitivity of forgetting to events prior to and accompanying the retention test, however, this approach may be useful only if it can be shown that degree of learning influences the effect of a reactivation treatment. Some preliminary evidence is consistent with the latter, although a final decision on this matter would be premature.

Finally, it is notable that a direct relationship between degree of learning and retention is not inevitable. The opposite relationship might be expected under some conditions of basic conditioning (Spear, 1973), and evidence of an opposite relationship has been found under certain circumstances of verbal memory processing. Runquist and his colleagues have found less forgetting over a 7-day interval for items given the fewest repetitions and having the lowest probability of immediate recall; perhaps, they suggest, this is because very weak items are discriminated more readily from alternative incorrect items (Runquist & Joinson, 1968; Runquist & Snyder, 1969).

Rehearsal

Rehearsal is conventionally identified as a means by which human subjects may increase symbolically the number of repetitions of an episode. Rehearsal may also be used to bridge a retention interval: Continuous repetition from the time of memory storage until the retention test permits errorless recall. Such continuous rehearsal seems unlikely under most circumstances, however, and once the chain of rehearsal is broken, we must account for how it might begin anew. Therefore, our concern with rehearsal at this point is the benefit it may bring to retention through increased repetition prior to a source of forgetting.

In the case of recognition, rote rehearsal has been identified as an effective means for improving accuracy (Woodward, Bjork, & Jongeward, 1973). In terms of application of the frequency theory of recognition, furthermore, rehearsal has been assigned a basic role in the establishment of the differential in frequency that leads subsequently to accurate recognition (Underwood, Reichardt, & Zimmerman, 1973; Wallace, 1972).

In the case of recall, there seems little doubt that rote repetition through rehearsal provides a benefit to retention after short intervals (Atkinson & Shiffrin, 1968; Estes, 1973). After long intervals, this benefit from repetition is less certain, and it is under these circumstances that we are led to consider different kinds or qualities of rehearsal. Indeed, it has become evident that differences in the opportunity for repetitive rehearsal may not influence retention measured after the interpolation of other tasks or a relatively long retention interval (Craik & Watkins, 1973; Light, 1974; Meunier, Kestner, Meunier, & Ritz, 1974; Woodward, Bjork, & Jongeward, 1973).

There are indications that the kind or quality of rehearsal used by subjects may differ depending on whether they anticipate an immediate or a delayed test of retention. Among subjects presented consecutively with a number of lists for free recall, some were informed about a later test to be given following the presentation and the immediate testing of all of the lists. When the later test was given, the subjects who had been forewarned had better recall than unwarned subjects (although this was accomplished at the expense of their poorer recall on the immediate test; Bellezza & Walker, 1974). Similarly, it is now clear that when subjects are presented a series of lists for free recall, the manner in which they rehearse the terminal items of each list (which ordinarily are forgotten rapidly) may enhance the long-term retention of those items. Mazuryk (1974) found that subjects given special instructions about how to process terminal items showed better long-term recall of those items, though again at the cost of poorer immediate recall. Tests with the Brown–Peterson paradigm for assessing short-term retention have shown a similar effect. Among subjects presented sets of five common nouns and tested after intervals ranging between 0 and 18 seconds, those given a particular set of rehearsal instructions ("form meaningful connections among the five words") showed significantly better retention then other subjects. The effect on test performance was greater after long intervals than after short ones, indicating a genuine effect on forgetting, not degree of learning. Finally, beyond the differential effect of rehearsal instructions on retention after short and long intervals, there are indications that if subjects are informed in advance of the length of the retention interval they may spontaneously adopt appropriate rehearsal mechanisms to optimize retention (Hinrichs & Grunke, 1975).

A major implication of this work, as suggested earlier, is that rote repetition is not the most important determinant of recall. This implication is supported by further evidence. For example, during the later trials of a multitrial free-recall task recall does not benefit from additional rehearsal repetitions; a similar lack of benefit from rehearsal repetitions can be found under some circumstances for the first few items in such a list (Einstein, Pellegrino, Mondani, & Battig, 1974; Jacoby 1973a). Furthermore, items treated so they stand out from others in the list (as in the Von Restorff effect) may be twice as likely to be recalled as comparable normal items even though they are rehearsed no more often (Einstein et al., 1974). A second implication is that some deficiencies in the processing of memories may be alleviated by applying proper rehearsal techniques. Indeed, it has become clear that age-related deficits in recall among preschool children and among retardates may be traced to their failure to apply effective rehearsal strategies, and these deficits may be reduced if these subjects learn to apply such strategies (e.g., Ellis, 1970; Flavell, 1970; Ornstein & Liberty, 1973; Winters & Ward, 1975).

Distribution of Repetitions

Since Jost inferred from Ebbinghaus' data that learning might be enhanced if practice were spaced (Jost, 1897, cited by Hintzman, 1974), it has seemed possible that one effective mode of mnemonic preparation might be to achieve some optimal distribution of study. Two phenomena indicate that this would be an effective strategy for enhancing retention of verbal materials. The first is the enhanced retention found following long intervals when, under special circumstances, lists of verbal units have been acquired under distributed rather than massed practice. The second is the dramatic benefit found for the free recall of repeated items when those repetitions are distributed rather than massed. It is useful to examine these phenomena in more detail.

Reduced forgetting of a list of verbal items following distributed practice. When a list of paired verbal units is learned after the acquisition of similar but conflicting memories—that is, when learning proceeds in spite of negative transfer from prior learning—subsequent forgetting of that list is slower with more widely distributed learning trials (Keppel, 1964; Underwood, Keppel, & Schulz, 1962; Wickelgren, 1972).

An experiment by Keppel (1964) provides an example. Subjects practiced a list of paired verbal items for eight trials, then were tested for retention after 1, 8, or 29 days. For "massed" practice, all eight trials were given on the same day with a 4-second intertrial interval; for "distributed" practice, two trials were given each day for four consecutive days. Prior to learning this list, each subject had learned three conflicting lists having the same stimuli but different responses, which probably contributed to the somewhat poorer learning found under the distributed condition.

In spite of their relatively poorer learning, recall by subjects in the distributed condition was nearly five times as great as in the massed condition when tested 24 hours after the final learning trial. This advantage was maintained over longer intervals: After 8 days, retention declined relatively little in the distributed condition, remaining four times better than that found after only a 1-day interval for subjects given massed training; 29 days after learning, retention among subjects given distributed practice remained about twice as effective as that shown only 24 hours after learning under the massed condition. While the magnitude of Keppel's results can probably be attributed in part to the lessening of proactive interference in the distributed condition owing to the subject's having acquired the prior conflicting lists under a very different trial distribution (massed practice; cf. Underwood & Ekstrand, 1966, 1967), and although distribution of practice may have much less influence on forgetting if proactive interference is absent, these results are notable nevertheless because it is so rare to find variables that so profoundly alter forgetting when the source of the forgetting is a retention interval.

Spaced versus massed repetitions within a list.   Repetitions of words in a list to be recalled are far more effective if they are spaced than if they are presented in massed fashion (between *spaced* repetitions, other items, unusual activities, or extraordinary long intervals are interpolated; no such events are interpolated between *massed* repetitions). Extensive study of this "spacing effect," inspired by the initial work of Melton (e.g., 1967), has shown it to be a phenomenon of remarkable generality. The spacing effect occurs whether the list items are words, nonword letter combinations, or pictures, whether they are single items or presented as paired associates or even as sentences, and whether the test requires recall or recognition. Underwood (1970) observed the spacing effect in each of five diverse experiments, which included an assortment of tasks, either children or adults as subjects, and different kinds of interpolated events to provide spacing of items. The regular occurrence of the spacing effect among these experiments prompted Underwood to suggest that "the very consistency of the results across conditions and materials makes theory spinning difficult" (1970, pp. 579–580). While the circumstances of this phenomenon do not permit a clear separation of effects on retention from those on learning, the importance of the spacing effect as a form of mnemonic preparation requires its consideration here.

The importance of the spacing effect for theory may be illustrated in terms of three anomalies that this effect creates for certain views and phenomena of memory processing. First, the spacing effect opposes the principle of better retention for more recent events. Holding constant the time between the last repetition of an item and testing, the spacing effect implies that the influence of the prior repetition is greater with a long than with a short interval between its occurrence and testing. Second, because spaced and massed items are equated in terms of total study time permitted, the spacing effect provides an exception to the general rule that the amount learned is a simple increasing function of the time devoted to study (the "total-time law"; see Cooper & Pantel, 1967; Underwood, 1970). Third, the spacing effect is in opposition to the general finding that physically unusual items within a list yield enhanced recall (the "Von Restorff effect"). Even when massed repetitions are quite rare relative to spaced repetitions, the former has less effect on recall; indeed, the repetition may be barely noticed when massed (Hintzman, 1974; Hintzman & Block, 1970).

A variety of explanations for the spacing effect have been proposed and tested, but elaboration of the consequences of these tests is beyond our present intentions (particularly insightful reviews of this material may be found in chapters by Hintzman, 1974, 1976). It is notable, however, that among the more promising explanations of the spacing effect are suggestions that an attentional deficit is associated with massed repetitions (Hintzman, 1974; Underwood, 1969, 1970). An explanation in terms of differential attention or habituation to massed and spaced presentations would address the processing of memories in only an indirect manner, and hence would be of relatively little interest for our concern with retention and forgetting. Present indications, however, are that habituation or attentional mechanisms are unlikely to account for the entire spacing effect (Elmes, Sanders, & Dowel, 1973; Hintzman, Summers, Eki, & Moore, 1975; Shaughnessy, Zimmerman, & Underwood, 1972). Moreover, theories with this view would appear to have particular difficulty accounting for the "lag effects" (better retention the more widely spaced the repetitions) that are found when huge lags of 30 to 40 interpolated items between repetitions yield differences in recall (Crowder, 1976; Glenberg, 1976).

Understanding of the spacing effect may be expected to clarify a variety of instances of mnemonic preparation.

Organization and Transformation

A nearly universal belief about learning and retention is that effectiveness in retrieving stored information depends on the organization of that information in storage. This is not the only plausible model. For example, one might suppose that only a limited amount of stored information may be held in an accessible state at any given moment, so to ensure that the desired information becomes accessible for retrieval one must force a great deal of new information into the inaccessible state, thus "pushing out" the required stored memories into accessibility. Such a model is unlikely to be adopted or even acceptable, however, because it is not consistent with our own experience or with ancient traditions of how best to process memories. As long as 2,000 years ago, mnemonic preparation through organizational schemes constituted a practical art passed on by educators as one of the important subareas of rhetoric. This "art" continued to be practiced and implemented widely among most educated persons until the past century or so.

Among the several varieties of mnemonic techniques practiced (for a description and analysis of some of these, see Bower, 1970;1972b), the origin of the "method of loci" was attributed by Cicero to the poet Simonides of Ceos, Greece, several hundred years earlier (Yates, 1966). The gist of this familiar technique is to align the sequence of events to be remembered with a sequence of very familiar events, such as objects regularly seen as one progresses on a familiar path through one's home. After achieving identification of each to-be-remembered event with one of the familiar objects, retrieval of the critical events in sequence may be achieved by mentally retracing the familiar pathway. Most other techniques similarly combine imagery and well-established memories in achieving optimal mnemonic preparation.

Such techniques must be viewed in proper perspective. First, they are not inevitably effective, and like learning in general, relative success in implementing them may depend on unspecified individual differences among subjects. Second, organizational techniques may be successful primarily because of the increased quantity of semantic or rote processing that accompanies implementation of the schemes, not necessarily because of the particular scheme of organization employed. Third, the benefit from certain reorganizational schemes may be restricted to certain aspects of memory processing while not affecting or impairing others; for example, some mnemonic aids may enhance learning but impair retention (see Postman & Burns, 1973).

Yet it is obvious that organizational and transformational modifications of materials to be learned are implemented by apparently all normal humans. One does not need a great deal of insight to determine that even a college sophomore in a verbal learning experiment is by no means merely an associative mechanism; rather, adult humans actively process the materials to be learned, sometimes reorganizing, sometimes transforming, and often elaborating them in terms of other memories. The information that has been gained through scientific investigation addresses the question of whether such activities are in fact fundamental to mnemonic preparation or whether, at the opposite extreme, these activities are merely adjunctive epiphenomena of the learning and retention that would occur regardless. We shall discuss some of this evidence.

Aspects of reorganization of learned materials.   We alluded earlier to the propensity for subjects to reorder items presented for free recall. For the most part, this organizational operation proceeds in an orderly and predictable manner and is sufficiently familiar so that we need not elaborate its characteristics and implications (for further discussion of theory and facts concerning this topic, see Mandler, 1967; Tulving, 1962, 1964, 1968, 1972). A useful illustration of this behavior is provided by a brief experiment reported by Underwood (1964). Subjects were presented with four lists of 16 words. Two of the lists included sets of 4 conceptually similar words (such as *France, Germany, England, Spain, dog, cat, horse, cow*), and two included words that were not obviously related to each other; the lists were presented in ABBA fashion.

Recall after a single presentation was of course better for the lists with high conceptual similarity: An average of about 15 items each were correctly recalled for these lists, compared to 11 items each for the lists of unrelated words; nearly one-third of the subjects correctly recalled all the words in the former lists, and only 3% of the subjects accomplished this for the lists of unrelated items. The manner in which the conceptually similar items were recalled provides the data that most starkly illustrate the human disposition for organizing verbal materials. In this case, subjects organize their recall around the categories of the words presented, even though the exemplars of each concept had been mixed among the other words when presented (i.e., the concept members were not presented contiguously). First, failure to show evidence for retention of a conceptual category was found on less than 1% of possible occurrences. Typically, all four items within a concept were given before any items of another concept, and no subjects gave more than four or less than three members of any recalled concept. Organizational features of recall are also apparent in the subjects' restriction in recall to the instances in a concept that actually appeared in the list: For every 73 correct responses, only about one intrusion occurred (and about 90% of these intrusions were members of one of the four concepts represented in the list; see Chapter 4 regarding the selector mechanism).

Does the reorganization engaged in by subjects facilitate recall? There seems to be little doubt that it does under some circumstances. Tulving (1965) compared recall of a list of words ordered in accordance with the output of subjects recalling that list in an earlier experiment and recall of the same list ordered in approximately the opposite manner. With a new set of subjects, he found better recall when the items were presented in the order that had resulted from reorganization by the previous subjects. Generally, reorganization of items recalled has been cited as a major mechanism for overcoming our limit capacities for memory storage (e.g., Mandler, 1967; Miller, 1956; Tulving, 1968, 1972). Yet discussions by both Postman (1972) and Wood (1972) suggest that experimental support for the mnemonic value of such organizational activity may have been overestimated in value. The principal doubts that remain are whether such organizational devices are necessary to overcome our limited capacity for processing memories and whether they may be applied to relatively new materials as effectively as to previously overlearned, tightly cohesive units such as conceptual categories.

Will reorganization of to-be-learned materials influence how rapidly they are forgotten? A general prediction has been difficult. Certain conceivable consequences of organizational devices may be beneficial, but others may be detrimental to retention following a source of forgetting. For example, regrouping of items by the subject may be accomplished in such a way as to make them less susceptible to interference from prior or subsequent learning. On the other hand, subjects not only can identify the idiosyncratic units they apply in their reorganization but also label them (Dong & Kintsch, 1968), and if the identification is not provided by the experimenter at the retention test, it might be subject to forgetting in the same way as list items. Similarly, the processing needed for retention of the idiosyncratic organizational units might preclude retention of list items following a source of forgetting.

There is limited evidence that organizational aids will facilitate retention following a source of forgetting even when the aids themselves are not completely available at the retention test. Such evidence provided by Barrett and Ekstrand (1975) indicates that when organization of a set of paired words is improved by the application of a conceptual rule, less forgetting of the pairs occurs over a 7-day interval than without such organization. Furthermore, this benefit to retention occurred even though subjects were provided at the retention test with only partial information concerning the conceptual rule. Notably, however, these investigators later tested the effect of certain organizational strategies and a mnemonic device (peg-word technique) on the free recall of words, and they found that forgetting over a 7-day interval was not affected by these organizational aids (Barrett, Maier, Ekstrand & Pellegrino, 1975).

Strand (1975) has produced other experimental evidence that another type of organization device may serve to lessen forgetting after intervals of several days. She found that later retention of words was significantly improved when subjects organized them during learning in terms of their physical attributes. This benefit to retention after a 5- or 7-day interval could not be attributed to differences in degree of original learning. This benefit was not found in terms of all measures of retention, however.

There is little clear evidence regarding whether organizational devices might facilitate retention following sources of forgetting other than a retention interval. By extrapolation, one might suppose that the reduction in retroactive interference produced by semantic cueing (Tulving & Psotka, 1971) may depend on the particular organizational scheme adopted by the subject during original learning. On the other hand, evidence and discussion by Postman (1972) and Wood (1972) that forgetting attributable to retroactive interference might be unaffected or even increased by the application of certain organizational schemes.

Transforming individual items.   The consequences of transforming individual verbal units through techniques such as reorganizing the order of letters has been studied for its effect on learning, but not with regard to the consequences of a source of forgetting. One form of such transformations has been termed *stimulus selection* and another *response coding*.

Humans and animals alike have been found to employ stimulus selection to increase the economy of processing a multicomponent stimulus. For instance, because a discriminative stimulus need only be recognized and not reproduced, subjects regularly select the most salient or most meaningful aspect of the nominal stimulus for use as the functional stimulus and devote little or no processing to its remaining components (Lawrence, 1963; Richardson, 1972a,b, 1976; Rudy, 1974; Underwood, 1963). It is unclear how forgetting might be affected by stimulus selection. To the extent that the hierarchy of salience or meaningfulness among the components of a stimulus item might be influenced by a source of forgetting, we might expect stimulus selection to be accompanied by a retention deficit. There are indications that forgetting over a long interval may be enhanced when the subject's interpretation (recoding) of stimulus items is relatively unstable (Hasher & Johnson, 1975).

A retention deficit might also be expected to accompany the other major case of item transformation: response coding (Podd & Spear, 1967; Underwood & Erlebacher, 1965). It is commonly observed that subjects rearrange the components of a response to form a more meaningful unit (e.g., the response *esmok* may be coded as "smoke" or the response emsuo as "mouse"). An equally common observation is that subjects may engage in such transformations to the actual detriment of their recall accuracy, owing to the difficulty in decoding when the original response is required (Underwood & Keppel, 1963b). If the decoding operation were impaired further by a source of forgetting, we would expect more forgetting when such response coding is applied than when it is not.

Elaborate transformations.   Devices of mnemonic preparation involving relatively elaborate strategies for the storage and retrieval of memories were mentioned earlier. There is no doubt that such strategies, which seem to guide "the overall conduct of the subject's search through memory" (Bower, 1972b, p. 111), can be very helpful in facilitating immediate recall. The common feature of such strategies is to represent items to be learned and certain extralist "peg words" used to guide their organization as visual images, particularly visual images in which these two kinds of items interact. As an illustration of the power of such a procedure, Wallace, Turner, and Perkins (1957, cited by Wood, 1967) presented subjects with pairs of words to be learned, with instructions to form visual images linking each pair. As the investigators increased the number of pairs in each list from 25 to 700, a remarkable capacity for recall was shown with this technique: For example, recall of a list containing 500 pairs was 99% accurate. Before discussing the influence of such a strategy on retention, we must consider briefly the consequences of such imagery instructions for immediate recall.

Some potential reasons for the effectiveness of imagery instructions on immediate recall may apply to considerations of their potential influence on forgetting. For example, perhaps by transforming verbal items into visual images sources of proactive or retroactive interference from similar verbal items may be alleviated. There is at present only mixed support for such a possibility, however (Nelson, Borden, & Wheeler, 1975; Nelson & Brooks, 1973). Another technique for eliminating sources of interference or reducing their effect might be to use images so bizarre as to be associated with relatively few conflicting memories. A series of experiments by Wollen and his associates indicate, however, that bizarreness is not a critical feature of this type of mnemonic preparation.

Noting that previous investigations had tended to confound bizarreness with the extent of imaginal interaction among the items to be associated, Wollen, Weber, and Lowry (1972) used an experimental design that separated these factors. They found that recall was better the greater the imaginal interaction among to-be-remembered items, but the relative bizarreness of the images used by subjects seemed to make no difference in recall. In a subsequent experiment, subjects were presented 48 pairs of nouns for recall. By a prearranged signal, they were instructed which pairs should be learned by forming bizarre images and which by common images (the effectiveness of this instructional variable was confirmed by a technique involving interrogation of the subjects and independent judges to assess bizarreness of images). Even though subjects used nearly twice as much time to form bizarre images as to form common ones, recall was only 65% accurate when using the former and 68% accurate with the latter. It would appear that the use of images that are bizarre carries no special advantage among the populations tested (college students), although it remains possible that some benefit exists for highly practiced subjects such as professional mnemonists.

The few experiments that have tested the influence of imagery on forgetting have failed to observe such an influence. Bower (1972c) presented subjects with five lists of 20 pairs of concrete nouns (e.g., *dog–bicycle*). Recall of each response item (e.g., *bicycle*) was tested upon presentation of each stimulus item (e.g., *dog*), both immediately after presentation of each list and after all five lists had been presented and tested. Subjects instructed to form their associations by "imagining a visual scene or mental picture in which these two objects are interacting" (Bower, 1972, p. 66) were nearly twice as accurate in their immediate recall as subjects not given these instructions. For the delayed test, this advantage was maintained but was no greater, suggesting that forgetting caused by the delay between learning and test was unaffected by the use of imagery during learning. A careful set of experiments by Hasher, Riebman, and Wren (1976) leads to the same conclusion. In two experiments involving several kinds of imagery instructions and separate tests given immediately and one or two weeks later, forgetting rate was found to be unaffected by imagery instructions.

Mnemonic Preparation for Special Forms of Testing

Jacoby (1973) tested systematically whether different forms of mnemonic preparation are particularly suited for different forms of the retention test or, in other words, whether test performance may be affected by how subjects expect to be tested. His results yielded an affirmative answer; for example, subjects expecting to be tested for free (uncued) recall of a list of 56 uncategorized words performed less well on cued-recall and recognition tests than subjects who expected the latter tests.

In spite of these results from Jacoby's thorough study, it would be premature to exaggerate the importance of "test-appropriate study strategies" as determinants of retention. Postman, Kruesi, and Regan (1975) had subjects learn paired-associate lists by either recognition (multiple choice) or cued recall (the proper response must be given when its stimulus occurs). The lists included single letters as stimuli and four-letter adjectives as responses, and the criterion of learning was one perfect recitation of the list. Procedures were selected to yield equal rates of learning for the two learning conditions. Seven days later, subjects were tested with either the same procedure used to establish original learning or the alternative (e.g., half the subjects who had learned under cued recall were tested for recognition and the other half were tested for cued recall).

The results gave no indication that learning by a special procedure, and hence probably expectation of the same procedure at the retention test, yielded better retention in terms of that procedure. Specifically, testing procedure during learning had no influence on retention, and there was no interaction between learning and retention test procedures. Postman and his associates note that other studies have also failed to find differences in mnemonic preparation (encoding) when subjects are led to anticipate a recall test rather than a recognition test (or vice versa). Perhaps the conclusion of Postman and his associates may have been more consistent with that of Jacoby (1973) had the 7-day retention interval not been included or if the former had compared recognition with free recall rather than cued recall. However, a firm conclusion regarding preparation for special forms of testing must await further study.

Another important discovery by Postman and his associates warrants mention before turning to another topic. These experimenters found that regardless of the learning conditions, retention after 7 days was dramatically more effective when measured by recognition than when measured by cued recall. Overall, cued recall yielded nearly 40% fewer correct responses than recognition. Seven days after learning by either the cued-recall or the multiple-choice techniques, average recognition performance was 9.18 out of 10 items given correctly, nearly perfect; subjects given the cued-recall test gave an average of 5.75 of the 10 items correctly. Because of the care taken by Postman and his colleagues to equate rate and degree of original learning, this is the clearest demonstration to my knowledge that recognition is more resistant to this source of forgetting (a long retention interval) than cued recall (for an overview of the characteristics of recall vs. recognition, see Brown, 1976).

Directed ("Intentional") Forgetting

One likely form of mnemonic preparation is to sort out useful memories from among those that are no longer accurate or those that interfere with the retrieval of more useful memories. Similar screening of information has been identified in terms of physiological and behavioral mechanisms operating at both the receptor level and afferently. These mechanisms may determine what information is processed to the level of perception. Yet much of the information remaining probably need not or should not be processed thoroughly as memories, so it is reasonable to look for additional screening procedures at this stage. Such a mechanism might be termed *intentional forgetting* (Bjork, 1972).

Unlike the similar Freudian mechanisms of suppression and repression, our present topic is not restricted to information of an emotional nature. Intentional forgetting seems to be more aptly considered as a special case of an organizational mechanism, although because of its singular significance I am treating it separately from those discussed in the previous section.

There is little doubt that intentional forgetting can readily be tested under experimental circumstances and is a robust phenomenon found in retention of both individual units and complete sentences (Geiselman, 1975). We therefore may be brief with respect to these issues.

Procedures and basic effects.   The basic paradigm for studying intentional forgetting is to accompany some of a list of verbal units with a prearranged signal indicating that these units are to be forgotten; for the other verbal units, a different signal indicates that they are to be remembered. To properly exclude contaminating effects on sensory or elementary perceptual processes, it is necessary to withhold presentation of the "forget" or "remember" instructions until *after* presentation of the verbal units in question. The length of this interval between the occurrence of the verbal unit and the processing instruction determines the effect of that instruction on retention, which is a good indication that important processing of a verbal unit occurs following its presentation (an example of such an effect may be found in Jongeward, Woodward, & Bjork, 1975, and in Timmins, 1974).

Items signaled to be forgotten generally are unlikely to be recalled. This fact is not due to a general damping of memory processing, however; the accompanying items, signaled to be remembered, are recalled as well or better than when no items are to be forgotten (for exceptions apparently attributable to special procedures, see Reitman, Malin, Bjork, & Higman, 1973, and Roediger & Crowder, 1972). At the same time, *recognition* of items signaled to be forgotten is only slightly impaired, if at all. This suggests that some attributes of the memory for such units are spared by the "forget" instruction, although the attributes spared are unlikely to support recall.

There is ample indication that intentional forgetting may serve to reduce the adverse effects of other sources of forgetting on to-be-remembered items. Bjork (1972) has reviewed evidence demonstrating that proactive interference of to-be-remembered items is reduced when potentionally interfering items, or entire lists of items, are cued to be forgotten. Similarly, the results of Reitman and his associates (1973) indicate that retroactive interference from items signaled to be forgotten is dramatically less than that obtained if these items are signaled to be remembered.

The most promising explanations as to how intentional forgetting is accomplished emphasize two factors: the differential in the extent and manner of rehearsal devoted to "remember" and "forget" items, and the effects of the separate classification or differential treatment that aids in the discrimination of "remember" and "forget" items. One consequence of the latter factor is to reduce the functional similarity between "remember" and "forget" items and hence to reduce the interference that the "forget" items otherwise might exert on retention of the "remember" items (and vice versa). For the former point, direct manipulation of the duration of processing allowed for particular items following instructions to forget or remember them indicates that the probability of recalling a "forget" word is proportional to the length of time that word was processed between its presentation and the "forget" instruction. The time allowed for processing after this instruction does not affect recall, suggesting that no special processing is applied to this case of forgetting.

Collectively, the evidence favors these two explanations over alternatives based on selective retrieval, output interference during recall, or momentary suppression of to-be-forgotten items.

Levels of Processing

Concerning rehearsal, I concluded earlier that recall is often more dependent on the manner in which a verbal unit is rehearsed than on the time or number of rote repetitions devoted to that rehearsal. "Levels of processing" incorporates a similar view toward analyzing the determinants of retention; actually, the level of processing is the fundamental unit of that analysis. In this view, the manner in which verbal units are perceived and analyzed when first presented determines subsequent retention and is a more important determinant than duration of the perception or analysis. Craik and Lockhart (1972) presented the first specific explication of this view, beginning with the principle that a memory representing an episode is essentially a by-product of perceptual processing. "Perceptual processing" is taken to be the continuum of stages or levels at which stimuli are analyzed by the perceiver (see also Sutherland, 1968; Treisman, 1964). The continuum begins at one extreme with initial detection and discrimination of fundamental sensory features, and at the other extreme is the extraction of meaning, or "semantic analysis." This continuum is characterized as one of "depth," with elaborate semantic analysis the deepest. According to the levels-of-processing view, retention depends on the depth of one's analysis—not speed of processing or total time spent processing at one particular level, but the most advanced (deepest) level of analysis attained after sensory reception.

Empirical support for this view has been produced by encouraging subjects to process verbal units at different levels, without explicitly asking that the verbal units be learned or even suggesting that subsequent recall might be requested. To induce a relatively deep level of processing, subjects might be asked, for example, "Is this word animate or inanimate?" or "Is this word an instance of the concept 'biological'?" To induce processing at lesser depths, subjects might be asked, "Does this word rhyme with *book*?" or "How many consonants are in this word?" Recall is better for words processed in terms of answers to the former questions, that is, at the deeper level (e.g., Hyde & Jenkins, 1969, 1973; Johnston & Jenkins, 1971).

Such an effect has been found often, under diverse circumstances. For example, recall of sentences is better when subjects have judged them in terms of semantic or affective content than when judgments about synactical or structural characteristics are required; similarly, a sentence is more likely to be recalled if subjects are asked about its logical relationship with a previous sentence than if they are merely asked whether or not it makes sense (Bobrow & Bower, 1969; Mistler-Lachman, 1975). Of particular interest here, Treisman and Tuxworth (1974) found that although immediate recall of sentences did not differ whether subjects had made phonemic or semantic judgments about them, delayed recall (after a number of sentences had been presented) was better when the semantic judgments were required. This suggests an effect of level of processing on forgetting.

The "levels-of-processing" position provides a general alternative to the "memory stores" position. The latter view, which assumes separate memory stores involving different kinds of processing of memories (e.g., short term and long term), has a number of weaknesses (see Chapter 4; see also Craik & Lockhart, 1972; Murdock, 1974; Wickelgren, 1975a,b). The levels-of-processing framework also includes some weaknesses, identified in a thoughtful review by Postman (1975). The basic shortcomings concern lack of predictive precision and operational means for indexing depth. Certainly depth must be defined independently of the measure of retention (manipulations of depth of processing that affect recall rarely have a similar effect on recognition).

There is also the question of whether temporally determined levels of processing really are different from temporally determined stores of memory. However, evidence has emerged in support of a clearer independence between depth of processing, which is the critical parameter of the levels view, and duration of processing, which is the critical parameter of the stores view. Gardiner (1974) found better recall for words semantically rather than structurally processed, even though the average duration of time required was significantly less for the semantic processing.

Generally, the view emphasizing levels of processing has provided a valuable and stimulating tool for the analysis of retention and forgetting. It should be remembered that this view was introduced by Craik and Lockhart as a general framework and not as a complete theory, which accounts for its apparent limitations. Work conducted within this framework has resulted in unexpected phenomena of potential importance; for example, Craik and Tulving (1975) found that regardless of type or duration of processing, verbal units for which subjects gave an affirmative answer were better recognized than those associated with a negative answer. Within this framework, we should continue to find new ideas introduced and previous ideas clarified. In this respect, a compelling clarification and extension of the levels-of-processing approach is found in a chapter by Lockhart, Craik, and Jacoby (1976).

Mnemonic Preparation in Animals

It is unlikely that a literal meaning of the term *mnemonic preparation* is applicable for animals. By the same reasoning, the literal meaning may be inappropriate for humans; it would appear that it is rare for humans to be completely aware of the future consequences they hope to achieve from the use of many aspects of mnemonic preparation. Yet it seems quite feasible that animals might employ variations in duration, frequency, or distribution of exposures to certain episodes to promote retention that might be especially adaptive. There is little clear evidence that these variables do influence forgetting in animals, but systematic tests are rare. Some evidence, however, encourages the view that aspects of mnemonic preparation warrant study with animals and that their understanding may be expected to enrich our knowledge of the biological foundations of the processing of memories.

In addition to subject-induced variation in basic physical parameters such as frequency or duration of exposure, some forms of mnemonic preparation may be quite similar in animals and humans. An example is stimulus selection (Rudy, 1974; Wagner, 1969). Other forms, such as the "rehearsal" studied in rabbits by Wagner, Rudy, and Whitlow (1973; see Chapter 5), probably have underlying behavioral and physiological mechanisms that are quite different from those found among humans, especially with regard to the human's processing of verbal materials. Nevertheless, to the extent that the rehearsal studied by Wagner and his associates involves posttrial memory processing that is separable from the more automatic consolidation process, this behavior holds obvious significance as an aspect of mnemonic preparation in animals.

It seems likely that forgetting by animals may be lessened when training trials are more widely distributed, but again, there is little evidence to support this (Chiszar & Spear, 1969; Kessler, 1976). A close analog to the spacing effect has been found, however, with apes. Robbins & Bush (1973) tested two gorillas, two orangutans, and two chimpanzees on a series of discrimination tasks. The three trials given for a particular discrimination problem occurred in fairly rapid succession (massed), or additional problems were interpolated between trials (spaced). There were two major results. First, the spacing effect occurred: Subjects who had unrelated problems interpolated between the first and second trials performed better on the third (test) trial than subjects for whom the first and second trials were massed. Second, the relative benefit of having had wider spacing between the first and second trials was greater when the subjects also had wide spacing between the second and third trials. In other words, the effect of trial distribution (between Trials 1 and 2) depended on length of the retention interval (between Trials 2 and 3). A similar interaction has been reported for short-term retention of verbal materials in humans (Glenberg, 1976; Peterson, 1966; Peterson, Hillner, & Saltzman, 1962), for delayed alternation with rats (Roberts, 1974b) and for delayed response with monkeys (Medin, 1975).

A final, apparent form of mnemonic preparation in animals must remain unspecified as to its foundations, but is particularly exciting. Following massive numbers of retention tests with a retention interval as the source of forgetting, test performance is improved selectively after relatively long intervals. D'Amato (1973; also see D'Amato & Cox, 1976) has found that with the accumulation of literally years of experience with a delayed-matching-to-sample task, the rate of forgetting over intervals of a few minutes declined independently of trivial performance factors. In other words, retention performance following a source of forgetting (retention interval) is more affected by this extensive experience than performance without the source of forgetting (i.e., on the immediate test). This indicates that the effect is on retention and not original perception or learning. A similar effect has been found with the delayed-response task—progressive improvements in accuracy of 20–25% have been reported over a series of 1,000 trials on various problems (Davis & Steele, 1963; Meyer & Harlow, 1962)— although it is less clear with this task that the effect is attributable to variation in forgetting per se.

Perhaps there are general techniques through which individuals may learn to cope more effectively with any source of forgetting. For example, we mentioned in Chapter 7 that forgetting caused by electroconvulsive shock was markedly reduced among animals experienced with it, although this is probably a special case quite unrelated to D'Amato's finding. It seems more likely that the progressive decline in forgetting with practice is both task specific and specific to the source of forgetting in question.

MAJOR ISSUE: DOES RETENTION DEPEND ON THE CONTENT OF A MEMORY?

The issue is whether retention is better for some events than for others. This issue may be restated in other ways: Are sources of forgetting especially detrimental to memories of certain kinds of events? When all other factors such as degree of original learning are equivalent, does the effectiveness of remembering depend on what is to be remembered? In terms of specific examples, the issue is whether, given equal learning before the intervention of a long interval, you are more likely to recall events surrounding purchase of your car than those surrounding purchase of a hamburger, more effective in remembering a list of nonsense syllables than in remembering a poem, or more likely to remember what a former friend looks like than what she or he sounds like.

By *content* of a memory we mean the operationally specifiable, material events that are to be represented memorially for learning and retention. Of special concern is the kind, not the number, of events represented; perhaps the number of attributes constituting a memory varies widely and perhaps this number determines retention, but this is a different issue.

The content of a memory has been studied experimentally in terms of two principal variables, the sensory modality through which information is acquired and the past experience or biological disposition of subjects in responding to such information. We therefore may address two general questions for which there is empirical evidence. The first is whether forgetting is affected by the experience or biological disposition of subjects with particular memory content when sensory modality is held constant. The second is the converse: With information content equated in terms of the subject's past experience or biological disposition, is forgetting affected by the sensory modality through which that information is conveyed to the subject? As an example of the first question with human subjects, we might test whether the contingency between a loud crash and a toddler's cry is forgotten more or less rapidly than that between a loud crash and a tone; for the second question, we might compare forgetting of the contingency between hearing a loud crash followed by a toddler's cry and that between a loud crash followed by *seeing* a toddler cry.

The first case to be discussed concerns the effect of semantic characteristics of verbal materials. One historic consideration within the study of memory processing is that for humans, all information might be coded linguistically (or perhaps only verbally). To remember a painting, perhaps persons do not store and retrieve visual images per se, but process only the verbal labels attached to the painting. If this were so, we would expect to find no retention differences associated with sensory modality per se and all effects of memory content attributable to differences in semantic characteristics of information. To anticipate our later discussion, it is notable (and probably not surprising) that retention in humans does occur with materials unlikely to be coded verbally. Yet it will also be seen that issues concerning sensory modality and biological disposition as variables in the content of memory may be answered more readily with animals than with humans as subjects.

Semantic Content of Verbal Memories

Let us adopt the convention of defining "meaning" in terms of the network of associations held by a particular verbal unit, and "meaningfulness" as the quantitative index reflected in, for example, the number of associates produced in response to a given verbal unit or the frequency with which that unit appears in the language. Viewed in this way, it is inevitable that meaning and meaningfulness are a product of prior experience. Our question is whether differential prior experience with a verbal unit yields differential forgetting when that unit becomes incorporated into a new memory.

While the ultimate index of meaningfulness has not been identified, it is quite clear that various scales of meaningfulness are rather well correlated (for review and discussion, see Goss & Nodine, 1965; Kausler, 1974; Underwood & Schulz, 1960). Thus, in terms of three-letter units of the form consonant–vowel–consonant, Archer's (1960) classification of CIJ and XEP as low in association value, NEF and BOH as medium, and BIM and CAT as high is in general agreement with other scales based on somewhat different operations.

It has been established that variation in meaningfulness within this range (e.g., XEP vs. BOH vs. BIM) does not yield differences in forgetting following a retention interval, provided that learning is equated prior to the interval (Underwood, 1954, 1964). This conclusion has been important methodologically and is also startling intuitively. Variation within this range of meaningfulness causes dramatic differences in rate of original learning, so this conclusion seems to oppose the common belief in a continuum of processes between learning and retention. According to this belief, products of the initial processing of different classes of materials should predict subsequent differences in their forgetting, as seems to be reflected in data gathered by Cavanagh (1972).

Cavanagh found that the rate with which verbal units were processed when first presented was a remarkably effective predictor of memory span. Across a wide range of materials—digits, letters, words, and syllables, as well as colors, geometric shapes, and random forms—average processing time associated with a particular class of memory content accounted for 99.5% of the variance in memory span for that class. By Cavanagh's index, for example, the wide difference in processing time required for words (e.g., *dog*) and nonsense syllables (e.g., *dof*)—.047 seconds compared to .073 seconds per item—was accompanied by a corresponding difference in memory span—5.5 compared to 3.4 items immediately recalled. Therefore, if initial processing time were a major determinant of retention generally, beyond the confines of the memory span test, we would expect that memory content should determine rate of forgetting.

But complexities arise. For example, items that initially require more processing time probably will also require special processing efforts by the subject to equate learning of these items with that of others prior to introducing a source of forgetting. This "special" processing may involve more repetitions or different levels of processing than otherwise occurs. Perhaps the achievement of equal learning is accompanied by achievement of equivalent processing time; initial processing time may well reflect degree of prior learning in a manner similar to that of other indexes of meaningfulness. The question would remain, however, whether the items differing in initial processing time would differ in their resistance to a source of forgetting. In other words, it is unclear whether the correlation between initial processing rate and retention performance is maintained if certain sources of forgetting intervene.

These are precisely the considerations that make uncertain the relationship between meaningfulness and forgetting. Furthermore, a systematic analysis of the role of interference in forgetting has led to a thorough investigation of this relationship. As a paradigmatic study of the influence of memory content on forgetting, we shall discuss briefly the course of this investigation.

The role of memory content in interference theory. In a now-classic paper, Underwood and Postman (1960) implicated memory content as a major determinant of forgetting. Based on convincing evidence that simple forgetting of a list of verbal items could be attributed to interference from prior or subsequent learning outside the laboratory, Underwood and Postman specified the features of memory content that seemed to be of special importance to this forgetting. At one extreme are items such as *icx,* of such low meaningfulness as to involve unusual letter sequences. It was suggested that subsequent retention for items of this class would be disrupted by "letter sequence interference" derived from prior or subsequent acquisition of similar memories involving more common sequences, such as *ibm* or *ice.* At the other extreme of the meaningfulness continuum—high frequency words such as *boy*—subsequent retention was expected to be disrupted by "unit sequence interference" arising from the many conflicting memories in which *boy* enters into other associations. The clear prediction was that for lists involving associated letters, the less common that particular sequence of letters, the more the forgetting; for lists involving associated words, the more common the word, the more the forgetting.

The Underwood–Postman theory was plausible, timely, and quite testable, so it attracted a good deal of experimental attention. The history of science predicts that the ultimate fate of testable theories is disconfirmation and modification. Of major interest here is the simple fact that from a wide spectrum of thorough tests no systematic evidence was found that memory content—in terms of the meaningfulness of verbal materials—is a major determinant of forgetting. (For the history of this work, see Keppel, 1968, 1972; Postman, 1971; Postman & Underwood, 1973; see also Chapter 4.)

A variety of important new facts and ideas evolved from tests of the Underwood–Postman theory. These products concerned mechanisms through which features of memory content might facilitate retention under some circumstances but be conducive to interference under others (e.g., Postman, 1963), and how memories acquired in the laboratory might be protected from interference caused by memories acquired elsewhere (e.g., Underwood & Ekstrand, 1966, 1967). In addition, the plausibility of the interference theory framework suggests that the Underwood–Postman approach is appropriate but that the form of the stored information most likely to interfere with retention may not be individual letters or small groups of letters.

Perhaps our system for processing memories is constructed adaptively so as to be more sensitive to abstracted features of events. By "abstracted features" we mean not only categories, concepts, and implicit organizations or groupings of events, but also sensory and affective abstractions, any of which might become the principal attributes for memorial representation of an event. Organisms are encumbered with large quantities of information for storage, even after attentional screening at the perceptual level. Some form of abstraction should increase efficiency in processing this information. If the storage and retrieval mechanisms responsible for retention do operate primarily on the basis of such abstractions, adaptive features such as interference may be demonstrated and studied most clearly in terms of such units of analysis. The question "Which units of behavior provide the most insightful and general analysis?" is historic (for a comparable issue concerning operant conditioning, see Collier, Hirsch, & Kanarek, 1976). The following evidence has implicated conceptual structure as a promising unit for the analysis of memory content.

Degree of hierarchical conceptual structure.   This variable has the unfortunate characteristic of being more difficult to describe than its effect on behavior. One example of differing levels of conceptual structure is most readily described in the manner of Underwood and Zimmerman (1973), by referring to the lists themselves as shown in Table 8.1. List 1 is constructed so that no apparent conceptual grouping can be used to order the items. In List 2, the first eight items may be distinguished conceptually from the last eight on a living–

TABLE 8.1
Lists Varying from Low (List 1) to High (List 5) Hierarchical
Conceptual Structure[a]

List 1	List 2	List 3	List 4	List 5
dog	dog	dog	dog	dog
banjo	bean	tiger	pony	pony
rifle	turnip	hyena	hyena	tiger
bugle	pony	pony	tiger	hyena
pony	carrot	bean	turnip	carrot
bean	hyena	turnip	carrot	turnip
hyena	tiger	carrot	bean	bean
pepper	pepper	pepper	pepper	pepper
violin	violin	violin	violin	violin
turnip	rifle	bugle	banjo	banjo
saber	knife	banjo	bugle	flute
knife	banjo	flute	flute	bugle
carrot	bugle	rifle	saber	knife
flute	saber	saber	knife	saber
tiger	flute	knife	rifle	rifle
mortar	mortar	mortar	mortar	mortar

[a]From Underwood & Zimmerman, 1973.

nonliving basis, a distinction maintained for Lists 3, 4, and 5. In addition, in List 3 the first of the four living items are animals and the second four vegetables, while the first four of the nonliving items are musical instruments and the last four are weapons. The further conceptual grouping in List 4 applies to each successive set of two words: *dog* and *pony* are domestic animals, *hyena* and *tiger* are wild; *turnip* and *carrot* are root vegetables, *bean* and *pepper* are pod vegetables; *violin* and *banjo* are stringed instruments, *flute* and *bugle* are wind instruments; *saber* and *knife* are cutting weapons, *rifle* and *mortar* are ballistic weapons. Carrying this structure into List 5, the additional distinction is that the first of each two successive words is a high-frequency word and the second a low-frequency word.

There is no doubt that learning is better with higher levels of conceptual structure; our concern here is with subsequent retention following an interval of onc or several days, once equivalent learning is attained. When words were ordered so as to be more congruent with previously learned conceptual groupings, less forgetting was found. For Lists 1–5 in Table 8.1, percent forgetting was estimated to be 29%, 15%, 11%, 8%, and 6% when learning had occurred with the numbers 1 through 16 as stimulus items and the pairs presented in a constant order; also, percent forgetting was 22%, 20%, 14%, 13%, and 9% when learning was by the serial learning procedure (Underwood & Zimmerman, 1973). These results were replicated in a subsequent experiment by Underwood, Shaughnessy, and Zimmerman (1974; but this replication did not occur when certain procedural changes were included, causing Underwood et al. to reevaluate this effect, as we shall see).

In a general sense, this effect of abstracted conceptual features of words on forgetting is precisely what had been predicted by Underwood and Postman in terms of simpler, direct associations between individual verbal units. As Underwood and his colleagues have pointed out, however, the generality of this effect may be limited. Internal evidence in these studies did not indicate that the greater forgetting with the less structured list was caused by interference from prior conceptual habits, and furthermore, Underwood believes that the benefit of hierarchical organization to retention may be restricted to certain methods of testing and have little importance for theory. Results by Underwood and his associates (1974) and Rogers and Underwood (1976) tend to support this judgment. In the latter study, using retroactive interference rather than an interval as the source of forgetting, higher levels of conceptual structure resulted in greater forgetting when the interfering list also had a high level of structure and had no influence on retention when the structure of the interfering list was low. Results reported by Wortman (1975) suggest better retention after a 1-week interval for lists with high rather than low hierarchical structure, but in this study it is unclear whether the method for equating original learning is adequate.

By way of speculation, perhaps processes underlying the forgetting ordinarily found after a retention interval function independently of level of conceptual structure, but under certain circumstances other events occurring during the interval *enhance* retention for a list with a high level of structure. With more concepts involved in ordering the list, there is higher probability of any particular concept's recurring in the subject's experience during the retention interval and thus reactivating the memory of the list learned in the laboratory. Each consequent retrieval of that memory is likely to have a rehearsal-like benefit for subsequent retention of the list. On this basis, one might expect under certain circumstances to find signs of better retention after 24 hours than earlier— "reminiscence"—for subjects who had learned the more highly structured list. Interestingly enough, such reminiscence has been detected. In the experiment by Underwood and Zimmerman, better relearning was found after 24 hours than immediately when a relatively large number of concepts were applicable to structuring the list. In the experiment by Underwood and his associates, the most highly structured list included three exemplars of each of eight concepts. When recall of this list was tested 24 hours later, the number of occasions on which exemplars of a concept were given correctly increased by nearly 40% (from 39% to 54%) in comparison to the last recall trial of original learning. While this increase is probably overestimated because it does not account for possible increases in performance resulting from the last recall trial of original learning (as noted by Underwood et al.), the magnitude of the effect makes reminiscence an enticing possibility.

Forgetting of Words That Differ in Level of Concreteness–Imagery

Throughout the hundreds of years in which mnemonic techniques have been applied, it has been supposed that events that more readily evoke a particularly vivid mental image are more readily retrieved from one's store of memories. For particular mnemonic devices, one therefore should expect that for optimal retention the "peg words" or "loci" used to organize the materials should be concrete and easily imaged. This characteristic has been presumed to be responsible for the effectiveness of devices such as the mnemonic rhyme "One is a bun, two is a shoe, etc." To apply this device to learning a list of ordered words (e.g., *dog, apple,* etc.), one would imagine the first word interacting with "bun" (e.g., a *dog* sandwich), the second with "shoe" (e.g., an *apple* wearing shoes), and so on. Accordingly, it has seemed that such a system would have decreased effectiveness for retention if the peg words were more abstract, less easily imaged in a consistent way (e.g., "One is fun, two is new"). Is retention poorer the more abstract the word?

Verbal items rated relatively high in concreteness–imagery have been accompanied by more rapid learning under a variety of circumstances, and explanations of this effect have led to parallel expectations concerning the influence of concreteness–imagery on retention.

Several characteristics of items with high concreteness–imagery seem to provide plausible reasons why such items might yield better retention. First, words high in concreteness–imagery may be organized with special effectiveness. For example, the words *black, ferocious, dog* may be unitized readily into an image, in contrast to items such as *unclear, basic, concept.* The former three words would seem to be simultaneously accessible for retrieval, while the latter three seem to be accessible only in serial succession, so perhaps the former take up less "memory space" than the latter (Begg, 1972, 1973). Second, words that are easily imaged may be coded visually as well as verbally, permitting twice as many access routes in retrieval than items that are not readily coded other than verbally (Paivio & Csapo, 1973; Lutz & Scheirer, 1974). A third possible explanation is that words high and low in concreteness–imagery are differentially susceptible to interference. Fourth, it has been suggested that, in comparison to purely verbal forms, visual images of words simply provide memories with greater "strength" and are more "memorable." Although hazy in its conceptualization, this remains a possibility. In addition, initial encoding seems more rapid the more concrete the item, and variability in encoding also is less for concrete items; nearly perfect negative correlations have been found between the scaled imagery value of a word and latency for subjects to report formation of an image, and between the imagery value of a word and the between-subject variance in this imagery rating (John Schmitt, personal communication, 1977). For further discussion of such differences between words high and low in concreteness–imagery, see Paivio (1975) and Postman & Burns (1974).

It may be apparent that none of these characteristics is sufficient to account for differential forgetting that might occur among items of high and low concreteness–imagery. Before considering their elaboration into proper explanations of the latter, we should consider the empirical evidence.

Tests of the influence of concreteness–imagery on retention and forgetting.   Conclusive tests of the effect of concreteness–imagery on retention with and without a source of forgetting have been conducted for words acquired with the paired-associate and free-recall paradigms. In each case, the source of forgetting has been a retention interval several days in length.

With the paired-associate paradigm, learning has generally been found to be more rapid with items of higher concreteness–imagery, and a larger effect has been found with variation in terms of the stimulus items than for the response items. Postman and Burns (1973) therefore tested the influence of concreteness–imagery on retention of paired-associate lists by comparing the retention of four groups of subjects, each of which had been assigned one of the four possible combinations of level of imagery–concreteness (high or low) and locus of that level (among the stimulus words or the response words). On the basis of a previous experiment, subjects given high levels of imagery–concreteness among both the stimulus and response words (Group HH) were known to require only about 4 study trials to attain the learning criterion of 12 correct among 16 items, subjects with low concreteness–imagery for both stimulus and response words (group LL) to require about 13 trials, and the remaining groups (L–H and H–L) to require about 9 and 6 trials, respectively, to attain the same criterion. Using this information to carefully equate degree of learning prior to the retention interval, a clearer assessment of the effect of concreteness–imagery on forgetting was possible than for previous studies (e.g., Butter & Palermo, 1970; Yuille, 1971). Accordingly, retention after an interval of 1 week yielded quite unambiguous results: Forgetting was least for items having stimuli of low and responses of high concreteness–imagery (Group LH); the greatest amount of forgetting was found when both the stimuli and responses were high in concreteness–imagery (Group HH); and for the remaining conditions, amount of forgetting fell about midway between these two extremes. These results are in opposition to the conventional notion that we may combat forgetting by using more concrete, easily imaged conceptual pegs (stimuli). They suggest that especially if the response terms we wish to retrieve also happen to be high in concreteness–imagery, more, not less, forgetting may result from this technique.

Using free-recall procedures, Begg and Robertson (1973) obtained results that seemed to show less forgetting over an interval of several days for words rated high in concreteness–imagery compared to those rated low on this scale. The firmness of these results is in doubt, however. Apparent methodological deficiencies in their experiments and the results of a similar experiment by Postman and Burns (1974) indicate at most a much more limited effect of concreteness–imagery on forgetting.

A major difficulty in the Begg and Robertson experiments was in establishing, prior to the source of forgetting (retention interval), equivalent learning for words high and low in concreteness–imagery. Limitations on the measurement of original learning were imposed by ceiling effects that may have masked differences in overlearning. The ceiling effect was eliminated in one experiment (Experiment 2, in which subjects were taken to a criterion of only 76% accuracy in acquisition), but in this experiment the anticipation method was used. With the anticipation procedure, each trial provides an opportunity for study by the subject as well as providing a test. Therefore, undetected differences in learning on the terminal acquisition trial may account for the differences in retention performance. Furthermore, study of the items in acquisition was self-paced, and it is unclear whether or not differences in concreteness–imagery were confounded by differences in study time. Postman (1974) has discussed further methodological problems with the Begg–Robertson experiments.

Postman and Burns (1974) found that forgetting may be reduced if words are relatively high in concreteness–imagery, but only under certain conditions that limit the theoretical importance of the effect. To understand this limitation, a brief description of their experiment is useful.

Following several practice trials in the free recall of abstract or concrete words, separate groups of subjects were tested for retention either 1 minute or 1 week later. For some subjects, all the words in their list were of one kind, either concrete or abstract. For other subjects, the words were presented in mixed-list fashion, with half the items concrete and the other half abstract. The amount of practice permitted originally was controlled carefully to equate the degree to which the abstract and concrete words were learned. In strictly numerical terms, Postman and Burns found greater forgetting between 1 minute and 1 week when the items were abstract than when they were concrete; but this critical interaction between type of word and length of the retention interval achieved statistical significance only with the mixed-list presentation. Postman and Burns (1974) judge this effect to be unimportant as an instance of the effect of memory content on forgetting, stating that their "results obtained with mixed lists are not likely to provide a good basis for generalizations about the influence of item attributes (abstract versus concrete) on the processes of storage and retrieval" (p. 708). They suggest that with the mixed-list procedure better recall of concrete than abstract words was due to the greater "strength" these items acquired during acquisition and consequent inhibition in the reproduction of the weaker, abstract words. In other words, they believe their effect with the mixed-list design was due not to relative concreteness–imagery per se but, rather, to more general processes responsible for inhibition of the recall of weaker items in the presence of stronger ones, as we discussed earlier (see also Tulving & Hastie, 1972).

Interpreting the effect of concreteness-imagery on memory processing.   Earlier we considered characteristics of words high in concreteness–imagery that might account for better retention of such words. We then noted that the best evidence seems to indicate that better retention either is not found for these items or, if it is obtained, as with the Postman-Burns finding with mixed lists, that the characteristics of concreteness–imagery per se may not provide a satisfactory explanation. For example, Postman and Burns found no indication that concrete items had more consistent subjective organization than abstract items, which limits the applicability of the organization-based interpretation that concrete words are somehow more cohesive or more easily unitized.

What of the contrary findings by Postman and Burns (1973) indicating more forgetting of paired associates when both the stimulus and response words are high in concreteness–imagery than when one or both members of the pair are low in this dimension? Postman and Burns explain this result in terms of two supposed consequences of associating the members of a pair by mediation through a composite visual image. The first is that the image linking the two words may be altered increasingly as the retention interval lengthens because of the subject's exposure during the interval to different representations involving either of the two words. The second is that as the retention interval lengthens, translation (decoding) of the composite visual image into the precise response word required by the experimenter becomes increasingly more difficult; most images may be described by a variety of words, and it is unlikely that the image selected in learning will maintain all of the distinguishing features of the specific word required. The latter suggestion is consistent with the extraordinarily large number of extralist intrusions found by Postman and Burns when both members of a paired-associate item had high values of concreteness–imagery.

To explain the excellent retention found for pairs low in concreteness–imagery on the stimulus side and high on the response side, Postman and Burns suggest why such pairs might be extra resistant to interference-produced forgetting: The ordering of an abstract word followed by a concrete word has a relatively low probability of occurrence in the language, which should reduce extraexperimental interference; at the same time, the high imagery of the responses may enhance their availability at recall.

A final point to be addressed is whether any effects of concreteness–imagery on the processing of memories can unequivocally be attributed to a unique advantage of "imagery" as a vivid sensory representation, as has been supposed in the application of mnemonic techniques. This issue may be considered with reference to the effect of scaled concreteness–imagery on learning. There is no doubt that learning is more rapid when items are higher in scaled concreteness–imagery, but what does this mean?

The difficulty in drawing conclusions about scaled properties of verbal units has been illustrated clearly in attempts to understand the fundamental properties of meaningfulness (see Underwood & Schulz, 1960). The common problem is that any scaled characteristic of verbal units is likely to be correlated with other characteristics, so differences that seem to be attributable to one characteristic may equally be due to its correlate.

With particular reference to the influence of scaled concreteness–imagery on learning, we may consider a reanalysis of data from the Postman–Burns (1973) study. In this experiment, when stimulus members of the pairs were high in concreteness–imagery, learning was completed within about 5 trials, while learning of pairs with low concreteness–imagery stimuli required nearly twice as many—11 trials. It may seem reasonable, therefore, to conclude that the advantage of having stimuli with high concreteness–imagery was due to their having more readily available images for use as "conceptual pegs." This interpretation, however, is not consistent with the replies given by subjects asked to identify the mediators they had used in learning each pair. Subjects given stimuli of low concreteness–imagery reported using almost as many imaginal mediators as those with stimuli high in concreteness–imagery; the average number of imaginal mediators reported were 7.5 and 9.0, respectively. Thus, while learning with high concreteness–imagery stimuli may be said to have been 120% more rapid than learning with low concreteness–imagery, the number of imaginal mediators used was only about 22% greater. This analysis is contrived only in the adoption of the common practice of assuming some validity for the subjects' reports and treating the trials-to-learn ratio as an index of relative learning rate. The suggestion is that differences in rate of learning words that vary in terms of scaled concreteness–imagery are not due entirely to differences in the application of imagery by the subjects.

The interpretation of the effects of imagery on memory processing have been discussed by Pylyshyn (1973) and need not be repeated here. But beyond the issues raised by Pylyshyn, we may note the convincing evidence that learning or retention differences attributable to differences in scaled concreteness–imagery may be attributed equally, or perhaps better, to their correlated differences in perceived frequency (Galbraith & Underwood, 1973; Wallace, Murphy, & Sawyer, 1973). Another possibility is that the "quality" of an image or its consistency may be especially important for any aid to learning, but scaling of these dimensions is difficult.

Two general conclusions emerge from the preceding discussion. First, whatever advantages the imagery potential of an event might have for memory processing are not likely to be due exclusively to something like imaginal "sensory memory" or the invoking of additional sensory systems. Second, for the practical purpose of developing more efficient mnemonic techniques, it would appear that dimensions other than concreteness–imagery may determine the effectiveness of peg words, and that sensory imagery may have some unexpected negative effects on retention.

Influence of Sensory Modality on Retention

The content of memories may differ in terms of the sensory modality through which the information in the memory is acquired. There are two general mechanisms through which this difference might influence retention. Different numbers or kinds of sensory modalities might serve as discriminative attributes of a memory, or the memorial representations of certain sensory modalities may be more readily accessible than others because, for example, they may be less susceptible to sources of interference. The critical question addressing the former mechanism is whether sensory modality is indeed represented as an attribute of memory; in other words, beyond other episodic information required at a retention test, can subjects also report the sensory modality through which the episode was perceived? For the latter mechanism, the question is whether retention for specified information is better when it was perceived in terms of one sensory modality than in terms of another. We shall address these issues in a moment, but first we must address a question of relevance particularly for humans: Is encoding of a linguistic form part of a central processing system wherein information is stripped of its sensory identity?

Sensory modality would be relatively unimportant for retention if the encoding of linguistic materials into and out of storage were common to all information regardless of the sensory channel through which it is received or disseminated at retrieval. Speaking now in evolutionary terms, if humans had developed a capacity for linguistic transformations of more importance than raw sensory capacities for any particular modality, so linguistic information was always processed in the same system regardless of the sensory mode of perception, then sensory deficiencies might yield relatively little disadvantage for an individual human. One problem with this reasoning is that biologically one might view this state of affairs equally well as an evolutionary disadvantage to survival of the species, even though it might be an advantage to individuals within the species. The sensory deficiencies might decrease the chance of survival to the age of reproduction, though increasing one's adaptability in adulthood through the possibly intellectual advantages of storing memories independent of sensory modality. Nevertheless, if all acquired information were stored in terms of its verbal representation, there would be little reason to expect retention to depend on sensory modality.

This leads us to two questions. The first is whether lexically identical verbal items such as words or letters have the same characteristics of retention whether they are received by visual, auditory, or somesthetic (e.g., by the blind) modalities. For the second question, we are concerned only with the visual modality and whether retention of pictures has the same characteristics as retention of the verbal labels of those pictures. These apply primarily to humans, although analogous questions might be plausible concerning memory processing by animals. Species differ greatly in the hierarchical ordering of the effectiveness of different sensory systems. For example, the visual capacities of birds and some primates may be greater in some ways than those of rodents, but the reverse is probably true for olfactory capacities. Perhaps we may evolve principles relating retention effectiveness for episodes involving certain sensory modalities to the relative effectiveness of that sensory modality in the animal's hierarchy. For example, the mere quantity of visual information handled by birds or primates might yield more interference in retention for their visually mediated memories than for olfactory or somesthetic memories, but the opposite may be true for rodents. Alternatively, birds and primates might show better retention for memories involving visual information simply because they have evolved a vastly more capable system for handling large quantities of information through this modality. There has been little systematic investigation of such effects with animals, but in the next section we shall address parallel possibilities in terms of human retention.

We now concentrate on two basic features of retention by humans. The first concerns the storage of sensory modality as a potential discriminative attribute of a memory. The second concerns the relationship between the sensory content of a memory and its retention.

Sensory modality may serve as an attribute of verbal memories. Underwood (1969) has suggested that a fundamental discriminative attribute of the memory representing the occurrence of a verbal unit is the modality through which that unit was perceived. Several studies have confirmed that humans are capable of reporting whether verbal items were presented acoustically or visually even when they had previously understood that this information was unnecessary; as far as the subjects were concerned, only correct recall of the verbal materials themselves was necessary (e.g., Bray & Batchelder, 1972; Hintzman, Block & Inskeep, 1972; Madigan & Doherty, 1972). There is further evidence that incidental sensory information, beyond that of the general acoustic–visual classification, may be stored as an attribute of the memory: Under a variety of conditions, humans are known to recall correctly whether an item had been presented as a picture or as a label of such a picture, and subjects asked only to learn sentences spoken through a tape recorder are quite adept at recalling also whether a particular sentence had been read in a male or a female voice (e.g., Light, Stansbury, Rubin, & Linde, 1973).

To store sensory features of a stimulus as an attribute of a memory is not necessarily to store redundant information. As discriminative attributes, this information may serve to facilitate retention through a variety of means, such as protecting against interference effects (for illustration of such protection, see Wickens, 1970). Therefore, if attributes representing sensory modality lose their effectiveness as a consequence of a source of forgetting, retention of other attributes of the memory may similarly be impaired. It is a different question, however, to ask whether information about the sensory modality of an episode is stored and forgotten independently of other memory attributes, compared to asking whether other aspects of the episode are forgotten at a particular rate because their input was mediated by a particular sensory modality. The latter question is considered next.

Retention and forgetting as a function of sensory modality.   For a variety of reasons, one might expect that the sensory modality through which an episode is perceived might influence subsequent forgetting of that episode. For example, because more frequently applied sensory modalities are represented as attributes of a number of memories, the discriminative function of these attributes may be weakened and memories acquired in terms of these modalities subjected thereby to more interference in retention. Retention of odor information may be unusually efficient in man, perhaps owing to the infrequent application of this sensory modality in memory processing by humans. Countering this hypothesis, however, is the possible existence of mechanisms acting to conserve memories involving organisms' more dominant sensory modalities. One such mechanism might be the reactivation of a memory's attributes whenever stimuli similar to those represented by the attributes are perceived through the same sensory modality as before. By promoting something like rehearsal, the consequence of this mechanism would be better retention.

It is conceivable also that something like "inherent memorability" differs for different sensory modalities. Such a concept appears often in the literature and appears to mean something akin to differential "decay." Although there is little evidence as to its operation after a source of forgetting, it remains a possible hypothesis. One may readily find evidence that iconic or sensory memories representing sensory events over very short intervals may be longer when the information is presented acoustically than when it is presented visually (for a review, see Crowder, 1976). Such differential decay might serve as a "sweeping device" to alleviate interference in retention by immediately eliminating redundant information involving more frequently used sensory modalities.

Finally, different forms of information processing are inherent in certain sensory modalities, and one might expect an influence of sensory modality on retention on this basis. To acquire the memory of a complex picture, the components of that picture must be presented simultaneously; it is not difficult to imagine how frustrating it would be to attempt such learning if various parts of the picture were presented successively. Moreover, the latter procedure would preclude the sources of visual contrast and spatial relationships needed to properly perceive such an item. In contrast, if a symphony or a simple melody is to be appreciated, or even recognized, its components must be presented sequentially. Sequential presentation of auditory or olfactory stimuli or simultaneous presentation of visual material is not always necessary. For example, we know that experienced musicians can make decisions about the nature of individual tones among a large number of tones presented simultaneously, and telegraph operators efficiently process sequentially presented letters as if they were presented simultaneously in the form of words. But in general, undeniable differences exist in how information through particular sensory modalities is typically processed, and this feature might be responsible for retention differences associated with sensory modality.

Modality-related differences in human retention of nonverbal episodes.   It is commonly believed that the retention of odors is extraordinarily effective. This belief has been encouraged by a series of experiments with human subjects by Engen and his colleagues. They initially tested retention of odors over short intervals ranging between 3 and 30 seconds (Engen, Kuisma, & Eimas, 1973). As events to be recalled, Engen and his associates developed a sample of 100 odors, which included "familiar household products such as garlic, vanilla, and floor wax; chemical compounds such as acetates, alcohols and aldehydes; perfume products such as neroli oil and Arpege perfume" (1973, p. 223). The odors were presented in a little ball of cotton placed under the nose of each subject. Two kinds of tests were given. For one, the subject was to reply whether or not each successive odor had previously been presented; for the other, subjects were initially presented five odors in succession, and then, after the retention interval, were presented a single odor and asked whether or not it had been among the previous five. Test performance was generally poor with the latter procedure; but for both conditions no significant decrements in retention were observed throughout the 30-second interval.

Similar tests after much longer retention intervals were conducted by Engen and Ross (1973). Subjects in the first experiment were tested for recognition of odors either immediately, 1 day, 7 days, or 30 days after their initial presentation. The results are simple, but rather astounding: The probability of a correct recognition did not change significantly after 30 days compared to the immediate test (although, curiously, performance was better after a 1-day interval than after the 30-day interval). Furthermore, Engen and Ross conducted two additional experiments that used slightly different procedures but did not test retention until 3 months after the odors had been presented. They found that in spite of this long interval, retention performance was comparable in absolute terms to that found in their first experiment (retention after short intervals was not assessed in the latter two experiments).

Other features of these experiments are also remarkable. In all of these experiments (Engel et al., 1973; Engen & Ross, 1973), the excellent retention occurred in spite of substantial opportunity for proactive interference by prior exposure to other odors in the same experiment (it may be noted, however, that proactive interference is ordinarily of little consequence in tests of *verbal* recognition also). Second, retention of odors was equally good whether or not a particular odor was judged to be familiar or unfamiliar to the subject. Finally, in the latter experiments by Engen and Ross, which tested retention after a 3-month interval, subjects were given no indication when the odors were presented that they would later be tested for retention. Apparently, the subjects believed that their only task was to make judgments of various sorts about the odors at the time they were presented. Finally, it should be noted that definite limitations have been identified for processing of memories with olfactory attributes, and it is quite premature to conclude that such olfactory information is especially resistant to forgetting (Davis, 1975, 1977).

Comparison of retention across different sensory modalities is, in many ways, as difficult to interpret as comparisons involving subject variables such as species, age, and so forth. So although it is notable that with a similar retention test by Shepard (1967), involving recognition of pictures, retention was found to decrease from about 100% to 50% accuracy over a 4-month retention interval, this does not permit us to conclude that visual information is forgotten more readily than olfactory information. To permit such a conclusion, we would need to draw such comparisons within a single experiment in which control is exerted over all factors other than sensory modality, such as degree of original learning, number of intramodality dimensions, and so forth. What we can investigate more readily is whether functional differences exist in retention involving different sensory modalities. For example, are some sources of forgetting more effective with auditory than with visual memories and others more effective with visual than with auditory memories? Evidence for such functional differences is limited, but we shall discuss some shortly.

The data of Engen and his colleagues also indicate that the mode of sensory stimulation is not inevitably translated, categorized, and stored in verbal form (for further study of this point, see Lawless & Engen, 1977). In tests of retention up to 30 seconds after presentation, recognition of odors was not found to differ among subjects given differential opportunity for rehearsal during the retention interval. We know that rehearsal of verbal units does improve retention under these circumstances, so it seems unlikely that the odors were remembered by the spontaneous assignment of verbal labels to the odors. Furthermore, when retention was tested after an interval of several weeks, providing explicit instructions to the subjects concerning labeling of the odors had little influence on their retention.

Further evidence agrees that retention of sensory events may proceed quite efficiently in the absence of verbal mediation. For example, Deutsch (1975) has summarized a large number of studies that have tested recognition of pure tones a few seconds or a few milliseconds after their presentation. By presenting a number of tests to each subject involving a number of different tones, effective verbal encoding (labeling) of each tone appears quite improbable. Similarly, a large number of investigations have been inspired by the suggestion of Crowder and Morton (1969) that a precategorical sensory representation of certain auditory characteristics of verbal units may be maintained over an interval of about 2 seconds (subsequent studies by Cole, 1973, and Springer, 1973, suggest that this interval might be as long as 4–8 seconds). Finally, there is the evidence with animals that sensory information may be maintained over long intervals when mediators (physical or verbal) are unlikely or impossible. The most striking example is the capacity for monkeys to recognize accurately a picture of a geometric figure for as long as 9 minutes after a single presentation (e.g., D'Amato, 1973; D'Amato & Cox, 1976). It is perhaps notable here that the same monkeys were so deficient in processing auditory stimuli for recognition that even when the sample and the test for "retention" were presented simultaneously recognition was not evident.

Most data relevant to the influence of memory content on retention and forgetting in humans is derived from comparison of different kinds of visual events or different kinds of auditory events. We shall first consider what these data tell us, and then we shall consider investigations of a more difficult problem—whether there are functional differences in retention of auditory compared to visual events.

The effect of visual content of a memory on retention and forgetting. Most of the pertinent evidence addresses the more specific question of whether retention for pictures has different functional characteristics than retention for words. For example, pictures of human faces might be processed differently than words because of their biological significance or because of extreme affective loading associated with a particular face. Shepherd and Ellis (1973) tested whether retention of pictures of young women's faces depends on the relative judged attractiveness of the women. Each of the subjects was presented 54 such pictures with the instruction that they should memorize them. Three minutes after studying the pictures, the subjects were presented with 9 pairs of faces; the task was to identify which member of each pair had actually been presented previously. Without prior warning, the subjects were asked to return 6 days later; 35 days later, they were asked to return once more. Each time, the subjects were presented 9 different pairs of faces and given a recognition test as before.

For some purposes, such a within-subject test of retention is inappropriate without proper control over new learning or reactivation effects, but the Shepherd–Ellis results warrant mention because of the interesting interaction found between the effects of type of face and length of the retention interval. As they had predicted, the faces judged to be of moderate attractiveness were forgotten more rapidly than those that were either very attractive or very unattractive. Although retention of the former pictures was slightly better than retention of the others at the 3-minute test, retention loss for these items 35 days later was nearly 50%, while only negligible loss was found for pictures of faces that were very attractive or very unattractive.

Shepherd and Ellis offer the interpretation that these differences in forgetting are attributable to the greater arousal felt by subjects when viewing the very attractive or very unattractive faces. However, in view of the inconsistency of the more general effects of arousal on forgetting, and the complexity of the processes underlying face recognition generally (see Harmon, 1973), an evaluation of this interpretation is premature. These data, though, remain the sort that give emphasis to the possibility of functional differences in the retention of words compared to pictures.

Most comparisons of the memory processing of words and pictures have used simple pictures with clearly identifiable labels. This permits a common verbal test of recall for the two kinds of items, and it avoids the problem of assessing the accuracy of subjects' drawings of the pictures at recall or the correspondingly more complex verbal reports of subjects asked to recall more complex pictures by describing them.

The latter problem is limited to the relatively few tests thus far conducted for recall of complex pictures. The results of these tests suggest, however, that it is with such items that functional differences in the retention of words and pictures are most likely to appear. Shiffrin (1973) devised an elaborate but apparently effective scoring system to assess free recall of complex pictures. In contrast to the nearly inevitable primacy and recency effects found in the free recall of words, Shiffrin found no such effects associated with the free recall of complex pictures throughout comparable variation in list length and rate of presentation. It is unlikely that complex pictures can be rehearsed effectively. It is this reduction or elimination of rehearsal that Shriffin believes is primarily responsible for the absence of primacy and recency effects in the recall of these items. This seems to be a likely explanation in view of the general agreement that differential rehearsal is largely responsible for the effect of primacy and perhaps also of recency and negative recency.

"A SMILING OLD MAN HOLDS
A LITTLE GIRL"

Figure 8.2 This illustrates the four versions of a common item tested for recognition after 7 minutes or 7 weeks following study of any one of these four items (from Nelson et al., 1974. Copyright 1974 by the American Psychological Association. Reprinted by permission.)

Other functional differences in the verbal recall of pictures and words have been reported. For example, Erdelyi and Becker (1974) found progressive improvement in the recall of pictures but not of words when repeated test trials were given without intervening study trials. As in several such studies, however, Erdelyi and Becker used simple, readily labeled pictures. Dual coding (visual image and verbal label) may be applied to such pictures. It is difficult to separate this feature from purely visual processing of the picture when drawing comparisons with the processing of words.

Equally notable are the functional similarities that have been shown for the recall of verbal and nonverbal materials. Using the Brown–Peterson paradigm, Yuille and Fox (1973) found that, like similar effects with words, proactive interference cumulated when successively tested objects were of a similar shape and was released upon tests with new objects differing in terms of certain critical dimensions. For example, proactive interference increased with successive tests of "cylindrical" objects such as a match and a nail, but was released upon presentation of "square" objects such as a book or an envelope. As another functional similarity, Frost (1971) found clustering in the recall of similar pictorial shapes, as is commonly found in the free recall of sets of similar words. Finally, in the experiment by Shiffrin (1973) it was found that the probability of recalling a particular complex picture grew progressively lower the longer the list of such items, a finding commonly reported when words are recalled.

Recognition and recall of pictures.   Even when the recall of easily labeled pictures is compared with that of the labels themselves, so the same responses are required of each at the retention test, there is an inherent confounding by physical change of the item between presentation and recall. One might therefore expect a bias in terms of recalling the verbal materials, because the (verbal) symbol required at recall is precisely the same as that presented previously. One solution has been simply to ignore the matter of recall and instead test in terms of recognition, requiring only identification, not reproduction, of the stimuli. With this procedure, it is commonly found that pictures are recognized better than words under a variety of circumstances. Before elaborating on this conclusion and its implications for forgetting, we should be aware of evidence that suggests that recalling a picture on the basis of its verbal label may involve a different process (or at least a different weighting of common processes) than recognizing whether or not that specific picture had been presented previously. In this case, the major point is appreciation of the issue, because the relevant evidence is only suggestive. I shall describe a study by Dallett, Wilcox, and D'Andrea (1968), more for its provocative value than its conclusiveness concerning this issue.

Dallett and his associates (1968) presented relatively complex pictures to subjects and asked them to rate each picture according to its esthetic value. Although they included a good deal of detail, the pictures could be described simply (e.g., "a bird sitting on a post," "a man with a rifle") and hence could easily be referenced by a short title. Either immediately or 1 week after presentation, the subjects were tested for recognition of these pictures from among an equal number of different pictures describable by the same titles as those of the original set. Variation in terms of tasks immediately preceding the retention test yielded two results of special interest.

First, before the recognition test, half the subjects were presented only the title of each critical picture and asked to rate how clearly they recalled it; the remaining subjects were not given this task. If we assume that such ratings require that subjects attempt to recall the pictures, and if recall is part of the requirement for recognition, then we would expect that the subjects attempting the ratings would have an advantage at the recognition test. However, producing these ratings did not influence subsequent recognition, whether the test was given immediately or 1 week after original learning. The second result is also relevant to whether accessibility of a picture's label and judged proficiency in recalling the picture influence recognition of the picture. A firm statement on this point is not possible because the data of Dallett and his associates are not treated by item analysis to address this question. Some inferences can be made, however, on the basis of their grouped data. On the immediate tests, it was found that the pictures rated as most clearly recalled were more likely to be recognized correctly; but after a 1-week retention interval all semblance of such a relationship was gone. The suggestion is that, following a source of forgetting, recognition cannot be predicted on the basis of how effectively subjects believe they could recall the pictures. Bahrick and Boucher (1968) have reported a similar dissociation between recognition of pictures and recall of their labels. They found no relationship between accuracy in recognizing a previously presented picture and the probability of correctly recalling its label. Future work determining the basis of this dissociation and whether it is especially affected by sources of forgetting should provide critical insights into the basis of memory processing in general.

What are the differences between words and pictures that might account for the consistently superior recognition of the latter on immediate tests (for an exception to this general rule, see Goldstein, Locke, and Fehr, 1972)? One explanation might be that pictures, real or imaged, involve more details than verbal labels. These extra details might themselves become memory attributes and enhance the probability of memory retrieval in accordance with some basic principle, such as the more attributes there are, the more likely it is that one will be aroused. A hypothesis of this sort was tested by Nelson, Metzler, and Reed (1974). Subjects were presented 120 items of one of four kinds: photographs, line drawings that included most of the details of the photographs, line drawings based on a one-sentence description of the photograph, or the one-sentence description itself. An example of this variation is shown in Figure 8.2. Recognition was tested either 7 minutes or 7 weeks after the subjects observed the items.

The results confirmed that recognition of the pictures was indeed better than recognition of the verbal descriptions. But among the different kinds of pictures

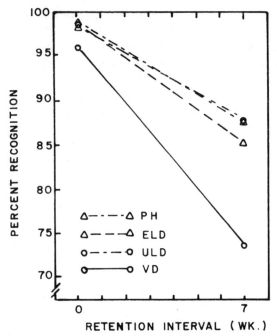

Figure 8.3   Retention in terms of percent recognition is shown for each of the four kinds of items illustrated in Figure 8.2; PH refers to photograph; ELD refers to embellished line drawing; ULD refers to unembellished line drawing, and VD refers to verbal description (adapted from Nelson et al., 1974. Copyright 1974 by the American Psychological Association. Reprinted by permission.)

amount of detail did not matter (see Figure 8.3). Furthermore, these relationships remained the same over the 7-week retention interval. It is notable that greater decrement in retention was found 7 weeks later for the verbal description than for any of the types of pictures, although this result is difficult to interpret because of possible differences in degree of original learning and the use of a within-subject variation in retention interval.

A final comment concerning the relative retention of visual–pictorial and visual–verbal stimuli: It is worth emphasis, again, that especially when comparison is made between simple pictures and their verbal labels, *both* visual and semantic transformations of information are likely to be employed by humans in their memory processing. A series of experiments by Frost (e.g., 1972) indicates that humans maintain parallel access to both kinds of information when processing the memories of simple pictures. Visual information seems to be employed for more rapid and efficient access during recognition tests, but verbal information is used when verbal recall is required. If recall of pictures could be assessed directly without verbal mediation, it is unclear whether the verbal information would be at all useful. Frost therefore suggests that, with simple pictures, visual and verbal transformations in memory processing are not really separable.

Characteristic memory processing of auditory events.   In the life cycle of probably all vertebrates, specific sequences of sounds predict important events, aversive or pleasant. The processing of these sequences of special importance for birds and many mammals, including especially the processing of speech by humans, requires an exceptional quality of memory processing (e.g., see Nottebom, 1972, esp. pp. 130–133). The special requirement is some form of maintenance or storage of auditory events for a period beyond their perception.

Lashley often noted, with characteristic eloquence, that the memory processing of a sequence of tones constituting a coherent melody or the sequence of sounds that yield a sensible idea seems almost intolerably complex. Although the basis of this processing clearly has significance of a general biological nature (Marler, 1967; Nottebom, 1972), the psychological analysis of related phenomena has advanced primarily within the study of human verbal memories (e.g., Estes, 1973). It is within this context that we shall discuss this issue.

This is the issue: Because auditory events must be processed sequentially and therefore the significance of a particular event is established in relation to the preceding one, have we evolved for the auditory system an especially effective mechanism for short-term retention to permit more effective retention of the preceding event in a sequence? This possibility is consistent with the observation by Conrad (1967) and others that auditory (phonetic) representation in memory storage occurs even when verbal materials are presented visually. Although it is quite possible to process verbal items such as letters entirely in visual form (as in the case of deaf–mute children), memory processing of these materials ordinarily is more efficient on a phonetic (auditory) basis (Conrad, 1972).

Yet if there is a special advantage in coding events phonetically for retention over very short intervals, it seems unlikely that it would be limited to sounds unique to speech, even if the special capacity for phonetic coding was evolved in humans for the precise purpose of processing speech sounds. From this reasoning, we now address the question of whether there is indeed a "sensory store" of acoustic attributes that holds a representation of nonlinguistic, raw auditory stimuli for some period longer than the duration of receptor stimulation.

A possibly unique system of memory storage for auditory stimuli has been considered by Crowder and Morton (1969; see also Morton, Crowder, & Prussin, 1971). Such a system seemed to be needed to account for three phenomena of retention found when verbal items are presented acoustically.

First, short-term retention of verbal items is generally better if they are presented acoustically than if they are presented visually. Although it is not a simple matter methodologically to design an experiment that permits clear conclusions about the influence of mode of presentation of verbal units, this phenomenon has been studied so extensively that one can safely assert that it is neither an artifactual nor a trivial effect (for reviews, see Crowder, 1976; Murdock, 1972, 1974; Penney, 1975; Watkins, Watkins & Crowder, 1974). Murdock has shown, for instance, that the effect cannot be understood in terms of the following simple explanations: that greater rehearsal time is available for auditory than for visual material; that spoken items are somehow greater in amplitude than written items; or that the most commonly used tests, which emphasize temporal associations, are more compatible with the auditory than with the visual mode of presentation.

The second phenomenon is that the recency effect in serial recall of verbal items is greater with auditory than with visual presentation of the items and is especially susceptible to interference from phonologically similar items.

Third, following presentation of a nearly supraspan verbal unit usually consisting of seven or eight consonants or words, retention of the last component presented is reduced markedly when an auditory suffix item is interpolated between presentation and recall. Because this effect occurs whether or not the suffix item is of the same class of linguistic material as the unit to be remembered, Crowder and his associates have referred to this as evidence of "precategorical acoustic storage."

Crowder and his associates originally estimated the capacity of precategorical acoustic storage to be 2 seconds in duration. Through the application of somewhat different techniques, this estimate ahs been revised upward. S.P. Springer (1973) gave subjects two presentations of a syllable with the instruction to determine as quickly as possible whether the items were the same or different. Either of two consonant–vowel syllables (BA or DA) were presented in either of two pitches (104 or 140 Hz). The interval between presentation of the two items was either .2, 1, or 4 seconds, and because so few errors were made, the primary response measure was reaction time. Springer found very little deterioration in performance after 4 seconds compared to the shorter intervals. This suggests that the distinctive characteristics of the first stimulus were maintained in storage for at least 4 seconds. With a similar technique, Cole (1973) found effective retention of other presumably raw auditory stimuli over intervals of 8 seconds.

These data, together with those collected in studies of the maintenance of a representation of raw visual stimuli (e.g., Posner, 1969; Posner & Boies, 1971; Sperling, 1960), suggest that retention of untransformed precategorical auditory events may remain evident after longer durations than is found for visual events. Yet it is difficult to be absolutely certain that a clear distinction has been drawn empirically between the processing of auditory stimuli and that of their linguistic characteristics, at least with the methods applied so far (for an analysis of this issue, see Crowder, 1971, 1974, 1975; Watkins, 1972, 1974).

The more general issue of whether phonetic signals represent unique acoustic events has become widespread and methodologically complex (e.g., Blechner, Day, & Cutting, 1976; Pastore, Ahroon, Puleo, Crimmins, Golowner, & Berger, 1976). At the moment, the safest conclusion is one that is rather indecisive: that precategorical processing of raw auditory information does exist, but that whether its duration is on the order of several milliseconds or several seconds depends on one's interpretation of several studies using tests of backward masking and other assessments of short-term retention when subjects are exposed to interfering auditory stimuli of different kinds, phonetic or nonphonetic (see Morton, 1970; Massaro, 1972). Finally, with certain tests of the retention of a tone or a sequence of tones, it appears that acoustic events of linguistic and nonlinguistic types may be processed in parallel (Deutsch, 1972). It is not yet clear whether this indicates a general capacity for the simultaneous memory processing of two or more acoustic events or whether this is primarily a reflection of the redundancy included in certain kinds of acoustical information, such as melodies.

Other possible differences in retention by humans attributable to differences in the content of memories.   Folklore holds that acquired motor skills—riding a bicycle, swimming, ice skating—are extraordinarily resistant to forgetting. Science has been unable to establish whether there is indeed a qualitative difference in the retention of verbal and motor skills because of methodological problems such as control over degree of learning and a clean separation between "motor per se" and "verbal per se." One analytical approach to studying the retention of motor skills has been to search for functional similarities or differences in comparison to retention of verbal skills. Thus, it has been determined that, as with verbal behavior, forgetting of motor skills may be enhanced by proactive or retroactive interference. Other functional similarities, such as the phenomenon of directed forgetting, also have been found (for example, Burwitz, 1974). Among the puzzles remaining is one identified by Posner (1967). Posner found that while information about spatial location could be disrupted by interpolated tasks that restricted rehearsal opportunities, kinesthetic information (amount or distance of movement) was forgotten over shorter intervals regardless of interpolated activity (Pepper & Herman, 1970, present further work on this complexity).

Comparison with retention of verbal materials is complicated further because verbal recall is ordinarily measured in terms of the probability of a perfect reproduction whereas retention of motor skills is typically measured in terms of degree of accuracy, usually on the basis of constant error. It is therefore premature to draw conclusions about possible retention differences attributable to the relative contribution of motor or verbal attributes in a memory, although the increasingly analytical study of motor skill retention constitutes an interesting and important body of literature (see Stelmach, 1969; Stelmach & Kelso, 1975).

Influence of Memory Content on Retention by Animals

There is probably unanimous agreement that an organism's specific prior experiences or general biological dispositions will cause some features of the conditioning environment to enter into the memorial representation of an episode more rapidly than others. Pavlov (1927) labeled this general phenomenon "overshadowing." A special case of this is "blocking," which may be shown when a dog conditioned to expect a footshock contingent upon a bell is later given the same bell together with a flashing light as a compound signal for footshock. "Blocking" is demonstrated when, in spite of a number of such conditioning trials, tests with the flashing light alone yield none of the foot withdrawal regularly elicited by the bell. Similarly, animals biologically or experientially disposed to visual processing of information, such as the pigeon or monkey, may be little affected by a tone that appears together with a color to signal the availability of food. The color will subsequently control the animal's behavior, while the tone probably will not. These phenomena might reflect the influence of the content of an event or episode on either retention or learning, but probably not. They are not of direct interest here, but I mention them to emphasize the question that is of interest: After learning is accomplished to a common level, will subsequent forgetting of some events differ from that of others?

Although with animal subjects there is little or no direct evidence that might bear on this question, there is reason to believe that an answer is forthcoming. Furthermore, because there is a broader scope of tests that may be applied to animals than to humans—for example, the wider range of affect that may be induced by using either aversive or appetitive tests with animals, and the clearer biological dispositions that cannot be mediated by a common linguistic processing—we may find that such studies will produce a richer body of information from which to evaluate the influence of memory content on retention. The following four examples illustrate the promise of study in this area:

1. In view of their relatively weak ability to use symbolism, animals may be particularly adept in retention of motor response components of a memory, that is, the animals' physical activities during learning. For example, the number of actual, physical avoidances emitted by a rat seems to be a better predictor of the influence of passive avoidance training on retention following retroactive interference than the number of punishments received for failing to avoid (Spear, Gordon, & Chiszar, 1972). An example that may reflect more directly the occurrence of differential retention of response attributes is found in a study conducted several years ago by Cowles (1940).

Cowles intended to compare the limits of retention by rats in a delayed-response task in terms of three different testing methods. These limits were assessed using a titration method that was very time-consuming in those precomputer days, and the study as a whole was an enormous undertaking. Although it was not Cowles' intention, the three methods may be viewed as differing in terms of the contribution of the response component to processing of the memory as a whole.

All the rats first learned a black–white discrimination in a Y-maze. Some animals were rewarded with food for choosing black and others for choosing white, with the rewarded alternative sometimes on the left side and sometimes on the right. For the delayed-response task, each rat first was permitted to observe which alternative was white and which black; then, following the delay, the rat was required to respond when both alternatives had been changed to a gray color. To the extent that the rat responded in accordance with the earlier location of the rewarded alternative, retention was established.

For Method 1, the rat was permitted to maintain its orientation toward the location of the correct alternative throughout the delay interval. But even if it actually did maintain this orientation, little was gained because the longest delay after which choices were more accurate than chance was about .5 seconds, and at this point response accuracy was only 57%. Rats tested with Method 2 were permitted the same opportunity to orient as those in Method 1 and, in addition, were permitted to run up to the correct alternative and touch the door prior to the onset of the delay interval. Also, these animals were permitted to remain at the door throughout the retention interval. These opportunities, too, were of surprisingly little benefit: The average delay tolerated for above-chance responding was 5 seconds, and on tests with this delay 73% accuracy was obtained.

The remarkable condition was Method 3. Prior to the delay with this method, the rat not only was allowed to observe and approach the correct alternative but also was permitted to enter the correct goal box. After entering, the rat did not find the usual reward (1 gr of wet mash) and, instead, was replaced immediately into the start compartment. Only then did the delay begin. In spite of all this jostling around from one part of the apparatus to the other, and although the rat's initial response prior to the delay was not rewarded—and thus constituted an extinction treatment—the average delay tolerated by these animals was 60 seconds and accuracy with this delay was 86%. One-third of these rats responded with consistent accuracy after delays of 3 minutes, and more than 10% were accurate with delays of 5 minutes or longer.

The precise reason for the superior retention found with Method 3 is unclear. Perhaps the advantage resulted from the rats' use of pheromone (odor) trials, or perhaps the extinction trial just prior to the delay strengthened responding through secondary reinforcement, although neither of these possibilities is particularly convincing. What seems more likely is that the integrated response of orienting, approaching, and entering the alternative, plus perhaps the emotional consequence of finding no reward there on some occasions, resulted in a memorial representation that was retained better over long intervals than the representations provided in the alternative methods.

2. A second case that illustrates the promise of further study is the possibility that memories resulting from Pavlovian conditioning may be more durable than those resulting from instrumental conditioning. There are many operational differences that might provide some basis for such a relationship—for example, more control over the eliciting stimulus is possible with Pavlovian conditioning—but few experiments have addressed this problem, and none have been sufficiently analytical to warrant conclusions concerning the possible basis of forgetting differences that might arise from these two conditioning procedures. Possibly relevant, however, is the evidence cited earlier concerning retrograde amnesia, suggesting that autonomic responding may be more resistant to the influence

of a source of forgetting than skeletal responding. To the extent that the former provides a more representative index of Pavlovian conditioning, less forgetting should be observed with that procedure. I am referring here to the study by Springer (1973), who found that when the conditions of the amnesic treatment were held constant, indexes of autonomic responding (heart rate and defecation) yielded better retention than the index of skeletal response (licking).

3. Certain contextual stimuli seem to be forgotten more rapidly than specific discriminative stimuli (e.g., McAllister & McAllister, 1971; Perkins & Weyant, 1958). This may be a consequence of a lower degree of original learning or of less attention to these stimuli; but this may also represent selective forgetting of memory content attributable to the difference in the contingencies of reinforcement associated with the contextual stimuli, as compared to the more predictive discriminative or conditioned stimuli.

4. Finally, in an earlier chapter our discussion of acquired aversions to specific tastes (poisoning) included mention of "long-delay conditioning." The delay of interest here is the intratrial retention interval, the interval between temporally separate events that become attributes of a common memory. For example, if you were to eat six chocolate éclairs and become ill an hour later, it is likely that the éclairs and the illness would be stored as a memory of a common episode. This memory might be manifested in later behavior by your reluctance to eat six chocolate éclairs at one time. In this context, it does not seem remarkable that rats that became ill an hour after consuming a novel substance, such as saccharin, later choose not to drink much saccharin. However, if rats are presented a novel exteroceptive event like a flashing light and later are given a footshock, they are unlikely to acquire an aversion to the flashing light if the intratrial interval exceeds a few seconds; realizing this, the acquired aversion to saccharin with the 1-hour intratrial interval becomes remarkable indeed.

In our earlier discussion concerning acquired aversions and long-delay conditioning, we described Revusky's interference theory, which explains why retention of novel events such as éclairs or saccharin might be exceptionally good at the time of illness. Our present concern is to what extent retention of the first event (the CS) depends on its content. We now turn to a further elaboration of this problem.

Does long-delay conditioning imply differential forgetting for differing contents of a memory? In terms of an analysis such as that of Revusky (1971), long-delay conditioning may provide an exemplary case for an influence of memory content on retention. In this view, conditioning depends on retention of the first-occurring event, the CS. When the second event (UCS) occurs, retention of the CS would be impaired by interference from biological dispositions or from prior or subsequent learning involving the same CS or a similar CS. Accordingly, the characteristic of the CS that has seemed to be the most important determinant of long-delay conditioning is its novelty. Revusky has compiled a good deal of evidence in support of this view. Subsequently, two classes of tests have frequently been applied, one dealing with the characteristics of the CS necessary for long-delay conditioning, the other with certain characteristics of the delay interval that might determine the degree of interference. Studies by Kalat (1974) and Rozin and Ree (1972) provide examples.

Kalat's investigation was intended to determine whether stimulus intensity or stimulus novelty was the more important dimension determining the effectiveness of a particular CS in long-delay conditioning. By orthogonal manipulation of the rats' prior experience in tasting certain flavors and the concentration (intensity) of a particular flavor, Kalat found that novelty of the CS was the more important factor determining long-delayed conditioning. Although an important feature of novelty probably is its resistance to interference from conflicting memories, at present it is unclear whether the more novel CS is merely subject to less negative transfer and hence is better learned, or if the more novel CS actually is more resistant to the source of forgetting (the long delay).

Rozin and Ree conducted tests addressed directly to factors influencing retention of the CS rather than to its original acquisition. After rats had consumed a novel substance (any of three flavors had the same effect), they were maintained under anesthesia for about 9 hours. Soon after the rats awoke from the anesthesia, lithium chloride was intubated intragastrically to induce toxicosis. The question was whether association of the novel taste (CS) and the illness (UCS) would be more likely when the animal was asleep during most of the CS–UCS interval: Compared to animals awake during this period, sleeping animals should be less likely to acquire competing memories that might interfere retroactively with retention of the CS (cf. Jenkins & Dallenbach, 1924; Ekstrand, 1967). From their many previous experiments with the same conditioning procedures, Rozin and Ree estimated that the maximal interval nonanesthetized (awake) rats could tolerate and still show conditioning would be 3 hours. On this basis, one would expect no conditioning to result for rats awake during the entire 9 hours between the CS and the UCS. In contrast, quite effective conditioning was found for rats *anesthetized* throughout the 9-hour CS–UCS interval, producing a conditioned aversion comparable to that found in nonanesthetized rats given only a 30-minute interval between the CS and the UCS.

Can general principles be established to indicate which kinds of events might a priori be more "memorable," more resistant than others to a source of forgetting? For example, are certain sensory classes of CS events more likely than others to be forgotten because of the sources of interference such as those apparently counteracted in the experiments by Rozin and Ree and by Lett (1974, 1975; see Chapter 5)? In the life history of laboratory animals, perhaps events like dull noises appear so often that retention of such an event would be especially subject to proactive interference of some other source of forgetting, whereas stimulus dimensions such as flavors may be sampled so infrequently that little interference in their retention is to be expected.

Although not necessarily novel, events involving eating or drinking provide cases of unusually good retention by laboratory animals. Capaldi and his colleagues (see Capaldi, 1967, 1971) have often demonstrated that over 24-hour intervals rats are quite proficient in remembering whether a food reward was present or absent following their last instrumental response. Holman (1973), capitalizing on the general tendency of rats to alternate between different tastes if permitted to do so, found that preference for a different flavor than the one most recently consumed persisted for durations of about 4 hours in one experiment and about 6 hours in another. Spear (1967) discussed abundant evidence indicating that the memory of a particular magnitude of a food reward, as well as its occurrence or nonoccurrence, can be important determinants of animal behavior. Pschirrer (1972) found that rats could learn to predict the occurrence of nonreward in the goal box of a straight runway depending on whether the reward obtained in the goal box 15 minutes earlier had been milk or food pellets, which indicates that certain qualitative characteristics of a reward may be maintained by the rat over relatively long intervals. Staddon (1974) has found that a good deal of data may be integrated under the simple assumption that food pellets are more "memorable" than exteroceptive events.

The following suggestion emerges when this evidence is combined with the dramatic retention shown for tastes in long-delay conditioned aversion: if one were to search for stimuli especially resistant to forgetting, a good place to start with animals would be substances they eat or drink. A promising set of studies in this regard has been conducted by Maki and his colleagues (e.g., Maki, Moe, & Bierley, 1977). Testing pigeons with the delayed-matching-to-sample paradigm, they found forgetting for samples consisting of the presence-versus-absence of food to be similar to that for samples consisting of different colors.

In conclusion, the evidence for an effect of memory content on forgetting and retention in animals has status similar to the corresponding evidence with human subjects. In both cases the logic and data implying the effect have been sufficient to inspire important theories that assume that forgetting depends on memory content. Yet, firm principles governing this effect have not emerged. Generally, memory content does not seem to have a particularly pervasive effect on retention and forgetting. Especially with animal subjects, however, with which a richer spectrum of memory contents may be sampled experimentally than with humans, the evidence is too incomplete to permit a definite conclusion.

SUMMARY AND CONCLUSIONS

This chapter discussed three major issues that I view as especially important for understanding the processing of memories: (1) What governs retrieval of a memory? (2) What is the nature and consequence of mnemonic preparation? (3) Does retention depend on the content of a memory?

What Governs Retrieval of a Memory?

By holding constant the conditions of memory storage and manipulating circumstances preceding or accompanying tests of retention, we may draw inferences concerning events that affect accessibility and retrieval of a memory. It is not necessary to be sympathetic with the use of the terms *accessibility* and *retrieval* to find value in the results of these manipulations. Nor is it necessary to assume that memories are permanently available, although with that assumption, interpretation of experiments in this area becomes simpler.

Experimental analysis of events that seem to alter retention by influencing memory retrieval includes manipulation of either "contemporary context" or "prior cueing." This distinction is not yet important for analysis of verbal memories because prior cueing, in which cueing events clearly precede the retention test, has not been applied. On the other hand, manipulations of contemporary context have had special importance for theoretical decisions in this area (some discussion of these effects may also be found in Chapter 2). Loosely speaking, the view labeled "encoding specificity" places a different emphasis on the importance of contemporary semantic context than the alternative, "tagging theory." The former interpretation views recognition and recall as about equally dependent on the retrieval process and hence predicts an influence of contemporary context for either method of assessing retention. Tagging theory is a less monolithic viewpoint, but the many separate versions agree that recall generally is a more complex process than recognition, and typically recognition is subsumed as one step in recall. The various versions of tagging theory also agree that variation in the context of verbal material, from one repetition of that material to the next, should have less effect on later recognition than on recall. The facts have led to modification and blurring in the distinctiveness of episodic and tagging theories.

Generally, increasing the similarity between the semantic context of learning and testing can enhance recall scores markedly. Certain negative consequences of cueing by semantic context may also impair recall, through mechanisms identified by some as "output interference" and by others as "cue overload." Changes in semantic context between learning and a test for recognition can have clear detrimental effects, and recognition sometimes is best when the context of learning and testing are most similar. But there are clear boundaries to this influence: Underwood and his associates have shown that for many cases of recognition learning much of the variance may be accounted for by a theory that emphasizes frequency judgments without reference to semantic context.

For understanding basic conditioning and learning with animal subjects, the prior cueing technique has become an increasingly important investigative tool. Manipulations of contemporary context are also useful (these were discussed at length in Chapter 2). A variety of prior cueing techniques have been found to alleviate forgetting from a variety of sources. Their application has led to reconsideration of the action of certain amnesic agents as primarily on memory retrieval rather than on memory storage; has provided an analytical paradigm comparing the properties of older, active or passive memories with those recently acquired; and has become increasingly relevant to understanding abnormal memory processing by persons with brain damage or Korsakoff symptoms and the behavior of neurotic persons with phobias.

Several largely unresolved but important issues of verbal memory processing were discussed. A basic problem is how one can understand the enhancement to recall caused by presenting semantically related words, in contrast to the apparent inefficiency in learning a list of words by storing together with each word a semantically related item that may later serve as a retrieval cue.

Other significant issues concern the fundamental action of reactivation events within the prior cueing procedure. One is whether reactivation treatments may alter the retrieval process as well as its effectiveness. Another is the role of new learning that may arise from reactivation treatments. Perhaps the most significant issue relevant to manipulations of either contemporary context or prior cueing is whether their primary effect is to promote discrimination among equally accessible memories or elicitation from among equally available (though not accessible) memories. The view represented by this book is the elicitation model. Elicitation is unlikely to be the primary mode of action of reactivation treatments in all cases, however, especially when there is reason to expect a variety of memories to be in an equally accessible state (this issue is also discussed in Spear, 1976).

What Is the Nature and Consequence of Mnemonic Preparation?

Even though an individual may be unable to control the circumstances of a retention test, events that precede it, or what is to be remembered, he or she typically is free to engage in a variety of activities that may alter retention or forgetting. Collectively, these activities are termed *mnemonic preparation.*

A conventional method for enhancing retention is to increase degree of learning. Tests of retention of discrete verbal units, the experimental paradigm that has yielded the most systematic evidence, do indicate less forgetting after higher degrees of learning. Only a few exceptions to this relationship may be found within this paradigm. Generality to broader classes of memory content and organisms tested is largely undetermined, although one may identify several instances of abnormal memory processing in which sources of forgetting are less effective for memories having a higher degree of original learning. Accordingly, we must be aware that many variables appearing to influence retention and forgetting may do so only indirectly by altering degree of learning.

Closely aligned to the concept of degree of learning is physical repetition of a perceived episode. It is in fact conventional to apply repetition toward enhancement of retention. This effect of repetition has been interpreted in terms of "strength" theory, in which strength is the fundamental dimension of a memory and cumulates with successive repetitions. This simplest version of strength theory has not worked because it assumes that individual repetitions lose their identity, and a great deal of data indicate that this is not so. Instead, frequency of repetition itself is stored as an important part of a memory. While it remains rather uncertain whether repetition directly acts to defend against later forgetting (or only indirectly by enhancing degree of original learning), spacing of repetitions clearly does have this direct effect, at least under some circumstances.

Human subjects are known to transform materials to be remembered in a variety of ways, including the classical mnemonic techniques (e.g., "method of loci"). There seems to be little doubt that such organizational or transformational techniques may enhance immediate recall, but whether they act to combat sources of forgetting is less clear. Some tests indicate that forgetting over a long interval may be lessened by applying certain conceptual rules as organizational devices, but this evidence is limited.

A promising conceptual framework for understanding retention has emphasized the importance of how episodes are processed during initial perception and thereafter. This "levels-of-processing" view has inspired several conceptual and empirical advances. This view is symptomatic of the increasing theoretical recognition that the nature of posttrial processing has special importance as a determinant of retention and forgetting. After many years of neglect, the rehearsal process has been studied directly. The general outcome has been increasing attention to kind rather than quantity of rehearsal as a determinant of long-term retention. Indeed, the interaction between kind of rehearsal and its influence after short compared to long retention intervals provides perhaps the most encouraging evidence for a temporally based theoretical distinction between "short-term memory" and "long-term memory."

Another type of posttrial processing among humans is termed *intentional forgetting*. Subjects directed to forget certain items after perceiving them show a clear deficit in recalling these items, though they often show adequate recognition of these same items. Beyond its intrinsic interest, this phenomenon has provided a useful tool for investigating rehearsal and posttrial processing in general.

Tests of mnemonic preparation in animals have lagged those with humans. Some comparable phenomena have been identified, including the benefit to retention from spaced repetitions and from the opportunity for posttrial processing.

Does Retention Depend on the Content of a Memory?

The content of an episode has seemed a likely determinant of how well the episode will be remembered. It has seemed especially reasonable that retention should be more effective for memories involving more familiar or more meaningful events, or involving dominant sensory modalities, or involving events of particular biological importance for the organism. For each of these instances, a body of systematic knowledge is under development.

As with so many other of the issues addressed in this book, the experimental analysis of memory content and its effect on retention and forgetting has progressed furthest with regard to the processing of verbal memories. The best evidence prior to 1960 indicated that forgetting of verbal units does not depend on their meaningfulness. This was unexpected, not only because more meaningful items are more rapidly learned but also because this finding conflicts with certain expectations of interference theory. Accordingly, a systematic theory was devised by Underwood and Postman (1960) to account simultaneously for previously determined absences and specific occurrences of an influence of meaningfulness on forgetting. A decade of study in response to this theory led to many new discoveries about memory processing and new ways of viewing meaningfulness (e.g., hierarchical conceptual structure). Yet the evidence consistently has indicated no direct influence of meaningfulness on forgetting.

Another property of verbal units, concreteness–imagery, has seemed likely to influence retention and forgetting because this dimension of "cue" or "peg" words has seemed important in classical mnemonic techniques. It has seemed, in short, that more concrete and readily imaged words should be more resistant to forgetting. Although immediate recall of words having higher concreteness–imagery often is more effective than that of words rated low in this dimension, it is unclear whether concreteness–imagery affects subsequent forgetting. The most careful studies have yielded mixed results. The evidence does not permit the conclusion that items of high concreteness–imagery are less prone to forgetting, and under some circumstances the converse has appeared (Postman & Burns, 1973).

When verbal information is processed, redundant sensory features associated with that information are stored as part of the memory. Perhaps, however, this adjunctive sensory information is not really redundant in effect, and acts to facilitate memory retrieval or to aid discrimination among alternative memories (for example, see Wickens, 1972). If so, the type and quantity of sensory information may influence retention. More direct effects of sensory modality on forgetting also are plausible. For example, the discriminative function of sensory attributes of a memory may be less effective if these attributes represent the most frequently applied sensory modalities and thus are subject to more interference from conflicting memories having the same sensory attributes. Or, certain processing characteristics inextricably linked to specific sensory modalities (e.g., sequential processing for most acoustic stimuli) may promote constraints on retention.

Experimental evidence has begun to suggest special characteristics of retention associated with certain sensory modalities (e.g., olfactory). Also, a "modality effect" in short-term retention with humans seems to be definite, with better immediate retention of items presented acoustically than presented visually. Like this "modality effect," two other considerations of sensory modality and forgetting have been prevalent. These topics concern relative retention and forgetting of pictures and their verbal labels, and whether acoustic stimuli are subject to important precategorical processing. Generally speaking, it has appeared that the processing of simple pictures typically incorporates the advantage of dual coding, visual and verbal–semantic, and this may affect forgetting relative to when only one type of encoding is applied. The forgetting and retention of complex pictures may have characteristics unlike those associated with simple verbal materials. Precategorical processing of acoustic units seems likely, although it is uncertain that phonetic signals associated with language are unique in terms of how they are processed and the behavioral products of their processing.

Among biologically oriented experiments with animals as subjects, analysis of the influence of memory content on forgetting is in its infancy but promises to provide a richer sampling of memory content than can be found with human subjects because of the greater experimental flexibility permitted with regard to tests of memories for aversive or even traumatic episodes. Studies so far have suggested some classes of events to which animals may respond with special characteristics of forgetting. Seemingly resistant to sources of forgetting are discrete overt responses, autonomic as contrasted with primarily skeletal responding, discriminative or conditioned stimuli as compared to less predictive contextual stimuli, and certain event combinations such as gustatory stimuli and visceral consequences.

9
Brief Comments on Selected Issues

It would be foolish to de-emphasize the importance of acquisition of a memory, because a memory's initial storage is so obviously a critical stage in its processing. The present viewpoint emphasizes, however, that it is at least equally useful to consider the processing that occurs afterward and leads to behavioral manifestation—or not—of that memory. This reflects an old message that bears repeating: Once acquired and stored, a memory does not maintain a steady probability of influencing behavior. Rather, accessibility of a memory fluctuates in a lawful manner, sometimes decreasing as the organism encounters sources of forgetting and sometimes increasing as the organism engages in the retrieval process. The focus of this book has been upon such post-acquisition processing of a memory.

The interest in forgetting and retention implies that analysis begin from a point of established acquisition of a memory. For the purpose of most empirical analyses, a further implication is that the characteristics of the acquired memory be specified precisely. Of special concern is quantification of one of these characteristics, "degree of learning", which often has been found to influence forgetting and retention.

The present viewpoint emphasizes that more than one source of forgetting may be specified empirically. "Forgetting", as defined operationally, may be induced by the occurrence of any of several events apart from the passage of time. A "source of forgetting" is any event that produces a decrement in learned performance. To qualify in this case, the decrement must be due to deficient memory processing and so cannot be attributable to performance deficits of a sensory, perceptual-motor or motivational nature. So long as forgetting from a specified source may be replicated with a variety of converging operations, the concept "source of forgetting" is no more tautological than conventional concepts such as "reinforcement". In this manner, therefore, "source of forgetting" is treated as an intervening variable, like the classical treatment of motivation, learning, and other concepts employed in psychobiology.

The intent of this book has been to consider retention and forgetting in terms of psychological processes common to both a variety of organisms and a reasonably broad spectrum of behaviors. We do not exclude the possibility of some common processes among all organisms and all behaviors. Major emphasis has been placed on normal processing of memories. Selected instances of abnormal processing were also considered in depth to provide perspective concerning the potential extremes of memory processing, biological limitations, and the inevitable advantage for understanding function by observing dysfunction.

To accomplish this purpose, it has been useful to examine memory processing among animals and humans. Phenomena associated with either animals or humans have been applied here rather interchangeably, but with caution, toward understanding areas and questions regarding memory processing. In doing so, we have not restricted our topic to the processing of verbal materials, nor have we restricted it to the processing of events that accompany basic conditioning. This is not meant to imply that in our attempts to understand memory processing we may ignore differences among organisms and among the events that constitute a memory. Indeed, general principles derived about our topic probably will require qualification in terms of both these factors and others, and each factor may constitute a major issue to be resolved in the course of understanding retention and forgetting. Note, however, that while it is likely that constraints on principles of memory processing will be required in terms of factors such as individual differences and the content of a memory, the specific nature of such limits, and whether they are needed at all, remains uncertain.

My intention has been to apply the soundest evidence available to evaluate issues of importance to understanding memory processing. While such an intention may seem inevitable (what is the alternative?), my point is to emphasize that evidence was selected conscientiously, largely on methodological grounds. Judgments of what is or is not "sound" evidence are not subjective; rather, there are recognized principles of methodology to govern experimental design (e.g., Underwood, 1957; Underwood & Shaughnessy, 1975). This reminder will seem trivial to most readers, but even a cursory survey of research on memory processing reveals that these principles are not always appreciated, even at the level of editorial review. On the other hand, the magnitude of information on memory processing is so vast that it is impossible to conduct a truly exhaustive search and summarization, and beyond that, there occasionally occur experiments that appear equally sound methodologically but yield conflicting conclusions. Some further selection clearly is necessary in determining which evidence to rely on.

Most of the predictions, theories, ideas, and hunches I have considered obviously have not arisen deductively from a framework of explicit postulates. Equally apparent has been my willingness to apply ideas evolved in one area of memory processing, such as verbal learning, to the analysis of phenomena evolved in a disparate area of research, such as basic conditioning with animal subjects. There are pitfalls with this approach, but it does seem both reasonable and desirable to apply ideas disciplined through systematic empirical evidence of some kind in preference to ideas not constrained by any empirical evidence. Fortunately, these extremes are not the sole alternatives.

Finally, the intention throughout these chapters has been to provide some degree of cohesion via a conceptual framework based on one of psychology's most ancient ideas. This is the notion, or principle, that a memory will be manifested in behavior in accordance with the presence of circumstances that accompanied its acquisition. This principle has been elaborated in earlier chapters, and elsewhere it has been considered as a guide to the design and interpretation of experiments believed to concern memory retrieval (e.g., Spear, 1971, 1973, 1976). Considerations of this particular application should not distract the reader from the value of the basic principle.

FURTHER ISSUES IN THE STUDY OF MEMORY PROCESSING

The selection and interpretation of evidence is more mechanical and less subjective than the selection of the important issues to be resolved in an area of knowledge. The particular issues judged most urgently to require attention for the understanding of memory processing reflect a judgment of the state of present knowledge about memory processing, the capacity of available techniques for resolving particular issues, and an estimate of how theories, or the general structure of knowledge, may develop in this area. What I wish to do now is to be more explicit about some remaining issues of importance that have not been identified in major headings or chapter titles earlier in the book.

None of the issues discussed here is particularly new—all have been discussed in some form by psychologists and philosophers for at least a century. There is, first, a set of issues that remain relatively intractable in terms of experimental investigation, so that their conceptual form has changed less than others over the years simply because we have not been able to learn about them through experimental tests.

Issues Relatively Intractable to Solution through Experimental Tests

One example from this first set of issues is the nature of the "specious present." This issue is interpreted here (perhaps differently than some have interpreted it) as the question of how an episode is delineated temporally for representation as a memory: If a memory represents a discrete set of events that has a beginning and an end, by what principles are the beginning and end determined? This issue cannot stand alone. It must be accompanied by the questions of whether the memorial representation of an episode actually includes a beginning and an end, and whether the beginning and end are represented explicitly (e.g., the beginning being a contextual or discriminative stimulus and the end being the reinforcer) or delineated in more implicit fashion (e.g., with an episode encapsulated as an example of a particular conceptual class of events such as *dinner* or *ballgame*). An alternative is that experiences are recorded continuously, as if the processing of memories includes a "recorder" or "camera" that runs uninterrupted from birth to death and has a "reel" with a capacity limited only by life span.

Another issue related closely to that of the specious present is how memories are structured. This issue may be viewed biologically in terms of the physiological basis of a memory and its processing, although this is not necessary. In strictly behavioral terms as well, we may ask what the dimensions of a memory might be, whether it is unitary, and if not unitary, how its components might be shared with other memories. The stability of this structure is yet another issue of importance, linked to questions raised within the Gestalt orientation that have received more direct experimental investigation (beginning with Bartlett, 1932) than the others mentioned in this section.

The final issue in this set concerns how a memory is evidenced most clearly in behavior. In other words, which unit of behavior corresponds best to the structure of a memory and thereby optimizes assessment of the influence of that memory on behavior? Should we consider the clearest indication of an accessible memory to be in the number of detailed separate events recalled about an episode, or in metaphorical reports of the nature (conceptual class, category) of the episode? Is a memory more "accessible" when the hungry animal performs the last thing it had done to attain food in training than when the sated animal has the same autonomic CNS reactions but without the overt skeletal behavior required in training? And if an episode involves dynamic separable events such as a series of training trials, is the better evidence of the memory of that episode shown by recollection (or other representative behavior) of the terminal trials, the initial trials, or some conceptual average of the trial events? Selection of the appropriate unit of analysis historically has been critical to the advancement of all areas of science.

The issues in this first set are not entirely immune to experimental test. For example, consider the case where a subject performs with 100% accuracy at the conclusion of discrimination learning but performs with only 60% accuracy on a retention test. The issue of the specious present arises when we ask whether the results of this test indicate failure to manifest in behavior the memory of the complete training episode or whether they indicate merely a failure to establish or to manifest a memory representing the *terminal* stages of training (when the animal responded with 100% accuracy). This question implies that different portions of training (e.g., early, middle, and late stages of training) may be represented as separable episodes in terms of discretely different memories. Further, it is conceivable that these results might faithfully reflect actual retrieval of the memory representing only the events that took place at the time early in training when the animal in fact was performing with 60% accuracy. My own opinion is that the latter possibility is most unlikely to be verified, although there is no empirical evidence on which to base this judgment. In any case, a test of these alternative interpretations could be made by accompanying each stage of training with a unique contextual stimulus, then determining whether performance at that stage could be reestablished in accordance with the particular contextual stimulus. Note that proper implementation of such an experiment would require a complex set of control conditions and carefully selected contextual stimuli, and its interpretation must be sensitive to the influence of proactive and retroactive interference, but it is not necessary to discuss this matter here.

In considering issues of this sort, which initially seem to be distant from the operations and capabilities of laboratory investigation, we have occasion to admire the ingenuity of experimental psychologists and so become optimistic about the development of proper tests. One of my most enjoyable moments in teaching is to describe the concepts of ''transsituational identity'' and ''automatic access'' and ask students how they might test these assumptions empirically (these concepts were discussed in Chapter 8; see also Watkins & Tulving, 1975). Students typically find this an impossible task and conclude (especially biologically oriented students) that before such assumptions can be judged empirically, complete knowledge of where and how a memory is represented physiologically is needed. At that point, it is a great pleasure to describe how these assumptions have been tested with scientific equipment consisting of only a sheet of paper, a pencil, and tests of recognition and recall with college sophomores as subjects.

Finally, we may touch briefly the issue of the structure of memory, for which tests have begun to be developed (Tulving & Watkins, 1975). Tulving and Bower (1974) present a discussion of considerable relevance to this issue, and the reader is referred to their chapter for elaboration.

Rejecting the characterization of memory either as a relatively precise copy of perceived events or as having the single dimension of strength, Tulving and Bower (1974) offer this conclusion about the structure of a memory:

> Many researchers agree now that (a) traces (memories) of individual events can be studied and described, (b) they are usefully conceptualized as collections of more elementary components or features, (c) these features and components differ from one another in some sense qualitatively, (d) they are at least, to some extent, independently manipulable and variable, and (e) the extent to which a particular feature is represented in a memory trace can be quantitatively assessed. (page 297)

Tulving and Bower suggest, however, that it is of far greater value to consider the properties of memories in terms of their function and processes such as retrieval, rather than persisting ''in the attempt to define or characterize memory traces in terms of what they *are*'' (1974, p. 293).

Important Experimentally Tractable Issues Rarely Tested: Degree of Learning and the Nature of Interference

The most obvious and inevitable source of forgetting, and certainly the most ubiquitous, is a temporal interval between learning and testing. The natural question is whether amount of forgetting per unit of time is a constant, and if not, which parameters determine rate of forgetting. Much of this book has addressed these questions in one way or another. We have considered, for example, the remarkable answers evolved within the boundaries imposed by certain tests of the retention of verbal materials: According to the analysis of Underwood (e.g., 1964, 1966, 1972), amount of forgetting over a given period is invariant if degree of original learning and amount of interference (i.e., acquired verbal associations that conflict with those to be remembered) can be fixed. With proper control exerted over these parameters, forgetting over a specified period of time theoretically could thus be predicted without reference to the meaningfulness of the items to be remembered, the nature of the interrelationships among these items, or individual differences among the subjects being tested, even though each of these three factors produce dramatic differences in the rate of learning verbal materials. The boundaries to which this conclusion applies were drawn carefully and minor exceptions, such as the modified rate of forgetting found with variation in intertrial interval during certain circumstances of learning, were noted. Subsequently, a few other exceptions have arisen in this context, such as those discussed earlier with reference to "mnemonic preparation," but for these the story is less complete. Moreover, it remains possible that all exceptions ultimately may be shown to influence either degree of learning or the effective amount of interference. The importance of the latter two variables will require some further elaboration, although we may be brief at this point.

Degree of learning.   Degree of learning is defined by the test performance of subjects in control conditions not given the source of forgetting. If training is so complete that performance in these control conditions is asymptotic—as good as can be measured—then although still further training may alter the influence of a source of forgetting, control of degree of learning is lost and so is the opportunity for proper analysis of retention and forgetting. These technical points are fairly obvious, although not always appreciated and implemented. *Conceptualization* of degree of learning is a different matter.

There appear to be two general alternatives. Degree of learning may reflect primarily the value of a "strength" attribute of a memory, or it may correspond to the number or configuration of the attributes of a memory. For example, the number of different contextual attributes may be the critical dimension of degree of learning that predicts retention; or perhaps when retention is manifested in terms of only a few attributes of a memory (e.g., a particular response emitted to a particular conditioned or discriminative stimulus), greater "degree of learning" may exist the more often that particular subset of attributes is held within separately stored memories (whether or not the assumption of transsituational identity is appropriate). It would appear that the latter conception of degree of learning must be accompanied by explicit assumptions concerning the structure of a memory. In my opinion, we are not yet near a resolution of these alternative views of degree of learning, but some further evidence and ideas will be discussed later in this chapter (see also, e.g., Hintzman, 1976).

Nature of interference.   We noted earlier that theories of how conflicting learning determines retention have evolved almost exclusively within the context of human verbal memory processing. Theorizing about this topic increasingly has tended to emphasize the role of the vast linguistic network possessed by humans and, more generally, the flexibility that our memory-processing systems must possess to deal with the massive amounts of information encountered daily.One might wonder whether such theorizing makes any contact with the memory processing of other organisms or with that of humans for episodes with minimal verbal content. There is little doubt that animals also possess associative networks of some range, and the same may be true for nonverbal behaviors in humans, but it is possible that the quantitative differences may effectively become qualitative for purposes of analysis.

My opinion is that the nature of interference in retention will be understood in terms of principles that, for the most part, have wide generality in their application. Confidence in this conjecture is increased by an observation discussed by Runquist (1975) in his theory of the nature and function of interference in verbal memory processing. He suggests that "activation of erroneous associations" is a primary mechanism through which conflicting learning influences retention of verbal associations (p. 156). With this, Runquist implies that the mere perception of a stimulus element associated with the material to be remembered is sufficient to activate competing memories having attributes representing the same stimulus element. The resulting competition among the activated conflicting memories may be resolved by a variety of mechanisms that ultimately reduce the influence of this interference on retention. Perhaps it is at this stage that a human's enormous flexibility in processing memories of a semantic nature is implemented in unique fashion.

Nevertheless, the point is that the basic characteristics of the interference effect may be similar for memories of quite different content or for memories acquired by nonverbal organisms.

A Final Word—On Individual Differences

A book on retention and forgetting might be expected to include summaries and charts indicating how much forgetting one should expect for a particular species after a particular source of forgetting. The reason I have not done so can be appreciated by considering the following samples of forgetting.

Wolves "tamed" to be approachable by humans, fed by them, touched, and so forth without retreat or hostile retaliation are reported to remain friendly to humans for nearly 2 years in the absence of such contact. Young wolf pups, however, fail to maintain this adaptation to humans over intervals longer than 6 months (Mech, 1970). Jackdaws raised by humans maintain "courting-like" responses to humans 6–8 months later even though they have traveled in the interim with a flock of other jackdaws, and they may even recognize individual humans after a similar interval (Eibl-Eibesfeldt, 1970; Tinbergen, 1963). Similarly, male turkeys that are allowed to follow humans at a critical young age and so continue to follow them later (i.e., are "imprinted" on humans) maintain preferential responses to humans for periods of 5 years (Eibl-Eibesfelt, 1970). Nice (1943) reported that a song sparrow that sang a species-specific defensive tune when brought into a room containing a stuffed owl emitted the same tune when returned to the room 18 months later, although the owl was absent. Salmon have been shown to retain odor discriminations over periods as long as 6 months, which tends to confirm the hypothesis of Hassler and his associates that distinctive odors guide the salmon back to its place of birth after intervals of 5 years (Hasler & Larsen, 1955); practical application of this principle has led to the restocking of salmon in several rivers in the eastern United States. Significant retention of a visual discrimination has been recorded in the octopus after a 27-day interval, in the carp after a 20-month interval, and in the trout after 150 days, and dolphins show significant retention of a learned visual discrimination after a 7-month interval (Kellogg & Rice, 1964). The crested newt exhibits excellent retention of a discrimination 10, 18, or 26 days after training, even when metamorphosis intervenes between training and testing (Hershkowitz & Samuel, 1973). Retention of apparent observational learning has been claimed for the parakeet after intervals of 3 months (Dawson & Foss, 1965). Gerbils that acquire a black–white discrimination to avoid aversive heat exhibit significant savings 180 days later (Neylon & Brosgole, 1974).

In systematic tests, the elephant has lived up to its reputation for "never forgetting": Rensch (1957) found that an elephant exhibited quite good retention (accuracy was 75% or better) 1 year after having acquired a series of visual discriminations and 1.5 years after acquiring auditory discriminations. Similarly, among three elephants tested 8 years after acquiring a light–dark discrimination, one made only 2 errors in reachieving the original criterion of 20 successive correct responses; although the other two elephants were seriously deficient, they were discovered to have suffered severe visual impairment during the interim (Markowitz, Schmidt, Nadal, & Squier, 1975).

Using a wide variety of tasks that might be characterized generally as variations on the delayed-response paradigm, Beritoff (1971) has compiled a great deal of data on forgetting in a variety of species. The maximal retention interval that could be tolerated for accuracy in returning to a particular location where the animals previously were fed was 8–10 seconds for goldfish; 3–4 minutes for summer frogs; 2–4 minutes for marsh turtles; 2 minutes for lizards when the ambient temperature was cold and 3 minutes when it was warm; 1–5 days for chickens; 1–2 months for rabbits, cats, and dogs; and 45 days for baboons. The maximal retention interval tolerated for accurate avoidance of a location in which an electric shock had previously been administered was 10–11 seconds for goldfish, 0 seconds for winter frogs, 3–4 hours for summer frogs, 4–5 minutes for marsh turtles and lizards, 1–2 weeks for chickens, and 3–4 weeks for dogs and cats; the maximal retention interval that could be tolerated with evidence of a maintained conditioned reflex was 1 week for rabbits, 2–4 weeks for goldfish, 3–4 weeks for lizards, and 4–6 weeks for marsh turtles.

How useful is this type of comparative information for developing principles of retention and forgetting? It does not require much study of these data to observe apparently huge differences from species to species in retention when there is a delay between training and testing. But enticing though it may be to grasp for inferences about phylogenetic orderings in forgetting, the ubiquitous "comparative problem" precludes meaningful conclusions about species differences, as with any subject variable (see, e.g., Bitterman, 1960; Underwood, 1957; Underwood & Shaughnessy, 1975). Without equating from species to species the specific value of parameters known or suspected to influence forgetting—for example, degree of learning, motivational factors, events occurring during the retention test, and so forth—we cannot know whether such differences in forgetting are really due to differences in species. This is elementary. But beyond problems of method—even if such parameter values were properly controlled, which may be impossible, unlikely, or too difficult to justify on economic grounds—it is unclear how such comparisons would help us achieve principles governing retention and forgetting, except in a quite indirect manner.

Perhaps the greatest value of experiments involving subject variables is to test the generality of phenomena of memory processing. Concurrently, important species differences may be determined through evidence that memory-processing phenomena observed in one class of subjects may not occur or may be different for another class of subjects.

Based on comparative investigations like those represented earlier, Beritoff (1971) has reported retention phenomena resembling those discussed earlier in this book, with respect to different species. A sample of these may be listed as follows:

1. Beritoff seems to assume that retention is some function of the number or kind of memory attributes representing an episode. Generally, he notes, if a dog's original perception of the location of food is based on a single sensory modality such as vision, significant retention is found only for relatively short intervals, from a few minutes to at most one or two hours. But when a larger number of attributes may have been stored as the memory of the episode, "complex perception" occurs "in which all sensory modalities, including olfaction and taste, participate, [and] the image of the location of food is retained for many days or weeks" (Beritoff, 1971, p. 6). Beritoff notes further that an animal's toleration of long retention intervals could be increased dramatically if it were permitted to go close enough to the food to smell it (but not permitted to eat it), in comparison to animals not permitted closer than a meter from the food. This may be viewed as indicating an influence of memory content on retention. Obvious questions arise concerning degree of original learning, secondary reinforcement, attention, and so forth, but the point is the relationship between Beritoff's evi-

dence and our earlier discussion concerning the effect of memory content on retention.

2. Beritoff reports treatments that enhance an animal's capacity for tolerating a retention interval; some of these may be interpreted as reactivation treatments that alleviate forgetting. Beritoff found that dogs taken out of their cages and walked about the room during the retention interval (presumably without being within sight or smell of the food) tolerated significantly longer retention intervals than dogs confined to their cages. Beritoff (1971) interpreted this enhanced retention after long intervals as due to "movement of the animal about the room [which] can lead to a reinforced production of the image of the location of the food" (p. 13). Another study by Beritoff showed that after an animal is allowed auditory or visual perception of food shifted to a new location in a particular room, feeding in *another* room may alleviate forgetting; that is, although a long retention interval passes from the time of original perception, retention remains efficient. Similarly, for a delayed-response task for which the retention capacity of chickens was 2–3 minutes, this capacity could be increased to 5–10 minutes if the chickens were fed during the retention interval.

3. An influence of apparently nonspecific retroactive interference, perhaps analogous to the influence of illumination on delayed matching to sample (see Chapter 3), is reported by Beritoff in terms of the animal's location during the retention interval. For example, a monkey presented food on several successive occasions in different locations within the same room typically had a retention capacity of 30 to 60 minutes; but if the monkey was presented food in a new place in the experimental room and then returned immediately to its home cage, efficient retention performance was evident as long as 1 week later. Further, if a piece of food was placed somewhere in a completely *new* room in the monkey's presence, efficient retention performance could occur 1 1/2 months later, reports Beritoff. As another indication of interference in retention, Beritoff reported a very rapid decline in the length of the retention interval tolerated by dogs if, within the same room on the same day, several tests were given with the food assigned different locations on each test. On the following day, however, the dog's retention capacity on the first trial would return to the higher level that was present at the beginning of the previous day. It is as if proactive interference built up throughout the day and when the context changed and a new day began, the proactive interference was released.

4. Suggestions concerning the ontogeny of retention among different species are also presented by Beritoff (see Chapter 5). When about 1 1/2 months of age, dogs permitted visual perception of the location of food could find it efficiently only if permitted to do so before 20 to 30 seconds had elapsed; but by the age of 3–4 months delays of 6 or 7 minutes could be tolerated. Similar improvement was noted in the retention capacity of kittens as they mature.

This use of subject variables for identifying which phenomena of retention and forgetting are particularly robust, and hence are probably most important, seems to me to be a great benefit from the testing of different species. But, especially with regard to construction of a phylogenetic ordering based on retention capacity, note that the effectiveness of memory processing need not have been favored throughout evolution. As Robin (1973) has argued, using intriguing evidence, species survival need not be linked to cognitive aptitudes; in some cases, effectiveness in learning and retention might be a disadvantage to survival.

Individual differences among humans in retention and forgetting. Underwood (1964) reported this startling inference: The most systematic data seemed to indicate little or no individual differences among human subjects in rate of forgetting. Among subjects learning a single list of verbal units and tested for retention a day or so later, so much of the variance in forgetting could be accounted for by differences in degree of original learning that little was left to attribute to differences among subjects. If this inference were verified generally, the implications for understanding retention and forgetting would be enormous. It would suggest not only that the fundamental source of forgetting is unitary but also that it is a biological constant, at least within species. It would suggest either that interference and reactivation events during the interval are of little consequence for retention or that these factors are equally present and equally effective among all individuals. Such crucial implications obviously could readily be multiplied. This illustrates the value of studying individual differences in retention and forgetting. The more general values of considering individual differences for evaluating theories has been discussed by Underwood (1975).

A further application of the study of individual differences is to identify the possibly unique characteristics of memory processing found in individuals who seem unusual in their capacity for retention or forgetting. Especially when obvious physiological abnormalities are discounted, such individuals may provide clues to critical features of retention and forgetting through identification of other abnormal features of their behavior. Correlational evidence of this kind obviously is inconclusive and often misleading, but it can also provide a source of relatively disciplined ideas for experimental tests.

Two systematic tests of exceptional mnemonists are now familiar to students of memory processing. These were conducted by Hunt and Love (1972) and Luria (1968). Some similarities between the individuals tested (VP and S) include the intriguing feature that both originated from a similar geographic location in Eastern Europe and had undergone early education that emphasized memorization.

The behavior of these mnemonists differed in interesting ways, also. A striking characteristic of S, unlike VP, was his capacity for synaesthesia. Synaesthesia is the perceptual capacity manifested when a given stimulus consistently arouses sensations unexpected on the basis of the physical properties of the stimulus. A common case is "chromaesthesia," the imaging of colors following sensation of apparently unrelated stimuli such as sound. A topic long of interest in psychology, examples of synaesthesia have been described for many years, as exemplified in a paper by Myers (1914). Myers describes two individuals who consistently reported a spectrum of colors in regular association with specific acoustic frequencies. One of these persons reported that although the highest frequency he heard was colorless, as the pitch of the tone was lowered, the colors imaged changed correspondingly to green, greenish blue, blue, pink, orange, and brown. The second case was an accomplished painter who experienced a quite different relationship between tone and color: For her, the highest frequencies were yellow and successively lower frequencies were blue, light green, "flame," deep golden, "clear purple," dark blue streaked with violet, and finally, clear blue. Both of these individuals were reported paradoxically to have poor visual imagery, and it is interesting that the painter enjoyed music in particular because of the visual sensations they aroused for different composers. For example, this individual reported that Chopin aroused "very translucent colors such as green leaves in the spring," while Schumann's compositions did not elicit primary colors but, rather, "give purples and the like—not transparent colors" (Myers, 1914, p. 123). Luria's S seemed to capitalize on such synaesthesia to optimize retention. Yet VP was reported not to possess this capacity, nor did he appear to have a special capacity for eidetic imagery. Rather, VP attributed much of his own success to the application of mnemonic techniques involving transformations of the material, although he tended more toward transformations involving verbal concepts than to the sensory transformations S employed.

We noted earlier that instances of mnemonic preparation might be more effective in the hands of some individuals than others, perhaps through experience or special perceptual capacities. Like their common early training in memorization, their special perceptual capacities constitute an interesting similarity between VP and S. While S apparently has exceptional gifts for imaging and for synaesthesia, VP was reported by Hunt and Love (1972) to be "unusually rapid at noticing small details between stimuli" (p. 257). This capacity was also manifested in terms of a high score on Guilford's test to isolate the factor of perceptual speed. Our earlier discussion of mnemonic preparation indicated that increasing theoretical attention is being given to the manner of initial perception or "level of processing" of materials to be learned, and there is evidence, impressive though largely indirect, showing that the nature of this initial perception may determine subsequent rate of forgetting. The importance of this initial processing for retention and forgetting may be exemplified by S and VP and is also consistent with Underwood's finding that when a retention interval is the source of forgetting and degree of original learning under highly structured circumstances is equated, individual differences in rate of forgetting are minimal. Further study of possible individual differences in retention and forgetting would appear to be not only an intriguing undertaking but a useful one as well for the purpose of developing general principles in this area.

SUMMARY AND CONCLUSIONS

This final chapter considered selected issues believed to be of particular importance for understanding how memories are processed and retention or forgetting achieved. Some of these issues seem beyond the reach of current research methods. Not difficult to generate and not ignored by philosophers and psychologists, examples of such experimentally intractable issues include the question of the specious present, whether experience is represented memorially in terms of discrete episodes, and if so, what principles might determine the beginning and end of an episodic memory. The related issue is how memories are structured, on the one hand in terms of physiological substrates (for which there is increasing suggestion but no definitive answers) and, on the other, in terms of the dimensions conceivable for a memory and for its processing. Another issue in this category is which unit of analysis is best suited for understanding the structure of a memory and the manner in which it is processed to influence behavior.

Some of the critical issues more susceptible to experimental tests have yet to receive the degree of investigation commensurate with their importance. These include the influence of degree of original learning on retention and forgetting and the precise mechanisms through which interference alters retention and forgetting among all species.

A final portion of this chapter concerned individual differences in retention and forgetting. It is concluded that the analytical advantage of comparing memory processing by individuals, between or within species, is limited for investigations directed at simple quantitative statements about relative forgetting. This approach promises to be increasingly useful, however, in terms of studies concentrated on interactions between subject variables and other variables known to influence retention and forgetting.

References

Aaronson, D. Temporal factors in perception and short-term memory. *Psychological Bulletin,* 1967, **67,** 130–144.

Adams, H. E. Extinction of the effect of one ECS. *Psychonomic Science,* 1966, **5,** 295–296.

Adams, H. E. & Calhoun, K. S. Indices of memory recovery following electroconvulsive shock. *Physiology and Behavior,* 1972, **9,** 783–787.

Adams, H. E., Calhoun, K. S., Davis, J. W. & Peters, R. D. Effects of isolation on retrograde amnesia produced by ECS in multiple trial learning. *Physiology and Behavior,* 1974, **12,** 499–501.

Adams, J. A. *Human memory.* New York: McGraw-Hill, 1967.

Adams, J. A. The second facet of forgetting: A review of warm-up decrement. *Psychological Bulletin,* 1961, **58,** 257–273.

Adams, W. Effect of pretraining on long-term memory improvement. *Developmental Psychology,* 1973, **9,** 433.

Agranoff, B. W., Effects of antibiotics on long-term memory formation in the goldfish. In W. K. Honig & P. H. R. James (Editors), *Animal Memory.* New York: Academic Press, 1971, 243–258.

Agranoff, B. W., & Klinger, P. D. Puromycin effect on memory fixation in the goldfish. *Science,* 1964, **146,** 952–953.

Aiken, E. G. & Gibson, K. L. Continuous and fixed ratio reinforcement effects in extinction one day and three weeks after acquisition. *Psychonomic Science,* 1965, **3,** 527–528.

Albert, D. J. The effect of spreading depression on the consolidation of learning. *Neuropsychologia,* 1966, **4,** 49–64.

Alloway, T. M. Learning and memory in insects. *Annual Review of Entomology,* 1972, **17,** 43–56.

Allport, G. W. *Personality: A psychological interpretation.* New York: Holt, 1937.

Alpern, H. P. Facilitation of learning by implantation of strychnine sulphate in the central nervous system. Unpublished doctoral dissertation, University of California, Irvine, 1968.

Alpern, H. P. & Crabbe, J. C. Facilitation of the long-term store of memory with strychnine. *Science,* 1972, **177,** 722–724.

Alpern, H. P. & Kimble, D. P. Retrograde amnesic effects of diethyl ether and bis (trifluoroethyl) ether. *Journal of Comparative and Physiological Psychology,* 1967, **63,** 168–171.

Alpern, H. P. & Marriott, J. G. Short-term memory: Facilitation and disruption with cholinergic agents. *Physiology and Behavior,* 1973, **11,** 571–575.

Ammons, R. B. Acquisition of motor skill: I. Quantitative analysis and theoretical formulation *Psychological Review,* 1947, **54,** 263–281.

Amsel, A. Selective association and the anticipatory goal response mechanism as explanatory concepts in learning theory. *Journal of Experimental Psychology,* 1949, **39,** 785–799.

485

Anderson, A. C., Evidences of Reminiscence in the Rat in Maze Learning, *Journal of Comparative Psychology*, 1940, **30**, 399–412.

Anderson, J. R. & Bower, G. H. Recognition and retrieval processes in free recall. *Psychological Review*, 1972, **79**, 97–123.

Anderson, J. R. & Bower, G. H. A propositional theory of recognition memory. *Memory and Cognition*, 1974, **2**, 406–412.

Anisman, H. Time-dependent variations in aversively motivated behaviors: Nonassociative effects of cholinergic and catecholaminergic activity. *Psychological Review*, 1975, **82**, 359–385.

Archer, E. J. A re-evaluation of the meaningfulness of all possible CVC trigrams. *Psychological Monographs*, 1960, **74**, (10, whole number 497).

Asratian, E. A. *Compensatory adaptations, reflex activity and the brain.* Oxford: Pergamon Press, 1965.

Atkinson, R. C. & Shiffrin, R. M. Human memory: A proposed system and its control processes. In K. W. Spence & J. T. Spence (Eds.), *The psychology of learning and motivation.* Vol. 2. New York: Academic Press, 1968, 89–105.

Auerbach, P. & Carlton, P. L. Retention deficits correlated with a deficit in the corticoid response to stress. *Science*, 1971, **173**, 1148–1149.

Averbach, E. & Sperling, G. Short-term storage of information in vision. In C. Cherry (Ed.) *Information theory.* London: Butterworths, London, 1961.

Avis, H. H. The effects of temporary disruption of electrical activity of the brain on retention. Unpublished Ph.D. dissertation, Rutgers University, 1969.

Azrin, N. H., Holz, W. C. & Hake, D. F. Fixed-ratio punishment. *Journal of the Experimental Analysis of Behavior*, 1963, **6**, 141–148.

Bacon, W. E. & Stanley, W. C. Avoidance learning in neonatal dogs. *Journal of Comparative and Physiological Psychology*, 1970, **70**, 448–452.

Baddeley, A. D. Theories of amnesia. In A. Kennedy & A. Wilkes (Eds.), *Studies in long-term memory,* New York: Wiley and Sons, 1975.

Baddeley, A. D., & Hitch, G. Working memory. In. G. H. Bower (Ed.), *The Psychology of Learning and Motivation. Vol. 8.* New York, Academic Press, 1974.

Baddeley, A. D. & Warrington, E. K. Amnesia and the distinction between long and short-term memory. *Journal of Verbal Learning and Verbal Behavior*, 1970, **9**, 176–189.

Baddeley, A. D. & Warrington, E. K. Memory coding and amnesia. *Neuropsychologia*, 1973, **11**, 159–165.

Bahrick, H. P. Two-phase model for prompted recall. *Psychological Review*, 1970, **77**, 215–222.

Bahrick, H. P., Bahrick, P. O., & Wittlinger, R. P. Fifty years of memory for names and faces: A cross-sectional approach. *Journal of Experimental Psychology: General*, 1975, **104**, 54–75.

Bahrick, H. P. & Boucher, B. Retention of visual and verbal codes of the same stimuli. *Journal of Experimental Psychology*, 1968, **78**, 417–422.

Bailey, C. J. The effectiveness of drives as cues. *Journal of Comparative and Physiological Psychology*, 1955, **48**, 183–187.

Bailey, C. J. & Porter, L. W. Relevant cues in drive discrimination in cats. *Journal of Comparative and Physiological Psychology*, 1955, **48**, 180–182.

Banker, G., Hunt, E. & Pagano, R. Evidence supporting the memory disruption hypothesis of electroconvulsive shock action. *Physiology and Behavior*, 1969, **4**, 895–899.

Barbizet, J. *Human memory and its Pathology,* San Francisco: W. H. Freeman & Company, 1970.

Barnes, J. M. & Underwood, B. J. "Fate" of first-list associations in transfer theory. *Journal of Experimental Psychology*, 1959, **58**, 97–105.

Barondes, S. H. Protein-synthesis dependent and protein-synthesis independent memory storage processes. In D. Deutsch and J. A. Deutsch (Eds.), *Short-term memory.* New York: Academic Press, 1975, 380–390.

Barondes, S. H. & Cohen, H. D. Delayed and sustained effects of acetoxycycloheximide on memory in mice. *Proceedings of the National Academy of Sciences*, 1967, **14**, 371–376.

Barondes, S. H. & Cohen, H. D. Memory impairment after subqutaneous injection of acetoxycy-cloheximide. *Science,* 1968, **160,** 556–557.

Barondes, S. H. & Jarvik, M. E. The influences of actinomycin-D on brain RNA synthesis and on memory. *Journal of Neurochemistry,* 1964, **11,** 187–195.

Barondes, S. H. & Squire, L. R. Slow biological processes in memory storage and "recovery" of memory. In J. L. McGaugh (Ed.), *The chemistry of mood, motivation and memory.* New York: Plenum Press, 1972.

Barrett, R. J., Leith, N. J. & Ray, O. S. The effects of pituitary-adrenal manipulations on time-dependent processes in avoidance learning. *Physiology and Behavior,* 1971, **7,** 663–665.

Barrett, R. J. & Ray, O. S. Attenuation of habituation by electroconvulsive shock. *Journal of Comparative and Physiological Psychology,* 1969, **69,** 133–135.

Barrett, T. R. & Ekstrand, B. R. Second-order associations in single-list retention. *Journal of Experimental Psychology: Human Learning and Memory,* 1975, **104,** 41–49.

Barrett, T. R., Maier, W., Ekstrand, B. R. & Pellegrino, K. W. Effects of experimenter-imposed organization on long-term forgetting. *Journal of Experimental Psychology: Human Learning and Memory,* 1975, **104,** 480–490.

Bartlett, S. C. *Remembering: A study in experimental and social psychology.* Cambridge: Cambridge University Press, 1932.

Beach, F. A., Hebb, D. O., Morgan, C. T. & Nissen, H. W. *The neuropsychology of Lashley: Selective papers of K. S. Lashley.* New York: McGraw Hill, 1960.

Begg, I. Imagery and integration in the recall of words. *Canadian Journal of Psychology,* 1973, **27,** 159–163.

Begg, I. Recall of meaningful phrases. *Journal of Verbal Learning and Verbal Behavior,* 1972, **11,** 431–439.

Begg, I. & Robertson, R. Imagery and long-term retention. *Journal of Verbal Learning and Verbal Behavior,* 1973, **12,** 689–700.

Bellezza, F. S. & Walker, R. J. Storage-coding trade-off in short-term store. *Journal of Experimental Psychology,* 1974, **102,** 629–633.

Benowitz, L. I. & Sperry, R. W. Amnesic effects of lithium chloride in chicks. *Experimental Neurology,* 1973, **40,** 540–546.

Berger, B. D. Learning in the anesthetized rat. Paper presented at meetings of the Eastern Psychological Association, Atlantic City, April 2–4, 1970.

Berger, B. D. Conditioning of food aversions by injections of psychoactive drugs. *Journal of Comparative and Physiological Psychology,* 1972, **81,** 21–26.

Beritoff, J. S. *Vertebrate memory: Characteristics and origin.* New York: Plenum Press, 1971.

Bessemer, D. W. Retention of object discriminations by learning set experienced monkeys. (Unpublished Doctoral Dissertation, University of Wisconsin, 1967, Cited by Bessemer & Stollnitz, 1971).

Bessemer, D. W. & Stollnitz, F. Retention of discriminations and an analysis of learning set. In A. M. Schrier and F. Stollnitz (Eds.), *Behavior of nonhuman primates: Modern research trends, Vol. 4.* New York: Academic Press, 1971, pp. 1–58.

Bickford, R., Mulder, D. W., Dodge, H. W., Svien, H. J. & Rome, H. P. Changes in memory function produced by electrical stimulation of the temporal lobes in man. *Research Publications of the Association for Research in Nervous and Mental Disease,* 1958, **36,** 227–257.

Bilodeau, E. A. Retention. In E. A. Bilodeau (Ed.), *Acquisition of skill.* New York: Academic Press, 1966, 315–350.

Bilodeau, E. A. (Editor) *Acquisition of skill.* New York: Academic Press, 1966.

Bindra, D. Stimulus change, reaction to novelty and response decrement. *Psychological Review,* 1959, **66,** 96–105.

Bindra, D. Components of general activity in the analysis of behavior. *Psychological Review,* 1961, **68,** 205–215.

Bindra, D. & Cameron, L. Changes in experimentally produced anxiety with the passage of time: Incubation effect. *Journal of Experimental Psychology,* 1953, **45,** 197–203.

Bindra, D., Nyman, K. & Wise, J. Barbituate-induced dissociation of acquisition and extinction: Role of movement initiation in processes. *Journal of Comparative and Physiological Psychology,* 1965, **60,** 223–228.

Bindra, D. & Reichert, H. Dissociation of movement initiation without dissociation of response choice. *Psychonomic Science,* 1966, **4,** 95–96.

Bintz, J. Effects of detention in and removal from the training environment on retention of aversively motivated behavior. *Learning and Motivation,* 1972, **3,** 44–50.

Birnbaum, I. M. Context stimuli in verbal learning and the persistance of associative factors. *Journal of Experimental Psychology,* 1966, **71,** 483–487.

Bitterman, M. E. Toward a comparative psychology of learning. *American Psychologist,* 1960, **15,** 704–712.

Bitterman, M. E. Phyletic differences in learning. *American Psychologist,* 1965, **20,** 396–410.

Bjork, R. A. Theoretical implications of directed forgetting. In A. W. Melton & E. Martin (Eds.), *Coding processes in human memory.* Washington, D. C.: Winston, 1972.

Black, A. H. The operant conditioning of central nervous system electrical activity. In G. H. Bower (Ed.), *The Psychology of Learning and Motivation.* Vol. 6 New York: Academic Press, 1972.

Blake, M. & Okada, R. Intralist cueing following retroactive inhibition of well-learned items. *Journal of Experimental Psychology,* 1973, **101,** 386–388.

Blechner, M. J., Day, R. S. & Cutting, J. E. Processing two dimensions of nonspeech stimuli: The auditory-phonetic distinction reconsidered. *Journal of Experimental Psychology: Human Perception and Performance,* 1976, **2,** 257–266.

Bliss, D. K. Dissociated learning and state-dependent retention induced by pentobarbital in the rhesus monkey. *Journal of Comparative and Physiological Psychology,* 1973, **84,** 149–161.

Bliss, D. K. Theoretical explanations of drug-dissociative behaviors. *Federation Proceedings,* 1974, **33,** 1787–1796.

Bliss, D. K., Sledjeski, M., & Leiman, A. L. State-dependent choice behavior in the rhesus monkey. *Neuropsychologia,* 1971, **9,** 51–58.

Bloch, V. Facts and hypothesis concerning memory consolidation processes. *Brain Research,* 1970, **24,** 561–575.

Bloch, V., deweer, B., & Hennevin, E. Suppression de l'Amnesia retrograde et consolidation d'un apprentissage a essai unique par stimulation reticulaire. *Physiology and Behavior,* 1970, **5,** 1235–1241.

Blough, D. S. Delayed matching in the pigeon. *Journal of the Experimental Analysis of Behavior,* 1959, **2,** 151–160.

Blum, G. S., Graef, J. R., Hauenstein, L. S. & Passini, F. T. Distinctive mental contexts in long-term memory. *International Journal of Clinical and Experimental Hypnosis,* 1971, **19,** 117–133.

Bobrow, S. A. & Bower, G. H. Comprehension and recall of sentences. *Journal of Experimental Psychology,* 1969, **80,** 455–461.

Booth, D. A. Protein synthesis and memory. In J. A. Deutsch (Ed.) *The physiological basis of memory.* New York: Academic Press, 1973, 27–58.

Booth, D. A. & Pilcher, C. W. T. Behavioral effects of protein synthesis inhibitors: Consolidation blockade or negative reinforcement. In G. B. Ansell & P. B. Bradley (Eds.), Macro molecules and behavior. London: McMillan, 1973.

Bower, G. H. Organizational factors in memory. *Cognitive Psychology,* 1970, **1,** 18–46.

Bower, G. H. A multi-component theory of the memory trace. In K. W. Spence & J. T. Spence (eds.), *The Psychology of Learning and Motivation.* Vol. 1. New York: Academic Press, 1967.

Bower, G. H. Stimulus-sampling theory of encoding variability. In A. W. Melton & E. Martin (Eds.), *Coding processes in human memory.* Washington, D.C.: Winston, 1972 (a).

Bower, G. H. A selective review of organizational factors in memory. In E. Tulving & W. Donaldson (Eds.), *Organization of Memory*. New York: Academic Press, 1972 (b).

Bower, G. H. Mental imagery and associative learning. In L. W. Gregg (ed.), *Cognition and learning in memory*. New York: Wiley, 1972, 51–88 (c).

Bray, N. W. & Batchelder, W. H. Effects of instructions and retention interval on memory of presentation mode. *Journal of Verbal Learning and Verbal Behavior*, 1972, **11**, 367–374.

Brennan, M. J. Modification of the effects of electroconvulsive shock as a function of prior foot-shock. Unpublished Masters Thesis, State University of New York at Binghamton, 1976.

Brennan, M. J., & Gordon, W. C. Modification of the effects of ECS as a function of prior footshock: The aversive properties of ECS. *Physiology and Behavior*, 1977, **18**, 819–824.

Bresnahan, E. & Routtenberg, A. Memory disruption by unilateral low level, subseizure stimulation of the medial amygdaloid nucleus. *Physiology and Behavior*, 1972, **9**, 513–525.

Breznitz, S. Incubation of threat: Duration of anticipation and false alarm as determinants of the fear reaction to an unavoidable frightening event. *Journal of Experimental Research in Personality*, 1967, **2**, 173–179.

Bronstein, P. M. & Spear, N. E. Acquisition of a spatial discrimination by rats as a function of age. *Journal of Comparative and Physiological Psychology*, 1972, **78**, 208–212.

Brown, A. In C. H. Graham (Ed.) *Vision and visual perception*. New York: Wiley, 1965.

Brown, J. (Ed.), *Recall and recognition*. New York: Wiley, 1976.

Brown, J. Some tests of the decay theory of immediate memory. *Quarterly Journal of Experimental Psychology*, 1958, **10**, 12–21.

Bruce, D. & Weaver, G. E. Retroactive facilitation and short-term retention of minimally learned paired-associates. *Journal of Experimental Psychology*, 1973, **100**, 9–17.

Brunner, R. L., Roth, T. G. & Rossi, R. R. Age differences in the development of the CER. *Psychonomic Science*, 1970, **21**, 135–136.

Brush, F. R. Retention of aversively motivated behavior. In F. R. Brush (Ed.), *Aversive conditioning and learning*. New York: Academic Press, 1971.

Brush, F. R. & Levine, S. Adrenocortical activity and avoidance behavior as a function of time after fear conditioning. *Physiology and Behavior*, 1966, **1**, 309–311.

Brush, F. R., Myer, J. S. & Palmer, M. E. Effects of kind of prior training and intersession interval upon subsequent avoidance learning. *Journal of Comparative and Physiological Psychology*, 1963, **56**, 539–545.

Bryan, R. G. & Spear, N. E. Forgetting of a discrimination after intervals of intermediate length: The Kamin effect with choice behavior. *Journal of Experimental Psychology: Animal Behavior Processes*, 1976, **2**, 221–234.

Bullock, D. H. Note on conditioned reinforcement and avoidance extinction. *Journal of the Experimental Analysis of Behavior*, 1960, **3**, 273.

Bures, J., & Buresova, O. The use of Laao's spreading depression in the study of inter-hemispheric transfer of memory traces. *Journal of Comparative and Physiological Psychology*, 1960, **53**, 558–565.

Bures, J. & Buresova, O. Cortical spreading depression as a memory disturbing factor. *Journal of Comparative and Physiological Psychology*, 1963, **56**, 268–272.

Bures, J. & Buresova, O. Inducing cortical spreading depression. In R. D. Myers (Ed.), *Methods in Psychobiology Vol. 2 Specialized laboratory techniques in neuropsychology and neurobiology*. New York: Academic Press, 1972, 319–344.

Buresova, O. & Bures, J. The effect of prolonged cortical spreading depression on learning and memory in rats. *Journal of Neurobiology*, 1969, **2**, 135–146.

Burr, D. E. S. & Thomas, D. R. Effect of proactive inhibition upon the post-discrimination generalization gradient. *Journal of Comparative and Physiological Psychology*, 1972, **81**, 441–448.

Burwitz, L. Proactive interference and directed forgetting in short-term motor memory. *Journal of Experimental Psychology*, 1974, **102**, 799–805.

Buschke, H. Short-term retention, learning and retrieval from long-term memory. In D. Deutsch and J. A. Deutsch (Editors), *Short-term memory*. New York: Academic Press, 1975.

Bustamante, J. A., Jordan, A., Vila, M., Gonzalez, A. & Insua, A. State-dependent learning in humans. *Physiology and Behavior*, 1970, **5**, 793–796.

Butter, M. J. & Palermo, D. S. Effects of imagery on paired-associate recall as a function of retention interval, list length, and trials. *Journal of Verbal Learning and Verbal Behavior*, 1970, **9**, 716–719.

Butters, N. & Cermak, L. S. The role of cognitive factors in the memory disorders of alcoholic patients with the Korsakoff syndrome. *Annals of the New York Academy of Sciences*, 1974, **233**,

Butters, N., & Cermak, L. S. Some analyses of amnesia syndromes in brain-damaged patients. In R. L. Isaacson and K. H. Pribram (Eds.), *The hippocampus Vol* **2**, New York: Plenum Press, 1975.

Butters, N., Lewis, R., Cermak, L. S. & Goodglass, H. Material-specific memory deficits in alcoholic Korsakoff patients. *Neuropsychologia*, 1973, **11**, 291–299.

Caldwell, D. F. & Werboff, J. Classical conditioning in newborn rats. *Science*, 1962, **136**, 1118–1119.

Calhoun, K. S., Prewett, M. J., Peters, R. D. & Adams, H. E. Factors in the modification by isolation of electroconvulsive shock-produced retrograde amnesia in the rat. *Journal of Comparative and Physiological Psychology*, 1975, **88**, 373–377.

Calhoun, W. H. Central nervous system stimulants. In E. Furchtgott (Editor), *Pharmacological and biophysical agents and behavior*. New York: Academic Press, 1971, 181–268.

Calhoun, W. H. Effect of level of external stimulation on rate of learning and interaction of this effect with strychnine treatment in mice. *Psychological Reports*, 1966, **18**, 715–722.

Calhoun, W. H. & Handley, G. W. Long-term memory following serial discrimination reversal learning. *Bulletin of the Psychonomic Society*, 1973, **1**, 354–356.

Campbell, B. A. Developmental studies of learning and motivation in infraprimate mammals. In H. W. Stevenson, E. H. Hess & H. L. Rheingold (Eds.), *Early behavior: Comparative and developmental approaches*. New York: Wiley, 1967.

Campbell, B. A. & Campbell, E. H. Retention and extinction of learned fear in infant and adult rats. *Journal of Comparative and Physiological Psychology*, 1962, **55**, 1–8.

Campbell, B. A. & Coulter, X. *Ontogeny of Learning and Memory*. Cambridge: MIT Press, 1976.

Campbell, B. A. & Jaynes, J. Effect of duration of reinstatement on retention of a visual discrimination learned in infancy. *Developmental Psychology*, 1969, **1**, 71–74.

Campbell, B. A. & Jaynes, J. Reinstatement. *Psychological Review*, 1966, **73**, 478–480.

Campbell, B. A., Lytle, L. D. & Fibiger, H. Ontogeny of adrenergic arousal and cholinergic inhibitory mechanisms in the rat. *Science*, 1969, **166**, 637–638.

Campbell, B. A. & Mabry, P. D. Ontogeny of behavioral arousal: A comparative study. *Journal of Comparative and Physiological Psychology*, 1972, **81**, 371–379.

Campbell, B. A. & Mabry, P. D. The role of catecholamines in behavioral arousal during ontogenesis. *Psychopharmacolgia*, 1973, **31**, 253–264.

Campbell, B. A., Jaynes, J. & Misanin, J. Retention of a light-dark discrimination in rats of different ages. *Journal of Comparative and Physiological Psychology*, 1968, **66**, 467–472.

Campbell, B. A., Misanin, J. R., White, B. C. & Lytle, L. D. Species differences in ontogeny of memory: indirect support for neural maturation as a determinant of forgetting. *Journal of Comparative and Physiological Psychology*, 1974, **87**, 193–202.

Campbell, B. A., Riccio, D. C. and Rohrbaugh, M. Ontogenesis of learning and memory: Research and theory. In M. E. Meyer (Ed.), *Second Washington symposium on learning: Early learning*. Bellingham, Washington: Western Washington State College, 1971, 76–109.

Campbell, B. A. & Spear, N. E. Ontogeny of memory. *Psychological Review*, 1972, **79**, 215–236.

Campbell, P. E., Phillips, E. L., Fixsen, D. L. & Crumbaugh, C. Free operant response reinstatement during extinction and time-contingent (DRO) reward. *Psychological Reports*, 1968, **22**, 263–269.

Capaldi, E. J. Memory and learning: A sequential viewpoint. In W. K. Honig & P. H. R. James (Eds.) *Animal Memory*. New York: Academic Press, 1971.

Capaldi, E. J. Partial reinforcement: A hypothesis of sequential effects. *Psychological Review,* 1966, **73,** 459–477.

Capaldi, E. J. A sequential hypothesis of instrumental learning. In K. W. Spence and J. T. Spence (Eds.), *The Psychology of Learning and Motivation Vol. 1.* New York: Academic Press, 1967, 67–156.

Carew, T. J. Do passive-avoidance tasks permit assessment of retrograde amnesia in rats? *Journal of Comparative and Physiological Psychology,* 1970, **72,** 267–271.

Carlton, P. L. Cholinergic mechanisms in the control of behavior by the brain. *Psychological Review,* 1963, **70,** 19–39.

Carlton, P. L. Brain, acetylcholine and inhibition. In J. T. Tapp (Ed.), *Reinforcement and behavior.* New York: Academic Press, 1969.

Carlton, P. L. & Markiewicz, B. Studies of the physiological bases of memory. In E. Stellar and J. M. Sprague (Eds.), *Progress in physiological psychology Vol. 5.* New York: Academic Press, 1973.

Carr, H. A. *Psychology: A study of mental activity.* New York: Longmans, Green, 1925.

Carter, E. E. & Bruno, L. J. J. Extinction and reconditioning of behavior generated by a DRL contingency of reinforcement. *Psychonomic Science,* 1968, **11,** 19–20.

Caul, W. F. & Barrett, R. J. Electroconvulsive shock effects on conditioned heart rate and repression of drinking. *Physiology and Behavior,* 1972, **8,** 287–290.

Cavanagh, J. P. Relation between the immediate memory span and the memory search rate. *Psychological Review,* 1972, **79,** 525–530.

Cermak, L. S. & Butters, N. The role of interference and encoding in the short-term memory deficit of Korsakoff patients. *Neuropsychologia,* 1972, **10,** 89–96.

Cermak, L. S., Butters, N. & Gerrein, J. The extent of the verbal encoding ability of Korsakoff patients. *Neuropsychologia,* 1973, **11,** 85–94.

Cermak, L. S., Naus, M. J., Reale, L. Rehearsal Strategy of Alcoholics, Korsakoff Patients. *Brain and Language,* 1976, **3,** 375–385.

Cermak, L. S., Butters, N. & Goodglass, H. The extent of memory loss in Korsakoff patients. *Neuropsychologia,* 1971, **9,** 307–315.

Cermak, L. S., Butters, N. & Moreines, J. Some analyses of the verbal encoding deficit of alcoholic Korsakoff patients. *Brain and Language,* 1974, **2,** 141–150.

Chen, W. Y., Aranda, L. C. & Luco, J. V. learning and long- and short-term memory in cockroaches. *Animal Behavior,* 1970, **18,** 725–732.

Cherkin, A. Retrograde amnesia: Role of temperature, dose and duration of amnesic agent. *Psychonomic Science,* 1968, **13,** 255–256.

Cherkin, A. Kinetics of memory consolidation: Role of amnesic parameters. *Proceedings of the National Academy of Sciences,* 1969, **63,** 1094–1101.

Cherkin, A. Biphasic time course of performance after one-trial avoidance training in the chick. *Communications in Behavioral Biology,* 1971, **5,** 379–381.

Cherkin, A. Retrograde amnesia in the chick: Resistance to the reminder effect. *Physiology and Behavior,* 1972, **8,** 949–955.

Cherkin, A. Effects of flurothyl (indoklon) upon memory in the chick. In M. Fink, S. Kety, J. McGaugh & T. A. Williams (Eds.), *Psychobiology of convulsive therapy.* Washington, D.C. V. H. Winston and Sons, 1974, 129–142.

Cherkin, A., Meinecke, R. O. & Garman, M. W. Retrograde enhancement of memory by mild flurothyl treatment in the chick. *Physiology and Behavior,* 1975, **14,** 151–158.

Chiszar, D. A. & Spear, N. E. Stimulus change, reversal learning and retention in the rat. *Journal of Comparative and Physiological Psychology,* 1969, **69,** 190–195.

Cholewiak, R. W., Hammond, R., Siegler, I. C. & Papsdorf, J. D. The effects of strychnine sulfate on the classically conditioned nictating membrane response of the rabbit. *Journal of Comparative and Physiological Psychology,* 1968, **66,** 77–81.

Chorover, S. L. & Schiller, P. H. Re-examination of prolonged retrograde amnesia in one-trial learning. *Journal of Comparative and Physiological Psychology,* 1966, **61,** 34–41.

Chorover, S. L. & Schiller, P. H. Short-term retrograde amnesia in rats. *Journal of Comparative and Physiological Psychology,* 1965, **59,** 73–78.

Chute, D. L. & Wright, D. C. Retrograde state-dependent learning. *Science,* 1973, **180,** 878–879.

Claparede, E. Recognition et moiite. *Arch. Psychol. Geneve,* 1911, 11, 79–90 (cited by Talland, G. A. *Deranged memory: A psychonomic study of the amnesic syndrome.* New York: Academic Press, 1965).

Clayton, K. N. The distinction between long- and short-term memory. Published in the Report Series of the Department of Psychology, Vanderbilt University, Nashville, Tennessee, 1974.

Clemente, C. D., Purpura, C. P. & Mayer, S. E. *Sleep and the maturing nervous system.* New York: Academic Press, 1972.

Cobb, S. *Borderlines of psychiatry.* Cambridge: Harvard University Press, 1946.

Cohen, H. D. & Barondes, S. H. Effects of acetoxycycloheximide on learning and memory of a light-dark discrimination. *Nature,* 1968, **218,** 271–273.

Cohen, L. B. & Gelber, E. R. Infant visual memory. In L. B. Cohen & Salbatek (Eds.), *Infant Perception: From Sensation to Cognition, Volume 1. Basic Visual Processes.* New York: Academic Press, 1975.

Cole, R. A. Different memory functions for consonants and vowels. *Cognitive Psychology,* 1973, **4,** 39–54.

Collier, G., Hirsch, E., & Kanarek, R. The operant revisited. In W. K. Honig and J. E. R. Staddon (Eds.), *Handbook of operant behavior.* Englewood Cliffs, N. J.: Prentice-Hall, 1977.

Connelly, J. J., Connelly, J. M. & Epps, J. O. Disruption of dissociated learning in a discrimination paradigm by emotionally important stimuli. *Psychopharmacologia,* (Berlin) 1973, **30,** 275–282.

Connor, J. B. & Meyer, D. R. Assessment of the role of transfer suppression in learning-set formation in monkeys. *Journal of Comparative and Physiological Psychology,* 1971, **75,** 141–145.

Conrad, R. Interference or decay over short intervals *Journal of Verbal Learning and Verbal Behavior,* 1967, **6,** 49–54.

Conrad, R. Speech and reading. In J. F. Kavanagh & I. G. Mattingly (Eds.), *Language by ear and by eye.* Cambridge, Mass: MIT Press, 1972.

Cooper, R. M. & Krass, M. Strychnine: Duration of the effects on maze learning. *Psychopharmacologia,* 1963, **4,** 472–475.

Cooper, E. H. & Pantle, A. J. The total-time hypothesis in verbal learning. *Psychological Bulletin,* 1967, **68,** 221–234.

Corey, S. N. An experimental study of retention in the white rat. *Journal of Experimental Psychology,* 1931, **14,** 252–259.

Corkin, F. Acquisition of motor skills after bilateral medial temporal-lobe excision. *Neuropsychologia,* 1968, **6,** 255–266.

Corsini, D. A. Memory: Interaction of stimulus and organismic factors. *Human Development,* 1971, **14,** 227–235.

Coulter, X., Collier, A. C. & Campbell, B. A. Long-term retention of early Pavlovian fear conditioning in infant rats. *Journal of Experimental Psychology: Animal Behavior Processes,* 1976, **2,** 48–56.

Cowles, A. T. & Nissen, H. W. Reward expectancy and delayed responses of chimpanzees. *Journal of Comparative Psychology,* 1937, **24,** 345–347.

Cowles, J. T. "Delayed response" as tested by three methods and its relation to other learning situations. *Journal of Psychology,* 1940, **9,** 103–130.

Crabbe, J. C. & Alpern, H. P. Facilitation and disruption of the long-term store of memory with neural excitants. *Pharmacology, Biochemistry and Behavior,* 1973, **1,** 197–202.

Craik, F. I. M. & Lockhart, R. S. Levels of processing: A framework for memory research. *Journal of Verbal Learning and Verbal Behavior,* 1972, **11,** 671–684.

Craik, F. I. M. & Tulving, E. Depth of processing and the retention of words in episodic memory. *Journal of Experimental Psychology: General,* 1975, **104,** 268–294.

Craik, F. I. M. & Watkins, M. J. The role of rehearsal in short-term memory. *Journal of Verbal Learning and Verbal Behavior*, 1973, **12**, 599–607.

Cronholm, B. Post-ECT amnesias. In G. A. Talland & N. C. Waugh (Editors), *The pathology of memory*. New York: Academic Press, 1969.

Cronholm, B. & Lagergren, A. Memory disturbances after electroconvulsive therapy. III. An experimental study of retrograde amnesia after electroconvulsive shock treatment. *ACTA Psychiatrica et Neurologica Scandinavica*, 1959, **34**, 283–310.

Cronholm, B. & Molander, L. Memory disturbances after electroconvulsive therapy. I Condition six hours after electroshock treatment. *ACTA Psychiatrica et Neurologica Scandinavica*, 1957, **32**, 280–306.

Crowder, R. G. *Principles of learning and memory*. Hillsdale, New Jersey: Lawrence Erlbaum Associates, 1976.

Crowder, R. G. The sound of vowels and consonants in immediate memory. *Journal of Verbal Learning and Verbal Behavior*, 1971, **10**, 587–596.

Crowder, R. G. Inferential problems in echoic memory. In P. Rabbitt & S. Dornic (Eds.), *Attention and performance V*. London: Academic Press, 1975, 218–229.

Crowder, R. G. & Morton, J. Precategorical acoustic storage (PAS). *Perception and Psychophysics*, 1969, **5**, 365–373.

D'Agostino, P. R. & DeRemer, T. Repetition effects as a function of rehearsal and encoding variability. *Journal of Verbal Learning and Verbal Behavior*, 1973, **12**, 108–113.

Dallett, K. & Wilcox, S. G. Contextual stimuli and proactive inhibition. *Journal of Experimental Psychology*, 1968, **78**, 475–480.

Dallett, K., Wilcox, S. G. & d'Andrea, L. Picture memory experiments. *Journal of Experimental Psychology*, 1968, **76**, 312–320.

D'Amato, M. R. *Experimental Psychology: Methodology, psychophysics and learning*. New York: McGraw-Hill, 1970.

D'Amato, M. R. Delayed matching and short-term memory in monkeys. In G. H. Bower (Ed.) *The psychology of learning and motivation: Advances in research and theory. Vol. 7*. New York: Academic Press, 1973.

D'Amato, M. R. & Cox, J. K. Delay of consequences in short-term memory in monkeys. In D. L. Medin, W. A. Roberts, and R. T. Davis (Eds.), *Processes of animal memory*. Hillsdale, N. J., Lawrence Erlbaum Associates, 1976.

D'Amato, M. R. & O'Neill, W. Effects of delay-interval illumination on matching behavior in the Capuchin monkey. *Journal of the Experimental Analysis of Behavior*, 1971, **15**, 327–333.

D'Amato, M. R. & Worsham, R. W. Delayed matching in the Capuchin monkey with brief sample durations *Learning and Motivation*, 1972, **3**, 304–312.

Daniels, D. Acquisition, storage and recall of memory for brightness discrimination by rats following intra-cerebral infusion of acetoxycycloheximide. *Journal of Comparative and Physiological Psychology*, 1971, **79**, 110–118.

DaPolito, F., Barker, D. & Wiant, J. The effects of contextual changes on component recognition. *American Journal of Psychology*, 1972, **85**, 431–440.

Davenport, J. W., Gonzalez, L. M., Hennies, R. S. & Hagquist, W. W. Severity and timing of early thyroid deficiency as factors in the induction of learning disorders in rats. *Hormones and Behavior*, 1976, **7**, 139–158.

David-Remacle, M. Attenuation of anoxia-induced retrograde amnesia in rats by pretraining placebo injection. *Physiology & Behavior*, 1973, **10**, 693–696.

Davis, R. E. & Holmes, P. A. ECS-produced retrograde amnesia of conditioned inhibition of respiration in cataleptic goldfish. *Physiology and Behavior*, 1971, **7**, 11–14.

Davis, R. G. Acquisition of verbal association to olfactory stimuli of varying familiarity and to abstract visual stimuli. *Journal of Experimental Psychology: Human Learning and Memory*, 1975, **1**, 134–142.

Davis, R. G. Acquisition and retention of verbal associations to olfactory and abstract visual stimuli of varying similarity. *Journal of Experimental Psychology: Human Learning and Memory,* 1977, **3**, 37–51.

Davis, R. T. Monkeys as perceivers. In L. A. Rosenbloom (Ed.), *Primate behavior, Vol. 3.* New York: Academic Press, 1973.

Davis, R. T. & Steele, J. P. Performance selection through radiation death in rhesus monkeys. *Journal of Psychology,* 1963, **56**, 119–136.

Dawkins, R. Selective neurone death as a possible memory mechanism. *Nature,* 1971, **229**, 118–119.

Dawson, B. V. & Foss, B. M. Observational learning in Budgerigaris. *Animal Behavior,* 1965, **13**, 470–477.

Dawson, R. G. & McGaugh, J. L. Drug facilitation of learning and memory. In J. A. Deutsch (Ed.), *The physiological basis of memory.* New York: Academic Press, 1973, 78–111.

Dawson, R. G. & McGaugh, J. L. Electroconvulsive shock-produced retrograde amnesia: Analysis of the familiarization effect. *Communications in Behavioral Biology,* 1969, **4**, 91–95.

Deets, A. C., Harlow, H. F. & Blomquist, A. J. Effects of intertrial interval and trial on reward during acquisition of an object-discrimination learning set in monkeys. *Journal of Comparative and Physiological Psychology,* 1970, **73**, 501–505.

d'Elia, G. (Ed.), Unilateral electroconvulsive therapy. *ACTA Psychiatrica Scandinavica,* 1970 **46** (supplement 215), 1–98.

d'Elia, G. Unilateral electroconvulsive therapy. In M. Fink, S. Kety, J. McGaugh, & T. A. Williams (Eds.), *Psychobiology of convulsive therapy.* New York: Wiley, 1974.

Denny, M. R. Recent explorations in a T-maze: Women's lib, long delays and all that. Presidential Address, Midwestern Psychological Association Meetings, Chicago, 1974.

Denti, A., McGaugh, J. L., Landfield, B. W. & Shinkman, P. T. Effects of posttrial electrical stimulation of the mesencephalic reticular formation on avoidance learning in rats. *Physiology and Behavior,* 1970, **5**, 659–662.

Detterman, D. K. Induced retrograde amnesia as retrieval failure. Presented at meetings of the Midwestern Psychological Association, Chicago, May, 1974 (1975a).

Detterman, D. K. Von Resteroff effect and induced amnesia: Production by manipulation of sound intensity. *Journal of Experimental Psychology: Human Learning and Memory,* 1975, **1**, 614–628b.

Detterman, D. K. & Ellis, N. R. Determinants of induced amnesia in short-term memory. *Journal of Experimental Psychology,* 1972, **95**, 308–316.

Deutsch, D. The effect of repetition of standard and comparison tones on recognition memory for pitch. *Journal of Experimental Psychology,* 1972, **93**, 156–162.

Deutsch, D. The organization of short-term memory for a single acoustic attribute. In D. Deutsch & J. A. Deutsch (Eds.), *Short-term memory.* New York: Academic Press, 1975.

Deutsch, J. A. The physiological basis of memory. *Annual Review of Psychology,* 1969, **20**, 85–104.

Deutsch, J. A. The cholinergic synapse and the site of memory. *Science,* 1971, **174**, 788–794.

Deutsch, J. A. The cholinergic synapse and the (site) of memory. In J. A. Deutsch (Ed.), *The physiological basis of memory.* New York: Academic Press, 1973.

Deutsch, J. A. The cholinergic synapse and the site of memory. In J. L. McGaugh (Ed.), *The chemistry of mood, motivation and memory.* New York: Plenum Press, 1972.

Deutsch, D. & Deutsch, J. A. (Eds.), *Short-Term Memory.* New York: Academic Press, 1975.

DeVietti, T. L. & Hopfer, T. M. ECS-induced amnesia: Retention function consistent with state-dependency predictions. *Physiological Psychology,* 1974, **2**, 35–37. (a)

DeVietti, T. L. & Hopfer, T. M. Reinstatement of memory in rats: Dependence upon two forms of retrieval deficit following electroconvulsive shock. Journal of Comparative and *Physiological Psychology,* 1974, **86**, 1090–1099. (b)

DeVietti, T. L. & Kallioinen, E. K. ECS-induced retrograde amnesia indicated by a heart rate measure of retention. *Psychonomic Science,* 1972, **27**, 35–36.

DeVietti, T. L. & Larson, R. C. ECS effects: Evidence supporting state-dependent learning in rats. *Journal of Comparative and Physiological Psychology,* 1971, **74,** 407–415.

DeVietti, T. L., Mayse, J. F. & Morris, L. W. Footshock/ECS induced state-dependent learning in rats: Parametric evaluation of ECS intensity and time of testing. *Learning and Motivation,* 1974, **5,** 70–79.

deWied, D. Pituitary-adrenal system hormones and behavior. In F. O. Schmitt & F. T. Worden (Eds.), *The neurosciences, Vol. 3.* Cambridge, Massachusetts: MIT Press, 1974.

deWied, D. & Weijnen, J. A. W. M. (Eds.) *Progress in brain research, Vol. 32: Pituitary, adrenal and the brain.* Amsterdam: Elsevier Publishing Company, 1970.

DiCara, L. D. & Miller, N. E. Long-term retention of instrumentally learned heart-rate changes in a curarized rat. *Communications in Behavioral Biology,* 1968, **2,** 19–23.

DiGiusto, E. L., Cairncross, K. & King, M. G. Hormonal influences on fear-motivated responses. *Psychological Bulletin,* 1971, **75,** 432–444.

Dinsmoor, J. A. Variable-interval escape from stimuli accompanied by shocks. *Journal of the Experimental Analysis of Behavior,* 1962, **5,** 41–47.

Diven, K. Certain determinants in the conditioning of anxiety reactions. *Journal of Psychology,* 1937, **3,** 291–308.

Dollard, J. & Miller, N. E. *Personality and psychotherapy* New York: McGraw Hill, 1950.

Dong, T. & Kintsch, W. Subjective retrieval cues in free recall. *Journal of Verbal Learning and Verbal Behavior,* 1968, **7,** 813–816.

Dornbush, R. L. & Williams, M. Memory and ECT. In M. Fink, S. Kety, J. McGaugh and T. A. Williams (Eds.), *Psychobiology of convulsive therapy.* New York: Wiley, 1974, 199–208.

Doty, B. A. Age and avoidance conditioning in rats. *Journal of Gerontology,* 1966, 287–290.

Drachman, D. A. & Arbit, J. Memory and hippocampal complex, II. *Archives of Neurology,* 1966, **15,** 52–61.

Dudycha, G. J. & Dudycha, M. M. Childhood memories: A review of the literature. *Psychological Bulletin,* 1941, **38,** 668–682.

Dudycha, G. J. & Dudycha, M. M. Some factors and characteristics of childhood memories. *Child Development,* 1933, **4,** 265–278.

Duncan, C. P. The retroactive effect of electroshock on learning. *Journal of Comparative and Physiological Psychology,* 1949, **42,** 32–44.

Duncan, C. P. Habit reversal induced by electroshock in the rat. *Journal of Comparative and Physiological Psychology,* 1948, **41,** 11–16.

Duncan, C. P. The effect of electroshock convulsions on the maze habit in the white rat. *Journal of Experimental Psychology,* 1945, **35,** 267–278.

Duncan, C. P. & Underwood, B. J. Retention of transfer in motor learning after 24 hours and after 14 months. *Journal of Experimental Psychology,* 1953, 46, 442–452.

Dusewicz, R. A. Strychnine performance: A learning or performance effect. *Journal of General Psychology,* 1972, **87,** 59–64.

Dyal, J. A. Transfer of behavioral bias and learning enhancement: A critique of specificity experiments. In G. Adam (Ed.), *Biology of memory.* New York: Plenum Press, 1971.

Ebbinghaus, H. Memory: A contribution to Experimental Psychology. Translated by Ruger, H. A. & Bussanius, C. E. New York: Bureau of Publications, Teachers College, Columbia University, 1913.

Egger, G. J., Livesey, P. J. & Dawson, R. G. Ontogenetic aspects of central cholinergic involvement in spontaneous alternation behavior. *Developmental Psychobiology,* 1973, **6,** 289–299.

Eibl-Eibesfeldt, I. Ethology: The biology of behavior. New York: Holt Reinhardt & Winston, 1970.

Eich, J., Weingartner, H., Stillman, R. & Gillin, J. State-dependent accessibility of retrieval cues and retention of a categorized list. *Journal of Verbal Learning and Verbal Behavior,* 1975, **14,** 408–417.

Einstein, G. O., Pellegrino, J. W., Mondani, M. S. & Battig, W. F. Free-recall performance as a function of overt rehearsal frequency. *Journal of Experimental Psychology,* 1974, **103,** 440–449.

Eisenson, J. *Adult aphasia: Assessment and treatment.* Englewood Cliffs, New Jersey: Prentice Hall, 1973.

Ekert, E. & Kanak, J. Verbal discrimination learning: A review of the acquisition, transfer, and retention literature through 1972. *Psychological Bulletin,* 1974, **81,** 582–607.

Ekstrand, B. R. The effect of sleep on memory. *Journal of Experimental Psychology,* 1967, **75,** 64–72.

Ekstrand, B. R. To sleep, perchance to dream (about why we forget). In C. P. Duncan, L. Sechrest & A. W. Melton (Editors), *Human memory: Festschrift in honor of Benton J. Underwood.* New York: Appleton-Century-Crofts, 1972.

Ekstrand, B. R., Wallace, W. P. & Underwood, B. J. A frequency theory of verbal-discrimination learning. *Psychological Review,* 1966, **73,** 566–578.

Ellis, N. R. Memory processes in retardates and normals. In N. R. Ellis (Ed.), *International Review of Research in Mental Retardation, Vol. 4* New York: Academic Press, 1970.

Elmes, D. G., Sanders, L. W. & Dovel, J. C. Isolation of massed- and distributed-practice items. *Memory and Cognition,* 1973, **1,** 77–79.

Engen, T., Quisma, J. E. & Eimas, P. Short-term memory of odors. *Journal of Experimental Psychology,* 1973, **99,** 222–225.

Engen, T. & Ross, B. M. Long-term memory of odors with and without verbal descriptions. *Journal of Experimental Psychology,* 1973, **100,** 221–227.

Epstein, W. Varieties of perceptual learning, New York: McGraw-Hill, 1967.

Erdelyi, M. H. & Becker, J. Hypermnesia for pictures: Incremental memory for pictures but not words in multiple recall trials. *Cognitive Psychology,* 1974, **6,** 159–171.

Erdelyi, M. H. & Kleinbard, J. Has Ebbinghaus decayed with time? The growth of recall (hypermnesia) over days. *Cognitive Psychology,* 1976, under review.

Erickson, C. K. & Patel, J. B. Facilitation of avoidance learning by posttrial hippocampal electrical stimulation. *Journal of Comparative and Physiological Psychology,* 1969, **68,** 400–411.

Essman, W. B. Neurochemical changes in ECS and ECT. *Seminars in psychiatry,* 1972, **4,** 67–77.

Essman, W. B. Age dependent effects of five-hydroxytryptamine upon memory consolidation and cerebral protein syntheses. *Pharmacology, Biochemistry & Behavior,* 1973, **1,** 7–14.

Essman, W. B. Effects of electroconvulsive shock on cerebral protein synthesis. In M. Fink, S. Kety, J. McGaugh & T. A. Williams (Eds.), *Psychobiology of convulsive therapy.* New York: Wiley, 1974, 237–250.

Essman, W. B. & Jarvik, M. E. Impairment of retention for a conditioned response by ether anesthesia in mice. *Psychopharmacologia,* 1961, **2,** 172–176.

Estes, W. K. Statistical theory of spontaneous recovery and regression. *Psychological Review,* 1955, **62,** 145–154.

Estes, W. K. Stimulus-response theory of drive. In M. R. Jones (Ed.), *Nebraska symposium on motivation.* Lincoln: University of Nebraska Press, 1958.

Estes, W. K. The statistical approach to learning theory. In S. Koch (Ed.), *Psychology: A study of a science.* Vol. 2. New York: McGraw-Hill, 1959.

Estes, W. K. *Learning theory and mental development.* New York: Academic Press, 1970.

Estes, W. K. Phonemic coding and rehearsal in short-term memory for letter strings. *Journal of Verbal Learning and Verbal Behavior,* 1973, **12,** 360–372.

Estes, W. K., Koch, S., MacCorquodale, K., Meehl, P., Mueller, C. G., Jr., Schoenfeld, W. N. & Verplanck, W. S. *Modern learning theory.* New York: Appleton-Century-Crofts, 1954.

Etkin, M. Light-induced interference in a delayed-matching task with Capuchin monkeys. *Learning and Motivation,* 1972, **3,** 317–324.

Etkin, M. & D'Amato, M. R. Delayed-matching-to-sample and short-term memory in the Capuchin monkey. *Journal of Comparative and Physiological Psychology,* 1969, **69,** 544–549.

Etkin, M. W. Ambient light-produced interference in a delayed matching task with capuchin monkeys. Unpublished doctoral dissertation, Rutgers University, 1970.

Eysenck, H. J. Single trial conditioning, neurosis and the Napalkov phenomenon. *Behavior Research and Therapy,* 1967, **5,** 63–65.

Fagan, J. F. Infants recognition memory for a series of visual stimuli. *Journal of Experimental Child Psychology*, 1971, **11**, 244–254.

Fagan, J. F. Memory in the infant. *Journal of Experimental Child Psychology*, 1970, **9**, 217–226.

Falkenberg, P. R. Recall improves in short-term memory the more recall context resembles learning context. *Journal of Experimental Psychology*, 1972, **95**, 39–47.

Farthing, G. W. & Hearst, E. Attention in the pigeon: testing with compounds for elements. *Learning and Motivation*, 1970, **1**, 65–78.

Feigley, D. A. Effects of scopolamine on active and passive avoidance learning in rats of different ages. *Journal of Comparative and Physiological Psychology*, 1974, **87**, 26–36.

Feigley, D. A. & Hamilton, L. W. Response to novel environment following septal lesions or cholinergic blockade in rats. *Journal of Comparative and Physiological Psychology*, 1971, **76**, 496–504.

Feigley, D. A., Parsons, P. J., Hamilton, L. W. & Spear, N. E. The development of habituation to novel environments in the rat. *Journal of Comparative and Physiological Psychology*, 1972, **79**, 443–452.

Feigley, D. A. & Spear, N. E. Effect of age and punishment condition on long-term retention by the rat of active and passive avoidance learning. *Journal of Comparative and Physiological Psychology*, 1970, **73**, 514–526.

Fibiger, H. C., Lytle, L. D. & Campbell, B. A. Cholinergic modulation of adrenergic arousal in the developing rat. *Journal of Comparative and Physiological Psychology*, 1970, **72**, 384–389.

Finan, J. L. Delayed response with a pre-delay reinforcement in monkeys after the removal of the frontal lobes. *American Journal of Psychology*, 1942, **55**, 202–214.

Fink, M., Kety, S., McGaugh, J. & Williams, T. A. (Eds.). *Psychobiology of convulsive therapy.* Washington, D.C.: V. H. Winston & Sons, 1974.

Fishbein, W. Interference with conversion of memory from short-term to long-term storage by partial sleep deprivation. *Communications in Behavioral Biology*, 1970, **5**, 171–175.

Fishbein, W. Paradoxical sleep and memory storage processes. In W. Fishbein & E. Weitzman (Eds.), *Advances in sleep research, Vol. 4.* New York: Spectrum Publications, 1977.

Flavell, J. H. Developmental studies of mediated memory. In L. P. Lipsitt & H. W. Reese (Eds.), *Advances in Child Development and Behavior.* New York: Academic Press, 1970, **5**, 182–211.

Fletcher, H. J. The delayed response problem. In Schrier, A. M., Harlow, H. F. & Stollnitz, F., *Behavior of non-human primates: Modern Research Trends, Vol. 1,* New York: Academic Press, 1965.

Fletcher, H. J. & Davis, J. K. Evidence supporting an intratrial interpretation of delayed response performance of monkeys. *Perceptual and Motor Skills*, 1965, **21**, 735–742.

Flexner, J. B. & Flexner, L. B. Pituitary-peptides and the suppression of memory by puromycin. *Proceedings of the National Academy of Sciences*, 1970, **68**, 2519–2521.

Flexner, J. B. & Flexner, L. B. Adrenalectomy and the suppression of memory by Auromycin. *Proceedings of the National Academy of Sciences*, 1970, **66**, 48–50.

Flexner, L. B., Flexner, J. B. & Roberts, R. B. Stages of memory in mice treated with acetoxycycloheximide before or immediately after learning. *Proceedings of the National Academy of Sciences*, 1966, **56**, 730–735.

Flood, J. F., Bennett, E. L., Rosenzweig, M. R. & Orme, A. E. Influence of training strength on amnesia induced by pretraining injections of cycloheximide. *Physiology and Behavior*, 1972, **9**, 589–600.

Foree, D. D. & LoLordo, V. M. Signalled and unsignalled free-operant avoidance in the pigeon. *Journal of the Experimental Analysis of Behavior*, 1970, **13**, 283–290.

Franchina, J. J. & Moore, M. H. Strychnine and the inhibition of previous performance. *Science*, 1968, **160**, 903–904.

French, G. M. Performance of squirrel monkeys on variants of delayed-response. *Journal of Comparative and Physiological Psychology*, 1959, **52**, 741–745.

Freud, S. *A general introduction to psychoanalysis.* New York: Clarion Books, 1935.

Frey, P. W. & Gavin, W. Overnight incubation of a partially conditioned eye blink response in rabbits. *Animal Learning and Behavior,* 1975, **3,** 114–118.

Frost, N. Clustering by visual shape in the free recall of pictorial stimuli. *Journal of Experimental Psychology,* 1971, **88,** 409–413.

Frost, N. Encoding and retrieval in visual memory tasks. *Journal of Experimental Psychology,* 1972, **95,** 317–326.

Fuchs, A. F. & Melton, A. W. Effects of frequency of presentation of stimulus lengths on retention in the Brown-Peterson paradigm. *Journal of Experimental Psychology,* 1974, **103,** 629–637.

Fuller, J. L., Easler, D. A. & Banks, E. M. Formation of conditioned avoidance responses in young puppies. *American Journal of Physiology,* 1950, **160,** 462–466.

Fuller, J. L. & Christake, A. Conditioning of leg flexion and cardio-acceleration in the puppy. *Federation Proceedings,* 1959, **18,** 98.

Gabriel, M. Incubation of avoidance produced by generalization to stimuli of the conditioning apparatus. *Topics in learning and performance.* New York: Academic Press, 1972, 59–84.

Gabriel, M. Effects of intersession delay and training level on avoidance, extinction and intertrial behavior. *Journal of Comparative and Physiological Psychology,* 1968, **66,** 412–416.

Gabriel, M. Intersession delay in avoidance extinction to training and generalization stimuli. *Psychonomic Science,* 1967, **9,** 243–244.

Gabriel, M. & Vogt, J. Incubation of avoidance CR's in the rabbit produced by increase over time in stimulus generalization to apparatus. *Behavioral Biology,* 1972, **7,** 113–125.

Gaffan, D. Recognition memory in animals. In J. Brown (Ed.), *Recall and Recognition.* New York: John Wiley & Son, 1976, 229–242.

Gaito, J. & Bonnet, K. Quantitative vs. qualitative RNA and protein changes in the brain during behavior. *Psychological bulletin,* 1971, **75,** 109–127.

Galbraith, R. C. & Underwood, B. J. Perceived frequency of concrete and abstract words. *Memory and Cognition,* 1973, **1,** 56–60.

Galosy, R. A. & Thompson, R. W. A further investigation of familiarization effects on ECS-produced retrograde amnesia. *Psychonomic Science,* 1971, **22,** 147–148.

Ganong, W. F. & Martini, L. *Frontiers in neuroendocrinology, 1969.* New York: Oxford University Press, 1969.

Garcia, J. & Ervin, F. R. Gustatory-visceral and telereceptor-cutaneous conditioning-adaptation in internal and external milieus. *Communications in Behavioral Biology,* 1968, **1,** 389–415.

Garcia, J., McGowan, B. K. & Green, K. F. Assumptions, theories, models. In A. H. Black & W. F. Prokasy (Eds.), *Classical conditioning II: Current research and theory.* New York: Appleton-Century-Crofts, 1972, 3–27.

Gardiner, J. M. Levels of processing in word recognition and subsequent free recall. *Journal of Experimental Psychology,* 1974, **102,** 101–105.

Gardiner, J. M., Craik, F. I. M. & Birtwistle, J. Retrieval cues and release from proactive inhibition. *Journal of Verbal Learning and Verbal Behavior,* 1972, **11,** 778–783.

Gardner, B. T. & Gardner, R. A. Evidence for sentence constituents in the early utterances of child and chimpanzee. *Journal of Experimental Psychology, General,* 1975, **104,** 244–267.

Gardner, E. L., Glick, S. D., & Jarvik, M. E. ECS dissociation of learning and one-way cross-dissociation with physostigmine and scopolamine. *Physiology and Behavior,* 1972, **8,** 11–15.

Gardner, H. Boller, F., Moreines, J. & Butters, N. Retrieving information from Korsakoff patients: Effects of categorical cues in reference to the task. *Cortex,* 1973, **9,** 165–175.

Geiselman, R. E. Semantic process of forgetting: Another cocktail party problem. *Journal of Verbal Learning and Verbal Behavior,* 1975, **14,** 73–81.

Geller, A. & Jarvik, M. E. The time relations of ECS-induced amnesia. *Psychonomic Science,* 1968, **12,** 169–170.

Geller, A. & Jarvik, M. E. The role of consolidation in memory. In R. E. Bowman & S. P. Datta (Eds.) *Biochemistry of brain and behavior,* New York: Plenum Press, 1970.

Geller, A., Jarvik, M. E. & Robustelli, F. Incubation and the Kamin effect. *Journal of Experimental Psychology,* 1970, **85,** 61–65.

Gerard, R. W. What is memory? *Scientific American*, 1953, **189**, 118–126.

Gidro-Frank, L. & Bowersbuch, M. K. A study of the plantar response in hypnotic aids regression. *Journal of Nervous and Mental Disease*, 1948, **107**, 443–458.

Girden, E. Cerebral mechanisms in conditioning under curare. *American Journal of Psychology*, 1940, **53**, 397–402.

Girden, E. & Culler, E. Conditioned responses in curarized striate muscle in dogs. *Journal of Comparative Psychology*, 1937, **23**, 261–268.

Gispen, W. H., Greidanns, T. B. V. W., Bohus, B. and deWied, D. *Hormones, homeostasis and the brain, Progress in brain research, Vol. 42.* New York: Elsevier Scientific Publishing Company, 1975.

Giurgea, C., Lefevre, D., Lescrenier, C. & David-Remacle, M. Pharmacological protection against hypoxia-induced amnesia in rats. *Psychopharmacologia*, 1971, **20**, 160–168.

Glanzer, M. Storage mechanisms in recall. In G. H. Bower & J. T. Spence (Eds.), *The psychology of learning and motivation Vol. 5.* New York: Academic Press, 1972, 129–193.

Glanzer, M. & Meinzer, A. The effects of intralist activity on free recall. *Journal of Verbal Learning and Verbal Behavior*, 1967, **6**, 928–935.

Gleitman, H. Forgetting of long-term memories in animals. In W. K. Honig and P. H. R. James (Eds.) *Animal memory* New York: Academic Press, 1971.

Gleitman, H. & Holmes, P. Retention of incompletely learned CER in rats. *Psychonomic Science*, 1967, **7**, 19–20.

Gleitman, H. & Steinman, F. Depression effect as a function of retention interval before and after shift in reward magnitude. *Journal of Comparative and Physiological Psychology*, 1964, **57**, 158–160.

Gleitman, H., Wilson, W. A., Jr., Herman, M. M. & Rescorla, R. A. Massing within-delayed position as factors in delayed-response performance. *Journal of Comparative and Physiological Psychology*, 1963, **56**, 445–451.

Glenberg, A. M., Monotonic and nonmonotonic lag effects in paired-associate and recognition memory paradigms. *Journal of Verbal Learning and Verbal Behavior*, 1976, **15**, 1–16.

Glick, S. D. & Zimmerberg, B. Amnesic effects of scopolamine. *Behavioral Biology*, 1972, **7**, 245–254.

Glickman, S. E. Perseverative neural processes and consolidation of the memory trace. *Psychological Bulletin*, 1961, **58**, 218–233.

Goddard, G. B. Amygdaloid stimulation and learning in the rat. *Journal of Comparative and Physiological Psychology*, 1964, **58**, 23–30.

Gold, P. E., Macri, J. & McGaugh, J. L. Retrograde amnesia effects: Effects of direct cortical stimulation. *Science*, 1973, **179**, 1343–1345.

Gold, P. E. & McGaugh, J. L. Relationship between amnesia and brain seizures in rats. *Physiology and Behavior*, 1973, **10**, 41–46.

Gold, P. E. & King, R. D. Retrograde amnesia: Storage failure versus retrieval failure. *Psychological Review*, 1974, **81**, 465–469.

Gold, P. E. & VanBuskirk, R. B. Facilitation of time-dependent memory processes with posttrial epinephrine injections. *Behavioral Biology*, 1975, **13**, 145–153.

Gold, P. E. & VanBuskirk, R. Enhancement of memory processes with posttrial hormone injections. *Hormones and Behavior*, 1976, **7**, 509–517.

Goldstein, J., Locke, J. L. & Fehr, F. S. Children's prerecall phonetic processing of pictures and printed words. *Psychonomic Science*, 1972, **26**, 314–316.

Golin, S. Incubation effect: Role of awareness in an immediate versus delayed test of conditioned emotionality. *Journal of Abnormal and Social Psychology*, 1961, **63**, 534–539.

Gollon, E. S. Developmental Studies A Visual recognition of incomplete objects. *Perceptual and motor skills*, 1960, **11**, 289–298.

Gomulicki, B. R. The development and the present status of the trace theory of memory. *British Journal of Psychology*, 1953, **29** (monograph suppl.).

Gonzales, R. C., Fernhoff, D. & David, F. G. Contrast, resistance to extinction, and forgetting in rats. *Journal of Comparative and Physiological Psychology*, 1973, **84,** 562–571.

Goodwin, D. W. Blackouts and alcohol-induced memory disfunction. In N. K. Mello & J. Mendelsohn (Eds.) *Recent advances in studies of alcoholism: An interdisciplinary symposium* GHS Publication No. (HSM) 71-9045, Washington, D.C. U.S. Government Printing Office, 1971.

Gordon, W. C. Similarities of short-term and reactivated memories. Unpublished doctoral dissertation, Rutgers University, 1973.

Gordon, W. C., Brennan, M. J., & Rose, R. C. Facilitation of the long-term memory store with strychnine: A re-examination. *Pharmacology, Biochemistry and Behavior*, 1975, **6,** 967–972.

Gordon, W. C. & Spear, N. E. The effects of strychnine on recently acquired and reactivated passive avoidance memories. *Physiology and Behavior*, 1973, **10,** 1071–1075.

Goss, A. E., Morgan, C. H. & Golin, S. J. Paired-associate learning as a function of percentage occurrence of response members (reinforcement). *Journal of Experimental Psychology*, 1959, **57,** 96–104.

Goss, A. E. & Nodine, C. F. *Paired-associates learning: The role of meaningfulness, similarity, and familiarization.* New York: Academic Press, 1965.

Gottlieb, G. (Ed.), *Studies of the development of behavior and the nervous system Vol. 2, Aspects of Neurogenesis,* New York: Academic Press, 1974.

Gottlieb, W. & Lindauer, M. S. The effect of contextual stimuli on retroactive inhibition. *Psychonomic Science*, 1967, **9,** 331–332.

Goulet, L. R. Verbal learning in children: Implications for developmental research. *Psychological Bulletin*, 1968, **59,** 359–376.

Grant, D. S. Effect of sample presentation time on long-delayed matching in the pigeon. *Learning and Motivation*, 1976, **7,** 580–590.

Grant, D. S. Proactive interference in pigeon short-term memory. *Journal of Experimental Psychology: Animal Behavior Processes*, 1975, **104,** 207–220.

Grant, D. S. & Roberts, W. A. Sources of retroactive inhibition in vision short-term memory. *Journal of Experimental Psychology, Animal Behavior Processes*, 1976, **1,** 1–16.

Grant, D. S. & Roberts, W. A. Sources of retroactive inhibition in pigeon short-term memory. *Journal of Experimental Psychology*, 1972, **94,** 74–83.

Grant, D. S. & Roberts, W. A. Trace interaction in pigeon short-term memory. *Journal of Experimental Psychology*, 1973, **101,** 21–29.

Gray, C. R. & Gummerman, K. The enigmatic eidetic image: A critical examination of methods, data and theory. *Psychological Bulletin*, 1975, **82,** 383–407.

Gray, P. Effect of adrenocorticotropic hormone on conditioned avoidance in rats interpreted as state-dependent learning. *Journal of comparative and Physiological Psychology*, 1975, **88,** 281–284.

Greeno, J. G., James, C. T. & DaPolito, F. J. A cognitive interpretation of negative transfer and forgetting of paired associates. *Journal of Verbal Learning and Verbal Behavior*, 1971, **10,** 331–345.

Greenough, W. T. & McGaugh, J. L. The effect of strychnine sulphate on learning as a function of time of administration. *Psychopharmacologia*, 1965, **8,** 290–294.

Greenspoon, J. & Ranyard, R. Stimulus conditions and retroactive inhibition. *Journal of Experimental Psychology*, 1957, **53,** 55–59.

Gregory, E. H. & Pfaff, D. W. Development of olfactory-guided behavior in infant rats. *Physiology and Behavior*, 1971, **6,** 575–576.

Grice, G. R. Relation of secondary reinforcement to delayed reward in visual discrimination learning. *Journal of Experimental Psychology*, 1948, **38,** 1–16.

Gross, C. G. Inferotemporal cortex and vision. In E. Stellar and J. M. Sprague (Eds.), *Progress in physiological psychology* Vol. 5. New York: Academic Press, 1973.

Gross, C. G., Cowey, A. & Manning, F. J. Further analysis of visual discrimination deficits following foveal prestriate and inferotemporal lesions in rhesus monkeys. *Journal of Comparative and Physiological Psychology*, 1971, **76,** 1–7.

Gross, C. G. & Zeigler, H. P. *Readings in physiological psychology: Learning and memory.* New York: Harper and Row, 1969.

Grossman, S. P. Facilitation of learning following intracranial injections of pentelene-tetrazol. *Physiology and Behavior,* 1969, **4,** 625–628.

Grossman, S. P. *A textbook of physiological psychology,* New York: Wiley & Sons, 1967.

Gudekunst, R. & Youniss, J. Interruption of imprinting following anesthesia. *Perceptual Motor Skills,* 1963, **16,** 348.

Gummerman, K. & Gray, C. R. Age, iconic storage and visual information processing. *Journal of Experimental Child Psychology,* 1972, **13,** 165–170.

Guthrie, E. R. *The psychology of learning (rev. ed.).* New York: Harper, 1952.

Guthrie, E. R. *The psychology of learning.* New York: Harper, 1935.

Haber, R. N. & Haber, R. B. Eidetic imagery: I. Frequency. *Perceptual and Motor Skills,* 1964, **19,** 131–138.

Hagen, J. W. Some thoughts on how children learn to remember. *Human Development,* 1971, **14,** 262–271.

Haith, M. M. Developmental changes in visual information processing and short-term visual memory. *Human Development,* 1971, **14,** 249–261.

Hake, D. F. & Azrin, N. H. Conditioned punishment. *Journal of the Experimental Analysis of Behavior.* 1965, **8,** 279–293.

Hale, G. A. & Taweel, S. S. Age differences in children's performance on measures of component selection and incidental learning. *Journal of Experimental Child Psychology,* 1974, **18,** 107–116.(a)

Hale, G. A. & Taweel, S. S. Children's component selection with varying degrees of training. *Journal of Experimental Child Psychology,* 1974, **17,** 229–241 (b)

Hall, J. F. *The psychology of learning.* Philadelphia: J. B. Lippincott Company, 1966.

Hall, J. W. & Halperin, M. S. The development of memory-encoding processes in young children. *Developmental Psychology,* 1972, **6,** 181.

Hall, J. W. & Pierce, J. W. Recognition and recall by children and adults as a function of variations in memory coding instructions. *Memory and Cognition,* 1974, **2,** 585.

Halstead, W. C. Brain and intelligence. In L. A. Jeffres (Ed.), *Cerebral mechanisms and Behavior.* New York: Wiley, 1951.

Hamburg, M. D. & Fulton, D. R. Influence of recall on an anticholinesterase induced retrograde amnesia. *Physiology and Behavior,* 1972, **9,** 409–418.

Hamilton, L. W. & Flaherty, C. F. Behavioral patterns associated with water intake in normal and septal rats. *Journal of Comparative and Physiological Psychology,* 1971, **76,** 165–174.

Hamilton, L. W. & Flaherty, C. F. Interactive effects of deprivation in the albino rat. *Learning and Motivation,* 1973, **4,** 148–162.

Harlow, H. F. Comparative behavior of primates: III Complicated delayed reaction tests on primates. *Journal of Comparative Psychology,* 1932, **14,** 241–252.

Harlow, H. F. Primate learning. In C. P. Stone (Ed.), *Comparative psychology, 3rd Edition.* New York: Prentice Hall, 1951.

Harlow, H. F. Learning set and error factor theory. In S. Koch (Ed.), *Psychology: A study of a science Vol. 2.* New York: McGraw-Hill, 1959, 492–537.

Harmon, L. D. The recognition of faces. *Scientific American.* 1973, **229,** 71–82.

Harrison, R. & Nissen, H. W. Spatial separation and the delayed response performance in chimpanzees. *Journal of Comparative Psychology,* 1941, **31,** 427–435.

Hasher, L. & Johnson, M. K. Interpretive factors in forgetting. *Journal of Experimental Psychology: Human Learning and Memory,* 1975, **1,** 567–575.

Hasher, L., Riebman, B., & Wren, F. Imagery and the retention of free-recall learning. *Journal of Experimental Psychology: Human Learning and Memory,* 1976, **2,** 172–181.

Hasher, L., Griffin, M. & Johnson, M. K. More on interpretive factors in forgetting. *Memory and Cognition,* **5,** 41–45.

Hasher, L., & Thomas, H. A developmental study of retention. *Developmental Psychology,* 1973, **9,** 281.

Hasler, A. D. & Larsen, J. A. The homing salmon. *Scientific American,* 1955, **193,** 72–76.

Hebb, D. O. *The organization of behavior.* New York: Wiley, 1949.

Hebb, D. O. Distinctive features of learning in the higher animal. In J. F. Delafresnaye (Ed.), *Brain mechanisms and learning.* London: Oxford University Press, 1961, 37–46.

Hecaen, H. Clinical-anatomical and neurolinguistic aspects of aphasia. In G. A. Talland & N. C. Waugh (Eds.), *The pathology of memory.* New York: Academic Press, 1969.

Heimann, H., Reed, C. F., & Witt, P. N. Some observations suggesting preservation of skilled motoacts despite drug-induced stress. *Psychopharmacologia,* 1968, **13,** 287–298.

Hellyer, S. Supplementary report: Frequency of stimulus presentation on short-term decrement in recall. *Journal of Experimental Psychology,* 1962, **64,** 650.

Henderson, R. W. Conditioned and unconditioned fear inhibition in rats. *Journal of Comparative and Physiological Psychology,* 1973, **84,** 554–561.

Henschen, G. & Kleist, K. *Gehirnpathologie Leipzig:* J. Barth, 1934.

Heron, W. T. Learning: General introduction. In C. P. Stone (Ed.), *Comparative psychology, 3rd Ed.* Englewood Cliffs, New Jersey: Prentice-Hall, 1951.

Hershkowitz, M. & Samuel D. The retention of learning during metamorphosis of the Crested Newt *(Triturus cristatus). Animal Behavior,* 1973, **21,** 83–85.

Herz, M. J. Interference with one-trial appetitive and aversive learning by ether and ECS. *Journal of Neurobiology,* 1969, 111–122.

Hicks, R. E. McDaniel, J. W. & Hensley, J. H. Forgetting of acquisition and extinction in an invertebrate. *The Journal of General Psychology,* 1973, **88,** 65–69.

Hilgard, E. R. & Bower, G. *Theories of learning, 4th ed.* New York: Appleton-Century-Crofts, 1974.

Hill, W. F., Cotton, J. W., Spear, N. E. & Duncan, C. P. Retention of T maze learning after varying intervals following partial and continuous reinforcement. *Journal of Experimental Psychology,* 1969, **79,** 584–585.

Hill, W. F., Erlebacher, A. & Spear, N. E. Reminiscence and forgetting in a runway. *Journal of Experimental Psychology,* 1965, **70,** 201–209.

Hill, W. F. & Spear, N. E. Resistance to extinction as a joint function of reward magnitude and spacing of extinction trials. *Journal of Experimental Psychology,* 1962, **64,** 636–639.

Himwich, W. A. (Ed.), *Developmental Neurobiology* Springfield, Illinois: C. C. Thomas, 1970.

Hinderliter, C. F., Smith, S. J. & Misanin, J. R. A reduction of ECS-produced amnesia through post-ECS sensory isolation. *Bulletin of the Psychonomic Society,* 1976, **7,** 542–544.

Hinderliter, C. F., Smith, S. L. & Misanin, J. R. Effects of pretraining experience on retention of a passive avoidance task following ECS. *Physiology & Behavior,* 1973, **10,** 671–675.

Hinderliter, C. F., Webster, T. & Riccio, D. C. Amnesia induced by hypothermia as a function of treatment-test interval and recooling in rats. *Animal Learning and Behavior,* 1975, **3,** 257–263.

Hine, B. & Paolino, R. M. Retrograde amnesia: Production of skeletal but not cardiac response gradient by electroconvulsive shock. *Science,* 1970, **169,** 1224–1226.

Hinrichs, J. V. & Grunke, M. E. Control processes in short-term memory: Use of retention interval information. *Journal of Experimental Psychology:* Human Learning and Memory, 1975, **104,** 229–237.

Hintzman, D. L. Theoretical implications of the spacing effect. In R. L. Solso (Ed.), *Theories in cognitive psychology: The loyola symposium.* Potomac, Maryland: Lawrence Erlbaum Associates, 1974.

Hintzman, D. L. Repetition and memory. In G. H. Bower (Ed.), *The psychology of learning and motivation Vol.* **10.** New York: Academic Press, 1976.

Hintzman, D. L. & Block, R. A. Memory judgments and the effects of spacing. *Journal of Verbal Learning and Verbal Behavior,* 1970, **9,** 561–566.

Hintzman, D. L. & Block, R. A. Repetition and memory: evidence for a multiple-traced hypothesis. *Journal of Experimental Psychology,* 1971, **88,** 297–306.

Hintzman, D. L., Block, R. A. & Inskeep, N. R. Memory for mode of input. *Journal of Verbal Learning and Verbal Behavior,* 1972, **11,** 741–749.

Hintzman, D. L., Block, R. A. & Summers, J. J. Modality tags in memory for repetitions: Locus of the spacing effect. *Journal of Verbal Learning and Verbal Behavior,* 1973, **12,** 229–238. (a)

Hintzman, D. L., Block, R. A. & Summers, J. J. Contextual associations in memory for serial position. *Journal of Experimental Psychology,* 1973, **97,** 220–229. (b)

Hintzman, D. L., Summers, J. J., Eki, N. T. & Moore, M. D. Voluntary attention and the spacing effect. *Memory and Cognition,* 1975, **3,** 576–580.

Hirsch, E. The influence of ovariectomy on avoidance learning in rats. Paper presented at meetings of the Eastern Psychological Association Philadelphia, 1969.

Ho, Y. H. Transfer and degree of integration. *Journal of Comparative Psychology,* 1928, 87–99.

Hodos, W. & Campbell, C. B. G. *Scala naturae:* Why there is no theory in comparative psychology. *Psychological Review.* 1969, **76,** 337–350.

Hofer, M. A. The effects of brief material separations on behavior and heart-rate of two week old rat pups. *Physiology and Behavior,* 1973, **10,** 423–427.

Hoffman, H. S. Stimulus factors in conditioned suppression. In B. A. Campbell & R. M. Church (Editors), *Punishment and aversive behavior.* New York: Appleton-Century-Crofts, 1969.

Hoffman, H. S., Fleshler, M. & Chorny, H. Discriminated bar-press avoidance. *Journal of the Experimental Analysis of Behavior,* 1961, **4,** 309–316.

Holloway, F. A. & Wansley, R. A. Multiple retention deficits at periodic intervals after passive avoidance learning. *Science,* 1973, **80,** 208–210.

Holman, E. W. Temporal properties of gustatory spontaneous alternation in rats. *Journal of Comparative and Physiological Psychology,* 1973, **85,** 536–539.

Homzie, M. J. Nonreward anticipated: Effects on extinction runway performance in the rat. *Animal Learning and Behavior,* 1974, **2,** 77–79.

Honig, W. K. A new method for the study of stimulus memory in pigeons. Meetings of the Psychonomics Society, Boston, November, 1974.

Honig, W. K. Effects of extradimensional discrimination training upon previously acquired stimulus control. *Learning and Motivation,* 1974, **5,** 1–15.

Houston, J. P. Proactive inhibition and undetected retention interval rehearsal. *Journal of Experimental Psychology,* 1969, **82,** 511–514.

Houston, J. P. Proactive inhibition and undetected rehearsal: A replication. *Journal of Experimental Psychology,* 1971, **90,** 156–157.

Howard, R. L., Glendenning, R. L. & Meyer, D. R. Motivational control of retrograde amnesia: Further explorations and effects. *Journal of Comparative and Physiological Psychology,* 1974, **86,** 187–192.

Huang, K. L. & Payne, R. B. Individual and sex differences in reminiscence. *Memory and Cognition,* 1975, **3,** 252–256.

Hudson, B. B. One-trial learning in the domestic rat. *Genetic Psychology Monographs,* 1950, **41,** 99–145.

Hughes, R. A. Retrograde amnesia in rats produced by hippocampal injections of potassium chloride: Gradient of effect and recovery. *Journal of Comparative and Physiological Psychology,* 1969, **68,** 637–644.

Hughes, R. A., Barrett, R. J. & Ray, O. S. Retrograde amnesia in rats increases as a function of ECS-test interval and ECS intensity. *Physiology and Behavior,* 1970, **5,** 27–30.

Hull, C. L. *Principles of behavior.* New York: Appleton-Century-Crofts, 1943.

Humphrey, G. *The nature of learning.* New York: Harcourt, Brace and Company, 1933.

Hunt, E. & Love, T. How good can memory be? In A. W. Melton & E. Martin (Eds.), *Coding processes in human memory.* Washington, D.C. Winston & Sons, 1972, 237–260.

Hunt, R. R. & Ellis, H. C. Recognition memory and degree of semantic contextual change. *Journal of Experimental Psychology,* 1974, **103,** 1153–1159.

Hunter, W. S. The delayed reaction in animals and children. *Behavior Monographs,* 1913, **2,** Serial #6.

Hunter, W. S. The delayed reaction in a child. *Psychological Review,* 1917, **24,** 74–87.

Hyde, T. F. & Jenkins, J. J. The differential effects of incidental tasks on the organization of recall of a list of highly associated words. *Journal of Experimental Psychology*, 1969, **82**, 472–481.

Hyde, T. F. & Jenkins, J. J. Recall for words is a function of semantic, graphic and syntactic orienting tasks. *Journal of Verbal Learning and Verbal Behavior*, 1973, **12**, 471–480.

Isaacson, R. L. Hippocampal destruction in man and other animals. *Neuropsychologia*, 1972, **10**, 47–64.

Ivanitsky, A. M. Development of the conditioned reflex activity in ontogenesis in rabbit. *Bull. Exp. Biol. Med.*, 1958, **46**, 27–30. Cited in Volokhov, A. A. The ontogenetic development of higher nervous activity in animals. In W. A. Himwich (Ed.), *Developmental Neurobiology*. Canfield: C. C Thomas, 1970.

Iversen, S. D. Brain lesions and memory in animals. In J. A. Deutsch (Ed.), *The physiological basis of memory*. New York: Academic Press, 1973, 305–364.

Jablonski, E. M. Free recall in children. *Psychological Bulletin*, 1974, **81**, 522–539.

Jacoby, L. L. Context effects on frequency judgments of words and sentences. *Journal of Experimental Psychology*, 1972, 255–260.

Jacoby, L. L. Encoding processes, rehearsal, and recall requirements. *Journal of Verbal Learning and Verbal Behavior*, 1973, **12**, 302–310. (a)

Jacoby, L. L. Test appropriate strategies in retention of categorized lists. *Journal of Verbal Learning and Verbal Behavior*, 1973, **12**, 675–682. (b)

James, W. *The principles of psychology, Vol. II*. New York: Holt, 1890.

Jarrard, L. E. Role of interference in retention by rats with hippocampal lesions. *Journal of Comparative and Physiological Psychology*, 1975, **89**, 400–408.

Jarrard, L. E. & Moise, S. L. Short-term memory in the stump tail (M. speciosa): Effect of physical restraint of behavior on performance. *Learning and Motivation*, 1970, **1**, 267–275.

Jarrard, L. E. & Moise, S. L. Short-term memory in the monkey. In L. E. Jarrard (Ed), *Cognitive Processes of non-human primates* New York: Academy, 1971.

Jarvik, M. E. Effects of chemical and physical treatments on learning and memory. *Annual Review of Psychology*, 1972, **23**, 457–486.

Jarvik, M. E., Goldfarb, T. L. & Carley, J. L. Influence of interference on delayed-matching in monkeys *Journal of Experimental Psychology*, 1969, **81**, 1–6.

Jenkins, J. B. & Dallenbach, K. M. Oblivescence during sleep and waking. *American Journal of Psychology*, 1924, **35**, 605–612.

Jensen, R. A. & Riccio, D. C. Effects of a prior experience upon retrograde amnesia produced by hypothermia. *Physiology and Behavior*, 1970, **5**, 1291–1294.

Jensen, R. A., Riccio, D. C. & Gehres, L. Effects of prior aversive experience upon retrograde amnesia induced by hypothermia. *Physiology and Behavior*, 1975, **15**, 165–169.

Jersild, A. T. and Holmes, F. B. Children's fears. *Child Development Monographs*, #20, New York: Bureau of Publications, Teachers College, Columbia University, 1935.

John, E. R. *Mechanisms of memory*. New York: Academic Press, 1967.

John, E. R. Switchboard versus statistical theories of learning and memory. *Science*, 1972, **2**, 177, 850–864.

Johnston, C. D. & Jenkins, J. J. Two more incidental tasks that differentially affect associative clustering in recall. *Journal of Experimental Psychology*, 1971, **89**, 92–95.

Jones, M. K. Imagery as a mnemonic aid after left temporal lobectomy: Contrast between material-specific and generalized memory disorders. *Neuropsychologia*, 1974, **12**, 21–30.

Jongeward, R. H., Jr., Woodward, A. E., Jr., and Bjork, R. A. The relative roles of input and output mechanisms in directed forgetting. *Memory and Cognition*, 1975, **3**, 51–57.

Jost, A. Die Assoziationsfestigkeit in ihrer Abhangigkeit der Verteilung der Wiederholungen. *Z. Psychology*, 1897, **14**, 436–472.

Joy, R. N. & Prinz, P. N. The effect of sleep altering environments upon the acquisition and retention of a conditioned avoidance response in rats. *Physiology and Behavior*, 1969, **4**, 809–814.

Jung, J. *Verbal learning*. New York: Holt, Rinehart & Winston, 1968.

Kagan, J. Do infants think? *Scientific American,* 1972, **226,** 74–82.

Kagan, J. & Lewis, M. Studies of attention in the human infant. *Merrill-Palmer Quarterly,* 1965, **11,** 95–127.

Kalat, J. W. Taste salience depends on novelty, not concentration, in taste-aversion learning in the rat. *Journal of Comparative and Physiological Psychology,* 1974, **86,** 47–50.

Kamil, A. C. & Mauldin, J. E. Intra-problem retention during learning-set acquisition in blue jays (*Cyanocitta cristata*). *Animal Learning and Behavior,* 1975, **3,** 125–130.

Kamin, L. J. Selective association in conditioning. In N. J. Mackintosh and W. K. Honig (Eds.), *Fundamental issues in associative learning.* Halifax: Dalhousie University Press, 1969.

Kamin, L. J. The retention of an incompletely learned avoidance response. *Journal of Comparative and Physiological Psychology,* 1957, **50,** 457–460.

Kamin, L. J. Retention of an incompletely learned avoidance response: Some further analysis. *Journal of Comparative and Physiological Psychology,* 1963, **56,** 713–718.

Kapp, B. S. & Schneider, A. M. Selective recovery from retrograde amnesia produced by hippocampal spreading depression. *Science,* 1971, **173,** 1149–1151.

Kaufman, H. M. & Wilson, M. Visual information processing in monkeys. Paper presented at the meetings of the Psychonomics Society, San Antonio, November, 1970.

Kausler, D. H. *Psychology of verbal learning and memory.* New York: Academic Press, 1974.

Kavanagh, J. P. Relation between the immediate memory span and the memory search rate. *Psychological Review,* 1972, **79,** 525–530.

Kay, H. Theories of learning and aging. In J. E. Birren (Ed.), *Handbook of aging and the individual: Psychological and Biological Aspects.* Chicago: University of Chicago Press, 1959.

Keane, T. & Lisman, S. Multiple task disruption of alcohol state-dependent retention. Paper presented at Eastern Psychological Association meetings, New York City, April, 1976.

Kellogg, W. N. & Rice, C. E. Visual problem-solving in a bottlenosed dolphin. *Science,* 1964, **143,** 1052–1055.

Kendler, H. H. The influence of simultaneous hunger and thirst drives upon the learning of two opposed spatial responses of the white rat. *Journal of Experimental Psychology,* 1946, **36,** 212–220.

Keppel, G. Facilitation in short and long-term retention of paired associates following distributed practice in learning. *Journal of Verbal Learning and Verbal Behavior,* 1964, **3,** 91–111.

Keppel, G. Forgetting. In L. Sechrist, C. P. Duncan and A. W. Melton (Eds.), *Human Memory: Festschrift for Benton J. Underwood,* New York: Appleton-Century-Crofts, 1972.

Keppel, G. Verbal learning in children. *Psychological Bulletin,* 1964, **61,** 63–80.

Keppel, G. Retroactive and proactive inhibition. In T. R. Dixon and D. L. Horton (Eds.), *Verbal behavior and general behavior theory.* Englewood Cliffs, New Jersey: Prentice-Hall, 1968, 172–213.

Keppel, G., Postman, L. & Zavortink, B. Studies of learning to learn: VIII The influence of maximum amounts of training upon the learning and retention of paired-associate lists. *Journal of Verbal Learning and Verbal Behavior,* 1968, **7,** 790–796.

Keppel, G. & Underwood, B. J. Proactive inhibition in short-term retention of single items. *Journal of Verbal Learning and Verbal Behavior,* 1962, **1,** 153–161.

Keppel, G. & Underwood, B. J. Reminiscence in the short-term retention of paired-associate lists. *Journal of Verbal Learning and Verbal Behavior,* 1967, **6,** 375–382.

Kesner, R. A neural system analysis of memory storage and retrieval. *Psychological Bulletin,* 1973, **80,** 177–203.

Kesner, R. P. & Conner, H. S. Effects of electrical stimulation of rat limbic system and midbrain reticular formation upon short- and long-term memory. *Physiology and Behavior,* 1974, **12,** 5–12.

Kesner, R. P. & Connor, H. S. Independence of short- and long-term memory: A neural systems analysis. *Science,* 1972, **176,** 432–434.

Kesner, R. P. & Doty, R. W. Amnesia produced in cats by local seizure activity initiated from the amygdala. *Experimental Neurology,* 1968, **21,** 58–68.

Kesner, R. P., McDonough, J. H. & Doty, R. W. Diminished amnestic effects of a second electroconvulsive seizure. *Experimental Neurology*, 1970, **27**, 527–533.

Kessler, P. G. Retention of early Pavlovian fear conditioning in infant rats: Effect of temporal variables in conditioning, Unpublished doctoral dissertation, State University of New York, Stony Brook, 1976.

Kimble, G. A. An experimental test of a two factor theory of inhibition. *Journal of Experimental Psychology*, 1949, **39**, 15–23.

King, R. A. & Glasser, R. L. Duration of electroconvulsive shock-induced retrograde amnesia in rats. *Physiology and Behavior*, 1970, **5**, 335–339.

King, R. A. & Glasser, R. L. Factors influencing one-trial passive avoidance behavior: Implications for studies of retrograde amnesia (RA). *Physiology and Behavior*, 1973, **10**, 817–819.

Kintsch, W. *Learning, memory and conceptual processes*. New York: Wiley, 1970.

Kintsch, W. *The representation of meaning in memory*. Hillsdale, New Jersey: Lawrence Erlbaum Associates, 1974.

Klein, S. B. Adrenal-pituitary influence in reactivation of avoidance-memory in the rat after immediate intervals. *Journal of Comparative and Physiological Psychology*, 1972, **79**, 341–359.

Klein, S. B. & Spear, N. E. Forgetting by the rat after intermediate intervals ("Kamin effect") as retrieval failure. *Journal of Comparative and Physiological Psychology*, 1970, **71**, 165–170 (a).

Klein, S. B. & Spear, N. E. Reactivation of avoidance-memory in the rat after intermediate intervals. *Journal of Comparative and Physiological Psychology*, 1970, **72**, 498–504 (b).

Klein, S. B., & Spear, N. E. Influence of age on short-term retention of active avoidance learning in rats. *Journal of Comparative and Physiological Psychology*, 1969, **69**, 383–389.

Kleinsmith, L. J. & Kaplan, S. Paired-associate learning as a function of arousal and interpolated intervals. *Journal of Experimental Psychology*, 1963, **65**, 190–193.

Kleinsmith, L. J. & Kaplan, S. Interaction of arousal and recall interval in nonsense syllable paired-associate learning. *Journal of Experimental Psychology*, 1964, **67**, 124–126.

Koffka, K. *Principles of Gestalt psychology* New York: Harcourt, Brace, 1935.

Kopp, R., Bohdanecky, Z. & Jarvik, M. E. Proactive effect of a single electroconvulsive shock (ECS) on one-trial learning in mice. *Journal of Comparative and Physiological Psychology*, 1968, **65**, 514–517.

Krane, R. V. & Wagner, A. R. Taste aversion learning with a delayed shock US: Implications for the "generality of the laws of learning". *Journal of Comparative and Physiological Psychology*, 1975, **88**, 882–889.

Krech, D. Discussion. In J. L. McGaugh (ed.), *Advances in behavioral biology Vol. 4: The chemistry of mood, motivation and memory*. New York: Plenum Press, 1972.

Krivanek, J. A. Facilitation of avoidance learning by pentylenetetrazol as a function of task difficulty, deprivation and shock level. *Psychopharmacologia*, 1971, **20**, 213–229.

Krivanek, J. & McGaugh, J. L. Effects of pentylenetetrazol on memory storage in mice. *Psychopharmacologia*, 1968, **12**, 303–321.

Krivanek, J. & McGaugh, J. L. Facilitating effects of pre and posttrial amphetamine administration on discrimination learning in mice. *Agents and Actions*, 1969, **1**, 36–42.

Kuhn, T. S. *The structure of scientific revolutions*. Chicago: University of Chicago Press, 1962.

Kuhn, T. S. *The structure of scientific revolutions*, Second edition, Chicago: University of Chicago Press, 1970.

Kulkarni, A. S. Avoidance acquisition and CNS stimulants. *Psychopharmacology*, 1972, **273**, 394–400.

Landauer, T. K. Consolidation in human memory: Retrograde amnestic effects of confusable items in paired-associate learnings. *Journal of Verbal Learning and Verbal Behavior*, 1974, **13**, 45–53.

Landauer, T. K. Reinforcement as consolidation. *Psychological Review*, 1969, **76**, 82–96.

Landfield, P. W. Neurobiological correlates of memory storage processes. Unpublished Ph.D. dissertation. University of California Irvine, 1971.

Landfield, P. W., McGaugh, J. L. & Tusa, R. J. Theta rythym: A temporal correlate of memory storage processes in the rat. *Science*, 1972, **175**, 87–89.

Lanier, L. P., Dunn, A. J. & VanHartesveldt, C. Development of neurotransmitters and their function in brain. In S. Ehrenpreis & I. J. Kopin (Editors), *Reviews of neuroscience Vol. 2.* New York: Raven Press, 1976.

Lashley, K. S. The effects of strychnine and caffeine upon the rate of learning. *Psychobiology,* 1917, **1,** 141–170.

Lashley, K. S. In search of the engram. *Symposia of the Society for Experimental Biology,* 1950, **4,** 454–582.

Lashley, K. S. Cerebral organization and the behavior. In *The brain and human behavior, proceedings of the Association for Research on Nervous and Mental Diseases,* 1958, **36,** 1–18.

Lashley, K. S. & Franz, S. I. The effects of cerebral destruction upon habit-formation and retention in the albino rat. *Psychobiology,* 1917, **1,** 71–140.

Lashley, K. S. & Wade, M. The Pavlovian theory of generalization. *Psychological Review,* 1946, **53,** 72–87.

Lawless, H. & Engen, T. Associations to odors: Interferences, mnemonics, and verbal labeling. *Journal of Experimental Psychology: Human Learning and Memory,* 1977, **3,** 52–59.

Lawrence, D. H. The nature of a stimulus: some relationships between learning and perception. In S. Koch (Ed.), *Psychology: A study of a science, Vol.* **5,** New York: McGraw Hill, 1963.

Layden, T. A. & Birch, H. The effect of electroconvulsive shock on body weight, food intake and water intake in the rat. *Physiology and Behavior,* 1969, **4,** 1015–1017.

Lazar, G. Warm-up before recall of paired adjectives. *Journal of Verbal Learning and Verbal Behavior,* 1967, **6,** 321–327.

LeBoeuf, B. J. & Peeke, H. V. S. The effect of strychnine administration during development on adult maze learning in the rat. *Psychopharmacologia,* 1969, **16,** 49–53.

Lee-Teng, E., Magnus, J. G., Kanner, M. & Hochman, H. Two separable phases of behaviorally manifest memory for 1-trial learning in chicks. *International Journal of Neuroscience,* 1970, **1,** 99–106.

Lefevre, D., David-Remacle, M., & Sara, S. J. Influence of differential rearing on ECS and anoxia effects: Seizure susceptibility and retrograde amnesia. Unpublished manuscript 1975.

Lehr, D. J. & Duncan, C. P. Effects of priming on spontaneous recovery of verbal lists. *Journal of Verbal Learning and Verbal Behavior,* 1970, **9,** 106–110.

Leiman, A. L., Bliss, D. K., Powers, J. B. and Rosenzweig, M. R. Electrical correlates of drug-dissociated learning. *Federation Proceedings,* 1967, **26,** 263–269.

Lett, B. T. Delayed reward learning: Disproof of the traditional theory. *Learning and Motivation,* 1973, **4,** 237–246.

Lett, B. T. Visual discrimination learning with a one-minute delay of reward. *Learning and Motivation,* 1974, **5,** 174–181.

Lett, B. T. Long-delayed learning in the T-maze. *Learning and Motivation,* 1975, **6,** 80–90.

Lett, B. T. Regarding Roberts reported failure to obtain visual discrimination learning with delayed reward. *Learning and Motivation,* 1977, **8,** 136–139.

Leukel, F. A comparison of the effects of ECS and anesthesia on acquisition of the maze habit. *Journal of Comparative and Physiological Psychology,* 1957, **50,** 300–306.

Levine, M. Hypothesis behavior. In A. M. Schrier, H. F. Harlow and F. Stollnitz (Editors), *Behavior of nonhuman primates, Vol. 1.* New York: Academic Press, 1965, pp. 97–127.

Levine, S. The role of irrelevant drive stimuli in learning. *Journal of Experimental Psychology,* 1953, **45,** 410–416.

Levine, S. Hormones in conditioning. In W. J. Arnold (Editor), *Nebraska symposium on motivation.* Lincoln University of Nebraska Press, 1968.

Levine, S. & Brush, F. R. Adrenocortical activity and avoidance learning as a function of time after avoidance training. *Physiology and Behavior,* 1967, **2,** 385–388.

Levine, S. & Mullins, F. F., Jr. Hormones in infancy. In: G. Newton and S. Levine (Eds.), *Early Experience and Behavior* Springfield, Illinois: Thomas, 1968. pp. 168–197.

Levy, D. M. The infant's earliest memory of innoculation: A contribution to public health procedures. *Journal of Genetic Psychology,* 1960, **96,** 3–46.

Lewis, D. J. Sources of experimental amnesia. *Psychological Review,* 1969, **76,** 461–472.

Lewis, D. J. A cognitive approach to experimental amnesia. *American Journal of Psychology,* 1976, **89,** 51–80.

Lewis, D. J., Bregman, N. J. & Mahan, J. J. Cue-dependent amnesia in rats. *Journal of Comparative and Physiological Psychology,* 1972, **81,** 243–247.

Lewis, D. J., Miller, R. R. & Misanin, J. R. Control of retrograde amnesia. *Journal of Comparative and Physiological Psychology,* 1968, **66,** 48–52.

Lewis, D. J., Miller, R. R. & Misanin, J. R. Selective amnesia in rats produced by electroconvulsive shock. *Journal of Comparative and Physiological Psychology,* 1969, **69,** 136–140.

Lewis, M. Q. & Bartz, W. H. Learning and memory stores. *Journal of Experimental Psychology,* 1970, **86,** 465—466.

Liberty, C. & Ornstein, P. A. Age differences in organization and recall: The effects of training and categorization. *Journal of Experimental Child Psychology,* 1973, **15,** 169–186.

Lidsky, A. & Slotnick, B. Effects of posttrial limbic stimulation on retention of one-trial passive avoidance response. *Journal of Comparative and Physiological Psychology,* 1971, **76,** 337–348.

Light, L. L. Incentives, information, rehearsal, and the negative frequency effects. *Memory and Cognition,* 1974, **2,** 295–300.

Light, L. L. & Carter-Sobell, L. Effects of changed semantic context on recognition memory. *Journal of Verbal Learning and Verbal Behavior,* 1970, **9,** 1–11.

Light, L. L., Kimble, G. A. & Pellegrino, J. W. Comments on "Episodic memory: When recognition fails" by Watkins and Tulving. *Journal of Experimental Psychology: General,* 1975, **104,** 30–36.

Light, L. L., Stansbury, C., Linde, S. & Rubin, C. Memory for modality of presentation: Within-modality discrimination. *Memory and Cognition,* 1973, **1,** 395–400.

Lindquist, N. Some notes on development of memory during the first years of life. *ACTA Paediatric,* Stockholm, 1945, **32,** 592–598.

Lockhart, R. S., Craik, F. I. M. and Jacoby, L. Depth of processing, recognition and recall. In J. Brown (Editor), *Recall and recognition.* New York: Wiley, 1976, 75–102.

Loeb, J. *Comparative physiology of the brain and comparative psychology.* Translated by Anne L. Loeb, New York: Putman's 1900.

Logan, F. A. *Incentive.* New Haven: Yale University Press, 1960.

Luce, G. G. *Biological Rhythms in Human and Animal Physiology,* Dover, N. Y. 1972.

Luria, A. R. *The mind of a mnemonist.* New York: Basic Books, Inc., 1968.

Lutz, W. J. & Schierer, C. J. Coding processes for pictures and words. *Journal of Verbal Learning & Verbal Behavior,* 1974, **13,** 316–320.

Lynch, S. & Yarnell, T. R. Retrograde amnesia: Delayed forgetting after concussion. *American Journal of Psychology,* 1973, **86,** 643–645.

Lyon, D. O. & Ozolins, D. Pavlovian conditioning of shock elicited aggression: A discrimination procedure. *Journal of the Experimental Analysis of Behavior,* 1970, **13,** 325–331.

Lytle, L. D., Moorcroft, W. H. & Campbell, B. A. Ontogeny of amphetamine anorexia and insulin hyperphagia in the rat. *Journal of Comparative and Physiological Psychology,* 1971, **77,** 388–393.

Mabry, P. D. & Campbell, B. A. Developmental psychopharmacology. In L. L. Iversen, S. D. Iversen & S. H. Snyder (Eds.), *Handbook of Psychopharmacology,* Volume 3 New York: Plenum Press, 1975.

MacCorquodale, K. An analysis of certain cues in the delayed response. *Journal of Comparative Psychology,* 1947, **40,** 239–253.

Mackintosh, N. J. *The psychology of animal learning.* London: Academic Press, 1974.

Madigan, S. A. Intraserial repetition and coding processes in free recall. *Journal of Verbal Learning and Verbal Behavior,* 1969, **8,** 828–835.

Madigan, S. & Doherty, L. Retention of item attributes in free recall. *Psychonomic Science,* 1972, **27,** 233–235.

Magdsick, W. K. The curve of retention of an incompletely learned problem in albino rats at various age levels. *Journal of Psychology,* 1936, **2,** 25–48.

Mah. C. J. & Albert, D. J. The attenuation of ECS-produced amnesia by re-establishing continuity with the training environment: A further examination. *Physiological Psychology*, 1974, **2**, 357-359.

Maier, N. R. F. Delayed retention and memory in rats. *Comparative Psychology Monographs*, 1929, **36**, 538-549.

Maki, W. S. Jr., Moe, J. C. & Bierley, C. M. Short-term memory for stimuli, responses, and reinforcers. *Journal of Experimental Psychology: Animal Behavior Processes*, 1977, **3**, 156-177.

Malmo, R. B. Interference factors in monkeys after removal of frontal lobe. *Journal of Neurophysiology*, 1942, **5**, 295-308.

Mandler, G. Organization and memory. In K. W. Spence & J. T. Spence (Eds.), *The Psychology of Learning and Motivation Vol. 1.* New York: Academic Press: 1967, 327-372.

Manning, F. J. Punishment for errors in visual-discrimination learning by monkeys with inferotemporal cortex lesions. *Journal of Comparative and Physiological Psychology*, 1971, **75**, 146-152.

Mare, W. *Early one morning.* New York: MacMillan, 1935.

Mark, R. F. & Watts, M. E. Drug inhibition of memory formation in chickens. I Long-term memory. *Proceedings of the Royal Society of London*, 1971, **178**, 439-454.

Markowitz, H., Schmidt, M., Nadal, L. & Squire, L. Do elephants ever forget? *Journal of Applied Behavior Analysis*, 1975, **8**, 333-335.

Marler, P. Animal communication signals. *Science*, 1967, **157**, 769-774.

Martin, E. Generation-recognition retrieval theory and the encoding specificity principle *Psychological Review*, 1975, **82**, 150-153.

Martin, E. Verbal learning theory and independent retrieval phenomena. *Psychological Review*, 1971, **78**, 314-332.

Martini, L. and Ganong, W. F. *Neuroendocrinology, Vol. 1.* New York: Academic Press, 1966.

Marx, M. H. The effects of cumulative training upon retroactive inhibition and transfer. *Comparative Psychology Monographs*, 1944, Whole No. 94.

Massaro, D. W. Preperceptual images, processing time and perceptual units in auditory perception. *Psychological Review*, 1972, **79**, 124-145.

Massaro, D. W. Preperceptual auditory images. *Journal of Experimental Psychology*, 1970, **85**, 411-417.

Mayes, A. R. & Cowey, A. The interhemispheric transfer of avoidance learning: An examination of the stimulus control hypothesis. *Behavioral Biology*, 1973, **8**, 193-205.

Mayor, S. J. Puromycin's effects on long-term memory and the acquisition of two successive visual discrimination tasks in Japanese quail. *Physiological Psychology*, 1973, **1**, 33-36.

Mazuryk, G. F. Positive recency in final free recall. *Journal of Experimental Psychology*, 1974, **103**, 812-813.

McAllister, W. R. & McAllister, D. E. Incubation of fear: An examination of the concept. *Journal of Experimental Research and Personality*, 1967, **3**, 80-90.

McAllister, W. R. & McAllister, D. E. Behavioral measurement of conditioned fear. In F. R. Brush (Ed.), *Aversive conditioning and learning.* New York: Academic Press, 1971.

McDowell, A. A., Gaylord, H. A. & Brown, W. L. Learning set formation by naive rhesus monkeys. *Journal of Genetic Psychology*, 1965, **106**, 253-257.

McEwen, B. S. & Weiss, J. M. The uptake and action of corticosterone: Regional and subcellular studies on rat brain. In: D. DeWied and J. A. W. M. Weijnen (Eds.), *Pituitary Adrenal and Brain: Progress in Brain Research. Volume 32.* Amsterdam, Elsevier, 1970.

McGaugh, J. L. Drug facilitation of learning and memory. *Annual Review of Pharmacology*, 1973, **13**, 229-241.

McGaugh, J. L. Time-dependent processes in memory storage. *Science*, 1966, **153**, 1351-1358.

McGaugh, J. L. & Alpern, H. P. Effects of electroshock on memory: Amnesia without convulsions. *Science*, 1966, **152**, 665-666.

McGaugh, J. L. & Dawson, R. G. Modification of memory storage processes. In W. K. Honig and P. H. R. James (Eds.), *Animal memory.* New York: Academic Press, 1971.

McGaugh, J. L. & Herz, M. J. *Memory consolidation*. San Francisco: Albion Publishing Company, 1972.

McGaugh, J. L. & Krivanek, J. Strychnine effects on discrimination learning in mice: Effects of dose and time of administration. *Physiology and Behavior*, 1970, **5**, 1437–1442.

McGaugh, J. L. & Landfield, P. W. Delayed development of amnesia following electroconvulsive shock. *Physiology and Behavior*, 1970, **5**, 751–755.

McGaugh, J. L. & Zornetzer, S. Amnesia and brain seizure activity in mice: Effects of diethyl ether anesthesia prior to electroshock stimulation. *Communications in Behavioral Biology*, 1970, **5**, 243–248.

McGeoch, G. O. The conditions of reminiscence. *American Journal of Psychology*, 1935, **47**, 65–89.

McGeoch, J. A. Forgetting and the law of disuse. *Psychological Review*, 1932, **39**, 352–370.

McGeoch, J. A. *The psychology of human learning: An introduction*. New York: Longmans, Green 1942.

McGeoch, J. A. & Irion, A. L. *The psychology of human learning*. New York: Longmans Green & Company, 1952.

McGovern, J. B. Extinction of associations in forced transfer paradigm. *Psychological Monographs*, 1964, **78** (16 Whole number 593).

McIntyre, D. C. & Reichert, H. State-dependent learning in rats induced by kindled convulsions. *Physiology and Behavior*, 1971, **7**, 15–20.

Means, M. H. Fears of 1,000 college women. *Journal of Abnormal and Social Psychology*, 1936, **31**, 291–311.

Mech, L. David. *The Wolf:* The Ecology and Behavior of an Endangered Species. Published for the American Museum of Natural History, The Natural History Press, Garden City, New York, 1970.

Mechanic, A. The responses involved in the rote learnings of verbal materials. *Journal of Verbal Learning and Verbal Behavior*, 1964, **3**, 30–36.

Medin, D. L. Form perception and pattern reproduction by monkeys. *Journal of Comparative and Physiological Psychology*, 1969, **68**, 412–419.

Medin, D. L. Animal models and memory models. In D. L. Medin, W. A. Roberts, and R. Davis (Eds.), *Processes in animal memory*. Hillsdale, New Jersey: Lawrence Erlbaum Associates, 1976.

Medin, D. L. A theory of context in discrimination learning. In G. H. Bower (Ed.), *The psychology of learning and motivation*, Vol. 9, New York: Academic Press, 1975.

Medin, D. L. & Davis, R. T. Memory. In A. M. Schrier and F. Stollnitz (Eds.), *Behavior of nonhuman primates: Modern research trends, Volume 5*. New York: Academic Press, 1974.

Mello, N. Alcohol effects on delayed matching-to-sample performance by Rhesus monkeys. Physiology & Behavior, 1971, **7**, 77–101.

Melton, A. W. Implications of short-term memory for general theory of memory. *Journal of Verbal Learning and Verbal Behavior*, 1963, **2**, 1–21.

Melton, A. W. Repetition and retrieval from memory. *Science*, 1967, **158**, 532.

Melton, A. W. & Irwin, J. M. The influence of degree of interpolated learning on retroactive inhibition and the overt transfer of specific responses. *American Journal of Psychology*, 1940, **53**, 173–203.

Melton, A. W. & Von Lackum, W. J. Retroactive and proactive inhibition in retention: evidence for a two factor theory of retroactive inhibition. *American Journal of Psychology*, 1941, **54**, 157–173.

Mendoza, M. E. & Adams, H. E. Does electroconvulsive shock produce retrograde amnesia: *Physiology and Behavior*, 1969, **4**, 307–309.

Messenger, J. B. Two-stage recovery of a response in *Sepia. Nature*, 1971, **232**, 202–203.

Meunier, G. F., Kestner, J., Meunier, J. A., & Ritz, D. Overt rehearsal and long-term retention. *Journal of Experimental Psychology*, 1974, **102**, 913–914.

Meyer, D. R. Access to engrams. *American Psychologist*, 1972, **27**, 124–133.

Meyer, D. R. & Harlow, H. F. Effects of multiple variables on delayed response performance by monkeys. *Journal of Genetic Psychology*, 1952, **81**, 53–61.

Meyer, D. R., Isaac, C. W. & Maher, B. A. The role of stimulation in spontaneous reorganization of visual habits. *Journal of Comparative and Physiological Psychology,* 1958, **51,** 546-548.

Michels, K. M. & Brown, D. R. The delayed-response performance of raccoons. *Journal of Comparative and Physiological Psychology,* 1959, **52,** 737-740.

Miller, A. J. Variations in retrograde amnesia with parameters of electroconvulsive shock and time of testing. *Journal of Comparative and Physiological Psychology,* 1968, **66,** 40-47.

Miller, B. V. & Levis, D. J. The effects of varying short visual exposure to a phobic test stimulus on subsequent avoidance behavior. *Behavior Research and Therapy,* 1971, **9,** 17-21.

Miller, G. A. The magical number 7 ± 2: Some limits on our capacity for processing information. *Psychological Review,* 1956, **63,** 81-97.

Miller, N. E. Learning resistance to pain and fear: Effects of overlearning, exposure and rewarded exposure in context. *Journal of Experimental Psychology,* 1960, **60,** 137-145.

Miller, N. E. Some recent studies of conflict behavior and drugs. *American Psychologist,* 1961, **16,** 12-24.

Miller, N. E. & Dollard, J. *Social learning and imitation.* New Haven: Yale University Press, 1941.

Miller, R. R. Effects of environmental complexity on amnesia induced by electroconvulsive shock in rats. *Journal of Comparative and Physiological Psychology,* 1970, **71,** 267-275.

Miller, R. R. & Berk, A. M. Retention over metamorphosis in the African claw-toed frog. *Journal of Experimental Psychology: Animal Behavior Processes,* 1977, **3,** 343-356.

Miller, R. R., Malinowski, B., Puk, G. & Springer, A. D. State-dependent models of ECS-induced amnesia in rats. *Journal of Comparative and Physiological Psychology,* 1972, **81,** 533-540.

Miller, R. R. & Misanin, J. R. Critique of electroconvulsive shock-induced retrograde amnesia: Analysis of the familiarization effect. *Communications in Behavioral Biology,* 1969, **4,** 255-256.

Miller, R. R., Ott, C. A., Berk, A. M. & Springer, A. D. Appetitive memory restoration after electroconvulsive shock in the rat. *Journal of Comparative and Physiological Psychology,* 1974, **87,** 717-723.

Miller, R. R. & Spear, N. E. Memory and the extensor phase of convulsions induced by electroconvulsive shock. *Psychonomic Science,* 1969, **15,** 164-166.

Miller, R. R. & Springer, A. D. Amnesia, consolidation and retrieval. *Psychological Review,* 1973, **80,** 69-79.

Miller, R. R. & Springer, A. D. Temporal course of amnesia in rats after electroconvulsive shock. *Physiology and Behavior,* 1971, **6,** 229-233.

Miller, R. R. & Springer, A. D. Induced recovery of memory in rats following electroconvulsive shock. *Physiology and Behavior,* 1972, **8,** 645-651.

Miller, R. R. & Springer, A. D. Implications of recovery from experimental amnesia. *Psychological Review,* 1974, **81,** 470-473.

Milner, B. Les troubles de la memoire accompagnant des lesions hippocampiques bilaterales. In *Physiologie de Phippocampe.* Paris: C.N.R.S., 257-272, 1962. [English translation in P. M. Milner & S. Glickman (Eds.), *Cognitive processes and the brain.* Princeton, N. J.: Van Nostrand, 97-111, 1965]

Milner, B. Amnesia following operation on the temporal lobes. In C. W. M. Whitty and O. L. Zangwill (Eds.), *Amnesia.* London: Butterworths, 1966, 109-133.

Milner, B., Corkin, S. & Teuber, H. L. Further analysis of the hippocampal-amnesic syndrome: 14 year follow-up study of H. M. Neuropsychologia, 1968, **6,** 215-234.

Misanin, J. R. The effects of ECS on ECT: Implications for behavioral research. *Psychonomic Science,* 1970, **20,** 159-161.

Misanin, J. R. Chubb, L. D., Quinn, S. A. & Schweikert, G. E. An apparatus and procedure for effective instrumental training of neonatal and infant rats. *Bulletin of the Psychonomics Society,* 1974, **4,** 171-173.

Misanin, J. R., Haigh, J. M., Hinderliter, C. F. and Nagy, Z. M. Analysis of response competition and nondiscriminated escape training of neonatal rats. *Journal of Comparative and Physiological Psychology,* 1973, **85,** 570-580.

Misanin, J. R. & Lewis, D. J. Sensitivity and reactivity to foot shock following electroconvulsive shock stimulation. *Physiology and Behavior,* 1970, **5,** 397–405.

Misanin, J. R., Nagy, Z. M., Keiser, E. F. & Bowen, W. Emergence of long-term memory in the neonatal rat. *Journal of Comparative and Physiological Psychology,* 1971, **77,** 188–199.

Misanin, J. R., Smith, F. & Miller, R. R. Memory of electroconvulsive shock as a function of intensity and duration. *Psychonomic Science,* 1971, **22,** 5–7.

Mishkin, M., Dunkel, R. D., Rosveld, H. E. Contact occluders: A method for restricting vision in animals. *Science,* 1959, **129,** 1220–1221.

Mistler-Lachman, J. L. Queer sentences, ambiguity and levels of processing. *Memory and Cognition,* 1975, **3,** 395–400.

Moffett, A. & Ettlinger, G. Opposite responding to position in the light and dark. *Neuropsychologia,* 1967, **5,** 59–65.

Moise, S. L. Short-term retention in *Macaca speciosa* following interpolated activity during delayed matching from sample. *Journal of Comparative and Physiological Psychology,* 1970, **73,** 506–514.

Moorcroft, W. H. Ontogeny of behavioral inhibition by forebrain structures in the rat. *Brain Research,* 1971, **35,** 513–522.

Moorcroft, W. H., Lytle, L. D. & Campbell, B. A. Ontogeny of starvation-induced behavioral arousal in the rat. *Journal of Comparative and Physiological Psychology,* 1971, **75,** 59–67.

Morrison, G. R. & Collyer, R. Taste-mediated conditioned adversion to an exteroceptive stimulus following LiCl poisoning. *Journal of Comparative and Physiological Psychology,* 1974, **86,** 51–55.

Morton, J. A functional model for memory. In D. A. Norman (Ed.), *Models of human memory.* New York: Academic Press, 1970, 203–254.

Morton, J., Crowder, R. G. & Prussin, H. A. Experiments with the stimulus suffix effect. *Journal of Experimental Psychology,* 1971, **91,** 169–190.

Müller, G. E. & Pilzecker, A. Experimentelle bietrage zur lehre bom gedachtnisses. *Zeitschrift fur Psychologie,* Erganzungsband 1, 1900.

Murdock, B. B., Jr. Short-term memory. In G. H. Bower (Ed.), *The psychology of learning and motivation: Advances in research and theory, Vol. 5.* New York: Academic Press, 1972.

Murdock, B., Jr., *Human memory: Theory and data.* Hillsdale, New Jersey: Lawrence Erlbaum Associates, 1974.

Murphy, J. M. & Nagy, Z. M. Neonatal thyroxine stimulation accelerates the maturation of locomotor and memory processes in mice. *Journal of Comparative and Physiological Psychology,* 1976, **90.**

Myers, C. S. Two cases of synaesthesia. *British Journal of Psychology,* 1914, **7,** 115–124.

Nachman, M. & Meinecke, R. O. Lack of retrograde amnesia effects of repeated electroconvulsive shock and carbon dioxide treatments. *Journal of Comparative and Physiological Psychology,* 1969, **68,** 631–636.

Nagy, Z. M. Escape learning in infant mice as a function of drive level and drive shift during acquisition. *Development Psychobiology,* 1976, **9,** 389–399.

Nagy, Z. M., Misanin, J. R., Newman, J. A., Olsen, P. L. & Hinderliter, C. F. Ontogeny of memory in the neonatal mouse. *Journal of Comparative and Physiological Psychology,* 1972, **81,** 380–393.

Nagy, Z. M., Misanin, J. R. & Wetzel, B. Inception of a 24-hour memory capacity in two mouse strains. *Developmental psychobiology,* 1973, **6,** 521–529.

Nagy, Z. M. & Mueller, P. M. Effects of amount of original training upon onset of a 24-hour memory capacity in neonatal mice. *Journal of Comparative and Physiological Psychology,* 1973, **85,** 151–159.

Nagy, Z. M. & Murphy, J. M. Learning and retention of a discriminated escape response in infant mice. *Developmental psychobiology,* 1974, **7,** 185–192.

Nagy, Z. M., Pagano, M. R. & Gable, T. Differential development of 24-hour retention capacities of two components of t maze escape learning by infant mice. *Animal Learning and Behavior*, 1976, **4**, 25–29.

Nagy, Z. M. & Sandmann, M. Development of learning and memory of T maze training in neonatal mice. *Journal of Comparative and Physiological Psychology*, 1973, **83**, 19–26.

Naitoh, P. Selective impairment of Pavlovian conditional responses by electroconvulsive shock. *Physiology and Behavior*, 1971, **7**, 291–296.

Nakajima, S. Amnesic effects of cycloheximide in the mouse mediated by adrenocortical hormones. *Journal of Comparative and Physiological Psychology*, 1975, **88**, 378–385.

Nakajima, S. Biochemical disruption of memory: A re-examination. In W. B. Essman & S. Nakajima (Eds.), *Current biochemical approaches to learning and memory*. New York: Halstead, 1973.

Nakamura, C. Y. & Anderson, N. H. Avoidance behavior differences within and between strains of rats. *Journal of Comparative and Physiological Psychology*, 1962, **55**, 740–747.

Neisser, Y. *Cognitive psychology*. New York: Appleton-Century-Crofts, 1967.

Nelson, D. L. & Borden, R. C. & Wheeler, J. W. Sensory features in the reduction of imaginal interference. *Memory and Cognition*, 1975, **3**, 239–242.

Nelson, D. L. & Brooks, D. H. Independence of phonetic and imaginal features. *Journal of Experimental Psychology*, 1973, **97**, 1–7.

Nelson, T. O., Metzler, J. & Reed, D. A. Role of details in the long-term recognition of pictures and verbal descriptions. *Journal of Experimental Psychology*, 1974, **102**, 184–186.

Neylon, A. & Brosgole, L. Long-term retention of heat training in mongolian gerbils. *Psychological Reports*, 1974, **34**, 511–514.

Ni, C. F. An experimental study of the influence of punishment for errors during learning upon retention. *Journal of Comparative Psychology*, 1934, **17**, 279–301.

Nice, M. M. Studies in the life history of the song sparrow II. Society, New York, 1943, **6**, 1–328.

Nielson, H. C. Evidence that electroconvulsive shock alters memory retrieval rather than memory consolidation. *Experimental Neurology*, 1968, **20**, 3–20.

Norman, D. A. & Rumelhart, D. E. A system for perception and memory. In D. A. Norman (Ed.), *Models of human memory*. New York: Academic Press, 1970.

Nottebom, F. The origins of vocal learning. *The American Naturalist*, 1972, **106**, 116–140.

Obrist, P. A., Black, A. H., Brener, J. & DiCara, L. V. (Eds.), *Cardio vascular psychophysiology: Current issues in response mechanisms, biofeedback, and methodology*. Chicago: Aldine, 1974.

O'Connell, D. N., Shor, R. E., & Orne, M. T. Hypnotic age regression: An empirical and methodological analysis. *Journal of Abnormal Psychology Monographs*, 1970, **76**, no. 3, part 2, 1–32.

Ornstein, P. A. & Liberty, C. Rehearsal processes in children's memory. Paper presented at meetings of the Society for Research and Child Development, Philadelphia, Spring, 1973.

Oscar-Berman, M. Hypothesis testing and focusing behavior during concept formation by amnesic Korsakoff patients. *Neuropsychologia*, 1973, **11**, 191–198.

Otis, L. F. Drive conditioning: Fear as a response to biogenic drive stimuli previously associated with painful stimulation. Unpublished Ph.D. thesis, University of Chicago, Chicago, Illinois, 1957.

Ottosson, J. O. (Ed.), Experimental studies on the mode of action of electroconvulsive therapy. *ACTA Psychiatrica Scandinavica*, 1960, **35** (supplement 145), 103–141.

Overmier, J. B. & Seligman, M. E. P. Effects of inescapable shock upon subsequent escape in avoidance responding. *Journal of Comparative and Physiological Psychology*, 1967, **63**, 28–33.

Overton, D. State-dependent or "dissociated" learning produced with pentobarbitol. *Journal of Comparative and Physiological Psychology*, 1964, **57**, 3–12.

Overton, D. A. Visual cues and shock sensitivity in the control of a T-maze choice by drug conditions. *Journal of Comparative and Physiological Psychology*, 1968, **66**, 216–219.

Overton, D. State-dependent learning produced by depressant and atropine-like drugs. *Psychopharmacologia*, 1966, **10**, 6–31.

Overton, D. A. Discriminative control of behavior by drug-states. In G. Thompson and R. Pickins (Eds.), *Stimulus properties of drugs*. New York: Appleton-Century-Crofts, 1971.

Overton, D. A. State-dependent learning produced by alcohol and its relevance to alcoholism. In B. Kissin & H. Begleiter (Eds.), *The biology of alcoholism*, Vol. 2, Physiology and Behavior. New York: Plenum Press, 1972.

Overton, D. A. Experimental methods for the study of state-dependent learning. *Federation Proceedings*, 1974, **33**, 1800–1813.

Paivio, A. Imagery and long-term memory. In A. Kennedy and A. Wilkes (Eds.), *Studies in long-term memory*. New York: Wiley, 1975.

Paivio, A. & Csapo, K. Picture superiority in free recall: Imagery or dual coding? *Cognitive Psychology*, 1973, **5**, 176–206.

Palfai, T. & Chillag, D. Time-dependent memory deficits produced by pentylenetetrazol (Metrazol)—The effect of reinforcement magnitude. *Physiology and Behavior*, 1971, **7**, 439–442.

Palfai, T. & Kurtz, P. Time-dependent effects of metrazol on memory. *Pharmacology, Biochemistry and Behavior*, 1973, **1**, 55–59.

Pancratz, C. N. & Cohen, L. B. Recovery of habituation in infants. *Journal of Experimental Child Psychology*, 1970, **9**, 208–216.

Paolino, R. M., Quartermain, D. & Miller, N. E. Different temporal gradients of retrograde amnesia produced by carbon dioxide anesthesia and electroconvulsive shock. *Journal of Comparative and Physiological Psychology*, 1966, **62**, 270–274.

Pappas, B. A. & Gray, P. Cue value ot dexamethasone for fear-motivated behavior. *Physiology and Behavior*, 1971, **6**, 127–130.

Papsdorf, J. D., Snyder, R. E., & Cholewiak, R. W. Effects of posttrial strychnine injections on the classically conditioned nicitating membrane response. Cited in McGaugh, J. L. Drug facilitation of memory and learning. *Proceedings of the sixth annual meeting of the American College of Neuropsychopharmacology*, D. H. Efron, (Ed.), 1968, 891–904.

Parsons, P. J., Fagan, T. & Spear, N. E. Short-term retention of habituation in the rat: A developmental study from infancy to old age. *Journal of Comparative and Physiological Psychology*, 1973, **84**, 545–553.

Parsons, P. J. & Spear, N. E. Long-term retention of avoidance learning by immature and adult rats as a function of environmental enrichment. *Journal of Comparative and Physiological Psychology*, 1972, **80**, 297–303.

Pastore, R. E. Categorical perception: A critical re-evaluation. In S. K. Hirsh, D. H. Eldredge, I. J. Hirsh and S. R. Silverman (Eds.), *Hearing and Davis: Essays honoring Hallowell Davis*. St. Louis: Washington University Press, 1976.

Pastore, R. E., Ahroon, W. A., Puleo, J. S., Crimmins, D. B., Golowner, L. & Berger, R. S. Processing interaction between two dimensions of nonphonetic auditory signals. *Journal of Experimental Psychology: Human Perception and Performance*, 1976, **2**, 267–276.

Pavlov, I. P. *Lectures on conditioned reflexes*. New York International Publishers Company, Inc. 1928.

Pavlov, I. P. *Conditioned reflexes*. T. V. Anrep (Translator). London: Oxford University Press, 1927.

Pearlman, C. Similar retrograde amnesia effects of ether and spreading cortical depression. *Journal of Comparative and Physiological Psychology*, 1966, **61**, 306–308.

Pearlman, C. A., Sharpless, S. K. & Jarvik, M. E. Retrograde amnesia produced by anesthetic and convulsant agents. *Journal of Comparative and Physiological Psychology*, 1961, **54**, 109–112.

Peeke, H. V. S. & Herz, M. J. Caudate neucleus stimulation retroactively impairs complex maze learning in the rat. *Science*, 1971, **173**, 80–82.

Peeke, H. V. S., LeBoeuf, B. J. & Herz, M. J. The effect of strychnine administration during development on adult maze learning in the rat. II: Drug Administration from day 51 to 70. *Psychopharmacologia*, 1971, **19**, 262–265.

Penney, C. G. Modality effects in short-term verbal memory. *Psychological Bulletin*, 1975, **82**, 68–84.

Pepper, R. L. & Herman, L. M. Decay and interference effects in a short-term retention of a discrete motor act. *Journal of Experimental Psychology Monographs Supplement,* 1970, **83.**

Perkins, C. C., Jr. The relation of secondary reward to gradients of reinforcement. *Journal of Experimental Psychology,* 1947, **37,** 377–392.

Perkins, C. C., Jr. A conceptual scheme for studies of stimulus generalization. In D. I. Mostofsky (Ed.), *Stimulus Generalization.* Stanford: Stanford University Press, 1965.

Perkins, C. C., Jr. & Weyant, R. G. The interval between training and test trials as determiner of the slope of generalization gradients. *Journal of Comparative and Physiological Psychology,* 1958, **51,** 596–600.

Peters, R. D., Calhoun, K. S. & Adams, H. E. Modification by environmental conditions of retrograde amnesia produced by ECS. *Physiology and Behavior,* 1973, **11,** 889–892.

Petersen, R. Isolation of processes involved in state-dependent recall in man. Paper presented at Federation of American Society for Experimental Biology meetings, Atlantic City, New Jersey, April, 1974.

Peterson, L. R. Reminiscence in short-term memory. *Journal of Experimental Psychology,* 1966, **71,** 115–118.

Peterson, L. R., Hillner, K. & Saltzman, D. Time between pairings in short-term retention. *Journal of Experimental Psychology,* 1962, **64,** 550–551.

Peterson, L. R. & Peterson, M. J. Short-term retention of individual verbal items. *Journal of Experimental Psychology,* 1959, **58,** 193–198.

Petrich, J. A. Retroactive inhibition under a multiple-choice procedure. *American Journal of Psychology,* 1974, **87,** 335–349.

Pinel, J. P. J., Malsbury, C. W., & Corcoran, M. E. The incubation effect in rats: Skin resistance changes after footshock. *Physiology and Behavior,* 1971, **6,** 111–114.

Podd, M. H. & Spear, N. E. Stimulus relatedness and response coding. *Journal of Verbal Learning and Verbal Behavior,* 1967, **6,** 55–60.

Posner, M. I. Short-term memory systems in human information processing. *ACTA Psychologica* 1967, **27,** 267–284.

Posner, M. I. Abstraction and the process of recognition. In G. Bower and J. T. Spence (Eds.), *Psychology of learning and motivation Vol. 3.* New York: Academic Press, 1969.

Posner, M. I. & Boies, S. J. Complements of attention. *Psychological Review,* 1971, **78,** 391–408.

Postman, L. Does interference theory predict too much forgetting? *Journal of Verbal Learning and Verbal Behavior,* 1963, **2,** 40–48.

Postman, L. Short-term memory and incidental learning. In A. W. Melton (Ed.), *Categories of human learning.* New York: Academic Press, 1964.

Postman, L. Association and performance in analysis of verbal learning. In T. R. Dixon and D. L. Horton (Eds.), *Verbal behavior and general behavior theory.* Englewood-Cliffs, New Jersey: Prentice-Hall, 1968.

Postman, L. Transfer, interference and forgetting. In J. W. Kling and L. A. Riggs (Eds.), *Woodworth and Schlosberg's experimental psychology.* New York: Holt, Rinehart and Winston, 1971.

Postman, L. Experimental analysis of learning to learn. In G. R. Bower and J. T. Spence (Eds.), *Psychology of learning and motivation Vol. 3.* New York: Academic Press, 1969.

Postman, L. Verbal learning and memory. *Annual Review of Psychology,* 1975, **26,** 291–335.

Postman, L. A pragmatic view of organization theory. In E. Tulving and W. Donaldson (Eds.), *Organization of memory.* New York: Academic Press, 1972, 4–50.

Postman, L. Does imagery enhance long-term retention? *Bulletin of the Psychonomic Society,* 1974, **3,** 375–377.

Postman, L. & Burns, S. Experimental analysis of coding processes. *Memory and Cognition,* 1973, **1,** 503–507.

Postman, L. & Burns, S. Long-term retention as a function of word concreteness under conditions of free recall. *Memory and Cognition,* 1974, **2,** 703–708.

Postman, L. & Hasher, L. Conditions of proactive inhibition in free recall. *Journal of Experimental Psychology,* 1972, **92,** 276–284.

Postman, L., Kreusi, E. & Regan, J. Recognition and recall as measures of long-term retention. *Quarterly Journal of Experimental Psychology,* 1975, **27**, 411-418.

Postman, L., Stark, K. & Burns, S. Sources of proactive inhibition on unpaced tests of retention. *American Journal of Psychology,* 1974, **87**, 33-56.

Postman, L., Stark, K. & Fraser, J. Temporal changes in interference. *Journal of Verbal Learning and Verbal Behavior,* 1968, **7**, 672-694.

Postman, L. & Underwood, B. J. Critical issues in interference theory. *Memory and Cognition,* 1973, **1**, 19-40.

Powell, B. J., Goodwin, D. W., James, C. L., & Hoine, H. State-dependent effects of alcohol on autonomic conditioning responses. *Psychonomic Sciences,* 1971, **25**, 305-306.

Powell, R. W. The effect of shock intensity upon responding under a multiple-avoidance schedule. *Journal of the Experimental Analysis of Behavior,* 1970, **14**, 321-329.

Powell, R. W. Analysis of warm-up effects during avoidance in wild and domesticated rodents. *Journal of Comparative and Physiological Psychology,* 1972, **78**, 311-316.

Powell, R. W. & Peck, S. Activity and avoidance in a Mongolian gerbil. *Journal of the Experimental Analysis of Behavior,* 1969, **12**, 779-787.

Prien, R. F., Wayner, M. J. & Kahan, S. A. Lack of facilitation in maze learning by picrotoxin and strychnine sulfate. *American Journal of Physiology,* 1963, **204**, 488-492.

Pryor, G. T., Peache, S. & Scott, M. K. The effect of repeated electroconvulsive shock on avoidance conditioning and brain monoamine oxidase activity. *Physiology & Behavior,* 1972, **9**, 623-628.

Pschirrer, M. Goal events as discriminative stimuli over extended intertrial intervals. *Journal of Experimental Psychology,* 1972, **80**, 425-432.

Pylyshyn, Z. W. What the mind's eye tells the mind's brain: A critique of mental imagery. *Psychological Bulletin,* 1973, **80**, 1-24.

Quartermain, D. & Botwinick, C. W. Role of biogenic amines in the reversal of cycloheximide-induced amnesia. *Journal of Comparative and Physiological Psychology,* 1975, **88**, 386-401.

Quartermain, D. & McEwen, B. S. Temporal characteristics of amnesia induced by inhibition of protein synthesis. *Nature,* 1970, **228**, 677-678.

Quartermain, D., McEwen, B. S. & Azmitia, E. Amnesia produced by electroconvulsive shock of cycloheximide: Conditions for recovery. *Science,* 1970, **169**, 683-686.

Quartermain, D., McEwen, B. S. & Azmitia, E. C. Recovery of memory following amnesia in the rat and mouse. *Journal of Comparative and Physiological Psychology,* 1972, **79**, 360-370.

Quinton, E. E. The cycloheximide-induced amnesia gradient of a passive avoidance task. *Psychonomic Science,* 1971, **25**, 295-296.

Quinton, E. Memory retrieval reactivation, and protein synthesis. Paper presented at the meetings of the Rocky Mountain Psychological Association, 1972.

Rand, G. & Wapner, S. Postural status as a factor in memory. *Journal of Verbal Learning and Verbal Behavior,* 1967, **6**, 268-271.

Randt, C. T., Barnett, B. M., McEwen, B. S. & Quartermain, D. Amnesic effects of cycloheximide on two strains of mice with different memory characteristics. *Experimental Neurology,* 1971, **30**, 467-474.

Ray, O. S. & Barrett, R. J. Disruptive effects of electroconvulsive shock as a function of current level and mode of delivery. *Journal of Comparative and Physiological Psychology,* 1969, **67**, 110-116.

Ray, O. S. & Bivens, L. W. Reinforcement magnitude as a determinant of performance decrement after electroconvulsive shock. *Science,* 1968, **160**, 330-332.

Ray, O. S. & Emley, T. Time factors in interhemispheric transfer of learning. *Science,* 1964, **144**, 76-78.

Razran, G. H. S. Extinction, spontaneous recovery and forgetting. *American Journal of Psychology,* 1939, **52**, 100-102.

Reder, L. M., Anderson, J. R. & Bjork, R. A. A semantic interpretation of encoding specificity. *Journal of Experimental Psychology,* 1974, **102**, 648-656.

Rego, M. The effects of thyroxine on learning and retention in neonatal rat. Unpublished Master's thesis, State University of New York at Binghamton, 1976.

Reid, R. L. The role of the reinforcer as a stimulant. *British Journal of Psychology*, 1958, **49**, 202–209.

Reiff, R. & Scheerer, M. *Memory and hypnotic age regression: Developmental aspects of cognitive function explored through hypnosis*. New York: International University Press, 1959.

Reinis, S. Indirect effect of puromycin on memory. *Psychonomic Science*, 1969, **14**, 44–45.

Reitman, J. S. Without surreptitious rehearsal, information in short-term memory decays. *Journal of Verbal Learning and Verbal Behavior*, 1974, **13**, 365–377.

Reitman, W., Malin, J. T., Bjork, R. A. & Higman, B. Strategy control and directed forgetting. *Journal of Verbal Learning and Verbal Behavior*, 1973, **12**, 140–149.

Rensch, B. The intelligence of elephants. *Scientific America*, 1957, **196**, 72–76.

Rescorla, R. A. Evidence for "unique stimulus" account of configural conditioning. *Journal of Comparative and Physiological Psychology*, 1973, **85**, 331–338.

Rescorla, R. A. & Heth, C. E. Reinstatement of fear to an extinguished conditioned stimulus. *Journal of Experimental Psychology: Animal Behavior Processes'* 1975, **104**, 88–96.

Rescorla, R. A. & Wagner, A. R. A theory of Pavlovian conditioning: Variations in the effectiveness of reinforcement and nonreinforcement. In A. H. Black and W. F. Prokasy (Eds.), *Classical conditioning II: Current research and theory*. New York: Appleton-Century-Crofts, 1972, 64–99.

Revusky, S. The role of interference in association over a delay. In W. K. Honig and P. H. R. James (Eds.), *Animal memory*. New York: Academic Press, 1971.

Revusky, S. Long-delay learning in rats: A black white discrimination. *Bulletin of the Psychonomic Society*, 1974, **4**, 526–528.

Revusky, S. & Garcia, J. Learned associations over long delays. In G. H. Bower (Ed.), *The psychology of learning and motivation: Advances in the research and theory Vol. 4*. New York: Academic Press, 1970.

Reynierse, J. H., Zerbolio, D. J. & Denny, M. R. Avoidance decrement: Replication and further analysis. *Psychonomic Science*, 1964, **1**, 401–402.

Riccio, D. C. The paradox of retrograde amnesia. Paper presented at meetings of the Midwestern Psychological Association, Chicago, May, 1975.

Riccio, D. C., Gaebelein, C. & Cohen, P. Some behavioral aspects of retrograde amnesia produced by hypothermia. *Physiology and Behavior*, 1968, **3**, 973–976.

Riccio, D. C., Hodges, L. A. & Randall, P. K. Retrograde amnesia produced by hypothermia in rats. *Journal of Comparative and Physiological Psychology*, 1968, **66**, 618–622.

Riccio, D. C. & Marrazo, M. J. Effects of punishing active avoidance in young and adult rats. *Journal of Comparative and Physiological Psychology*, 1972, **79**, 453–458.

Riccio, D. C. Rohrbaugh, M. & Hodges, L. A. Developmental aspects of passive and active avoidance learning in rats. *Developmental Psychobiology*, 1968, **1**, 108–111.

Riccio, D. C. & Stikes, E. R. Persistent but modifiable retrograde amnesia produced by hypothermia. *Physiology and Behavior*, 1969, **4**, 649–652.

Riccio, D. C., Urda, M. & Thomas, D. R. Stimulus control in pigeons based on proprioceptive stimuli from the floor inclination. *Science*, 1966, **153**, 434–436.

Richardson, J. Encoding as stimulus selection in paired associates verbal learning. In A. W. Melton and E. Martin (Eds.), *Coding processes in human memory*. Washington, D. C.: Winston, 1972. (a)

Richardson, J. Encoding as stimulus selection in paired associates verbal learning. In L. M. Secrest, C. P. Duncan & A. W. Melton (Eds.), *Human memory: Feshrift for Benton J. Underwood*. New York: Appleton-Century-Crofts, 1972 (b).

Richardson, J. Component selection and paired-associated learning: Research and theory. *American Journal of Psychology*, 1976, **89**, 3–49.

Richter, C. P. Sleep and activity: their relation to the 24-hour clock. In S. S. Kety, E. V. Evarts and H. L. Williams (Eds.), *Proceedings of the Association for Research in Nervous and Mental Diseases*. Baltimore: Williams and Wilkins Co., 1967.

Riege, W. H. & Cherkin, A. Retroactive facilitation of memory in goldfish by flurothyl. *Psychopharmacologia,* 1973, 195–204.

Riesen, A. H. (Ed.), *The developmental neuropsychology of sensory deprivation.* New York: Academic Press, 1975.

Rigter, H. & van Riezen, H. Anti-amnesic effect of $ACTH_{4-10}$: Its independence of the nature of the amnesic agent and the behavioral test. *Physiology and Behavior,* 1975, **14,** 563–566.

Rigter, H., van Riezen, H. & deWied, D. The effects of ACTH and vasopressin-analogue on CO_2-induced retrograde amnesia in rats. *Physiology and Behavior,* 1974, **13,** 381–388.

Riopelle, A. J. Performance of rhesus monkeys on spatial delayed response (indirect method). *Journal of Comparative and Physiological Psychology,* 1959, **52,** 746–750.

Robbins, D. & Bush, C. T. Memory in great apes. *Journal of Experimental Psychology,* 1973, **97,** 344–348.

Roberts, R. B., Flexner, J. B. & Flexner, L. B. Some evidence for the involvement of adrenergic sites in the memory trace. *Proceedings of the National Academy of Science,* 1970, **66,** 310–313.

Roberts, W. A. Still no evidence for visual discrimination learning: A reply to Lett. *Learning and Motivation,* 1977, **8,** 140–144.

Roberts, W. A. Failure to replicate visual discrimination learning with a one-minute delay of reward. *Learning and Motivation,* 1974, 393–408. (a)

Roberts, W. A. Short-term memory in the pigeon: Effects of repetition and spacing. *Journal of Experimental Psychology,* 1972, **94,** 74–83.

Roberts, W. A. Short-term memory in the pigeon with presentation time precisely controlled. *Learning and Motivation,* 1974, 393–408.

Roberts, W. A. Spaced repetition facilitates short-term retention in the rat. *Journal of Comparative and Physiological Psychology,* 1974, **86,** 164–171. (b)

Roberts, W. A. & Grant, D. S. Short-term memory in the pigeon with presentation time precisely controlled. *Learning and Motivation,* 1974, **5,** 393–408.

Robin, E. D. The evolutionary advantages of being stupid. *Perspectives in Biology and Medicine,* 1973, **16,** 369–380.

Robustelli, F., Geller, A. & Jarvik, M. E. Potentiation of the amnesic effect of electroconvulsive shock by detention. *Psychonomic Science,* 1968, **12,** 85–86.

Rodnick, E. H. The effect of a metrazol shock on habit systems. *Journal of Abnormal and Social Psychology,* 1942, **37,** 560–565.

Roediger, H. L. III. Inhibition in recall from cueing with recall targets. *Journal of Verbal Learning and Verbal Behavior,* 1973, **12,** 644–657.

Roediger, H. L. III. Inhibiting effects of recall. *Memory and Cognition,* 1974, **2,** 261–269.

Roediger, H. L. III, & Crowder, R. G. Instructed forgetting: Rehearsal control or retrieval inhibition (repression)? *Cognitive Psychology,* 1972, **3,** 244–254.

Rogers, J. L., Jr. & Underwood, B. J. Retroactive inhibition as a function of the conceptual structure of original and interpolated lists. *Memory and Cognition,* 1976, **4,** 190–216.

Rohrbaugh, M. & Riccio, D. C. Paradoxical enhancement of learned fear. *Journal of Abnormal Psychology,* 1970, **75,** 210–216.

Rohwer, W. D., Jr. Elaboration and learning in childhood and adolescence. In H. W. Reese (Ed.), *Advances in child development and behavior, Vol. 8.* New York: Academic Press, 1973.

Rohwer, W. D., Jr., Shuell, T. J. & Levin, J. R. Context effects in the initial storage and retrieval of noun pairs. *Journal of Verbal Learning and Verbal Behavior,* 1967, **6,** 796–801.

Rosenblatt, J. F. Learning in newborn kittens. *Scientific American,* 1972, **277,** 18–25.

Rosenblatt, J. S. Suckling and home orientation in the kitten: A comparative developmental study. In E. Tobach, L. R. Aronson and E. Shaw (Eds.), *The biopsychology of development.* New York: Academic Press, 1971, 345–410.

Rosenzweig, M. R. & Bennett, E. L. (Eds.), *Neural mechanisms of learning and memory.* Cambridge, Mass.: The MIT Press, 1976.

Rosenzweig, M. R., Mollgaard, K., Diamond, M. C. & Bennett, E. L. Negative as well as positive synaptic changes may store memory. *Psychological Review,* 1972, **79,** 93–96.

Routtenberg, A. & Kay, K. E. Effect of one electroconvulsive seizure on rat behavior. *Journal of Comparative and Physiological Psychology*, 1965, **59**, 285–288.

Rozin, P. & Ree, P. Long extension of effective CS-US as interval by anesthesia between CS and US. *Journal of Comparative and Physiological Psychology*, 1972, **80**, 43–48.

Rudy, J. W. Stimulus selection in animal learning and paired-associate learning: Variations in the associative process. *Journal of Verbal Learning and Verbal Behavior*, 1974, **13**, 282–296.

Runquist, W. N. Interference among memory traces. *Memory and Cognition*, 1975, **3**, 143–159.

Runquist, W. N. & Joinson, P. A. Predictions of terminal acquisition performance for individual subjects. *Journal of Verbal Learning and Verbal Behavior*, 1968, **7**, 98–105.

Runquist, W. N. & Snyder, R. A. Forgetting of verbal paired associates after low degrees of learning. *Journal of Verbal Learning and Verbal Behavior*, 1969, **8**, 512–517.

Russell, W. R. Traumatic amnesia. *Quarterly Journal of Experimental Psychology*, 1948, **1**, 2–6.

Russell, W. R. & Nathan, P. Traumatic amnesia. *Brain*, 1946, **69**, 280–300.

Sachs, E. Dissociation of learning in rats and its similarities to dissociative states in man. In J. Zubin and H. Hunt (Eds.), *Comparative psychopathology, animal and human*. New York: Grune and Stratton, 1967.

Saltz, E. & Asdourian, D. Incubation of anxiety as a function of cognitive differentiation. *Journal of Experimental Psychology*, 1963, **66**, 17–22.

Sanders, G. D. & Barlow, J. J. Variations in retention performance during long-term memory formation. *Nature*, 1971, **232**, 203–204.

Sanders, H. I. & Warrington, E. K. Memory for remote events in amnesic patients. *Brain*, 1971, **94**, 661–668.

Santa, J. L. & Lamwers, L. L. Where does the confusion lie: Comments on the Wiseman and Tulving paper. *Journal of Verbal Learning and Verbal Behavior*, 1976, **15**, 35–38.

Santa, J. L. & Lamwers, L. L. Encoding specificity: Fact or artifact. *Journal of Verbal Learning and Verbal Behavior*, 1974, **13**, 412–423.

Sara, S. Retrograde amnesia: Consolidation failure or retrieval dysfunction? Unpublished dissertation for the degree of Doctor of Psychology, Psychology Faculty, University of Louvain, Belgium, 1975.

Sara, S. and Lefevre, D. Hypoxia induced amnesia in one-trial learning and pharmacological protection by Piracetam. *Psychopharmacologia*, 1972, **25**, 32–40.

Sara, S. J. & Lefevre, D. Re-examination of role of familiarization in retrograde amnesia in the rat. *Journal of Comparative and Physiological Psychology*, 1973, **84**, 361–364.

Sara, S. J. Delayed development of amnestic behavior after hypoxia. *Physiology and Behavior*, 1974, **13**, 693–696.

Saufley, W. H. Jr. & Winograd, E. Retrograde amnesia and priority instructions in free recall. *Journal of Experimental Psychology*, 1970, **85**, 150–152.

Schachtel, E. G. On memory and childhood amnesia. *Psychiatry*, 1947, **10**, 1–26.

Schapiro, S. & Erdelyi, M. H. Hypermnesia for pictures but not words. *Journal of Experimental Psychology*, 1974, **103**, 1218–1219.

Schapiro, S. & Salas, M. Behavioral response of infant rats to maternal odor. *Physiology and Behavior*, 1970, **5**, 815–817.

Schapiro, S. Hormonal and environmental influences on rats' brain development and behavior. In: M. B. Sterman, D. J. McGuinty, and A. M. Adinolfi (Eds.), *Brain Development and Behavior*. New York: Academic Press, 1971.

Schapiro, S. Maturation of the neuroendocrine response to stress in the rat. In G. Newton and S. Levine (Eds.), *Early experience and behavior*. Springfield, Illinois: C. C. Thomas, 1968.

Schierer, C. J. & Voss, J. F. Reminiscence in short-term memory. *Journal of Experimental Psychology*, 1969, **80**, 262–270.

Scherrer, J. Electrophysiological aspects of cortical development. In E. A. Asratyon (Ed.), *Progress in Brain Research*. Amsterdam: Elsevier, 1967, **22**, 480–489.

Schmidt, R. A. & Nacson, J. Further tests of the activity-set hypothesis for warm-up decrement. *Journal of Experimental Psychology*, 1971, **90**, 56–64.

Schneider, A. M. Control of memory by spreading cortical depression: A case for stimulus control. *Psychological Review*, 1967, **74**, 201–215.

Schneider, A. M. Spreading depression: A behavioral analysis. In J. A. Deutsch (Ed.), *The physiological basis of memory*. New York: Academic Press, 1973, 271–304.

Schneider, A. M., Advokat, C., Kapp, B. & Sherman, W. Retrograde amnesic effects of unilateral spreading depression. Paper presented at meetings of the Eastern Psychological Association, Philadelphia, 1969.

Schneirla, T. C. The process and mechanism of ant learning: The combination-problem and the successive-presentation problem. *Journal of Comparative Psychology*, 1934, **17**, 303–328.

Schoel, W. M. & Agranoff, B. W. The effect of puromycin on retention of conditioned cardiac deceleration in goldfish. *Behavioral Biology*, 1972, **7**, 553–565.

Scobie, S. R. & Bliss, D. K. Ethyl alcohol: Relationships to memory for aversive learning in goldfish (*Carassius auratus*). *Journal of Comparative and Physiological Psychology*, 1974, **86**, 867–874.

Scott, J. P. & Fuller, J. L. *Genetics and the social behavior of the dog*. Chicago: University of Chicago Press, 1965.

Scoville, W. B. & Milner, B. Loss of recent memory after bilateral hippocampal lesions. *Journal of Neurological Neurosurgery and Psychiatry*, 1957, **20**, 11–21.

Sechenov, I. M. *Reflexes of the brain*. Cambridge: MIT Press, 1965 (originally published in 1863).

Segal, D. S., Squire, L. R. & Barondes, S. H. Cycloheximide: its effects on activity is dissociable from its effects on memory. *Science*, 1971, **172**, 82–84.

Seligman, M. E. P. On the generality of the laws of learning. *Psychological Review*, 1970, **77**, 406–418.

Seligman, M. E. P. & Hager, J. L. (Eds.), *Biological boundaries of learning*. New York: Appleton-Century-Crofts, 1972.

Seligman, M. E. P., Ives, C. E., Ames, H. & Mineka, S. Conditioned drinking and its failure to extinguish: Avoidance preparedness, or functional autonomy. *Journal of Comparative and Physiological Psychology*, 1970, **71**, 411–419.

Seligman, M. E. P., Maier, S. F. & Solomon, R. L. Unpredictable and uncontrollable aversive events. In F. R. Brush (Ed.), *Aversive conditioning and learning*. New York: Academic Press, 1971.

Selye, H. The general adaptation syndrome and the diseases of adaptation. *Endocrinology*, 1946, **36**, 217–230.

Serota, R. G., Roberts, R. B. & Flexner, L. B. Acetoxycycloheximide-induced transient amnesia: Protective effects of adrenergic stimulants. *Proceedings of the National Academy of Science*, 1972, **69**, 340–342.

Shaffer, W. O. & Shiffrin, R. M. Rehearsal and storage of visual information. *Journal of Experimental Psychology*, 1972, **92**, 292–296.

Shallice, T. & Warrington, E. K. Independent functioning of verbal memory stores: A neuropsychological study. *Quarterly Journal of Experimental Psychology*, 1970, **22**, 261–273.

Shaughnessy, J. J., Zimmerman, J. & Underwood, B. J. Further evidence on the MP-DP effect in free recall learning. *Journal of Verbal Learning and Verbal Behavior*, 1972, **11**, 1–12.

Shepard, J. W. & Ellis, H. D. The effect of attractiveness on recognition memory for faces. *American Journal of Psychology*, 1973, **87**, 627–633.

Shepard, R. N. Recognition memory for words, sentences, and pictures. *Journal of Verbal Learning and Verbal Behavior*, 1967, **6**, 156–163.

Shiffrin, R. A. Visual free recall. *Science*, 1973, **180**, 980–982.

Sidman, M. Two temporal parameters of the maintenance of avoidance behavior by the white rat. *Journal of Comparative and Physiological Psychology*, 1953, **46**, 253–261.

Sidman, M. Reduction of shock frequency as reinforcement for avoidance behavior. *Journal of the Experimental Analysis of Behavior*, 1962, **5**, 247–257.

Sidman, M., Stoddard, L. T. & Mohr, J. P. Some additional quantitative observations of immediate memory in a patient with bilateral hippocampal lesions. *Neuropsychologia*, 1968, **6**, 245–254.

Silvestri, R., Rohrbaugh, M. J. & Riccio, D. C. Conditions influencing the retention of learned fear in young rats. *Developmental Psychology,* 1970, **2,** 380–395.

Singh, P. J., Sakellaris, P. C. & Brush, F. R. Retention of active and passive avoidance responses tested in extinction. *Learning and Motivation,* 1971, **2,** 305–321.

Skinner, B. F. *The behavior of organisms: An experimental analysis.* New York: Appleton-Century-Crofts, 1938.

Skinner, B. F. Are theories of learning necessary? *Psychological Review,* 1950, **57,** 193–216.

Slamecka, N. J. Testing for associative storage in multi-trial free recall. *Journal of Experimental Psychology,* 1969, **81,** 557–560.

Slamecka, N. J. An examination of trace storage in free recall. *Journal of Experimental Psychology,* 1968, **76,** 504–513.

Spear, N. E. Retention of reinforcer magnitude. *Psychological Review,* 1967, **74,** 216–234.

Spear, N. E. Forgetting as retrieval failure. In W. K. Honig and P. H. R. James (Eds.), *Animal memory.* New York: Academic Press, 1971.

Spear, N. E. Retrieval of memory in animals. *Psychological Review,* 1973, **80,** 163–194.

Spear, N. E. Verbal learning and retention. In M. R. D'Amato, *Experimental psychology: Psychophysics, methodology and learning.* New York: McGraw-Hill, 1970.

Spear, N. E. Retrieval of memory: A psychobiological approach. In W. K. Estes (Ed.), *Handbook of Learning and cognitive processes, Vol. 4, Memory processes.* Hillsdale, New Jersey: Lawrence Erlbaum Associates, 1976.

Spear, N. E., Bryan, R. G., Gordon, W. C., Chiszar, D. A. & Timmons, R. Manuscript in preparation.

Spear, N. E. & Gordon, W. C. Sleep, dreaming and the retrieval of memories. In W. Fishbein and E. Weitzman (Eds.), *Advances in sleep research, Vol. 4.* New York: Spectrum Publications, 1977.

Spear, N. E., Gordon, W. C., & Chiszar, D. A. Interaction between memories in the rat: Effect of degree of prior coinflicting learning on forgetting after short intervals. *Journal of Comparative and Physiological Psychology,* 1972, **78,** 471–477.

Spear, N. E., Gordon, W. C. & Martin, P. A. Warm-up decrement as failure in memory retrieval in the rat. *Journal of Comparative and Physiological Psychology,* 1973, **85,** 601–614.

Spear, N. E., Klein, S. B. & Riley, E. P. The Kamin effect as "state-dependent" learning: Memory retrieval failure in the rat. *Journal of Comparative and Physiological Psychology,* 1971, **74,** 416–425.

Spear, N. E. & Parsons, P. Analysis of a reactivation treatment: Ontogeny and alleviated forgetting. In D. Medin, R. Davis & W. Roberts (Eds.), *Coding processes in animal memory.* Hillsdale, New Jersey: Lawrence Erlbaum Associates, 1976.

Spear, N. E. & Spitzner, J. H. Effective initial nonrewarded trials: Factors responsible for increased resistance to extinction. *Journal of Experimental Psychology,* 1967, **74,** 525–537.

Spence, K. W. *Behavior theory and conditioning.* New Haven: Yale University Press, 1956.

Spence, K. W. The nature of theory construction in psychology. *Psychological Review,* 1944, **51,** 47–68.

Spence, K. W. & Taylor, J. Anxiety and strength of the UCS as determinants of the amount of eyelid conditioning. *Journal of Experimental Psychology,* 1951, **42,** 183–188.

Spence, K. W., Taylor, J. & Ketchel, R. Anxiety (drive) level and degree of competition in paired-associate learning. *Journal of Experimental Psychology,* 1956, **52,** 306–310.

Sperling, G. The information available in brief visual presentations. *Psychological Monographs,* 1960, **74** (whole no. 498).

Sperling, G. Successive approximations to a model for short-term memory. *ACTA Psychologia,* 1967, **27,** 285–292.

Sperling, G. A. A model for visual memory tasks. *Human Factors,* 1963, **5,** 19–31.

Sperry, R. W., Stamm, J. S. & Miner, N. Relearning tests for interocular transfer following division of optic chiasma and corpus callosum in cats. *Journal of Comparative and Physiological Psychology,* 1956, **49,** 529–533.

Spevack, A. A. & Suboski, M. D. Retrograde effects of electroconvulsive shock on learned responses. *Psychological Bulletin,* 1969, **72,** 66–76.

Springer, A. D. Vulnerability of skeletal and autonomic manifestations of a CER to the amnesic effects of ECS. Unpublished Ph.D. dissertation, Brooklyn College of the City University of New York, 1973.

Springer, A. D. Vulnerability of skeletal and autonomic manifestations of memory in the rat through electroconvulsive shock. *Journal of Comparative and Physiological Psychology,* 1975, **88,** 890–903.

Springer, A. D., Schoel, W. M., Klinger, P. D. & Agranoff, B. W. Anterograde and retrograde effects of electroconvulsive shock and of puromycin on memory formation in the goldfish. *Behavioral Biology,* 1975, **13,** 467–481.

Springer, A. D. & Miller, R. R. Retrieval failure induced by electroconvulsive shock: Reversal with dissimilar training and recovery agents. *Science,* 1972, **177,** 628–630.

Springer, S. P. Memory for linguistic and nonlinguistic dimensions of the same acoustic stimulus. *Journal of Experimental Psychology,* 1973, **101,** 159–163.

Squire, L., Smith, G. A. & Barondes, S. H. Cycloheximide affects memory within minutes after the onset of training. *Nature,* 1973, **242,** 201–202.

Squire, L. R. Amnesia for remote events following electroconvulsive therapy. *Behavioral Biology,* 1974, **12,** 119–125.

Squire, L. R. Short-term memory as a biological entity. In D. Deutsch and J. A. Deutsch (Eds.), *Short-Term Memory.* New York: Academic Press, 1975, 1–42.

Squire, L. R. & Miller, P. L. Diminution of anterograde amnesia following electroconvulsive therapy. *The British Journal of Psychiatry,* 1974, **125,** 490–495.

Squire, L. R., Slater, P. C. & Chace, P. M. Retrograde amnesia: Temporal gradient in very long-term memory following electroconvulsive therapy. *Science,* 1975, **187,** 77–79.

Staddon, J. E. R. Temporal control, attention, and memory. *Psychological Review,* 1974, **81,** 375–391.

Stalnaker, J. M. & Riddle, E. E. The effects of hypnosis on long-delayed recall. *Journal of General Psychology,* 1932, **6,** 429–439.

Stanley, W. C. Feeding behavior and learning in neonatal dogs. In J. F. Bosma (Ed.), *Second symposium on oral sensation and perception.* Springfield, Illinois: C. C. Thomas, 1970.

Starr, A. & Phillips, L. Verbal and motor memory in the amnesic syndrome. *Neuropsychologia,* 1970, **8,** 75–88.

Stedman's Medical Dictionary. Baltimore: Williams and Wilkins Company, 1972.

Stein, D. G. & Chorover, S. L. Effects of posttrial electrical stimulation of hippocampus and candate nucleus on maze learning in the rat. *Physiology and Behavior,* 1968, **3,** 787–791.

Stein, D. G. & Kimble, D. P. Effects of hippocampal lesions and posttrial strychnine administration on maze behavior in the rat. *Journal of Comparative and Physiological Psychology,* 1966, **62,** 243–249.

Steiner, F. A. Effects of ACTH and corticosterone on single neurons in the hypothalamus. In D. DeWied, & J. A. W. M. Weijnen, *Progress in Brain Research, Volume 32, Pituitary Adrenal and Brain.* Amsterdam, Elsevier, 1970.

Steinman, F. Retention of alley brightness in the rat. *Journal of Comparative and Physiological Psychology,* 1967, **64,** 105–109.

Stelmach, G. & Kelso, J. A. S. Memory trace strength and response biasing in short-term motor memory. *Memory and Cognition,* 1975, **3,** 58–62.

Stelmach, G. Short-term motor retention as a function of response similarity. *Journal of Motor Behavior,* 1969, **1,** 37–44.

Stengel, E. Psychogenic loss of memory. In C. W. M. Whitty and O. L. Zangwill (Eds.), *Amnesia.* London: Butterworths, 1966.

Sterman, M. B., McGinty, D. J. & Adinolfi, A. M. (Eds.), *Brain development and behavior,* New York: Academic Press, 1971.

Stern, W. C. & Morgane, P. J. Theoretical view of REM sleep function: Maintenance of catecholamine systems in the central nervous system. *Behavioral Biology,* 1974, **11,** 1–32.

Stollnitz, F. Forgetting of discrimination learning set by rhesus monkeys. Paper presented at meetings of the Psychonomics Society, San Antonio, November, 1970.

Stone, J. M. & Greenough, W. T. Excess neonatal thyroxine: Effects on learning in infant and adolescent rats. *Developmental Psychobiology,* 1975, **8,** 479–488.

Strand, B. Z. Change of context and retroactive inhibition. *Journal of Verbal Learning and Verbal Behavior,* 1970, **9,** 202–206.

Strand, B. Z. Effects of instructions for category organization on long-term retention. *Journal of Experimental Psychology: Human Learning and Memory,* 1975, **1,** 780–786.

Stratton, G. M. Retroactive hypermnesia and other emotional effects on memory. *Psychological Review,* 1919, **26,** 774–786.

Stroebel, C. F. Behavioral aspects of Circadean rhythms. In J. Zubin and H. F. Hunt (Eds.), *Comparative psychopathology.* New York: Grune & Stratton, 1967.

Sutherland, N. S. Outlines of a theory of visual pattern recognition in animals and man. *Proceedings of the Royal Society. Series B,* 1968, **171,** 297–317.

Sutherland, N. S. & Mackintosh, N. J. *Mechanisms of animal discrimination learning.* London: Academic Press, 1971.

Swanson, R., McGaugh, J. L., & Cotman, C. Acetoxycycloheximide effects on one-trial inhibitory avoidance learning. *Communications in Behavioral Biology,* 1969, **4,** 239–245.

Talland, G. A. *Deranged memory.* New York: Academic Press, 1965.

Taylor, J. A. The relationship of anxiety to the conditioned eyelid response. *Journal of Experimental Psychology,* 1951, **41,** 81–92.

Taylor, J. A. & Spence, K. W. The relationship of anxiety level to performance in serial learning. *Journal of Experimental Psychology,* 1952, **44,** 61–64.

Terrace, H. S. Stimulus control. In W. K. Honig (Ed.), *Operant behavior: Areas of research and application.* New York: Appleton-Century-Crofts, 1966.

Terry, W. S. & Wagner, A. R. Short-term memory for "surprising" vs "expected" unconditioned stimuli in Pavlovian conditioning. *Journal of Experimental Psychology: Animal Behavior Processes,* 1975, **104,** 122–133.

Thompson, C. I. & Grossman, L. B. Loss and recovery of long-term memory after ECS in rats: Evidence for state-dependent recall. *Journal of Comparative Psychology,* 1972, **78,** 248–254.

Thompson, C. I. & Neely, J. E. Dissociated learning in rats produced by electroconvulsive shock. *Physiology and Behavior,* 1970, **5,** 783–786.

Thompson, R. F. & Spencer, W. A. Habituation: A model phenomenon for the study of neuronal substrates of behavior. *Psychological Review,* 1966, **73,** 16–43.

Thompson, R. W., Koenigsberg, L. A. & Tennison, J. C. Effects of age on learning and retention of an avoidance response in rats. *Journal of Comparative and Physiological Psychology,* 1965, **60,** 457–459.

Thorndike, E. L. *Human learning.* New York: Century, 1931.

Thorndike, E. L. *The psychology of learning.* New York: Teachers College, Columbia University Press, 1913.

Thune, L. E. & Underwood, B. J. Retroactive inhibition as a function of degree of interpolated learning. *Journal of Experimental Psychology,* 1943, **32,** 185–200.

Timmins, W. K. Varying processing time in directed forgetting. *Journal of Verbal Learning and Verbal Behavior,* 1974, **13,** 539–544.

Tinbergen, N. The herring gull's world. London: Collins, 1963.

Tinklepaugh, O. L. An experimental study of representative factors in monkeys. *Journal of Comparative Psychology,* 1928, **8,** 197.

Titus, H. E. & Costanzo, D. J. Effects of puromycin on learning in the toad. *Psychological Reports,* 1972, **30,** 627–630.

Tolman, E. C. *Purposive behavior in animals and men.* New York: Appleton-Century-Crofts, 1932.

Tompkins, S. S. A theory of memory. In J. S. Antrobus (Ed.), *Cognition and affect*. Boston: Little, Brown, 1970.

Treisman, A. Monitoring and storage of irrelevant passages in selective attention. *Journal of Verbal Learning and Verbal Behavior*, 1964, **3**, 449–459.

Treisman, A. & Tuxworth, J. Immediate and delayed recall of sentences after perceptual processing of different levels. *Journal of Verbal Learning and Verbal Behavior*, 1974, **13**, 38–44.

Tribhowan, T., Rucker, W. B. & McDiarmid, C. G. Demonstration of a Kamin-like effect after appetitive training. *Psychonomic Science*, 1971, **23**, 41–42.

Troshikhin, V. A. Influence of age and rearing on the mobility of nervous processes in dogs. *Proc. Pavlov. Inst. Physiol SSSR. Acad. Sci.* 1957, **5**, 165–173. Cited in Volokhov, A. A. The ontogenetic development of higher nervous activity in animals. In W. A. Himwich (Ed.) *Developmental Neurobiology*. Canfield: C. C Thomas, 1970.

True, R. M. & Stephenson, C. W. Controlled experiments correlating electroencephalogram, pulse, and plantar reflexes with hypnotic age regression and induced emotional states. *Personality*, 1951, **1**, 252–263.

Tulving, E. Retrograde amnesia in free recall. *Science*, 1969, **164**, 88–90.

Tulving, E. Subjective organization in free recall of "unrelated" words. *Psychological Review*, 1962, **69**, 344–354.

Tulving, E. Intratrial and intertrial retention: Notes towards a theory of free-recall verbal learning. *Psychological Review*, 1964, **71**, 219–237.

Tulving, E. The effect of order of presentation on learning of "unrelated" words. *Psychosomatic Science, 1965*, **3**, 337–388.

Tulving, E. Theoretical issues in free recall. In T. R. Dixon & D. L. Horton (Eds.), *Verbal behavior and general behavior theory*. Englewood Cliffs, New Jersey: Prentice Hall, 1968.

Tulving, E. Episodic and semantic memory. In E. Tulving and W. Donaldson (Eds.), *Organization of memory*. New York: Academic Press, 1972, 381–403.

Tulving, E. & Bower, G. H. The logic of memory representations. In G. H. Bower (Ed.), *The psychology of learning and motivation: Advances in research and theory Vol. 8*. New York: Academic Press, 1974.

Tulving, E. & Hastie, R. Inhibition effects of intralist repetition in free recall. *Journal of Experimental Psychology*, 1972, **92**, 297–304.

Tulving, E. & Osler, S. Effectiveness of retrieval cues in memory for words. *Journal of Experimental Psychology*, 1968, **77**, 593–601.

Tulving, E. & Psotka, J. Retroactive inhibition and free-recall: Inaccessibility of information available in the memory store. *Journal of Experimental Psychology*, 1971, **87**, 1–8.

Tulving, E. & Thomson, D. M. Retrieval processes in recognition memory: Effects of associative context. *Journal of Experimental Psychology*, 1971, **87**, 116–124.

Tulving, E. & Thomson, D. M. Encoding specificity and retrieval processes in episodic memory. *Psychological Review*, 1973, **80**, 352–373.

Tulving, E. & Watkins, M. J. Structure of memory traces. *Psychological Review*, 1975, **82**, 261–275.

Tulving, E. & Wiseman, S. Relation between recognition and recognition failure of recallable words. *Bulletin of the Psychonomic Society*, 1975, in press.

Ulrich, R. E., Holz, W. C. & Azrin, N. H. Stimulus control of avoidance behavior. *Journal of the Experimental Analysis of Behavior*, 1964, **7**, 129–133.

Underwood, B. J. The effects of successive interpolations on retroactive and proactive inhibition. *Psychological Monographs*, 1945, **59** (3, whole #273).

Underwood, B. J. Speed of learning and amount retained: A consideration of methodology. *Psychological Bulletin*, 1954, **51**, 276–282.

Underwood, B. J. Interference and forgetting. Psychological Review, 1957, **64**, 49–60.

Underwood, B. J. Stimulus selection in verbal learning. C. N. Cofer & B. S. Musgrave (Eds.), *Verbal behavior and learning*. New York: McGraw Hill, 1963.

Underwood, B. J. Degree of learning and the measurement of forgetting. *Journal of Verbal Learning and Verbal Behavior,* 1964, **3,** 112–129.

Underwood, B. J. False recognition produced by implicit verbal responses. *Journal of Experimental Psychology,* 1965, **70,** 122–129.

Underwood, B. J. *Experimental Psychology (second edition)* New York: Appleton-Century-Crofts, 1966. (a)

Underwood, B. J. Motor-skills learning and verbal learning: Some observations. In E. A. Bilodeau (Ed.), *Acquisition of skill.* New York: Academic Press, 1966 (b).

Underwood, B. J. Attributes of memory. *Psychological Review,* 1969, **76,** 559–573.

Underwood, B. J. A breakdown of the total-time law in free-recall learning. *Journal of Verbal Learning and Verbal Behavior,* 1970, **9,** 573–580.

Underwood, B. J. Recognition memory. In H. H. Kendler and J. T. Spence (Eds.), *Essays in neobehaviorism: A memorial volume to Kenneth W. Spence.* New York: Appleton-Century-Crofts, 1971.

Underwood, B. J. Are we overloading memory? In A. W. Melton and E. Martin (Eds.), *Coding processes in human memory.* Washington, D.C.: Winston, 1972.

Underwood, B. J. The role of association in recognition memory. *Journal of Experimental Psychology Monograph,* 1974, **102,** 917–939.

Underwood, B. J. Individual differences as a crucible for theory construction. *American Psychologist,* 1975, **30,** 128–134.

Underwood, B. J. Recognition memory for pairs of words as a function of associative context. *Journal of Experimental Psychology: Human Learning and Memory,* 1976, **2,** 404–412.

Underwood, B. J. & Ekstrand, B. R. Studies of distributive practice: XXIV. Differentiation and proactive inhibition. *Journal of Experimental Psychology,* 1967, **74,** 574–580.

Underwood, B. J. & Ekstrand, B. R. An analysis of some shortcomings in the interference theory of forgetting. *Psychological Review,* 1966, **73,** 540–549.

Underwood, B. J. & Erlebacher, A. H. Studies of coding in verbal learning. *Psychological Monographs,* 1965, **79** (13, whole number 606).

Underwood, B. J. & Freund, J. S. Relative frequency judgment and verbal discrimination learning. *Journal of Experimental Psychology,* 1970, **83,** 279–285.

Underwood, B. J. & Freund, J. S. Effect of temporal separation of two tasks on proactive inhibition. *Journal of Experimental Psychology,* 1968, **78,** 50–54.

Underwood, B. J. & Keppel, G. Retention as a function of degree of learning and letter-sequence interference. *Psychological Monographs,* 1963, **77** (4, whole No. 567). (a)

Underwood, B. J. and Keppel, G. Coding processes in verbal learning. *Journal of Verbal Learning and Verbal Behavior,* 1963, **1,** 250–257 (b).

Underwood, B. J., Keppel, G. & Schulz, R. W. Studies of distributed practice: XXII. Some considerations which enhance retention. *Journal of Experimental Psychology,* 1962, **64,** 228–235.

Underwood, B. J., Patterson, M. & Freund, J. S. Recognition and number of incorrect alternatives presented during learning. *Journal of Educational Psychology,* 1972, **63,** 1–7.

Underwood, B. J. & Postman, L. Extra-experimental sources of interference in forgetting. *Psychological Review,* 1960, **67,** 73–95.

Underwood, B. J., Reichardt, C. S. & Malmi, R. A. Sources of facilitation in learning conceptually structured paired-associate lists. *Journal of Experimental Psychology: Human Learning and Memory,* 1975, **104,** 160–166.

Underwood, B. J., Reichardt, C. S. & Zimmerman, J. Conceptual associations in verbal discrimination learning. *American Journal of Psychology,* 1973, **86,** 613–615.

Underwood, B. J., Runquist, W. N. & Schulz, R. W. Response learning in paired-associate lists as a function of intralist similarity. *Journal of Experimental Psychology,* 1959, **58,** 70–78.

Underwood, B. J. & Schulz, R. W. *Meaningfulness and verbal learning.* Philadelphia, Pennsylvania: Lippincott, 1960.

Underwood, B. J. & Shaughnessy, J. J. *Experimentation in psychology.* New York: Wiley, 1975.

Underwood, B. J., Shaughnessy, J. J. & Zimmerman, J. The locus of the retention differences associated with degree of hierarchical conceptual structure. *Journal of Experimental Psychology.*

Underwood, B. J. & Zimmerman, J. Serial retention as a function of hierarchical structure. *Journal of Experimental Psychology,* 1973, **99,** 236–242.

Underwood, B. J., Zimmerman, J. & Freund, J. S. Retention of frequency information with observations on recognition and recall. *Journal of Experimental Psychology,* 1971, **87,** 149–162.

Vacher, J. M., King, R. A. & Miller, A. T. Failure of hypoxia to produce retrograde amnesia. *Journal of Comparative and Physiological Psychology,* 1968, **66,** 179–181.

Vardaris, R. M. & Schwartz, K. E. Retrograde amnesia for passive avoidance produced by stimulation of dorsal hippocampus. *Physiology and Behavior,* 1971, **6,** 131–135.

Verplanck, W. S. & Hayes, J. R. Eating and drinking as a function of maintenance schedule. *Journal of Comparative and Physiological Psychology,* 1953, **46,** 327–333.

Volokhov, A. A. The ontogenetic development of higher nervous activity in animals. In W. A. Himwich (Ed.), *Developmental neurobiology.* Canfield: C. C Thomas, 1970.

von Kries, J., Ueber die Abhangigkeit der Dammerungswerthe vom Adaptationsgrade. Z. Psychol., 1901, **25,** 225–238, (cited by Gomulicki, 1953).

vonWright, J. M. The effect of systematic changes of context stimuli on repeated recall. *ACTA Psychologia,* 1959, **16,** 59–68.

Voronin, L. G., Leontiev, A. N., Luria, A. R., Sokolov, E. N., and Vinogradova, O. D. (Eds.), *Orienting reflex and exploratory behavior.* (Translated by V. Shmelev and K. Hanes; edited by D. B. Lindsley). Washington, D.C.: American Institute of Biological Sciences and the American Psychological Association, 1965.

Wagner, A. R. Elementary associations. In H. H. Kendler and J. T. Spence (Eds.), *Essays in neobehaviorism: A memorial volume to Kenneth W. Spence.* New York: Appleton-Century-Crofts, 1971, 187–216.

Wagner, A. R. Stimulus validity and stimulus selection in associative learning. In J. N. Mackintosh and W. K. Honig (Eds.), *Fundamental issues in associative learning.* Halifax: Dalhousie University Press, 1969.

Wagner, A. R. & Rescorla, R. A. Inhibition in Pavlovian conditioning: Application of a theory. In R. A. Boakes and M. S. Halliday (Eds.), *Inhibition and learning.* London: Academic Press, 1972, 301–336.

Wagner, A. R., Rudy, J. W. & Whitlow, J. W., Jr. Rehearsal in animal conditioning. *Journal of Experimental Psychology Monograph,* 1973, **97,** 407–426.

Waldfogel, S. The frequency and affective character of childhood amnesias. *Psychological Monographs,* 1948, **62** (4,291).

Walen, S. R. Recall in children and adults. *Journal of Verbal Learning and Verbal Behavior,* 1970, **9,** 94–98.

Wallace, W. P. Review of the historical, empirical and theoretical status of the von Restorff phenomenon. *Psychological Bulletin,* 1965, **63,** 410–424.

Wallace, W. P. Verbal discrimination. In C. P. Duncan, L. Sechrist & A. W. Melton (Eds.), *Human memory: Festschrift in honor of Benton J. Underwood.* New York: Appleton-Century-Crofts, 1972.

Wallace, W. P., Murphy, M. D., & Sawyer, T. J. Imagery and frequency in verbal discrimination learning. *Journal of Experimental Psychology Monograph* 1973, **101,** 201–219.

Wallace, W. H., Turner, S. H. & Perkins, C. C. Preliminary studies of human information storage. Signal Corps Project Number 1320, 1957, Institute for Cooperative Research, University of Pennsylvania.

Wansley, R. A. & Holloway, F. A. Multiple retention deficits following one-trial appetitive training. *Behavioral Biology,* 1975, **14,** 135–149.

Ward, L. B. Reminiscence and role learning. *Psychological Monographs,* 1937, **49,** No. 220.

Warrington, E. K. & Baddeley, A. D. Amnesia and memory for visual location. *Neuropsychologia,* 1974, **12,** 257–263.

Warrington, E. K. & Sanders, H. I. The fate of old memories. *Quarterly Journal of Experimental Psychology*, 1971, **23**, 432–442.

Warrington, E. K. & Shallice, T. The selective impairment of auditory verbal short-term memory. *Brain*, 1969, **92**, 885–896.

Warrington, E. K. & Weiskrantz, L. Organisational aspects of memory in amnesic patients. *Neuropsychologia*, 1971, **9**, 283–291.

Warrington, E. K. & Weiskrantz, L. Amnesic syndrome: Consolidation or retrieval? *Nature* (London) 1970, 228, 628–630.

Warrington, E. K. & Weiskrantz, L. A study of learning and retention in amnesic patients. *Neuropsychologia*, 1968, **6**, 283–291.

Warrington, E. K. & Weiskrantz, L. An analysis of short-term and long-term memory defects in man. In J. A. Deutsch (Ed.), *The physiological basis of memory*. New York and London: Academic Press, 1973, pp. 365–395.

Warrington, E. K. & Weiskrantz, L. The effect of prior learning on subsequent retention in amnesic patients. *Neuropsychologia*, 1974, **12**, 419–428.

Waters, R. H. & Vitale, A. G. Degree of interpolated learning and retroactive inhibition in maze learning I. Animal subjects. *Journal of Comparative Psychology*, 1945, **38**, 119–126.

Watkins, M. J. The concept and measurement of primary memory. *Psychological Bulletin*, 1974, **81**, 695–711.

Watkins, M. J. Locus of the modality effect in free recall. *Journal of Verbal Learning and Verbal Behavior*, 1972, **11**, 644–648.

Watkins, M. J. & Tulving, E. Episodic memory: When recognition fails. *Journal of Experimental Psychology:* General, 1975, **104**, 5–29.

Watkins, M. J., Watkins, O. C. & Crowder, R. G. The modality effect in free and serial recall as a function of phonological similarity. *Journal of Verbal Learning and Verbal Behavior*, 1974, **13**, 430–447.

Watkins, O. C. & Watkins, M. J. Built up of proactive inhibition as a cue-overload effect. *Journal of Experimental Psychology: Human Learning and Memory*, 1975, **104**, 442–452.

Watson, J. B. An attempted formulation of the scope of behavior psychology, *Psychological Review*, 1917, **24**, 329–352.

Watts, M. E. & Mark, R. F. Drug inhibition of memory formation in chickens. II Short-term memory. *Proceedings of the Royal Society of London: B*. 1971, **178**, 455–464.

Weaver, G. E. Effects of poststimulus study time on recognition of pictures. *Journal of Experimental Psychology*, 1974, **103**, 799–801.

Weingartner, H., Adefris, W., Eich, J. E. & Murphy, D. L. Encoding-imagery specificity in alcohol state-dependent learning. *Journal of Experimental Psychology: Human Learning and Memory*, 1976, **2**, 83–87.

Weiskrantz, L. Experimental studies of amnesia. In C. W. M. Whitty and O. L. Zangwill (Eds.), *Amnesia*. London: Butterworths, 1966, 1–35.

Weiskrantz, L. Experiments on the r.n.s. (real nervous system) and monkey memory. *Proceedings of the Royal Society of Britain*, 1968, **171**, 335–352.

Weiskrantz, L. Comparison of amnesic states in monkey and man. In L. E. Jarrard (Ed.), *Cognitive processes of nonhuman primates*. New York and London: Academic Press, 1971, pp. 25–46.

Weiskrantz, L. A long-term view of short-term memory in psychology. In G. Horn and R. A. Hinde (Eds.), *Short-Term Changes in Neural Activity and Behavior*. Cambridge: Cambridge University Press, 1970.

Weiskrantz, L. & Warrington, E. K. Verbal learning and retention by amnesic patients using partial information. *Psychonomic Science*, 1970, **20**, 210–211 (a).

Weiskrantz, L. & Warrington, E. K. A study of forgetting in amnesic patients. *Neuropsychologia*, 1970, **8**, 281–288. (b)

Weiskrantz, L. & Warrington, E. K. The problem of the amnesic syndrome in man and animals. In

R. L. Isaacson and K. H. Pribram (Eds.), *The Hippocampus Volume 2*. New York: Plenum Press, 1975. (a)

Weiskrantz, L. & Warrington, E. K. Some comments on Woods' and Piercy's claim of a similarity between amnesic memory and normal forgetting. *Neuropsychologia*, 1975, **13**, 365–368. (b)

Weiss, B. A. & Schneirla, T. C. Inter-situational transfer in the ant *Formica schaufussi* as tested in a t-phase single choice point maze. *Behaviour*, 1967, **28**, 269–279.

Weiss, J. M., McEwen, B. S., Silva, M. T. A. & Kalkut, M. F. Pituitary-adrenal influence on fear responding. *Science*, 1969, **163**, 197–199.

Weiss, S. J. Stimulus compounding in free-operant and classical conditioning: A review and analysis. *Psychological Bulletin*, 1972, **78**, 189–208.

Welker, R. L., Tomie, A., Davitt, G. A. & Thomas, D. R. Contextual stimulus control over operant responding in pigeons. *Journal of Comparative and Physiological Psychology*, 1974, **86**, 549–562.

Wendt, G. R. Two and one-half year retention of a conditioned response. *Journal of General Psychology*, 1937, **17**, 178–180.

Werber, M. Effect of hypothermia on a T-maze habit in the grain beetle (Tenebrio Molitor). *Journal of Comparative and Physiological Psychology*, 1974, **87**, 188–192.

Whitely, P. L. & Blankenship, A. B. The influence of certain conditions prior to learning upon subsequent recall. *Journal of Experimental Psychology*, 1936, **19**, 496–504.

Whitlow, Jr., J. W. & Wagner, A. R. Negative patterning in classical conditioning: Summation of response tendencies to isolate and configural components. *Psychonomic Science*, 1972, **27**, 299–301.

Whitty, C. W. M. & Lishman, W. A. Amnesia in cerebral disease. In C. W. M. Whitty & O. L. Zangwill (Eds.), *Amnesia*. London: Butterworths, 1966.

Wickelgren, W. A. Sparing of short-term memory in an amnesic patient: Implications for strength theory of memory. *Neuropsychologia*, 1968, **6**, 235–244.

Wickelgren, W. A. Trace resistance and the decay of long-term memory. *Journal of Mathematical Psychology*, 1972, **9**, 418–455.

Wickelgren, W. A. The long and short of memory. *Psychological Bulletin*, 1973, **80**, 425–438.

Wickelgren, W. A. The long and the short of memory. In D. Deutsch & J. A. Deutsch (Eds.), *Short-term memory*. New York: Academic Press, 1975, 43–65. (a)

Wickelgren, W. A. More on the long and short of memory. In D. Deutsch & J. A. Deutsch (Eds.), *Short-Term Memory*. New York: Academic Press, 1975, 66–75. (b)

Wickelgren, W. A. & Norman, D. A. Invariance of forgetting rate with number of repetitions in verbal short-term recognition memory. *Psychonomic Science*, 1971, **22**, 363–364.

Wickens, D. D. Encoding categories of words: An empirical approach to meanings. *Psychological Review*, 1970, **77**, 1–15.

Wickens, D. D. Characteristics of work encoding. In A. W. Melton & E. Martin (Eds.), *Coding Processes in Human Memory*. Washington, D. C.: V. H. Winston & Sons, 1972.

Wickens, D. D. Classical conditioning as it contributes to basic psychological processes. In J. McGuigan (Ed.), *Current problems in learning and conditioning*. New York: Winston and Sons, 1973.

Wickens, D. D. & Dalezman, J. Spontaneous recovery and clustering of first-list responses. *Journal of Experimental Psychology*, 1974, **103**, 1067–1073.

Wickens, D. D., Tuber, D. S., Nield, A. F. & Wickens, C. Memory for the conditioned response: The effects of potential interference introduced before and after original conditioning. *Journal of Experimental Psychology: General*, 1977, **106**, 47–70.

Wiener, N. I. & Messer, J. Scopolamine-induced impairment of retention in rats. *Behavioral Biology*, 1973, **9**, 227–234.

Wilburn, M. W. & Kesner, R. P. Differential amnestic effects produced by electrical stimulation of the caudate neucleus in nonspecific thalamic system. *Experimental Neurology*, 1972, **34**, 45–50.

Williams, J. M., Hamilton, L. W. & Carlton, P. L. Ontogenetic dissociation of two classes of habituation. *Journal of Comparative and Physiological Psychology*, 1975, **89**, 733–737.

Williams, M. Traumatic retrograde amnesia and normal forgetting. In G. Talland and N. Waugh (Eds.), *The pathology of memory*. New York: Academic Press, 1969.

Wilson, E. H. Reinstatement of extinguished avoidance in the rat: Feeling states as US-specific mediators. Unpublished doctoral dissertation, Department of Psychology, Indiana University, 1971.

Wilson, L. M. & Riccio, D. C. CS familiarization and condition suppression in weanling and adult albino rats. *Bulletin of the Psychonomic Society*, 1973, **1**, 184–186.

Wilson, M. Kaufman, H. M., Zieler, R. E. & Lieb, J. P. Visual identification and memory in monkeys with circumscribed infratemporal lesions. *Journal of Comparative and Physiological Psychology*, 1972, **78**, 173–183.

Wimer, R. E. & Huston, C. Facilitation of learning performance by posttrial etherization. *Behavioral Biology*, 1974, **10**, 385–389.

Winocur, G. & Weiskrantz, L. An investigation of paired-associate learning in amnesic patients. *Neuropsychologia*, 1976, **14**, 97–110.

Winograd, E. List differentiation as a function of frequency and retention interval. *Journal of Experimental Psychology Monograph Supplement*, 1968, **76** (Part II).

Winograd, E. Some issues relating animal memory to human memory. In W. K. Honig and P. H. R. James (Eds.), *Animal memory*. New York: Academic Press, 1971, 259–278.

Winograd, E. & Conn, C. P. Evidence from recognition memory for specific encoding of unmodified homographs. *Journal of Verbal Learning and Verbal Behavior*, 1971, **10**, 702–706.

Winters, J. J., Jr. & Ward, T. B. The effects of induced passive rehearsal and the von Restorff phenomenon on the free recall of normals and retardates. *Memory and Cognition*, 1975, **4**, 421–426.

Wiseman, S. & Tulving, E. A test of confusion theory of encoding specificity. *Journal of Verbal Learning and Verbal Behavior*, 1975, **14**, 370–381.

Wiseman, S. & Tulving, E. Encoding specificity: Relation between recall superiority and recognition failure. *Journal of Experimental Psychology: Human Learning and Memory*, 1976, **2**, 349, 361.

Wollen, K. A., Weber, A. & Lowry, B. H. Bizarreness vs interaction of mental images as determinants of learning. *Cognitive Psychology*, 1972, **3**, 518–523.

Wood, G. Menmonic systems in recall. *Journal of Education Psychology Monographs*, 1967, **58** (6, Part 2).

Wood, G. Organizational processes and free-recall. In E. Tulving & W. Donaldson (Eds.), *Organization of memory*. New York: Academic Press, 1972.

Woods, R. T. & Piercy, M. A similarity between amnesic memory and normal forgetting. *Neuropsychologia*, 1974, **12**, 437–445.

Woodward, A. E., Jr., Bjork, R. A. & Jongeward, R. H. Recall and recognition as a function of primary rehearsal. *Journal of Verbal Learning and Verbal Behavior*, 1973, **12**, 608–617.

Worsham, R. W. & D'Amato, M. R. Ambient light, white noise and monkey vocalization as sources of interference in visual short-term memory of monkeys. *Journal of Experimental Psychology*, 1973, **99**, 99–105.

Wortman, P. M. Long-term retention of information as a function of its organization. *Journal of Experimental Psychology: Human Learning and Memory*, 1975, **1**, 576–583.

Wright, D. C. & Chute, D. L. State-dependent learning produced by posttrial intrathoracic administration of sodium pentobarbitol. *Psychopharmacologia*, 1973, **31**, 91–94.

Wright, D. C., Chute, D. L., & McCullom, G. C. Drug induced retrieval control of one trial discrimination learning. Unpublished manuscript, 1973.

Wyers, E. J. & Deadwyler, S. A. Duration and nature of retrograde amnesia produced by stimulation of caudate neucleus. *Physiology and Behavior*, 1971, **6**, 97–103.

Yaginuma, S. & Iwahara, S. Retrograde effects of electroconvulsive shock on a passive avoidance response and conditioned emotionality (defecation) in rats. *The Annual of Animal Psychology*, 1971, **21**, 1–9.

Yamaguchi, H. G. Gradients of drive stimulus (S_D) intensity generalization. *Journal of Experimental Psychology*, 1952, **43**, 298–304.

Yates, F. A. *The art of memory*. Chicago: University of Chicago Press, 1966.

Yerkes, R. M. The mind of a gorilla: Part III. Memory. *Comparative Psychology Monographs*, 1928, **5(24)**, 1–92.

Yuille, J. C. Does the concreteness effect reverse with delay? *Journal of Experimental Psychology*, 1971, **88**, 147–148.

Yuille, J. C. & Fox, C. Proactive inhibition in short-term retention of pictures. *Journal of Experimental Psychology*, 1973, **101**, 388–390.

Zammit-Montebello, A., Black, M., Marquis, H. A. & Suboski, M. D. Incubation of passive avoidance in rats: Shock intensity and pre-training. *Journal of Comparative and Physiological Psychology*, 1969, **69**, 579–582.

Zangwill, O. L. Remembering revisited. *Quarterly Journal of Experimental Psychology*, 1972, **24**, 123–138.

Zentall, T. R. Effects of context change on forgetting in rats. *Journal of Experimental Psychology*, 1970, **86**, 440–448.

Zentall, T. R. Memory in the pigeon: Retroactive inhibition in a delayed matching task. *Bulletin of the Psychonomics Society*, 1973, **1**, 126–128.

Zentall, T. R., & Hogan, D. E. Memory in the pigeon: Proactive inhibition in a delayed matching task. *Bulletin of the Psychonomic Society*, 1974, **4**, 109–112.

Zentall, T. R. & Hogan, D. E. Short-term Proactive Inhibition in the Pigeon. *Learning and Motivation*, 1977, **8**, 367–386.

Zerbolio, D. J. The proactive effect of electroconvulsive shock on memory storage with and without convulsion. *Communications in Behavioral Biology*, 1969, **4**, 23–27.

Zimmerman, R. R. Effects of age, experience and malnutrition on object retention in learning set. *Perceptual and Motor Skills*, 1969, **28**, 867–876.

Zinkin, S. & Miller, A. J. Recovery of memory after amnesia induced by electroconvulsive shock. *Science*, 1967, **155**, 102–104.

Zornetzer, S. F. Brain stimulation in retrograde amnesia in rats: A neuro-anatomical approach. *Physiology and Behavior*, 1972, **8**, 239–244.

Zornetzer, S. F. & Chronister, R. B. Neural and anatomical localization of memory disruption: Relationship between brain structure and learning task. *Physiology and Behavior*, 1973, **10**, 747–750.

Zornetzer, S. F., Chronister, R. B. & Ross, B. The hippocampus in retrograde amnesia: Localization of some positive and negative memory disruption sights. *Behavioral Biology*, 1973, **8**, 507–518.

Zornetzer, S. F. & McGaugh, J. L. Electrophysiological correlates of frontal cortex-induced retrograde amnesia in rats. *Physiology and Behavior*, 1972, **8**, 233–238.

Zornetzer, S. & McGaugh, J. L. Retrograde amnesia and brain seizures in mice. *Physiology and Behavior*, 1971, **7**, 401–408.

Author Index

The numbers in *italics* refer to the pages on which the complete reference is cited.

A

Aaronson, D., 145, *485*
Adams, H. E., 348, 361, 362, 370, 371, 372, *485, 490, 510, 514*
Adams, J. A., 250, 251, 252, 301, *485*
Adams, W., 246, *485*
Adefris, W., 92, *526*
Adinolfi, A. M., 239, *522*
Advokat, C., 329, *519*
Agranoff, B. W., 335, 344, 362, 367, 368, 382, *485, 519, 521*
Ahroon, W. A., 460, *514*
Aiken, E. G., 114, *485*
Albert, D. J., 328, 372, *485, 508*
Alloway, T. M., 82, 96, *485*
Allport, G. W., 228, 241, *485*
Alpern, H. P., 331, 357, 389, 391, 392, 394, 396, 397, *485, 492, 509*
Ames, H., 115, *519*
Ammons, R. B., 29, *485*
Amsel, A., 80, *485*
Anderson, A. C., 166, 167, *486*
Anderson, J. R., 48, 406, 407, *486, 516*
Anderson, N. H., 251, 253, 254, *512*
Anisman, H., 179, 181, *486*
Aranda, L. C., 55, *491*
Arbit, J., *495*
Archer, E. J., 439, *486*
Asdourian, D., 173, *518*
Asratian, D., 173, *518*

B

Asratian, E. A., 55, 69, 70, *486*
Atkinson, R. C., 296, 423, *486*
Auerbach, P., 362, *486*
Averbach, E., 138, *486*
Avis, H. H., 362, *486*
Azmitia, E. C., 336, 367, *515, 516*
Azrin, N. H., 253, 255, *486, 501, 523*

B

Bacon, W. E., 223, *486*
Baddeley, A. D., 286, 289, 290, 293, 294, 301, 306, 418, *486*
Bahrick, H. P., 272, 409, 457, *486*
Bahrick, P. O., 272, *486*
Bailey, C. J., 81, 82, *486*
Banker, G., 353, 361, *486*
Banks, E. M., 222, *497*
Barbizet, J., 6, 287, 314, *486*
Barker, D., 408, *493*
Barlow, J. J., 160, 162, *518*
Barnes, J. M., 35, 198, *486*
Barnett, B. M., 368, *516*
Barondes, S. H., 335, 336, 337, 344, 367, 368, 369, 375, *486, 487, 492, 519, 521*
Barrett, R. J., 162, 181, 349, 356, 362, 369, *487, 491, 503, 516*
Barrett, T. R., 429, *487*
Bartlett, S. C., 20, 401, 475, *487*
Bartz, W. H., 421, *507*

531

Subject Index